ON THE RAILS
AROUND
FRANCE
BELGIUM
THE NETHERLANDS
and
LUXEMBOURG

The practical guide to holidays by train

Edited by Roger Thomas

A Thomas Cook Touring Handbook

Published by Thomas Cook Publishing
The Thomas Cook Group Ltd
PO Box 227
Peterborough PE3 8BQ
United Kingdom

ISBN 0 906273 56 0

British Library Cataloguing in Publication Data.
A catalogue record for this book is available
from the British Library.

*Whilst every care has been taken in compiling
this publication, using the most up-to-date
information available at the time of going to
press, all details are liable to change and cannot
be guaranteed. The Thomas Cook Group Ltd
cannot accept any liability whatsoever arising
from errors or omissions, however caused. The
views and opinions expressed in this book are
not necessarily those of the Thomas Cook
Group Ltd.*

Managing Editor: Stephen York
Project Editor: Deborah Parker
Map and Timetable Editor: Bernard Horton

Cover design by Greene Moore Lowenhoff
Cover illustration by Michael Benallack-Hart
Text typeset in Frutiger using Advent 3B2
  desk-top publishing system
Maps and diagrams created using GST
  Designworks
Printed in Great Britain by Bell & Bain Ltd,
  Glasgow

The Writing Team

Book Editor: **Roger Thomas**
Series Editor: **Melissa Shales**

Written and researched by:
Stephen Blyth
Sarah Jarvis
Jim Keeble
Lucy Koserski
Carol Sykes
Nia Williams

Acknowledgements

The authors and publishers would like to thank
the following people and organisations for their
assistance during the preparation of this book:

Marielle Albers, Netherlands Board of Tourism,
London; Herman ter Balkt, VVV, Amsterdam;
Pierre Claus, Belgian Tourist Office, London; the
Davis family; Tony Evans; Brendan Fox, Thomas
Cook Publishing, Peterborough; Laëtitia Le Fur,
Thomas Cook Bankers France, Paris; W der Flier,
NS, London; Anita Gajdecki; Iain Gellatly, APT
Marketing, UK; Ben Haines; Richard Jarvis;
Mme Ann Lacroix, Tourist Office, Namur; Jim
Livesey; Peter Mills and Christine Lagardère,
SNCF, London; Dominique and Pauline Misconi;
Serge Moes, Luxembourg Tourist Office, Lon-
don; Marieke van Peer, Thomas Cook Neder-
land, Amsterdam; Jacqueline van Rijn, Euro-
mast, Rotterdam; Dag Scher, Rail Europe, White
Plains USA; Christophe Sturzel; Gemma Uden,
Holland Rail, Ropley; Rosi Velander-Davis, IYHF,
London; Sacha Vogler, Maritiem Museum Prins
Hendrik, Rotterdam; Jon Wakefield; Lema van
der Weghe, IYHF, Bruges; Jaap Westerhuijs and
Bert Wever, Top of Holland, Netherlands.

CONTENTS

Routes and Cities – France

To find a town or city not listed here, look it up in the Index, pp. 349–351. Routes are listed twice – in the direction in which they are named and described in the book and again in the reverse direction, in *italic* type. For example, the route from Bordeaux to Toulouse listed under BORDEAUX is also shown as a reminder under TOULOUSE as *Toulouse to Bordeaux*.

CONTENTS

Routes and Cities – Belgium, The Netherlands and Luxembourg

Reference Section

INTRODUCTION

At high speed or low speed, by futuristic TGV train or traditional branch line, France and the Benelux countries offer great scope for rail travellers. You can spent just a few hours on a rapid city-to-city journey, or take days – even weeks – exploring the rural backwaters of these beguiling countries. France's scenic diversity adds a special dimension to the experience of rail travel. Lines claw their way through the high Alps as well as clinging to glitzy coastlines and running along sylvan river valleys

This book is geared to the traveller who wants to enjoy the best of France and the Benelux countries by train. The routes have been carefully planned to make the journey an attractive and interesting one. Although the routes demand time if you want to enjoy them to the full, we also give a 'fast track' option for those in a hurry. Mention of high-speed transit prompts a reference to the opening of the Channel Tunnel, which heralds a new era in rail travel.

Whether you choose to dash across France, the Netherlands, Belgium and Luxembourg, explore smaller areas in detail, or make a more ambitious attempt to see everything from Calais to Cannes by train, then this book will point you in the right direction. Some of the information might appear to relate to the young and impecunious; but we all like a bargain, and the money-saving advice we give applies to a wide band of travellers.

To make your journey smoother, we advise that you also take a copy of the latest, monthly *Thomas Cook European Timetable* (*ETT*), which has much more detailed timetabling (see p. 21). Remember always to check station timetables, because there are many more short-distance trains available than the ETT has room for.

This book is a product of exhaustive research. We have gone to great lengths to make it as accurate as possible – but things do change. We apologise in advance if you find any errors, and would be very grateful if you could write to us with alterations, additions and suggestions to help us improve the next edition.

HOW TO USE THIS BOOK

ROUTES AND CITIES

The book's format is based around 21 key cities and towns, with 39 linking recommended routes. These are arranged in alphabetical order country by country, beginning with France (34 routes), then the Netherlands (2 routes), followed by Belgium (3 routes). Unlike their French equivalents, most of the routes in the Benelux countries are cross-border ones.

The key towns and cities are followed by the routes which begin there. Smaller cities and towns are described along the route on which they lie. Flexibility of travel is built into the book, for there are clear cross-references throughout the text and on the route diagrams. To avoid repetition, each route is described only once. We have tried to use the most logical direction, but they are designed to be used either way, e.g. Biarritz to Toulouse can just as easily be followed by those travelling from Toulouse to Biarritz.

WITHIN EACH ROUTE

 Fast Track

This describes the quickest and most direct journey between the key cities/towns and the beginning and end of each route.

 On Track

This introduces the full route, with times and other train details along the series of recommended stops. Train frequencies, approximate schedules and journey times are given for each segment. Details are deliberately general, so they will not date too fast, but they should give you a clear idea of how convenient any section of the journey will be. The On Track routing does not necessarily follow the shortest line between key cities/towns and there may be major differences to the Fast Track alternative.

Obviously, you do not have to stop at every town we mention and you can often find faster trains to take you from town A to town C without stopping in town B. There simply isn't space to give every combination of these, but local information and the *ETT* will fill in the gaps.

Route Diagrams

These show, in visual form, the line of the route; the various stops; the fastest time between the two end points; journey times

---

Abbreviations used in the book

av.	avenue	pl.	place
blvd.	boulevard	r.	rue
hr(s)	hour(s)	rte	route
km	kilometres	sq.	square
m	metres	tel:	telephone
min(s)	minute(s)		

Jan, Feb are January, February,etc
Sun, Mon are Sunday, Monday, etc

---

between stops; inter-connecting routes (marked by a black arrow); side-tracks (a white arrow); and border crossings.

Recommended Stops

Train details are followed by descriptions, of varying length and detail, of recommended stops. These highlight the best options available on the route, but do not cover everything. Ask the local tourist office for more details on surrounding options.

Side Tracks from . . .

You will frequently find this heading at the end of a stop. It is used to describe the very best sights, towns and places to visit off the main route. Some side tracks are given a full description; others are mentioned more briefly (usually for reasons of space) so that you are at least aware of their existence.

THE REST OF THE BOOK

Travel Essentials is a brief alphabetical section of general advice for the traveller. **Travelling by Train** takes a more detailed look at how the rail network works in France and the Benelux countries, with information and advice on everything from rail passes to sleeping cars. **Country by Country** provides a brief and basic rundown on the four countries covered in the book. The selection of **Themed Itineraries** shows the potential of rail travel for tours which follow a particular theme.

The quickest way to find information on any place, large or small, and on general topics, is to look it up in the Index. The easiest way to look up a route is to consult the Rail Route Maps overleaf. People who wish to reach their destination in a hurry, but don't want to fly, should turn to **Through Routes** at the end of the Route Maps, which details additional direct long-distance routes.

ROUTE MAP

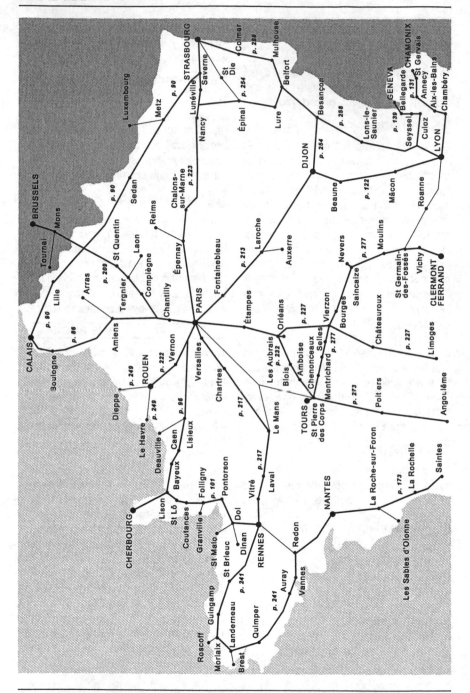

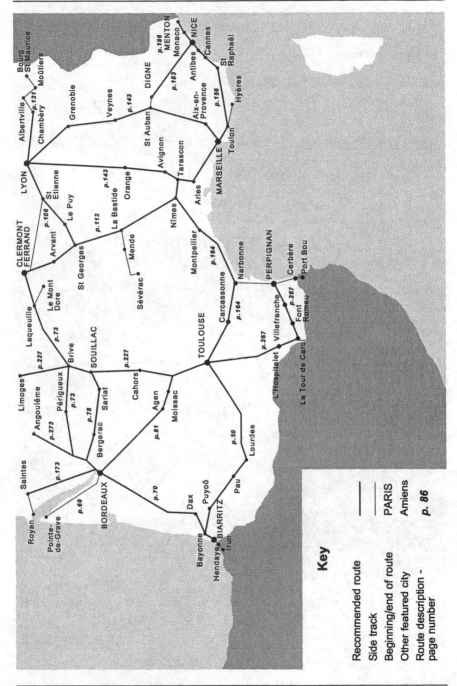

Key

——	Recommended route
——	Side track
●	Beginning/end of route
PARIS	
Amiens	Other featured city
p. 86	Route description - page number

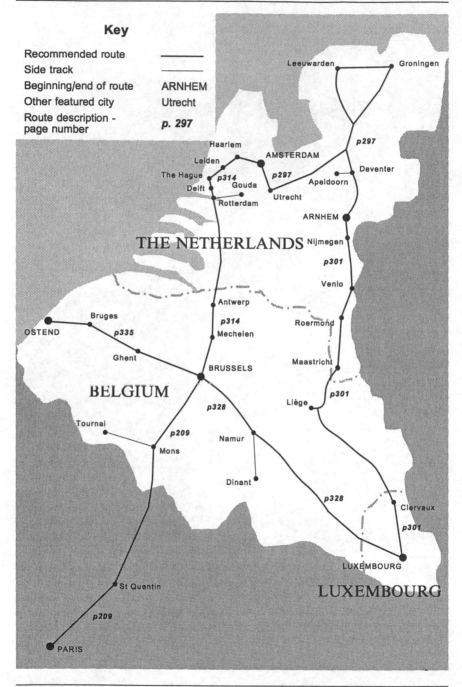

Key

Recommended route	————
Side track	———
Beginning/end of route	ARNHEM
Other featured city	Utrecht
Route description - page number	*p. 297*

Leeuwarden   **Groningen**

p297

Haarlem

AMSTERDAM

Leiden   Deventer

The Hague   *p314*

Delft   Gouda   *p297*   Apeldoorn

Rotterdam   Utrecht

ARNHEM

THE NETHERLANDS Nijmegen

p301

Venlo

Antwerp

p314   Roermond

Bruges   Mechelen

OSTEND   *p335*

Ghent   Maastricht

BRUSSELS

BELGIUM   *p301*

p328   Liège

Tournai

p209   Namur

Mons

Dinant

p328

Clervaux

p301

LUXEMBOURG

LUXEMBOURG

St Quentin

p209

PARIS

THROUGH ROUTES

Some travellers wish to make their way as quickly as possible to a chosen city to begin their more leisurely travel from that point. This will often mean going through two or more consecutive routes in this book without stopping.

The following table shows a selection of possible longer 'through routes', as an aid to journey planning, with approximate summer frequencies and journey times. All these through routes may also be taken in the reverse direction to that shown but number of trains per day may differ. Some of the trains require payment of supplements and many involve overnight travel. Not all services are daily. Always consult the latest issue of the Thomas Cook European Timetable (ETT), which gives up-to-date schedules for these and many other long-distance trains.

Through route	ETT table number	Approx journey time	Trains per day	Notes
Amsterdam–Basel	28	8 hrs	2	Direct (additional services available by changing trains in Cologne)
Amsterdam–Marseille	48	15 hrs	1	Overnight, summer only (additional services available by changing trains in Paris)
Amsterdam–Paris	18	6 hrs	5	Direct (additional services available by changing trains in Brussels)
Bordeaux–Lyon	140	7½ hrs	4	Direct (1 overnight)
Bordeaux–Marseille	139	6 hrs	5	Direct (1 overnight)
Bordeaux–Nantes	134	4 hrs	6	Direct
Bordeaux–Paris	136	3–3½ hrs	14	Direct TGVs
Brussels–Marseille	48	12–13 hrs	1	Overnight (additional services available by changing trains in Paris)
Brussels–Strasbourg	40	5 hrs	3	Direct
Lyon–Nantes	150a/127	5 hrs	3	Direct TGVs (also 1 overnight)
Lyon–Paris	150	2 hrs	20	Direct TGVs
Lyon–Toulouse	151	5½ hrs	3	Direct (1 overnight)
Marseille–Nantes	139	11 hrs	2	Direct (1 overnight)
Marseille–Paris	151	4 hrs	11	Direct TGVs (also 2 overnight)
Paris–Geneva	159	3½ hrs	5	Direct TGVs
Paris–Luxembourg	173	4 hrs	4	Direct (additional services available by changing trains in Metz)
Paris–Nice	164	6½ hrs	2	Direct TGVs (additional services available by changing trains in Marseille, also 2 overnight)
Paris–Perpignan	163	10 hrs	2	Direct (1 overnight)

TRAVEL ESSENTIALS

The following is an alphabetical listing of helpful tips for those planning a holiday to France and the Benelux countries by rail.

Accommodation

This part of Europe offers all kinds of accommodation at all price ranges, from spartan youth hostels to unashamed five-star luxury. The Continental practice of paying by the room – as opposed to per person in the UK – can help budget travellers. But room rates in the big cities and along the glittering Côte d'Azur can be high, especially in the summer months. Rural areas offer by far the best value for money: you can stay within an hour of the sea in inland Provence, for example, for half the cost of a room on the coast. If you are travelling on a budget, look out for the less expensive areas to stay in recommended in this book, and the advice we give on areas of a city/town where budget accommodation can be found.

The tourist offices mentioned in the text will usually help you find, and often reserve, hotel and other accommodation. This is almost always your best starting point if you haven't pre-booked. Don't be afraid to make clear to them your price horizons. If you prefer to reserve some or all of your hotel rooms in advance, this can usually be arranged by Thomas Cook or another good travel agent (best done at the same time you buy your air ticket, if you are travelling from outside Europe).

For those travellers who like to stay in hotels belonging to one of the branded international or national chains, we have indicated in the text which chains are represented in a city by means of initials in the 'Accommodation' section: e.g. *BW, Ho, Nv* means that the city has Best Western, Holiday Inn and Novotel properties (the initials used are explained in the box on p 13). Further details can then be obtained from the chain's central reservation phone number in your own country, or through your travel agent.

Hostelling International (HI)

The best bet, for those on a tight budget, is to join **HI** (Hostelling International), the new name for the IYHF (International Youth Hostel Federation). There is no age limit, membership of a national association will entitle you to use over 5,000 HI member association hostels in 60 different countries, and, besides camping, they are often the cheapest form of accommodation available. Sleeping arrangements are usually in dormitory-style rooms, though some hostels also have smaller one- and two-bedded rooms. Many also have excellent-value dining, cooking and, in some cases, laundry facilities. Membership for those over/under 18 is currently: A$40/ free (Australia); C$25/12 (Canada); NZ $24 plus $10 joining fee (New Zealand); £9/£3 (UK); $25/12 (USA). A directory *Budget Accommodation You Can Trust* (£6.99) is also available, which lists addresses, contact numbers, locations and facilities of all HI member associations. Buy this upon joining, or from bookshops. Hostels are graded according to their standard of comfort and facilities. Some, especially those in larger cities, are open 24 hours daily, while others have lock-out times. You are usually allowed to stay in a hostel for as long as you require but in peak periods, if

Hotel Chains

The following abbreviations have been used throughout the book to denote the particular chain to which a hotel belongs.

BW	Best Western
Ca	Campanile
Cd	Concorde
Cl	Climat
Co	Confort
Dm	Demeure
Ex	Excelsior
F1	Formule 1
Fo	Forum
FP	Forte Post House
GT	Golden Tulip
Hn	Hilton
Ho	Holiday Inn
Hy	Hyatt
Ib	Ibis
Ic	Intercontinental
IH	InterHotel
Ma	Marriott
Md	Meridian
Me	Mercure
Mp	Metropole
Nv	Novotel
Pe	Penta
Pr	Primavere
Pu	Pullman
Ra	Ramada
RC	Ritz Carlton
SA	SAS
Sf	Sofitel
Sh	Sheraton
TH	TimHôtel

you have not already booked to stay for more than three days, you may be asked to vacate your bed to make way for newcomers.

Although it is not usually compulsory to reserve accommodation, hostels are often full in summer so you should book as far ahead as possible. In winter (except around Christmas) bookings can be slow, so it's worth asking if they have any special price deals. For information, to join, and for advance booking: Australia *tel: (02) 261 1111*; Canada *tel: (0800) 663 5777*; New Zealand *tel: (09) 379 4224*; UK *tel (0171) 836 1036*; USA *tel: (0202) 783 6161*.

Where accommodation details are given, we have included hostels where relevant (represented by the initials HI). There may also be hostels in towns we have mentioned in less detail, so always check.

Camping

There are good campsites right across the area covered in this book (the French, in particular, have a passion for camping, with even the smaller towns having good local sites). Facilities range from basic (clean toilets and showers) to luxury sites with dining rooms and swimming pools and even vast complexes of permanent tents. The one drawback is that in most of the large cities, campsites can be miles from the centre.

The various national tourist offices can provide listings (see the relevant Country by Country entries, pp. 31–50). Either contact them before you leave home or trust to luck, but make sure that you always arrive in a new town with plenty of daylight to spare and ask at the local tourist office when you get there.

Bicycles

Cycling is very popular in the part of Europe covered by this book. It's often the best way to explore locally, and you can sometimes hire a bike at one train station and leave it at another. This can even be cheaper than going to bike-hire shops. You may also be able to carry bikes on some trains, but advance notice may be required. If you are interested in cycling, contact the relevant national tourist office for information before you leave (see Country by Country section for addresses).

Borders

The European Union (EU) has technically agreed to open borders between member states. When travelling around the Continent, you'll find that while most borders still remain in place, checks are perfunctory at most. Britain and Ireland take a different view, and continue to maintain a vigilant attitude to cross-border traffic.

Children

Travelling by train with children is easier than you might think – as long as you have someone to help you haul bags and pushchairs up the inevitable steps. Most children even find train travel a great novelty, and thoroughly enjoy themselves. However, they can become get bored on long journeys, so make sure you're not short of ideas to keep them amused and have plenty of food and drink at hand. If children are old enough, ask them to keep a travel diary. This will focus their attention on what they see and do, and make them think about the whole experience.

Most popular tourist destinations are reasonably well adapted for children, with hygienic facilities, plenty of baby food and nappies. Baby-sitters are not that hard to find if you ask around – try the local tourist office or possibly the church. Many hotels will offer family rooms or provide a cot in a normal double. If you can't find suitable restaurants, you can always call at a coffee shop, snack bar or fast-food place which serves a children's menu or, at the very

least, the sort of food they'll be inclined to try. Many sights, hotels and forms of transport will accept babies for free, and those under 12 for half-price. For useful reading try Maureen Wheeler's *Travel with Children*, (Lonely Planet, £5.95/$10.95).

Climate

Apart from the South of France and the Alps, the climate in this part of Europe is not renowned for its excesses. Summer in Brittany and along the shores of Normandy, Belgium and the Netherlands is usually pleasantly warm without being stifling, and winters are not unbearably cold. Inland, temperatures can plunge – the mountains of the Massif Central, although not high by Alpine standards, have their ski resorts. Western France comes under the influences of the Atlantic, so summer showers in the Dordogne and Lot areas are not unknown. Further south, the Mediterranean climate almost guarantees blue skies from May to mid-Aug, though inland Provence is always at the mercy of the howling *mistral* wind which can blow for days on end. If you have the flexibility, try to travel in May/June or Sept. The climate should be pleasant, and you have the added advantage of avoiding school holiday crowds.

Clothing

Most of Europe is very informal these days so you'll rarely need evening clothes, or even a smart suit. You should make sure that you have some smart casual clothes (not jeans and trainers) for evening wear. People wearing shorts or sleeveless tops may be excluded from some churches, the most traditional of which still expect you to cover your head, so pack a long-sleeved shirt or blouse and a shawl or large scarf. You can encounter rain or cool weather no matter where you go, so at least one sweater or jacket and some sort of rainwear are essential.

In addition, take at least two pairs of trousers, or skirts; a pair of shorts; three or four shorts or blouses and three sets of underwear and non-synthetic socks (one on, one in the wash, one spare). For women, a huge t-shirt is useful for a beach cover-up and sleeping in, as well as during the day. Shoes should be comfortable, light and well broken-in, and a pair of flip-flops is useful for unhygienic showers and overnight travel.

Pack a tube of Travel Wash (available from most camping shops and chemists) and a piece of string, to serve as a washing line, so you can wash clothes through as you travel and save on the expense and inconvenience of using a launderette.

Currency

European Union countries place no limit on the import/export of currency between member states (though you may be asked to declare large amounts – over FFr.50,000 at French customs, for example). That said, it is never advisable to carry more cash than necessary, and it is sensible to take most of money in the form of Eurocheques, travellers' cheques and credit cards. The latter are particularly convenient and widely accepted for most transactions, and often represent the best value in terms of commissions/charges.

The Thomas Cook offices listed throughout this book will cash any type of Eurocheque/travellers' cheque and will replace Thomas Cook travellers' cheques if yours are lost or stolen.

Customs

Importing narcotics and offensive weapons is banned through Europe – and penalties for carrying them can be very severe; so, in you own interests, do not be tempted, and do not carry things for anyone else, especially when you are crossing borders. Professional crooks are very good at passing themselves off as harmless and in need of help, and some people are languishing in jail today because they believed a hard-luck story or did someone a 'small' favour. Pornography is also banned in many countries and, since it is notoriously difficult to define, it is better to avoid carrying anything that might offend. If you are taking a prescribed drug on a regular basis, carry something (such as a doctor's letter) that will prove it is legitimate.

There are often restrictions on the import and export of plants and fresh foodstuffs and you might be asked to abandon them at borders, so be careful about stocking up just before leaving a country.

Customs allowances in the EU

Travellers in the areas of Europe featured in this book, will, to all intents and purposes, face no restrictions in respect of goods bought in ordinary shops. However, you may be questioned if you have excessive amounts. Allowances (which apply to anyone aged 17 or over) are:
800 cigarettes, 200 cigars, 400 cigarillos and 1 kg tobacco
+ 90 litres wine (max. 60 litres sparkling)
+ 10 litres alcohol over 22% volume (e.g. most spirits)
+ 20 litres alcohol under 22% volume (e.g. port and sherry)
+ 110 litres beer.

Allowances for those returning home

Australia: goods to the value of A$400 (half for those under 18) plus 250 cigarettes or 250 g tobacco and 1 litre alcohol.

Canada: goods to the value of C$300, provided you have been away for over a week and have not already used up part of your allowance for that year. You are also allowed 50 cigars plus 200 cigarettes and 1 kg tobacco (if over 16) and 40 oz/1 litre alcohol.

New Zealand: goods to the value of NZ$700. Anyone over 17 may also take 200 cigarettes or 250 g tobacco or 50 cigars or combination of tobacco products not exceeding 250 g in all, plus 4½ litres of beer or wine and 1.125 litres spirits.

UK: standard EU regulations apply.

USA: goods to the value of US$400 as long as you have been out of the country for at least 48 hrs and only use your allowance once every 30 days. Anyone over 21 is allowed 1 litre alcohol plus 100 (non-Cuban) cigars and 100 cigarettes.

Disabled Travellers

Europe, in theory, provides more facilities for the disabled than most parts of the world. In practice, those facilities that do exist often fall short of real needs and expectations. Travel is feasible, but it will almost inevitably be more expensive, as it is usually only the modern trains, and the more up-market hotels which are able to cater for the disabled. You will also have to make meticulous plans, always writing and phoning ahead to make sure you have a reservation and that there is someone on hand to help you.

There are two main problems to face in respect of trains – how to get onto them, and whether there is space for you once on board. Although modern rolling stock tends not to have wide gaps between train and platform, in many Continental stations the platforms are quite low and passengers have to climb steps to board trains. Once aboard, only the more modern carriages provide space for a wheelchair; otherwise, space will be provided in the baggage car. The new express services, such as the French TGV, do provide proper facilities for the disabled.

Some national railway offices and tourist offices have leaflets about rail travel for the disabled, while the Dutch also have a telephone information line (*tel: (030) 35 55 55*). Ask also about any discount passes for the disabled which may be available.

UK information: RADAR (Royal Society for Disability and Rehabilitation), *Unit 12, City Forum, 250 City Road, London EC1V 8AF, tel: (0171) 250 3222* publishes a useful annual guide called *Holidays and Travel Abroad* (£5 inclusive of post and packing).

US information: SATH (Society for the Advancement of Travel for the Handicapped), *347 5th Avenue, Suite 610, New York NY 10016; tel: (212) 447 7284.*

For useful reading try: *The AA Guide for the Disabled Traveller* (AA Publishing, £3.95); Susan Abbott and Mary Ann Tyrrell, *The World Wheelchair Traveller* (also AA Publishing, £3.95; you may have to hunt around for a copy); Alison Walsh, *Nothing Ventured: A Rough Guide Special* (Penguin, £7.99).

Discounts

In many countries reductions are available on public transport and on entrance fees for senior citizens, students and the young. The concessionary rate is often given in brackets after the full price in this book, but even if no reduced rate is quoted it may be worth asking is any discount is available. Some proof of your eligibility is usually required. Students should obtain an International Student Identity Card (ISIC) from their union, as this is recognised everywhere and offers a wider range of discounts than the national union card. For a small fee, some destinations also offer a book of discount vouchers available to everyone, covering anything from museums to restaurants. In many cases, discount passes for tourists, including some national rail passes, must be purchased before you leave home. Contact the relevant national tourist office(s) for details.

Driving

To hire a vehicle (with the exception of a moped) in most European countries, you usually have to be over 21 (25 with some hire companies) and in possession of a valid driving licence with one or two years' driving experience. Always check the condition of the hire car before you set out. There is a wide network of motor-rail services across Europe for those who wish to avoid the hassle of long-distance driving but have their own car available during their holiday. Contact the relevant national railway(s) for details.

Electricity

With few exceptions (notably the UK, which uses 240V), the European countries use 220V. The shape of the plugs varies so, if you are taking any sort of electrical gadget, you will need a travel adaptor (these are inexpensive and widely available). It is unlikely that you will face power cuts, but a small torch (flashlight) is a useful back-up and essential if camping.

Health

The countries in this book, on the whole, are clean and hygienic, and there are no compulsory vaccination requirements. However, it is always advisable to keep your tetanus and polio protection up to date. You must be able to produce a certificate against yellow fever if you have

been in a yellow fever endemic zone in the six days before entering Europe. It is a good idea to visit your dentist for a check-up before you leave home.

If you are a UK citizen, you should fill in Form E111 before you leave (available from your local health authority/doctor/post office). This form entitles you to treatment under the reciprocal arrangements that exist across most of Europe. However, the procedure is a bureaucratic one and you may have to pay up-front for treatment and reclaim the costs when you return home; additionally, you are only covered for medical care, not repatriation, so you are strongly advised to take out travel insurance (which will also cover you for other items – see Insurance on p. 18).

If you happen to feel unwell while you are away, try visiting the pharmacy first before you make an appointment with the doctor, as European pharmacists tend to be well trained and may be able to advise you and prescribe treatment on the spot.

Dangers

Although we tend to think of parts of Europe as being cool and grey, there is a severe risk of sunburn in the south and in the high mountain areas. Don't spend hours outdoors without using a high-factor sunblock.

Holiday romances are all very well, but don't get so carried away that you forget all about AIDS – and all the other sexually transmitted diseases. If casual sex is your scene, fine, but do take precautions.

Rabies exists across much of Continental Europe and, while the risk is very small, you should be wary of stray animals.

Hitchhiking

If you are on a budget, you may want to try hitchhiking around local towns rather than use public transport. This can be fun and a good way to meet the locals, but it can also be dangerous. To avoid trouble, don't hitch alone, or take any ride when you are outnumbered or clearly physically weaker than the people in the car.

Insurance

You must take out travel insurance that covers your health as well as your belongings. It should also give cover in case of cancellation and include an emergency flight home if something goes wrong. If you are likely to do something that might be classified as risky (e.g. ski, drive a moped, dive), make sure that your insurance covers you for the activity concerned. The Thomas Cook Recommended Travel Insurance Package offers comprehensive medical insurance and is available from all Thomas Cook retail travel shops in the UK.

Language

You might arm yourself with a copy of the *Thomas Cook European Rail Traveller's Phrasebook*. It contains over three hundred phrases, covering the needs of the rail traveller, each translated into a number of European languages (including French) with their phonetic spellings. In the UK the phrasebook costs £3.95 and is available from any branch of Thomas Cook, many UK bookshops or by *tel: (01733) 268943*.

Before you go, learn one or two very basic phrases in a few languages, such as: 'Hello. I'm sorry but I don't speak ... Does anyone here speak English?' Don't be too self-conscious. Even if you only have the most rudimentary grasp of the language, your efforts to speak it will usually be appreciated. It's sensible to have a pen and paper handy at all times, so that you can ask people to write down figures like times and prices.

Luggage

The amount of space available to store luggage on trains varies considerably from country to country, but it is always sensible to travel as light as possible.

Soft-sided bags may not be as secure as cases, but they are light, easy to carry and can be squeezed into cramped spaces. Backpacks are the best option if you have to do a lot of carrying; otherwise go for a large, zippable canvas or plastic bag, with a shoulder strap to leave your hands free. If you've never used a backpack before, shop carefully before making your choice. It's worth spending a bit more money to ensure comfort and durability (the best have a lifetime guarantee). Essential features are a strong internal frame, padded shoulder straps and a hip strap, to lift the bulk away from your neck.

Most major stations have left luggage offices and many will also let you register your bags and send them on ahead to your destination.

Opening Hours

A rough guide to opening hours of banks, shops and museums is given in the Country by Country section, but even then, there is a lot of variation. Don't, for instance, assume that every bank will be open during the banking hours listed – and you may find some that actually stay open longer. Although Sun is the usual closing day, many tourist attractions remain open – but will close on Mon or Tues. Timings are also subject to seasonal variations, with many places closing altogether in winter.

Passports and Visas

Although EU citizens can, in theory, travel to other member countries on a National Identity Card (or British Visitor's Passport until Jan 1996), it makes sense to have a full passport which should have at least six months' validity left. As for non-European travellers, this book concentrates on requirements for citizens of Australia, Canada, New Zealand and the USA; others should check with their nearest embassy before they travel. If you are plan to stay more than 90 days in a single country, check to see if you need a visa. It is most advisable to sort out your visa requirements before you travel; while, in theory, you can obtain a visa at the border, in practice it is better to get it in advance. In the UK, **Thomas Cook**, *45 Berkeley Street, London W1A 1EB, tel: (0171) 499 4000*, operates a visa service which will order and collect your documents for you.

Public Holidays

These have been listed under the individual headings in the Country by Country section. Many are religious holidays, whose dates vary from year to year: the principal ones are Good Friday and Easter Monday (Mar/April), Ascension Day (the 6th Thurs after Easter); Whitsun/Pentecost (on Monday, 11 days after Ascension); Corpus Christi (early June); and Midsummer Day (late June). If an official holiday falls on a weekend, the following Mon or Tues often becomes a holiday as well.

There are many local festivals (e.g. saints' days) which are celebrated in only one town or locality. Train services are liable to considerable alteration on holiday dates.

Sales Tax

Value Added Tax (VAT in the UK) is automatically added to most goods on the Continent. Non-residents can claim the

---

tax back, though there is the deterrent of the usual impenetrable bureaucracy to contend with. Refunds can be reclaimed on major items of expenditure, with limits which vary from country to country. At the time of your purchase you must ask the shop assistant to fill in a tax refund form for you to initiate the refund process (not all shops operate this service).

Security

The best way to avoid becoming a victim of theft is to try and give the impression that you are not worth robbing (e.g. do not flash expensive jewellery or rolls of bank-notes). Use a hidden money-belt for your valuables, travel documents and spare cash. Never carry a wallet in your back pocket or leave your handbag open, and use a bag with a shoulder strap slung horizontally. In all public places – especially crowded markets – take precautions with anything that is obviously worth stealing. Never leave luggage unattended – if it isn't stolen, European countries are nowadays very terrorist-conscious, and chances are that it will be reported as a possible bomb.

When sleeping rough, in any sort of dormitory, or on trains, the safest place for your small valuables is at the bottom of your sleeping bag. In sleeping cars, padlock your luggage to the seat. In both sleepers and couchettes ask the attendant to show you how to lock the door at night. Be particularly safety conscious in areas around stations, especially large cities.

Women travelling on their own should, to avoid irritation, dress on the conservative side, walk purposefully and confidently, and avoid direct eye contact with proble-matic men. Be careful to whom you speak, and while you can be perfectly friendly, keep it cool and off-limits. If you feel the need, carry a rape alarm.

Exercise the usual rules of caution when abroad. Don't go off with people who have been drinking or get into cars with strangers. Avoid dark alleys and lonely, or red-light areas, make sure you have a clear view all round you and, if in doubt, scream first and think later. If you feel threatened, head for the nearest hotel and ask for help.

Mugging is a problem in some areas, but as a rule it is not rife in European city centres, although pickpockets are a real danger there. If you are attacked, it is safer to let go of your bag or hand over the small amount of obvious money – you are more likely to be attacked physically if the thief meets with resistance. If you do run into trouble, you must report it to the local police, even if it is only to get a copy of their report for your insurance company.

Finally, take half a dozen passport photos (useful for all kinds of purposes) and photocopy the important pages and any visa stamps in your passport. Store these safely, together with a note of the numbers of your travellers' cheques, credit cards and insurance documents (keep them separate from the items themselves). If you are unfortunate enough to be robbed, you will at least have some identification, and replacing the documents will be much easier.

Telephones

You should have few problems finding a phone in European towns and everywhere is on direct-dial. Useful telephone numbers are provided throughout the book and in the Country by Country section you will find advice on how to make calls.

Time

There are several time zones within Europe. The following list includes only the countries covered in this book. The UK uses

Greenwich Mean Time in winter, but is GMT + 1 hr in summer. Belgium, France, Luxembourg and the Netherlands are GMT + 1 hr in winter, GMT + 2 hrs in summer. The *Thomas Cook European Timetable* (see p. 346) also has a time-zone guide.

Toilets/WCs

There are public toilets at railway and bus stations, in public buildings and in stores. In some countries (e.g. France) you may come across places where both sexes use the same facilities. Quality varies considerably, from modern and clean to the infamous hole-in-the-ground variety. Be prepared for anything, and always carry some paper.

Useful Reading

The *Thomas Cook Rail Timetable of Britain, France and Benelux Summer Special* (see p. 5) is published in May each year, costs £7.95, and has summer timings for most rail services and some shipping services in France and Benelux. It is essential both for pre-planning and making on-the-spot decisions about independent rail travel and is available from UK bookshops. For up to-date details of European rail services year round, *The Thomas Cook European Timetable* (ETT), published monthly at £7.90, is invaluable. A useful companion to either timetable is the *Thomas Cook New Rail Map of Europe* (£4.95). Both of these publications are obtainable from some stations, any UK branch of Thomas Cook or by phoning (01733) 268943. In North America, contact the Forsyth Travel Library Inc., *9154 West 57th Street, PO Box 2975, Shawnee Mission, Kansas 66201; tel: (800) 367 7984 (toll-free)*, see also advertisement pp. 343–345.

The *Thomas Cook Travellers* worldwide series (£6.99/7.99), published in the USA as

Passport's Illustrated Travel Guides ($12.95/14.95), covers many European destinations, including the following: Amsterdam, Belgium, Normandy, Paris and Provence. These guides and the *Thomas Cook European Rail Traveller's Phrasebook* are available from any UK branch of Thomas Cook, most UK bookshops, or by phoning (01733) 268943. In the USA, they are available from bookstores and published by Passport Books, Chicago.

What to Take

A few things that really are useful are: water-bottle, muesli-type bars, Swiss Army pocket knife, torch (flashlight), sewing kit, padlock and bicycle chain (for anchoring your luggage), small first-aid kit (including insect repellent and antihistamine cream, sun-screen cream, after-sun lotion, something for headaches and tummy troubles, antiseptic spray or cream, medicated wet wipes, plasters, bandages), contraceptives and tampons, safety matches, mug and basic cutlery, small towel, soap, toothbrush, travel wash, string (for a washing-line), travel adapter, universal plug (often missing from wash-basins), dental floss, sunglasses, alarm clock, note pad and pen, pocket calculator (to convert money), a money-belt and a good book (for long waits at stations and train journeys). If you wear spectacles, take a spare pair and copy of your prescription.

If you're not sure what you're doing about accommodation, take a lightweight sleeping bag, a sheet liner, inflatable travel pillow and eye-mask (invaluable for comfort on long train journeys, even if you look a total idiot).

Finally, pack a large supply of plastic bags, useful for all sorts of things, plus one or two rubber bands to seal them.

Time–Toilets–Useful Reading–What to Take

TRAVELLING by TRAIN

This chapter provides hints to help you plan your rail journey and includes a section on rail passes that cover the countries featured in this book.

FRANCE

The French are justly proud of their efficient and extensive national rail network, which is run by the state-owned *Société National de Chemins de Fer Français* (**SNCF**) *tel: (1) 45 82 50 50*. Their TGV services are among the fastest in the world.

SNCF is changing the separate telephone numbers for information and booking for each département to one central number; *tel: 36 35 35 35*. Calls are charged at FFr.2.19 per minute.

In the UK, a wide range of tickets and passes (see p. 25) can be obtained in person from **French Railways House**, *179 Piccadilly, London W1V 0BA*. For information, *tel: 0891 515477* (calls cost £0.49 per minute peak rate, £0.39 at other times); to make credit card bookings call their Rail Shop, *tel: 0345 300003*. See advertisement on p. 343 for tickets and passes in the US.

Many stations now have automatic ticket machines with touch-screen terminals on which you can order tickets and make seat reservations, and pay with coins (up to FFr.100) or credit/charge cards. They also provide timetable information. Touch the flag logo in the top right hand corner of the screen to change the instruction language.

Wander away from the main lines, however, and a different aspect of French Railways becomes apparent. Long, single-track branch lines give an insight into rural, pastoral France.

Trains

The TGV (*Train à Grande-Vitesse*) is the flagship of modern train travel, with a maximum speed of 300 kph. It is currently operating on three major routes from Paris. The Sud Est, in orange livery, the original TGV line, now extends beyond Lyon and soon will reach the Mediterranean. The Atlantique, with blue and silver livery, serves Brittany and the Atlantic coast. The TGV Nord stretches from Paris to Lille, Calais and the Channel Tunnel.

Seat reservation is compulsory for travel on TGV trains, but can be obtained at the last minute, if space is available, from ticket machines on the platform; supplements are payable on all TGV services.

Away from the TGV routes, French expresses are similar to inter-city trains throughout western Europe, generally fast and comfortable, but in France they are not always very frequent. TER trains run on local lines, often financed by the local region, and vary from slow, stopping trains to fast modern trains filling in the gaps left by the limited-stop TGV network.

International trains from France can normally be used for local journeys although EuroCity trains require additional supplements.

First- and second-class seats are available on most trains except for some second-class only local services and a few first-class only TGVs. Some overnight sleeping car and couchette car trains do not have any seating accommodation.

Overnight Trains

Sleeping cars (*voiture-lits*) in France are designed for night travel with little daytime use. As such the compartments are little larger than the beds they contain, with room only for a small wash-basin and limited, though ingeniously arranged, storage space. Toilets and, increasingly, showers are located at the ends of carriages and every car has an attendant. First-class accommodation is in single or double cabins, second-class in two- or three-bed cabins.

Couchettes, which are less expensive than sleeping cabins, have up to four people per compartment in first-class, and up to six in second-class. Compartments are mixed sex, clothing is not removed, and each carriage has washrooms and toilets.

Some trains have second-class bunks – *Cabine 8* or *Sièges à dossier inclinable* – for the same fare as a seat. Advance booking is necessary for overnight trains.

Timetables

SNCF produce a national rail timetable in three volumes, not suitable for taking with you. However, the *Ville à Ville* timetable which contains details of every train linking 230 towns and cities is available from SNCF. If you intend to cover large areas of France the *Thomas Cook European Timetable* is best (see p. 346).

For smaller areas SNCF and the local governments publish handy regional transport guides giving information about train services, bus connections and plans of local train routes (available from tourist offices and main stations).

Timetables are a must for travelling in France; whereas most European countries run trains at regular intervals throughout the day, French services are more erratic.

Meals on Trains

The traditional restaurant cars are disappearing as fast from France as elsewhere. Modern three-course meals are served at the passenger's seat in the carriage close to the kitchen. For this reason it is important when reserving seats to state that a full meal is required. Full meal services are often restricted to first-class passengers.

Gril-express (*libre-service*) cars offer self-service buffets on some expresses. Bars, where food and drink is bought at a counter and taken back to your seat, are found on the majority of long-distance expresses. Increasingly the catering on French trains is provided by trolleys (*vente ambulante*) pushed through the train.

Fares

Fares are based on the distance travelled, class of carriage and tariff period. Tariff periods for non-TGV services are based on a system of blue (off-peak) and white (peak) periods. Travel is cheaper and tends to be quieter and more comfortable in blue periods. SNCF issue a *calendrier voyageurs*, which tells you when the different tariffs apply. Expensive white period fares usually operate from Fri at noon to Sat at noon, from Sun from 1500 until noon on Mon and in peak periods around some public holidays. The TGV supplement works differently involving four levels of tariff (yellow, grey, green and pink, which is the busiest and most expensive period to travel) which can be found on the the the timetable. Guides are produced for each line, giving timetable and tariff information.

All tickets bought in France must be validated by the automatic date-stamping machines (*composteur*) at the entrance to platforms (if not you're liable to be fined).

Rail Passes and Discounts

If your return journey is over 1000 km and you're travelling out on a blue day, you can get a reduction of 25% on the ordinary return fare.

Carrissimo is a discount card for people between the ages of 12 and 25, giving 50% off blue day fares and 20% off for white days. Up to three friends (between the ages of 12 and 25) can claim the same discount. There are two types of card, each of which is valid for one year: the four single journeys card costs £23 and the eight journey card costs £43.

Carte Couple gives couples a 25% reduction for journeys commencing on a blue day. The card is free but you need to show proof of marriage or cohabitation and a photograph of both people.

Carte Vermeille is the discount card for people over 60, entitling holders to a discount of 50% on blue day fares and 20% discounts on white days. The card is valid for one year and comes in two forms: *Carte Vermeil Quatre Temps*, which covers four journeys and costs £17, and *Carte Vermeil Plein Temps*, which costs £31, is valid for an unlimited number of journeys and gives a 30% reduction on some international journeys commencing on blue days.

Children under 16 can get a **Carte Kiwi**, which gives the holder, plus four relations or friends, up to a 50% reduction on fares on blue or white days. There are two types of Carte Kiwi: one for four single journeys within one year, which costs £34, the other, for which you need a photo, giving unlimited travel within one year in Europe (£52). The blue and white discounted periods are applicable on ordinary trains, but subject to availability on TGVs.

The **France Railpass** is available in the USA. Prices range from US$115–$185, depending on the class of travel and the number of people travelling together, giving three days travel in any month. Additional days can be added for US$30 per person. Also available in the US are the **France Rail and Drive Pass** and the **France Rail and Fly Pass**. These can be obtained from **The Forsyth Travel Library Inc**; *tel: 1-800-367-7984* (toll-free) or **Rail Europe**; *tel: 1-800-4-EURAIL* (toll-free) in the USA or *tel: 1-800-361-RAIL* (toll-free) in Canada.

Passes give the advantage of not having to pay for reservations or some supplements, but where reservations are required, such as on TGVs, there is only a limited number of seats available for people holding passes, and if you don't book early you may miss the quota of seats.

BELGIUM

The Belgian national railway system, like most things in Belgium, uses two names, one French and one Flemish. *Société Nationale des Chemins de fer Belges* (**SNCB**) is the French version, *Nationale Maatschappij der Belgische Spoorwegen* (**NMBS**) the Flemish. For nationwide enquiries; *tel: (02) 219 28 80* and *(02) 219 26 40*, manned 0600–2230.

The rail logo is 'B' in an oval. Information kiosks with this logo are in all sizable stations, but (except in the rare instances where there are signs to the contrary) they give information about trains only.

Trains

Belgium's rail network is comprehensive and reliable, with *IC* and *IR* fast services linking the major cities.

All trains operate at regular intervals (usually hourly) and the timetable is integrated to avoid long waits.

Stations

Stations have pictograms to indicate their facilities. Bear in mind that the word for platform varies: *spoor*, *voie* and *quai* are all used. Be aware that it's not unusual for two trains to leave different ends of the same platform at the same time, so always check the train information signs at both ends of the platform and board carriages only at the end that shows your destination. If you can't see the stop you want, ask an official. Very small stations, the type with only two platforms, usually have permanent boards on each saying '*Vers* ... (the next major town)', so you can check you are heading in the right direction.

The smallest stations have few, if any, facilities. All the others have at least WCs, telephones, a left-luggage facility, a train information booth and snacks. You can hire bicycles at 35 stations for BFr.280 per calendar day – or just BFr.150 if you're travelling by train.

Train tickets should be bought in advance but you can buy them on the train – *provided* you tell the conductor *before* you board (and pay an extra BFr.60). If you board without clearing it first, you are liable for a fine of BFr.500–5000. Tickets can be purchased up to five days in advance, but you must specify the date of travel. You can upgrade your class of travel once you are on the train, by paying the difference to the conductor.

Timetables

All stations have large yellow timetables for departures (white ones for arrivals), which include platform numbers and arrival times at each stop. There's usually one set for Mon–Fri (Ⓐ) and another for Sat, Sun and holidays (Ⓒ), so check the top line to ensure you're consulting the right one.

Most train information gives both French and Flemish versions of names.

Luggage

At manned left-luggage offices, the rate is BFr.60 per case per calendar day. At the old-style lockers you pay BFr.15 for 24 hrs and take the key away with you, but these are insecure and few are still in working order – check for a key before inserting money. The new electronic lockers cost BFr.60/80/100 (depending on size) for 24 hrs. You can usually keep them for 72 hrs (sometimes only 48, so check) and pay any excess when you return. In some cases you take a key, but the latest models give you a slip of paper: when you return, peel off the top layer and key in the number revealed.

Rail Passes

For those aged 12–25, **Go Pass** (BFr.1290) is valid six months and provides ten second-class journeys within Belgium, but not before 0800 on working weekdays.

The **50% Reduction Card** (BFr.570) is valid for one month's unlimited rail travel at half the normal fares. The **Belgian Tourrail Card** (BFr.1980 second-class, BFr.2970 first-class) gives unlimited train travel for any 5 days in a one-month period.

If you have the type of ticket where you nominate your own days of travel, you must fill in each date before you board. Failure to do this can result in a fine of BFr.500.

A free brochure (available at all stations) offers a complete range of B-Daytrips: all-inclusive rail excursions.

THE NETHERLANDS

The national rail company is **Nederlandse Spoorwegen (NS)**. The NS logo is prominently displayed on everything connected with it and is sometimes the only exterior indication of a station.

Trains

The rail service is fast and comfortable, but there are gaps in the network. You seldom have to wait longer than 30 mins and the vast majority of trains run on time. Intercity and *Sneltreins* have a few stops, while *stoptreins* serve all stations en route.

Sleepers/couchettes are the standard European type, but needed only for some international journeys. Some intercity trains have a trolley service with food and drink. Reservations are possible only for international journeys, but you are can upgrade to first-class if you are sure second-class is full.

There's often a big gap between the train and platform, so watch your step.

Stations

Rail stations are usually central and invariably adjoin the main bus/tram terminals. Most display large yellow timetables (with platform numbers) for the regular trains. If your journey involves a change, ask for details at the ticket office and get a print-out.

Only the longest trains use both ends of a platform, so the a/b suffix is as important as the platform number and you should ensure you are at the correct end.

All but the very smallest stations have takeaways, good-quality cafés, vending machines for snacks, WCs and luggage lockers. Large stations also have baggage trolleys, VVV booths, manned left-luggage offices and bookshops.

The **GWK** bank has exchange offices at 35 stations, including all the big ones. They open all week and for extended hours.

The stations have extensive pictograms and, if you remember that *spoor* means 'platform' and *Uit* 'exit' (also indicated by a

square with an arrow pointing out of the bottom), you won't go far wrong.

Luggage

Luggage lockers (indicated by a case with a key beneath it) come in two sizes: quite large (DG4) and really large (DG6). Close the door, feed in coins and wait for a ticket (there's often a longish pause). When you return, insert the ticket and the door will open – or you will be told the amount of excess due. The initial payment covers 24 hrs, but your belongings are safe for up to 72 hrs. The machines take DG1 (or smaller) coins. They will accept DG5 pieces, but do not give change. At manned luggage offices you have to pay (DG4) per item.

Rail Passes

The **Netherlands Rail Rover** can be purchased for first/second-class travel and is valid for one day's unlimited rail travel (DG97.50/65). Rovers can be extended to cover all buses, trams and metros (DG7 for one day; DG17 for ten). In the UK contact **Holland Rail**, *Gilbert Street, Ropley, Hampshire, SO24 0BY; tel: (01962) 773646.*

LUXEMBOURG

The national rail company is **CFL**, *9 pl. de la Gare, Luxembourg; tel: 49 24 24.* The network is limited, but CFL also run long-distance buses on which passes are valid.

Trains

The standard of rolling-stock varies considerably, but most trains are comfortable. On long-distance trains the doors may be automatic (or opened with buttons), on local ones you simply use the handles.

Stations

Most stations are small and have little in

the way of facilities, although you can expect WCs, timetables and a manned ticket office which may (or may not) let you leave your baggage at the station for a while: the staff in small stations are usually helpful.

Tickets

Billet Réseau is a day-card (LFr.140) for unlimited second-class travel on any bus or train in the country (a day is considered to end at 0800 on the following day). *Oeko-Carnet* is a block of five one-day cards (LFr.540). Both are available from CFL offices and must be validated for the first journey of the day: on boarding buses or at rail stations before boarding trains. Border travel is excluded, so buy a separate ticket to cover the journey between the border and whichever station is closest.

EUROPEAN RAIL PASSES

The passes below allow reduced rate travel in more than one country, including at least one of the counties covered in this book, and can usually be purchased from any branch of the national railway and its appointed agents.

In order to buy rail passes, you will often have to supply one or two passport-size photos and show your passport or other relevant identification. The passes generally cover all the ordinary services of the national rail companies and can be used on most of the special services provided you pay a supplement. A few, such as Eurail, cover the supplement. In addition, many give free or discounted travel on private railways (such as steam trains and cog railways), buses and/or ferries. A few even give free entrance to transport museums. You will get full details of the 'extras' when you buy the pass.

Inter-Rail Pass

The Inter-Rail Pass has launched generations of young people into the travelling life. A well-established scheme, it provides a practical and ultra-cheap way of seeing most of Europe by train. It can be bought by anyone who will be under 26 on the first day for which it is valid, provided that they can prove that they have lived for at least six months in one of the European countries where the pass is valid, or are a national of that country, and that they hold a valid passport. It can be purchased up to two months before travel begins. The current cost is £249 for a month and you can buy two consecutive passes for longer journeys. You will not get free travel in the country where you buy the pass, but you may get some discount.

At present, an Inter-Rail pass gives you unlimited second-class rail travel for a month on most European national railways, including Belgium, France, Luxembourg and the Netherlands. It also gives free or discounted crossings on many other ferries, so check before you travel.

In the UK, Inter-Rail provides a discount on the rail portion of tickets between London and the Continental ports, plus 30% or 50% discount (depending on the company) on most of the ferries to Europe.

Zonal Inter-Rail Passes

These regional variations on the Inter-Rail Pass are for those under 26. The same rules about eligibility apply. For zonal passes, Europe has been divided into seven geographical zones including one covering France, Belgium, the Netherlands and Luxembourg.

Passes are available for 1 zone (15 days only; £179); 2 zones (1 month; £209); and 3 zones (1 month; £229). If you are only travelling in France, Belgium, the Netherlands and Luxembourg, these can offer savings over the standard Europe-wide pass.

Inter-Rail 26+ Pass

This is the same as the Inter-Rail Pass, except that it is for people over 26 and does not cover travel in Belgium or France. The current cost is £269 for a month or £209 for 15 days.

Benelux Tourrail Pass

This can be bought in the UK and the USA and provides unlimited rail travel throughout Belgium, Luxembourg and the Netherlands for any 5 days in a one-month period. For those over 26, prices are £125/US$230 in first class and £84/US$153 in second class. If you are under 26, you will only be able to purchase a pass in second class, at a cost of £63/US$115.

Eurail Passes

These can be purchased only by people living outside Europe. It is possible to get the passes once you've arrived, but they will be much more expensive. As you can buy one up to six months before you use it you should try and buy in advance. Eurail passes offer unlimited travel on most European national railways including Belgium, France, Luxembourg and the Netherlands. They also cover some private railways and selected ferries. A complete list of bonuses is included on the complimentary map issued with your tickets.

The basic **Eurail Pass** has no age limit. It provides first-class travel on all services and even covers most of the supplements for travelling on express and de luxe trains. It also gives free or reduced travel on many lake steamers, ferries and buses. There are several versions, valid for 15 days, 21 days,

1 month, 2 months or 3 months. Current prices range from US$498 for 15 days to US$1398 for 3 months, children under 12 half price.

The **Eurail Youth Pass** is much the same, but cheaper, as it is designed for those under 26 and is based on second-class travel. There are versions valid for either 15 days (US$398) or up to two months (US$768).

The **Eurail Flexipass** is similar to the basic Eurail pass, but allows you to travel for any 5 days (US$348), any 10 days (US$560) or any 15 days (US$740) within a two-month period.

The **Eurail Youth Flexipass** allows second-class travel for those under 26 within a two-month period for 5 days (US$255), 10 days (US$398) and 15 days (US$540).

The **Eurail Saverpass** is designed for groups of 3–5 people travelling together at all times (between 1 Oct and 31 Mar two people travelling together is accepted) and offers first-class rail travel over a 15-day period at US$430, 21 days at US$550 and 1 month at US$678.

Euro-Domino Freedom Pass

This is a catch-all title for a whole series of passes allowing unlimited travel on the national railway of an individual country (including most high-speed train supplements). They are not valid for travel in your own country. Conditions of use are the same everywhere and the options available are for any 3, 5 or 10 days within a period of one month. The passes can be purchased by non-Europeans but only upon reaching a country for which the pass applies.

There is no age limit, but the price varies according to age. Those under 26 pay less but are restricted to second-class, while those over 26 can opt for either first- or second-class. Children pay half (the age at which they qualify for the reduction varies in different countries). The price also varies according to the size of the railway network in the country chosen.

Passes can be purchased up to two months before travel begins. Countries currently offering them include: Belgium, where prices range from £32 (£42 for those over 26) for 3 days second-class travel to £129 for 10 days first-class travel; in France prices range from £96 for 3 days second-class travel (£118 for those over 26) to £352 for 10 days first-class travel; and Luxembourg, from £11 (£16 for those over 26) for 3 days second-class travel to £55 for 10 days first-class travel. For the Netherlands prices range from £25 (£34 if over 26) for 3 days second-class travel to £130 for 10 days travelling first-class, and a **Public Transport Link** pass can be purchased to supplement the Euro Domino pass, allowing unlimited travel on the bus, tram and metro systems, starting at £7 for 3 days.

In the UK, holders of any Euro-Domino Freedom pass can get up to 50% discount off the rail/ferry ticket from London to a Continental port. Other ferry discounts are available (details with the ticket).

Europass

Available in the USA only, this pass allows flexible first-class rail travel for those over 26 in France (also Germany, Italy and Switzerland). If you purchase a 5-day pass (the minimum), you receive unlimited rail travel in your choice of three of the above countries. The more travel days you purchase, the more countries you can visit. The maximum number of rail-travel days you can choose is 15, and however many you choose, you must travel within a 2-month period. Countries must border each other and travel days may be used consecutively or non-consecutively.

A special second-class Europass Youth is available for those under 26. Prices range from US$280 for 5 days (Europass Youth: US$198) to US$660 for 15 days (US$478). Various bonuses are available and listed on the map which accompanies the rail pass.

Rail Europe-Senior Card

This card is for women over 60 and men over 60 or 65 (depending on the age at which they are classed as a senior citizen in their own country). It offers a discount of 30% (sometimes more) off the cost of rail travel (excluding supplements) in most countrys in Europe, including Belgium, France, Luxembourg and the Netherlands. The card is not available to US citizens.

Most countries have a rail card for their senior citizens, which is needed to buy the Rail Europe-Senior Card. In the UK the Senior Railcard is available to people over 60 (costs £16 p.a.) The Rail Europe-Senior Card, available from British Rail International, costs an extra £5. It becomes valid on the day of purchase and expires on the same date as the domestic card.

Youth Passes

If you are under 26, there are many other discounted tickets and passes available. Some are to single destinations or for travel in single countries, others (like the examples above) to whole groups of countries. Passes come under many different names such as Euro-Youth, Explorer Pass and BIJ (*Billets International de Jeunesse*).

If the Inter-Rail/Eurail passes are too general for your needs, contact an organisation that specialises in youth travel such as **Campus,** *tel: (0171) 730 3402* or **Wasteels,** *tel: (0171) 834 7066.*

COUNTRY
by
COUNTRY

FRANCE

Capital: Paris. **Language**: French; quite a few people can speak or understand a little English, particularly in Paris. Always try to speak at least a little French. Even though you may not have much command of the language, your efforts will be appreciated. **Currency**: The currency of France is the French Franc (FFr), which is divided into 100 centimes. There are 5, 10, 20 and 50 centime coins and FFr.1, 2, 5 and 10 coins. Notes come in FFr.20, 50, 100, 200 and 500 denominations. (There are plans to replace the FFr.20 note with a coin in the near future).

Customs

For customs allowances in the European Union (EU), see p.15. There is no limit on the amount of money you can take into France, but you must declare banknotes totalling in excess of FFr.50,000 taken out of the country. There are restrictions on the importation of items such as recreational drugs, weapons and animals; for up-to-date regulations, contact the French consulate.

EU residents are liable to local sales taxes, but there are no extra duties for tax-paid goods for individual consumption. A sales tax is applied to most items bought in France. The tax on staple items is quite modest, but luxury goods tend to attract a higher rate. If you spend more than FFr.2,000 in one shop, ask for a TVA reclaim form, which must be completed and stamped by the sales person. When you leave France you will need to present the form(s) at Customs for verification before reclaiming any refund. Non-EU residents may be liable to customs duty when they import the goods. If in doubt check with home tax authorities.

Passports and Visas

British visitors to France need a valid passport (or, until Jan 1996, a British Visitor's Passport). EU nationals do not need visas for stays of less than three months; for longer visits a residence permit (*carte de séjour*) is required, either from the French consulate at home or from the Service des Étrangers at local *préfectures de police* in France. Visitors from the USA, Canada and New Zealand only require visas for stays of over 90 days. Australians and South Africans should obtain visas from their French consulate and may be required to show proof of adequate funds for the visit. Entry regulations and visa charges are liable to change, so check with the consulate before leaving.

Tourist Information

Thousands of tourist offices in France provide information on local accommodation, where to eat, attractions, transport and entertainment. In most towns they're known as *Syndicats d'Initiatives* or *Offices de Tourisme*; offices in larger centres are called *Acceuil de France*. These are the best places to help you get your bearings in a new town, especially if you don't speak any French. A number of regions and *départments* have tourist offices in Paris (see p. 32) which provide information and advice about travel. Some offices also operate hotel reservation services.

Maison Alpes-Dauphiné, *2 pl. André Malraux, Paris; tel: 42 96 08 43 and 42 96 08 56*. **Maison de l'Alsace**, *39 av. des Champs Elysées, Paris; tel: 42 25 93 42 and 42 56 15 94*. **Maison de l'Auvergne**, *194 bis, r. de Rivoli, Paris; tel: 44 55 33 33*.

Maison de l'Aveyron, *46 r. Berger, Paris; tel: 42 36 84 63*. **Maison de la Bretagne**, *17 r. Arrivée, Paris; tel: 45 38 73 15*. **Maison de la Franche-Comté**, *2 blvd de la Madeleine, Paris; tel: 42 66 26 28*. **Maison du Gard**, *53 av. F Roosevelt, Paris; tel: 40 76 07 14*.

Maison des Hautes-Alpes, *4 av. de l'Opéra, Paris; tel: 42 96 05 08*. **Maison du Limousin**, *30 r. Caumartin, Paris; tel: 40 07 04 67*. **Maison du Lot et Garonne**, *15-17 pass Choiseul, Paris; tel: 42 96 51 43 or 42 97 51 43*. **Maison de la Lozère**, *4 r. Hautefeuille, Paris; tel: 43 54 26 64*.

Maison du Nord-Pas de Calais, *1 r. de Châteaudun, Paris; tel: 40 16 07 07*. **Maison du Périgord**, *6 r. Gomboust, Paris; tel: 42 60 38 77*. **Maison Poitou-Charentes**, *68 r. du Cherche Midi, Paris; tel: 42 22 83 74*. **Maison des Pyrenées**, *15 r. Saint Augustin, Paris; tel: 42 86 51 86*. **Maison de la Savoie**, *31, av. de l'Opéra, Paris; tel: 42 61 74 73*.

Useful Addresses in the UK

Consulate General, *21 Cromwell Road, London SW7 2DQ; tel: (0171) 838 2000*. **Maison de la France (Tourist Office)**, *178 Piccadilly, London W1V 0BA; tel: (0171) 244 123*. **French Railways Ltd (SCNF)**, *French Railways House, 179 Piccadilly, London W1V 0BA; tel: (0171) 495 4433*.

Useful Addresses in Ireland

Embassy, *36 Ailesbury Road, Dublin 4; tel: (1) 694 777*. **French Government Tourist Office**, *35 Lower Abbey Street, Dublin 1; tel: (1) 77 18 71*.

Useful Addresses in the USA

Embassy, *4101 Reservoir Road NW, Washington DC 20007; tel: (202) 944 6000*. **French Government Tourist Office**, *610 Fifth Ave., New York, NY 10020-25452; tel: (212) 757 1125*. **Rail enquiries** *Raileurope Inc 226-230 Westchester Ave., White Plains, NY 10604; tel: (800) 682 2999*.

Useful Addresses in Canada

Embassy, *42 Promenade Sussex, Ottawa, Ontario K1M 2C9; tel: (613) 512 1715*. **French Government Tourist Office**, *1 Dundas Street West, Suite 24005, Box 8, Toronto, Ontario; tel: (416) 593 4722*. **Rail enquiries**, *Raileurope Inc, 2087 Dundas East, Suite 100, Mississauga, Ontario L4X IM2; tel: (416) 602 4195*.

Useful Addresses in Australia

Consulate, *31 Market St, Level 26, Sydney NSW 2000; tel: (2) 261 5779*. **French Government Tourist Office**, *BNP House, 12 Castlereagh St, Sydney NSW 2000; tel: (2) 231 5244*. **Thomas Cook Limited**, *175 Pitt St, GPO Box 3590, Sydney NSW 2000; tel: (2) 229 6611 for SNCF tickets* .

Useful Addresses in South Africa

Consulate, *35th Floor, Carlton Centre, Commissioners St, Johannesburg 2001; tel: (11) 333 468*. **French Government Tourist Office**, *PO Box 41022, Craig Hall, Johannesburg 2024; tel: (11) 880 8062*. **SNCF**, *World Travel Agency, PO Box 4568, Johannesburg 2000; tel: (11) 403 2606*.

Arriving and Departing

Air

There is no shortage of choice of flights to France, but the national carrier, Air France, offers the most comprehensive service. Most international flights arrive at the Paris airports, Roissy/Charles-de-Gaulle (*tel: 48 62 22 80*) and Orly (*tel: 49 75 15 15*). There is also a well-developed network of scheduled flights, especially from other European cities, to France's major provincial airports: Bordeaux Merignac (*tel: 56 34 84 84*); Lyon-Satolas (*tel: 72 72 72 21*); Marseille (*tel: 42 89 90 10*); Nice (*tel: 93 21 30 12*); Strasbourg-Entzheim (*tel: 88 78 40 99*), and Toulouse-Blagnac (*tel: 61 42 40 00*).

The national rail company, SNCF (*Société Nationale des Chemins de Fer Français*), produces a useful leaflet, *Pour prendre l'avion, prenez le train* ('To catch your plane, use the train'), available from tourist offices, airports and rail information offices, giving details of current timetables, tariffs and connections to mainline stations.

Coach

Eurolines, *52 Grosvenor Gardens, Victoria, London SW1W 0AU; tel: 0171 730 0202*, run services from London to many destinations in France. There is a daily service between London and Paris with reductions for travellers under 25.

Sea

Ferries tend to be cheaper than the faster SeaCat and Hovercraft crossings. All fares are cheaper from Nov to Easter and most expensive in the peak holiday period, from mid-July to early Sept. Reductions are usually available for children under 14. See p. 55 for details of sailings. The main ferry companies based in Britain are:

Brittany Ferries, *The Brittany Centre, Wharf Road, Portsmouth PO2 8RW; tel: 01705 827701, and Millbay Docks, Plymouth PL1 3EW; tel: 01752 221321*

Stena-Sealink, *Charter House, Park Street, Ashford TN24 8EX; tel: 01233 647047.*

P & O European Ferries, *Channel House, Channel View Road, Dover CT17 9TJ; tel: 01304 203388.*

Sally Line, *81 Piccadilly, London W1V 9HF; tel: 0171 409 2240*

Folkestone Boulogne Ferries, *Tontine House, Tontine Street, Folkestone, Kent CT20 1UB; tel: 01303 24 6880.*

Irish Ferries, *2–4 Merrion Row, Dublin 2; tel: 01 661 0551.*

Hovercraft services between Dover and Calais and Folkestone and Boulogne are operated by **Hoverspeed**, *Western Docks, Dover CT17 9TG; tel: 01304 240241.*

Train

The opening of the Channel Tunnel in 1994 made it possible to take an uninterrupted train journey from Britain to France on **Eurostar**'s specially designed trains. Further details are given on p. 56.

Staying in France

Accommodation

Hotels: prices vary according to facilities, location and season. By law, the tariff must be displayed at the reception and in the rooms. Prices are usually quoted per room; a small supplement may be charges for three or four persons sharing the room. Breakfast (*petit déjeuner*) is generally extra. Hotels with restaurants may offer half board (*demi-pension*) and full board (*pension*).

Local authorities classify hotels on a five-grade scale. 'IC' (*Instance de classement*) against a hotel in information leaflets means that the hotel is waiting for its grade to be awarded. Hotels that are unstarred (*sans étoile*) don't have the facilities required for one star, but might still be good value: look at a room before taking it.

Several organisations in France represent independent hotels, specialist and self-catering accommodation. **Logis de France,** *83 av. d'Italie, 75013 Paris; tel: 45 84 70 00,* lists over 4000 family-run hotels, usually one- or two-star. Members display the Logis' yellow fireplace logo and are often good places to eat, especially for regional specialities. The **Fédération National des Gîtes Ruraux,** *35 r. Godot de Mauroy, 75009 Paris; tel: 47 42 20 20,* can provide information on renting holiday cottages in France. **Relais et Châteaux,** *av. Marceau 9, 75116 Paris; tel: 47 23 41 42,* offer luxurious stays in converted châteaux and manor houses.

Information about **Bed and Breakfast** is available at local tourist offices, and *French Country Welcome,* published annually, gives details of around 14,000 establishments throughout France; copies are available from **Gîtes de France,** *178 Piccadilly, London W1V 9DB* for £10.85 (plus postage).

Youth hostels are open to people of all ages and are a good budget, no-frills option. Membership of a youth hostel association in your own country allows you to use any of the 200-plus hostels in France run by the **Fédération Unie des Auberges de Jeunesse,** *27 r. Pajol, 75018 Paris; tel: 44 89 87 27.* Members of Hostelling International (HI) (the new name for the International Youth Hostel Federation) can also book hostel rooms in advance by letter or fax or using the IBN (International Booking Network; details from local associations). Booking ahead is advisable for popular destinations such as Paris and the south coast, and in peak periods. If you are not a member of an association and a hostel has a vacancy you

can usually buy a Hostelling International Card on the spot.

Some hostels in Paris are open 24 hrs, but the usual opening hours are 0700–1000 and 1700–2200 (later in summer).

The **Ligue Française pour les Auberges de la Jeunesse** also runs more than 90 hostels in France. Details of hostels and membership are available from their head office at *38 blvd Raspail, 75007 Paris; tel: 45 48 69 84.*

Camping: tourist campsites are classified from one to four stars, according to facilities. At the top of the scale many campsites have swimming pools and entertainment. Camping is popular in France, and it's a good idea to book ahead or avoid popular areas in Aug, when the French flock to the coast. Farm campsites (*camping à la ferme*) are an alternative to the more developed sites. By law they are restricted to a maximum of six plots (20 people).

The national camping organisation is the **Fédération Française de Camping et Caravanning,** *r. de Rivoli 78, 75004 Paris; tel: 42 72 84 08.*

Camping Qualité France, *105 r. Lafayette, 75010 Paris; tel: 48 78 13 77,* operates 200 sites throughout France and **Etampes André Trigano,** *111 r. de Reuilly, 75012 Paris; tel: 43 46 07 91,* runs 150 three- and four-star sites.

Don't camp uninvited on private land: always check with the owner and obtain permission first, or you may be liable to prosecution for trespassing.

Cards and Currency

Most major banks, large rail stations and hotels, as well as the Thomas Cook offices listed throughout this book, can exchange foreign currency and travellers' cheques (commission-free if Thomas Cook Travellers

Cheques at Thomas Cook bureaux). If you intend to travel outside the main towns take FFr. travellers' cheques, as exchange facilities are likely to be thinner on the ground. In case of loss or theft of Thomas Cook Travellers Cheques *tel: 05 90 83 30* (toll-free 24-hr line).

Price tags and receipts use a comma between the francs and the centimes, rather than a decimal point.

Credit cards are accepted at most hotels, shops and restaurants, although some smaller establishments may not take them. The Carte Bleue/Visa is ubiquitous, and other major cards such as Eurocard/Access/Mastercard and American Express are also widely accepted.

To report lost or stolen cards phone the following numbers: **VISA/Carte Bleue** *tel: 42 77 11 90* (Paris) or *54 42 12 12* (Provinces); **American Express** *tel: 47 77 72 00*; **MasterCard/Eurocard** *tel: 45 67 84 84.*

Climate

The French climate varies widely according to the region. The south has hot, dry summers and warm, wet winters; northern areas such as Brittany and Normandy are much cooler; and inland, eastern regions tend to have hot summers and cold winters. Local factors such as mountain systems can complicate matters; for instance, the northern Massif Central suffers severe storms in the middle of summer; and the bitingly cold *Mistral* blows down the generally mild Rhône valley in the winter.

Three telephone weather information services are available: a general forecast on *36 68 02* plus the *département* number (France has over 90 administrative regions and each is given a two-digit number that is included in the postal code and found in the telephone directory and post office); coastal weather on *36 68 08* and mountain information on *36 68 04 04.*

Crime

Theft can be a problem in popular tourist areas; don't leave bags and belongings unattended, and don't wander alone into deserted or dubious areas, especially after dark. If anything is stolen, report it to the police (either *Gendarmeries Nationales* or *Police Nationale*) immediately – this is often a requirement of insurance policies. Police have a right to stop anyone at any time to request and inspect identity documents.

Disabled Travellers

A guide for travellers with a disability, *Touristes Quand-Même*, is available from *28 blvd Raspail, 75007 Paris; tel: 45 48 90 13*, providing general information on facilities and acccess in France. See p. 16 for information details in the UK and USA.

People who are registered blind can take a companion free of charge on SNCF journeys with a full fare return ticket (an official certificate is provided when you buy the ticket).

Food and Drink

Eating out is one of the great pleasures of France. Although in recent years a little complacency – and a touch of Euro-standardisation – has crept in, France can still offer unparalleled eating experiences. If you avoid the obvious tourist traps, you can eat extremely well for surprisingly few francs, especially if you choose the set-price menus, usually based on three courses.

Breakfast, served in cafés and restaurants, is usually a light meal – a baguette or croissant with butter or jam, and coffee or hot chocolate. Lunch is served from midday until around 1400, and for dinner restaurants take orders from about 1900, with the rush coming between 2000 and 2100. Outside major tourist centres it's unusual for orders to be taken after 2100. **Brasseries** tend to be more flexible than restaurants, though they offer a more limited choice of food.

Cafés usually charge less to eat or drink while standing at the counter (*comptoir*) than to sit at a table (*salle*) or outside (*terrasse*).

Restaurants offer a range of set-price meals (*menu*) as well as the full menu choice (*à la carte*), which is usually more expensive. In some restaurants, especially in summer and in prime tourist locations, only the more expensive menus are on offer if you sit outside.

Prices displayed outside restaurants should include all charges, including service, usually 15%. Customers can leave tips if they are especially pleased with the service.

Under recent legislation smoking is restricted in cafés and restaurants, which are supposed to provide non-smoking areas – but don't bank on it.

France has its own well-established fast food tradition – baguette sandwiches at cafés, *crêpes* and *frites* (chips) at roadside stalls; the Quick chain is a French answer to McDonalds and Burger King, who also have a firm foothold in major cities.

Health

Travellers from EU countries and North America do not need vaccinations. Rabies is present in France and there are restrictions on the importation of animals. Don't approach stray animals or animals behaving strangely, especially in the wild.

Tourist offices have lists of doctors, dentists and pharmacists (and can tell you which ones speak English). French pharmacists are qualified dispensers and can sell a wide range of drugs without prescription and provide advice about minor health problems. There is an emergency rota – *Pharmacie de grade* – which is usually displayed on the door of every pharmacy, in local newspapers and in the police station.

If you need medication regularly take an up-to-date prescription with details of the trade name and pharmaceutical name of the drug(s) you require, the name of the manufacturer and details of the precise dosage (it may be useful to get a French translation of the prescription as well). You may also be asked for your address as part of the dispensing procedure.

If you already have private medical insurance check that it will cover you while you are in France; if not, you may be able to extend the cover to include your visit for an additional premium. EU residents are entitled to reduced cost health care in France under reciprocal arrangements between member states. To claim this get form E111 from the social security authorities before travelling. To reclaim money after treatment you need an authorised form from the doctor to present to the local sickness insurance office (*Caisse Primaries d'Assurance Malade*).

Maps

The *Institut Géographique National* (IGN) is the official cartographic body in France; the IGN Map 901, a general map of France (scale 1 cm = 10 km), is good for planning countrywide routes. Specialist maps include Map 902 (1 cm = 10 km), showing major historic sites; Map 903 (1 cm = 10 km), which traces the national long distance footpaths; Map 906 (1 cm = 1 km), designed for cyclists; and various Outdoor

Activities maps (1 cm = 1 km) for national parks and tourist areas.

The most useful regional maps are the *Série Verte* (Green Series), covering mainland France in 74 sheets (scale 1 cm = 1 km) and, for cycling or walking, the *Série Bleue* (Blue Series), with 2000 sheets and a detailed scale of 4 cm = 1 km.

Local maps and plans can usually be bought at tourist offices, which often have perfectly adequate free town maps as well.

Opening Hours

Banks: Mon–Fri or Tues–Sat 0900–1200 and 1400–1600 or 1700. Banks usually close early on the day before a public holiday.

Shops: Mon–Sat 0900–1200 and 1430–1830; food shops tend to open earlier and on Sun mornings. In the south and country areas the midday break is longer and evening opening hours are longer, especially in the summer.

Museums: Generally 0900–1600 (extended evening hours may operate in the summer). Most national museums close on Tues; municipal museums tend to close on Mon. On Sun, entrance is often free or for a reduced fee. All museums tend to close on public holidays, Easter Sun and Mon and at Christmas.

Post Offices

Post offices open Mon–Fri 0800–1200 and 1430–1900, Sat 0800–1200; offices in town and city centres don't usually close for lunch. They're easily recognised by their yellow signs with *La Poste* in blue. Post boxes, small metal boxes fixed to the wall, are also yellow.

There can be long queues at post office counters, but many now have self-service franking machines which weigh letters and packages and print franked stickers (there's usually an English-language instructions option). Coin-operated stamp machines provide FFr.20 booklets (it costs FFr.2.80 to send a postcard within the EU, FFr.4.30 to the USA). Stamps can also be bought from shops and cafés showing the red diamond-shaped Tabac sign.

You can have post sent for collection c/o Poste Restante, Poste Centrale, in most towns, and offices will hold mail for up to a month. To collect you have to show proof of identity – usually a passport or driver's licence – and pay a small fee.

Public Holidays

France has 11 official public holidays, most of which mark religious occasions, though some celebrate historical events.

New Year 1 Jan; **Easter Monday** late Mar or early Apr; **Labour Day** 1 May; **VE Day** 8 May; **Ascension Day** five weeks after Easter Day; **Whit Monday** late May; **Bastille Day** 14 July; **Assumption** 15 Aug; **All Saints** 1 Nov; **Armistice Day** 11 Nov; and **Christmas** 25 Dec.

Holidays are sometimes extended by shops and cafés if they fall on Tues or Thurs, to include the preceding Mon or following Fri.

Telephones

The French telephone system, run by the state-owned France Telecom, is considered one of the best in the world. Public phone boxes, which are widely available, are free-standing clear glass cabins with *Téléphone* signs or the France Telecom logo (a digital dialling pad enclosed in an oval) on the handle. In city centres and major tourist centres phones have instructions in English and French (including current tariff and international dialling codes). There are some coin-operated phone boxes but most now take only phone cards (*télécartes*), sold at post offices and newsagents. A 50 unit card costs FFr.40 and a 120 unit card costs FFr.96.

There are two telephone regions within France: Paris and the Provinces. All numbers have eight digits. Paris numbers start with a 4, provincial numbers with either a 3 or a 6. The prefix for calls from Paris to the provinces is 16, and from the provinces to Paris 161. Domestic calls are cheaper on weekdays between 2230 and 0800 and at weekends after 1400 on Saturday. For the operator call 13 and dial 12 for Directory Enquiries.

International calls can be made from phone boxes and some large post offices have a metered call service, where you book a booth, make the call and then pay. To dial abroad dial 00 and wait for the dialling tone, then dial the country code (44 for the UK, 353 for Ireland, 1 for USA or Canada, 61 for Australia, 64 for New Zealand, 27 for South Africa) and finally the area code (excluding the first 0) and the number. For the international operator, dial 00, wait for the dialling tone and then dial 33 12 and the country code. France Telecom produces a credit card-sized leaflet, *Call home with télécarte*, which explains how to use a phone card and how to phone internationally, and gives current tariff and country dialling codes.

To phone France from abroad dial your own international code, e.g. 00 from the UK, 011 from the USA then 33, except for Paris, which is 331, then the eight-digit number.

Emergency calls are free. For the police, dial 17; for the fire service (*Pompiers*), dial 18; and for ambulance and emergency medical care (SAMU), dial 15.

Toilets

Toilets are usually single-sex (Men: *Messieurs*; women: *Dames*), but automatic coin-operated unisex cabins are now a familiar feature in streets and parks.

In public places such as stations, there is often an attendant collecting money at the entrance; you may be expected to pay for toilet paper.

Transport

Coaches and buses: Most long-distance coaches are international services in transit through France. Bus and coach lines tend to provide local and regional transport, supplementing rail services. Information and timetables are available locally from tourist information offices and bus stations (*gares routières*). Regional transport authorities and SNCF produce a free regional service guide, *Guide Regional des Transports*, which provides information about train and bus services between major towns.

Taxis pick up from ranks (*stations de taxi*) on main streets, stations etc. Before getting in, check that the cab is licensed and has a meter. The conventional tip is 10–15 per cent of the fare.

Bicycles can usually be taken on the train free of charge, but on some busy services and inter-city trains space is limited and there may be restrictions or a supplement to pay. SNCF publishes a leaflet, *Guide du Train et du Vélo*, which gives details. Cycles can be hired in most towns and villages, and in many SCNF stations. The three types of bikes available are basic, 'Rover' 10-speed bikes (FFr.44 a day with a deposit of FFr.1000), and mountain bikes (FFr.55 a day and a FFr.1500 deposit).

For more information on cycling in France contact the **Fédération Française de Cyclotourisme**, *8 r. Jean-Marie Jégo 75013 Paris*; *tel: 45 80 30 21.*

BELGIUM

Capital: Brussels (Bruxelles/Brussel). **Language:** Belgium has three official language areas: some small regions to the east are German-speaking, the north is Flemish and the south is French, with Brussels being bilingual. Most Belgians speak both French and Flemish and many (especially the young) also speak reasonable English and/or German. English usually receives a better response in the Flemish areas. **Currency:** Belgian Francs (BFr.). The 5-franc and 20-franc pieces are very similar in size and colour, so be careful until you learn to distinguish between them. Some machines accept a variety of coins, but all take 5-franc pieces (many exclusively), so keep a reasonable supply. Credit cards are widely recognised, but generally unwelcome unless you are spending major sums.

Passports and Visas

A British Visitor's Passport (available until Jan 1996) is sufficient, as are EU National Identity Cards. All other travellers need full passports. Visas are not needed by nationals of the EU, Australia, Canada, New Zealand or the USA. Others should check.

Customs

Standard EU regulations apply (see p. 15), but there's an extra allowance of 8 litres of Luxembourg wines, if imported directly across the Luxembourg border.

Tourist Information

Two full-colour brochures which are very useful are *Guide to Tourist Attractions* and the more detailed *Belgium Historic Cities*, both of which cover the whole of Belgium and are available from Belgian tourist offices both inside and outside the country. The latter costs BFr.50 if you don't get it in advance.

In French areas, tourist offices are **Office du Tourisme**, in Flemish areas **Toerisme**, in German areas **Verkehrsamt**, but it's usually easier to spot the universal logo: a white 'i' on a green background. An 'i' on a blue background indicates information of some kind, but seldom a tourist office. Opening hours in smaller places should be regarded as flexible, especially out of peak seasons, since it's not at all unusual for them to open late or take a break when things are quiet.

They provide every type of information, but usually charge for such detailed literature as walking itineraries and good street maps. There's an English-language version of almost all literature and most tourist offices have English-speaking staff.

A weekly English-language publication called *The Bulletin* (and its supplement *What's On*) is available from newsagents for BFr.80 and lists everything from films in English to job opportunities throughout the country.

Useful Addresses in the UK

Belgian Embassy, *103 Eaton Square, Victoria, London SW1W 9AB; tel: (0171) 235 5422.* **Belgian Tourist Office**, *29 Princes St, London W1R 7RG; tel: (0171) 629 0230.*

Useful Addresses in the USA

Belgian Embassy, *3330 Garfield St NW, Washington DC 20008; tel: (202) 333-6900.* **Belgian Tourist Office and National Railroads**, *780 Third Avenue (Suite 1501), New York, NY 10017; tel: (212) 758-8130.*

Useful Address in Australia

Embassy, *Arkana Street, Yarralumla, Canberra, ACT 2600; tel: (6) 273 2501.*

Useful Address in Canada

Embassy, *80 Elgin Street, 4th Floor, Ottawa, Ontario K1P 1B7; tel: (613) 236 7267.*

Useful Address in New Zealand

Embassy, *Willis Coroon House, 2th Floor, 1–3 Willeston Street, Wellington; tel: (4) 472 9558.*

Useful Address in South Africa

Embassy, *625 Leyds Street, Muckleneuk, 0002 Pretoria; tel: (12) 44 3201.*

Staying in Belgium

Accommodation

The Benelux countries (Belgium, the Netherlands and Luxembourg) have a common hotel-rating system and all hotels must display a blue plaque showing their rating. The lowest rating is 'O' (accommodation only, but meeting minimum requirements of hygiene and comfort); the next is 'H' (moderately comfortable, with at least one bathroom per ten rooms). After that, you're onto the usual star system, one-star places being obliged (as a minimum) to have a wash-stand in every room and to serve breakfast. Hotel rates must be displayed in reception and also in bedrooms, the rates shown including VAT and service charges. Breakfast may, or may not, be included.

Hotel accommodation in Belgium tends to be pricey and you're unlikely to get anything anywhere for less than BFr.1000 (BFr.700 single). Tourist offices don't charge for booking hotels (they take a deposit which is deducted from your bill) and can often get reduced rates.

Literature about accommodation is almost always free. Campsites and hostels are normally included in the hotel brochures, while bed and breakfast places are listed separately. Tourist offices can sometimes be persuaded to check availability. Rough camping (on beaches, etc.) is not permitted and you must use official campsites, unless you can get permission from a farmer to camp on his land.

In summer, accommodation of all kinds can be hard to find and it's sensible to pre-book, especially in Bruges and on the coast. **Belgium Tourist Reservations**, *blvd Anspach 111; tel: (02) 513 74 84; fax (02) 513 92 77*, offer a free service for hotel reservations throughout Belgium.

You can get a leaflet listing star-rated campsites from your nearest Belgian tourist office. For further information, contact the provincial tourist authorities.

Discounts

Belgium offers a wide range of discounts, especially on travel and entertainment, for the old and the young, so always check.

Escalators

Escalators are activated by weight, with signs indicating their direction. If nothing happens when you step on (quite common in the Brussels metro), it's out of order and you'll have to walk.

Food and Drink

Belgian food is very varied and the cuisines of most countries are represented – at a price. You get what you pay for, and top quality (which is as good as you can get anywhere) demands a generous budget.

Most restaurants have fixed-price *menus* (*plat du jour, tourist menu, dagschotel*) which are much cheaper than à la carte. There's a wide variation in prices and establishments in the main squares often charge two or three times as much as similar places in nearby side streets. Try the waffles (*wafels/gaufres*), mussels (*moules*), ice cream, savoury pancakes (*crêpes*), freshly-baked *petit pain au chocolat* (croissants with chocolate) and other pastries. The most common snack is (*fritures/frituurs/frites*), a cross between french fries and English-style chips with mayonnaise or other sauces.

Sweets of all kinds are ubiquitous, notably nougat and the deservedly famous chocolates: note that the ones containing cream have a short shelf-life and check the sell-by date of pre-packaged ones – whatever the salesperson says.

Tea is usually with lemon unless you specify milk (you get cream), but the coffee and hot chocolate are delicious. It is easy (though not cheap) to get freshly squeezed orange and lemon. Many bottled juices are low in sugar and refreshing. Belgium produces over three hundred beers (both dark and light).

Opening Hours

Banks: Mon–Fri 0900–1600, but some close for lunch. **Shops:** Mon–Sat 0900/1000–1800/1900 (often later Fri/Sat), but some close 1200–1400.

Museums: there's considerable variation, but most open six days a week: 1000–1700 (many closing for two hours over lunch). Last tickets are often sold 30 mins or more before closing time. The official closing day is usually Mon or Tues, but smaller places are unpredictable and can be closed at any time, so it's inadvisable to go too far out of your way. **Churches:** as a rule of thumb, these open at much the same times as museums (except when there are services), but few (other than the major places that charge an entrance fee) specify opening times and, even if they do, you can't count on them,

---

Belgian Beers

Beer is to the Belgians what wine is to the French, and is one aspect of life in which all the nation's language-groups are united.

The art of beer-making in Belgium, much of it derived from a long and surviving tradition of monastic brewing, has produced a variety found nowhere else. The range of highly individual beers still associated with abbey breweries includes the strong Chimay and the ultra-dry Leffe. The standard light lager type of beer is ubiquitous and made to a high standard, including such well-known brands as Stella Artois, but it would be a shame to visit Belgium and not to sample the more individual brews, such as *lambic*, made with wheat and fermented by natural airborne yeast, or *kriek* (*lambic* flavoured strongly with bitter cherries – tasting as unusual as it sounds).

Belgian beers are generally strong, and some are very strong, being preferred to spirits to round off an evening at the café.

---

so which are open is largely a matter of luck.

Postage

Major **post offices** (*Postes/Posterijen/De Post*) are open Mon–Fri 0900–1700 (some also open Fri evening and Sat morning), but the counters for special services often open for shorter hours. Smaller branches usually close 1200–1400. Stamps can be purchased at most places that sell postcards.

Post boxes are bright red and attached to walls or free-standing poles.

Public Holidays

1 Jan; Easter Monday; 1 May; Ascension Day; Whit Monday; 21 July; 15 Aug; 1, 11 Nov; 25 Dec. Nothing opens 1 Jan or 25 Dec. On other holidays many places close, but others open (Sun hours), so check locally.

Tipping

Restaurant bills include a service charge (16.5%) and you need not leave anything extra. Similarly, tip taxi drivers only if you want to. Porters at rail stations (if you can find one) expect BFr.60 per piece. If you are shown to your seat in a theatre, etc., tip BFr.20 per person. Cloakroom attendants should be given BFr.50–100 per garment. Hotel bills include service, but long-term guests usually give something extra to (at least) the room maid. The norm for manned WCs is BFr.10 and that's what you should leave if there's no sign (slot machines need BFr.5).

Telephones

The national company is **Belgacom**. There are coin boxes (which take 5-franc and 20-franc coins) and Telecard booths (which don't accept credit cards). Telecards can be purchased at rail stations, post offices and some tobacconists. All booths have English instructions. Numbers prefixed 077 are at premium rates.

Calls to North America and the British Isles are at reduced rates Mon–Sat 2000–0800 and all day Sun.

To call abroad from Belgium: *tel: 00*. To call Belgium from abroad: *tel: 32*. For the national operator: *tel: 1307 (1207* in Flemish areas). For the European operator: *tel: 1304 (1204* in Flemish areas). For the international operator: *tel: 1323 (1223* in Flemish areas). International operators speak English. **Emergencies:** Police: *tel: 101*; Fire/Ambulance: *tel: 100*; Red Cross: *tel: 1050*

Transport

The national bus companies are **De Lijn** in Flemish areas and **Tec** in French areas, but there are few long-distance buses except in areas where the rail network is scanty. The main rail and bus stations are usually close together.

Buses, Trams and **Metros:** You generally open the doors yourself. When there are no handles, there's a pictogram by a button close to the doors, or beside a black strip (usually on the outside) which you have to push. If you have a ticket you can board buses/trams by whichever door is nearest. If not, board at the front and buy one from the driver. Get off by any other door.

Each city offers **multi-ride cards** (valid nowhere else), which are normally for ten rides and pay their way if you make more than six journeys. You must validate them in the yellow box whenever you board a new bus/tram or at the entrance to a metro, but each is valid for an hour (i.e. travel must be completed within 60 mins – if it isn't, you must re-validate) and nothing is deducted if your last journey was less than 60 mins before. Drivers issue single tickets, but you should get multi-ride cards from rail stations, bus-line offices or tourist offices before boarding. It is in order for more than one person to use a multi-ride card: just validate it once per person.

Taxis have roof signs. It's legal to hail them in the street, but drivers tend to ignore signals and it's better to find a rank (there's invariably one at the rail station), or to telephone. The rate per km varies, but it always doubles if you go outside the city limits.

THE NETHERLANDS

Capital: The Netherlands has two capitals. Amsterdam is administrative and The Hague (Den Haag) is legislative. **Language**: Dutch is the official language. English is almost universal, German is widely spoken and French to a lesser degree. The universal greeting is *Dag* (pronounded like 'dark' with the 'k' catching in the throat). If you say this in a friendly manner and then continue in English, etiquette is observed and you need not feel awkward about speaking no Dutch. The chief problem with pronunciation is the guttural 'g'. It helps to remember that *ui* is pronounced 'ow' and *ij* is the equivalent of 'y' (and interchangeable with it). **Currency**: Guilders; 1 guilder = 100 cents. Guilders were once known as florins and price tags usually show 'f' or 'fl', although 'Dfl', 'Hfl' and 'NLG' are sometimes used in literature. This book uses 'DG'. Major credit cards are recognised, but their acceptance is fairly limited.

Passports and Visas

A British Visitor's Passport (until Jan 1996) is sufficient, as are EU National Identity Cards. Other travellers need full passports. Visas are not needed by nationals of the EU, Australia, Canada, New Zealand or the USA. Others should check.

Tourist Information

Tourist bureaux within the Netherlands are **Vereniging voor Vreemdelingenverkeer**, universally known as **VVV** (pronounced *Vay-vay-vay*), with offices in virtually every town: signs show a triangle with three Vs. They have English-speaking staff and most literature has an English section. VVV provide a comprehensive service, but charge (DG4) for making bookings. Mini-mum opening times (except public holidays): Mon–Fri 0900–1700, Sat 1000–1200. Most open longer.

Very little literature is free, but there's usually a general-purpose leaflet for around DG3 which includes an outline map. The suggested walking routes average 1 hr 30 mins and provide an excellent way of seeing the things of major architectural and historical significance, but seldom include other attractions.

Many attractions close Oct–Easter, while Apr–May is tulip time and the country is crowded, so (unless you want to see the tulips) June–Sept is the best time to visit.

Plan to spend Sun–Mon in large places with a variety of attractions: on Sun public transport can be sparse, some VVV offices are closed and most attractions open for only short hours; on Mon many museums are closed.

Electronic information machines are understandable if you remember that *gesloten* means 'closed' and know the days of the week: *Zo(ndag)* – Sun, *Ma(andag)* – Mon, *Di(nsdag)* – Tues, *Wo(ensdag)* – Wed, *Do(nderdag)* – Thur, *Vr(ijdag)* – Fri and *Za(terdag)* – Sat. So: *ma t/m vr* is Mon–Fri.

Geen and *verboden* indicate prohibitions: *Geen toegang* means 'No entry'. It's worth noting that *uit/uitgang* may not mean an exit: sometimes they just indicate the next place on a suggested route.

If signposts run out before you reach your objective, continue in the same direction. An arrow pointing at the ground means you should go straight ahead: for descents to a different level the arrow is generally at an angle.

Useful Addresses in the UK

Netherlands Embassy, *38 Hyde Park Gate, London SW7 5DP; tel: (0171) 584 5040.*

Netherlands Board of Tourism (NBT), *Egginton House, 25/28 Buckingham Gate, London SW1E 6LD; tel: (0891) 200 277. Or: PO Box 523, London SW1E 6NT.* **Netherlands Railways**, *c/o Board of Tourism; tel: (0171) 630 1735.*

Useful Addresses in the USA

Embassy, *4200 Linnean Avenue NW, Washington, DC 20008-1848; tel: (202) 244 5304.* **Netherlands Board of Tourism**, *355 Lexington Avenue (21st Floor), New York, NY 10017; tel: (212) 370 7367.*

Useful Addresses in Australia

Embassy, *120 Empire Circuit, Yarralumla, Canberra, ACT 2600; tel: (06) 273 3111.*

Useful Addresses in Canada

Embassy, *Suite 2020, 350 Albert Street, Ottawa, Ontario, KIR 1A4; tel: (613) 237 5030.* **Tourist Office**, *25 Adelaide St E., Suite 710, Toronto, Ontario, M5C 1Y2; tel: (416) 363 1577.*

Useful Addresses in Ireland

Embassy, *160 Merrion Rd, Dublin 4; tel: (01) 269 3444.*

Useful Addresses in South Africa

Embassy, *PO Box 117, Pretoria 0001; tel: (012) 344 3910.*

Embassies in The Netherlands

Unusually, these are not all in the same city. **Australia:** *Carnegielaan 14, The Hague; tel: (070) 310 8200.* **Canada:** *Sophialaan 7, The Hague; tel: (070) 361 4111.* **New Zealand:** *Mauritskade 25, The Hague; tel: (070) 346 9324.* **Republic of Ireland:** *dr. Kuyperstraat 9, The Hague; tel: (070) 363 0993.* **UK:** *Koningslaan 44, Amsterdam; tel: (020) 676 4343.* **USA:** *Museumplein 19, Amsterdam; tel: (020) 664 5661.*

Staying in The Netherlands

Accommodation

The Netherlands participates in the Benelux hotel-classification scheme (see Belgium, p. 40). NBT produce full-colour brochures listing hotels (all grades) and campsites.

Standards are high: low prices reflect limited facilities rather than lack of cleanliness or comfort. Room rates start around DG45 single (DG65 double), so hostels and camping represent a considerable saving.

Advance booking is advisable. There's a free central booking service: **Netherlands Reservation Centre (NRC)**, *PO Box 404, 2260 AK Leidschendam; English-language tel: (070) 320 2500.* NRC have a London branch (*in NBT; tel: (0171) 931 0801*), but they do charge (£7).

The HQ of the **Dutch Youth Hostels Association (NJHC)** is *Prof. Tulpplein 4, 1018 GX Amsterdam; tel: (020) 551 3155.*

Rooms in private houses (from around DG25) can be booked through **Bed and Breakfast Holland**, *Warmondstraat 129 1e; tel: (020) 615 7527.* It's always worth asking, but this type of accommodation is common only in coastal areas and Gelderland.

Disabled Travellers

The Dutch are sympathetic to the problems of disabled people and many attractions have special facilities. For information, *tel: (030) 355 555.*

Discounts

Many passes require a passport photo, so always carry a couple with you. If you are a senior citizen, student or young (under 18 is the norm), ask whether you are entitled to a discount.

The **Museumjaarkaart** (from VVV and all participating museums; DG40) is valid for a year and provides free entry to the majority of museums and even to some special exhibitions. If you are not particularly into museums, consider getting a **Kortingkaart** (DG12.50), which provides reductions for museum entry.

Anyone under 26 can ask VVV for a **CJP (Cultureel Jongeren Paspoort)**, which costs DG20 and provides discounts on museums and some cultural events.

Food and Drink

The *Nederlands Dis* sign (featuring a red, white and blue soup tureen) indicates somewhere offering Dutch specialities. There are many Indonesian restaurants, for spicy food, and the cities offer a good variety of international cuisine. Bars and food stalls abound.

Mensas are subsidised student canteens (very cheap and not restricted to students), found in all university towns, but open only during term-time. Most eating-places stay open all day. Outside towns, many restaurants take last orders by 2100.

Some establishments offer a *dagschotel* (one course for around DG12.50) or a *tourist menu* (three courses for DG25). For good value, try a 'brown café': a traditional pub that serves food.

Dutch cuisine is simple and substantial. Try the ubiquitous apple pie (heavy on cinnamon and sultanas), herring marinated in brine, steamed eels, white asparagus, *poffertjes* (tiny puff-pancakes with icing sugar), *pannekoeken* (pancakes with sweet and/or savoury fillings: try bacon with syrup). Everywhere you go you will find *frites/patats* (a cross between thin french fries and English-style chips), usually served with mayonnaise (25c extra), but in Limburg you may have the option of *zurvlees* (a slightly sour regional speciality). Vending machines at stations sell croquettes (DG1.50) – *bami* and *nasi* are spicy.

Excellent coffee is ubiquitous, as are tea and hot chocolate. Chocolate is usually delicious (often topped with whipped cream – *slagroom*). Tea is a glass of hot water with (usually) a choice of teabags and you have to ask specifically for milk.

Dutch beer is served with two fingers of froth on top. Most of the local liqueurs are excellent. The main spirit is *jenever*, a strong gin made from juniper berries.

Opening Hours

Banks: Mon–Fri 0900–1600/1700, later on Thur. **Shops:** Mon–Sat 0900/0930–1730/1800 (till 2100 Thur or Fri), Sat 0900/0930–1600/1700. Many close Mon morning and one afternoon a week. Non-EU citizens can reclaim VAT (18.5%) if they spend DG300 in one go. **Museums:** These vary, but the norm is Tues–Sat 1000–1700, Sun 1100–1700.

In many public places, such as post offices, you take a ticket from a machine and wait until your number comes up. In others you queue – behind the line if one is marked, otherwise at least a metre from the person being served. It's considered impolite to crowd someone who's doing business.

Postage

The **post office** logo is *ptt post*. Post offices open Mon–Fri 0830–1700, but some larger ones also open Sat 0830–1200. There's an information number about postal services and charges: *tel: (06) 0417*. Most places that sell postcards also sell the stamps .

Public Holidays

1 Jan; Good Friday; Easter Sun–Mon; 30 Apr; 5 May (Liberation Day); Ascension Day; Whit Sunday–Mon; 25, 26 Dec.

Almost nothing opens on 25 Dec or 1 Jan. On other public holidays, expect Sun hours and check locally.

Telephones

The Dutch telephone system is being standardised to ten digit numbers (including the area code). This process is expected to be complete by Oct 1995 and any number consisting of less than ten digits should be changing in the immediate future.

Most hotel rooms have phones, but don't use them unless you have checked the charges or are prepared to pay well over the odds. You should also check the rates at telephone service centres.

Phone booths have instructions in English. Coin boxes take 25c and DG1 coins. Any excess goes towards another call provided you replace the receiver for less than a second. Card-operated boxes accept major credit cards, as well as *telefoonkaarten* (available from post offices, VVV and NS).

Reduced rates for international calls apply Sat–Sun and weekday evenings. For the British Isles, the cheap time is 2000–0800; for North America 1900–1000; for Australia and New Zealand midnight–0700 and 1500–2000.

If you get a recorded message in Dutch, hold on – it will probably be repeated in English.

To call abroad from the Netherlands: *tel: 00*. To call the Netherlands from abroad: *tel: 31*. For the operator: *tel: (06) 0410*. For international directory enquiries: *tel: (06) 0418*. For national directory enquiries: *tel: (06) 8008*.

Emergencies: Police/Fire/Ambulance: *06 11* (no charge).

There is an increasing tendency for information numbers to be centralised and prefixed by '06', with premium rates (usually 50c per min, but occasionally DG1 per min).

Tipping

Fifteen per cent, on top of VAT (18.5%), is usually included in hotel and restaurant bills and no tip is needed. Give DG1 to guides/skippers of small boats. Doormen expect 50c–DG1 if they call a cab, hotel bellhops DG1 per bag, but rail porters look for DG2.50 per bag.

Toilets

For machines, you require 25c coins. Where there's an attendant, the going rate is usually 40–50c. Street public conveniences are non-existent, but every museum and department store has them, so does every café – for customers.

Transport

Centralised numbers cover all enquiries. For domestic services, *tel: (06) 9292*; for international journeys, *tel: (06) 9293*. Computers check the connections, so the service is fast and accurate, but calls are at premium rates.

Trains, metros, buses and trams are equipped with (yellow) buttons, inside and out, so you can open the doors yourself if necessary.

Buses and Trams: stops are identified by yellow squares showing the numbers and destinations of all lines using them, so you can check you are waiting in the right place. Most also display a (white) timetable. Sometimes terminals have more than one stop for the same bus number (depending on direction), so check the route and, if your destination isn't shown, look for another stop – or ask.

Most buses are boarded by the front door, the driver validating tickets, and you get off by the middle or rear doors. City buses and trams, however, carry little yellow boxes in which you validate your own ticket, so board by whichever door is nearest. When you want to get off, ring the bell.

Tell drivers where you're going and ask them to call out when you reach the stop – many will then point you in the right direction for the museum, etc. Ask which stop you will need for your return/onward journey, because this is often far from obvious.

On Sun (and holidays) bus services are erratic and often stop early, so check details for your return journey (including bus numbers, which can vary during the day) before you set out.

Politeness prevails, the young and healthy being expected to give up their seats to the old and infirm.

All **taxis** have a sign on the roof and it is customary to phone, or board them at ranks. You can try hailing them in the street, but you'll be lucky if one stops. They are expensive and it's usual to round the metered fare up to the next guilder.

Treintaxis also have a rank at stations and a roof sign. No money changes hands: you buy treintaxi tickets for specific towns from any rail ticket office. The fare is a flat DG6 for anywhere within the city limits. They have to wait 10 mins unless there's a full load (four passengers), but are good value if you are staying on the outskirts (likely if you're using hostels). They are not available in Amsterdam, The Hague or Rotterdam.

Tickets and Passes: Strippenkaart is a strip ticket (DG12.50 for 15 strips, DG32.25 for 45 strips) available from stations, post offices, VVV (sometimes) and city transport companies. Strips are valid on all bus, tram and metro services country-wide: you use one section to board plus one for each travel zone. Once stamped, a strip is valid for an hour, even if you change from one form of transport to another (unless you increase the number of zones). You need only the minimum two strips for travel within any city centre (*Centrum*).

Individual tickets, also valid for an hour, can be purchased on boarding, but this is uneconomical.

Inspectors operate checks and impose hefty on-the-spot fines if you cannot produce a valid ticket. They are unimpressed by foreigners' pleas of ignorance.

Bicycles: if you're in shape, cycling is undoubtedly the best way to get around quieter areas and travelling by train entitles you to a discount on bikes hired at rail stations. Contact your nearest Dutch tourist office for information about hiring or taking your own bicycle on trains. If you don't usually cycle, try a couple of short rides before you get ambitious.

Walking

Non-walkers should ask for elaboration when told somewhere is 'not far', but there's no shortage of benches and other perches for a brief rest. There are also plenty of alfresco cafés.

Unless there are 'don't walk' symbols, pedestrians have the right of way at marked crossings and most cars stop even before you start to cross. The same cannot be said for bicycles, but they're adept at avoiding you.

Where there are separate areas for cyclists and pedestrians, they are largely ignored – so always glance over your shoulder before changing direction.

If there's a green light at the end of a stationary escalator, step on: your weight will make it start.

The Netherlands have a hard-drugs problem and the police are very alert, so leave fast if a street dealer tries to engage your attention.

LUXEMBOURG

Capital: Luxembourg City (Ville de Luxembourg). **Language**: Lëtzebuergesch is the national tongue (a German language with some French words that's a bit like Dutch), but almost everybody also speaks fluent French and/or German and a great number speak at least some English. **Currency**: Luxembourg Francs (LFr.). Belgian and Luxembourg francs are co-rated and Belgian money is accepted everywhere. It works less easily the other way round, however, so try not to get left with Luxembourg francs when you leave. Credit cards are widely recognised, but often refused unless you are spending sizable amounts.

Passports and Visas

The same as for Belgium; see p. 39. Those needing to check if a visa is required should do so – with their nearest Belgian consulate if Luxembourg has no representation in their country.

Customs

Standard EU regulations apply; see p. 15.

Tourist Information

As it is such a small country, literature covering the whole Grand Duchy is the norm and you can get most of it from any tourist office in (or outside) the country. They produce an annual *Calendar of Events* and *Grand Duchy of Luxembourg*, a brochure containing miscellaneous information for visitors.

Most tourist literature is free and, unless you want detailed information, this will be more than adequate.

Useful Addresses in the UK

Embassy, *27 Wilton Crescent, London SW1X 8SD; tel: (0171) 235 6961.* **Luxembourg National Tourist Office**, *122 Regent Street, London W1R 5FE; tel: (0171) 434 2800.*

Useful Addresses in the USA

Embassy, *2200 Massachusetts Avenue NW, Washington DC 20008; tel: (202) 265 4171.* **Luxembourg National Tourist Office**, *17 Beekman Place, New York, NY 10022; tel: (212) 935 8888.*

Staying in Luxembourg

Accommodation

Your nearest branch of the Luxembourg National Tourist Office should be able to provide free brochures covering hotels, apartments, farm holidays and camping in the Grand Duchy and a bed and breakfast booklet that covers the Benelux countries.

Camping Guidage (tel: *48 11 99*) keeps a day-to-day record of where there are vacancies. It's manned daily 1100–1930 at times when space is likely to be a problem.

Food and Drink

Most hotels serve breakfast until 1000. Lunch is around 1200–1400 and dinner 1900–2200.

Luxembourg cuisine is pithily described as 'French quality, German quantity', but eating out is expensive. Keep costs down by making lunch your main meal and looking for the special deals: *plat du jour* (single course) or *menu* (two or three courses). Some local specialities are: Ardennes ham, *treipen* (black pudding), *quenelles* (calf's liver dumplings), *thüringer* (the standard local sausage), *grompere-kichelcher* (fried potato patties) and (in Sept) *quetschentaart* (a flan featuring dark-violet plums).

Luxembourg produces a variety of lagers, liqueurs and white wines. Sugar may not be added while making wine, so the Moselles are drier and fruitier than their German equivalents.

Opening Hours

Banks: Usually Mon–Fri 0800/0900–1200 and 1300–1600, but some stay open a little later and many don't close for lunch. **Shops:** Mon 1300/1400–1800; Tues–Sat 0900–1800, but some close for lunch. **Museums:** Vary, but most open six days a week (Mon being the usual closing day) and (except in peak season) close over lunch.

Postage

Post offices *(Poste)* usually open Mon–Fri 0800–1200 and 1400–1700. Post boxes (small, bright yellow and attached to walls) are marked *Postes*.

Tipping

Hotel and restaurant bills include service charges, but you can round up to the nearest LFr.50–100. Bellhops and doormen expect LFr.50–100 (depending on the grade of hotel), more if they do something special. Cloakroom attendants are usually left LFr.20 per coat. Unless otherwise stated, the charge in WCs is LFr.10 when there's an attendant (the slot machines take 5-franc pieces). Give taxi drivers LFr.100–200 on top of the metered fare.

Public Holidays

1 Jan (New Year), Feb (Carnival*), Easter Monday*, 1 May (May Day), Ascension*, Whit Monday*, 23 June (National Day), 15

Festivals

In Luxembourg every town has its own traditional feasts, but several are celebrated nationwide.

The February Carnival is the most widespread; the major venues are Vianden and Woreldange on the Monday, Echternach and Steinsel on the Tuesday, but there are few towns without celebrations. The usual pattern is for afternoon processions to be followed by masked balls and the Carnival Prince reigns supreme.

At Easter local boys go through the street shaking rattles, summoning citizens to prayer – they then call at each house to be rewarded with Easter eggs.

23 June is National Day. The holiday is marked by colourful parades, concerts, religious services and dances.

On the Sunday prior to 6 Dec, most towns hav a colourful procession featuring St Nicholas, after which the Saint distributes sweets.

Aug (Assumption), 1 Nov (All Saints' Day) and 25 Dec.

*Movable. When holidays fall on Sun, the Mon usually becomes a holiday.

Telephones

Public phone booths on the street and in post offices are cheaper than the ones in such establishments as restaurants. The instructions are in the form of pictograms, usually with the addition of text in French and German. Most coin boxes take all the denominations, but card boxes take only *télécartes*. You can get *télécartes* from post offices and some CFL offices.

There are reduced rates for some international calls at the weekends and in the evenings: to North America 2200–1000; to the British Isles 1900–0800.

To call abroad from Luxembourg: *tel: 00*. To call Luxembourg from abroad: *tel: 352* – there are no area codes. For local operators: *tel: 017*. For international operators (they speak English) *tel: 016*. **Emergencies:** for the police *tel: 113*; for fire, ambulance, doctor, dentist and late-opening pharmacies *tel: 112*. The emergency operators speak English.

Transport

The national rail company, **CFL**, *9 pl. de la Gare, Luxembourg; tel: 49 24 24*, also runs buses to fill the gaps on the rail network.

CFL have no connection with city buses (although the multi-ride passes cover them) and for details of local services you will have to consult the bus companies directly – or ask the tourist office. Most bus-stops show a blue oblong with an illustration of a bus. At terminals the different stops are numbered without any relevance to the buses using them. If you see 'quai . . .' that is simply the number of the 'platform' and you must consult the other signs (the ones with destinations as well as numbers) to find out which stop your bus will use. The norm is to board buses at the front and validate your ticket there (or buy one from the driver) and to disembark by a rear door.

The cost of single bus tickets is LFr.35. Multi-ride tickets must be validated each time you board a bus, but no charge is made within an hour of the previous journey. For details of tickets covering both rail and bus travel, see p. 28.

THEMED ITINERARIES

Here are five themed tours using some of the recommended routes. There are digressions in some cases and a lot of travelling in others. You can adapt the basic idea to plan itineraries which take in your own interests, or pace, and some of the themes here. Use the sightseeing information provided throughout this book to make up your own themed tour. For example, devise your own itinerary that covers Roman France, taking in towns such towns as Orange, Nîmes and Arles with their Roman attractions, or pick out the museums or cathedrals that you most want to see and build an itinerary around them.

For convenience sake, all the tours listed below are based on a circular idea, starting and finishing in Paris. The suggested overnight stop is always in **bold type**.

PLANNING AN ITINERARY

Themes can make a trip more fun but to make sure tours are practical, here are some tips.

1. Work out train times with the detailed leaflets available free at most rail stations, or take an up-to-date copy of the *Thomas Cook European Timetable* (see p. 346). Do pay attention to footnotes, as they may refer to days when train services are not operating to the usual time. Ask the staff at the rail station to double-check anything you do not understand, or just to reassure your-

self. A copy of the *Thomas Cook New Rail Map of Europe* will also help when planning a tour.
2. If the place you are planning to visit is very small and you have luggage with you, check beforehand if there is somewhere to leave your bags.
3. Allow plenty of time for your visit to the attraction or town. This may be quite a distance from the rail station, so do not plan quick change-overs. Stay longer to look around or build time for a meal or coffee break into your stay. Double-check the opening times of a museum or gallery which you definitely want to see so that you don't miss the whole point of your visit.
4. Pre-book accommodation if you plan to arrive fairly late in the evening or after the tourist office is closed.
5. Try to pick places with frequent train services. If you are a real enthusiast about the theme you have chosen, then an obscure place that is a real gem might be worth all the waiting around, otherwise it might be interesting to fit in a couple of other more accessible locations.
6. Be flexible. If you discover that real gem, stay longer to explore it and discard something else planned for another day.
7. Allow plenty of time to get back to your departure point, whether it's an airport, station or ferry port.

1. CHÂTEAUX TRAIL (10 days)

The Loire Valley is the top region for extensive sightseeing of châteaux, some of which can be reached by train or bus.

Day 1, 2: **Paris**. Using Paris as a base, make two day trips, one to Reuil-

Malmaison (p. 208) to see two Napoleonic manor houses, the other to see Fontaine-bleau (p. 213). Day 3: Paris–**Orlèans**: using Orlèans (p. 233) as a base, take the SNCF bus to Chateaudun (p. 235). Day 4: Orlèans–**Blois**. Blois (p. 235) has a magnificent château, and there is a tour bus to Chambord. Day 5: Blois–**Amboise**: The château at Amboise (p. 236) is furnished. Day 6: Amboise–**Tours**. Tours (p. 270) is a good base, using the leaflet available from the station about getting to châteaux by train or SNCF bus service, such as the route which takes in Loches, Azay-Le Rideau and Chinon (p. 272). It is also possible to visit famous Chenonceau (p. 278). Day 7: Tours–**Saumur**. Within the château at Saumur (p. 281) are two museums; near the area are the châteaux of Villandry and Langeais (p. 281). Day 8: Saumur–**Angers**. From Angers (p. 283) several châteaux are accessible by bus or on a tour from the local tourist office. Day 9: Angers–**Nantes**. At Nantes (p. 170) is the château of the dukes of Brittany. Day 10: Nantes–**Paris**.

---

2. FOR WINE-BUFFS (10 days)

The places featured here are good bases for make excursions into the vineyard-filled countryside, either by train, bus or through excursions offered at the tourist offices. Some places en route have their own wine tasting cellars or wine-making museums.

Day 1: Paris–**Reims** (p. 224). Tours of the cellars of famous champagne *maisons* take place here (and at Épernay, p. 224). Day 2: Reims–**Strasbourg** (p. 250): For details of public transport to places along the Route du Vin d'Alsace (The Alsace Wine Route – p. 259) visit the tourist office at Strasbourg. Day 3: Strasbourg–**Dijon** (p. 120). Tours of the Burgundy vineyards are

available from the tourist office. Day 4: Dijon–**Lyon** (p. 122). Break the journey by stopping at Beaune (p. 123), where wine tastings are the main entertainment and there is also a wine museum. Day 5: Lyon–**Marseille** (p. 143). A good base for the wines of Provence and the Mediterranean vineyards. Day 6: Marseille–Narbonne, Narbonne–**Perpignan** (p. 237). This is the other Mediterranean wine region, Languedoc-Roussillon. Day 7, 8: Perpignan–Narbonne, Narbonne–**Bordeaux**. Allow a day to get to Bordeaux (p. 64) and choose one of the famous wines from this region to go with an evening meal. Well-organised tours to the wine-producing châteaux are offered by the Bordeaux tourist office and there are wine tastings with the experts at the Maison du Vin (p. 66). Alternatively, take the train service from Bordeaux to Pointe-de-Graves (p. 69), which stops at wine-producing villages such as Margaux and Pauillac. Day 9: Bordeaux–**Tours** (p. 273). With Tours as a base you can visit a wine-producing chateau of the Loire Valley. Ask at the tourist office for public transport details. Day 10: Tours–**Paris** (p. 192). Head for a Left-Bank brasserie and choose a favourite wine based on the knowledge you've picked up on this route. Santé!

---

3. FOR GASTRONOMES (10 days)

This extravaganza of a trip means a different regional cuisine or speciality for dinner every evening. For a more leisurely pace, choose a cuisine or region which appeals most and fit in those routes and destinations with the rest of your sightseeing programme.

Day 1: **Paris**. Get into the spirit by trying one of the city's famous restaurants. Day 2: Paris–**Strasbourg** (see route p. 223). Solid

---

Germanic cooking in Alsace-Lorraine is based on cabbages, sausages and stews. *Charcoute garnie* is a mixture of ham and sausage, on a bed of pickled cabbage with boiled potatoes. The famous *quiche Lorraine* is often served as a starter. For dessert, try *vacherin glacé*. Day 3: Strasbourg–**Lyon** (see route p. 258). In the Burgundy wine-making area, cooking takes advantage of the flavour of the region's wines, for instance, *boeuf bourguignonne* is slow-cooked with red wine, bacon, onions, *bouquet garni* and mushrooms. Also try *coq au vin*. *Gougère* is a delicate cake of cheese-flavoured *choux* pastry. French onion soup is said to have been created in Lyon. Day 4: Lyon–Clermont-Ferrand, Clermont Ferrand–**Pèrigeux** (p. 74). The town is famous for its truffles and *foie gras*. Day 5: Pèrigeux–Bordeaux, change at Bordeaux, Bordeaux–**Biarritz** (p. 57). Basque specialities at the seaside resort of Biarritz. Day 6: Biarritz–**Toulouse** (see route p. 60). In Toulouse (p. 262), try *cassoulet*, which is made with leg of lamb, local sausage, confit and haricot beans. *Tourain* is a hearty soup cased on *foie gras* and garlic with onions or tomatoes. Day 7: Toulouse–Narbonne, change at Narbonne, Narbonne–**Perpignan** (p. 237), for its Catalan specialities. Day 8: Perpignan–Narbonne, change at Narbonne, Narbonne–**Marseille** (p. 151). *Bouillabaise* is a must, especially in the old port area. Day 9: Marseille–**Nice** (p. 177). Anchovy or olive paste in dishes is popular in provençal cooking. Try *salade niçoise* (anchovies are a main ingredient) and *soupe de pistou* (flavoured with a basil paste), grilled sea bass and *ratatouille*. Day 10: Nice–Paris. Another chance to sample a haute cuisine restaurant in **Paris**. (Or finish this route by continuing to Monaco, p. 188, another sophisticated background for eating-out).

4. NORTHERN FRANCE (10 days)

By staying in the north-west of the country, mostly above the Loire valley, sightseeing on this route includes a grand château, Disneyland and the high-tech Futuroscope theme park, William the Conqueror and World War II historical sites, an Atlantic coastal town, famous cathedral cities and a royal palace.

Day 1, 2: **Paris**. Using the capital as a base, take two day trips, one to either Disneyland Paris or Parc Asterix (p. 208), the other to Fontainebleau (p. 213), for the ultimate of châteaux. Day 3: Paris–Vernon, Vernon–**Rouen**. From Vernon take the bus to nearby Giverny to see Monet's home and garden, then on to the city where he painted his famous series of works showing Rouen cathedral (see route p. 222). Day 4: Rouen–Èvereux, Èvereux–**Caen** (p. 99), where there are links with William the Conqueror and the Memorial based on histories of the two World Wars. From Caen take a trip to Bayeux (p. 97) to see the fine medieval centre and the world's most famous tapestry. Day 5: Caen–**Nantes** (p. 170) with a bevy of important museums. Day 6: Nantes–**La Rochelle** (p. 174), a cheerful, bustling Atlantic coast port, with lots to do, including a museum about immigration to the New World. Day 7: La Rochelle–**Poitiers** (p. 273). See the restoration work in progress on the cathedral, and take a trip north to Futuroscope, a theme park using state-of-the-art cinematic technology (p. 275). Day 8. Poitiers–**Tours**. Tours (p. 270) is a good base for visiting a Loire Valley château. Day 9. Tours–**Chartres** (p. 218), for the magnificent cathedral. Day 10. Chartres–Versailles (p. 218), to visit Louis X1V's sumptuous palace, Versailles–**Paris**.

5. SOUTHERN FRANCE (7 days)

Below the Loire Valley, this route takes in a porcelain centre, three walled towns, the astonishing architecture of Le Puy, plus the major centres of Toulouse, Clermont-Ferrand and Lyon.

Day 1: Paris–**Limoges** (p. 229). Follow up the porcelain and enamel-making art in the museums and shops. Day 2: Limoges–Cahors, Cahors–**Toulouse**. The little Cathar town of Cahors has a dramatic setting, some ramparts and a fortress bridge (p. 231). There is fine dining-out in Toulouse (p. 262), with its many local specialities.

Day 3: Toulouse–Carcassone, Carcassone–**Avignon**. Carcassone is a compact medieval walled town. Avignon (p. 144) has substantial walls and a papal palace as well as the famous bridge. Day 4: Avignon–**Lyon**. Lyon (p. 125) is a busy city with lots to enjoy. Day 5: Lyon–Le Puy, Le Puy–**Clermont-Ferrand** (see route on p. 108). Le Puy (p. 109) has colossal religious monuments on volcanic peaks. Day 6: **Clermont-Ferrand** (p. 105). Take the train service for a day-trip to the mountain-top town of Le Mont-Dore via Laqueuille (p. 77), or take a bus excursion to the Le Puy de Dome mountain peak (p. 109). Day 7: Clermont-Ferrand–**Paris.**

SEA CROSSINGS

These pages list ferries operating between Britain and Ireland and France and the Benelux Countries, at the time of going to press. Frequencies and journey times from port to port are those of the summer season.

UK–FRANCE

From . . . To	No. of Sailings	Journey Time	Operating Company	Tel. for further details
Since the opening of the Channel Tunnel in November 1994 there has been a thorough reorganisation of the ferry services linking Britain and Ireland to Europe. Ferry companies have introduced bigger, faster ships to compete with Le Shuttle.				
PLYMOUTH to . . .				
Roscoff	1 per day	6 hrs	Brittany Ferries	*tel: (01752) 221321*
PORTSMOUTH to . . .				
St Malo	1 per day	9 hrs	Brittany Ferries	*tel: (01752) 221321*
Ouistreham	2 per day	6 hrs	Brittany Ferries	*tel: (01752) 221321*
Le Havre	3 per day	6 hrs	P & O European Ferries	*tel: (01304) 203388*
Cherbourg	4 per day	5 hrs	P & O European Ferries	*tel: (01304) 203388*
POOLE to . . .				
St Malo	4 per week	8 hrs	Brittany Ferries	*tel: (01752) 221321*
Cherbourg	2 per day	4¼ hrs	Truckline	*tel: (01752 221321*
CORK to . . .				
Roscoff	2 per week	14 hrs	Brittany Ferries	*tel: (01752) 221321*
St Malo	1 per week	18 hrs	Brittany Ferries	*tel: (01752) 221321*
Cherbourg	1 per week	20 hrs	Irish Ferries	*tel: (01) 855 2222*
Le Havre	1 per week	20 hrs	Irish Ferries	*tel: (01) 855 2222*
DOVER to . . .				
Calais (catamaran)	12 per day	35 mins	Hoverspeed	*tel: (01304) 240241*
Calais	25 per day	75 mins	P & O European Ferries	*tel: (01304) 203388*
Calais	25 per day	1½ hrs	Stena Sealink	*tel: (01233) 647047*
FOLKESTONE to . . .				
Boulogne	6 per day	55 mins	Hoverspeed	*tel: (01304) 240241*
ROSSLARE to . . .				
Cherbourg	2 per week	17 hrs	Irish Ferries	*tel: (01) 855 2222*
Le Havre	3 per week	21 hrs	Irish Ferries	*tel: (01) 855 2222*
RAMSGATE to . . .				
Dunkerque	5 per day	2½ hrs	Sally Ferries	*tel: (01843) 595522*
NEWHAVEN to . . .				
Dieppe (ship)	4 per day	4 hrs	Stena Sealink	*tel: (01233) 647047*
Dieppe (catamaran)	4 per day	2 hrs	Stena Sealink	*tel: (01233) 647047*
SOUTHAMPTON to . . .				
Cherbourg	2 per day	5 hrs	Stena Sealink	*tel: (01233) 647047*

SEA CROSSINGS

UK–BELGIUM/NETHERLANDS			
From . . . To	No. of Sailings	Journey Time	Operating Company	Tel. for further details
HULL to . . .				
Rotterdam Europoort	daily	13 hrs	North Sea Ferries	tel: (01482) 377177
Zeebrugge	daily	13 hrs	North Sea Ferries	tel: (01482) 377177
RAMSGATE to . . .				
Ostend (ship)	5 per day	4 hrs	Oostende Lines	tel: (01843) 595522
Ostend (jetfoil)	5 per day	1½ hrs	Oostende Lines	tel: (01843) 595522
FELIXSTOWE to . . .				
Zeebrugge	2 per day	5½ hrs	P & O European Ferries	tel: (01304) 203388
HARWICH to . . .				
Hoek van Holland	2 per day	7 hrs	Stena Sealink	tel: (01233) 647047

The Channel Tunnel

The idea of a cross-Channel tunnel was first proposed as long ago as 1802. Early attempts were stopped for fear of invasion and the project only got the green light in 1985. This feat of engineering actually consists of three tunnels (two for trains and one for services and safety), each one 50 km long. Eurostar rail services began in late 1994 and the car-carrying service started at Christmas the same year.

Le Shuttle, running from Folkestone to Calais, is the car transporter service. The aim is to have trains leave every 15 mins throughout the day, with a maximum journey time of 1 hr, including waiting, loading and unloading. Customs and immigration are passed before boarding. The carriages have toilet facilities, but no refreshments or seats – passengers remain in or near their car.

Eurostar Passenger Services currently concentrate on two routes. **London (Waterloo)–Paris (Nord)** takes 3 hrs (2 hrs 30 mins when the British rail link to the channel opens around the year 2000). **London (Waterloo)–Lille (Europe)–Brussels (Midi/Zuid)** takes 3 hrs 15 mins (2 hrs 40 mins after the completion of the new Belgian high-speed link; 2 hrs 10 mins by 2000). Additional trains will run at peak periods. Connections can be made at Brussels for trains to Amsterdam, Germany etc., and at Lille for TGVs to the rest of France. The trains have first- and standard-class accommodation. There are also family compartments with baby-changing facilities. First-class tickets include a full meal, while in the rest of the train there are two bar-buffet coaches and a trolley service. Passengers clear customs before boarding and immigration checks are carried out on board.

From 1996 services will also run from Edinburgh and Birmingham (with stops en route) to Brussels, Lille and Paris. Overnight services will include trains from London to Amsterdam (via Rotterdam, The Hague); and from Glasgow to Paris and Brussels, Swansea to Paris and Plymouth to Brussels. A new international tickets and reservation system will allow ticketing through travel agents and most UK stations, for the Eurostar (see also p. 22) and most other major European routes.

BIARRITZ

The smart set have been coming here since the splendid beaches and mild climate were 'discovered' in the mid-19th century by European royalty and English aristocrats, who introduced golf to the resort. Movie stars joined in the high life of the 1950s and 60s. Deborah Kerr's husband brought a surfboard to try the high-rolling Atlantic waves, thus leading to the resort's status as an international surfing centre. Visitors come for its 'sun, sea and sand' attractions as well as seawater therapy, sports and gambling.

Tourist Information

Tourist Office: *1 sq. d'Ixelles, 64200 Biarritz; tel: 59 24 20 24.* Open daily 0800–2000 (June–Sept); 0900–1845 (Oct–May). Provides free maps and information on the Basque region.

Arriving and Departing

Gare de Biarritz-La Négresse, *allée du Mouna; tel: 36 35 35 35.* Information, lockers. Tourist information open 0915–1245, 1415–1830 (mid-June–mid-Sept), free maps. The town centre is 3 km away down a winding road, about a 40-min walk. Take bus no. 2 for a 15-min ride to the town hall. Bus no. 9 also goes there via a longer route.

The **STAB** bus network links the town with outlying villages and towns. The bus kiosk and terminus is next to the tourist office at *r. L. Barthou; tel: 59 24 26 59.* The drivers give expert tips on how to manipulate surfboards through the bus doors.

Getting Around

Within a few minutes' walking distance of each other, the main attractions, hotels, restaurants and entertainment places are in the streets just off the beach.

STAB buses also go through the town centre (some routes leave from the town hall). Bus no. 4 goes past many beaches and golf courses and the **Chiberta Forest**. Tickets are FFr.7; a book of ten FFr.58.

The main taxi rank is at the corner of *av. du Mar. Foch* and *av. de Verdun; tel: 59 23 62 62* or *59 24 16 13.* Fare to station (10 mins) is FFr.45.

Staying in Biarritz

Accommodation

Hotel accommodation is mostly in the compact centre. Economy hotels are scarce but there are moderate-priced ones. Advance booking is recommended in July and Aug. Among the luxury hotels is the former summer palace of Napoléon III and the Empress Eugénie, **Hôtel du Palais**, *1 av. de l'Impératrice; tel: 59 41 64 00.* Chain hotels include *Ca, Cl, Co* and *Nv.* There are self-catering apartments, usually let on a weekly basis.

HI: *19 rte des Vignes 64699, Anglet; tel: 59 63 86 49.* Open Feb–Nov, it is about 4 km outside Biarritz; bus no. 4 from the tourist office.

Biarritz Camping, *r. d'Harcel; tel: 59 23 00 12,* is open Apr–Oct, in the town outskirts. Take bus no. 9, a 15-min journey, from the rail station (or from the town hall).

Eating and Drinking

From up-market seafood restaurants to bistros, brasseries, cafés, crêperies, pizzerias and tapas bars, there is a wide choice of places to eat. The Basque *piperade* is a

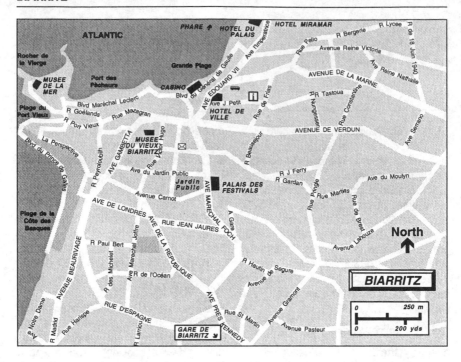

spicy omelette-style dish. Delicatessens, pâtisseries and baker's shops are plentiful for picnics on the beaches. The central market, *av. Mar. Joffre*, is open every morning.

Communications

Main **Post Office**: *r. de Postes; tel: 59 24 23 71.* Open Mon–Fri 0830–1900; Sat 0830–1200; poste restante facilities.

Thomas Cook bureau de change: *3 av. Edouard VII; tel: 59 24 71 40.* Open Tues–Sat 1000–1245 and 1400–1930.

Entertainment

A bustling nightlife includes a dozen discos and the newly refurbished **Casino Municipal**, *Grande Plage; tel: 59 22 77 77.* Open daily 1100–0300.

Biarritzscope, a free monthly listings leaflet, is published by the tourist office. The town's rich cultural life includes seasons of ballet, opera, rock and classical music and an annual international cinema festival. Many events can be booked at the box office of the **Palais des Festivals**, *23 av. Mar. Foch; tel: 59 22 12 21.* There are many golf tournaments and two international surfing competitions in July and Sept. Sports events include matches of **cesta punta**, a fierce variation of the Basque ball game *pelota*.

Shopping

Designer boutiques jostle with surf and sportswear shops. Antique shops nestle next to the bucket-and-spade and souvenir emporiums. A posh regional souvenir is a *makhila*, a handmade walking stick. Handcrafts such as ceramics and pottery are also

Sightseeing

The **Grande Plage** (main beach) is bedecked with brightly striped beach tents, trampolines and other beach activities, including surfing instruction. The large **Plage de la Côte des Basques** stretches in front of a backdrop of white cliffs. In between is the little, cliff-sheltered **Plage du Port-Vieux** and **Port des Pêcheurs** (fishermen's port). A bridge leads to the **Rocher de la Vierge** (Virgin's Rock), a rocky promontory with a good viewpoint. The **Petit Train Touristique,** 15 av. du Jardin Public; tel: 59 24 48 43, leaves on half-hour tours, Apr–Oct. Adults FFr.25 (concessions FFr.15).

On a hill-top behind an art deco façade is the renovated, five-storey **Musée de la Mer** (maritime museum and aquarium), 89 plateau de l'Atalaye; tel: 59 22 33 34.

Open daily 0930–1900 (July–Sept); until 2200 (mid-July–mid-Aug); daily 0930–1230, 1400–1800 (Oct–June). FFr.42 (FFr.22). With displays about the town's English history, the redundant Anglican church, **St-Andrew's**, is the **Musée du Vieux Biarritz** (Old Biarritz museum), r. Broquedis; tel: 59 24 56 88. Open daily except Thur and Sun, 1000–1200 and 1500–1800; FFr.15 (FFr.5).

A 15-min walk along the cliff-top fringed with tamarisk trees leads to the 44-m high **phare** (lighthouse), built 1831; tel: 59 24 01 29. Open 1000–1200, 1400–1800 (June–mid-Oct), admission free.

Seawater health treatments can be arranged at the **Institut de Thalasso-thérapie**, Hotel Miramar, 11 r. Louison Bobet; tel: 59 24 20 80, or without prior appointment at **Les Thermes Marins**, 80 r. de Madrid; tel: 59 23 01 22.

BIARRITZ to TOULOUSE

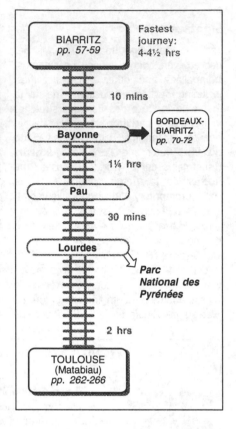

From the flat land and regimented forest plantations around Bayonne to the majestic Pyrenees mountain ranges, this 4½-hr journey takes in some very contrasting places before it reaches the cosmopolitan city of Toulouse. Flashy Biarritz, medieval Bayonne (see Bordeaux–Biarritz route, p. 72), graceful Pau, and hectic Lourdes are on the way; so are peaceful hamlets, hillside farms and sunlit woods.

TRAINS

ETT tables: 139.

 Fast Track

Just three trains a day (all with buffet cars) run through from Biarritz to Toulouse Matabiau, with an extra journey available Mon–Fri by changing trains at Bayonne. The journey takes 4–4½ hrs.

On Track

Biarritz–Bayonne

About a dozen trains a day make the 10-min run from Bayonne to Biarritz.

Bayonne–Pau

Five or six trains a day run between Bayonne and Pau; the journey takes about 1¼ hrs.

Pau–Lourdes

The 30-min trip from Pau to Lourdes is

covered by as many as 15 trains each day, including 3 TGV services.

Lourdes–Toulouse

Six or seven trains a day run between Lourdes and Toulouse Matabiau. The journey takes just over 2 hrs.

PAU

Station: *av. Gaston Lacoste; tel: 36 35 35 35.* Buffet, lockers, but no tourist information. Take the funicular railway opposite the station to reach the town centre (see under 'Sightseeing', p. 61). **Bus station:**

Citram, *30 r. Gachet; tel: 59 27 22 22*, runs buses to the Basque country (July–Aug). **Taxi**: *tel: 59 02 22 22.*
Tourist Office: *pl. Royale, 64000 Pau; tel: 59 27 27 08.* Open Mon–Sat 0900–1830 (July–Aug); Mon–Sat 0900–1200, 1400–1800. Offers information, hotel reservations and guided tours in French.

Accommodation and Food

Popular as a setting-off point for mountain drives, Pau has a good choice of hotels, especially in the moderate price range (around *r. Mar. Joffre, r. L. Barthou*). Chain hotels include *BW, Ca, Cl, F1, Ic, Me* and *Nv*.

HI: Auberge de la Jeunesse, *r. Michel Hounau; tel: 59 72 61 00.* A 15-min walk past the funicular: follow *r. M. Foch, cours Bosquet, r. E. Garet*, then left on *r. M. Hounau*. For the other hostel, **Logis des Jeunes**, *Base de Plein Air, 64110 Gélos; tel: 50 06 53 02,* take bus no. 1 from *pl. Clémenceau* (stop: *Gélos)* and then a 30-min walk to the Gélos district on the other side of the river. **Camping**: *blvd Cami Salié: tel: 59 02 30 49.* Bus no. 4 from *pl. Clémenceau* (stop: *Palais des Sports).* There are many restaurants in all price ranges, try *r. du Parlement* and *r. des Cordeliers.*

Sightseeing

This elegant city on a cliff, population 90,000, has panoramic views of the snow-capped Pyrenees mountains. Fortunately, opposite the station, there is a free funicular railway up the palm-fringed and hydrangea-frilled hillside – otherwise it is a challenging 15-min walk up. **Le Funiculaire** operates Mon–Sat 0700–1230, 1255–1930; Sat 1330–1930; Sun and holidays 1330–1930, 1955–2100. It ascends to the grand swathe of landscaped terrace overlooking the rushing river below and the mountains beyond. Almost immediately to the right is the handsome square, **pl. Royale**. Pau's attractions are within easy walking distance of each other; a free map is available from the tourist office.

Straight ahead is the town's most impressive sight, **Le Château**; *tel: 59 83 38 00.* Open daily 0930–1145, 1400–1715. FFr.27 (concessions FFr.18). There can be queues on summer afternoons at this former residence of that charismatic French monarch, Henri IV, with its tapestries, furniture and royal personal possessions. *Son et Lumière* productions about his court are held in July. Guided tours of the château are in French but there are English notes. In the château is **Le Musée Béarn** (the provincial museum) about the lives of ordinary citizens, admission FFr.8.

The old town streets are found near here, just beside the commercial centre with its modern fountains and many shops. Tucked beside the new town is **Le Musée Bernadotte**, *r. Tran* (enter from a courtyard in the next street, *r. St-Serviez); tel: 59 27 48 42.* Open Tues–Sun, 1000–1200, 1400–1800. FFr.10 (FFr.5). The polished wood and deeply tranquil ambiance make this old town house a pleasurable browse. It is the birthplace of one of Napoleon's marshals, who became King of Sweden in 1818, founding the House of Bernadotte. His descendants are today's royal family.

The town's fine arts museum, **Le Musée des Beaux Arts,** *r. M. Lalanne; tel: 59 27 33 02,* is rich in Spanish and French paintings including Degas and Latour. Open Wed–Tues, 1000–1200, 1400–1800. FFr.10 (FFr.5). Pau's English heritage is reflected in the landscaped **Beaumont Park**, where the winter palace is now the **Casino Municipal**. British soldiers settled here after the Spanish wars.

Pau

LOURDES

Station: *av. de la Gare; tel: 36 35 35 35.* Facilities include a buffet and luggage lockers, but no tourist information. It is a 15-min walk to the town centre, or you can take bus no. 1 (get off at stop: *Grotto*). **Bus station:** *av. du Paradis* (by the riverside); *tel: 62 42 22 90*, runs trips to the border country with Spain.

Tourist Office: *pl. Peyramale, BP17, 65101 Lourdes; tel: 62 42 77 40.* This is a well-stocked office which gets hectic during the summer and does not always have time to make hotel reservations, but offers free information, including well-compiled lists of all types of accommodation and maps.

Getting Around

TCVL, *tel: 62 94 31 30*, run the town's bus network. From the rail station, bus no. 1 goes to the centre and the grotto-shrine every 15 mins, daily 0745–1145, 1345–1815 (June–Oct). The fare to the centre is FFr.5, and to the grotto FFr.9. From the grotto, bus no. 2 goes to the **Pic du Jer** (a viaduct just outside the town); bus no. 3 takes a route that includes two bridges, **Pont Peyramale** and **Pont Vieux.**

Accommodation and Food

There are lots of hotels, self-catering accommodation and fixed price *tables d'hôtes*. Cheap and reasonable hotels are found beside the station. Chains include *Ca* and *Ib*. Hostel accommodation can be found at **Centre Pax Christi**, *rte de la Fôret; tel: 62 94 00 66*, walking distance (500m) behind the grotto (booking ahead essential). The **Camp des Jeunes** is in this area, a few mins walk from the Peyramale Bridge. **Camping:** There are 16 campsites in and around Lourdes, including two along the *rte de la Fôret* – **Camping du**

Loup, *tel: 62 94 23 60*, and **Camping de la Fôret**, *tel: 62 94 94 38.* **Camping de la Poste**, *26 r. de Langelle, tel: 62 94 40 35* is an 8-min walk from the station, or you can take bus no. 1 (stop: *pl. Peyramale*).

Catering for the masses means that the streets of Lourdes are lined with cafés, snackbars, pizzerias and crêperies.

Sightseeing

In its mountainous riverside setting the town is surrounded by natural beauty, but its buildings are tacky and it is overwhelmed by its status as a religious centre. The truly devout glow with awe and appreciation, the curious gawk in amazement. Lourdes, population 17,000, receives 6,000,000 Catholic pilgrims a year, mostly in the summer, when the streets are so crowded that a 5-min bus journey can crawl up to 15 mins.

Every other building is a shop overflowing with religious kitsch, blue and white figurines of St Bernadette in candle form or as plastic bottles with which to gather the holy drinking water. Bernadette was the 14-year-old who saw a vision of the Virgin Mary in the local grotto 18 times from 1848, inspiring worship here, especially after miracle cures started to take place.

The grotto area is huge and complicated, with seven church buildings. A free map is given at its information centre, the **Forum**, just inside the entrance of **St Joseph's Gate**, off *pl. Mgr Laurence*. The buildings include the **Basilica of the Rosary**, with its massive curved entrance ramps, the **Crypt**, which was the first chapel, and the **upper basilica**. Elsewhere is the **St Pius X Underground Basilica**, which holds up to 30,000 pilgrims. The complex includes an **Esplanade**, where nightly torchlight processions begin at

2045 (summer). There are Masses in English, daily 0900 (May–mid-Sept) in the **Hemicycle Mont Carmel** beside the church of **Ste-Bernadette**.

The spring, which is credited with healing powers, still flows and water is collected to supply the Baths and the drinking fountains. The **Baths**, rebuilt in 1955, are open for visits from the public and hundreds of people, both the sick and the healthy, are plunged into the 14 separate baths daily. The **Way of the Cross** is also used for prayers, winding its way over the hilltop, with stunning views of the river below. Each stop on the route has a group of statues, wrought in metal in 1912.

There are town attractions connected with the legend. The **Boly Mill**, r. Bernadette Soubirous, where the saint was born, is open daily 0900–1200, 1330–1800. The **Cachot** (or jail), r. des Petits Fossés, where the family later lived, is open daily, 0930–1200, 1400–1900. These are free, considered to be part of the pilgrimage.

The town has joined together eight other attractions to offer **Visa Lourdes**, a pass which costs FFr.160, children FFr.80. (The total cost of the attractions individually would be FFr.215.) Most of these are within a couple of minutes' walk of each other, and three are 'tableau-style'. The following attractions are included. The **Château-Fort**, which contains the **Musée Pyrénéen** (about local life), open daily 0900–1100, 1400–1800 (summer); Wed–Mon 0900–1100, 1400–1700 (winter), FFr.26 (FFr.13). **Le Musée du Petit Lourdes**, 68 av. Peyramale, with miniature town layouts, open Mon–Sat 0900–1145 (opens Sun at 1000), 1330–1845, and 2030–2200 (July–Aug only), FFr.27 (FFr.10). **Le Musée de la Nativité**, quai St-Jean, tableaux of the Christmas story,

open daily 0900–1200, 1430–1900 and 2030–2200 (July–Aug), FFr.27 (FFr.10). **Le Musée Grevin**, 87 r. de la Grotte, a wax museum of bible scenes, open daily 0900–1200, 1330–1830; also from 2030–2200 (July–Aug), FFr.30 (FFr.10). **Le Musée de Lourdes**, at car park de l'Égalité, tableaux of local life, open 0900–1145, 1330–1815; also from 2030–2200 (July–Aug). FFr.28 (FFr.10). The **Petit Train**, which has guided tours of the town, departs from pl. Mgr Laurence outside the grotto, 0900–1200, 1330–1830, 2030, FFr.25 (FFr.15). The **Funiculaire du pic du Jer**, 59 av. F. Lacardére, runs 0900–1200, 1330–1820 (last ascent to the ramparts is 1730). The fare, FFr.42 (FFr.21), includes the return trip and a visit to the caverns.

Out of Town

Many bus excursions are organised from Lourdes, departing from the bus station at av. du Paradis. One-day journeys leave at 0800 to **Parc National des Pyrénées** (Tues–Thurs, cost FFr.117). The park follows the French–Spanish borders for 100 km with magnificent views, the snow-capped mountain peaks in contrast to flower-bedecked terrain, popular with walkers, who sometimes follow gentian and columbine 'trails' to look for the rare varieties found in the area. One-day excursions also go to the **Basque country** and **St-Jean de Luz** (Wed, Fri, FFr.130). Half-day trips (depart 1330, 1400, or 1430) include **Bartres** and the Lac du Lourdes, FFr.32; **Cavarnie**, FFr.75; and **Col du Tourmalet**, FFr.80. The trip to the **Grottes de Betharram** departs at 0830 and 1430, FFr.38. These vast underground caverns offer train and boat rides to view the strange landscape of limestone formations. On excursions, any admission charges to attractions are extra.

BORDEAUX

Sprawling Bordeaux, population 213,000, spreads out boisterously on the banks of the Garonne. Three bridges span the majestic river before it meets the Dordogne, to merge into the Gironde, finally flowing into the Atlantic 97 km away. The city boasts a mixture of splendid 18th-century architecture on grand thoroughfares and atmospheric old neighbourhoods with narrow, run-down streets and unexpected monuments. It is in the heart of the Gironde region, famous for great wines.

Tourist Information

Tourist Office: 12 cours du XXX Juillet, 33080 Bordeaux; tel: 56 44 28 41. Open Mon–Sat 0900–2000, Sun and holidays 0900–1900 (June–Sept); daily 0900–1900 (Oct–May).

Maison du Tourisme de la Gironde, 21 Cours de l'Intendance; tel: 56 52 61 40. Open Mon–Sat 0900–1900. Free information, some in English, about the region (no hotel reservations).

Arriving and Departing

Airport

Aéroport International Bordeaux–Mérignac, av. Kennedy, Mérignac; tel: 56 34 84 84. It is 12 km west of the city and is France's fifth largest airport. A regular bus service, **Navette Aéroport,** tel: 56 34 50 50, departs from the airport Mon–Fri 0610–0030, Sat 0610–2230, Sun 0615–2245. From the rail station, Mon–Fri 0530–2245, Sat–Sun 0530–2200 (also picking up

at the main tourist office) the fare is FFr.33 (concessions FFr.20). and journey time 30–45 mins. The three-storey airport has a bank (open Mon–Sat 0845–1230, 1300–1700), money-changing machine (accepts £, Can$, US$), post office, lockers, snack bars, caféteria, restaurant and taxi rank, tel: 56 97 11 27. Fare FFr.100 to city centre. Tourist information desk is open Mon–Sat 0800–1900, Sun 0845–1230, 1315–1900; tel: 56 34 39 39.

Station

Gare St-Jean, r. Charles Domercq, a 35-min walk to the city centre's pl. Gambetta (or the pl. de la Comédie for the tourist office). Take bus nos 7 or 8, a 15-min journey. Rail enquiries and reservations; tel: 36 35 35 35. The station has automatic cash dispensers, a large caféteria and snack bars. Lockers are FFr.15–20; showers FFr.14. Entrance to tourist information office is from outside the station; tel: 56 91 64 70. Open daily 0900–1200, 1245–1900 (June–Sept); in winter from 1000 on Sun. With its grandiose proportions and sculpted decorations, the station is one of the greats of rail architecture and boasted the largest station concourse in the world when it was built at the end of the 19th century.

Buses

Citram, 14 r. Fondaudège; tel: 56 43 04 04. Information desk open Mon–Sat 0900–1200, 1400–1800. Buses depart for many regional towns (St-Emilion, Bergerac) and coastal beaches, such as Arachon or Cap Ferret (journey takes under 2 hrs; return fare FFr.110).

Eurolines, 32 r. Charles Domercq (opposite the rail station); tel: 56 92 50 42. Open Mon–Sat 0900–1900. Buses depart for cities in other countries.

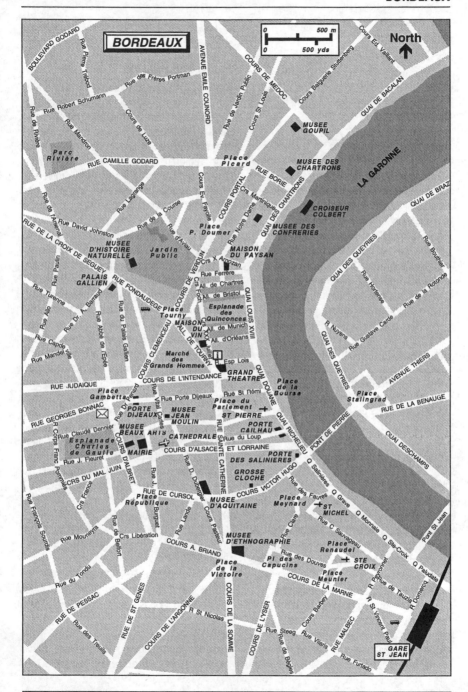

Getting Around

In the centre, the cathedral, main museums and the heart of the shopping area are within easy walking distance of each other but the sprawling city makes the bus network a necessity.

Buses

CGFTE buses cover the city extensively; *tel: 57 57 88 88*. Single journey FFr.7. The *Carte Bordeaux Découverte* travel pass allows unlimited journeys on all bus routes with one-day or three-day tickets, FFr.21 or FFr.50; a three-day youth version is FFr.25. Buy the pass at CGFTE office adjacent to the rail station or *4 r. Georges Bonnac* (off *pl. Gambetta*) or *1 pl. Jean Jaurès*. *Plan Poche* is a free routes map; there are leaflets of individual routes.

Taxis

Taxi rank at rail station; *tel: 56 91 48 11*. Fare to city centre FFr.50 (night fare FFr.65). Other ranks include: *allée de Tourny; tel: 56 48 03 25; pl. de la République; tel: 56 44 35 61; pl. de la Victoire; tel: 56 91 47 05*.

Staying in Bordeaux

Accommodation

There is a wide choice of hotels in all price brackets and no problem in finding a room except during the one-week June wine fair. Large modern hotels are on the outskirts. Hotel chains include *BW, Ca, Cl, Ib, Ho, Me, Pu* and *Sf*.

Cheap and moderate hotels cluster in streets near the rail station, a ramshackle but lively area. Central hotels of all categories are located in streets near the *pl. Gambetta* (including *r. de la Boétie, r. de la Vieille Tour*).

HI: *22 cours Barbey* (8-min walk from the rail station), *tel: 56 91 59 51*.

Eating and Drinking

Reflecting the region's fame for wine and cuisine, Bordeaux has a wide range of highly rated restaurants and many brasseries and bistros, with three-course menus from FFr.65 easy to find. Gourmet menus with regional specialities are priced from about FFr.125. Thanks to the university student population, there are lots of places to gather for some *moules* or *frites* and a beer as well as crêperies, pizzerias and burger bars, especially near the **Porte d'Aquitaine**, the 18th-century arch at *pl. de la Victoire*. Outdoor brasseries are in the *r. Victor Hugo, pl. du Parlement*, in streets off *pl. Gambetta*, around the cathedral (*r. du Loup*) and just across from the rail station. International cuisine includes Mexican, Japanese, Russian and Vietnamese. In a bustling city, picnic spots are rare but the large **Jardin Public**, *cours de Verdun*, open daily 0700–2000, is close to the centre and has a botanic garden and boat cruises around the islands of its lake. There are many food markets (closed Sun) with the main **Marché des Capucins**, off *cours de la Marne*, open 0400–1300. Wine tastings with experts take place at the **Maison du Vin**, *3 cours du XXX Juillet; tel: 56 00 22 88*. Open Mon–Fri 0830–1800; also Sat 0900–1230, 1400–1700 (mid-May–mid-Oct).

Communications

Main **Post Office**, *52 r. G. Bonnac; tel: 56 48 85 23*. Open Mon–Fri 0800–1900, Sat 0800–1200, it has poste restante facilities.

Money

Thomas Cook bureau de change, *Parvis Louis Armand, Gare St-Jean; tel: 56 91 58*

80. Open daily 0800–2000. It is the only money-changing bureau at the station. There is a wide choice of banks in the city centre.

Consulates

UK: *33 blvd Wilson; tel: 56 42 34 13.* (stop: *Carnot*).
USA: *22 cours Mar. Foch; tel: 56 52 65 95.* (stop: *Jardin Public*).

Entertainment

Besides an international musical festival each May, the cultural scene in Bordeaux is busy, from opera seasons to rock festivals and symphony orchestra concerts at such venues as the **Palais de Sports**. Bookings at **Box Office,** *24 Galerie Bordelaise; tel: 56 48 26 26*; **FNAC,** *Centre St-Christoly; tel: 56 00 21 30*; **Virgin Megastore,** *pl. Gambetta; tel: 56 56 05 56.*

The night life is lively. A bi-monthly booklet in French, *Clubs and Concerts,* lists musical events and venues including jazz, blues and rock pubs, bars and brasseries. Free at tourist office. *Confetti* is a bi-monthly listings magazine, FFr.2, available at news kiosks, with arts, theatre, music and cinema sections plus listings of restaurants, discos, pubs, bars and clubs.

From cabaret dinner shows to striptease joints, the city has something for everyone. Informal bar clubs (no membership required) and 'pubs' are found in most districts but in general around the restaurant areas. Country and folk music is popular, including several Irish pubs (the **Connemara**, *18 cours d'Albret; tel: 56 52 82 59*, has quiz nights in English). Discos are found anywhere from the quayside to the *r. d'Ornano*, with a variety of music including African, reggae and salsa. Some cocktail bars have dance areas.

Classical drama, opera and dance have a spectacular background at the **Grand Théâtre,** *pl. de la Comédie; tel: 56 48 58 54.* Opened in 1780 with a façade of Corinthian columns, it is a landmark of the city. Its opulent, recently restored interior complete with domed staircase is open for tours (book in person at the main tourist office), which include English commentary, Mon–Sat, times vary but hourly some days. Adults FFr.25 (concessions FFr.20). Nearby, the **Théâtre Fémina,** *29 r. de Grassi; tel: 56 81 02 07*, is used for concerts, musical, plays and repertory productions. There are several other theatres.

The cinema scene (in French only) includes the **CGR Français,** with 14 screens in a converted theatre with a handsome corner front at *rond-point de l'Intendance* (off *r. Montesquieu); tel: 36 68 01 22.* Around the corner is the **Gaumont,** *9 cours G. Clémenceau; tel: 36 68 75 55.*

Soccer matches are held at the **Stade Municipal,** *pl. David Johnson; tel: 56 16 11 11*; (match days) *56 93 25 83.*

Events

Major events include a carnival in Mar, an international music festival in May, a summer festival of arts in July/Aug and a wine festival in Oct.

Shopping

For international designers and smart shops, head for 'the triangle', an area bordered by *cours de l'Intendance, cours G. Clémenceau* and *allée de Tourny*. In its centre is **Galerie des Grands Hommes**, a chic shopping mall. There is an English-only bookshop, **Bradley's,** *32 pl. Gambetta; tel: 56 52 10 57.* For antique shops, browse along the picturesque *r. Bouffard.* Other covered shopping centres are the modern **Centre St-Christoly** and the arcaded

Galerie Bordelaise. For cheaper shopping and a long stroll, the pedestrianised *r. Ste-Catherine* starts at *pl. de la Comédie* and has interesting off-shoots like *r. de la Porte Dijeaux*. The large **Mériadeck** shopping mall has a supermarket, snack bars and useful services such as shoe repairs.

Sightseeing

Guided tours in French and English include: panoramic tour by bus, Wed and Sat 1000 (mid-May–mid-Oct), FFr.55; **Old Bordeaux** walking tour, daily 1000 except Wed and Sat (July–mid-Sept) FFr.32 (concessions FFr.27); **Old Bordeaux by Night** walking tour (French only) Sat 2115 (July–Aug) FFr.32 (FFr.27). Starting point for all tours is the main tourist office. Walking tours of individual quarters take place on regular days at 1430 (July–mid-Sept) from various starting points. FFr.32 (FFr.27).

Bordeaux by Bus, a CGFTE brochure in English, outlines four routes for hop-on/hop-off exploration of main and off-the-beaten-track sights, each route takes 40–70 mins.

The city centre attractions include the twin-spired **Cathédrale St-André**, *pl. Pey Berland*, with its **Tour Pey-Berland**, a detached belfry tower, 51 m tall, which can be climbed. The cathedral has weekly organ concerts. **Le Musée d'Aquitaine**, *20 cours Pasteur; tel: 56 01 51 00*, is open Tues–Sat 1000–1800. FFr.18 (FFr.9), free admission Wed (stop: *cours Pasteur)*. It gives an imaginatively presented introduction to local history including the city's heyday as a great port. **Le Musée des Beaux Arts**, *20 cours d'Albret; tel: 56 10 16 93*. Open Wed–Mon 1000–1800, closed holidays. FFr.18 (FFr.9), free on Wed, (stop: *cours d'Albret)*. It has a collection of European masters. **Le Musée des Arts Decoratifs**, *39 r. Bouffard; tel: 56*

10 15 62. Open Wed–Mon 1400–1800, closed holidays. FFr.18 (FFr.9), free on Wed. (stop: *pl. Pey Berland)*. There are three storeys filled with fine furniture, porcelain, miniatures and prints.

Dotted throughout the city are museums on subjects such as the liberation, art printing in the 19th century, military uniforms and natural history as well as Goya's last residence.

For nautical heritage, there are two contrasting museums. At the riverside is **Croiseur Colbert** (a French navy cruiser), *60 quai des Chartrons; tel: 56 44 96 11*, with admiral's quarters, navigation bridge, engine room and sailors' mess desks. Open Mon–Fri 1000–1800, Sat–Sun and holidays 1000–1900 (April–Sept); Wed–Fri 1000–1800; Sat, Sun and holidays 1000–1900 (Oct–March). Admission FFr.42 (FFr.25) (stop: *Les Chartrons)*. **Conservatoire International de Plaisance** (pleasure boat museum), *bassin à flot, blvd Alfred Daney; tel: 56 11 11 50*. Open Wed–Fri 1300–1900, Sat and Sun 1000–1900 (Mar–mid-Nov), FFr.30 (FFr.15), stop: *blvd A. Daney*. The 70 sail and power boats, some world champions, are displayed in the old submarine hall.

Many of the city's interesting quarters adjoin the waterfront. Closest to the rail station is the sadly neglected neighbourhood around the stunningly simple Romanesque **Église Ste-Croix** (St Croix Church), in a quiet square with the romantic ruins of an 18th-century fountain set into 14th-century wall remnants. The **St-Michel** quarter is evocative of a provincial town, with grannies chatting in the old streets, men playing cards in the rustic bars, the sturdy late-Gothic **Église St-Michel** (St Michael's Church) with its detached, spired bell-tower where a flea market gathers most mornings. In the **St-Pierre** quarter is **Porte Cailhu**, a turretted former royal gateway of 1495 (exhibition open daily in summer, Wed and Sat in winter) and the Gothic **Église St-Pierre** (St Peter's Church). Next, at the finely designed 18th-century square, **pl. de la Bourse**, one of the elegant buildings is the **Musée des Douanes** (museum of customs and excise) tracing the port's history (closed Mon). Then, the **Esplanade des Quinconces**, a spacious 19th-century garden square, has colossal statuary including the **Monuments aux Girondins**. Further along is the old wine merchants' district of **Chartrons** with the **Musée des Chartrons**, *41 r. Borie; tel: 56 44 27 77.* It portrays the wine trade (closed Sun, Mon).

Boat cruises run from *Embarcadère des Quinconces, quai Louis XVIII.* **Le Ville de Bordeaux** departs daily 1500, returns 1630 (June–Sept) FFr.50 (FFr.40). There are Sun lunch cruises in summer to **Blaye** and **Cadillac**, depart 1230, return 1800, menus from FFr.95, *tel: 56 52 88 88.* **Aliènor** offers cruises all year, except Feb, in the harbour and along the Gironde (to Blaye), the Dordogne (to Libourne) and the Garonne (to Langon); phone for individual availability as departures depend on group bookings, *tel: 56 52 17 67.*

Out of Town

The famous wine regions of Bordeaux can be reached by train. The electrified line that runs north from Bordeaux St-Jean to **Pointe-de-Grave** (see *ETT* table 132) travels through the Medoc area and passes some of the best known vineyards in France. **Château Margaux** is not far from the eponymous station and **Château Mouton Rothchild** and **Château Lafitte** can be reached from **Pauillac** station.

Another option is to take a guided bus tour (French and English) from the main

Canal du Midi

The canals of southern France link the Atlantic Ocean with the Mediterranean Sea along a 450-km route. They are better-known as the **Canal du Midi**, a network now used for pleasure boating. Originally they were built as a means of transporting supplies and manufactured goods in greater quantities without hazarding treacherous, or non-existent, roads and mountain passes. The **Canal Latéral à la Garonne** (the canal beside the Garonne River), built in 1856, flows between Bordeaux and Toulouse, the last of the network which dates back 300 years. The architect of this grand scheme in the 1600s was Pierre-Paul Riquet, a businessman and salt-tax collector who had a great interest in water-linked engineering projects.

As well as canal boat cruising, there are barge hotels. Information about **Le Mark Twain** (at Bordeaux) from *Continentale de Croisières Francaises, 19 r. d'Athènes, 75009 Paris; tel: (1) 40 20 02 04.* Contact **Carabosse**, *Pont des Demoiselles, 31400 Toulouse; tel: 61 53 07 82.*

tourist office. These depart daily 1330, return 1830 (mid-May–mid-Oct), FFr.130 (FFr.110). All-day tours take in the city's wine merchant quarter, lunch with wine tasting and a château; Wed and Sat, depart 0930, return 1830, FFr.240 (FFr.220). Shorter wine tasting tours depart Tues, Fri 1030, Thurs 1700, FFr.130 (FFr.110). About twice a month (May–Aug) there are guided wine tasting tours with a candlelit dinner in a château. FFr.250.

BORDEAUX to BIARRITZ

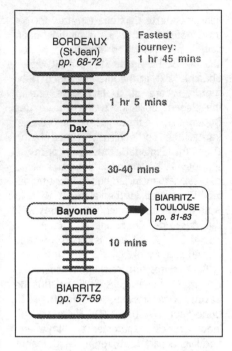

BORDEAUX (St-Jean) pp. 68-72

Fastest journey: 1 hr 45 mins

1 hr 5 mins

Dax

30-40 mins

Bayonne

BIARRITZ-TOULOUSE pp. 81-83

10 mins

BIARRITZ pp. 57-59

After the built-up suburbs of Bordeaux, the scenery changes quickly to flat stretches of sunflowers and cornfields. Here and there farm machinery with delicate irrigation wings sprays the crops. Forests of spindly trees, the ground luxuriant with bright green ferns, start dominating the views. Some 60 per cent of Les Landes district is cultivated for its timber, wood pulp and resin, an industry started in the mid-19th century when the locals drained the flat heathland. It is a soothing 2-hr journey all the way to the jet-set resort of Biarritz, with no hint of the sandy Atlantic beaches stretching nearby.

TRAINS

ETT table: 137.

→ **Fast Track**

Six trains link Bordeaux St-Jean with Biarritz each day, journey times varying from 1 hr 45 mins for the TGVs to 2 hrs 30 mins for the local services.

 On Track

Bordeaux–Dax

Up to a dozen services run daily between Bordeaux St-Jean and Dax, mostly TGVs, with journey times of around 1 hr 5 mins.

Dax–Bayonne

Eight or nine trains a day run between Dax

and Bayonne, the journey taking 30–40 mins.

Bayonne–Biarritz

About a dozen trains each day make the 10-min run from Bayonne to Biarritz.

This route can be continued into Spain via Hendaye to Irún, for connections to destinations throughout Spain; see ETT tables 137 and 430/440.

DAX

Station: *av. de la Gare: tel: 36 35 35 35.* Facilities include an automatic cash dispenser, buffet and lockers. The 20-min walk to the centre crosses over the River Adour which divides the town. Bus no. 1E runs to the centre (stop: *pl. St-Pierre*). **Taxi:** *tel: 58 91 20 60,* fare to centre: FFr.30. **Bus Station:** *pl. de la Gare; tel: 58 74 19*

76. Local bus lines are run by **Urbus**. Single fare FFr.5, ten for FFr.32. For destinations further afield, **Régie Départemental des Transports des Landes**, *tel: 58 56 80 80*, has bus services to towns in the Les Landes forest area (Seignosse, Soustons).

Tourist Office: *pl. Thiers, BP177, 40100 Dax; tel: 58 90 20 00*. Open daily 0930–1230, 1400–1900 (June–Aug); 0930–1230, 1400–1800 (Sept–Nov); Mon–Fri 0930–1230, 1400–1800; Sat 0930–1230 (Dec–Feb); Mon–Fri 0930–1230, Sat 1400–1800 (Mar–May). English leaflets, hotel lists (no reservations). Guided tours in French.

Accommodation and Food

Dax, population 20,000, is spread-out, noisy and busy. Hydrotherapy and thermal treatments are the backbone of its tourist industry. There are aerobaths, underwater massage, steam treatment, high-pressure showers and treatments using special local mud called *peloide*. The hotel brochure, *Dax Guide*, lists doctors specialising in such treatments. One outlet is **Thermes des Arènes**, *blvd A. Camus, 40100 Dax; tel: 58 56 01 83*. It joins up with an organisation offering studio-style accommodation, but will give free transport to people taking treatment who are staying elsewhere.

Many of the hotels and apartment residences are based on residents using their pools, showers and equipment, so are not cheap, although rates are usually arranged for a week or two. There is a wide range of studio accommodation for one or two people and *chambres d'hôtes*.

Camping: *Du Bois de Boulogne, Pierre Abaladejo, Les Chênes; tel: 58 90 05 53*, 1500 m from the town centre, 600 m from hydrotherapy outlets, take bus no. 1B (stop: *Bois de Boulogne*).

There are many places to eat from traditional and gourmet (try *r. des Pénitents* and *blvd St-Pierre*) to brasseries, salad bars and cafés (around *pl. Thiers* and *cours de Verdun*) and there are excellent charcuteries selling hams, *foies gras*, duck conserves and other local specialities. **Charcutier Roger Junca**, *22 pl. de la Fontaine Chaude; tel: 58 74 06 72*, has take-away dishes of the day; a picnic can be enjoyed in the park, **Parc Théodore Dennis**, set in the city walls opposite.

Sightseeing

As part of the Basque region, Dax enjoys a strong Spanish influence, with *féria* (festive events) held in Aug, including bullfighting, folk dancing, music and parades and the ball game, *pelote basque*. Information from **Régie Municipal des Fêtes et des Spectacles**, *pl. de la Fontaine Chaude, 40100 Dax; tel: 58 74 13 98*. An active nightlife includes a casino in the suburbs 3 kms away, **César Palace**, *allée de Christus, 40990, St-Paul-Lès-Dax; tel: 58 91 52 72*.

Its historic attractions and old streets are all within walking distance of one another. **La Fontaine Chaude** (hot water spring), 64°C, which has inspired the hydrotherapy industry and once attracted the Romans is in public view, and still bubbles away in a handsome pool with a Romanesque arched wall, part of the old quarter, next to a maze of streets (*r. des Carmes, r. St-Pierre*). At its heart is the **Cathédrale Notre-Dame**, in the classical style of the late 17th–18th centuries, with some Gothic ruins and a 13th-century apostles' door.

Away from the centre is **Le Musée de l'Aviation Legère de l'Armée de Terre-ALAT** (a collection of light aircraft, helicopters and associated objects), *58 de l'Aérodrome; tel: 58 74 66 19*. Open Mon–Sat 1430–1730 (closed Dec–mid-Feb), admission FFr.25. Guided tours (in French), Sat and Tues. Take bus no. 1B from *pl. de St-Pierre* (stop: *Musée d'ALAT*).

For cruises on the **River Adour, La Hire,** *quai du 28ème Battalion de Chasseurs; tel: 58 74 87 07,* (Mar–mid-Nov). Afternoon trips go to **Saubusse**, depart 1400 and return 1830. FFr.60. Day trips go to **Port-de-Lanne**, depart 1000, return 1900; FFr.230 (including a meal at a port of call).

BAYONNE

Station: *pl. Periere* (facing *pl. de la République*); *tel: 36 35 35 35.* There is a buffet, lockers and tourist information; *tel: 59 55 20 45.* Open Mon–Sat 0930–1230, 1400–1830 (July–Aug). The local bus network is run by **Stab**, which runs the service in nearby Biarritz, and some lines link the two towns.

Tourist Office: *pl. des Basques, 64100 Bayonne; tel: 59 46 01 46,* provides guided tours in French. It has leaflets, souvenirs, T-shirts and ticket booth for Aug festival. Open Mon–Sat 0900–1900, Sun 1300–1900 (summer); Mon–Fri 0900–1830, Sat 0930–1800 (winter).

Accommodation and Food

There are cheap and medium-priced hotels opposite the station and in the old quarter. Chains include: *Ca, F1, Ib,* and *Me*.

The nicest spots to eat line both banks of the **River Nive** with outdoor tables giving a pleasant outlook. The old streets tend to be quieter and you need time to explore before coming across a tucked-away restaurant or snack bar (*blvd Tour du Sault, r. Thiers*). There are several restaurants opposite the station and the tree-lined *pl. de la République*. Many good food shops sell Bayonne ham.

Sightseeing

Guided walking tours (French-language) leave the tourist office Tues, Fri, Sat 1000, also Sat 1500 (July–Aug), FFr.30. Bayonne centre is best seen on foot, as the narrow streets are mostly pedestrian.

Stunningly medieval, this grey stone city is surrounded by its old defence walls and stands commandingly over the banks of the wide **River Adour**. A second, narrower river, the **Nive**, flows along most of the old town. The twin spires of the cathedral top off the historical core of the city. **Cathédrale Ste-Marie**, built in the 13th–16th centuries, is a fine Gothic building, with its stonework bearing the coat of arms of England (three leopards) and the French *fleur-de-lys*. England occupied Bayonne for three centuries. In a separate entrance at the back are the 14th-century cloisters with intricately carved arches. These are open Mon–Sat 0930–1230, 1400–1800 (Apr–Oct); 0930–1230, 1400–1700 (Nov–Mar); FFr.7. There is an English leaflet to borrow.

Probably because most tourists have headed for the 106 km of sandy beaches for which this region is famous, Bayonne seems untouched, its inhabitants going about their business against a splendid backdrop of narrow streets, half-timbered houses and riverside. Beside the **citadel** near the station, the bulky ramparts make up a park, promenade and a venue for open-air concerts. They were constructed by Vauban in 1670. Around the same time Bayonne gave its name to another local military invention, the bayonet. On the station side of the rivers, **Le Musée Bonnat**, *r. J. Lafitte; tel: 59 59 08 52,* is open Wed–Mon 1000–1200, 1500–1900, Fri 1000–1200 (summer); Wed–Mon, 1000–1200, 1430–1830 (winter). There is a collection of paintings by Greco, Goya, Rubens and Ingrès as well as by Léon Bonnat, a native of Bayonne. Admission FFr.15 (concessions FFr.5).

BORDEAUX to CLERMONT-FERRAND

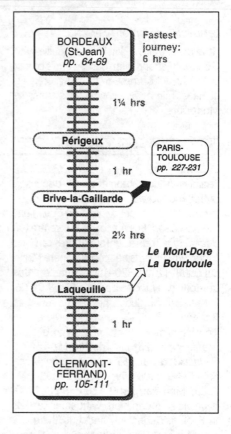

From the great port of Bordeaux and its wide Garonne river to the volcanic mountain range, the Chaîne de Puys, around Clermont-Ferrand, this route takes in many contrasts. At first there are are farmlands and vineyards, then pine forests on either side, with occasional returns to industry at the bigger centres, but it finishes with dramatic distant views of mountains which are soon right outside the windows.

TRAINS

ETT tables: 140, 140b.

 Fast Track

Only one train a day operates between Bordeaux St-Jean and Clermont-Ferrand, although even this train has been restricted to Fri only during the winter months. Other services are available by changing at Gannat or St Germain-des-Fossés. Journey times by either route are around 6 hrs.

 On Track

Bordeaux–Périgueux

Up to a dozen trains a day run between Bordeaux St-Jean and Périgueux although most run during the early morning and early evening peak periods and there are long gaps in the service during the rest of the day. The journey takes around 1¼ hrs.

Périgueux–Brive-la-Gaillarde

Four or five trains a day run between Périgueux and Brive-la-Gaillarde taking around 1 hr.

Brive-la-Gaillarde–Laqueuille

Le Ventadour leaves Brive-la-Gaillarde midmorning for the 2½-hr journey to Laqueuille. This train was running on Fri only for most of the 1994/5 winter season, so check the timetables carefully before travelling. The only alternative is an early morning local train.

Laqueuille–Clermont-Ferrand

At least six trains a day link Laqueuille with Clermont-Ferrand with journey times of just over 1 hr. All of these trains either start at, or have train or bus connections from, Le Mont-Dore.

PÉRIGEUX

Station: *r. de Papin, tel: 36 35 35 35.* Facilities include automatic cash dispenser, buffet and lockers. The 15-min walk to the centre follows *r. des Mobile-de-Coulmiers,* then *r. Wilson.* Bus A goes to the centre (*pl. Bugeaud).* Tourist information can be found in an outside booth, open Mon–Sat 0900–1200, 1330–1800 (summer). **Bus station:** *pl. Francheville; tel: 53 08 91 06.* Destinations include the pretty town of Brantôme.

Tourist Office: *Rond point de la Tour Mataguerre, 26 pl. Francheville, 24070 Périgeux; tel: 53 53 10 63.* Open Mon–Sat, 0900–1900, Sun 1000–1700 (July–Aug); Mon–Sat, 0900–1200, 1400–1900. It provides information, with some leaflets in English. During July and Aug there is a tourist information kiosk opposite St Front Cathedral.

Regional information is available from the **Comité Départemental de Tourisme de la Dordogne,** *16 r. Wilson, 24009 Périgeux; tel: 53 53 44 35.* Open Mon–Fri 0900–1200, 1400–1630. Information, but no hotel reservations.

Getting Around

Walking is the best way to see the sights. The local bus system is run by **Péribus,** *pl. Montaigne; tel: 53 53 30 37.* Open Mon–Fri 0845–1200, 1400–1800. Single ticket FFr.6.50; a book of ten, FFr.42. **Taxi**: *tel: 53 09 09 09.*

Accommodation and Food

Cheap and reasonable hotels face the station and are found throughout the centre. Chains include *Ca, Cl* and *F1.* **HI: FJT Rèsidense Lakanal,** *blvd Lakanal; tel: 53 53 52 05.* Bus A from station to *pl. Villefranche,* then bus no. 5 from the bus station (stop: *Lakanal).* **Camping:** *Barnabé-Plage, 80 r. des Bain; tel: 53 53 41 45.* Bus D from *pl. Montaigne* (bus stop: *r. des Bains).*

The many cheap places to eat (around *av. Gambetta* and *blvd Montaigne)* are backed with a good choice of gourmet restaurants. A pleasant square for outdoor eating, with perhaps a classical string quartet of music students giving an impromptu concert under the plane trees, is *pl. Louis.* Besides duck, pork and goose specialities, fish dishes include salt cod brandade, carp stuffed with *foie gras* and eel in red wine. Périgeux sauce is based on finely chopped truffles in madeira.

Food shopping is important and the town blossoms when its markets are in business. These are dotted here and there throughout the town, the main one beside St Front Cathedral on Wed and Sat. A farmer's market with tastings of *foie gras* is in *pl. St-Louis,* Wed and Sat mornings (mid-Nov–Mar). The town shops overflow with pâtés and walnut cakes, with the show-piece products being *foie gras, confit* of goose, duck or pork and truffles. Confectionery includes stuffed prunes and walnuts, sugar-coated chestnuts and chocolate truffles. Most products are available in tins.

Events

Périgeux is constantly *en fête* in summer, with many musical and theatrical events and an international annual mime festival in Aug.

Sightseeing

Guided tours, in French and English, leave the tourist office Tues–Fri (July–Aug). The Gallo-Romano route departs 1000, FFr.22 (concessions FFr.16) ; the medieval-Renaissance route departs 1430, FFr.22 (FFr.16). The **Tour Mataguerre** visit (opposite the tourist office) includes a slide show of the town in the tower, 1030, FFr.10 (FFr.8). There are other themes, including a bus tour, FFr.22 (FFr.18).

Périgeux is easily divided into two areas, with an old town (based around **Cathédral St-Front**) and an even older town (based around the crumbling St Stephen's Church, **Église St-Étienne-de-la-Cité**). With a free English route map from the tourist office, the latter district is easily explored on foot in an hour or so. Known as Vesunna in its prosperous Roman heyday, this area has a clutch of Roman remains, enhanced by the atmosphere of the austere streets; this is not the area for restaurants or shopping.

The *cité's* focus is the huge church, once the cathedral, truncated now with only two domes, 11th–12th century, of the original four left. From here, *r. Romaine*, with Roman wall vestiges, leads to the **Jardin de Vésone,** with the wonderful Roman tower, 27 m high, 20 m wide, standing in the middle of a shaded restful garden with giant plane trees, and landscaped with other bits of Roman ruins. Behind the garden, on the other side of the rail tracks, are extensive excavations of the Roman **Villa de Pompeïus**, visible from behind a wire fence and accessible only with a guide from the tourist office.

In this area are also the **Château de Barriére,** a mansion built using Roman remains, the **Porte Normande**, a Roman arch, and the **Arènes** (the Roman amphitheatre), now only a distinctive outline

in a lively park with a fountain used as a wading pool.

In the main town centre, St Front cathedral bustles with domes, cupolas and belfry towers, looming splendidly over shopping and restaurant streets. The white-stoned building has Romanesque beginnings but was largely rebuilt from 1852.

Handsome stone town mansions, medieval and Renaissance, add to the charm of the old streets (*r. Aubergerie, r. du Calvaire, r. de la Sagesse, r. Limogeanne, r. de la Constitution*). Beside the bridge, **Pont des Barris**, are interesting old quayside houses, including **Maison des Consuls**, facing the **River L'Isle**. To get an overview of the town's history, visit the airy former Augustinian convent, **Le Musée du Périgord** (museum of the Périgord district), *cours Tourny, tel: 53 53 16 42*. Open Wed–Mon 1000–1200, 1400–1700 (until 1800 in summer). FFr.12 (FFr.6).

BRIVE-LA-GAILLARDE

Station: *av. J. Jaurès; tel: 36 35 35 35*. Buffet, lockers and automatic cash dispenser. For the 15-min walk to the centre, take *av. J. Jaurès*, then turn right and follow an inner circle of town boulevards (*blvd M. Lyautey, de Puyblanc, J. Ferry, du Salans*) to *pl. du 14 Juillet*. Alternatively take bus no. 8 (stop: *pl. du 14 Juillet*).

Tourist Office: *pl. du 14 Juillet, 19100 Brive; tel: 55 24 08 80*. Open Mon–Sat, 0900–1230, 1400–1900, Sun 1000–1300 (July–Aug); Mon–Sat 1000–1200, 1430–1800 (Sept–June). Housed in an old water tower, it has information in English. No hotel reservations.

STUB bus station is at *pl. du 1 Juillet; tel: 55 24 29 93*. Single ticket FFr.6.60; book of ten, FFr.35.

Accommodation and Food

There are moderate hotels near the station and a good choice in the centre, but chain hotels are found on the outskirts. Chains include: *BW, Ca, Cl, Ib* and *Me*. **HI**: *56 av. M. Bugeaud, Parc Monjauze; tel: 55 24 34 00*. An almost 20-min walk from the station; follow the route for the town centre, but turn right into *av. Bugeaud* off *blvd du Salan*. Or take bus no. 8 to *pl. du 14 Juillet*, then bus nos 2 or 4 (stop: *Nautique*).

Camping Municipal: *Les Iles, blvd Michelet; tel: 55 24 34 74*. No bus, it is a 20-min walk from the station. Follow the directions for the youth hostel, from there take *blvd Cal Dubois, blvd Michelet* (about 5 mins away).

Restaurants in all price ranges are found in the centre around *r. de Toulzac* and *pl. de la Gaulle*. Markets are frequent, with the main one on Tues, Thurs, Sat, 0800–1200, at *pl. du 14 Juillet*. Look for the same food specialities as in Périgeux (see p. 74). An antique fair at *r. du Cap. Galinat* is held on the first and third Tues every month.

Sightseeing

Brive gives a refreshing welcome with its wide avenues of plane trees, which have replaced the city's defence walls, and which have many brasseries and restaurants on the way to the centre (*blvds de Puyblanc, J. Ferry*). Walking tours (including English) leave from the tourist office in July–Aug, Tues, Thurs, 1000; FFr.20. Booking necessary.

Across the road from the tourist office is the **Théâtre Municipal**, beside which is *av. de Paris* which leads into the old town with its pedestrianised shopping streets encircling **Église St-Martin** (St Martin's Church), a simple, Romanesque church with a lovely 14th-century nave. Nearby are the town mansions with handsome façades (*r. des Échevins, pl. Latreille*) and the town hall, built from 1650.

With undramatic but pleasant sights, the town gives an opportunity to indulge in a look at an interesting local industry. Two liqueur distilleries are open (although the staff speak French only, the open-plan layout puts the distilling procedure on view, the products are on sale and visitors are welcome). **Demoix**, *9 blvd du M. Lyautey; tel: 55 74 34 27*. This is just a few mins from the station at the end of *av. J. Jaurès*. Open Tues–Sat 0845–2000, 1430–1900 (also Mon in July–Aug). Hazelnut, chocolate, strawberry and orange are among the many flavours of liqueurs, along with mustard and chocolate truffles, produced against a background of gleaming wood and copper vats in this atmospheric distillery, established in 1839. A smaller, cosier establishment is **Bellet**, *3 av. M. Bugeaud, tel: 55 24 18 07*. It is just off the *blvd du Salin* on the walk into the centre. Open Mon–Sat 0900–1200, 1400–1800. Founded in 1899 and still run by the same family, the premises, reminiscent of an apothecary with so many bottles of beautifully coloured liquids, make liqueurs from aromatic plants and herbs (thyme, angelica, the pungent gentian) and fruit-berry combinations (e.g. raspberry-peach).

There are two good museums. **Le Musée Labenche,** *26 bis blvd J. Ferry; tel: 55 24 19 05*. Open Wed–Mon 1000–1830 (Apr–Oct); Wed–Mon 1330–1800 (Nov–Mar); FFr.12.50. In this mansion (with additions from the 16th–18th centuries) are Aubusson tapestries and English-made, 17th-century ones from Mortlake along with archeological finds and art objects. The Edmond Michelin museum is the **Centre National de la Résistance et** de la Déportation Edmond Michelet, *4 r. Champanatier, tel: 55 74 06 08.* Open Mon–Sat, 1000–1200, 1400–1800. Free. A short walk to the left of the station, this is more ambitious than many local liberation museums and has an in-depth look at the resistance movement, including paintings, and has been inspired by a local Brive man who was a resistance leader.

LAQUEUILLE

Regular connections from the branch line at Laqueuille go to **Le Mont-Dore**, a 25-min journey which gets right into the heart of the volcanic peaks.

Side Tracks from Laqueuille

The train to Le Mont-Dore stops at **La Bourboule**, where old houses with fabulous views hug the mountain sides and a cable car wends its way to the top. Both places are spa towns, winter sports resorts and the lively major resorts of the **Monts-Dore** chain, complete with casinos and discos as well as wooded walks to get away from it all.

LE MONT-DORE

Tourist Office: *av. de la Libération, 63240 Le Mont-Dore; tel: 73 65 20 21.* Open Mon–Sat 0900–1230, Sun, holidays 1000–1200, 11400–1830. Leaflets in English available. It is a straight 10-min walk from the little station down *av. Michel Bertrand* to *pl. C. de Gaulle*, the centre of this jaunty village in the mountains with a fabulous view in every direction. A book of 38 discount vouchers, called *Le Pass Sports-Loisirs*, sold at the tourist office, gives up to 10–30 per cent discounts off the prices of local attractions, excursions and sports facilities; FFr.200.

There is a good range of accommodation including self-catering apartments, whose residents have many good food shops to choose from. Day trippers can have picnics by the river. There are many places to eat plus bars, discos and a casino. The **Funiculaire du Capucin**, *tel: 73 65 01 25*, near the tourist office, runs every 20 mins, 0940–1140 and 1410–1810.

The funicular, built in 1898, is charmingly restored with its original features brightly painted in yellow and red. It climbs through beech and fir trees to the **Salon du Capucin**, an informal restaurant and coffee stop, in a clearing which overlooks the town and is also the crossroad for many footpaths.

Le Musée Joseph Forêt, *av. M. Bertrand* (telephone the tourist office for information), is open Tues–Sun 1630–1830; FFr.10. This off-beat museum's central display is the replica of 'the largest book in the world', compiled by Joseph Forêt. It is a modern interpretation of the Apocalypse, with illustrated pages by artists such as Dali, and text by Cocteau and his contemporaries.

The most unusual attraction is the lovely, neo-Byzantine building, **Les Thermes**, still busy dispensing water cures. There are 30-min guided tours Mon–Sat, leaving from 1115–1130 and 1500–1530, FFr.8. It is all right just to step in to view the marble-walled **Hall des Sources** and its fountain of therapeutic water. Full and half-day excursions depart from Le Mont-Dore, May–Sept, run by **Tourisme Verney**, *tel: 73 37 31 06*, or **Volcatours**, *tel: 73 65 57 07* (or ask at the tourist office).

BORDEAUX to SOUILLAC

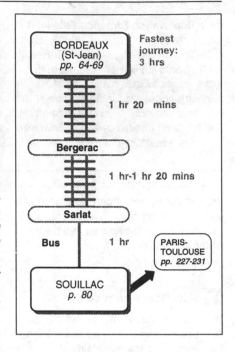

From Bordeaux, an industrial city, to the medieval showpiece of Sarlat, en route to Souillac, the two-carriage train heads through hamlets, villages and some tiny stations. There are stops every few minutes and a very rural feel as the train passes solid farmhouses with dormer roofs and old turetted buildings or square houses. The journey is completed by bus. The scenery starts off with gentle hills and vineyards, some growing in regimented lines, others flowing over into leafy geometric patterns. It ends up with steep stone cliffsides, chock-a-block with sunflowers, more vineyards, and steep hills dotted with houses and stone walls enclosing flocks of geese.

TRAINS

ETT table: 140a.

 Fast Track

Four trains a day link Bordeaux St-Jean with Sarlat, with journey times of 2–3 hrs. The bus ride from Sarlat to Souillac takes 1 hr.

 On Track

Bordeaux–Bergerac

Up to eight trains a day run between Bordeaux and Bergerac. The journey takes around 1 hr 20 mins.

Bergerac–Sarlat

Four trains each day make the journey

from Bergerac to Sarlat, taking 1 hr–1 hr 20 mins.

Sarlat–Souillac

These towns are linked by bus. From Sarlat station or *pl. Pasteur*, there is a bus daily (frequency depending on the day) to Souillac rail station. The almost hour-long journey costs FFr.25.50. This service is run by **SCETA Voyageurs,** *24 r. Aristide Briand, 87000 Limoges; tel: 55 77 57 65.* Souillac also appears on the Paris–Toulouse route; see p. 227.

BERGERAC

Station: *av. du 108e Régiment; tel: 36 35 35 35.* It is a 15-min walk to the modern centre, 20–25 mins to the old quarter and quays. Follow *cours Alsace Lorraine, r. Ste-Catherine* to *pl. de Lattre de Tassigny.* **Taxi:**

tel: 53 57 17 06. Fare to centre, FFr.30.
Tourist Office: *97 r. Neuve d'Argenson, 24100 Bergerac; tel: 53 57 03 11.* Open Mon–Sat 0900–2100, Sun 1600–1900 (July–mid-Sept); Mon 1400–1800, Tues–Sat 0900–1200, 1400–1800 (mid-Sept–June). Provides hotel reservations (July–mid-Sept), information and guided walks.

Accommodation and Food

On the expensive side, the town's hotels are scattered, mostly in the commercial centre and the outskirts of town, but there are a few opposite the station. Chains include *Ca* and *Cl.* **Camping Municipal**: *de la Pelouse, au bord de la Dordogne; tel: 53 57 06 67.* No bus; it is a short walk along the old quayside.

The greatest choice of restaurants, cafés and brasseries is found in the commercial centre (*pl. Gambetta*). In the old town, the streets add to pleasure of dining out (*pl. du Dr Cayla, r. de l'Ancien Port, pl. Pélissière*).

Sightseeing

Guided walks available include some given in English. As one of the largest towns along this route, Bergerac has an interesting history. In its old quarter and quayside the attractions are very close to one another.

Its museums include two about local produce and industry. **Le Musée d'Intérêt National du Tabac** (the tobacco museum), *10 r. de Ancien Port; tel: 53 63 04 13,* is open Tues–Fri 1000–1200, 1400–1800, Sat until 1700, Sun 1430–1830. FFr.15. **Le Musée du Vin et de la Batallerie** (museum of wine and canal transport), *r. des Conferences; tel: 53 57 80 92.* Open Tues–Fri 1000–1200, 1400–1730; Sat 1000–1200, 1400–1700 (mid-Nov–mid-Mar); same hours plus Sun 1430–1830 (mid-Mar–mid-Nov); admission FFr.5.

Also exploring the theme of wine is **Le Cloître des Récollects** (Convent of the Recollects), *2 pl. du Dr. Cayla; tel: 53 57 12 57.* It houses the **Maison du Vin**, which displays information about the region's famous vineyards. Open Mon–Sat 0900–1200, 1300–1800 (summer); Tues–Fri 0830–1230, 1330–1730 (winter), FFr.10.

Situated on a wide sweep of the Dordogne, Bergerac has pleasant riverside walks. From the **Vieux Port** (old port) there are regular hour-long boat excursions, daily 1100–1900 (May–Oct) FFr.20–35; *tel: 53 24 58 80.*

SARLAT

Station: *av. de la Gare; tel: 36 35 35 35.* A small, rural station well outside the town. Ticket booth only. No buffet, no lockers. It is a 20-min walk to the town; follow the *av. de la Gare* to *Le Pontet*, turn right and keep straight on until the *r. de la République.* At *Le Pontet*, Sarlat's two bus lines, A and B, both stop, Mon–Sat, 0822–1734; then both go to **pl. du 14 Juillet**, the square at the entrance to the historic centre. Single fare FFr.3.50. (Only Line B stops at the station, but does not go immediately to the town centre). **CFTA** bus information: *tel: 53 59 01 48.* **Taxi**: *tel: 53 59 02 43* or *53 59 00 49.*
Tourist Office: *pl. de la Liberté, 24200 Sarlat; tel: 53 59 27 67.* Open Mon–Sat 0900–1900; Sun 1000–1200, 1400–1800 (but closed Sun, Oct–May). Provides guided tours and information about farmhouse accommodation and *chambres d'hôtes.*

Accommodation and Food

There is a good choice of hotels in the centre and more on roads outside. Booking ahead in Aug advised. **HI:** *77 av. de Selves, rte de Périgueux, Sarlat; tel: 53 59 47 59.*

Open Mar–Nov. About half an hour's walk from the station. **Camping**: *Les Périères, BP 98, 24203 Sarlat.* This is the closest campsite, 800 m from the station.

Sarlat has lots of places to eat, including many inexpensive snackbars, cafés and pizzerias. Many food shops sell *foie gras, confit de canard,* hazelnut cake, liqueurs and other specialities.

Entertainment

Despite its small size, Sarlat has several discos. Its many cultural events include a theatre festival in July, and an annual international film festival in Nov. There is a crafts market in the *pl. André Malraux,* daily, 1000–2200 (May–mid-Sept).

Sightseeing

The medieval town of Sarlat, population 10,650, enchants all visitors with its well-conserved pedestrian streets and can get very crowded in summer, even on Sun. It has two distinct sides flanking the **r. de La République**, the main street, with the cathedral, most restaurants and attractions on one side in streets off the **pl. de la Liberté**. But the very quiet residential backwater on the other side, although quaintly dilapidated, makes for an interesting walk though history (especially *r. Jean Jacques Rousseau* and *r. des Armes*).

On the conservation side is the **Cathédrale St-Sacredos**, mostly 16th–17th century but retaining some of its Romanesque abbey features including its arcades and a tower. It is in *pl. du Peyrou* where the most photographed of its town houses is located, the 16th century **Maison Natale d'Etienne de la Boétie**. Look behind the cathedral garden for the 12th-century, beehive-shaped tower, the **Lantern of the Dead**. A newly opened museum gives a chance to see inside one of the old town mansions, including furniture, costumes and armour. It is **Manoir d'Aillac,** *L'Hôtel des Mirepoises, 13 r. Fénelon; tel: 53 59 02 63.* Open daily 1000–2000; on Wed, Sat until 2300 (May–Sept); daily 1000–1200, 1400–1800 (Oct–Apr); FFr.15–25. Other picturesque streets are *r. des Consuls* and *r. de la Salamandre.*

SOUILLAC

Station: *pl. de la Gare; tel: 36 35 35 35.* No buffet or lockers, this is a small rural station well out of the town centre, a 25-min walk. No bus. Follow *av. J. Jaurès* straight to *av. Gén. de Gaulle,* which becomes *blvd L. J. Malvy.* **Taxi:** *tel: 65 37 80 31.* Fare to the centre is FFr.30.

Tourist Office: *blvd L. J. Malvy, BP 99, 46200 Souillac; tel: 65 37 81 56.* Open Mon–Fri 0930–1230, 1400–1900, Sat 0930–1230, 1400–1700, Sun 0930–1230 (July–Sept); Mon–Sat 1000–1200, 1400–1700 (Oct–June). It has leaflets and hotel information (but no reservations).

Souillac is a market town and a popular starting point for walking holidays in the Dordogne Valley. There are many eating places and a wide choice of hotel accommodation in all price brackets.

The town has a busy main street with many good food shops and a quieter historic core around *ch. de St-Jacques-de-Compostelle,* with the splendid domed Romanesque **L'Église Abbatiale Ste-Marie** (the abbey church) which has some evocative carvings such as a dancing Isaiah. Right next door is the **Musée de l'Automatique** (museum of automatons), *pl. de l'abbaye; tel: 65 37 07 07.* Open daily 1000–1900 (July–Aug); daily 1000–1200, 1500–1800 (Apr–Oct, but closed Mon in Apr, May and Oct); Wed–Sun 1400–1700 (Jan–Mar, Nov and Dec). FFr.20–25.

BORDEAUX to TOULOUSE

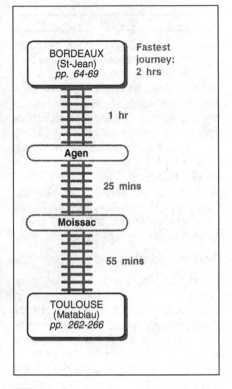

At the begining of this 2½-hr journey is the grand architecture of Bordeaux, at the end is the vivacious ambiance of Toulouse. Enhancing the scenery on the way are views of the canal linking the two. Although man-made, the canal fits in naturally with the fields of plum trees and vineyards, its calm water reflecting the trees along its banks in summer, the trees deep green in summer, richly varied in autumn.

Its construction has an intriguing appeal, with the canal actually higher than the train as it passes the small towns after Agen. Industrial areas with warehouses and transport equipment for the fruit crops of the region dot the route, but mostly the little towns exude a quiet charm and some are gateways to national parks. The last stretch, from Montauban, follows the Paris–Toulouse route (see p. 227).

TRAINS

ETT tables: 139.

→ Fast Track

Ten trains a day run between Bordeaux St-Jean and Toulouse Matabiau. Journey times are 2 hrs for Le Grand Sud express (supplementary fare payable), 2 hrs 7 mins for the three TGV trains and 2 hrs 20 mins for the ordinary expresses.

∿ On Track

Bordeaux–Agen

All the through trains between Bordeaux and Toulouse call at Agen en route with the sole exception of Le Grand Sud. The journey from Bordeaux St-Jean to Agen takes just over 1 hr.

Agen–Moissac–Toulouse

In addition to the 'Fast Track' expresses, a local train service runs between Agen and Toulouse between three and six times a day. These local trains call at Moissac en route. Agen to Moissac takes 25 mins and Moissac to Toulouse Matabiau takes 55 mins.

AGEN

Station: *blvd Sylvain Dumon; tel: 36 35 35 35.* It has buffet and lockers and is less than a 10-min walk to the old centre. Cross over and walk along the *av. Carnot,* turn right at *blvd de la République* to *pl. J. B. Durand,* or take bus nos 1 and 11 (stop: *Stadium).* **Bus** information: *tel: 53 98 15 00.* Single trip fare, FFr.5, ten tickets for FFr.40. **Taxi:** *tel: 53 66 39 14.*

Tourist Office: *107 blvd Carnot, 47000 Agen; tel: 53 47 36 09.* Open Mon–Sat 0900–1900, Sun 1000–1200 (July–Aug); Mon–Sat 0900–1230, 1400–1830 (Sept–June). It supplies leaflets and guided tours.

Accommodation

Accommodation is available in all price ranges, starting with the station area. Hotel chains include: *Ca, Cl, F1, Ib* and *Pr.* **HI:** *17 r. Léo Lagrange; tel: 53 66 18 98.* Bus no. 2 to Lalande (stop: *Léon Blum).* **Camping Municipal:** *A Bon Encontre; tel: 53 96 61 18.* This is near the youth hostel, so the directions are the same.

Sightseeing

Free guided tours in French (English translation on request) leave from the cathedral, Mon 1830, Thurs 2100 (mid-July–Aug). Agen seems an uneventful town but has a historic old quarter with timbered houses, a lively culinary heritage, the grand sweep of the Garonne river and the calm backwater of the canal. In the *pl. Esquirol* are the town hall theatre and **Le Musée d'Agen** (museum of Agen), which occupies four town mansions dating from the 16th–17th centuries and has Roman archaeological finds, several Goyas and a Greek marble sculpture from the 1st century BC of *Venus de Mas.* Open Wed–Mon 1100–1800 (summer); 1100–1700 (winter); FFr.15.

Nearby, other town mansions add to the charm of narrow streets such as *r. Beauville,* with its timber-framed houses with overhanging storeys in old-style brickwork. Named after the English Plantagenet king, Richard the Lion Heart, *r. R. Coeur de Lion* has the 18th-century house, **Hôtel Montesquieu-Suffolk,** with a courtyard and classic front staircase. Adjoining this street is *pl. des Jacobins,* a little square dominated by the Dominican church of the same name, **Église des Jacobins.**

Two main streets divide Agen, *av. Carnot,* uninteresting but with banks and the post office, and *blvd la République,* with many shops and restaurants, cafés and brasseries (especially around *pl. Jasmine).* The confectionery shops are a delight, with two traditional ones on *av. de Carnot,* very near the station. With stained glass windows, **P. Boisson** was founded in 1835, and is at no. 171, *tel: 53 66 20 61;* **J. Caban,** is at no. 175, *tel: 53 47 20 68.* The local specialities are the Agen plum, transformed by drying into the prized delicacy, and the Agen prune, stuffed or glacé, used in confectionery but also in savoury cooking.

For a quiet off-the-beaten-track walk (1–1½ hrs), follow the **Canal Latéral à la Garonne** (see also p. 69) from behind the station, along the quaysides to the Garonne where the canal continues its path over the river as **Le Pont Canal** (a canal bridge of water) with a pedestrian path. Completed in 1843, it has 23 arches. The grassy bank is fine for a picnic with a view of bridge, river and canal. Return via a different route by following *av. Gén. de Gaulle,* which joins *blvd la République.* For information about hiring a canal boat for a week's cruising, contact **Locaboat Plaisance,** *Port de la Gare du Pin, av. de la Stalingrad, 47000 Agen: tel: 53 66 00 74.*

Another bridge over the Garonne, the suspension bridge, **Passerelle**, is beside a landscaped park, **Esplanade du Gravier**.

MOISSAC

Station: *av. Pierre Chabrié; tel: 36 35 35 35.* A small rural station without lockers or bus service. For the 15-min walk to the centre follow *av. P. Chabrié*, then *av. de Brienne* to the historic centre, reached by some stairs. **Taxi:** *tel: 63 04 00 69.*

Tourist Office: *6 pl. Durand de Bredon, 82200 Moissac; tel: 63 04 01 85.* Open daily 0900–1900 (mid-July–Aug); daily 0900–1200, 1400–1800 (mid-Mar–June, Sept–mid-Oct); daily 0900–1200, 1400–1700 (mid-Oct–mid-Mar). It does not make hotel reservations.

Accommodation and Food

Accommodation is limited but reasonably priced. **Camping**: **Île du Moulin du Bidounet**; *tel: 63 32 29 96.* This also has 15 *gîte d'étape* places (overnight stops for walkers). From the station, walk along *av. P. Chabrié*, turn right at *blvd Lakenal*, straight over the bridge (Pont Napoléon), then first right.

Restaurants, including crêperies, are easy to find around the main square (*pl. R. Delthil*). Food shopping is colourful, with speciality shops and a market, Sat and Sun morning, at *pl. des Récollects*. The vineyards in the region grow the famous Chasselais grapes, available from Aug. Other fruit grown in abundance includes pears, melons, cherries and strawberries.

Sightseeing

Guided tours in French of the town leave from the tourist office all year, booking necessary, price FFr.11. A combined tour of the town, cloisters and the abbey museum is FFr.32. Cloisters only, FFr.19; cloisters and museum, FFr.21.

A little town, population 11,500, with a lively air, Moissac's great treasure is the carving on the capitals of the cloister and on the tympanum of the main doorway of the **Église St-Pierre** (St Peter's Abbey Church), which is the focus of the town centre. **Le Cloître** (cloister) is open the same hours as the adjoining tourist office from which it is entered; FFr.20 (concessions FFr.11). There is an abundance of carvings on the 66 columns, reflecting the craftsmanship of the sculptors of the 1100s. The guided tour is in French, as is an introductory exhibition, but there is an English guidebook, FFr.24. Nearby is the museum about the town's heritage, **Le Musée des Arts et Traditions Populaires**, *ancien palais abbatial; tel: 63 04 03 08.* Open Tues, FFr.5. There is a combined ticket for the cloisters and the museum, FFr.24 (FFr.12.50). The town's important religious buildings reflect its significance as a stop on the great medieval pilgrims' way (to Santiago de Compostela in Spain).

A 5-min walk away is **Le Musée St-Jacques**, *r. de l'Indonation; tel: 63 04 10 34.* Follow *r. de la République*, then *r. J. Moura*. Open daily 1500–1900 (summer); daily 1400–1800 (winter); FFr.10 (FFr.4). Within the redundant **Église St-Jacques**, the museum has displays on the three diverse themes of the railway, religious art and the region's traditions and crafts.

The **Canal Latéral à la Garonne** crosses through the town, making a pleasant walk along the towpath. Boat excursions, daily July–Aug, depart from **l'Uvarium** or **Le Port**. There are also small boats to hire for the half-day, day or weekend. Information from **Moissac Navigation Plaisance**, *Port de Plaisance, quai C. de Gaulle, tel: 63 04 48 28.*

CALAIS

Largely destroyed by bombing during World War II, Calais appears to offer little to detain the visitor. Most of the 16 million passengers who pass through Calais' ferry terminal en route to or from England also pass rapidly through the town. However, it is possible to pass a pleasant few hours in Calais if one is not put off by the more overt trappings of mass tourism; Calais is probably the most English of French towns.

Tourist Information

Tourist Office: *12 blvd G. Clémenceau; 62100 Calais, tel: 21 96 62 40.* Open Mon–Sat 0900–1930, Sun 1000–1300 and 1500–1930 (Apr–Aug); Mon–Sat 0900–1900, Sun closed (Sept–May). Turn left out of the rail station; the tourist office is 100 m to the right. There is an **information kiosk** at the ferry terminal, open daily 0900–2100 (July–Aug), closed Sept–June.

Arriving and Departing

Stations

Calais Ville, *blvd Jacquard; tel: 21 46 82 31*, opposite the Hôtel de Ville about 400 m south of the main tourist area. There is a daily TGV service to Paris Nord from Calais Ville, except on Sun.

Calais Fréthun station lies between Calais and Boulogne on the high-speed rail link to the Channel Tunnel. The daily TGV services to Calais and Boulogne from Paris both stop at Fréthun. There is a bus link between Calais Fréthun and Calais Ville.

Ferries

Sealink, *tel: 21 34 55 00*, and **P&O**, *tel: 21 46 04 40*, both operate regular sailings between Calais and Dover from the car ferry terminal.

Hoverspeed, *tel: 05 26 03 60* or *21 96 67 10*, operate SeaCats and hovercraft from the Hoverport, which is 2 km east of the ferry terminal. All companies run free shuttle buses between Calais Ville station and the ferry terminal to connect with ferry sailings.

Getting Around

Calais town centre is fairly compact and easily explored on foot; most interesting sights lie within a few hundred metres of Calais Ville station.

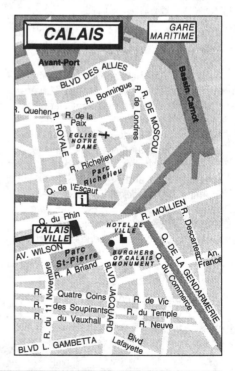

Staying in Calais

Accommodation

The number of travellers passing through Calais makes hotel reservations advisable but not essential; there is a reasonable supply of hotel rooms in the town although prices tend to be higher than elsewhere in northern France.

Hotel chains in Calais include *Ca, Ho, Ib* and *Mp*. The hostel **Maison pour Tous**, *blvd Jacquard; tel: 21 34 69 53*, is open June–Sept.

Eating and Drinking

There are numerous reasonable, if fairly unremarkable, brasseries and restaurants along *blvd Clémenceau* and its extension *r. Royale*, especially around *pl. d'Armes*. There are the usual supermarkets on *blvd Jacquard*, a few hundred metres south of the tourist office.

Communications

The main **post office** is at *pl. d'Alsace; tel: 21 85 52 80*, south of the rail station. A more convenient branch is at the *Tour du Guet; tel: 21 34 49 45*.

Shopping

Calais caters to thousands of British visitors who cross the channel to stock up on cheap beer and wine. Apart from the standard supermarkets there are hypermarkets slightly out of town on *av. Toumaniantz* and *av. Roger Salengo*; ask at the tourist office for bus details. Many new alcohol sales outlets, often no more than sheds, are being opened by French and British entrepreneurs.

Sightseeing

Visible from miles around, the distinctive **Hôtel de Ville** is Calais' most prominent landmark, a slightly garish early 20th-century reconstruction.

In front stands the original cast of Rodin's **The Six Burghers of Calais**. The statue depicts the six Calais townsmen who offered the keys of the city and their lives to Edward III in 1347, during the siege of the city. The town remained English until 1558 when it reverted to France, and Mary Tudor sadly commented, 'When I am dead and opened, you shall find 'Calais' lying in my heart'.

Opposite the Hôtel de Ville in the immaculate **Parc St-Pierre** is the **Musée de la Guerre** (War Museum), *tel: 21 34 21 57*, which concentrates on World War II and the damage inflicted upon Calais. Open daily 1000–1730 Mar–mid-Dec.

The **Musée des Beaux-Arts et de la Dentelle** (Fine Arts and Lace Museum), *25 r. Richelieu; tel: 21 46 62 00*, north of the tourist office, displays a collection of the type of lace for which Calais is renowned. Open Mon, Wed–Sun 1000–1200 and 1400–1730, closed Tues.

Heading north on *r. Royale* one passes the 13th-century **Tour du Guet**, one of the few buildings in Calais to survive the wars. Another, the **Église de Notre Dame**, (Church of Our Lady) *r. de Notre-Dame*, was built during the English rule of Calais; it is the only Tudor-style church in continental Europe, although otherwise unremarkable. About 1 km further north is the town beach, a good place to watch the ferries arrive.

Out of Calais off the A16 autoroute by the French Channel Tunnel terminal is the **EuroTunnel Information Centre** (*tel: 21 00 69 00*), where you can find out all about the great project. Open daily 1000–1900 (Apr–Sept); daily 1000–1800 (Oct–Mar).

CALAIS to PARIS

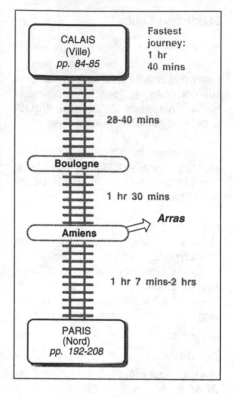

This route links Paris with the Channel ports of Boulogne and Calais, and is much used by travellers to and from Britain. The route runs through areas of northern France underexplored by travellers rapidly heading to the capital. Particularly noteworthy is Amiens, capital of Picardy and home to the largest cathedral in France.

TRAINS

ETT tables: 108, 102.

Fast Track

The opening of the fast rail line from Paris to the Channel Tunnel has allowed TGV trains to reach the Pas de Calais. At the moment services are limited, with an early morning train from Boulogne Ville to Paris Nord, calling at Calais Fréthun, returning in the evening. A second service runs from Paris Nord in the morning to Calais Ville, returning at lunchtime. The TGV takes only about 1 hr 40 mins between Calais and Paris, but a supplement is payable and the service is reduced on Sat and Sun. Ordinary trains run four times a day between Calais and Paris but take around 3¼ hrs.

~~> On Track

Calais–Boulogne

A frequent but erratic local service operates between Calais Ville and Boulogne Ville. Long gaps can occur between trains,

especially mid-morning. The journey takes between 28 and 40 mins.

Boulogne–Amiens

Five to seven trains each day operate between Boulogne Ville and Amiens, with journey times of about 1½ hrs.

Amiens–Paris

At least eight trains a day travel between Amiens and Paris Nord, with journey times varying between 1 hr 7 mins and 2 hrs.

BOULOGNE

Station: Boulogne Ville, blvd Voltaire; tel: 21 80 50 50, 1 km south of the town centre.

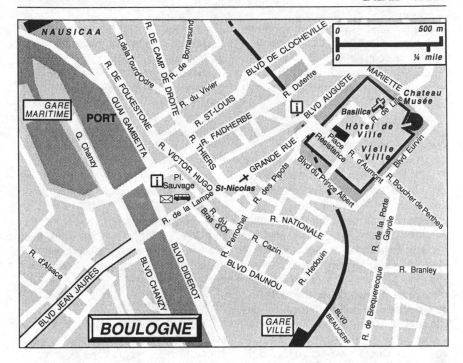

Ferries: Hoverspeed, *Gare Maritime; tel: 21 30 27 26*, run SeaCats to Folkestone.
Tourist Office: *Quai de la Poste 62200 Boulogne; tel: 21 31 68 38.* Open Mon–Thurs, Sun 0900–1900, Fri, Sat 0900–2000 (July–Aug); Mon–Sat 0900–1900, Sun 1000–1300, 1400–1700 (Sept–June). The accommodation booking service is free.

Getting Around

Most of central Boulogne is easily accessible on foot. To get from Boulogne Ville station to the tourist office, turn right on *blvd Voltaire* and then left on *blvd Daunou*. All bus routes serving Boulogne Ville go to the town centre. The central bus station is at *pl. de France*, near the tourist office.

Accommodation

Boulogne has a slightly less touristy feel to it than Calais, and the accommodation scene is more favourable as a result. Reasonably cheap and well-maintained hotels can be found right in the heart of town. Hotel chains in Boulogne include *Ch, Ib, Mp*.

HI: *36 r. Porte Gayole; tel: 21 31 48 22*, about 800 m north of the station, close to the old town.

Eating and Drinking

As befits a major fishing port, Boulogne's speciality is seafood. There are numerous reasonable restaurants down by the waterfront along *blvd Gambetta*. For more peaceful and serene surroundings, head up to the *Vieille Ville*; along *r. de Lille* and in front of the Hôtel de Ville in *pl. de Bouillon* there is a sequence of brasseries and restaurants whose fixed-price menus

---

offer good value. The pleasant surroundings make the hike uphill worthwhile. There is a centrally located supermarket on *r. de la Lampe*, and on Wed and Sat mornings you can pick up cheap food at the market on *pl. Dalton*.

Sightseeing

The **Vieille Ville** (Old Town) of Boulogne sits above the largely unremarkable modern city. The walk around the 13th-century **city walls** affords fine views of the town and harbour.

Within the ramparts, the 19th-century **Basilique Notre-Dame** draws together elements from St Paul's in London and St Peter's in Rome. Some interesting crypts from the 12th century survive below the more modern structure. At the south end of *r. de Lille* is **Le Beffroi** (The Belfry); one can climb its tower for even finer views of the surroundings (access through the Hôtel de Ville). Open Mon–Sat 0800–1730, closed Sun.

At the eastern corner of the walled town is the **Château-Musée**, *r. de Bernet; tel: 21 80 56 78*, which contains an eclectic collection of artifacts from Aleutian masks to Greek amphora. Open Mon, Wed–Sun 1000–1800, closed Tues.

The premier modern addition to Boulogne's tourist attractions is **Nausicaa**, on the seafront at *blvd Ste-Beuve; tel: 21 30 98 98*, the largest aquarium in France. It is equipped with underwater observation tanks from where you can view the sharks and other inhabitants. Open daily 1000–2000 (mid-May–mid-Sept); Mon–Fri 1000–1800, Sat, Sun 1000–1900 (mid-Sept–mid-May). Admission FFr.48.

AMIENS

Station: Gare du Nord, *pl. Alphonse Fiquet; tel: 22 92 50 50*, is Amiens' main station and is about 500 m south-east of the cathedral. One can easily locate the station: the grim Tour Perret provides a readily seen marker.

Tourist Office: *12 r. du Chapeau de Violettes, 80000 Amiens; tel: 22 91 79 28*. Open Mon–Sat 0900–1230 and 1400–1900, Sun closed (summer); Mon–Sat 0900–1230 and 1400–1830, Sun closed (winter). There is a convenient **branch office** at the rail station; *tel: 22 92 65 04*, open Mon–Sat 0800–2000, Sun 0930–2000 (summer); Mon–Sat 0800–1900, Sun 0930–1900 (winter). In summer only there is a fully equipped information **kiosk** right in front of the cathedral in *pl. Notre-Dame*, open daily 1000–1900.

Getting Around

To get to the cathedral from the rail station, turn right on *blvd d'Alsace Lorraine* and then second left on *r. Gloriette*. A colour-coded bus map is available from the tourist office. Buses are the only vehicles allowed into the pedestrianised heart of town; however it is virtually as fast to walk from the station. Much of the town centre and the St-Leu quarter are best explored on foot.

Accommodation

Amiens is a substantial town which is not deluged by tourists, so finding somewhere to stay is likely to be not too difficult.

Hotel chains in Amiens include *BW, Ca, Ib*. There are a number of bearable cheap hotels around the rail station. **HI:** *r. St-Fuscien; tel: 22 89 69 10*.

Eating and Drinking

Amiens' central area around *pl. Gambetta* and *r. Delambre* is packed with businesslike unpretentious eateries. For more elaborate but more tourist-oriented fare, head to the St-Leu district. There are some stylish restaurants along either bank of the river Somme, on *r. Belu* or *pl. du Don*. The surroundings are more dignified and the prices are higher. **Les Halles** food market, in a futuristic sloped-roof building opposite the main tourist office, sells colourful fresh produce ideal for a picnic. There is also a supermarket right by the rail station.

Sightseeing

The **Cathédrale de Notre-Dame** is the largest in France and arguably the purest example of Gothic architecture in the country. The relative quickness of its construction – 50 years in the 13th century – resulted in a coherence of style seldom found in such mammoth buildings. The west doorway, a 'book in stone', features the famous **Beau Dieu** portal. The interior of the cathedral is as impressive as its exterior. Exhibits describe the architectural evolution of the six great Gothic cathedrals in Picardy: Noyon, Senlis, Laon, Soissons, Beauvais and Amiens. Open daily 0730–1200 and 1400–1900 (Apr–Sept); daily 0730–1200 and 1400–1700 (Oct–Mar). The **Picardy Museum**, *48 r. de la République; tel: 22 91 36 44*, contains artifacts from the cathedral, in addition to other local archaeological exhibits and a substantial collection of medieval art. Open Tues–Sun 1000–1230 and 1400–1800, closed Mon.

The **St-Leu** district, straddling the Somme just north of the cathedral, dates from the Middle Ages. Most of the houses on the winding streets have been restored or are currently being renovated, but the area maintains a distinct medieval character. Beyond Parc St-Pierre are **Les Hortillonnages**, reclaimed marshlands which have provided food for Amiens since the Middle Ages. Enquire at the tourist office for details about barge tours.

Jules Verne wrote some of his pioneering science fiction works whilst living at *2 r. Charles Dubois*, which is now the **Jules Verne Information Centre** (*tel: 22 45 37 84*), an attraction more for the serious fan than for the curious, open Tues–Sat 0930–1200 and 1400–1800, closed Mon.

 Side Track from Amiens

ARRAS

Station: *pl. Maréchal Foch; tel: 21 73 50 50*, 500 m south-east of the town centre. Around 8 trains a day make the 40–50 min journey from Amiens.

Tourist Office: *pl. des Héros, 62000 Arras; tel: 21 51 26 95*, in the Hôtel de Ville. Open Mon–Sat 0900–1800, Sun 1000–1830 (summer); Mon–Sat 0900–1200 and 1400–1800, closed Sun (winter).

Arras is renowned for its Flemish houses which line the impressive *Grande pl.* and *pl. des Héros*. The rows of houses have been comprehensively reconstructed following damage in the two world wars. From the Hôtel de Ville it is possible to view Arras from above – at the top of the 75 m-high belfry (open the same hours as the tourist office) – or from below, in the 20 km of tunnels which stretch out from under the town centre. Known as **Les Boves**, they provided shelter during the numerous wars which passed through Arras. Contact the tourist office for details of the various guided tours. The **Musée des Beaux-Arts**, inside the Abbaye St-Vaast at *22 r. Paul Doumer*, contains some fine tapestries (for which the town was famous) and paintings including a selection from the Arras School.

CALAIS to STRASBOURG

This route links the Channel with the German border. It winds along the northern borders of France, from Calais through Flanders into the Ardennes and on to Strasbourg in Alsace.

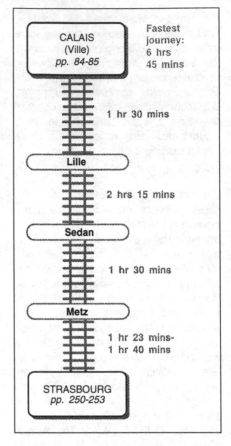

TRAINS

ETT tables: 108, 177, 176.

→ Fast Track

No through service operates from Calais to Strasbourg but there is one through train each day from Lille Flandres to Strasbourg, taking 5¼ hrs for the journey.

⌁ On Track

Calais–Lille

Six trains a day operate between Calais Ville and Lille Flandres, with journey times of around 1½ hrs.

Lille–Sedan–Metz

Two trains a day operate between Lille and Metz but only one of these calls at Sedan. Lille to Sedan takes 2¼ hrs and Sedan to Metz takes 1½ hrs.

Metz–Strasbourg

At least five trains daily link Metz and Strasbourg including two EuroCity Expresses with restaurant cars and on which supplements are payable. Timings range from 1 hr 23 mins on the EuroCity trains to 1 hr 40 mins on ordinary trains.

To continue into Germany, services run from Strasbourg to both Karlsruhe and Offenburg: see *ETT* table 727.

LILLE

Stations: Lille Flandres, *pl. de la Gare; tel: 20 74 50 50*, is the busiest station in France outside Paris. It handles all local trains, all non-TGV services and some TGV trains to and from Paris Gare du Nord. The brand new **Lille Europe**, *av. le Corbusier at blvd*

---

de Turin; tel: 20 74 50 50, part of the massive EuraLille development, is dedicated exclusively to TGV services. Lille Europe lies at the heart of the high-speed network between London, Paris and Brussels. The two stations are only 400 m apart, linked by av. le Corbusier. Alternatively you can take the metro one stop (see Getting Around below). Lille Flandres is about 400 m south-east of the town centre.

Tourist Office: Palais Rihour, pl. Rihour, 59000 Lille; tel: 20 30 81 00 (metro: Rihour). Open Mon–Sat 0900–1900, Sun 1000–1200 and 1400–1700. The office provides details of self-guided tours (see Sightseeing, p. 92).

Getting Around

Central Lille is compact and easily explored on foot. Flandres rail station, the tourist office, the old town and the town hall area are all a few minutes' walk from each other. To get to the tourist office from Flandres station head north-west along r. Faidherbe, then turn left and pass through pl. Gén. de Gaulle.

The Lille metropolitan area, however, stretches as far north as Roubaix and Tourcoing, and has a combined population of over 1 million. The city has developed an impressive public transport system. Information on all the local transport can be obtained from the **Transpole information office**, underneath Flandres station; tel: 20 98 50 50. Open Mon–Fri 0700–1900, Sat 0900–1700, closed Sun.

Métro

The Lille Metro opened in 1983. There are now two fully automated lines served by driverless trains. The metro serves both rail stations and pl. Rihour, although distances in the centre of town are short. Tickets cost FFr.7.50. A carnet of ten is available for

FFr.58.50 and a weekly pass costs FFr.67.00.

Trams

The tramway caters mostly to suburban commuters. There are two lines linking Tourcoing and Roubaix to Flandres station.

Buses

Complementing the metro and tramway is an extensive network of local buses. Route maps are on display at the Transpole information office. The major stop in the centre of town is at pl. des Buisses by Flandres station.

Staying in Lille

Accommodation

Whilst Lille has plenty of upmarket hotels, and will get more with the construction of EuraLille, there are few really pleasant cheap hotels. Hotel chains in Lille include Ca, Ch, Ib, Me, Nv, Sf. In the centre of town, the luxurious **Grand Hôtel Bellevue** is marvellously positioned by pl. Gén. de Gaulle. There is a gaggle of cheapish hotels around Flandres station, including **Hôtel Faid-herbe**, tel: 20 06 27 93, and **Hôtel des Voyageurs**, tel: 20 06 43 14, but this area is not the most salubrious. The **Auberge de Jeunesse** is at 1 av. Julien Destrée; tel: 20 52 98 94.

Eating and Drinking

South of the tourist office, pedestrianised r. de Béthune and the streets off it have a high concentration of reasonable restaurants and food stalls. There are also a number of eateries in the old town north of pl. Rihour around r. Royale and r. des Trois Mollettes. Places to eat around the station are fairly ordinary; there is a supermarket at r. du Molinel round the corner from

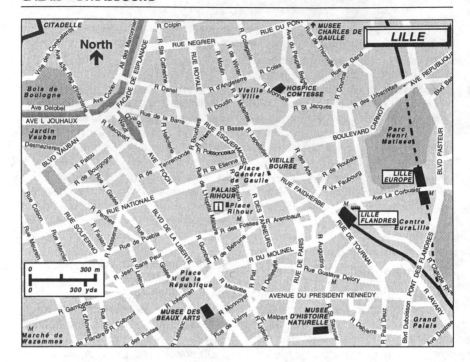

Flandres station. The place to go for really fresh produce is the market at Wazemmes, *pl. de la Nouvelle Aventure* (metro: *Gambetta*).

Money

Thomas Cook bureau de change: *Lille Flandres station; tel: 20 55 32 52.* Open daily 0800–*2000*.

Sightseeing

Lille has been a trade centre and transport hub since the Middle Ages, and remains the industrial powerhouse of Northern France. Lille is not immediately attractive to those in search of charm or refinement. However, the city has some fine old Flemish buildings, a collection of interesting museums, a lively nightlife, and may yet appeal to travellers from England tempted by the quick trip through the Channel Tunnel.

The tourist office itself is housed in the **Palais Rihour**, built by Philip the Good, Duke of Burgundy, as a stopping-off point en route between Burgundy and Holland. Details of four self-guided tours of central Lille, all starting at *pl. Rihour*, are available from the office. Probably the best is the one that winds through the *vieille ville* (old town). On this route is the **Ancienne Bourse** (old exchange), between *pl. Gén. de Gaulle* and *pl. du Théatre*, a splendid 17th-century example of the Lille-Flemish architectural style. The bourse, once France's sole stock exchange, is made up of 24 identical houses surrounding a yard which now is a book and flower market. Further north in the old town is the **Hospice Comtesse**, *32 r. de la Monnaie; tel: 20 49 50 90*, founded in the 13th century by the Countess of Flanders as a home for the poor. The current collection of ornate

15th–17th century buildings is now a museum of antiques and Flemish artwork. In addition the museum currently displays a small selection of paintings from the **Musée des Beaux Arts**, *pl. de la République; tel: 20 57 01 84.* The museum, which housed an outstanding collection of paintings including works by Rubens, Renoir and Van Gogh, is being refurbished and is now due to reopen in Spring 1995, although the reopening date has already been delayed a number of times. Hospice open Mon, Wed–Sun 1000–1230, 1400–1800, closed Tues. Admission FFr.10.

Charles de Gaulle was born in Lille in 1890 at *9 r. Princesse*, north of the Hospice Comtesse. His birthplace is now the **Musée Charles-de-Gaulle**, *tel: 20 31 96 03*, which contains documents and artifacts relating to his life, including a car used in an assassination attempt in 1962. Open Wed–Sun 1000–1200 and 1400–1700, closed Mon and Tues.

The Lille **Citadelle**, north of the town centre, was built, inevitably, by Vauban in the 17th century, and still serves as an army base. The massive five-pointed fortress can be toured on Sun in summer; enquire at the tourist office for details.

South of Flandres station is the Town Hall and the **Musée d'Histoire Naturelle et de Geologie**, *19 r. de Bruxelles; tel: 20 85 28 60* (metro: *Mairie de Lille*). Open Mon, Wed–Sat 0900–1200 and 1400–1700, Sun 1000–1700, closed Tues.

The area around Lille Europe station is undergoing massive reconstruction. The development, known as **EuraLille**, will eventually include Lille **Grand Palais**, a huge convention centre, plus high-rise hotels and offices, all centred around the TGV station at the hub of the European high-speed network. Construction began in 1991 and the progress is fascinating. The tourist office provides updates to the current state of the building works.

SEDAN

Station: *pl. de la Gare; tel: 24 33 50 50*, about 1.8 km south-west of the town centre. There is no baggage storage at the station.
Tourist Office: *pl. du Château, 08200 Sedan; tel: 24 27 73 73*, opposite the fortress.

Situated in the Meuse valley, Sedan has been a target of invaders for centuries. Most recently it was severely damaged in World War II. The town's main draw is the massive **Château-Fort**, built over five centuries from the 11th, which is the largest fortress (in terms of area) in Europe, stretching over 35,000 sq. m. Open daily 1000–1800 (mid-Mar–mid-Sept); 1300–1730 (mid-Sept–mid-Mar). There are also torch-lit visits to the château at 2200 (mid-June–Aug 31) and 2100 (Sept 1–15).

Out of Town

Sedan lies on the **Routes des Fortifications**, one of *Les Itinéraires Ardennais*, which runs from **Givet**, at the northern end of the wedge of France tucked into Belgium, via **Charleville-Mèziéres** and Sedan towards Metz and Lorraine. Along the route, which roughly follows the Meuse valley and the edge of the Ardennes forest, are fortifications dating from the time of Charlemagne right through to World War II. In addition to the one at Sedan, the tourist offices in Givet, *tel: 24 42 03 54*, Charleville-Mèziéres, *tel: 24 32 44 80*, and Fumay, *tel: 24 21 10 25*, can provide further details of the Ardennes area.

METZ

Station: *pl. Général de Gaulle; tel: 87 63 50 50*, 1 km south of the town centre.
Tourist Office: *pl. d'Armes; tel: 87 55 53 76*, opposite the cathedral. Open Mon–Sat 0900–2100, Sun 1000–1300, 1400–1700 (summer); Mon–Sat 0900–1900, Sun 1000–1300 (winter). There is a **branch office** in the rail station, open Mon–Fri 1100–1220, 1335–2000, closed Sat and Sun.

Getting Around

A large block of central Metz is pedestrianised and only accessible by bus or on foot. None of the bus routes individually has a particularly frequent service, although since about eight lines run between station and town centre a long wait is unlikely. Virtually all the buses serve *pl. République* at the edge of the pedestrianised area and most go to *pl. d'Armes*, 300 m further. Tickets cost FFr.5 and are available from the driver. There is a bus map at the rail station, although currently *pl. Gén. de Gaulle* is undergoing major works as part of the construction of an underground bus station, and buses presently stop in the streets around the station.

Accommodation

Metz has a number of mid-range to upmarket hotels and a couple of good youth hostels, but limited possibilities in the way of cheap hotels. Hotel chains in Metz include *Ca, Ib, Me, Nv*. There are many pleasant mid-range hotels around the station, and a few located in the central area.
HI: Auberge de Jeunesse Carrefour, *6 r. Marchant; tel: 87 75 07 26*. **Auberge de Jeunesse Metz-Plage**, *1 allée de Metz-Plage, pl. du Pontiffroy; tel: 87 30 44 02*.

Take bus nos 3 or 11 to the *pl. du Pontiffroy* stop.

Sightseeing

Metz is one of a number of cities claiming to be at the crossroads of Europe, and its credentials are better than most. A Roman settlement at the intersection of trade routes from Strasbourg to Reims and from the Mediterranean to the North Sea, Metz underwent two periods of German occupation before finally reverting to French control after World War II.

Opposite the tourist office is the Gothic **Cathédrale St-Etienne** (St Stephen's), built between the 13th and 16th centuries out of the distinctive local mustard-coloured sandstone. The cathedral, one of the largest in France, earned the name of the Lantern of God because of its outstanding stained glass, ranging from Munster in the 14th century to 20th-century Chagall. Further uses of local sandstone are evident around the cathedral and in the fine collection of buildings across across the Moselle canal by the 18th-century **Théâtre**.

Heading south from *pl. d'Armes* along *r. des Clercs*, you reach the **Esplanade**, a French garden looking over the Moselle. The **Église St-Pierre-aux-Nonnains** nearby, one of the oldest churches in France, dates from the 4th century, although it has been substantially rebuilt over the years.

North of *pl d'Armes* is the **Cour D'Or**, the **Musée d'Art et d'Histoire**, *2 r. du Haut-Poirier; tel: 87 75 10 18*. Here you can see the Roman baths on which the museum was built, and other local antiquities including the chancel from the St-Pierre-aux-Nonnains church. Open Mon, Wed–Sun 1000–1200 and 1400–1800, closed Tues (summer); Mon, Wed–Sun 1000–1200 and 1400–1700, closed Tues (winter).

CHERBOURG

Ever since the construction of its huge breakwaters Cherbourg has been an important military and commercial port. It was liberated by American troops three weeks after the landings on Utah beach – 17 days later than planned – to give the Allies a deep-water port for bringing in more heavy vehicles. Most people do not come to Cherbourg to stay, but if you have time there are a couple of interesting museums.

Tourist Information

Tourist Office: *2 quai Alexandre III, 50100 Cherbourg; tel: 33 93 52 02*. On the far side of the Bassin du Commerce, between the lifting bridge and the *r. Mar. Foch*.

Arriving and Departing

Station

Gare SNCF, *pl. Jean Jaurès; tel: 33 57 50 50*, at the end of the Bassin de Commerce. The Gare Routière (bus station) is opposite.

Ferries

Cherbourg has a greater choice of connections than any other French port, if not as many departures. All leave from the Gare Maritime.

Sealink: from Southampton (Apr–Dec only and limited service outside summer months); *tel: 33 20 43 38*.

P&O: from Portsmouth (year-round, but limited Jan–Mar); *tel: 33 88 65 70*.

Brittany Ferries (Truckline): from Poole (year-round); *tel: 31 36 36 00*.

Irish Ferries: from Cork (June–Aug only) and Rosslare; *tel: 33 44 28 99*.

Staying in Cherbourg

There is a large new three-star *Me* at the Gare Maritime, otherwise there are several small hotels in town.

HI: *av. L Lumière; tel: 33 44 26 31*, open mid-Apr–mid-Oct, 1.5 km from SNCF station (bus no. 5 to stop *Jean Moulin*).

Good areas to try for places to eat include *quai de Caligny*, the streets around the market hall and, for a more upmarket meal, *r. de l'Abbaye* (by the *Parc Emmanuel Liais*).

Sightseeing

South-east of the SNCF station the **Fort du Roule** overlooks town and the port. Inside, the **Museum of War and Liberation** commemorates the Allied landings and the liberation of Cherbourg and the Cotentin with models, photographs and Nazi propaganda recalling life under the occupation (open 0930–1730 Apr–Sept, 0900–1200, 1400–1800 Nov–Mar, admission FFr.10).

Behind *quai Alexandre III* the cultural centre houses **Musée Thomas Henry**, whose collection of 15th–19th-century fine arts features the Manche painter Millet (open 0900–1200, 1400–1800, admission FFr.10).

Side Tracks from Cherbourg

A bus service heads down the Cotentin to **Coutances** (see p. 102) via the villages of **Martinvast,** which has a 19th-century château with 11th-century keep, and **Bricquebec**, whose much older fortress also has a mighty keep and a museum of local life.

CHERBOURG to PARIS

This route, from the coast to the capital, takes you through the rolling countryside of Basse-Normandie, homeland of William the Conqueror, whose exploits are recorded in the Bayeux tapestry.

TRAINS

ETT table: 120

 Fast Track

Six or seven through trains run from Cherbourg to Paris St-Lazare each day, with journey times of 3½–4 hrs. A few of these trains require supplements. Connections can be made by changing at Caen; particularly useful with the long gap in the through-train services around midday.

On Track

Cherbourg–Bayeux–Caen

The Cherbourg to Paris trains also provide the service between Cherbourg and Caen, with nearly all trains calling at Bayeux en route. Cherbourg to Bayeux takes just over 1 hr and Bayeux to Caen 20 mins.

Caen–Lisieux

Around a dozen services operate between Caen and Lisieux each day, taking 32 mins, but after 1700 services are hard to find.

Lisieux–Paris

Ten or so trains link Lisieux to Paris St-

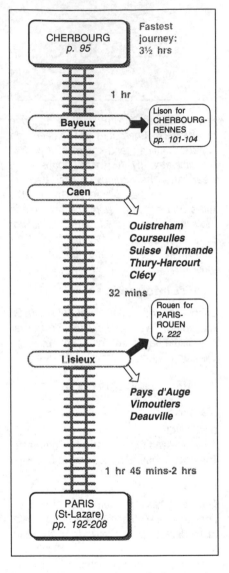

CHERBOURG
p. 95

Fastest journey: 3½ hrs

1 hr

Bayeux

Lison for CHERBOURG-RENNES
pp. 101-104

Caen

**Ouistreham
Courseulles
Suisse Normande
Thury-Harcourt
Clécy**

32 mins

Rouen for PARIS-ROUEN
p. 222

Lisieux

**Pays d'Auge
Vimoutiers
Deauville**

1 hr 45 mins-2 hrs

PARIS (St-Lazare)
pp. 192-208

Lazare, with journey times of 1 hrs 45 mins to 2 hrs.

BAYEUX

Station: *tel: 31 83 50 50.* Ten mins walk

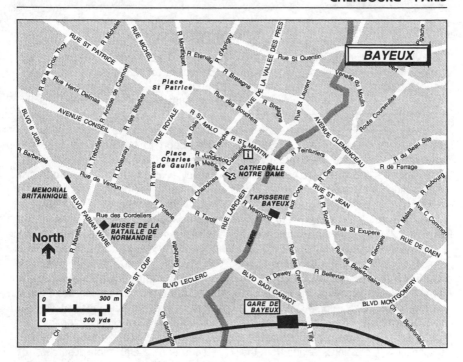

from the centre; turn left on *blvd Sadi Carnot* and bear right onto *r. Larcher*. Turn left onto *r. St-Martin* for the tourist office. **Tourist Office:** *1 r. des Cuisiniers, 14400 Bayeux; tel: 31 92 16 26*, found in a half-timbered 14th-century house on the corner with *r. St-Martin*.

Accommodation and Food

There is a wide selection of hotels and restaurants in the town centre, including a privately-run hostel, **Family Home**, *36 r. du Gén. Dais; tel: 31 92 55 72*. **HI: Centre d'Accueil Municipal**, *21 r. des Marettes; tel: 31 92 08 19*, south of the centre. **Campsite**, *blvd d'Eindhoven, tel: 31 92 08 43*, open 15 Mar–15 Oct.

Sightseeing

The dignified town of Bayeux was one of the first towns to be liberated by the Allies, on 7 June 1944, and escaped much damage to its fine medieval centre, which is dominated by the spires of the magnificent Gothic **Cathédrale Notre-Dame**. *R. St-Jean* is the main, bustling shopping street, but it is also worth exploring the quiet streets along the **Aure** where cloth dyers (*teinturiers*) had their water mills and where lace-making still flourishes.

Save plenty of energy for the world's most famous **tapestry**, in fact 70 m of embroidered linen and probably made not by Queen Mathilda but in England. The exhibition centre, well sign-posted on *r. de Nesmond*, presents an excellent interpretation of the story, using a life-size facsimile and models, so that by the time you see the embroidery itself it is quite familiar and easy to 'read'. Open daily 0900–1900 mid-

Jun–mid-Sept, 0900–1230, 1400–1830 mid-Mar–May, mid-Sept–mid-Oct, 0930–1230, 1400–1800, mid-Oct–mid-Mar; admission FFr.30, audio guide, in English FFr.5. Last tickets sold 1 hr before closing.

CAEN

Station: *pl. de la Gare; tel: 31 83 50 50.* Buses run the 1.5 km to the centre. Coach excursions offer the chance to visit several of the region's most interesting villages and châteaux.
Tourist Office: *pl. St-Pierre, 14000 Caen; tel: 31 86 27 65.* In the Renaissance **Hôtel d'Escouville** next to the church of St-Pierre. Regional information: the **Calvados tourist office** *pl. du Canada; tel: 31 86 53 30.*
Ferries: Brittany Ferries from Portsmouth sail year round (*tel: 31 36 36 00*). The port is at **Ouistreham**, 15 km north of Caen: *Bus Verts* bus no. 1 makes the 30-min trip to connect with crossings, leaving from the bus station next to the SNCF station.

Accommodation and Food

There are several hotel-restaurants opposite the SNCF station south of the centre and also around *pl. Courtonne* and *quai Vendeuvre* near the marina. International hotel chains in Caen include: *Ho, Me, Nv, Ib.* **HI:** *Résidence Robert Rème, 68 r. Eustache Restout; tel: 31 52 19 96.* Open June–Sept, 2 km from the SNCF station, bus nos 5 or 17 to stop *Lycée Fresnel.*

Caen has a good selection of restaurants, from international cooking to classic Norman cuisine. There are many to choose from in *r. de Geôle* and the *quartier Le Vaugueux* below the castle, but if you want to try somewhere special, check with the tourist office for full listings. In the capital of gastronomic Lower Normandy, the speciality is *tripe à la mode de Caen.*

Sightseeing

Caen is capital of Basse-Normandie and the *département* of Calvados. It is a busy, modern town, extensively rebuilt after heavy damage in World War II – as the bus-ride from the station shows. However, it is an excellent centre for both shopping and transport to the surrounding region, and there are still several traces of the town ruled by William the Conqueror. Just beyond the **Église de St-Pierre** (St Peter's Church) the curtain walls of William's **castle** now protect two museums. In the Governor's lodgings, the **Musée de Normandie** (open daily except Tues 1000–1230, 1400–1800, admission FFr.10) recalls the region's history, crafts and costume and the **Musée des Beaux-Arts** has a wide representation of Flemish, Italian and French schools (open daily except Tues 1000–1800, admission FFr.25).

There are several more churches of interest, including the Romanesque **St-Nicholas** and the Gothic **St-Sauveur** (St Saviour's), but most impressive are the two abbeys, one on either side of town, built by William the Conqueror and his wife Mathilda. The queen is buried in the **Abbaye aux Dames** (Ladies' abbey) on the east side of town (open daily 1430–1600, admission free) and the king in the beautiful **Église de St-Etienne** (St Stephen's) at the vast **Abbaye aux Hommes** (Men's abbey) (open daily 0900–1200, 1400–1700, admission FFr.10).

Fast becoming Caen's most famous attraction, **Mémorial** is a 'museum for peace'. The simple, windowless building on a windy plain north of town is a high-tech museum which charts world history from 1918 to the present. It has an excellent specialist bookshop, open daily 0900–1900, (until 2100 May–Sept), last tickets

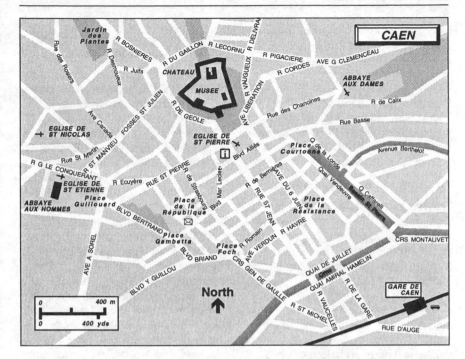

sold 1 hr 15 mins before closing, admission FFr.58, FFr.48 for over-60s and students, free to World War II veterans and under-10s. Closed 1–15 Jan and 19 Mar. Bus no. 12 from the SNCF station or town centre.

Side Tracks from Caen

There are memorials throughout the region to the Allied landings and liberation of the region, not least in Caen, but to see the beaches without a car is not easy as bus services are infrequent. **Ouistreham** and **Courseulles** can be reached by bus from Caen: check with **Bus Verts** at the bus station, *tel: 31 44 77 44.*

South from Caen the **River Orne** twists through the deep, wooded gorges of the **Suisse Normande** ('Norman Switzerland'), a region for those who enjoy the great

outdoors – whether it's canoeing, fishing, climbing or walking – which you need a car to explore fully, although Bus Verts no. 34 passes through, en route to Flers, allowing travellers to explore on foot.

There is a choice of bases. **Thury-Harcourt** is a small market town whose tourist office (*pl. St-Sauveur; tel: 31 79 70 45)* organises walks and events throughout summer. There are two campsites, three-star **Trapsy**, *tel: 31 79 61 80* and two-star **Bord de l'Orne**, *tel: 31 79 70 78*, both open Apr–mid-Oct. Further south in the village of **Clécy** a couple of hotels, a small art museum and the tourist office (*tel: 31 69 79 95)* cluster around the church. The campsite (open Easter–Sept; *tel: 31 69 80 20)* is in the neighbouring hamlet of **Le Vey** which lies on the GR 36 long-distance footpath. There is a narrow gauge train which runs very infrequently from Caen to

---

Caen

Clécy, details from the **gare de Thury-Harcourt**; *tel: 31 79 02 02.*

LISIEUX

Station: *pl. de la Gare; tel: 31 83 50 50.*
Tourist Information: *11 r. d'Alençon, 14100 Lisieux; tel: 31 62 08 41.* Follow *r. de la Gare* from the station and cross *pl. Fournet* for *r. d'Alençon.*

Accommodation and Food

The villages of the Pays d'Auge may be more appealing but this can be a useful base, with a choice of two-star hotel-restaurants in the town centre. Also try *r. au Char*, near the cathedral, or *blvd H. Fournet* for restaurants.

Sightseeing

Since the tragic wartime destruction of many of its half-timbered houses, most visitors to Lisieux are pilgrims. On a hill above town an enormous white **basilica** built in the 1950s commemorates **Ste-Thérèse**, a young Carmelite nun who died here aged only 24 at the end of the 19th century. Thérèse Martin was still a child when she saw her first vision of the Virgin Mary. She pleaded personally with Pope Leo XII to be allowed to enter the Carmelite convent at 15 instead of 21. Her book *The Story of a Soul* was published after her death from TB and she was canonised after reports throughout Europe of miraculous interventions. The main annual pilgrimages are on 15 Aug and the last Sun in Sept.

In contrast in the centre of town are the more restrained Norman Gothic **Cathédrale St-Pierre** and Bishop's Palace, which stand near a pleasant public garden. *R. Henri Cheron* leads west towards the **Musée du Vieux Lisieux** at *38 blvd de Pasteur* (daily except Tues 1400–1800).

 Side Tracks from Lisieux

Lisieux is the starting point for expeditions into the **Pays d'Auge,** Normandy's cheese and cider country, as well as to the fashionable resorts of the Côte Fleurie.

The bus service to **Vimoutiers** (Bus Verts no. 53) heads south via the village of **St-Germain de Livret** with its delightful chequerboard-patterned **château** (open daily except Tues, 1000–1200, 1400–1900 Apr–Sept, 1000–1200, 1400–1700 Oct–Mar) and **Livarot,** famous for its pungent round, orange-crusted cheese. The **Musée du Fromage de Livarot** at Manoir de l'Isle (*tel: 31 63 43 13)* is open Mon–Sat 1000–1200, 1400–1800, Sun and holidays 1400–1800 Apr–Oct. **Vimoutiers** in the pretty valley of the River Vie has another museum: the **Musée du Camembert,** *10 av. du Gaulle,* celebrates the best-known Normandy cheese. Camembert dates from 1791 and is credited to Marie Harel, a farmer's wife from a tiny village to the south of Vimioutiers, who was given the recipe by a priest whom she sheltered during the Revolution.

Pont l'Evêque, a creamy, square cheese is named after the town in the northern Pays d'Auge. As well as tasting the local cheese you can visit the calvados distillery of **Chais du Père Magloire** which stands next to the **Musée du Calvados et des Métiers Anciens**. From Pont l'Evêque the railway line continues to the unusual half-timbered station at **Deauville**, the Parisians' favourite summer 'retreat', famous for its *planches* (boardwalks), its film festival in early Sept and its horse racing May–Oct (tourist information at *pl de la Mairie; tel: 31 88 21 43).*

CHERBOURG to RENNES

From Normandy's liberated Cotentin to the capital of Brittany, this route has some particularly special side tracks to explore the delightful coast.

TRAINS

ETT table: 120, 119.

→ Fast Track

No fast trains run on these lines and the trains that do run are infrequent, with only one early morning and one evening journey available on most days, although weekend services are more frequent. The through journey from Cherbourg to Rennes takes over 3½ hrs, with a change of train at Lison.

∿ On Track

Cherbourg–St-Lô–Coutances

A few local trains and SNCF buses from Lison to Coutances supplement the rare through-trains and connect with trains from Cherbourg and Caen. All services call at St-Lô en route. Cherbourg to St-Lô, with a change of trains at Lison, takes just over 2 hrs, St-Lô to Coutances takes 20 mins.

Coutances–Folligny–Pontorson–Dol

The infrequent through trains offer the only service on this part of the route. Coutances to Folligny takes 20–25 mins, Folligny to

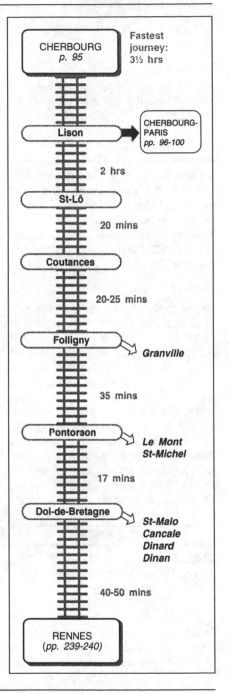

CHERBOURG p. 95 — Fastest journey: 3½ hrs

Lison → CHERBOURG-PARIS pp. 96-100

2 hrs

St-Lô

20 mins

Coutances

20-25 mins

Folligny → Granville

35 mins

Pontorson → Le Mont St-Michel

17 mins

Dol-de-Bretagne → St-Malo / Cancale / Dinard / Dinan

40-50 mins

RENNES (pp. 239-240)

Pontorson takes 35 mins and Pontorson to Dol takes 17 mins.

Dol–Rennes

Around ten trains a day run between Dol and Rennes, the journey taking 40–50 mins.

ST-LÔ

Station: *tel: 33 57 50 50.* Cross the River Vire for the town centre. The more expensive hotels are near the station on *pl. de la Préfecture.*
Tourist Office: *2 r. Havin, 50000 St-Lô; tel: 33 05 02 0*9. Open Tues–Sat 0900–1200, 1400–1800.

Sightseeing

Capital of the *départment* of La Manche, St-Lô was also known as the 'capital of ruins' after being devasted in the struggle for its liberation in 1944. The rebuilt town is still protected by its old ramparts and the 15th-century **Eglise de Notre-Dame** (Church of Our Lady) with its outdoor pulpit, has also been restored. On *pl. du Champ de Mars* the spacious new cultural centre houses an excellent **Musée des Beaux Arts**, with a fine collection of tapestries and French paintings, open daily except Tues, 1000–1200, 1400–1800 (Apr–Oct), admission FFr.10.

COUTANCES

Station: *tel; 33 57 50 50.*
Tourist Office: *pl. Georges Leclerc, 50200 Coutances; tel: 33 45 17 79.*

Sightseeing

This attractive town is dominated by its Gothic **Cathédrale Notre-Dame** whose elegant towers soar above the rooftops.

Behind the 17th-century Hôtel de Ville, a lovely stone mansion houses a small **museum** of local ceramics, paintings and costume and opens onto a beautiful landscaped **park**. Open daily except Tues 1000–1200, 1400–1800 (July–mid-Sept), daily except Wed and Sun morning 1000–1200, 1400–1700 (mid Sept–June).

Side Tracks from Coutances

An SNCF bus service runs direct to the popular coastal resort of **Granville** (by train, change at **Folligny**), whose long and fascinating history is documented in the **Musée du Vieux Granville**, open daily except Tues 1000–1200, 1400–1600 (July–Sept), Wed, Sat and Sun afternoon out of season; admission FFr.8. There are daily boat trips in summer to the offshore **Îles Chausey**. East from Granville and Folligny, **Villedieu-les-Poêles** has been known since the Middle Ages for its copper industry.

PONTORSON

Station: *tel: 33 57 50 50.*
Tourist Office: *pl. de l'Église, 50170 Pontorson; tel: 33 60 08 18.*
Pontorson is the nearest SNCF station to the abbey of **Le Mont St-Michel**, 9 km away. You can also take a bus (*tel: 33 50 08 99*) or rent a bicycle.

 Side Tracks from Pontorson

LE MONT ST-MICHEL

Tourist Office: *tel: 33 60 14 30*; at the foot of the *mont* (open Feb–Nov). Ask for a list of hotels.

The familiar spire-topped outline of the enormous church and fortified monastic buildings, known as the *Merveille*, sit above shops, hotels and restaurants clambering up the *Grand rue*, now thronged with visitors as it once was with pilgrims. Visits to the abbey are guided only, given in English in summer. Open 0900–1130, 1330–1800 (until 1600 Oct–mid-May), guided visit of 1 hr, FFr. 36; longer *Visite Conférence* of 2 hrs (July–Sept) FFr.56. On summer nights there is a *Son et Lumière* but this is much later than the last bus to Pontorson. From the abbey gardens there is a view both of the church and across the vast bay, which is renowned for the speed of its tides. Annual events include a pilgrimage across the sands in mid-July, as well as the feast of Spring Michaelmas in May and the festival of the Archangel Michael in late Sept.

DOL-DE-BRETAGNE

Station: *tel: 99 65 50 50.* South of town; follow *av. A. Briand* and *blvd Planson* to *pl. de la Mairie.*

Tourist Office: Hotel de Ville, *pl. de la Mairie, 35120 Dol; tel: 98 48 15 47.*

Accommodation and Food

If you want to make this small town your base, there is a good two-star hotel and restaurant, the **Hôtel de Bretagne**, on *pl. Chateaubriand, tel: 99 48 02 03*, and a couple of simple restaurants near the cathedral. The weekly market is on Sat mornings.

Sightseeing

Now little more than a large village on the edge of extensive reclaimed marshland,

Dol's days as an important bishopric on Brittany's frontier are evident from the huge granite **Cathédral de St-Sampson.** The walls of the stone house opposite are decorated with an assortment of signs and coats of armour advertising the **Musée Historique** inside. The historical museum tells the story of Dol from the prehistoric mammoths onwards, (open 0930–1230, 1330–1800, Easter–Oct, admission FFr.20). A walk along the **Promenade des Douves** gives a good view of **Mont Dol** rising from the flat marsh 2 km away. Site of the remains of ancient mammoths, it also bears what are said to be the traces of a violent struggle between the Devil and St Michael.

Side Tracks from Dol

From Dol there are train connections for both St-Malo/Dinard and Dinan. A bus service between Dinard and Dinan creates a circular connection.

A boat from St-Malo crosses the Rance estuary to the fashionable resort of **Dinard** whose main sandy beach is backed by expensive hotels and a casino. An enjoyable coastal walk, known as the *Promenade du Clair du Lune*, leads to a second beach via an **aquarium** and **maritime museum**, (open Mon–Sat 1030–1230, 1530–1930, Sun 1430–1930 mid-May–mid-Sept).

The SNCF bus from St-Malo to Dol and Fougères stops in **Cancale** which is still a fishing port as well as a holiday resort. The local speciality is oysters and there are plenty of places to try them.

Emeraude Lines (see p. 54) run a river trip along the Rance estuary from St-Malo to the medieval town of **Dinan** (FFr.85 one-way, FFr.115 return). There are also rail connections from Dol.

ST-MALO

Station: *tel: 99 65 50 50*. Two km east of the walled town (called *intra-muros*, 'within the walls', to distinguish it form the suburbs of Paramé and St-Servan); follow *av. Louis Martin* or take a bus.

Tourist Office: *esplanade St-Vincent, 35400 St-Malo; tel: 99 56 64 48.*

Sightseeing

The lively port of St-Malo makes an excellent base from which to explore this corner of Brittany. Although largely rebuilt after World War II, it is still easy to imagine this as the 18th-century town of the **privateers** Surcouf and Duguay-Trouin. Their exploits are recalled in the **Musée Historique** in the château to the right of the Porte St-Vincent, open daily 1000–1200, 1400–1800 Apr–Oct, (until 1700 Nov–Mar), closed Tues, admission FFr.18. In summer when the hot streets are bustling the **Cathédral de St-Vincent** is a sanctuary of coolness and peace, its walls and pillars alight with the dancing colours of the vivid windows. Nearby **St-Servan** has a good swimming beach and a spectacular cliff walk around the old fort known as the **Corniche d'Aleth**. **Tour Solidor** houses the maritime **Cape Horners' Museum**, open daily 1000–1200, 1400–1800 Apr–Oct, (until 1700 Nov–Mar), closed Tues, admission FFr. 18.

St-Malo is also a busy ferry port, with services from Portsmouth (**Brittany Ferries**; *tel: 98 82 41 41*, see p. 56) and the Channel Islands (**Condor Lines** *tel: 99 56 42 29*, **Emeraude Lines**, *tel: 99 40 48 40* and **Channiland**, *tel: 99 40 40 90*).

DINAN

Station: *tel: 99 65 50 50*. Ten mins from the historic centre: take *r. Carnot* to *pl. Gén. Leclerc*, then right along *r. Thiers* to follow the walls to *pl. Duclos*.

Tourist Office: *6 r. de l'Horloge, 22100 Dinan; tel: 96 39 75 40.*

From the town's port *r. du Petit Fort* climbs to the **Porte du Jerzual**; continue climbing the steps to the left for the views from the **Jardin Anglais.** From here the *promenade de la Duchesse Anne* follows the high ramparts or you can head to the heart of town around the **Basilique St-Sauveur**. In summer the nearby **Tour de l'Horloge** (clock tower) is open for visitors who want a better view over town. Once a year, on the weekend nearest to the start of Oct, the locals celebrate their Medieval heritage in the **Fête des Remparts**, when the streets are filled with jugglers, fire-eaters and nobles on horseback.

CLERMONT-FERRAND

The double-barrelled name is significant. There is hectic Clermont and staid Montferrand, with a combined population of 151,000. Industrial it may be but Clermont has a stunning location over volcanic mountain tops and an extensive old town where local heroes, the author Blaise Pascal, the Gallic chieftain Vercingétorix, and the Pope Urbain II have medallions of their likenesses embedded in the pedestrianised streets.

Tourist Information

Tourist Office: 69 blvd Gergovia, 63000 Clermont-Ferrand; tel: 73 93 30 20. Open Mon–Fri 0845–1830, Sat 0900–1200, 1400–1800 (Oct–end of May); Mon–Sat 0830–1900, Sun 0900–1200, 1400–1800 (June–end of Sept). Free maps, walking routes in English and leaflets and regional information are available. Rail travel desk.

Comité Régional du Tourisme d'Auvergne, 43 av. Julien; tel: 73 93 04 03. Open Mon–Fri 0800-1830.

Conseil General du Puy-de-Dôme, 24 r. St-Esprit; tel: 73 42 20 20. Open Mon–Sat 1000–1800 (mid July–Oct).

Arriving and Departing

Station

Gare SNCF av. de l'Union Soviétique: tel: 36 35 35 35. Buffet, lockers, automatic cash dispenser and an adjoining tourist office, which is open Mon–Sat 0915–1130, 1215–1700: tel: 73 91 87 89.

Buses

Bus Station, 69 blvd Gergovia (next to the main tourist office); tel: 73 93 13 61. Buses depart for Riom and Volvic.

Getting Around

The **T2C** buses mainly follow the circle of thoroughfares around Clermont and all, except bus no. 17, stop at pl. de Jaude, where the **T2C Boutique,** tel: 73 26 44 90, at the terminus sells books of 10 tickets, FFr.47 (also available at selected newsagents), and one-day tickets, FFr.22. Closed Sun and holidays.

Taxi ranks are outside the rail station (FFr.40 to the pl. de Jaude) and at the pl. de la Victoire, tel: 73 92 57 58.

Staying in Clermont-Ferrand

Accommodation

There are no luxury hotels but a wide choice of moderate hotels mainly in two areas – the streets spreading out from the rail station and around pl. de Jaude. There is a selection in the outskirts towards the local airport plus a couple of hotels in old Montferrand. Hotel chains include Ca, Co, Ib, IH, Me, and Nv.

HI: 55 av. de l'Union Soviétique; tel: 73 92 26 39. Open Mar–end of Oct. It is a couple of minutes' walk from the rail station. **Foyer International des Jeunes,** Home Dôme, 12 pl. Regensburg; tel:73 93 07 82. Take bus no. 13 (stop: 8 Mai), a 15-min journey from the Esplanade stop on r. de Grande Bretagne (a couple of minutes' walk from the rail station). In the suburb town of Ceyrat is **Le Chanset** campsite, av. Jean Baptiste Marrou; tel; 73 61 30 73. Bus no. 4c (bus no. 4 on Sun) from the rail station to bus stop Préguille, 30 min journey. Open all year.

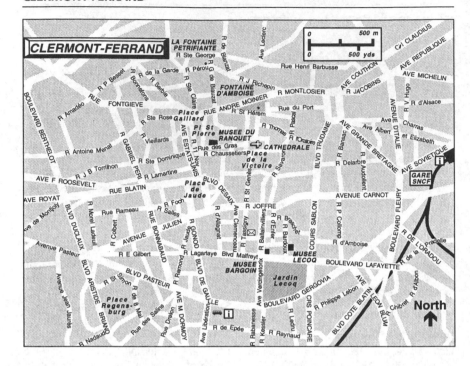

Eating and Drinking

From Canadian to Vietnamese, Clermont's many restaurants reflect international cuisine as well as traditional regional specialities from the Auvergne. As expected in a university town, there are many cheap places to eat and a good choice of delicatessens, pizzerias and snack bars with take-away specialities. The market at **pl. St-Pierre** is open daily except Sun and holidays. For picnics, head for the benches in the leafy avenues of the well-landscaped **Jardin Lecoq**, a popular background for wedding day photo sessions, which also has a caféteria overlooking a small lake.

Communications

Main **post office**, *17 r. Maréchal de Lattre de Tassigny; tel: 73 30 60 00.* Poste restante available.

Money

There is no money-changing bureau at the station. Cross over to the av. *Charras* where there are two banks, **BNP** (closed Sat and Sun) and **Crédit Agricole** (closed Sun and Mon).

Entertainment

Piano bars and pubs with rock, jazz and blues nights are popular. Hotels, restaurants, discos and clubs are listed in a brochure, *Étape du bon vivre,* free from the tourist office.

A quarterly magazine, *Demain,* in French only (FFr.6; free at tourist offices), includes listings of the many events, concerts, film seasons, theatre productions, art exhibitions and sports competitions. Tickets for musical events are available at **FNAC** at the *Centre Jaude; tel: 73 93 44 86.*

Shopping

Centre Jaude, a modern mall in the wide expanse of *pl. de Jaude*, is the focus of the main shopping area, which includes *r. Blatin*. Leading north off this large square is *r. de 11 Novembre*, the beginning of the narrow, mostly pedestrianised streets of the old town with speciality and craft shops, fashion boutiques and antique showrooms.

Sightseeing

The brochure *Welcome to Clermont-Ferrand*, in English, outlines walking routes in Clermont and Montferrand (to get to the old centre, take bus no. 6 outside the rail station to stop: *pl. de la Fontaine*, a 10-min journey). A charming way to explore both on foot is with the illustrated English map-leaflet, *Tour of Fountains*, including the landmark **Amboise Fountain**, overlooking splendid views. On the route is the unusual **La Fontaine Pétrifiante**, *13 r. du Pérou; tel: 73 37 15 58*. Open daily 0900–1200, 1400–1800 (Sept–June); daily 0800–1930 (July and Aug). It has English guided tours of the springs, the exhibition gallery and the garden with many life-sized models of people and animals, given an alabaster-like translucence by immersion in the mineral waters; free. **Le Musée du Ranquet,** *34 r. des Gras; tel: 73 37 38 63*. (bus stop: *Gaillard*). Open 1000–1200, 1400–1700 (until 1800, June–Sept; closed Mon, Sun mornings and holidays), admission FFr.12.

A museum of natural history, **Le Musée Lecoq,** *15 r. Bardoux; tel: 73 91 93 78* (bus stop: *Baillainvilliers*), is open Tues–Sat, 1000–1200, 1400–1700, Sun afternoon (until 1800 May–end of Sept; closed Mon, Sun morning). FFr.21 (FFr.11.30). **Le Musée Bargoin,** *45 r. Ballainvilliers; tel: 73 91 37 31*. (bus stop: *Baillainvilliers*).

Open 1000–1200, 1400–1700 (Oct–end of Apr); until 1800 (May–end of Sept); closed Mon, Sun morning and holidays. FFr.21 (FFr.11.30). It features archaeological finds, especially from the Roman era. In the same building is the new **Musée éducatif du Tapis d'Art** displaying Oriental carpets.

In Montferrand is the modern **Musée des Beaux-Arts,** *pl. Louis Deteix; tel: 73 23 08 49*. (bus stop: *Montesquieu*). It has paintings from the Middle Ages to the 20th century. Open Tues–Sun 1000–1800 (closed some hols) FFr.21 (FFr.11.30).

Guided walking tours take place mid-June–mid-Sept; in Clermont on Wed, Fri, Sat at 1500 from the Musee du Ranquet; evening tour on Mon at 2030 from the tourism kiosk at *pl. de Jaude*, and in Montferrand on Tues, Thurs, Sat at 1500 from the Musée des Beaux-Arts.

Out of Town

Le Puy de Dôme, 1465 m, the highest of the surrounding mountain peaks, has panoramic views, Roman ruins and an information centre, with video, commentary and an exhibition. *Tel: 73 62 21 46*. Open daily 0900–1900 (June–Sept); 0830–2000 (July–Aug). Coach excursions to the summit take place on Mon afternoon (Apr–mid-Oct); also on Thurs afternoon (July–Aug). Make reservations at **Voyages Maisonneuve,** *24 r. G. Clémenceau; tel: 73 93 16 72*. Open Mon–Fri 0830–1200, 1400–1830; Sat 0900–1200. Bookings can be made to visit other peaks.

Other excursions, leaving from the rail station, include a visit to the 18th-century apartments of **Château de Ravel**, Thurs afternoon, and a variety of one-off themed tours such as a cruise on **Lake Vassivière** or **Circuit George Sand**, which includes visit to the author's home and a museum in her honour.

CLERMONT-FERRAND to LYON

From the mountain ranges of Clermont-Ferrand to the bustling activity of Lyon set between two rivers, this route goes through a fantastic landscape as it heads south, especially when it reaches the volcanic hills of Le Velay. The most dramatically pointed outcrops have inspired religious edifices, two with colossal statues, one at Espaly and one at Le Puy,

both seen from the train. Fortified hamlets also top high points and agriculture remains part of the ever-changing terrain, with fields of sunflowers and wheat as well as vineyards on flat land or sloping hills beside the tracks as the train passes Brassac, Arvant and Brioude. A misted mountainous silhouette looms in the background.

This route requires a change of train at St Georges d'Aurac. The train heads north again after Le Puy.

TRAINS

ETT table: 140c, 145a, 148.

 Fast Track

Through trains between Clermont-Ferrand and Lyon Part-Dieu or Lyon Perrache take either of two different routes although

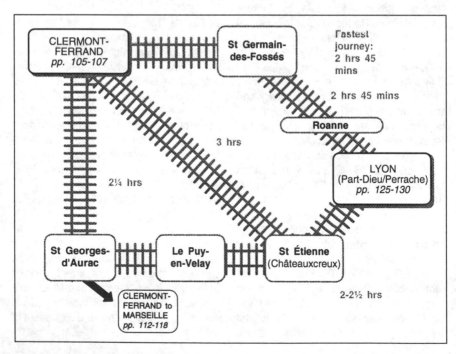

none go via Le Puy. The fastest services go via Roanne and take about 2 hr 45 mins, others go via St Étienne and take a little more than 3 hrs. Even with two routes to choose from there are no more than five or six through trains a day. Other journeys can be made by changing trains at St-Germain-des-Fossés.

On Track

Clermont-Ferrand–Le Puy-en-Velay

Two through trains run between Clermont-Ferrand and Le Puy, one morning and one evening, taking 2¼ hrs. Otherwise a change of train is required at St Georges-d'Aurac or Langeac (bus connection).

Le Puy-en-Velay–Lyon

Four trains a day run from Le Puy to Lyon Perrache with another two or three services available by changing trains at St-Étienne Châteaucreux. Journey times are between 2 and 2½ hrs.

LE PUY-EN-VELAY

Station: *av. Charles Dupuy; tel: 36 35 35 35.* About a 15-min walk to centre, turn left, follow *av. C. Dupuy,* to *sq. Coiffier,* then left on *blvd Mar. Fayolle* to *pl. du Breuil.* There is no bus from the station but lines nos 1 and 3 leave from *sq. Coiffier* (stop: *pl. Michelet).* **Taxi:** at station, *tel: 71 09 21 10;* at *pl. du Breuil, tel: 71 09 33 68.* **Bus station:** *pl. Mar. Leclerc; tel: 71 09 25 60.*

Tourist Office: *pl. du Breuil, 43000 Le Puy-en-Velay; tel: 71 09 38 41.* Open daily 0830–1200, 1345–1839 (Easter–Sept) with extended continuous hours 0830–1930 (July–Aug); Mon–Sat 0830–1200, 1345–1830 (Oct–Easter). Thers is leaflet information about the town and region, but the

tourist office does not make hotel reservations.

Getting Around

For the local bus network, go to the ticket booth **TUDIP**, *pl. Michelet; tel: 71 05 41 11.* Single journey FFr.5.40; ten tickets for FFr.39. The narrow street layout means it is more practical to walk to the attractions within the historic core, despite heavily cobbled, steep climbs.

Accommodation and Food

There is limited accommodation, with restricted choice at the lower-priced end. There are hotels near the station, near *pl. du Breuil (av. C. Charbonnier)* but not many in the old town. Hotel chains include *Ib.* **HI:** *centre Pierre Cardinal, 9 r. Jules Vallès; tel: 71 05 52 40.* A 15-min walk from the station, it is near the cathedral. **Camping:** *Bouthezard, ch. de Roderie, tel: 71 09 55 09.* Bus 6 from *pl. Michelet* (stop: *Parc Quincieu*), a 5-min journey.

There is a good choice of restaurants, many featuring local specialities, with some offering set price menus from FFr.55 (*pl. de la Halle, blvd St-Louis).* From salads to casseroles, many dishes feature the green Puy lentil, a plant which thrives in the volcanic soil of the Velay region. There are brasseries, pizzerias (*pl. du Breuil),* crêperies (*r. Vibert*) and gourmet restaurants (*r. Chènbouterie).*

Events

Festival events, involving costumed performers and residents, take place mid-Sept. Other festivals include a musical gathering of street musicians in June and a folklore celebration with costumed performers in mid-July. The spectacular **Les Fêtes Renaissance du Roi de l'Oiseau** (The Bird King Renaissance Festival), dates back to an

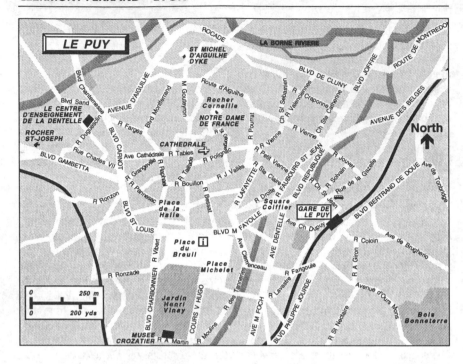

archery competition in 1524. A free special supplement, in French, details the varied events including concerts, exhibitions and re-enactments. The festival takes place anytime from mid-Aug to mid–Sept. Besides the tourist office, information is available from **Boutique Renaissance**, *44 r. Raphaël; tel: 71 09 23 78.*

Sightseeing

Guided tours (in French) leave from the tourist office daily 1000–1600 (first three weeks Aug); daily 1600 (last two weeks July; end-Aug–mid-Sept). Evening walks on Wed, Fri, 2100 (mid-July–Aug). FFr.30.

This most unusual town makes a striking skyline with its massive cathedral, its monumental statue and its solitary 11th-century chapel, all dominating rocky volcanic peaks or hills. Spread out flat, it would be easy to visit Le Puy's attractions in an afternoon, but the many steep climbs are quite punishing and set a slow pace, albeit in a historically evocative setting.

A free brochure, *Historical Visits*, is printed in English and is available from the tourist office. It outlines two walking routes of 2–3 hrs plus a 2-hr evening one, which pass all the historic sites.

It is always fascinating, especially since a turn of a corner often means coming across a lacemaker sitting outside a shop, bobbins clicking over intricate *dentelle* (lace) spread on a cushion (*r. St-Georges*). Traditional lacemaking is an industry in the town, population 26,000, which trains new craftsmen in the profession at an education centre with an exhibition and demonstration room open for viewing. It is **Le Centre d'Enseignement de la Dentelle du**

Puy (lace-making information centre), *2 r. Duguesclin; tel: 71 02 01 68.* Open Mon–Fri 0900–1130, 1400–1730 (and also on Sat, June–Sept); admission FFr.10.

Bobbin lace work from the 16th–20th centuries is on display at the **Le Musée Crozatier,** *jardin Henri Vinay* (off *pl. du Breuil*); *tel: 71 09 38 90.* Open Wed–Mon 1000–1200, 1400–1800 (May–Sept); Wed–Mon 1000–1200, 1400–1600 (Oct–Apr). FFr.12 (concessions FFr.6). Free on Sun, 1400–1600 (Oct–Apr). Geology, archaeology and folk traditions form part of the displays of this museum, founded in 1828, which also has early mechanical prototypes, such as a sewing machine, as well as many fine paintings from the 15th–18th centuries and medieval sculptures and furniture.

The peak-top attractions of Le Puy give breathtaking views. On **Rocher Corneille** (Corneille Rock) is the statue of **Notre-Dame de France** (Our Lady of France), with an internal staircase. An engineering feat completed in 1859, using cannons from the battle of Sebastopol, the Mother holds the Child blessing the town. The unusual red colour was chosen to make it even more visible from a distance and to match the red roofs of the houses of the town. The statue's dimensions are colossal. The hair is 7 m long and its foot is on a serpent 17 m long. The crowned head weights 110 tons and 18 people can fit inside the chest. Open daily 0900–1900 (May–Sept); daily 1000–1700, but closed Tues from Nov (Oct–mid-Mar); daily 0900–1800 (mid-Mar–Apr). Closed Dec; FFr.9.50.

There are 268 steps to **St-Michel d'Aiguile Dyke** (St Michael on a needle), built in the 11th century. It is open daily all year but with variable times 1000–1200, 1400–1800 (Apr–May); 0900–1200, 1400–1900 (June–mid-July); 0900–1900

(mid-June–mid-Sept); 0930–1200, 1400–1730 (mid-Sept–mid-Nov); 1400–1600 (end-Dec–beginning of Jan, mid-Feb–mid-Mar); 1000–1200; 1400–1700 (mid-Mar–end-Mar).

To reach the **cathedral**, follow *r. des Tables* to the 134 steps leading to the massive arched entrance, with carvings of the nativity and the death of Christ on the grand door within the porch. The cathedral is based on a Roman site and was a major medieval pilgrimage stop. **Le Cloître** (cloister) is open daily 0930–1230, 1400–1800 (Apr–June); daily 0930–1930 (July–Sept); Mon–Sat 0930–1200, 1400–1630, Sun, holidays 0930–1630 (Oct–Dec). FFr.20 (FFr.13). This includes a museum of sacred art. A combined ticket for the cloister, the statue, the chapel and the museum is available (Apr–Sept). FFr.32 (instead of FFr.51.50). It is sold at the tourist office and the attractions. One of the cathedral's famous objects is the Black Madonna, a 19th-century copy of a statue carved in dark cedar wood and said to have been brought back from the Crusades. The High Altar serves as its pedestal and ithe statue is carried in a procession during the mid-Aug Feast of the Assumption.

At **Espaly St-Marcel**, 2 km away, is **Rocher St-Joseph** (rock of St Joseph), with a diorama. Open daily 0900–1200, 1400–1800 (mid-July–Aug). FFr.7. Bus 4 from *pl. Michelet* (stop: *Arbrouset* in Espaly).

Out of Town

Guided excursions (in French) to the Velay region depart Tues 1400 (July–Aug) offering three routes, each 2½ hrs, to explore the volcanic landscape. They leave from the tourist office which sells the tickets and are a combination of bus travel and walks to volcano tops such as **Cheyrac** and **La Denise**.

CLERMONT-FERRAND to MARSEILLE

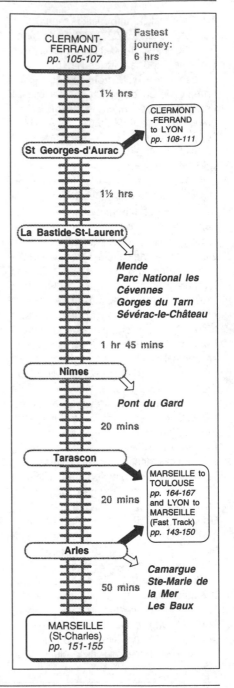

From the natural splendour of the mountains around Clermont-Ferrand, to the important Roman monuments of Nîmes, this route starts off flirting with the River Allier and there are many sightings of brightly coloured kayaks in the rushing waters of its gorges as well as occasional beaches and campsites. The first leg of this route, as far as St-Georges d'Aurac, is the same as Clermont-Ferrand–Lyon (see p. 108). It passes through small villages, some of which are tempting stopping-off points to explore the mountainous terrain.

TRAINS

ETT table: 145a.

 Fast Track

One train a day runs from Clermont-Ferrand to Marseille. *Le Cévenol*, with a buffet car, leaves Clermont around lunchtime and arrives at Marseille St-Charles over 6 hrs later. Two other services are available by changing trains at Nîmes.

On Track

Clermont-Ferrand–St Georges d'Aurac–La Bastide

Three trains a day run from Clermont-Ferrand to La Bastide-St-Laurent, with journey times of around 3 hrs. One of these trains calls at St Georges d'Aurac, which is 1½ hrs from both Clermont-Ferrand and La Bastide-St Laurent.

La Bastide–Nîmes

The three trains from Clermont-Ferrand are supplemented by three trains from Mende, giving six services for the 1 hr 45 mins journey between La Bastide-St-Laurent and Nîmes.

Nîmes–Tarascon

There is a train roughly every 2 hrs between Nîmes and Tarascon sur Rhône. The journey takes about 20 mins.

Tarascon–Arles

Around eight services link Tarascon sur Rhône and Arles each day, although there are long periods during the day with no trains. The journey takes 20 mins.

Arles–Marseille

As many as sixteen trains run between Arles and Marseille St-Charles each day with journey times of around 50 mins.

LA BASTIDE-ST-LAURENT

Change at La Bastide for the almost hour-long journey to Mende, and continue on by bus to visit Sévérac-le-Château.

 Side Tracks from La Bastide

MENDE

Station: *av. de la Gare; tel: 67 58 50 50* (information), *67 58 43 06* (sales). After June 1995, one number for both services: *tel: 36 35 35 35.* A small rural station. No lockers but it may be possible to leave luggage behind the counter. It is a 15-min walk to the centre. Follow the *av. de la Gare* to the bridge over the River Lot, turn right on *allée Piencourt* to *pl. Ch de Gaulle*, turn right into the town centre or go straight on the *blvd du Soubeyron*, leading to the tourist office.

Tourist Office: *14 blvd Henri Bourrillon, 48000 Mende; tel: 66 65 02 69.* Open daily 0830–2000 (July–Aug); Mon–Fri 0830–1230, 1400–1900, Sat 0900–1200 (Easter–June, Sept). Mon–Fri 0830–1230, 1400–1800, Sat 0900–1200 (Oct–Easter). Information about the town and region including accommodation such as *gîtes d'étapes* (overnight stops for walkers, often bed and breakfast in family homes) and camping sites; no hotel reservations.

Sightseeing

Dating from the 14th–16th centuries, **Cathédrale de St-Pierre**, *pl. Urbain V*, presides importantly over the centre of this little town with lots of ancient character. The cathedral has eight Aubusson tapestries.

The old streets have interesting houses, many from the 17th–18th centuries (*pl. du Mazel, r. l'Orange, r. des Mulets*). The tourist office provides a brochure outlining two walking routes that pass interesting town house façades and buildings in the town. The local history museum, *tel: 66 65 05 02*, is open Mon–Fri 1000–1200, 1500–1800.

Mende is gateway to **Le Parc National Les Cévennes**, the largest national park in France and very popular with walkers. Leaflets from the tourist office, prepared by the **Office Municipal de la Culture de Mende**, describe walking routes from Mende, half-day and full-day, which take in architecturally interesting hamlets (**Alteyrac, Badaroux**) or historic monuments like the 12th-century chapel at **La Rouvière**. On the periphery of the Cévennes park is yet more outstanding countryside, **Les Gorges du Tarn**, a canyon valley whose river is popular with canoeists.

Some bus services which run in the summer to the national park have schedules which allow for return day trips. **SNCF**: *tel: 66 49 00 39* (for Barjac and Chanac), has departures from the station. **Autocars Boulet**; *tel: 66 65 19 88* (to Balsièges, La Canourgue) with departures from *pl. du Forail*.

After making the trip to Mende, it is possible to continue to the medieval town of **Sévérac**, 64 km further west. Mende is the terminus for the little train but an SNCF bus goes to **Marvejols** (a 40-min journey) to connect with trains (almost a 40-min journey) to Sévérac.

Note that from Sévérac, there are trains to Clermont-Ferrand (see p. 105) to the north or Béziers to the south. Sévérac is a small station, so there are usually only two direct trains to either destination; otherwise change at Neussargues for Clermont-Ferrand and at Millau for Béziers.

SÉVÉRAC-LE-CHÂTEAU

Station: *pl. Salvador Allende; tel: 65 71 61 19*. A small rural station. No lockers (the staff may let you leave bags for a short time). No tourist information. The walk to the old historic town, 30 mins, is up the long hill road, *r. Serge Duhourquet* (which is very busy and without pavements) to *r. des Douves*. **Taxi**: *tel: 65 71 67 79*. **Tourist Office:** *r. des Douves, 12150 Sévérac-le-Château; tel: 65 47 67 31*. Open Tues–Sat 1000–1200, 1500–1900; Sun, Mon 1000–1200 (summer only). Information, not all free. No hotel reservations.

The town, population 5000, has five hotels, reasonably priced; three are opposite the station, which is a lively section of the lower town, especially as matches of *petanque* go on into the night in the floodlit playing area next to the station. The restaurants here are also popular, but for ambience, try the crêperie in the old town (*r. de la Ville*). The other two hotels are also up the hill.

This is another town with its charming old quarter high on a hill, this one overlooked by large romantic château ruins, and with a lower commercial centre where the modern facilities are located.

Le Château de Sévérac offers sweeping views over the valley of the Aveyron. Open daily 0900–1900 (mid-June–mid-Sept). FFr.10. Guided visits in French. A leaflet with brief highlights in English is given. Certain towers are accessible, including an ancient chapel and the restored kitchen, which displays old photographs about local life. Dating to the 11th century and once integral to the defence of the town, it fell into ruin after it was no longer occupied after the French Revolution. It is slightly further up the road than the old town, which is a compact, picturesque cluster of narrow pedestrian streets lined with ancient stone houses.

NÎMES

Station: Gare de Nîmes, *blvd Sergent Triaire*. South-east of the centre, 5 mins walk to central attractions. Train information 0800–1800, Sat 0900–1215, 1400–1800; *tel: 66 23 50 50*; for reservations *tel: 66 78 79 79*. For the town centre head straight down *av. Feuchères* opposite the station to *esplanade Charles de Gaulle*, then along *blvd Victor Hugo* to the tourist office. Tourist office in station, open 0930–

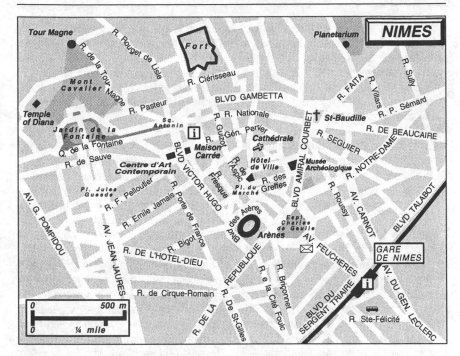

1230, 1430–1830 daily, *tel: 66 84 18 13.* Station closed 0100–0400. Left luggage open 0800–2000; bike hire available at the left luggage counter, *tel: 66 29 72 41.*
Bus Station: *r. Ste-Félicité* behind the station, *tel: 66 29 52 00.* Regular bus services run to Uzès, Pont du Gard and the Camargue.
Tourist Office: *6 r. Auguste, 30000 Nîmes; tel: 66 67 29 11,* in the town centre, open 0800–1900 in summer, closed lunch time in winter. Currency exchange.

Getting Around

Nîmes first came to prominence as a Roman town, and whilst 20th-century high-tech expansion has led to a dramatic growth in its size, the main tourist attractions are all easily accessible by foot. Free maps are available from the tourist office, including a map for disabled visitors.

Staying in Nîmes

Accommodation

Nîmes has been looking after guests since Caesar first rode into town, and offers a wide selection of hotels, from the grandiose **Hôtel Impérator Concorde**, *quai de la Fontaine*, favourite of the top toreadors during the bullfighting *ferias*, and the newly opened neo-classical **Le Cheval Blanc**, to simple family-run *auberges*.

Nîmes hosts conferences all year round, so booking is advisable in larger chain hotels. In summer months the city can get crowded with tourists, but the only real time you need worry about is during the bullfighting contests. Nîmes is crazy about bulls, and the biggest *ferias* at carnival time in Feb and the third week in Sept attract more party-goers than Munich's beer festival.

Inexpensive accommodation is best found near the bullfighting arena, along *blvd des Arènes*, or around *blvd Amiral Courbet* running north from *esplanade Charles de Gaulle*, 5 mins walk from the train station.

HI: *chemin de la Cigale; tel: 66 23 25 04*. Two km from the centre, bus no. 20 from the station. **Camping**: **Domaine de la Bastide**: *rte de Générac; tel: 66 38 09 21*. Take bus no. 4 in the direction of Bastide, get off at *Générac*.

Eating and Drinking

Traditionally Nîmes has been considered a culinary backwater, although local special-ities exist and should be sampled. *Branade de Mor*, a cod paste mixed with olive oil, and *tapenade d'olives*, an appetiser of ground olives, anchovies and herbs, both date back to Roman times. Goat's cheese from the surrounding hills is amongst the best in France, while sweeter tooths will appreciate the *croquants Villarets*, small almond biscuits.

For good-quality, inexpensive restau-rants head to the side streets off *blvd Victor Hugo* between the arena and Maison Carrée. Other possibilities abound along *r. Fresque* and *r. de l'Etoile*.

Communications

Post Office: *blvd de Bruxelles*, near *pl. de la Libération, tel: 66 76 67 06*. Open 0830–1800.

Entertainment

Nîmes is proud of its cultural heritage, and opera, dance, theatre and live music are all commonplace. A 24-hr information line gives details of current events, *tel: 66 36 27 27*.

For animated bars head for the places around the arena, *blvd Victor Hugo* and *blvd des Arènes*. During the **feria** this area is full of life and colour.

Ferias, or bullfighting festivals, take place all through the summer, but the biggest are in Feb, May and Sept. July sees the annual Jazz Festival grace the arenas.

Sightseeing

A key town on the Roman route between Italy and Spain, Nîmes quickly became a centre of opulence, culture and gladiatorial combat. In later years Nîmois textile merchants invented a durable blue cloth which was later discovered by Levi Strauss in California – the cloth was known as *de Nîmes*, or as the Americans called it, denim. Most recently Nîmes has been growing at a spectacular rate, thanks to an influx of high-tech industry and the building aspira-tions of mayor Jean Bousquet, whose *petits projets*, including a new 400 million franc art museum, rival the *grands projets* of President Mitterand in Paris.

The tourist office sells a three-day pass to all sights and museums at FFr.50, or FFr.25 for students. Museums in Nîmes are synchronised: opening times at time of writing were 1100–1800, closed Mon. Walking tours run daily July–Aug at 1430 from the tourist office, cost FFr.20.

Nîmes' fame is based on its Roman bits – the **Arènes** are perhaps the best preserved of all remaining Roman arenas and still host *feria* bullfights, when would-be Heming-ways flock to Nîmes. Elsewhere **Tour Magne** in the park on the slopes of Mont Cavalier is the oldest Roman monument in France, a bizarre tower whose original purpose is unknown. Steps lead to the top for fine views.

Ancient meets modern at the **Maison Carrée**, *r. Nationale; tel: 66 36 26 76*, the world's best preserved Roman temple (open 0900–1900, 0900–1730 Oct–Apr) standing next to the futuristic **Centre d'Art Contemporain**, Nîmes' new art-Mecca designed by Norman Foster. The art museum contain works by the 20th-century's greatest – Picasso, Braque, Jasper Johns etc. It is also on *r. Nationale; tel: 66 76 35 70*, open daily 1100–2000, closed Mon, and 1100–1800 Oct–Apr.

To the west, **Jardin de la Fontaine** was France's first public garden, complete with the romantic **Temple of Diana**.

Nîmes boasts an illustrious 17th-century history, when the local textile emperors enjoyed great wealth and power. A century earlier the crocodile was adopted as the city's emblem (following even earlier Roman usage as a symbol of victory after Augustus' victories in Egypt) and many of the impressive *hôtels particuliers*, or town houses, carry a carved reptile.

Nîmes' museums are somewhat disappointing. The **Musée d'Histoire Naturelle** and the **Musée Archéologique** are both housed at *13 bis av. Amiral Courbet; tel: 66 67 39 14*, for Natural History and *tel: 66 67 25 57*, for Archaeology. Children of any age will enjoy the local **Planetarium** on *av. Peladan; tel: 66 67 60 94*.

⌒ Side Track from Nîmes

A spectacular roman aqueduct, the **Pont du Gard**, stands 48 m above the River Gard. The site is being redeveloped to cope with its 2 million visitors a year. Buses run eight times a day from Nîmes.

TARASCON

Station: *pl. de la Gare*. For information *tel: 90 91 04 82*, open 0900–1200 and 1400–1800. Tarascon is not big. For its centre head right from the station. For the river and château head left.

Tourist Office: *59 r. des Halles, 13150 Tarascon; tel: 90 91 03 52.*

Accommodation and Food

Remarkably friendly, inexpensive hotels hug the square by the station. **Youth Hostel**: *31 blvd Gambetta; tel: 90 91 04 08*. A cluster of reasonable and sometimes lively restaurants is also found near the station.

Sightseeing

Tarascon is considered by many to be little more than a drab town on the Rhône. However, its does have its saving graces – cheap places to stay and a dramatic big fort, the **Château du Roi Réné**, a fairy-tale castle on the river (guided tours, closed Tues). The **House of Tartarin** is based on Daudet's famous fictional character. Here too is a model of the **Tarasque** dragon, which lived in the Rhône and was banished to its depths by St Martha's crucifix.

ARLES

Station: *av. Talabot*. Information 0900–1800 (closed lunch during winter) *tel: 90 96 43 94*. For the town centre walk down *av. Talabot*, through the walls at *pl. Lamartine*, along *r. Laclavière* to the arena. Otherwise take bus no. 4 to *blvd des Lices* and the tourist office. Tourist information open 0900–2000, Sun 0900–1400 summer, 0900–1300, 1400–1800 winter, closed Sun, *tel: 90 49 36 90*. The station and luggage lockers are closed 0100–0430.

Tourist Office: *Esplanade des Lices, 13200 Arles*, the other side of town from the station, 0900–1900 summer, 0900–1200, 1400–1800 winter.

Bus Station: opposite the station; *tel: 90 49 38 01*, runs regular buses to the Camargue, **Cars de Camargue**, *tel: 90 96 36 25.*

Getting Around

Arles is a town for walking: it takes 10 mins to walk from one side to another. **Taxis:** *blvd des Lices; tel: 90 96 90 03.* **Bike Hire**, at the station; *tel: 90 96 43 94*, or **DallOppio**; *10 r. Portagnel*, inside the walls then left from the station, *tel: 90 96 46 83.* Bikes are a perfect way to see the neighbouring flatlands of the Camargue.

Staying in Arles

Accommodation

Arles can be tight for accommodation, but is usually less expensive than its more grandiose neighbours. Be sure to reserve in advance in busy summer months. **HI:** *20 av. Foch, tel: 90 96 18 25*, south of the town, bus no. 4 from the station, then bus no. 3 from *blvd des Lices* to *Fournier*. In the centre, several inexpensive hotels cluster around *pl. du Forum* and *pl. Voltaire*.

Eating and Drinking

Numerous small but good quality restaurants grace Arles' streets. Try around *pl. du Forum*, and *r. du 4 Septembre* at the end of *r. d'Hôtel de Ville*. Cafés are liveliest around *pl. du Forum* and *pl. Voltaire*.

Communications

Post office: *5 blvd des Lices; tel: 90 96 07 80.*

Entertainment

In winter months Arles is a quiet country town. It takes the summer bullfights and the July music, dance and theatre festival to fill the streets and enliven the scattering of bars.

Sightseeing

The spiritual heart of Provence and a perfect place to relax and drink up history, Arles is one of the best preserved Roman towns in the world. To visit all the monuments and museums buy a global ticket from the tourist office. All major sights are included on the **Forfait 3** pass, FFr.44, students FFr.35. The **Forfait 2** takes in the Roman monuments at FFr.30, students FFr.20. The **Forfait 1** pass gives access to three of the museums at FFr.25, students FFr.19.

The **Arènes** is a mini Colosseum, still used for bullfights from Easter to Sept (*tel: 90 96 03 70*, open 1000–1800). The **Théâtre Antique**, *tel: 90 96 93 30*, is also still used for productions. In the town centre, **Musée Arlaten,** *r. de la République; tel: 90 96 08 23*, is dedicated to local history and traditions, whilst **Musée Réattu** *r. du Grand Prieuré; tel: 90 49 37 58*, has a collection of Picasso drawings. The tourist office runs Van Gogh tours, but none of the artist's works are here in the town where he cut off his ear.

- - - - - - - - - - - - - - - - - - - -

⤴ Side Tracks from Arles

A wild marshland and rice fields roamed by white horses and black bulls, lagoons pink with flamingos, **La Camargue** is best seen by bike or horse (bike hire in Arles, horse hire throughout the area). On the coast, **Saintes-Maries-de-la-Mer** is a gypsy shrine and site of an international gypsy festival in May. The church in the town is particularly spooky. Buses depart hourly from Arles.

To the north-east, **Les Baux** is a rock rising from the Crau plain, a windswept medieval bastion, now chic and endowed with expensive hotel and restaurants.

- - - - - - - - - - - - - - - - - - - -

DIJON

Dijon lies in the heartland of France, ancient capital of the Dukes of Burgundy from 1364 to 1477. Famed for its riches, its medieval architecture and most of all for its food and wine, Dijon is a place in which to indulge yourself. Many of its buildings date from the Middle Ages and the city centre is a dictionary definition of 'picturesque'. Architecture aside, the wines and gastronomy of Burgundy are reason enough to spend time in Dijon – while not cheap, a meal and bottle at one of the local restaurants is an unforgettable experience.

Tourist Information

Tourist Office: pl. Darcy, 21000 Dijon; tel: 80 43 42 12. Helpful and multi-lingual – ask for the Divio brochure, which contains practical details on Dijon. Free but almost useless maps. Accommodation booking service, FFr.15. Currency exchange. Open 0900–2100 summer, 0900–1200, 1400–1900 winter. **Branch Office:** 34 r. des Forges; tel: 80 30 35 39, administration office, but also supplies free maps with suggested walking itineraries etc.
CIJB (Centre Information Jeunesse de Bourgogne); 22 r. Audra; tel: 80 30 35 56, for student and youth information.

Arriving and Departing

Station

Gare Ville av. du Maréchal Foch; tel: 80 41 50 50 (information), 80 43 52 56 (reservations). The station is a 5-min walk from the city centre along av. Foch. Café/

bar: just outside station, open 0730–2000; left luggage open 0800–2000. **SOS Voyageurs:** help to travellers tel: 80 43 16 34. Open Mon–Sat 0830–1800.

Buses

Gare Routière de Dijon, av. Mar. Foch (outside train station) tel: 80 42 11 00 for information. Information office open Mon–Sat 0730–1200, 1400–1830, Sat 0730–1230. Buses to Beaune eight times a day.

Getting Around

Dijon is made for walking, as most of its streets and buildings were built at a time when feet were the main form of transport. The bus service is highly efficient, although unless you want to get out to Lac Kir, you will not need to use it. For the lake take line 18 from pl. Darcy – **STRD** information booth at pl. Grangier; tel: 80 30 60 90. Tickets FFr.5, five trip pass FFr.23.
Taxis are reliable and relatively honest. Main taxi ranks are at the station and pl. Darcy, tel: 80 43 31 30/80 41 11 12.

Staying in Dijon

Accommodation

There is no shortage of hotels, although many are geared towards the business traveller, but accommodation can be tight in the high summer season. Most are in the two-star category. Lower-priced hotels are dotted around the old town; try r. Monge.
HI: Centres de Rencontres Internationales, 1 blvd Champollion; tel: 80 71 32 12. Four km from the station. Take bus no. 5 from pl. Grangier just east of pl. Darcy.

Eating and Drinking

The citizens of Burgundy are renowned for their love of food and drink, and Dijon caters for them in every department. Kir

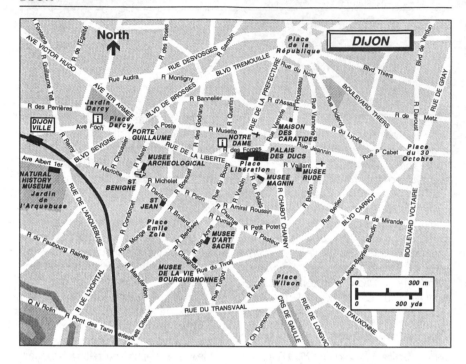

(the world famous apéritif of white wine and a dash of *crème de cassis* – blackcurrant liqueur) was invented in Dijon and named after one of the town's mayors. *Hors d'oeuvres* include *jambon persillé* (ham and parsley pâté) and snails – the latter basted in garlic butter. Classic main courses are *coq au vin* (chicken in red wine sauce) and *boeuf bourguignonne* (beef in thick red wine sauce). And the town gives its name to the traditional mustard, made from white wine rather than vinegar.

Restaurant prices in Dijon are somewhat elevated. In the old town, every second building is a restaurant, so shop around. Try the streets around *pl. Émile Zola*. If prices seem too much, head to one of the *charcuteries* which provide pâtés, pies, quiches and salads.

Burgundy wine is amongst the best in the world. Tours of the extensive surrounding vineyards are available from the tourist office (one-day FFr.150). For the best in white wine head to L'Yonne, where the renowned Chablis is produced, or Nièvre, home of the drier Pouilly-sur-Loire. Red wine fans will not be disappointed – Burgundy red is full-bodied with a series of distinct flavours. Seek out the Côte d'Or region, 60 km of vineyards between Dijon and Santenay south of Beaune. The area is subdivided into the Côte de Nuits area, home to such famous vintages as Musigny, Clos de Vougeot and Chambertin wines, while the Côte de Beaune region produces more delicate Corton, Beaune and Pommard reds.

Communications

Post Office: *pl. Grangier; tel: 80 50 62 19.*

Poste restante, telephones; open 0800–1900 Mon–Fri, 0800–1200 Sat.

Entertainment

Dijon is a student town, with a cultural scene to match, yet for some reason it may appear a dull provincial capital.

Theatre is strong, the best performances being at the **Nouveau Théâtre de Bourgogne**, r. Danton; tel: 80 30 12 12, situated in a converted church. Opera and classical music grace the **Théâtre de Dijon**; pl. du Théâtre; tel: 80 67 20 21, an 18th-century gem of an opera house (seats FFr.75–250).

Those in search of more frenetic night-life should wander around the old town. Try r. Berbisey behind pl. Emile Zola, or the streets around pl. Ste-Benigne.

Events

Each June **Été musical** is a summer festival of classical music, with top symphony orchestras, choirs and bands.

During mid-June and Aug the **Estivade** festival of music, dance and theatre takes over the streets; tel: 80 30 31 00.

In Sept the grape harvest is celebrated in **Fête de la Vigne**; tel: 80 30 37 95.

Sightseeing

The not-too-inclusive maps from the tourist office do set out a convenient walking tour of the town. A FFr.15 daily pass gets you in to all the museums (available from any museum).

Dijon's most impressive building, at the geographical and political centre of town, is the **Palais des Ducs de Bourgogne**. In their time (1364–1477) the dukes of Burgundy rivalled the Kings of France for control of eastern France. The oldest portion of the palace is the **Tour Philippe le Bon**, dating from the 15th century, rising in the midst of the extravagant palace. Most of the palace itself was built during the 17th century, designed by the architect of Versailles.

Much of the palace is now used by the Burgundy regional government, but the east wing is accessible to the public – this is the **Musée des Beaux Arts**, one of the finest in France; pl. de la Chapelle; tel: 80 74 52 70, open 1000–1800, closed Tues. Inside, to the left is the **Salle des Gardes**, the magnificent mausoleum of the famous dukes, their sarcophagi encrusted with gold. In the museum's galleries there are impressive collections of European art from the 14th–18th century. Upstairs is a fine collection of 19th–20th century art, including works by Picasso, Dufy and Bonnard.

From the palace head around the oldest streets in the town, including r. de la Houette, where the patron bird of Dijon is carved on the pillars of **Église de Notre Dame**, (Church of Our Lady) pl. Notre Dame; tel: 80 30 11 77. Rub the brass owl and good luck shall be yours. Outside, high above the impressive gargoyles, is the 14th-century **Horloge de Jacquemart**. Life-size figures chime every quarter hour.

Fine-art and fine furniture combine at the **Musée Magnin**, 4 r. des Bons Enfants; tel: 80 67 11 10, in a former mansion house (open 1000–1800 summer, 1000–1200, 1400–1800, closed Mon).

Outdoor relief from museums and churches comes at the **Jardin de l'Arquebuse**, Dijon's botanical gardens, 1 r. Albert 1er; tel: 80 76 82 76, open 0730–2000 summer, 0730–1800 winter, complete with 3500 different plants, streams and ponds. Nearby, the **Musée Grevin de Bourgogne** at 13 r. Albert 1er; tel: 80 42 03 03, contains displays of Burgundy's history, from the 6th century BC to the present (open 0930–1200, 1400–1900).

DIJON to LYON

Through the gastronomic heart of France, this route takes you along the banks of the Saône, a river mighty enough to rival the Rhône. From Dijon, capital of Burgundy, the route travels south past the great vineyards of Beaune, and on to the city of Cluny and its dramatic abbey, model for many of the cathedrals of Europe. The journey is gentle, past rolling cornfields and herds of cows in green pastures. In many ways this is the utopian picture of rural France – picturesque small towns, beautiful farmhouses, vineyards and lush meadows. All is calm, and somewhat monotonous, until the sudden appearance of the suburbs of France's second city, the frenetic metropolis of Lyon (see p. 125).

DIJON (Ville) pp. 119-121

Fastest journey: 1½ hrs

25 mins

Beaune

1 hr

Mâcon-Loché TGV for TGVs to PARIS

Mâcon (Ville) ⟹ Cluny

30-45 mins

LYON (Part-Dieu/Perrache) pp. 125-130

TRAINS

ETT table: 149.

 Fast Track

Nine or ten expresses operate each day between Dijon Ville and Lyon Part-Dieu; the journey takes between 1½ and 2 hrs.

 On Track

Dijon–Beaune

Up to a dozen services link Dijon Ville and Beaune each day with usually no more than 2 hrs between trains. Journey time is around 25 mins.

Beaune–Mâcon

No more than six trains run between Beaune and Mâcon Ville each day and these trains are concentrated on the morning and evening peak periods. There is nothing between 0930 and 1640. Those trains that do run take around 1 hr.

Mâcon–Lyon

A roughly hourly service operates for most of the day although trains are rare in the afternoon. The journey from Mâcon Ville to Lyon Part-Dieu or Perrache takes 30–45 mins.

BEAUNE

Station: *av. 8 Septembre; tel: 80 44 50 50,* for information. Provides luggage lockers; the station is closed 2400–0500.

Tourist Office: *r. de l'Hôtel de Ville, 21200 Beaune; tel: 80 22 24 51.* Free maps and accommodation service, lists and maps of vineyards and suggested tours. Currency exchange. Free guided tours of the town (in French) July–Aug at 1500. Open 0900–1000 in summer, 0900–1900 in winter.

Getting Around

The town is small and easily accessible by foot. Most of the sights are contained within the walls. Maps suggesting walking tours are available from the tourist office.

Bus Station: *Transco: tel: 80 42 11 00* (based in Dijon). Schedules from tourist office; many buses follow wine routes through the Côte d'Or region.

Accommodation and Food

Popular with foreign tourists, Beaune fills up quickly in summer. Reservations are recommended. There are no youth hostels (better to base yourself in Dijon, 30 mins away by train). Budget hotels are on the streets near the train station.

Camping: **Les Cent-Vignes**; *10 r. Dubois; tel: 80 22 03 91.* A walk of 20 mins from the centre – north on *r. Lorraine* from *pl. Monge.* Open Mar–15 Oct.

In Beaune drinking comes before eating, but this is still Burgundy and the dedication to the stomach persists. There are plenty of good value restaurants, serving local dishes such as snails, paté and distinct cheeses. Try the streets around *pl. Madeleine.*

Entertainment

The main entertainment in Beaune is wine. This is centre of the *Côtes de Beaune* vineyards, some of the finest in Burgundy. The tourist office has lists of local *caves* offering tasting sessions (*dégustations*). The only problem is that you are expected to leave with a bottle or two, purchased at often higher prices than you would pay in supermarkets. Yet the whole experience of wine-tasting is worth any purchase, and in many *caves* you will have consumed more than the price of a bottle before getting to the boutique at the end of the tour.

Welcoming wine cellars include:

Marché aux Vins, *r. Nicolas-Rolin; tel: 80 22 27 69,* in a 15th-century church just behind the Hôtel Dieu. Open 0930–1130, 1430–1800, admission FFr. 40.

Maison Calvet, *6 blvd Perpreuil; tel: 80 22 06 32.* In buildings dating from the 14th century, endless tunnelled cellars and fine wines make this a crowd-pleaser, for FFr. 25 a tour. Open 0900–1330, 1400–1700, closed Tues.

Halles Aux Vins, *28 r. Sylvestre Chauvelot; tel: 80 22 18 34,* in a 13th-century crypt, with 18 wines on offer, right down to the oldest *grands crus.* Admission FFr. 40, open 1000–1200 and 1400–1800.

Sightseeing

Beaune was once home to the dukes of Burgundy. The 15th-century ramparts still impress today, protecting a charming old town of cobbled streets and fine mansions.

The tourist office runs informative tours of the town (in French). Otherwise wander with the aid of their map.

The wealth gained from taxing both wine-growers and river traffic along the Saône went into many of Beaune's buildings. The **Hôtel Dieu**, *r. des Epinoches,* was built by a wealthy tax collector in 1443. Today it is a museum, offering a tour around medieval hospital wards and exquisite courtyards. Open 0900–1830.

The dukes of Burgundy left behind a grandiose palace when they departed for bigger and brassier Dijon. The palace now houses a museum dedicated to the life-blood of the area, the **Musée du Vin**, displaying antique wine-pressing machines and casks, as well as thousands of bottles (empty), at *r. d'Enfer; tel: 80 22 08 19.* Open 0930–1800, admission FFr. 20.

In the **Musée des Beaux Arts**; *r. de l'Hôtel de Ville; tel: 80 24 56 92*, a small collection of Dutch and Flemish artists mingle with better-known 19th and 20th-century French painters. Open 0930–1300, 1400–1800 summer, 1400–1800 winter.

MÂCON

Station: *r. Victor Hugo.* For information (0900–1900, closed for lunch), *tel: 80 93 50 50;* for reservations, *tel: 80 43 52 56.* For the town centre and the river turn left along *Victor Hugo* to *pl. de la Barre.* The old town and river are further east.

Tourist Office: *187 r. Carnot, 71000 Mâcon; tel: 85 39 71 37*, has information about local wine and vineyards.

On the banks of the Sâone, the heart of wine country, Mâcon deserves a brief glimpse, if only for an afternoon.

The **old town** is worth a wander amongst impressive Renaissance architecture. Pause at the **Musée des Ursulines** for an eclectic mix of archaeology and 17th-century art; *r. des Ursulines.* **Pl. des Herbes** is seductive, hosting a daily market.

- - - - - - - - - - - - - - - - - - -

 Side Track from Mâcon

CLUNY

Bus station: **SCETA Voyageurs** runs buses from Mâcon and Chalon-sur-Saône three times a day (45 mins–1½ hrs, FFr. 45, rail passes accepted), *tel: 85 93 50 50.*

Tourist Office: *6 r. Mercière, 71250 Cluny; tel: 85 59 05 34.* Distributes maps and organises tours of the abbey during summer. Open 1000–1900 summer, 1000–1200, 1400–1800 winter. Currency exchange available outside banking hours.

Accommodation

Accommodation can be tight in Cluny, especially at Easter and in high season (June–Sept) – it is best to book ahead. The best bet for budget accommodation is **Cluny Séjour**; *r. Porte de Pans; tel: 85 59 08 83*, behind the bus stop.

Camping: Camping municipal St-Vital; *r. des Griottins; tel: 85 59 08 34*, near the bus station. Open June–Sept.

Sightseeing

Cluny has been revered for over 1000 years as the site of one of Europe's most impressive churches. The town is quiet, pretty and welcoming – an ideal stop-over on the journey south.

The main sight is the abbey and its associated museum. Tours run every hour during summer, from the **Musée Ochier**.

The **Abbey of Cluny** was founded in 910 and grew to control monasteries from Portugal to the Russian border. It was the biggest church in the world until the construction of St Peter's in Rome. In the 14th and 15th centuries the abbots of Cluny rivalled papal emissaries for access to the kings of France. Yet little remains of the splendours of the past – greed and revolution tore down much of the great Abbey.

The remaining towers give an idea of former magnificence. Treasures collected by the monks are displayed in the **Museé Ochier**, in the former Bishop's palace.

- - - - - - - - - - - - - - - - - - -

LYON

France's second biggest city has long been forgotten by the powers-that-be in Paris. Lyonnais, the people of the city, are reputed by their fellow citizens to be the unfriendliest in France. Fog and pollution are said to reign supreme. For many French people, Lyon is just somewhere to get through on their way south.

Yet this great metropolis at the junction of two of Europe's mightiest rivers – the Saône and the Rhône – is far from uninviting. The people are hard-working and proud (this was the centre of the French Resistance during World War II), but also courteous and sociable. Lyon has been a crossroads since early Roman occupation in 43 BC and is used to greeting strangers.

The bustling city has much to offer the visitor – in particular its cuisine, served in historic bouchons, or inns. Many consider the city to be the capital of gastronomy, and restaurants abound, from three Michelin stars to simple one-room family establishments. Once fed, Lyon will offer you art, museums, dance, and a thriving student-oriented nightlife. Given all this, it is easy enough to forgive Lyon its weather.

Tourist Information

Tourist Office: pl. Bellecour, 69000 Lyon (east of Lyon-Perrache rail station); tel: 78 42 25 75. It provides free guides and maps to the city. Open Mon–Fri 0900–1900, Sat 0900–1800 and Sun 1000–1700.

Branch office: pl. St-Jean; av. Adolphe Max; tel: 78 42 25 75. Just across the Saône from pl. Bellecour. New tourist information with same maps etc as the main office, very efficient.

Centre d'Échange (Lyon-Perrache) at the rail station, for accommodation, maps etc. Open Mon–Fri 0900–1230 and 1400–1800, Sat 0900–1700. **Bureau des Guides:** 5 pl. St-Jean; tel: 78 42 25 75. Qualified multi-lingual guides for tours of Lyon, organised by the tourist office.

Centre Régional d'Information Jeunesse: 9 quai des Célestins; tel: 78 37 15 28. Open Mon 1200–1900, Tues–Fri 1000–1900. For student and youth information including jobs, accommodation, transport.

Arriving and Departing

Airport

Aéroport Lyon-Satolas: 25 km east of Lyon; tel: 72 22 72 21. Facilities include restaurants, exchange office and tourist information. From the airport a regular bus service runs every 20 mins between 0600 and 2300 to and from Perrache rail station (via Part-Dieu rail station, FFr.50).

Stations

There are two mainline stations in Lyon. Many trains stop at both stations, so check on your final destination. **Lyon-Perrache** is the more central, a 5-min walk from the tourist office; tel: 78 92 50 50. It provides tourist information and money exchange offices, luggage lockers, a restaurant and bar as well as **SOS Voyageurs** – an information and practical assistance service for passengers (tel: 78 37 03 31). The station is closed 2400–0500. For the tourist office head north from pl. Carnot, along av. Victor Hugo to pl. Bellecour.

Lyon-Part-Dieu is on the east bank of the Rhône and serves the business district (same telephone number as Lyon-Perrache for information). It has a restaurant and luggage lockers. **SOS Voyageurs** *tel: 72 34 12 16*. Station closed 2400–0500.

Buses

Perrache Station: services to Vienne, Annecy and Grenoble. *tel: 78 71 70 00*. Open 0630–1700.

Getting Around

Lyon is big (population 1.5 million). Nature, in the form of the two rivers, the Saône and the Rhône, has divided the city into thirds. On the west bank of the Saône is **Vieux Lyon** (Old Lyon), with its medieval streets. On the east bank of the Rhône is the **business centre**, the Part-Dieu rail station and shopping centre and many of Lyon's apartment blocks. In between, bordered by the Saône and Rhône, is the mainly **pedestrianised** centre of the city, from *pl. Bellecour* and Perrache rail station, to the Hôtel de Ville and the ancient quarter of **Les Terreaux.**

The central area between Perrache and the **Hôtel de Ville**, and across the Saône to **Vieux Lyon**, is accessible by foot.

Any further afield, take a bus, funicular (*funiculaires*) or subway train (*métro*), run by **TCL** (*Transports en commun lyonnais*); *tel: 78 62 67 69*, for information. Information booths can be found everywhere, including the rail stations and the main metro stops. Get the *plan de réseau* from the tourist office or any TCL branch.

Lyon is a relatively safe city. Wander anywhere during the day. At night some care is needed around the Perrache station and *pl. des Terreaux.*

Tickets

Tickets last 1 hr, good for buses and trolleys, and metro FFr.7; a book of six is FFr.38, students FFr.31. A single ticket covers unlimited travel for one-day on all TCL services. The *Ticket Liberté* costs FFr.20 from the tourist office, TCL booths or automatic vending machines.

Métro

The metro is fast, clean and safe. There are four lines, A, B, C and D which criss-cross the city. The metro operates 0500–2400.

Funicular Railway

Funiculaires depart from *pl. St-Jean* to the Roman theatre at St-Just and the **Fourvière Esplanade** high above the city.

Buses

Buses cover every corner of Lyon, 0500–2400 with a limited night bus service. Same ticket price as above.

Taxis

For 24-hr taxis *tel: 78 28 23 23*. Fare to the airport is FFr.200.

Staying in Lyon

Accommodation

Lyon is a business town, and during the week it fills with briefcases and expense-accounts. The central hotels are booked out Mon–Thurs but this is a big city – try around the Perrache rail station or north in **Le Terreaux** (take metro line A north from the rail station to **Hôtel de Ville**).

Chain hotels in Lyon include *Ca, Ho, Ib, Me, Nv, Pu,* and *Sf*. Budget accommodation abounds – try *cours de Verdun, r. Victor Hugo* near the Perrache rail station; *pl. Croix-Paquet* in Les Terreaux, near the Hôtel de Ville; and *r. Lainerie* in Vieux Lyon.

HI: *51 r. Roger Salengro Vénissieux; tel: 78 76 39 23*. Just outside the city – take bus no. 35 (last bus at 2100) from *pl. Bellecour* to stop: *George-Lévy* (30-min journey).

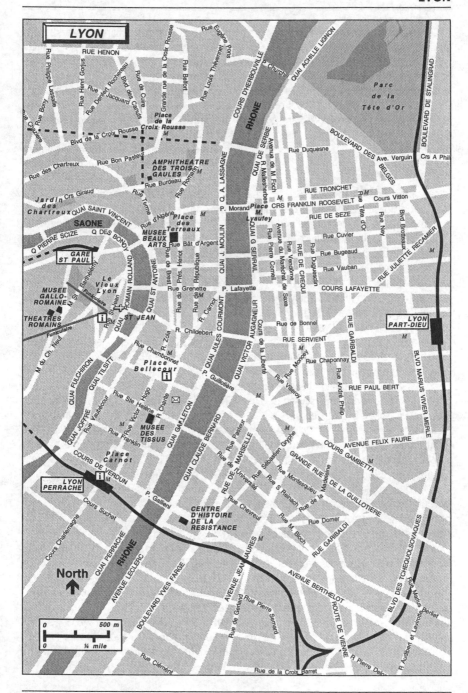

Centre International de Séjour: *46 r. du Commandant Pegoud; tel: 78 01 23 45.* Take bus no. 53 from Perrache, direction *St-Priest*, to stop: *États-Unis Beauvisage.*

Camping: **Dardilly**; *Ecully-Dardilly; tel: 78 35 64 55.* take bus no. 19 from the Hôtel de Ville, direction *Ecully-Dardilly* and get off at stop *Parc d'affaires.* Open year-round.

Eating and Drinking

Some visitors come to Lyon just for the food. Lyon boasts more famous chefs than almost any other city in Europe and some of the best restaurants in France. Yet good food is not the preserve of the wealthy. Countless small *restos* exist, often not serving set menus, but rather a *plat du jour*, the chef's whim of the day. Food is serious business here and even on a tight budget you can eat very well.

The most traditional of Lyonnais restaurants are the *bouchons*, travellers' inns. Twenty or so survive, mainly in the Les Terreaux quarter, serving hearty meals based on tripe, pork and sausages. The oldest is **Le Soleil**, *2 r. St-Georges.*

Lyonnais cuisine is very much based on meat dishes, particularly pork and poultry, sausage, creamy sauces and potatoes. Onions are also an important ingredient The food is undeniably rich, and full of flavour. Cooking is never fancy, but always performed with great attention to detail. Apart from the great array of sausages, expect to find hot pâtés, sea-food and chicken, all with accompanying sauces.

For good eateries away from Lyon's tourist areas try *r. des Marroniers* just to the east of *pl. Bellecour*, or the streets around the **Cordeliers** metro stop. *R. de la République* is also a good bet.

To discover where all the wonderful fresh produce comes from, take a wander through Lyon's great markets. Markets are open daily, except Mon, when, not entirely coincidentally, many of the restaurants are also closed.

The largest and most animated markets are at *quai St Antoine* on the Saône, west of metro Cordeliers, and along *blvd de la Croix-Rousse*, north of Les Terreaux. The covered market at **Les Halles** is more grandiose and expensive, but more varied, with meat joining the fruit and vegetables at *102 cours Lafayette; tel: 78 62 39 33*, for food-tasting information.

Do not miss **Renée Richard** cheeses in the market, the best in France; *tel: 78 62 30 78.*

Communications

Post Office: *pl. Antonin Poncet; tel: 78 42 60 50.* Next to *pl. Bellecour*, facilities include poste restante, photocopying, telephones and currency exchange. Open Mon–Fri 0800–1900, Sat 0800–1200.

Money

There are **Thomas Cook** bureaux de change at both Lyon-Part-Dieu and Lyon-Perrache stations. The bureaux at Part-Dieu is open daily 0800–2000 (summer), Mon–Sat 0800–1915, Sun 1000–1915 (winter). **AOC** money exchange is at the tourist offices in *pl. Bellecour* and at Perrache station.

Consulates

Canada: *74 r. de Bonnet; tel: 72 61 15 25*, near to Part-Dieu. Open Mon–Fri 1000–1200.

Republic of Ireland: *4 r. Jean Desparmet; tel: 78 76 44 85.*

UK: *24 r. Childebert; tel: 78 37 59 67.* Follow *r. de la République* to metro: Bellecour. Open Mon–Fri 1000–1200 and 1430–1700.

Entertainment

Theatre, a resident opera company, film, dance and dancing late into the night – Lyon has all the big-city attractions. A weekly publication *Lyon Poche* outlines the week's events (FFr.9 from news stands).

Cinemas

Lyon was birthplace of the brothers Lumière, inventors of cinema. Their legacy survives in numerous cinemas, and the **Institut Lumière**, *r. du Premier Film; tel: 78 00 86 88*, south-east of the centre in *Montplaisir* (metro: *Montplaisir-Lumière*). The institute shows free films during the summer.

Clubs

Lyon is a student city and naturally clubs abound. The best areas are near the Hôtel de Ville – *r. Algérie, pl. des Terreaux*. These do not get going until after midnight – head to a bar first. Most discos/clubs charge entry, up to FFr.100 at weekends (including your first drink).

Dance and Opera

Maison de la Danse; *Théâtre du 8ème, 8 av. Jean Mermoz; tel: 78 75 88 88*. For modern dance, Latin and African, as well as classical ballet.

Recently enlarged, the **Lyon Opera** now soars up to 18 different seating levels. Under the direction of Kent Nagano the company is now one of Europe's finest. The opera house is at *9 quai Jean Moulin*, just to the east of the Hôtel de Ville. Reservations *tel: 72 00 45 45*, from 1100–1900. Seats cost between FFr.50–250, depending on proximity to the stage.

Puppets

Lyon was birthplace of **Guignol**, the French equivalent of 'Punch', who proceeds through series of stock adventures, usually beating fellow puppets on the head as he goes. The **Nouvel Guignol de Lyon**, *2 r. Louis Carrand* in the old town, *tel: 78 28 92 57*, puts on classical performances for kids and adults alike.

Theatre

The Lyonnais love their theatre, and boast 15 different stages throughout the city. The most illustrious is **Théâtre des Célestins** at *4 r. Charles Dullin; tel: 78 37 50 51*, just north-west of *pl. Bellecour*. *Tel: 78 42 17 67*, for programme details; tickets run from FFr.70–250. Cheapest tickets on sale the evening of the performance.

Events

May: **Rencontres Internationales Théâtre et Jeunes Spectateurs**; *tel: 78 62 90 13*. International theatre and improvisation festival.

June: **Pennons de Lyon**; *tel: 78 92 86 33*. Horse races and traditional costumes.

July: **Festival du Jazz à Vienne**; *tel: 74 85 00 05*. International jazz stars at Vienne, a small town south of Lyon.

Sept: Chamber Music Festival **'Les Musicades'**; *tel: 78 93 29 86*.

Oct: **Grand Prix de Tennis**, *Palais des Sports; tel: 78 93 29 86*.

Nov: **Festival de Musique du Vieux Lyon:** *tel: 78 83 50 23*. Sacred music takes over the churches of the town, with Gregorian chanting and organ recitals.

Dec: **Illuminations** on 8 Dec, when every window contains a lit candle. For information *tel: 78 27 71 31*.

Sightseeing

Guided tours are available all year round from the Tourist Office, departing 1430, cost FFr.50. A general tour of the city by bus runs from Apr–Oct – useful if you have little time for sightseeing. Contact **Cars Philibert**, *tel: 78 23 10 56.*

One of the most pleasant ways to see Lyon is from the river – the *Bâteaux-Mouches* run from Apr–Oct, departing hourly 1400–1800 from *quai des Célestins; tel: 78 42 96 81.* Trip lasts 1–1½ hrs, FFr.45 round trip, students FFr.30. A longer day trip takes you down the river to Vienne (FFr.140, students FFr.65).

To see more than one of Lyon's museums purchase a one-day museum pass at FFr.30 (FFr.15 for students).

Like Paris, the best way to see Lyon is to stroll it. Start at the tourist office in *pl. Bellecour* and head north. *Pl. des Terreaux* is a bustling landmark. Here is the best of Lyon's museums – **Musée des Beaux Arts**, *pl. des Terreaux; tel: 78 28 07 66,* France's second-largest fine arts museum. It contains the usual collections of Italian Renaissance, 19th- and 20th-century French masters, sculpture and tapestry (Open 1030–1800, closed Mon, Tues, admission FFr.20). Next door is the **Musée d'Art Contemporain**; *16 r. Président Edouard Herriot; tel: 78 30 50 66,* a continuation of its neighbour, containing works post-1960 (open 1200–1800 closed Mon, Tues).

North of *pl. des Terreaux* is a vestige of the city's Roman past – **L'Amphithéâtre des Trois Gaules** in Croix-Rousse; *Jardin des Plantes* (open dawn–dusk, admission free). This was the site of an altar built to Rome and Emperor Augustus, the founder of Lyon.

South of *pl. Bellecour* is a monument to Lyon's textile history, and its role as Europe's silk capital – **Musée des Tissus**; *34 r. de la Charité; tel: 78 37 15 05.* Open 1000–1730, closed Mon, admission FFr.20. Silk made Lyon one of Europe's wealthiest cities in the 18th century, with 28,000 looms run by *canuts* or silk-weavers.

The oldest quarters of Lyon lie across the river, in **Vieux Lyon**. This was the heart of the Roman city, and subsequently core of the medieval settlement, and the best preserved Renaissance district in France. Renovated Renaissance mansions abound in **St Jean**, **St Paul** and **St George**, while the **Cathédrale St-Jean**, started in 1180, contains a unique mixture of building styles, including a 14th-century astronomical clock. Linked by covered passageways and courtyards called *Traboules* these streets are an intricate maze. A touring map is available from the tourist office.

Julius Caesar was responsible for developing the Roman town of *Lugdunum*, centred on the hillside of **Fourvière** above the old town. A trolley car pulls you up the hill to the **Esplanade** for a fine view of the city. The **Musée Gallo-Romain** at *17 r. Cléberg; tel: 78 25 94 68,* has an impressive collection of mosaics, coins and swords (open 0930–1200 and 1400–1800, closed Mon, Tues, admission FFr.20), but the most interesting sight is the **Théâtre Romain**, the oldest in France, just down the hill from the museum, with seating intact, and remains of gigantic columns (open 0700–2100 summer, 0700–1900 winter).

East of the Rhône is modern Lyon, the business centre, the new Part-Dieu development and the even newer **Cité Internationale** north of the **Parc de la Tête d'Or**, which houses Interpol's HQ. Just across **Pont Gallieni** from the tourist office is the most poignant museum in Lyon – **Le Centre d'Histoire de la Résistance et de la Déportation**, *14 r. Berthelot; tel: 78 72 23 11,* marking the history of Lyon during German occupation. (open 0900–1700, closed Mon, Tues, admission FFr.20).

LYON to CHAMONIX

For soaring alpine scenery, ice blue lakes and vertigo, the route from Lyon into the high Alps and the world famous ski resort of Chamonix is difficult to surpass. In winter this can be the coldest train in France, so wrap warmly. Snow lies thick in the fir forests and the landscape is a magical kingdom of ice. Yet summer brings its own attractions – lush meadows, alpine flowers and cow bells. The route passes through two of France's most beautiful towns – the historic spa of Aix-les-Bains, and the 'Venice of the Alps', the canal-riddled town of Annecy.

TRAINS

ETT tables: 167, 268.

→ Fast Track

Four through services a day run from Lyon Part-Dieu to St-Gervais-Le Fayet, where passengers must change onto a narrow gauge train for the journey to Chamonix.

A few extra services are available at weekends and by changing at Aix-les-Bains. The through journey takes around 4½ hrs.

∿ On Track

Lyon–Chambéry

Eight trains a day run from Lyon Part-Dieu or Perrache to Chambéry, with journey times of about 1½ hrs.

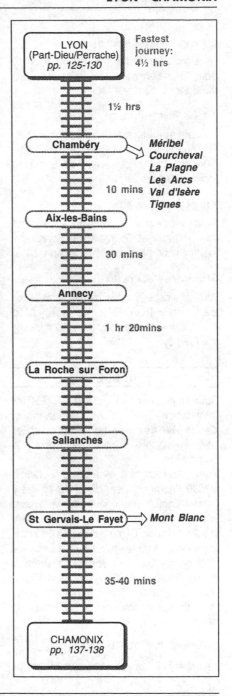

LYON (Part-Dieu/Perrache) pp. 125-130

Fastest journey: 4½ hrs

1½ hrs

Chambéry → Méribel / Courcheval / La Plagne / Les Arcs / Val d'Isère / Tignes

10 mins

Aix-les-Bains

30 mins

Annecy

1 hr 20mins

La Roche sur Foron

Sallanches

St Gervais-Le Fayet ⟹ Mont Blanc

35-40 mins

CHAMONIX pp. 137-138

Chambéry–Aix-les-Bains

Frequent trains make the 10 min journey from Chambéry to Aix-les-Bains-le-Revard throughout the day.

Aix-les-Bains–Annecy

A frequent if irregular (be careful between 1000 and 1300) service links Aix-les-Bains-le-Revard to Annecy, with trains taking around 30 mins for the journey.

Annecy–St-Gervais

Eight trains a day run between Annecy and the terminus at St-Gervais-Le Fayet, the journey taking between 1 hr 20 and 2 hrs.

St-Gervais–Chamonix

Around a dozen narrow gauge trains make the journey from St-Gervais-Le Fayet to Chamonix each day, taking 35–40 mins for the journey.

CHAMBÉRY

Station: *pl. de la Gare; tel: 79 85 50 50* for information; *79 62 35 26* for reservations. *Centre Ville* (town centre) is just south of the rail station, 5 mins walk down *r. Sommeiller.*
Tourist Office: *24 blvd de la Colonne, 73000 Chambéry; tel: 79 33 42 47.* Very helpful English speaking staff, free maps, walking tour maps. In the same building try the **Association Départementale de Tourisme de la Savoie;** *tel: 79 85 12 45,* for information on ski resorts and summer hiking. Both open 0900–1200 and 1330–1800 Mon–Sat.
CIDJ: Youth information, *4 pl. de la Gare; tel: 79 62 66 87.*

Satying in Chambéry

Chambéry is never as crowded as its neighbours, and has a good selection of attractive hotels. Chain Hotels include: *Ca, Ib, IH, Me, Nv.*

Hotels in the central area are surprisingly affordable; the area around the château is a good bet – *pl. St-Léger, pl. Hôtel de Ville.* There are no campsites in the area.

The heartland of Savoie, Chambéry offers fine regional cuisine at affordable prices. There are numerous low-priced restaurants throughout the old town – try *pl. Monge, pl. Hôtel de Ville* and *r. Croix d'Or.*

Communications

Post office: *pl. Paul Vidal; tel: 79 69 92 10.* Poste Restante, telephones, and currency exchange facilities.

Sightseeing

Ancient capital of Savoie, Chambéry is the epitome of an Alpine town. Quiet compared to the tourist Meccas of Annecy and Aix, it is pretty, welcoming and a good base for exploring the villages of the higher Alps.

Eminently walkable, most of Chambéry's sights are within the central district. Excellent guided tours of the château and the old town, daily in summer, weekends Oct–Apr (FFr.30), for reservations try the tourist office, and **Association des Guides**, *pl. du Château; tel: 79 85 93 73.*

Chambéry's role as home to the Dukes of Savoy brought the town great riches. The old town abounds with magnificent mansions, especially along *r. Croix d'Or*; tours start from the tourist office.

The **Château des Ducs de Savoie** is the highlight of the town, *pl. du Château.* Guided tours are obligatory, as the building now contains the regional Government HQ. The château was first built in the 15th century, and updated in the late 19th century.

Just outside the tourist office is the famous **Fontaine des Elephants**, a monument to General de Boigne and his victories in India. Elsewhere, two museums are worth seeing: the **Musée des Beaux Arts**, *pl. du Palais de Justice; tel: 79 33 75 03*, presenting the best collection of Italian paintings in France outside the Louvre, and the **Musée Savoisien**, *blvd du Théâtre; tel: 79 33 44 48*, in a former convent, displaying local archaeology, antiquities and historical displays.

Two km outside town along a marked trail, the **Sentier Jean-Jacques Rousseau**, is the **Musée Rousseau** in the beautiful country house where the French philosopher lived. There are plenty of memorabilia, but the garden is the most seductive attraction (*Les Charmettes; tel: 79 33 39 44*, open 1000–1200, 1400–1800 summer; 1000–1200, 1400–1630 winter, closed Tues, admission FFr.20).

〽 Side Tracks from Chambéry

From Chambéry a TGV line runs as far as **Bourg St-Maurice**, through the heart of the Alps. This serves some of the best skiing and hiking areas, including site of the 1992 winter Olympics – **Albertville** – and the world famous ski resorts of **Méribel**, **Courcheval**, **Tignes** and **Val d'Isère**. Train stations serving the resorts are **Moûtiers** (for Méribel) **Aime-la-Plagne** (for La Plagne) and **Bourg-St-Maurice** (for Les Arcs, Tignes and Val d'Isère).

MÉRIBEL/COURCHEVAL

Station: Gare SNCF Moûtiers; *tel: 79 85 50 50* for information; *79 62 40 60* for reservations. Train services to **Moûtiers**, then regular bus services run to Méribel

(journey time 40 mins) and Courcheval (55 mins). **Bus: Trans Savoie**; *tel: 79 24 03 31.* **Tourist Office:** *tel: 79 08 60 01.*

Accommodation: The best selection in the region, a wide range of prices. Central booking; *tel: 79 00 50 00.*

Winter: Expensive, excellent skiing, a very British atmosphere at Méribel, more European and more snooty at Courcheval. Pass available for the **Trois Vallées**, linking Méribel and Courcheval.

Summer: Good hiking, small alpine villages and wild flowers. Numerous sports, plus the best golf course in the Alps.

LA PLAGNE

Station: Gare SNCF Aime-la-Plagne; *tel: 79 09 77 04.*

Train services to **Aime-la-Plagne**, then regular bus to La Plagne (30–40 mins). **Bus: Voyages Bérard;** *tel: 79 09 73 45.* **Tourist Information:** For all resorts; *tel: 79 09 79 79.*

Accommodation: Fairly expensive. Central booking; *tel: 79 09 79 79.*

Winter: Combining ten ski stations, six at high altitude, all linked. This is a skiers paradise. Very sporty, a lot of families, except for **Belle-Plagne**, preferred by young wealthy couples.

Summer: Good hiking, also summer glacier skiing at 3000 m.

LES ARCS

Station: Gare SNCF Bourg-St-Maurice; *tel: 79 85 50 50.*

Train services to **Bourg-St-Maurice**, then funicular railway to **Arc 1800**, a mere 5 mins. Les Arcs is therefore the most easily accessible ski resort by train.

Tourist Office: *Maison des Arcs; tel: 79 07 26 00*, and Freephone *05 02 40 25.*

Accommodation is plentiful and reasonably priced. Central booking; *tel: 79 07 26 00*.

Winter: Incredible views up to **Mt Blanc** (the highest runs are at 3200 m) and 200 km of *pistes*. The resort for the young, free and single, with more eye-balling than skiing, and attitudes to match. Plan your runs for maximum sun-tanning.

Summer: Hiking, and water-sports – Bourg-St-Maurice is the alpine capital of water-sports, from rafting and jet-skiing to canoe-kayaking.

VAL D'ISÈRE/TIGNES

Station: Gare SNCF Bourg-St-Maurice; *tel: 79 85 50 50.*

Train services to **Bourg-St-Maurice**, then regular buses to Tignes and Val d'Isère (50-mins journey). **Bus: Autobus Martin;** *tel: 79 07 04 49.*

Tourist Information: Val d'Isère; *tel: 79 06 06 60*; Tignes; tel: 79 06 15 55.

Accommodation: Not inexpensive, but plenty of choice. Central booking; Val d'Isère; *tel: 79 06 18 90*; Tignes; *tel: 79 06 35 60.*

Winter: A long winter season, from late Oct to May. Superb skiing, good value ski passes, very expensive food.

Summer: Hiking, renowned mountain-biking and the best summer skiing in Europe. You can ski in Tignes 365 days a year, with 50 km of glacier skiing.

– – – – – – – – – – – – – – – – – – – –

AIX-LES-BAINS

Station: Gare SNCF, *pl. de la Gare; tel: 79 85 50 50* for information; *tel: 79 62 40 60* for reservations. Information open Mon–Sat 0830–1200, 1400–1730. Lockers available. For the tourist office cross *blvd*

Wilson, head down *av. de Gaulle,* cross the square and the office is on the left around the corner. For the lake head left out of the station to *av. du Grand Port.*

Tourist Office: *pl. Maurice Mollard, 73100 Aix-les-Baines; tel: 79 35 05 92.* Housed in a national monument, which was once a Roman temple. Excellent information service, free map and guide to town. Hotel information provided on an electronic board. Open Mon–Sat 0900–1215, 1400–1900, Sun 0930–1230, 1400–1800.

Getting Around

Central sights are easily accessible by foot – the **Thermes Nationaux** (central baths), the **Musée Faure** and **Casino**. For the lakeshore it is best to take a bus (bus no. 2 from the centre, direction Aix-Plage).

The bus service is highly efficient: an inclusive map is available from the tourist office (FFr.10). A single journey costs FFr.7.

Staying in Aix-les-Bains

Accommodation

For such a deluxe spa town, Aix boasts a pleasant selection of budget hotels. Easter and high summer season are crowded periods. Budget accommodation is plentiful along *blvd Wilson* and *av. du Tresserve* (to the east of the station).

HI: *promenade de Sierroz; tel: 79 88 32 88*. Bus no. 2 towards the lake, get off at *Camping*. Reservations necessary, as it fills up with groups. Reception 0700–1000 and 1800–2200.

Camping Municipal Sierroz *promenade de Sierroz; tel; 79 61 21 43.* Open Mar 15–Nov 15. Reservations imperative July–Aug.

Eating and Drinking

Aix has a wide range of eateries, although more in the upper price range, and the town centre contains numerous smaller restaurants and places to buy sandwiches. Picnics are popular, down at the lakeside.

Bars are expensive. For an introduction to local wines, the tourist office runs tours of the vineyards.

Communications

Post Office: *av. Victoria; tel: 79 33 15 15.* Poste restante facilities are at *av. Marie de Solms.*

Money

Banks with currency exchange can be found on *pl. Carnot.*

Entertainment

Aix Poche gives details of cultural and other events in Aix, available free from the tourist office.

In July, opera takes place at the **Casino** (*tel: 79 88 09 99* for information). Classical music takes place throughout the summer at the **Théâtre de Verdure**, with larger concerts at the **Palais du Congrès**. In autumn, a Berlioz concert opens the **Festival des Nuits Romantiques**, while winter sees theatre and music continue at the Palais du Congrès and Casino.

The pink and white Casino, *18 r. du Casino; tel: 79 35 16 16,* is open to over 18s. Clubs and bars in Aix are expensive, congregating around the Casino and *pl. du Revard.*

Sightseeing

Water is the essence of Aix-les-Bains – the Romans first built thermal baths here 2000 years ago, and today the spas of Aix are still thriving, attracting the same kind of wealthy citizens they did in Caesar's day. Aix is also **Lac du Bourget**, the largest natural lake in France, and an inspiration to poets, monks, fishermen and jet-skiers.

Organised tours of the city and/or bath complexes run from the tourist office at 1430 most afternoons from Easter–Sept.

The **Thermes Nationaux** are the birthplace of the city – tours run Tues–Sat at 1500 from the tourist office, cost FFr.10. Inaugurated in 1784, the baths have continued a tradition of welcoming royalty, begun in Roman days. Queen Victoria was a regular. Lesser baths include **Les Thermes d'Aix-Marlioz** to the east of the centre.

Musée Faure, *blvd des Côtes; tel: 76 61 06 57,* on a small hill to the west of the centre, contains an impressive array of Impressionist art, including works by Cézanne, Sisley, Degas, Bonnard and Renoir.

If you were wondering what lives in France's largest freshwater lake, look no further than **L'Aquarium d'Aix**, with 45 fish species on display (*Le Petit Port; tel: 79 61 08 22,* admission FFr.20, open 1000–1800, closed Mon).

No trip to Aix is complete without an excursion to **L'Abbaye d'Hautecombe**, a boat ride across the lake to a mystical monastery on the west shore (Open Mon and Wed–Sat 1000–1130 and 1400–1700, Sunday 1400–1700). Inspiration for the poet Lamartine, this haunting building houses the tombs of the Dukes of Savoy. Catch an early morning boat from **le Grand Port**, departures morning and afternoon, 1–2 hrs, free at the monastery, FFr.50 return. Other boat tours are available; **Bateaux du Lac du Bourget**; *Le Grand Port, Les Belles Rives; tel: 79 63 45 00.*

ANNECY

Station: *pl. de la Gare; tel: 50 66 50 50* (information); *50 51 50 60* (reservations). Most sights and amenities are towards the lake. Take *r. Sommeiller* to *r. Président Favre*, turn right to the **Bonlieu** shopping centre at *pl. de la Libération*. Information open 0830–1900 Mon–Sat, and 0900–1900 Sun. Lockers available.

Tourist Office: *1 r. Jean Jaurès, 74000 Annecy*, at *pl. de la Libération; tel: 50 45 00 33*. Situated in the **Bonlieu** shopping centre, with helpful staff, and lots of good information, including maps and the useful *Guide Pratique d'Annecy*.

Getting Around

Annecy is accessible by foot. For the lakeside beaches take a bus from *r. de la Préfecture*. Bus information at the kiosk on *r. de la Préfecture; tel: 50 51 70 33*.

Boats serve the towns around Lac d'Annecy – FFr.67 for the round trip, with the possibility of stopping off en route. Departures from 1030 at *pl. des Bois*, near the château. Open Apr–Oct. **Compagnie des Bateaux du Lac d'Annecy**, *tel: 50 51 08 40*.

Staying in Annecy

Accommodation

Annecy lives up to its nickname of 'Venice of the Alps' in more ways than one. Accommodation is expensive, and over-subscribed. From Easter–Sept reservations are necessary. Hotel chains in Annecy include; *Ca, IH, Me*, and *Nv*.

Cheaper options cluster around the station – try *av. Berthollet* to *av. de Cran*. Several hostels exist in Annecy, with larger four-bed or dormitory rooms. Try *r. des Marquisats*, south-east of the Château. **HI:** *La Grande Jeanne, 16 rte de Semnoz; tel: 50 45 33 19*. Bus no. 19 from the Hôtel de Ville (direction *Semnoz*, last bus 1900, fare FFr.7). **Camping:** *rte de Semnoz; tel: 50 45 48 30*. Open Jan–Oct. Very popular.

Eating and Drinking

Like elsewhere in Savoie, Annecy cooks up a good *fondue*, but at a price. Restaurants are expensive, so picnics might be the best option. There are markets around *pl. Ste-Claire* near the château, on Tues, Fri and Sun.

For less expensive restaurants head into the old town and towards the canal. While catering for tourists a number of small family-run restaurants serve good-value fare like *fondue savoyarde* and *raclette*.

Communications

Post Office: *4 r. des Glières; tel: 50 33 67 00*. Currency exchange, telephones and poste restante. Open 0800–1900, Sat 0800–1200.

Money

There are numerous money exchanges in the old town. It may be better to change at a bank, as these can offer far better rates.

Events

The first fortnight in July sees the **Festival de la Vieille Ville** – the old town festival, with music, eating and dancing and traditional costumes.

On the first Sat in Aug the **Fête du Lac** is the biggest bash of the year, with fireworks, floats and music, all on the lake.

Sightseeing

Convinced of its reputation as the prettiest town in France, Annecy greets myriads of tourists every summer. The canal runs through the heart of the town, hence the nickname 'Venice of the Alps'. Tours run at 1500 daily in summer from the tourist office, in English at 1430 Tues.

Divide your time between the lakeside and the old town. The lakeside promenade is a must, and offers ample picnic opportunities. Boats can be rented in the park at **Champ du Mars**. The nearest public beach is found at *r. des Marquisats*.

The pleasure of the Old Town lies in wandering. From the tourist office, start along *r. Royale*, then cut down to the canal. The Quays along the canal are supremely picturesque. Cross the canal to the **Palais de l'Île**, a triangular 12th-century building jutting out into the water. Formerly a royal residence, courthouse and prison, it now houses exhibitions. Annecy's main attraction is the **château**, *tel: 50 45 29 66* (open 1000–1200, 1400–1800, closed Tues; open daily July–Aug, admission FFr.30), offering a fine view down over the waterways of the town. The château museum houses the usual eclectic antiquities and folklore.

Out of Town

Near Annecy are the famous **Gorges du Fier**, 10 km west of town. Waterfalls crash over narrow gorges, a sight much favoured by 19th-century Romantics. Admission is charged (FFr.22) for the walk up to the waterfalls. *Tel: 50 46 23 07*, open Easter–Oct 0900–1800. Five mins onwards from the gorges is the **Château de Montrottier**, a medieval castle containing an interesting museum of 17th–18th century artifacts (*tel: 50 46 23 02*, open 0900–1200 and 1400–1800 closed Tues, obligatory tour FFr.25). Bus excursions are available from **Voyages Crolard**; *tel: 50 45 09 12*, adjacent to Annecy's rail station.

ST-GERVAIS

Station: **Gare de St-Gervais:** *tel: 50 78 05 33*.
Tourist Ofice: *av. Mont-Paccard, 74170 St-Gervais-les-Bains; tel: 50 78 22 43*.

Side Track from St-Gervais

From the small station of St-Gervais the world famous **Tramway de Mont Blanc** pulls passengers up to 2400 m. A one-way trip takes 1½ hrs (FFr.70 each way). This is also a prime skiing region and an alternative base to Chamonix with access to many of the same runs. Accommodation, however, is not as plentiful. **Tramway de Mont Blanc**, *tel: 50 78 27 23*.

CHAMONIX

Station: SNCF Chamonix; *av. de la Gare; tel: 50 53 00 44*. Five mins walk to the centre – follow *av. Michel Croz* into town, turn left on *r. du Docteur Paccard*. Information office open 0900–1200 and 1400–1715.
Tourist Office: *pl. Triangle de l'Amitié, 74400 Chamonix; tel: 50 53 00 24*. Modern centre with hotel listings, computerised information service. Sells hiking map and guide to what's on in Chamonix. Currency exchange. Open 0830–1930 summer; 0830–1230, 1400–1900 winter.

Bureau des Guides de Chamonix; *tel: 50 53 00 88*. **Club des Sports**; *tel: 50 53 11 57*. **Maison de la Montagne**; *pl. de l'Église; 50 53 22 08*. All you need to know about hiking routes and weather conditions and has helpful staff. Open similar hours to tourist office.

Getting Around

During the ski season, the service to the ski runs is highly efficient. Buses depart every 15 mins from the tourist office up and down the valley from Les Chavands to Le Tour; *pl. de l'Église; tel: 50 53 05 55*. Tickets FFr.7, *carnet* of 10, FFr.55

Taxis: expensive; *tel: 50 53 13 94*.

Annecy–St-Gervais–Chamonix

Staying in Chamonix

Accommodation

There is no lack of accommodation in Chamonix, from the sumptuous **Majestic** and **Savoy** hotels to countless *gîtes*, hostels and cheap hotels. The tourist office can book accommodation; otherwise call the central reservation service, *tel: 50 53 23 33*, a 30% deposit is required. A bed in a dormitory hostel costs around FFr.60; a room in a one-star hotel about FFr.180.

HI: *127 montée Jacques Balmat; tel: 50 53 14 52*, in les Pélerins, 25 mins walk (follow *rte des Pélerins*) or 10 mins by bus from *pl. de l'Église* (FFr.7, direction *Pélerins École*).

Eating and Drinking

Restaurants abound, although those in the pedestrian zone of the town are little more than tourist traps. Try to explore beyond the tourist hordes as small family restaurants are common, serving local specialities like *fondue*, *raclette* and fresh pasta.

Après-ski drinks are had in the centre of town at any of the bars in the pedestrian zone. The atmosphere is often raucous – bars stay open until 0400.

Entertainment

Après-ski is impressive in Chamonix – bars fill up by about 2300, with the numerous clubs getting going after 0100 (try **Le Refuge** in the town centre). In summer the town is quieter and entertainment becomes more cultural, with classical music concerts and film showings.

Sports

You can exercise in numerous ways – **parapente** is popular, parascending for beginners and experts – **Ecole Parapente de Chamonix**; *79 r. Whymper; tel: 50 55 99 49*. There is an 18-hole golf course, tennis and an olympic-size ice skating rink.

In summer **hiking** is excellent around Chamonix, with countless trails for every fitness level. Obtain maps from the **Maison de la Montagne** by the tourist office.

Chamonix is a centre of world **skiing**, and as such serves both professional and novice. The French National Ski Team is based here and the **Grands Montets** runs are considered by many to be the most beautiful in the world. A ski pass costs FFr.200 a day for access to all runs.

Sightseeing

As the train leaves Annecy and starts to climb, the soaring peaks of Europe's highest mountains come into view. Soon you are craning to see their summits, to catch a glimpse of the pinnacle of the greatest of them all: Mt Blanc which at (4807 m) is the highest peak in the Alps and second-highest in Europe.

Téléphérique cable cars head to the higher regions of the Alps, and are generally pricey. **Téléphérique de l'Aiguille du Midi** is the highest cable car in the world, ascending over thick forests to the needle rock of the summit at 3800 m. (Open 0700–1700 winter, 0800–1700 summer). One way to the very top takes 1½ hrs; FFr.140 one-way, FFr.180 return, although a mid-way stage at **Plan de l'Aiguille** is a mere FFr.55 one-way, FFr.70 return. Many cable car it to here then hike down (2 hrs). Air is thin up here – take it gently and pause for rest, as altitude sickness is not uncommon.

The most accessible **glacier** is the **Mer de Glace**, served by special trains from the small station by the Gare SNCF May–Sept, round trip FFr.55, journey time 1½ hrs. Nearby is **Grotte de Glace**, a cave containing ice sculptures.

LYON to GENEVA

This route takes you along the banks of the Rhône into Switzerland. While Lyon is consummately French, Geneva is umistakably Swiss – clean, efficient and intense. The border crossing is invisible from the train – at Geneva you have to pass through Swiss immigration and customs before entering the station.

From Lyon, the route initially crosses industrial countryside before veering southeast into gently rolling hills and on past the Marshes of Chautagne and Lavours. At Culoz the route rejoins the Rhône, following dramatic steep gorges, to the town of Seyssel. The Franco-Swiss border lies at Bellegarde.

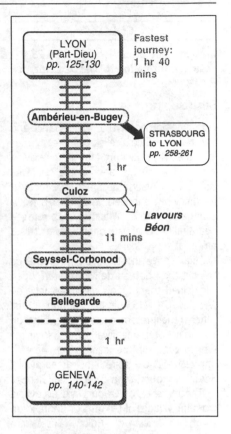

TRAINS

ETT table: 159.

 Fast Track

Seven or eight trains a day run between Lyon Part-Dieu and Geneva. Journey times vary from 1 hr 40 mins for the one daily non-stop TGV service to around 2 hrs for normal expresses. Most trains have buffets.

 On Track

Lyon–Culoz

A half dozen trains link Lyon Part-Dieu to Culoz most days with long gaps between trains in the morning and afternoon. The journey takes around 1 hr.

Culoz–Seyssel

The journey from Culoz to Seyssel-Corbonod only takes 11 mins but trains are few and far between, with no more than five a day.

Seyssel–Bellegarde

The local trains from Culoz to Seyssel-Corbonod continue on to Bellegarde, taking 20 mins for the journey.

Bellegarde–Geneva

Around a dozen trains link Bellegarde to Geneva each day. The journey takes 25 mins.

CULOZ

Station: *Gare SNCF; tel: 79 87 00 28*
Tourist Information: *Mairie de Culoz; tel: 79 87 00 30.*

Sightseeing

One-time border town between France and Switzerland, Culoz developed greatly during the 19th century. In its heyday it attracted such literary people as Paul Bourget and Gertrude Stein, but today it is somewhat subdued. The town is however gateway to the **Marshes of Lavours**, a beautiful national park offering river cruises amongst the wildlife.

High above the town on the *route de Béon* is the **Château de Montvéran**, open for guided tours if you call in advance on *tel: 79 87 01 33* (inquire at the tourist office). The present château was built on the ruins of a medieval castle, some of which can still be seen. The view is impressive and inspired the great pianist Sergei Prokofiev, who used to stay here.

The marshes of Lavours are accessible from the villages of **Lavours** or **Béon**, 2 km south or west of Culoz. Buses are infrequent, so a leisurely walk might be in order. Boat trips depart from Lavours, run by the *Association des amis du marais de Lavours*, Apr–Sept (again contact the tourist office for details).

SEYSSEL

Station: *Gare SNCF; tel: 50 56 12 78*
Tourist Office: *tel: 50 59 26 56*

Sightseeing

Seyssel was for centuries a major port on the Rhône, fought over between the French and Swiss. Today it is quiet, with pleasant medieval streets and quaysides

where barges are still loaded wih cargo for transportation down the Rhône.

From the station, cross the river on the new stone bridge (which replaced the original wooden as late as 1987). The bridge's **statue** used to be revered by the Rhône's sailors, who would come to make offerings on the bridge. Wander along the quaysides, where fine 18th-century houses are a reminder of Seyssel's glory days. Above the river the **Couvent des Capucins**, a former convent, is in a state of disrepair, but offers a good view over the town.

In the town centre at *pl. de la République* Seyssel's museum, **le Musée du Bois**, marks the region's historical dependence on the great mountain forests which provided timber for both homes and boats; *tel: 50 59 26 56.* Open 0900–1200, 1400–1800 July–Sept, admission FFr.10.

BELLEGARDE

Station: Gare SNCF; *tel: 50 56 02 36*
Tourist Office: *24 pl. Victor Bérard, 01200 Bellegarde; tel: 50 48 48 68.*

Bellegarde is not renowned for its attractiveness, having developed into an industrial town. Now a major transport cross-roads, with TGVs making frequent stops, Bellegarde is looking to redevelop – many citizens of Grenoble have second homes in the region.

GENEVA (GENÈVE)

Stations: Gare de Cornavin, *tel: (022) 731 64 50*, is the main terminal, 10mins walk north of the centre (bus nos. 5/6/9). **Gare Genève Eaux-Vives,** *tel: (022) 736 16 20*, on the eastern edge of the city, is the terminal for SNCF services from Annecy and St Gervais (bus no. 12).
Tourist Office: In Cornavin; *tel: (022) 738*

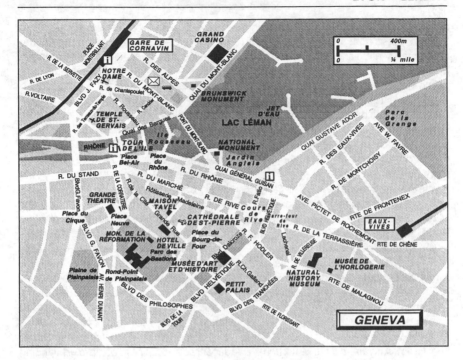

52 00. Open Mon–Fri 0800–2000, Sat–Sun 0800–1800 (mid-June–mid-Sept); Mon–Sat 0900–1800 (mid-Sept to mid-June). *What's On in Geneva* is an entertainment guide.

Getting Around

Geneva's sights are fairly scattered and a bit of route-planning is worthwhile, with a good network of buses to get you between the areas of interest. During May–Sept **Compagnie Generale de Navigation (CGN)** operate regular **lake ferries** from *quai du Mont Blanc; tel: (022) 722 39 16.*

Accommodation

Most hotels are expensive, but there are plenty of hostels and private rooms. Hotel chains with property in the city include: *Ch, Pe, Fo, Ic, Hn, Ra, Ex, Pu.* **HI**: *30 r.*

Rothschild; tel: (022) 732 62 60, 15 mins from Cornavin (bus no. 1). **Campsite:** *chemin de Conches 10; tel: (022) 347 06 03,* 4 km east of town (bus no. 8).

Sightseeing

Geneva is at the western tip of **Lake Geneva (Lac Léman)**, and split by the River Rhône into two distinct sections. The international area is on the **Rive Droite** (north side) and the old town on the **Rive Gauche** (south side).

Rive Droite

Well to the north of the centre (bus nos. 5/8/14/F/Z) is *pl. des Nations,* close to most of the international organisations.

The **Musée International de la Croix-Rouge**, *av. de la Paix 17,* is a stern building with high-tech exhibits tracing the history of the Red Cross and its Islamic offshoot, the Red Crescent. Profoundly moving, it covers man's inhumanity to man as well as natural disasters.

The **Palais des Nations**, *av. de la Paix 14*, was built 1929–37 to house the League of Nations, which was dissolved in 1940. When it was replaced by the **UN** in 1945, Geneva was chosen as the headquarters of the European section. There are guided tours.

The **Musée Ariana**, *av. de la Paix 10*, next to the UN building, now houses the **Musée Suisse de la Céramique et du Verre**, with some 18,000 objects covering seven centuries of glassware and ceramics.

Between here and the lake is the lovely **Jardin Botanique**, a perfect place for a quiet stroll. It includes a deer and llama park and an aviary.

Rive Gauche

The **Jardin Anglais**, on the waterfront, is famous for its **Horloge Fleurie** (floral clock), while the city's trade mark, the 140m fountain known as **Jet d'Eau**, spouts from a nearby pier.

The 12th-century **Maison Tavel**, *r. du Puits St-Pierre 6*, is now an excellent museum, with several period rooms and exhibits covering the 14th to 19th centuries, including a relief map of Geneva as it was around 1850.

The original 12th/13th-century Gothic façade of the **Cathédrale St-Pierre** was not improved by 18th-century additions. Most interior decorations were stripped out in the Reformation, but there are some frescos in the neo-Gothic *Chapelle des Maccabées*. Calvin preached here, his chair having been saved for posterity. The north tower, reached by a 157-step spiral staircase, offers a great view of the old town.

In the fascinating **Site Archéologique**, catwalks allow you to see the result of extensive 1980s excavations beneath the cathedral. The layers include a 4th-century baptistery and 5th-century mosaic floor. Sculptures found during the digs are also on display.

Two blocks south, the vast marble **Musée d'Art et d'Histoire**, *r. Charles Galland 2*, has several rooms in period style, a whole room devoted to Hodler landscapes and some woodcuts by the local artist Valloton, as well as large sections on such diverse subjects as arms and porcelain. The extraordinary painting *The Fishing Miracle*, by Witz, portrays Christ walking on the water – of Lake Geneva!

The 19th-century **Petit Palais**, *Terrasse St-Victor 2*, has an impressive array of art, including works by Cézanne, Renoir and the Surrealists. The nearby **Collection Baur**, *r. Munier-Romilly 8*, contains some lovely Japanese and Chinese *objets d'art*, ranging from Samurai swords to jade and porcelain.

Don't miss the amazing assortment of time-pieces in the **Musée de l'Horlogerie et de l'Emaillerie**, *rte de Malagnou 15*. It's an experience to be there when they sound the hour.

West of the cathedral, **Parc des Bastions** houses the university (founded by Calvin in 1599) and the vast **Monument de la Réformation**, erected in 1917. This is a 90 m-long wall with four central characters (Farel, Calvin, Bèze and Knox), each over 4.5 m high, flanked by the comparatively modest 2.75 m statues of lesser figures of the Reformation, plus varied bas-reliefs.

Carouge, south of the River Arve (20 mins by bus no. 12), is a baroque suburb with fine 18th-century architecture. Centred on the plane-shaded *pl. du Marché* is a picturesque area of Italian-style arcaded buildings, many restored.

LYON to MARSEILLE

Linking France's second and third largest cities of Lyon and Marseille, this route takes you along the banks the mighty Rhône. As you travel south lavender fields line the tracks; small hilltop settlements loom high above, fortress villages built in the Middle Ages. Soon you are in Provence. Passing the Étang de Berre, the great industrial zone of Marseille, you descend to the sprawling mass of the city itself.

The slower route takes you via Grenoble, high-tech city of the Alps, to Aix-en-Provence, Roman capital and intellectual centre of Provence. This train passes from the southern Alps into the rugged hinterland of Upper Provence and on through the vineyards of the Vaucluse.

TRAINS

ETT tables: 151, 154, 158, 166.

→ Fast Track

The fast track travels down the Rhône valley via Orange with three TGV services a day taking 2½ hrs for the journey. Five ordinary trains also make the journey, taking 3 hrs but not requiring the TGV supplementary fare.

On Track

Lyon–Orange

Four services a day link Lyon Perrache or Part-Dieu with Orange. More services are

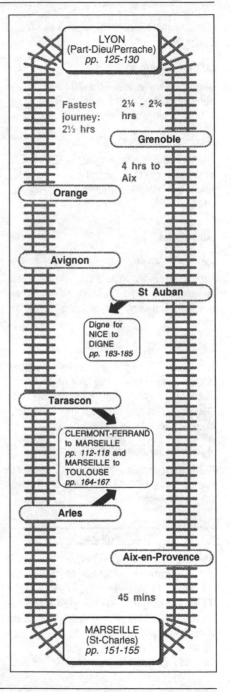

LYON (Part-Dieu/Perrache) pp. 125-130

Fastest journey: 2½ hrs   2¼ - 2¾ hrs

Grenoble

4 hrs to Aix

Orange

Avignon

St Auban

Digne for NICE to DIGNE pp. 183-185

Tarascon

CLERMONT-FERRAND to MARSEILLE pp. 112-118 and MARSEILLE to TOULOUSE pp. 164-167

Arles

Aix-en-Provence

45 mins

MARSEILLE (St-Charles) pp. 151-155

available by changing at Valence or Mont-élimar. The journey takes around 2 hrs.

Orange–Avignon

About ten trains make the 20-min journey between Orange and Avignon each day, with long gaps between services.

Avignon–Marseille

The service between Avignon and Marseille St-Charles operates throughout the day, some by TGV; the journey takes 50–70 mins.

Alternative route:

Lyon–Grenoble

Around a dozen trains a day run between Lyon Part-Dieu and Grenoble, with journey times of between 2¼ hrs and 2 hrs 45 mins.

Grenoble–Aix-en-Provence

Just one through service is available between Grenoble and Aix-en-Provence involving a change of trains at Veynes-Dévoluy. The journey, leaving Grenoble around noon, takes just over 4 hrs.

Aix-en-Provence–Marseille

A frequent local service operates between Aix-en-Provence and Marseille St-Charles, taking 45 mins.

ORANGE

Station: *av. Frédéric Mistral; tel: 90 82 50 50* (Avignon), local number *tel: 90 34 17 82*. Information open 0800–1200, 1400–1700. For the town centre head along *av. Frédéric Mistral/r. de la République* outside the station and turn into *r. St-Martin* after *pl. de la République*.

Tourist Office: *cours Aristide Briand, 84100 Orange*, (from *r. St-Martin); tel: 90 34 70 88*. Open 0900–1900.

Bus Station: *cours Pourtoules* next to the post office; *tel: 90 34 15 59*. Buses run to Carpentras, Vaison-la-Romaine, Avignon.

Post Office: *blvd E. Daladier*, off *cours Portoulles*; *tel: 90 34 08 70*.

Staying in Orange

The nearest youth hostel is 20 km away, so hostellers would do best to move on to Avignon. Try the area around *pl. aux Herbes* in the centre for inexpensive hotels.

Restaurants: *pl. aux Herbes* has inexpensive takeaways, whilst *pl. Sylvian* offers several good-value restaurants.

Sightseeing

Blessed with an impressive Roman **theatre** and little else, Orange is the gateway to Provence from the North. The theatre is the reason to come here, open daily 0900–1830, admission FFr.25, students FFr.20. Dating from the 1st century AD, it has the best preserved back wall in the Roman Empire – and still hosts a summer drama and opera festival. The **Triumphal Arch** inspired Napoleon to do better in Paris.

AVIGNON

Station: *porte de la République; tel: 90 82 50 50*, for reservations *tel: 90 82 56 29*, just outside the city walls to the south. Information open 0900–1830. For the town centre head through *porte de la République* and straight up (north) *cours Jean Jaurès*. Tourist information; *tel: 90 82 05 81*. Open 0900–2000 summer, 0900–1800 winter, closed Sun. Station closed 0100–0430.

Tourist Office: *41 cours Jean Jaurès, 84000 Avignon; tel: 90 82 65 11*. Open same hours as station office.

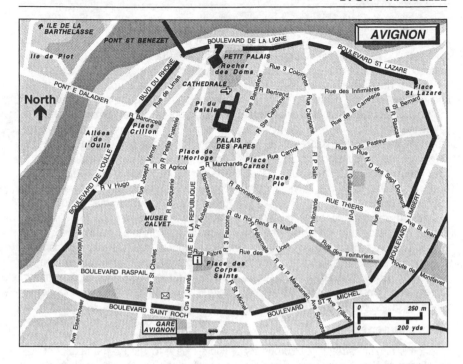

Bus Station: *tel: 90 82 07 35.* Just right from the rail station on *blvd St-Roch.* Regular buses run to Fontaine-de-Vaucluse, Vaison-la-Romaine and the Lubéron.

Getting Around

Like most Provençal towns, Avignon is entirely accessible by foot. Distances are small and free walking tour maps are graciously supplied by the tourist office. Boat tours along the Rhône are popular, with a lunch cruise available from **Le Mirério** at *allées de l'Oulle; tel: 90 85 62 25.* **Bike Hire: Cycles Peugeot**, *pl. Pie; tel: 90 82 32 19.* **Ardam Location**, *garage St-Valéry*, near the station; *tel: 90 86 81 11.* **Taxis**: *tel: 90 82 20 20.*

Staying in Avignon

In summer reservations are essential. Avignon is very difficult to miss by train and is a backpack honeypot in high season (July–Aug). Hotel chains in Avignon include: *Ca, Me* and *Ib.* Within the great walls of Avignon try *r. Joseph Vernet* (left off *Jean Jaurès*) and *r. Perdiguier* (right off *Jean Jaurès*) for reasonably priced hotels.

Youth Hostels; there is no **HI** hostel. Unaffiliated hostels include: **Foyer Bagatelle:** *Île de la Barthelasse; tel: 90 86 30 39.* Take bus no. 10 from the station. The hostel is in the midst of a large campsite on an island in the Rhône. **The Squash Club:** *32 blvd Limbert; tel: 90 85 27 78.* Take bus no. 1 from the station, get off at *Hôpital* stop. These are squash courts, but there are also 16 rooms. **Foyer YMCA:** *7 chemin de la Justice; tel: 90 25 90 20.* Take bus no. 10 from the station, get off at stop *Monteau.* Open Apr–Sept; swimming pool.

Campsites: Camping Bagatelle, *Île de la Barthelasse; tel: 90 86 30 39.* The same place as the youth hostel. **Camping St. Bénezet,** *Île de la Barthelasse; tel: 90 82 63 50:* further down the road from Bagatelle (an extra 10-min walk).

Avignon has enjoyed its food since papal days, and still offers a fine selection of Provençal and ethnic restaurants. *R. des Teinturiers* has several good choices – fast food abounds on *cours Jean Jaurès. Pl. de l'Horloge* by the Palais des Papes is good for bars and cafés.

Post Office: *cours Kennedy; tel: 90 86 78 00,* just inside the walls from the rail station. Poste restante upstairs.

Banks are found along *r. de la République.* **Chaix Conseil,** *43 cours Jean Jaurès.* **24-hr Doctor:** *tel: 90 82 77 77.* **Emergency:** *tel: 90 82 65 00.*

Entertainment

Avignon is famous throughout Europe for its summer festival, a jamboree of theatre which takes over the streets and halls of the city. Begun in 1946 by actor Jean Vilar, this now ranks as one of the world's great theatrical gatherings. There is also an active fringe programme. For festival bookings and further details contact **Bureau du Festival d'Avignon,** *8 bis r. de Mons; tel: 90 82 67 08.*

For year-round **bar-life,** *pl. des Corps Saints* to the east of the tourist office is lively, as is *pl. Pie.*

Sightseeing

City of Popes, Petrarch, and popular dissent, Avignon is a curious cultural centre on the banks of the Rhone. It appeared on the world map in 1303 when the papal powers decided to move shop from the anarchic violence of Rome to the peaceful pastures of Provence. Wealth followed the Popes and remained after they moved back to Rome 70 years later.

Tourist attractions in Avignon are generally massive. The ancient **city walls,** built by the Popes to protect their assets, surround the city. Jutting from the northeastern section is the **Pont St-Bénézet** of song fame – four arches tumbling into the Rhône. The bridge was originally 22 arches and ½ mile long. Its toll-collecting brought sizeable riches to the town – you still have to pay to walk to the end and dance back (open 0900–1800 summer, 0900–1300, 1400–1700 winter; *tel: 90 85 60 16).*

Inside the city's battlements the most photographed sight is the gargantuan **Palais des Papes** (Papal Palace), *tel: 90 86 03 32* (open 0900–1800 summer, 0900–1200, 1400–1700 winter, admission FFr.48, students FFr.38), boasting a 50 m-long banqueting hall, the **Grand Tinel,** where electors would meet after a Pope's death to choose the new pontiff.

Next door to the palace, Avignon's cathedral, **Notre-Dame-de-Doms,** is mildly interesting, with its strange square tower. More stimulating is the view from the gardens of **Rocher-des-Doms,** accessible from steps by the cathedral.

At the end of the *pl. des Papes* is the **Petit Palais,** *tel: 90 86 44 58,* a lesser palace which now contains Avignon's impressive collection of Renaissance art (open 0930–1200, 1400–1800; closed Tues).

In the centre of the city, **Musée Calvet,** *tel: 90 86 33 84,* on *r. Joseph Vernet,* has something for everyone, with an eclectic mixture of Impressionist art, Egyptian mummies and other artistic curios (open 1000–1200 and 1400–1800 closed Tues).

Shipwrecked in the midst of the Rhône is the **Île de Barthelasse,** Avignon's playground for as long as people have played. During the Papacy this was home to prostitutes and thieves, whilst in the 19th-century Provençal poets, the *Félibres* led by Frédéric Mistral, would recite verses beneath the weeping willows. Today it is a favourite picnic spot – there is also a large summer swimming pool.

Out of Town

To the east of Avignon are the rolling hills of the Lubéron, made famous by Peter Mayle's best-selling novel, *A Year in Provence*. Several companies run day trips from Avignon. Call **Rapides Sud-Est**; *tel: 90 82 48 50*, or ask at the tourist office.

GRENOBLE

Station: *pl. de la Gare; tel: 76 47 50 50*, (information); *76 47 54 27* (reservations). Information office open Mon–Fri 0830–1830, Sat 0900–1800. Luggage lockers. For central Grenoble take *av. Félix Viallet* to the *jardin de Ville* and turn right onto *r. de la République*. Otherwise catch a tram (line B, fare FFr.7).

Tourist Office: *14 r. de la République, 38000 Grenoble; tel: 76 42 41 41*, in a modern glass building, with excellent maps and the free *Grenoble Magazine*.

Centre Informations Montagnes et Sentiers: *Maison de la Randonnée, 7 r. Voltaire; tel: 76 51 76 00*, has information on hiking, biking and cross-country skiing.

Centre Régional d'Information Jeunesse; *8 r. Voltaire; tel: 76 54 70 38*, provides student and youth information.

Getting Around

It is possible to cover Grenoble on foot, while the **Bastille** is served by a regular cable car from **quai Stéphane Jay**. The local transport system, **TAG**, is excellent, and the tram and bus service very efficient. Maps and information from the office in *pl.*

de la Gare. Fares are FFr.7 a journey, a 10-journey *carnet* is FFr.45.

Staying in Grenoble

Accommodation

Accommodation is plentiful, from large business hotels to budget establishments. For lower-price hotels try the pedestrian zone around *r. de la République*.

HI: *18 av. du Grésivaudan; tel: 76 09 33 52*. Four km from Grenoble. From the rail station walk to *cours Jean Jaurès* along *av. Alsace Lorraine*. Turn right onto the *cours*, bus stop no. 8 (direction *La Quinzaine*).

Camping: *Les 3 Pucelles, Seyssins; tel: 76 96 45 73*. In Seyssins, south-west of the centre, near the youth hostel. Bus no. 8, as to HI.

Eating and Drinking

Grenoble offers food from all over the world – regional cuisine, including alpine specialities, North African, Italian, Indian and Vietnamese. The town's most famous dish is *gratin dauphinois* – sliced potatoes baked in a garlic and cream sauce.

Try the streets around the **Jardin de Ville** for regional food, with North African cuisine a little way further east. Vietnamese places are found around the station. Cafés and bars abound on *pl. St-André*.

Communications and Money

Post Office, *7 blvd Maréchal Lyautey; tel: 76 43 53 31*. Facilities include poste restante and currency exchange. **Money: Comptoir de Change**, *r. Philis de la Charce*, near the tourist office.

Entertainment

Grenoble is proud of its cultural heritage, and there is no shortage of music, theatre and art. To find out what's on, buy the official guide *Les Loisirs à Grenoble* (FFr.5) from the tourist office or bookshops. Plays, opera and dance take place at the **Théâtre de Grenoble**, *2 r. Hector Berlioz; tel: 76 54 03 08*, and **Théâtre Action** *8 r. Pierre Duclot; tel: 76 44 60 92*.

The **Festival of European Theatre** takes place every July, centred on the Théâtre Action (information; *tel: 76 44 60 92*).

Clubs and discos are popular (this is a university town). Buy *Guide DAHU*, written by Grenoble students, for what's new and improved (FFr.20 from the tourist office).

Sightseeing

An historic city, home to the great writer Stendhal, and now one of France's leading high-tech cities, Grenoble has adapted to the times. The university is now one of the most famous for sciences in Europe, while surrounding the glittering glass of the city are the mighty Alps and their ski resorts.

A trip up to the stark rock overlooking the city and its even starker prison fortress, **La Bastille**, is the highlight of a trip to Grenoble. The 6-min ride takes you across the river and up to the Bastille in a spherical car.

At the top, a view extends over Grenoble and up to the Alps. **Téléphérique Grenoble-Bastille**, *quai Stéphane Jay; tel: 76 44 33 65*; one-way FFr.19, return FFr.30, students FFr.10.50 and FFr.16.

Down the hill from the Bastille is the **Musée Dauphinois**, *30 r. Maurice Gignoux; tel: 76 85 19 00*, tracing the history of the region, from neanderthal man to the winter Olympics of 1992. The building is a listed monument, formerly a convent built in the 17th century.

The new building of the **Musée de Grenoble** combines medieval ramparts with 21st-century glass on *pl. Lavalette* just to the south of the river. This is one of the best museums in Europe, founded during the Revolution, with vast collections of 18th–19th-century art, by Impressionists and the very best of the modern age, including paintings by Rubens, Delacroix, Picasso, Matisse, Miro and Ernst (*Tel: 76 63 44 44*, open daily 1100–1900, Wed 1100–2200, closed Tues).

Ultra-modern art is found in **Le Magasin**, *155 cours Berriat; tel: 76 21 95 84*, a national art centre and museum converted from a warehouse designed by Gustave Eiffel of tower fame; open Tues–Sun 1200–1900 admission FFr.15.

Wander along the river bank and its 18th-century streets, the so-called **Village St-Hughes**. The **Jardin de Ville** is a finely manicured garden, perfect for picnics. Grenoble's most famous son, writer and Napoleon-admirer Marie Henri Beyle, better known as Stendhal, was born at the end of the 18th century, and is remembered in his own museum, **Musée Stendhal**, *1 r. Hector Berlioz; tel: 76 54 44 14*, open daily 1400–1800, closed Mon.

AIX-EN-PROVENCE

Station: *av. Victor-Hugo; tel: 42 89 09 79* or *91 08 50 50*, has hourly connections to Marseille. For the town centre walk up (north) *av. Victor Hugo* to La Rotonde and the tourist office (250 m). Shop/left luggage open 0800–1900.

Tourist Office: *pl. du Gén. de Gaulle, 13100 Aix-en-Provence; tel: 42 16 11 61*, guided tours of Aix daily in summer at 1000, 1530, and 2100; in English Wed at 1000 (FFr.50). Usually remarkably helpful, with English-speaking staff.

French-American Centre: *9 blvd Jean Jaurès; tel: 42 23 23 36*. Organises language courses, temporary jobs and exchanges. Good English-language library.

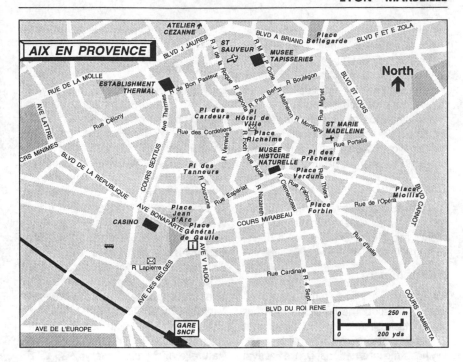

Getting Around

Aix is entirely accessible by foot and most of the central area is pedestrianised. The tourist office provides maps which present a variety of themed routes. For the energetic, bicycle hire is a good way of maximising your time: **Cycles Naddéo**, *av. de Lattre de Tassigny; tel: 42 21 06 93.*

Bus Station: *r. Lapierre; tel: 42 27 17 91.* Access to the surrounding Provençal countryside is restricted to local bus services, which are often erratic but highly entertaining. The bus station is located 5 mins walk west of the rail station. **Taxis:** *tel: 42 27 71 11.*

Staying in Aix

Aix has a good selection of hotels, from luxury down to basic student hostels. Cheaper accommodation tends to be found hugging the ring road, *blvd Carnot*. In the centre, a few venerable convents and manor houses are now attractive hotels, for those on higher budgets.

HI: *av. Marcel Pagnol, Jas de Bouffan; tel: 42 20 15 99 .* A 25-min walk from the centre of town, it is best to take a bus from **La Rotonde**, *pl. du Gén. de Gaulle*, the grandiose fountain/statue at the heart of Aix. Bus no. 12 departs every 30 mins until 1730, FFr.7, direction *Vasarely.*

Camping: Arc-en-Ciel; *Pont des Trois Sautets, route de Nice; tel: 42 26 14 28.* Take bus no. 3 from La Rotonde to *Trois Sautets.* Open all year.

Traditionally a gastronomic wilderness, Aix is now beginning to pull its culinary socks up. A thriving university crowd supports some good small ethnic places – try *r. de la Verrerie* and *pl. des Cardeurs* in

---

the old town centre. For more classical French fare head up *r. de la Couronne.*

There is only one place in Aix to drink during the day, *cours Mirabeau*, the most pretentious and stylish strip of cafés outside Paris. For those wanting a less studied ambience, try *pl. de l'Hôtel de Ville* and *Forum des Cardeurs.* Students keep Aix lively at night: *cours Sextius* and its back streets host numerous bars.

Communications

Post Office: *2 r. Lapierre; tel: 42 27 68 00.* Poste restante, currency exchange, telephones and photocopying. Open Mon–Fri 0830–1900 and Sat 0830–1200.

Entertainment

Aix is the region's cultural centre and nightlife hotspot. The numerous churches house classical music concerts throughout the year. Summer sees a series of festivals: July hosts the **International Dance Festival** and **International Music Festival**. Information on Aix's festivals from the **Comité Officiel des Fêtes**, *Complexe Forbin, cours Gambetta; tel: 42 63 06 75.*

Throughout the year students keep Aix happening with numerous jazz and rock bars, not to mention dance clubs. **Jazz Bars: Hot Brass**, *rte d'Eguilles Célony; tel: 42 21 05 57.* **Le Scat**, *11 r. Verrerie; tel: 42 23 00 23.* **Clubs/Bars: L'I.P.N**, *23 cours Sextius; tel: 42 26 98 00.* **Le Richèlme**, *24 r. Verrerie; tel: 42 23 49 29.*

Shopping

Aix is a shopper's paradise, with the bourgeois of the town supporting a dazzling array of speciality food shops and designer boutiques. The central area is littered with luxury bakers, butchers and grocers, not to mention fashion outlets. Aix's markets are a delight. Head to *pl. des Prêcheurs* for flowers, *pl. Richèlme* for vegetables.

Sightseeing

Forty mins from Marseille, but a world apart, Aix is a town of culture, grace and charm, housing one of France's premier universities. You cannot get lost in Aix. Wander at will, through the honey-coloured streets, past elegant façades and haughty statues. Aix is a Roman town, although little remains of its imperial past. *Cours Mirabeau* is Aix's strolling ground. When you've done the promenade, sit, sip coffee and people-watch (**Les Deux Garçons** is the most famous café, with an attitude to rival any Parisian establishment).

Aix's museums are dull, the best being **Musée des Tapisseries**, *pl. de l'Université; tel: 42 23 09 91*, open 1000–1200, 1400–1745, closed Tues, with beautiful textiles. Other museums include **Musée d'Histoire Naturelle**, *6 r. Espariat; tel: 42 26 23 67*, open 1000–1200, 1400–1800, closed Sun morning, with a few prehistoric remains, and the **Musée du Vieil Aix**, *17 r. de Saporta; tel: 42 21 43 55*, open 1000–1200, 1400–1700 closed Mon, in a magnificent building housing antiques, paintings and *santons* (Provençal figurines).

Aix was the birthplace of painter Cézanne. He despised his home town, which has never quite recovered from the ignominy of having ridiculed him and his art, but his **studio** is lovingly preserved: walk up *av. Pasteur* from the Cathedral (500 m) to **L'Atelier Cézanne**, *9 av. Cézanne; tel: 42 21 06 53*, open 1000–1200, 1400–1700 closed Tues. Otherwise follow the **Cézanne Trail** brochure from the tourist office, or hire a bike and take off into the countryside that stars in his paintings, along D17 to Le Tholonet, or D10 to Vauvenargues (and Picasso's grave).

MARSEILLE

Marseille is France's secret city. One of the oldest settlements in Europe, dating back over 2600 years, the old queen of the Mediterranean will surprise and invigorate. Sprawling along the sea shore, Marseille is a place to explore, comprising 100 different 'quartiers' or quarters teeming with traditions, cuisines and languages from around the world. Its museums are amongst the best in Provence, its opera halls and theatres rivalling anything Paris has to offer. A vast port, Marseille is a city ruled by the sea – boat trips from the Vieux Port (Old Port) to nearby islands, or simply along the stunning coastline, are a perfect way to idle away a sunfilled day.

Tourist Information

Tourist Office: 4 La Canebière, 13001 Marseille; tel: 91 54 91 11, open all week 0900–1930, Sun 1000–1700; 0830–2000 summer. Very helpful; book here for city tours, exhibitions and museums. **Branch office**: Gare St-Charles, tel: 91 50 59 18. Open 0800–2000 summer, 0800–1200 and 1400–1800 winter, closed weekends.

For student and youth information: **Centre Information Jeunesse**: 4, r. de la Visitation; tel: 91 49 91 55.

Arriving and Departing

Airport

Marseille-Marignan Airport Information, tel: 42 89 09 74 or 42 78 21 00. The single terminal takes international and national flights.

Airport to City: 25 km to Marseille, 25 km to Aix-en-Provence; 75 km to Avignon. Taxis to downtown Marseille cost about FFr.200 (FFr.270 at night and on Sun). Airport bus to main SNCF station in Marseille (St-Charles) runs every 20 mins from 0630–2400, the 25-min journey, costs FFr.37, destination: Gare St-Charles.

Car hire companies at the airport include Avis, Budget, Citer, Eurodollar, Europcar, Eurorent and Hertz.

Stations

Main station: Gare St-Charles: av. P. Semard; tel: 91 08 50 50 (for reservations); tel: 91 08 84 12 (for information) 0600–2200. The station, just west of the town centre, is closed 0100–0400. The information desk open 0900–1900, is closed Sun.

For the town centre, head down the monumental 'Marseillaise' steps, continue straight along blvd D'Athènes/blvd Dugommier to La Canebière, turn right to Vieux Port (800 m). Otherwise take the metro to Vieux Port (see under 'Getting Around'). Station services include currency exchange (open 0800–2000); left luggage (24 hrs), luggage lockers (closed 0100–0400) and showers, open 0400–2400.

SNCF office also at the tourist office on La Canebière; tel: 91 95 14 31 for information and reservations (often less stressful than St-Charles).

Ferries: sail from Corsica, North Africa, Italy; **SNCM**, 61 blvd des Dames; (metro: Joliette) tel: 91 56 32 00. Walking distance from Vieux Port (800 m).

Buses

Inter-City Bus Station: next door to St-Charles (out of station turn right and head for the buses) with connections to most towns in the South of France. Buses to

Marseille-Marignan airport run every 30 mins, from the station exit (FFr.35).

Getting Around

Marseille sprawls, and getting around all the sights is best by public transport, run by **RTM** (*Réseau de Transport Marseillais*). The metro is clean, efficient and very safe, but only has two lines. The local bus service is extensive and equally efficient. FFr.8.50 tickets are valid for both metro and bus – a carnet of six tickets costs FFr.40.

RTM also has guided tour buses: the **Histobus**, which encompasses all of Marseille's sights in one tour, and the **Bus Pagnol**, for sites associated with the childhood of the great writer and author of *Jean de Florette* and *Manon des Sources*, Marcel Pagnol.

Metro and bus network (RTM) – there are two metro lines, intersecting at Gare St-Charles (down the escalators), serving most of the city. Easy, efficient, and safe. **Line 1** (blue) runs east–west, and serves the Vieux Port area. **Line 2** (orange) runs north–south. Tickets at all metro stations, and on all buses, are transferable between the two. For the city centre take metro line 1, direction *La Timone*, and descend at *Vieux Port-Hôtel de Ville*. The metro stops running at 2100.

Local buses – most local buses pass through the Vieux Port/Canebière area. Night buses run from La Bourse, just north of La Canebière. (*Plan du Réseau* for bus and metro routes from the tourist office or RTM office at La Bourse, *6–8 r. de Fabres; tel: 91 91 92 10*).

Taxis: are available from the station exit, or *tel: 91 03 60 03*. Taxi ranks are found throughout the city – flagging down cabs is not usual. Taxis are expensive in the South of France and overcharging is not uncommon.

Staying in Marseille

Accommodation

There is accommodation to suit all pockets in Marseille, from four-star luxury to simple hostels. Hotels are busier in summer months, although this is a business city and rooms are taken all year round.

Hotel chains in Marseille include: *Ca, Ho, Ib, Me, Nv, Pu* and *Sf*. For cheap, functional and tranquil hotels try the areas between *blvd Garibaldi* and Réformés Canebière Metro (*allées Léon Gambetta*), and around the Préfecture (*r. Montgrand*). Accommodation is more expensive on the Vieux Port. It is best to avoid streets to the west of the station.

HI: There are two **youth hostels** in Marseille: the more attractive and less expensive is **Bois-Luzy** in the north, *76 av. Bois-Luzy; tel: 91 49 06 18*, bus no. 8 from the Bourse (closed 1030–1700). It is an old château overlooking the sea.

Bonneveine: *47 av. J. Vidal; tel: 91 73 21 81*, to the south, near the beach in a quite residential district, metro to *Castellane*, then bus no. 19 or 44 to *Vidal-Collet*.

Eating and Drinking

Marseille offers cuisine for all tastes and all pockets, from the street vendor to the most lavish *belle époque* restaurant. As Europe's most diverse cultural melting pot, the city offers a staggering array of ethnic eating places – North African, Vietnamese, Italian, Russian, Indian, Mongolian and even Corsican. Markets and delicatessens abound from which to stock up for picnics.

For *bouillabaisse*, the famous fish stew synonymous with Marseille, head to the **Vieux Port**, and the restaurants of **Quai de Rive Neuve**. Bouillabaisse does not come cheap, with an average rendering costing FFr. 200, but it is a meal in itself, containing

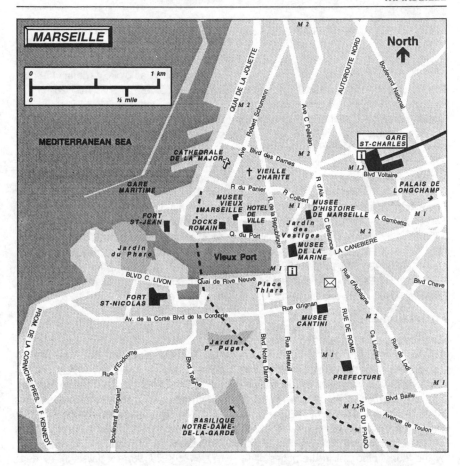

mussels, lobster, eel and the requisite for an authentic version – rascasse, an ugly red fish only found in the Mediterranean.

Oyster bars are found around *pl. Thiars* off the Quai, along with the hub of Marseille's nightlife, and several ethnic and fast-food restaurants. The other centre of culinary Marseille is at *cours Julien* and *cours D'Estienne d'Orves* – couscous, Vietnamese, Iranian, Russian . . . and old-fashioned French. More opulent restaurants are found along the *Corniche J. F. Kennedy*. For on-the-hoof fare, most street corners host pizza vans which cook fresh pizzas to order on charcoal ovens.

Drinking is a subject close to Marseille's heart: the life-blood of the city is the aniseed-flavoured *pastis*, produced by local firm Ricard. The bars and cafés of the Vieux Port house an older crowd, the young and hip head to *pl. Thiars* and *cours Julien*.

Communications

Post Office: *pl. de l'Hôtel des Postes; tel: 91 90 31 33*, near the Bourse. It has poste restante and currency exchange facilities and is open Mon–Fri 0800–1900, Sat 0800–1200.

Money

There is no shortage of money-changing facilities in Marseille. Major banks are found along *La Canebière*, along with bureaux de change.

Consulates

Canada: *24 av. du Prado; tel: 91 37 19 37.* Open 0900–1200 and 1400–1700.
Republic of Ireland: *148 r. Sainte; tel: 91 54 92 29.* open 0900–1230 and 1430–1700.
UK: *24 av. du Prado; tel: 91 53 43 32.* Open 0900–1200 and 1400–1700.
USA: *12 blvd Paul Peytral; tel: 91 54 92 00.* Open 0900–1200 and 1400–1730.

Entertainment

Marseille's nightlife is safe and notoriously dull. To be extra cautious, avoid streets to the south-west of the rail station (north of La Canebière), in particular *cours Bélsunce* and *blvd d'Athènes*. The **Opéra** district is Marseille's historical red-light venue – often lively but not dangerous. You can find out what's happening in *Taktik*, distributed free by the tourist office, or in the pages of *La Marseillaise*, *Le Provençal* or the Wed edition of *Le Méridional*. Or try the book and record chain **FNAC**, in the Centre Bourse, which not only has information on events, but sells tickets as well.

Music

The **Opéra Municipal** in *pl. Reyer (1er), tel: 91 54 70 54,* is one of the finest in France.
  L'Abbaye de St-Victoire hosts classical music concerts; *tel: 91 33 25 86.*
  Jazz, rock, dance and theatre are all on offer at **Espace Julien**; *33 cours Julien (6e); tel: 91 47 09 64.*

La Maison Hantée; *10 r. Vian,* off *r. des Trois Mages; tel: 91 92 09 40,* has a wide variety of rock and R & B.
  Jazz is found at **Le Pele-Mele**; *45 cours d'Etienne d'Orves, tel 91 54 85 26.*
  Pl. Thiars, off the Vieux Port, is the centre of nocturnal festivities, with trendy bars, restaurants and mediocre night-clubs. Try **L'Ascenseur**, *tel: 91 33 13 27.*
  Otherwise try the live music haunts around **cours Julien – Côte-Cours**, *40 r. des Trois Rois; tel: 91 48 97 48,* is a popular haunt.
  The city's football team – **L'Olympique de Marseille** – is Marseille's number one religion. On match days, the city is a ghost town until final whistle. Tickets start around FFr.100, from **Stade Vélodrome**, *blvd Michelet tel: 91 07 77 28,* (metro: *Rond Point du Prado).*

Theatre

The **Théâtre National de Marseille la Criée**, *30 r. de Rive-Neuve (7e); tel: 91 54 70 54* is amongst the finest in Europe.
  Bernadines, *17 blvd Garibaldi (1er); tel: 91 42 45 33,* puts on experimental dance and theatre.
  Théâtre du Merlan, a*v. Raimu (14e); tel: 91 98 28 98,* specialise in modern plays.

Cinema

Breteuil, *120 blvd de Notre-Dame (6e); tel: 91 37 88 18.* **Nouveau Paris**, *31 r. Pavillon (1er); tel: 91 33 15 59.* These cinemas show films both in French (indicated by V. F. – Version Française) and English (V. O. – Version Originale).

Shopping

A daily market enlivens the quarter around *Noailles* metro station. On the Vieux Port, the fish market is always vibrant and a glimpse of Marseillais temperament at its most entertaining.

Sightseeing

Vieux Port: there has been a port here for 2600 years. Remains of the Roman version are found in **Le Jardin des Vestiges** behind the Bourse shopping complex, which houses **Le Musée d'Histoire de Marseille**, an insight into Marseilles turbulent history (metro: *Vieux Port*) *12 r. Henri Barbusse; tel: 91 90 42 22*, open 1200–1900, closed Sun, admission FFr.10.

La Canebière ('Can o beer' to English sailors last century) is the second most famous street in France (after the Champs-Elysées). At *7, La Canebière; tel: 91 39 33 33*, **Le Musée de la Marine**, charts Marseilles relationship with the sea, with a series of paintings, carvings and models. Open 1000–1200 and 1400–1900, closed Tues, admission Free.

One of the oldest quarters in Marseille is the **Panier District**, north of the port, where narrow tortuous streets house families that have lived there for centuries. In many ways this is the heart of Marseille, and the people of Le Panier consider themselves the real *Marseillais*. It was here during German Occupation in World War II that the *résistance* was based, until the Nazis blew up many of the old houses. The modern concrete replacements are poignant reminders of this recent past.

In Le Panier the **Musée du Vieux Marseille**, *r. de la Prison; tel: 91 55 10 19*, exhibits two centuries worth of Marseille's fascinating junk in a 16th-century mansion house spared by the War.

The **Musée des Docks Romains** was a result of German explosives in 1943, which revealed ancient Roman docks, *pl. de Vivaux; tel: 91 91 24 62*. The museum displays pots and wine casks exported from Rome, a symbol of Marseille's seemingly eternal rapport with the sea.

Vieille Charité, once a lunatic asylum, is a fine baroque church now housing innovative art exhibitions; *2 r. de la Vieille Charité; tel: 91 56 28 38*, open 1000–1700, 1200–1900 Sat and Sun.

South of the Canebière, **Musée Cantini** boasts a fine collection of modern art at *19 r. de Grignan; 91 54 77 75*, open 1000–1700, 1200–1900 Sat and Sun, admission FFr.10. Works by Picasso, Miro, Bacon and Ernst in an impressively opulent 17th-century mansion.

Marseille's finest museum is the **Musée des Beaux Arts** to the east; *Palais Longchamp, tel: 91 62 21 17*, (metro: *Longchamp/Cinq Avenues*); offering an interesting mix of stoically classical works and lively impressionists.

End any visit to Marseille at **Basilique Notre-Dame-de-la-Garde**, the white church with a spectacular view down over the city (bus no. 60 from Vieux Port). From here a gold-leafed Virgin casts her benign influence over the city and the sea – sailors come here to give thanks for surviving shipwrecks, and paintings of their ordeals and models of the ships that went down, decorate the church interior. The church's real draw is its view – out over the entire sprawl of Marseille and across to the **Islands of Frioul**. In the distance, on *blvd Michelet*, you can just glimpse Le Corbusiers **Unité d'habitation**, a giant minimalist apartment complex built in 1945.

Given time, visit **Château d'If**, the skeletal island in the bay (boats depart regularly from *quai des Belges* at the Vieux Port; *tel: 91 59 02 30*) home of Dumas' Count of Monte Cristo. The neighbouring **Isle de Frioul** houses Marseille's former leper colony, now being converted into a museum.

MARSEILLE to NICE

One of France's most beautiful train rides, this route links the two great rivals of the South. The route leaves Marseille for the white hills of Aubagne, home to writer Marcel Pagnol and setting for his famous novels Jean de Florette and Manon des Sources. Heading towards the coast you catch glimpses of the cliffs behind the pretty port of Cassis. The end of the coastal route is in Toulon, France's biggest navy town. Here, the route heads inland, into the vineyards and farm fields of the Central Var, in many ways the epitome of traditional Provence. South of the tracks is the Massif des Maures, a string of mountains protecting the coast between Toulon and St-Tropez, the latter accessible by bus from Toulon. From Fréjus, Roman city and present-day resort, you follow the coast once more, along the ochre cliffs of the Estérel, dotted with warm sandy coves. The final leg of the journey takes you along a glittering but over-developed coastline to Nice.

TRAINS

ETT table: 164, 169.

 Fast Track

Over a dozen trains link Marseille St-Charles with Nice Ville each day but there are no trains between 0930 and 1200. The journey takes between takes 2 hrs 30 mins and 2 hrs 45 mins.

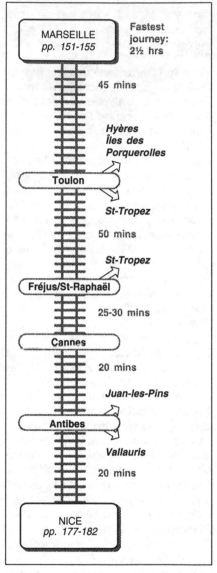

MARSEILLE pp. 151-155	Fastest journey: 2½ hrs

45 mins

Hyères
Îles des
Porquerolles

Toulon

St-Tropez

50 mins

St-Tropez

Fréjus/St-Raphaël

25-30 mins

Cannes

20 mins

Juan-les-Pins

Antibes

Vallauris

20 mins

NICE pp. 177-182

On Track

Marseille–Toulon

Through express trains between Marseille St-Charles and Toulon are supplemented by frequent local trains. Journey times vary from 40 mins for the expresses to 1 hr for the local trains.

Toulon–Fréjus–St-Raphaël–Cannes

The through Marseille to Nice trains form the service between Toulon and Cannes with all trains also calling at St-Raphaël-Valescure. Very few trains call at Fréjus. Toulon to St-Raphaël takes 50 mins, St Raphaël to Cannes takes 25 mins.

Cannes–Juan-les-Pins–Antibes–Nice

The through trains also form the Cannes to Nice fast service with all trains calling at Antibes. Additional frequent local trains run between Cannes and Nice and, as well as calling at Antibes, these trains call at Juan-les-Pins. Cannes to Juan-les-Pins takes 10 mins, Juan-les-Pins to Antibes takes 2–3 mins and Antibes to Nice Ville takes 15–25 mins.

TOULON

Station: *pl. Albert I; tel: 94 91 50 50, reservations: 94 22 39 19.* North of the centre, information 0900 1900. For town centre, exit the station, cross *pl. Albert 1er*, and head south down *av. Vauban*. The old town and seafront are south of *av. Mar. Leclerc*. The station is closed 0100–0400. Left luggage available 0730–2400, currency exchange open Mon–Fri 0900–1200 and 1400–1900 in summer.
Tourist Office: *8 av. Colbert, 83000 Toulon* (just south of the railway station); *tel: 94 22 08 22,* open 0800–1900 summer, 0830–1830 winter. Small and less used to dealing with tourists than other coastal offices.

The station tourist office, *tel: 94 62 73 87,* is open 0730–2000 summer, 0830–1200, 1400–1830 Sept–June, closed Sun.

Getting Around

Bus station: (next to the rail station); *tel: 94 93 11 39.* **Sodetrav** buses head coastward to St-Tropez (seven a day, 2 hrs 30 min journey, fare FFr.80).
Ferries: SNCM, *quai Stalingrad; tel: 94 16 66 66.* Two daily sailings to Corsica (FFr.490 return), weekly sailings to Sardinia. **SITCATC;** *tel: 94 46 35 46,* for ferries departing *quai Stalingrad* for tours of Toulon's harbour to La Seyne. **Transmed 2000:** *tel: 94 92 96 82,* offer summer trips to the Porquerolles islands (see p. 159); FFr.70 return.
Bike Hire: AAL Alliance Location, *238 blvd de Tessé* (exit station to left, 200 m); *tel: 94 09 22 22* (closed Sun). **Taxis:** *tel: 94 93 51 51.*

Communications

Post office: *r. Prosper Ferrero; tel: 94 92 36 04.* Open Mon–Fri 0800–1900, it has telephones and poste restante.

Staying in Toulon

Accommodation

Toulon is a cheap place to stay, but quality is not high. *R. Jean Jaurès* (down *Jean Moulin* from *Leclerc*) has several acceptable hotels.

Eating and Drinking

R. Jean Jaurès has a few good value restaurants. The old town offers dingy pizza places, and a less than welcoming atmosphere. Otherwise try the corniche road to the east (bus no. 23 from the station). Fish is the best bet, and several establishments put on a passable *bouillabaisse* for less than in neighbouring Marseille. Toulon's nightlife is desultory – most Toulonnais go to *Hyères*.

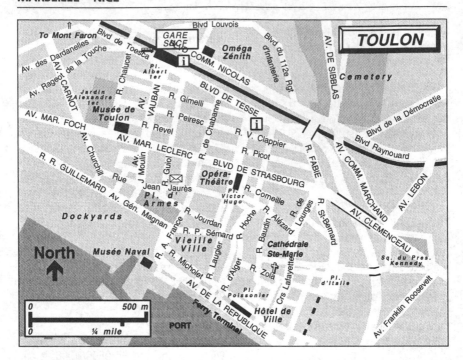

Entertainment

Traditional Toulonnais entertainment used to involve wine, women and song. Things have changed with the extravagant new **Zénith-Oméga** rock concert hall, the biggest in the South of France, *blvd Commandant Nicolas; tel: 94 22 66 66,.* Everyone plays here, from Elton John and Lenny Kravitz to Peter Gabriel.

The **Grand Opéra-Théâtre**, *blvd Strasbourg; tel: 94 92 70 78*, hosts opera and plays.

Events

Festival de la Danse et de l'Image is France's premier dance festival in a large amphitheatre/auditorium north-west of Toulon, *tel: 94 24 11 76*. The festival begins in July and runs for one month.

Sightseeing

France's number two naval base, suffering economic hardship, can be a depressing place. But the old town has a quirky potential, and for those in search of old-fashioned seediness it cannot be beaten. Toulon's naval past survives in the great docks, the fading extravagant architecture and the great ethnic diversity of its inhabitants. Although the huge ship-building yards of La Seyne are under constant threat of closure, Toulon itself has seen something of a regeneration in recent years.

There is not too much to see in Toulon. The **Musée Naval**, *pl. Monsenergue; tel: 94 02 02 01*, open 1000–1200, 1330–1800 closed Tues, traces Toulon's marine development. The **Musée de Toulon**, *113* av. Vauban; tel: 94 93 15 54, boasts a good painting collection. Lovers of sleaze will enjoy the quarter around **pl. des Armes**.

Toulon is best viewed from **Mont Faron**, 500 m above the Mediterranean, where there is a **zoo**, and the **Musée Mémorial du Débarquement** *tel: 94 88 08 09* open 0930–1200 and 1430–1900, recalling the allied invasion of Provence in 1944 (bus no. 40 from the station to where a **téléphérique** winches up to the summit).

 Side Tracks from Toulon

HYÈRES

Station: Gare SNCF; *tel: 94 38 82 97*. An infrequent rail service runs from Toulon to Hyères taking 20 mins.
Tourist Office: *rotonde Jean Salusse, av. de Belgique, 83400 Hyères; tel: 94 65 18 55.*

Sightseeing

Hyères first attracted visitors as a winter resort for royalty in the late 19th century. Tolstoy, Queen Victoria and Robert Louis Stevenson all enjoyed its mild climate. Today the town offers few specific attractions – the main draw is its beach, stretching from the pleasure port. The sea is 10 mins walk from the station, 15 mins from the town centre.

The best reason to stop in Hyères is to catch a ferry to the islands of the same name, just offshore. Buses run to the **Presqui'Île de Giens** and the port at **La Tour Fondue**, from where hourly ferries depart in summer to **Île de Porquerolles**, **Île de Port Cros** and **Île du Levant**. All three offer some of the most beautiful beaches in the Mediterranean. For ferry information, *tel: 94 58 21 81*.

ST-TROPEZ

Accessible only by Sodetrav bus from St-Raphaël or Toulon, or by boat from Ste-Maxime across the bay, 'St-Trop' ('Saint Too Much') can be a disappointment. The legendary beaches are in fact 5 km from the town. Bike hire is advisable to explore the pretty villages of **Ramatuelle** and **Gassin**, as well as 20 km of beaches.
Bus station: *av. de Gaulle; tel: 94 95 24 82*. Close to the port.

Accommodation and Food

Hotels: Expensive. Try campsites to the south along the coast. **Restaurants:** Likewise expensive, but still some small good places further away from the port – take *r. de la Citadelle.*

Bars: The **Sénéquier** on the port is still the place to be seen (at the back, the front is for tourists). Inland from the port, **pl. des Lices** is a must, with its plane trees and gnarled boules players. The **Café des Arts** was painted by Signac, and is still just about bohemian.

Sightseeing

Strolling is what Tropeziennes do best. But find time for **Musée de l'Annociade**, the region's finest art museum, in a converted chapel on the west side of the port, boasting a dazzling array of impressionists from Cézanne and Matisse to Dufy; *pl. Grammont; tel: 94 97 04 01*, open 1000–1200, 1500–1800, closed Tues and Nov.

A walk up to the **Citadelle** offers good views, and a confrontation with the town's haughty peacocks. There are two small **beaches** in town. From the base of the Citadelle and the seaside cemetery, continue along the path to **Plage des Graniers**, the closest real beach. Otherwise hitch or cycle the D93 south. **Tahiti**

---

beach has the jet-set crowd, **Pampelonne** the older stalwarts.

FRÉJUS/ST-RAPHAËL

Station: Gare de St-Raphaël, *pl. de la Gare; tel: 94 91 50 50*; for reservations, *tel: 94 22 39 19*. Information open 0900–1900. Station closed 0100–0400. For the sea, exit the station and head right 200 m. **Bus station St-Raphaël** (behind the rail station) *tel: 94 95 24 82*. To Nice/Marseille: **Cars Phocéens**, *tel: 93 85 66 61*. To St-Tropez (inaccessible by train) and Toulon: **Sodetrav**, *tel: 94 95 24 82*. Buses inland for Bagnols, Fayence and Les Adrets: **Gagnard**, *tel: 93 36 27 97*. **St-Raphaël Tourist Office:** *r. W. Rousseau, 83700 St-Raphaël; tel: 94 95 16 87*, opposite the station, across the road, open 0900–1900 summer, 0900–1800 winter. Currency exchange 0900–1200, 1400–1900 Easter–Oct. **Station: Gare de Fréjus**, *r. du Capitaine Blazy; tel: 94 95 16 90*. **Fréjus Tourist Office:** *325 r. Jean Jaurès, 83600 Fréjus; tel: 94 51 54 14*.

Fréjus-Plage Tourist Office: *blvd de la Libération; tel: 94 51 48 42*.

Accommodation and Food

HI: *chemin du Counillier; tel: 94 52 18 75*, is in a large park 2 km from Fréjus town, 4.5 km from the sea on the RN7 towards Cannes. A bus leaves quay 6 at St-Raphaël bus station at 1800 each night, and returns each morning (FFr.7).

Centre International du Manoir, *Boulouris; tel: 94 95 20 58*, 5 km from St-Raphaël, by the sea on *chemin l'Escale* next to the station at Boulouris. Buses run every 30 mins from St-Raphaël bus station – the beach is 100 m away.

Camping: Parc de Camping de St-Aygulf; *St-Aygulf; tel: 94 81 20 14*. To the west of Fréjus off the RN 98, between a small estuary and the beach, 4 km from the station at Fréjus (bus no. 29 direction *St-Aygulf* from St-Raphaël bus station).

Holiday Green; *rte de bagnols; tel: 94 40 88 20*. This is an anglophile campsite 6 km north of the sea (bus no. 11 direction Bagnols, from St-Raphaël). Otherwise accommodation is not cheap. The best bets are back from the sea in Fréjus-Plage.

St-Raphaël's daily fish market is fun, at *pl. Ortolan*. Best value food is found in Fréjus town, around *pl. Agricola* (pizzerias and creperies). In St-Raphaël, try to the east of the casino and just back from the sea, on *promenade R. Coty*. Otherwise, Fréjus-Plage is littered with fast-food stands. Dance and drink at St-Raphaël: the new port and casino area are liveliest.

Sightseeing

Barely a kilometre apart, these two communes have their own individual stations and tourist offices. Fréjus-Plage is a strip of tacky bars and restaurants, St-Raphaël its more up-market continuation, and Fréjus town an interesting, if not schizophrenic, historic resort.

Fréjus was a Roman port, created by Julius Caesar in the 49th century BC. The **Roman remains** are scattered, only one is organised (the **Arènes**, open morning and afternoon, but a glimpse through the fence is enough). Fréjus tourist office has a guide to the sites. Fréjus **Cathedral** was the first Gothic church in Provence; *pl. J. C. Formige; tel: 94 51 26 30*.

CANNES

Station: *r. Jean Jaurès; tel: 93 99 50 50*, *reservations tel: 93 88 89 93*. Information open 0800–2100, the station is closed

0100–0500. Change: 0800–2000 (closed lunch and weekends in winter). Luggage lockers are closed 0100–0500, left luggage available 0730–2400.

Bus stations: There are two bus stations in Cannes: one next to the rail station has buses to Vallauris, Golfe-Juan, Mougins, Grasse *tel: 93 39 31 37*, the other, at *pl. de l'Hôtel de Ville*, has buses to Juan-les-Pins, Antibes, Nice, Grasse, Vallauris and local buses, *tel: 93 39 11 39*.

Tourist Office: *Palais de Festivals, esplanade Georges Pompidou, 06400 Cannes; tel: 93 39 01 01*. For *La Croisette* and Palais des Festivals exit station and head straight (south) down *r. des Serbes*, to the sea (250 m). Tourist office at the **station**: *tel: 93 99 19 77*. Open 0900–2000 summer, 0900–1230, 1400–1830 Mon–Sat winter.

Getting Around

Orientation is easy in Cannes. From the station head south to the sea. The town stretches around the Baie de Lérins and the Mediterranean is a constant reference point. Everything is within walking distance, and anyway there are not many specific sights to see in Cannes. This is a place to stroll and soak up glamour.

If the glitz begins to pall, the perfect antidote is available just off-shore – the **Îles de Lérins** are two pine-clad islands offering small beaches and extensive woodland paths. Boats depart hourly during summer from the quays next to the Palais des Festivals Casino; *tel: 93 39 11 82*.

Staying in Cannes

Accommodation

Hotels: Inexpensive hotels do exist, away from the sea. Try *r. Maréchal Joffre*, from *pl. du 18 Juin* (turn right from the station), *r. Fortville*, and surrounding side-streets. In summer the town is packed full, so reservations are imperative. The film festival is even more busy – book hotel rooms a year in advance. Chain hotels in Cannes include: *Ca, Ho, Ic, Me, Nv*.

At the top end of the market, Cannes' hotels are amongst the most luxurious in the world. Made famous by famous visitors during the film festival, these seaside palaces survive mainly on a diet of conferences for the rest of the year. The most famous of the famous is **The Carlton**, *58 La Croisette; tel: 93 68 91 68*, a white extravaganza halfway along *La Croisette*. Its two black cupolas are said to be formed after the breasts of a notorious flamenco dancer who befriended royalty.

Camping: Le Grand Saule; *24 blvd Jean Moulin; tel: 93 90 55 10*. Take bus no. 9 from the Hôtel de Ville, direction *Grasse*, get off in *Ranguin* (FFr.7). Open Apr–Oct.

Eating and Drinking

Good food abounds in Cannes, but avoid the tourist traps along the seafront. *R. Félix Faure* runs parallel to the sea and has several good eateries. Also try *quai St-Pierre* by the port. Fish and sea-food is naturally excellent. For those splashing out, the hotel restaurants along *La Croisette* offer some of the finest cuisine in the South of France – at a lavish price. Lesser budgets will head to pizza places by the western end of *La Croisette* at *quai St-Pierre*.

Communications

Post Office: *22 Bivouac Napoléon; tel: 93 39 14 11*. Open 0800–1900, 0800–1200 Sat. Telephones, poste restante facilities.

Entertainment

Cannes proudly upholds the Riviera's reputation as an overpriced, overcrowded fleshpot. Entertainment here consists of

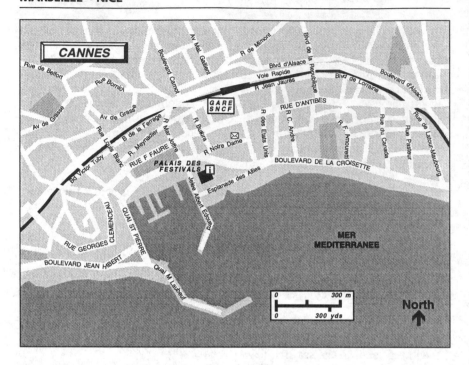

looking good, spending money and sleeping little. The bars and clubs are expensive, while the casinos attract some of Europe's most upmarket gamblers. Casinos are free to get in, but a dress code is upheld.

With towns all along the coast competing for custom, Cannes has recently begun to put on more and more cultural events – classical concerts, jazz and blues galas, even chess tournaments. Barely a day goes by without some conference or festival, usually centred upon the hideous concrete **Palais des Festivals**.

Cannes' nightlife can be fun. Those with less money and more sense will head to *r. Macé* and *r. Félix Faure*, where bars are reasonably priced. Otherwise, promenade along *La Croisette* and spend wisely on drinks at the most happening café.

The Film Festival takes place annually beginning the second week in May, in the Palais des Festivals. Public tickets for films outside the main competition are sold daily from the office next to the tourist office.

Sightseeing

Glitzy Cannes, twinned with Beverley Hills, is surprisingly welcoming to those without MGM contracts or family jewels. Wander away from the glamorous Croisette to small winding streets and hidden squares.

Cannes specialises in second-hand glamour – promenades along the Croisette are the favourite pastime. Begin at the **Palais des Festivals**, built in 1982 and christened 'the bunker'. It is here each May that the red carpets are unrolled, the Rollers polished up, and the world of cinema pats itself on the back. Glimpses of stars are frequent (practise climbing lamp posts).

If you miss the festival, do not despair: your favourite stars' handprint may well be cast in the concrete around the festival hall.

Elsewhere, there are few specific sights. Climb r. St-Antoine to the hill of **Le Suquet**, the oldest quarter. Here, **Musée de la Castre**, tel: 93 38 55 26, open 1000–1200 and 1400–1700, in the château has antiquities and a history of the town. Off Cannes, the **Îles de Lérins** are an antidote to chic. **Île de Ste-Marguerite** is the larger of the two, with better beaches. At the north end, the **Fort Royal** is an impressively stark fortress built by Vauban in 1712, and legendary home of the Man in the Iron Mask (whose identity is debated to this day). Smaller **Île de St-Honorat** houses a small working monastery. There are daily departures from the quay.

ANTIBES

Station: av. Robert Soleau; tel: 93 99 50 50, reservations tel: 93 88 89 93, information 0830–1900. Station closed 0100–0500. Regular trains to Nice, Cannes, stop on TGV route. For the town centre head down av. Robert Soleau to pl. de Gaulle. From here blvd Albert 1er leads to the sea.
Bus Station: Local coastal buses from pl. Gén. de Gaulle, others from the Gare Routière, r. de la République.
Tourist Office: 11 pl. du Gén. de Gaulle, 06600 Antibes; tel: 93 33 95 64. Open 0900–2000 and Sun morning in summer, 0900–1200, 1400–1800 and Sat morning in winter.

Accommodation and Food

Try around the bus station for places to stay. HI: blvd de la Garoupe; tel: 93 61 34 40, 3 km from Antibes, under pines by the sea on Cap d'Antibes, bus from pl. Gén. de Gaulle. Full in summer.

For restaurants pl. Nationale and surrounding side streets, two blocks inland from the Picasso museum, offer several inexpensive restaurants. R. Aubernon, just up from the port, has many bistros often frequented by yachting types.

Sightseeing

Mixing chic and tackiness, Antibes is a pleasure port, not for Anglophobes, with a thick history and a relaxed atmosphere. Take a walk along the port; the biggest boats in the Northern Med moor here. Do not miss the **Musée Picasso**, in the Château Grimaldi above the sea, pl. Mariejol; tel: 93 34 91 91. This excellent museum displays some of Picasso's most entertaining pottery. Open 1000–1200, 1500–1900 summer, 1000–1200, 1400–1800 winter, closed Tues and Nov.

The **Musée Archéologique** contains traces of Antibes' Greek and Roman past in the bastion St-André at the southern end of the sea wall; tel: 93 34 48 01, open 1000–1200, 1500–1900 summer, 1000–1200, 1400–1800 winter.

Side Tracks from Antibes

Juan-les-Pins. The playground of the coast, where the Côte d'Azur originated one summer in 1921, it has beaches, bars, discos and a Jazz festival in July. Buses depart from Antibes pl. Charles de Gaulle. Many of the beaches are private, but there is still public space.

Just inland to the west of Antibes, **Vallauris** is pottery capital of the Riviera, famous for ceramics since 1500. Picasso came here in 1946 to make pots. Today his huge fresco War and Peace is in the small **Picasso museum** (closed Tues and lunch).

MARSEILLE to TOULOUSE

This route travels west, from the vineyards and sunshine of Provence to the vineyards and sunshine of the Midi and its capital, the historic rugby-playing city of Toulouse. From Marseille the train heads north-west, past the murky waters of the Étang de Berre and its chemical complexes. Crossing the flat plains of the Crau, with the low hills of the Alpilles (the little Alps) to the north, the train calls at the Roman towns of Arles and Nîmes, which, along with Tarascon, are described in the Clermont-Ferrand–Marseille route, p. 112. The route continues on to Montpellier, another high-tech city of the Midi, with a renowned university and requisite Roman remains. The route then passes through the rolling hills of Languedoc, covered with vineyards and medieval châteaux. Passing the great walled city of Carcassonne, the route continues to Toulouse.

TRAINS

ETT tables: 163, 139.

 Fast Track

Six or seven trains a day make the journey between Marseille St-Charles and Toulouse Matabiau. The trains take around 4 hrs with the exception of *Le Grand Sud* (supplementary fare payable) leaving Marseille at lunchtime which takes 3 hrs 15 mins for the journey. Most trains have buffet cars, *Le Grand Sud* a restaurant car.

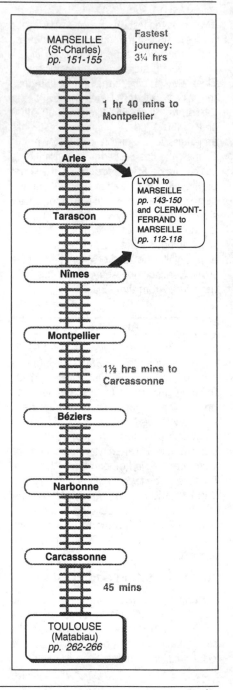

MARSEILLE (St-Charles) pp. 151-155

Fastest journey: 3¼ hrs

1 hr 40 mins to Montpellier

Arles

LYON to MARSEILLE pp. 143-150 and CLERMONT-FERRAND to MARSEILLE pp. 112-118

Tarascon

Nîmes

Montpellier

1½ hrs mins to Carcassonne

Béziers

Narbonne

Carcassonne

45 mins

TOULOUSE (Matabiau) pp. 262-266

∿ On Track

Marseille–Montpellier

Six trains a day link Marseille St-Charles with Montpellier. Journeys take around 1 hr 40 mins, with most trains having buffets.

Montpellier–Carcassonne

Eight trains run each day between Montpellier and Carcassonne with additional journeys made available by changing at Narbonne. The journey takes approximately 1½ hrs.

Carcassonne–Toulouse

Eleven services a day run between Carcassonne and Toulouse Matabiau with an average journey time of 45 mins.

MONTPELLIER

Station: *pl. Auguste Gibert; tel: 67 58 50 50* (information); *tel: 67 58 43 06* (sales). From June 1995, one number for both: *tel: 36 35 35 35*. Buffet, lockers. Tourist information; *tel: 67 92 90 03*; open Mon–Sat 1000–1300, 1530–1900. Automatic cash dispenser. Bureau de change open daily 0800–2000.

For the town centre, walk across to *r. Maguelone*, which leads straight to *pl. de la Comédie*. Bus nos 1–4 run to the centre. **Bus station:** *r. J. Ferry; tel: 67 92 01 43*, runs summer services to the coastal beaches (Palavas-les-Flots, Carnon and La Grand Motte). **Taxi:** *tel: 67 58 74 82.*

Tourist Office: *Le Triangle, allée du Tourisme, 34000 Montpellier; tel: 67 58 67 58.* Open Mon–Fri 0900–1300, 1400–1900, Sat 1000–1300, usually closed Sun (summer); Mon–Fri 0900–1300, 1400–1800, Sat 1000–1300, 1400–1800, Sun 1000–1300, 1400–1700 (winter). It provides free maps, leaflets and guided tours.

Getting Around

For local destinations, **SMTU**, *23 bis r. Maguelone; tel: 67 22 87 87*. Lines 1–4 go to the centre, passing the rail station. Single journey fare FFr.6. Main attractions are within walking distance of each other.

Accommodation and Food

There are hotels in all price ranges, several in the station area (*r. de la République, r. de Verdun*). Chains include: *Ca, Cl, F1, Ib, IH, Nv, Me, SF*. **HI:** *r. des Écoles Laïques 34000 Montpellier; tel: 67 60 32 22.* A 15-min walk from the station or bus nos 2 or 3 (stop: *Ursulines*). Restaurants in all price ranges enliven many streets (especially *r. de l'Ancien Courrier, r. Roucher*).

Sightseeing

Guided tours in French of the old centre depart from the tourist office Mon–Sat 1000, 1700 (July–Sept). FFr.50 (concessions FFr.35). From the *Esplanade*, the **Petit Train** leaves for a tour of the town every 45 mins from 1400; FFr.25 (FFr.10). On a summer Sun the streets are empty as the residents head for the beaches but otherwise it is lively and elegant, with Renaissance mansions, although the commercial centre, **Le Polygone**, is modern. The heart of the town is **pl. de la Comédie**, with the **Fountain of the Three Graces** and the famous theatre, **L'Opéra Comédie**.

A splendid place to stroll and enjoy the view of the Garrigue River and the Cévennes mountains is **pl. Promenade Royale de Peyrou**, first laid out in 1688 but developed into terraces in 1753 when an aqueduct was built. In grand style is **l'Arc de Triomphe** (triumphal arch), in honour of Louis XIV. The promenade is almost next to **Jardin des Plantes** (botanical garden), *163 r. A. Broussonet; tel: 67*

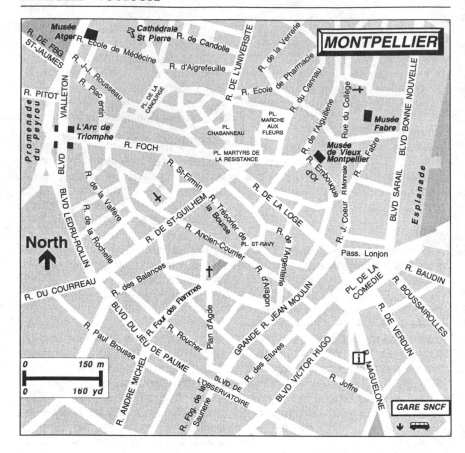

MONTPELLIER

63 43 22. Open Mon–Sat, 0800–1200, 1400–1800 (Apr–Oct); Mon-Sat 0800–1200, 1400–1730 (Nov–Mar); admission free. There is also an entrance off *blvd Henri IV*, opposite **Le Musée Atger**, *Faculté de Médicine, r. École de Médicine; tel: 67 60 73 71.* Actually inside the school of medicine, the museum is named after Xavier Atger, who collected Italian and French drawings in the 18th century. Open Mon–Fri 1330–1630; admission free. The building also has a museum of anatomy. Other university faculties have specialist museums on diverse subjects such as pharmacy and milling. These are listed in the free tourist map. The medical faculty is beside the **Cathédrale St-Pierre**, with its immense Gothic porch.

An important museum of fine arts is **Le Musée Fabre**, *blvd Sarrail; tel: 67 16 83 00.* Open Tues–Sun 0900–1730 (closes 1700 Sat, Sun). It is in a fine mansion (also a university library) facing the Esplanade, and has paintings from the 16th–18th centuries of the French, Flemish, Dutch and Italian schools. Admission FFr.18. **Le Musée du Vieux Montpellier** (museum of the old city), *Hôtel de Varenne,* *pl. Pétrarque, tel: 67 66 02 94.* Open Mon–Sat 1330–1700; admission free.

CARCASSONE

Station: *av. du Mar. Joffre; tel: 68 47 50 50 (information); tel: 58 34 73 11 (sales).* From June 1995, one number for both services, *tel: 36 35 35 35.* Buffet and lockers. It is a long walk, the last part up-hill, to the old town. Turn left on to *blvd J. Jaurès,* straight along to *sq. Gambetta,* then take *r. du Pont-Vieux,* over the Pont Vieux (old bridge) across the Aude river. Bus no. 4 goes from the station to the entrance of the old town. **Taxi:** *tel: 68 71 50 50.* **Bus station:** *Halte Centrale pl. Gambetta; tel: 68 47 82 22.* Single fare FFr.5, ten for FFr.42.
Tourist Office: *15 blvd Camille Pelletan,* (off *sq. Gambetta), BP842, 11012 Carcassone; tel: 68 25 07 04.* It is in the lower city. Open Mon–Sat 0900–1215, 1345–1900 (Apr–June, Sept); Mon–Sat 0900–1900 (July–Aug); 0900–1200, 1400–1830 (Oct–Mar). Bureau de change service outside banking hours. In the old town, the tourist office is at *Tour Narbonnaises; tel: 68 25 68 81.* Open daily 0900–1230, 1330–1800 (Easter–June, mid-Sept–Oct), daily 0900–1900 (July–mid-Sept).

Accommodation and Food

Hotels in the picturesque old city cost more but there is a reasonable choice in the lower city, including hotels in streets near the station (*r. de la Liberté, r. de Verdun*). Chains include: BW, Ca, Cl, F1, Ib, Me.
HI: *r. du Vicomte Trencavel 11000 Carcassone; tel: 68 25 23 16.* Open Feb–Nov. It is in the middle of the old city; take bus no. 4 from the station (stop: *La Cité),* then walk. **Camping:** *rte de Ste-Hilaire; tel: 68 25 11 77.* Open Mar–mid-Oct. A 10-min walk on the road adjoining the old city.
Restaurants are plentiful, with a choice of reasonably-priced places (*r. du Plô, pl. du Château*).

Sightseeing

Guided tours, some in English, are organised in summer. The fortress town of Carcassone, with 50 towers and a double medieval wall, high on a cliff-top overlooking the River Aude and the modern centre below, is a stunning sight. Helped by Victorian restoration, the remarkably preserved old part, **La Cité**, has two gates, the **Porte d'Aude** and the main entrance, the 13th-century **Porte Narbonnaise**. It is floodlit at night and looks spectacular for medieval re-enactments in Aug.

Although undeniably charming, it can get extremely crowded in summer. It is less hectic around **Église St-Nazaire**, a beautiful church with an 11th-century nave and fine 14th–15th century stained glass.

Dominating the centre is **Château Comtal** (the count's castle), *r. Viollet-Le Duc; tel: 68 25 01 66.* Open daily 0900–1900 (June–Sept); daily 1000–1230, 1400–1700 (Oct–Mar); daily 0930–1230, 1400–1800 (Apr–May). Two tickets available, both with a guide. One tour takes 40 mins around the château and its ramparts; FFr.26 (FFr.17). The other, 1½ hrs, also includes the monuments of the old city; FFr.46 (FFr.37). Opposite the château is **Le Musée Le Moyen Age dans la Cité** (museum of the Middle Ages), *r. Viollet-Le Duc; tel: 68 47 35 06.* Open daily 0930–2100 (mid-July–Aug) 1000–1800 (Apr–Oct); FFr.20 (FFr.15).

For a change of pace, visit **Le Musée de l'École** (the school museum), *3 r. du Plô, tel: 68 25 95 14.* Open daily 1000–1800 (Apr–Oct). It recreates an old-fashioned school-room; FFr.10.

MENTON

Almost in Italy, Menton is a town with charm, long stony beaches and a lemon festival. This is the warmest place in France (average temperature 17°C in Jan), hence the proliferation of lemon and orange trees, and retired people. The pace here is slow, but the town is attractive and boasts one of the Riviera's most enjoyable markets. The Italian border crossing, just to the east of the town, is anachronistic – you can cross without showing a passport.

Tourist Information

Tourist Office: *Palais de l'Europe, av. Boyer, 06500 Menton; tel: 93 57 57 00* (left from station then right) open 0900–1800. There is also a summer bureau at the **Bus Station**, *esplanade du Careï; tel: 93 28 43 27*.

Arriving and Departing

Station: *pl. de La Gare; tel: 93 87 50 50.* Open 0900–1830. For the sea head down *r. Edouard VII* from *pl. des Victoires*. Luggage storage: 0830–1200, 1500–1900.

Bus Station: *esplanade du Careï, av. de Sospel; tel: 93 55 24 00*, (north of the station, it has buses to the hinterland).

Getting Around

Menton is very walkable, with the main town and sights concentrated at the eastern end of the long beach, just before the Italian border. To visit the Menton hinterland and its dramatic perched villages, buses run regularly from the *esplanade du Careï* bus station.

Staying in Menton

Accommodation

Menton's hotels are a disappointment. Once a resort for Europe's monied classes, and host to Queen Victoria and her entourage, the town has slipped into relative slumber. The once palatial hotels are now retirement apartments. Remaining accommodation is not spectacular. For lower budget hotels try around the station, especially *r. Albert 1er*.

HI: *plateau St-Michel, rte des Ciappes de Castellar; tel: 93 35 93 14*. Open Feb–Nov.

Camping: **Camping Municipal du Plateau St-Michel**; *rte des Ciappes de Castellar; tel: 93 35 81 23*. Campsite next to the youth hostel, with a superb sea view.

Eating and Drinking

Menton is synonymous with lemons and oranges, and the town's most popular fruit is practically its only claim to gastronomic fame. Lemonade is a speciality, as are marzipan sweets in the shape of the hallowed citrus.

For dining, Italian-influenced places are best, in the old town around *r. St-Michel*. For picnics the market in *pl. aux Herbes* (opposite the Hôtel de Ville) is excellent, with a colourful array of fruit and vegetables, as well as Italian sausage and cheese. The surrounding hill villages offer small family-run restaurants specialising in local country cuisine. **Ste-Agnès** is the place to head to, with good-value establishments boasting gargantuan meals.

Communications

Post Office, *cours Georges V; tel: 93 28 64 84*, has poste restante, currency exchange.

Entertainment

For a night out in Menton, head to Monaco

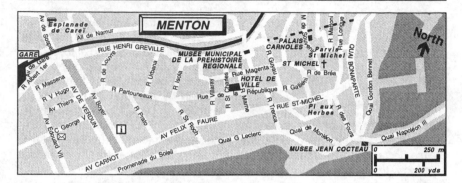

or Nice. Even local Mentonnais admit to the lack of entertainment in Menton. Café society does exist in the bars and cafés lining the sea, although this tends to be a summer attraction. The **Lemon Festival** is the highlight of the year, and a programme of associated cultural events offers classical music and theatre. It takes place in Feb, with a week of fireworks and parades of thousands of lemons on mobile floats. Temporary lemon and orange sculptures decorate the town. The main events are paying, with charges between FFr.50 and FFr.150 for seating.

Sightseeing

Begin by heading along the sea wall that marks the small port, with views back to the pastel façades of the old town. Wander up the steps from the port to the **Parvis St-Michel** and views down over the sea. The town's narrow streets and some of the houses were constructed by the Grimaldis (the family of the Princes of Monaco) in the 15th century. **Église St-Michel** (St Michael's church), built in 1640, is particularly impressive.

To the west on *av. de la Madone*, the **Palais Carnolès** once belonged to a Prince of Monaco and now houses an interesting art collection featuring Impressionist and modern paintings; *tel: 93 35 49 71*, open

1000–1230, 1500–1830, admission FFr.10.

In the town centre, off *r. de la République*, the **Hôtel de Ville** contains a **Salle des Mariages** lavishly decorated by Jean Cocteau (*tel: 93 57 87 87*, open 0930–1230, 1330–1700, closed weekends, admission FFr.10). There is also a colourful **Musée Jean Cocteau**, at the east end of the beaches, containing mosaics, pastels and pottery by the artist who took inspiration from the 'loves of the fishermen of Menton'; *bastion du Vieux-Port, quai Napoléon III; tel: 93 57 72 30*, open 1000–1200, 1500–1800, closed Tues, admission free.

The **Musée Municipale de Préhistoire Régionale**, *r. Lorédan-Larchey; tel: 93 35 84 64*, exhibits remains of humans who lived here 80,000 years ago. Here is the skeleton of Menton man, found in nearby caves, born 30,000 years ago, and dioramas of cave life. Open 1000–1200, 1400–1800, closed Tues. Admission free.

Out of Town

A short bus ride or a beautiful but strenuous walk from Menton, **Ste-Agnès** is the highest village on the French coast, at 650 m. The path takes 3 hrs up and 2 hrs down, while buses run daily – one in the morning, one in the afternoon (last bus back from Ste-Agnès 1740).

NANTES

Although Nantes officially left Brittany to join the Pays de la Loire in the 1960s, the Breton heritage is still apparent here, together with the international influences from a rich life of overseas trade. If you have time, it is worth looking beyond the medieval streets and museums in the centre to see something of the modern city beyond. The sleek, silent trams make it easy to explore.

Tourist Information

Nantes-Atlantique Tourist Office is in the city centre at *pl. du Commerce, 44000 Nantes* (tram stop: *Commerce*); *tel: 40 47 04 51, fax: 40 89 11 99*. Open Mon–Sat 0900–1900. An **annexe** opposite the château (and nearer to the SNCF station) is open all year Wed–Sun 1000–1900. Both have an accommodation booking service.

Arriving and Departing

Station

Gare de Nantes, *blvd Stalingrad; tel: 40 08 50 50*. Luggage lockers and café-restaurant. To reach the city centre, leave the station by the northerly exit, signposted as *Accès Nord*. On foot, turn left and follow *cours John Kennedy* for the Château des Ducs (7 mins), or take the tram (direction *Bellevue*) which continues to *pl. du Commerce*. TGV services leave from the modern **Gare Sud**.

Getting Around

Nantes' central sights can easily be reached on foot or by tram from the SNCF station. The **Gare Routière** (bus station) for longer distance journeys is at *av. Carnot; tel: 40 47 62 70*. Urban bus routes centre on *pl. du Commerce*, and like the trams are run by **SEMITAN**, *tel: 40 29 39 39*. Tickets can be bought from machines at the stops for FFr.7 each, or FFr.29 for a *carnet* of five, and are valid for an hour from the first time they are used. Services are less frequent at weekends.

Taxi: there is a rank outside SNCF station, Accès Nord, or *tel: 40 69 22 22 / 40 63 66 66*.

Staying in Nantes

Accommodation

Accommodation covers a wide range of prices, with several good value one- and two-star hotels in the city centre.

There is a choice of **hostel** accommodation: the most central is at *2 pl. de la Manu, tel. 40 20 57 25* (open end-June–mid-Sept, 400 m east of the SNCF station or tram to: *Manufacture*); two **Foyers de Jeunes Travailleurs**: **Residence Porte Neuve**, *1 pl. Ste-Elisabeth; tel: 40 20 00 80* (tram or bus no. 40/41); *Port Beaulieu* at *9 blvd Vincent Gache; tel: 40 12 24 00* (tram or bus no. 24). **Campsite**: **Le Val du Cens**, *blvd du Petit Port; tel: 40 74 47 94* (tram to *Petit Port* or bus nos 51/53).

International hotel chains include: *Ho, Ib, IH, Me, Nv*. There are one or two hotels near the SNCF station (Accès Nord) and many more in the pedestrianised streets of the old centre.

Eating and Drinking

City café-life centres on the spacious *pl. du Commerce*, with grills, pizzas and fast-food, while a short walk away the pedestrianised streets of the *Ste-Croix* and

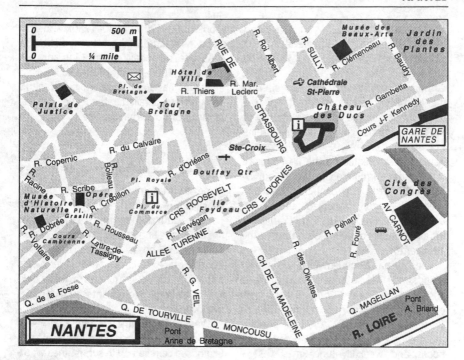

Bouffay quarter, such as *r. de la Juiverie* and *r. des Petits Ecuries*, are crammed with cafés and bistrots offering Greek and Chinese cuisine alongside traditional French and Breton food.

Entertainment

The elegant façade of the **Opéra de Nantes** dominates *pl. Graslin*, which also has cinemas, including the Katorza. A new multi-screen Gaumont cinema is being built on *pl. du Commerce*.

The renowned *Floralies Internationales* next takes place in 1999. Annual events include *Les Allumées* in Oct, the Spring Arts Festival in May and June, and the *Fêtes de l'Été* in July.

Shopping

Boutiques and branches of national chain stores are well represented in the streets west of *pl. Royale*, centring on *r. Crébillon*. *Pl. Bouffay* has a morning market (daily except Mon), where a stone plaque set into the ground commemorates those defenders of Breton liberty who were executed in the square on 26 March 1720.

One shopping experience doubles as a sightseeing destination: *le passage Pommeraye* (off *r. Crébillon*), an astonishing arcade on three levels dominated by a central staircase lined with lamp-topped white statues.

Sightseeing

Central Nantes' attractions fall into three broad categories – monuments, museums and gardens – all of which can be visited on foot or by public transport. The tourist office leads occasional walking tours of medieval Nantes in English.

Monuments in the city are grouped into

historic and architectural 'islands'. Nearest the SNCF station, the medieval quarter includes the **Château des Ducs de Bretagne** and the soaring Gothic **Cathédrale de St-Pierre** (St Peter's), with the animated pedestrian streets of the Bouffay quarter leading to the church of **Ste-Croix,** topped by its larger-than-life trumpeting angels. Eighteenth-century Nantes is represented by the **Île Feydeau** – no longer surrounded by water, but by busy boulevards – its central *r. Kervegan* lined with elegant balconied houses. The *pl. Royale, pl. Graslin* and *pl. du Commerce* are all reminders of bourgeois Nantes in the 19th century.

The city has a modern face too, which includes the **Mediathèque** on *quai de la Fosse* and the **Cité des Congrès**. For a view of it all, the **Tour Bretagne** (*pl. de Bretagne*) allows visitors onto its panoramic viewing platform on Saturday afternoons and weekday lunchtimes, 1215–1345.

There is a wide spectrum of **museums**, to which the *Carte Musées*, (FFr.50), gives unlimited access (except the **Planetarium**, *8 r. des Acadiens*). These are the most central: the **Château des Ducs**, which has played an important role in Brittany's history, now houses two collections – the **Salorges** museum of Nantes' maritime and commercial history, and the **Museum of Regional Popular Art**, open daily except Tues, 1000–1200, 1400–1800. You can visit the courtyard for free. Nearby at *10 r. G. Clémenceau* is the **Beaux-Arts** museum, open daily except Tues, 1000–1800, Sun 1100–1800. The **Musée Thomas Dobrée** open daily except Tues, 1000–1200, 1330–1730, is an interesting private collection in a remarkable building on *pl. Jean V*, near the *cours Cambronne*. Next door is the **Musée Archéologique** (open daily except

Mon, 1000–1200, 1330–1730) and just along *r. Voltaire* is the **Musée d'Histoire Naturelle**, open daily except Mon and Sun mornings, 1000–1200, 1400–1800.

Nantes has some excellent public parks and **gardens** detailed in the leaflet *Parcs et Jardins* from the tourist office.

⟲ Side Tracks from Nantes

Some of western France's most popular beaches are easily accessible by train from Nantes. South of the Loire estuary stretches the Côte Jade and **Pornic**, an attractive port with fishing boats and medieval castle (tourist office: *quai du Cdt L'Herminier, tel: 40 82 04 40*). There is a local train service to Pornic from Nantes, which takes just over an hour.

West of **St-Nazaire** – where a corner of the huge shipyards has been turned into an Ecomusée complete with submarine (*av. St-Hubert, tel: 40 22 35 33*) – the Côte d'Amour is a huge sandy crescent on which **Pornichet** and **Le Pouliguen** stand either side of **La Baule**, with its up-market hotels, shops and casino – and even a film festival in early Oct (tourist office: *pl. de la Victoire, tel: 40 24 34 44*). Frequent train services run from Nantes to St-Nazaire and La Baule.

The train continues to the rocky peninsula of **Le Croisic**, a small port with a lively seafront. Attractions include an aquarium, **Océarium** on *av. de St-Goustan* and a small *boucherie* where they claim to hold the world record for making *crêpes* (320 in an hour). Tourist information opposite the station at *pl. du 18 juin 1940, tel: 40 23 00 70*. North of **Batz-sur-Mer** look out for the *marais salants*, salt flats, whose unrefined product is sold throughout the region.

NANTES to BORDEAUX

Long sandy beaches, oyster-beds and vines are interspersed with handsome, historic towns in this region of western France, whch is a favourite holiday destination for the French and visitors alike. Side track exploration of the coast and the islands will be well rewarded.

TRAINS

ETT tables: 134.

 Fast Track

There are four day trains and one overnight train running between Nantes and Bordeaux St-Jean each day. The day trains all have buffets and take 4 hrs for the journey, while the overnight train with couchette cars takes 5½ hrs.

 On Track

Nantes–La Roche-sur-Yon–La Rochelle –Saintes–Bordeaux

The four through trains between Nantes and Bordeaux St-Jean also call at La Roche-sur-Yon, La Rochelle Ville and Saintes. Nantes to La Roche-sur-Yon takes around 45 mins, La Roche-sur-Yon to La Rochelle takes 40 mins, La Rochelle to Saintes takes 50 mins and Saintes to Bordeaux takes 1¼ hrs. A few additional trains run from Nantes to La Roche-sur-Yon, and from Saintes to Bordeaux, with longer travel times.

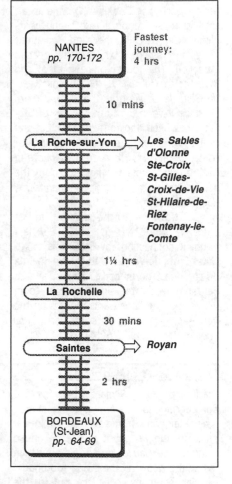

NANTES
pp. 170-172

Fastest journey: 4 hrs

10 mins

La Roche-sur-Yon ⟹ **Les Sables d'Olonne Ste-Croix St-Gilles-Croix-de-Vie St-Hilaire-de-Riez Fontenay-le-Comte**

1¼ hrs

La Rochelle

30 mins

Saintes ⟹ *Royan*

2 hrs

BORDEAUX (St-Jean) pp. 64-69

LA ROCHE-SUR-YON

La Roche-sur-Yon is the junction for the branch to Les Sables-d'Olonne. The journey takes 35 mins.

 Side Tracks from La Roche-sur-Yon

With a sheltered marina, casinos and

Trains–La-Roche-sur-Yon

fishing port, **Les Sables d'Olonne** is an established and popular resort, and as its name suggests, it is the sand – a great sweeping crescent – which is the greatest attraction. The tourist office is at *av. du Mar. Leclerc* (*tel: 51 32 03 28*): follow *av. du Gén. de Gaulle* from the SNCF station. On *r. de Verdun* the former abbey of **Ste-Croix** has been transformed into a cultural centre with an interesting museum of contemporary art. **HI:** *r. du Sémaphore* in La Chaume, across the harbour from the beach. Bus no. 2 to stop: *Armandèche*, open April–Sept, *tel: 51 95 76 21*.

Also from **La Roche-sur-Yon** (tourist office: *r. Joffre, tel: 51 36 00 85)*, less frequent connections by SNCF bus to **St-Gilles-Croix-de-Vie** and **St-Hilaire-de-Riez** on the coast north of Les Sables, and to **Fontenay-le-Comte**, an attractive town with some fine Renaissance houses on the Vendée river (tourist information: *quai Poey-d'Avant, tel: 51 69 44 99*).

- - - - - - - - - - - - - - - - - -

LA ROCHELLE

Station: *pl. Pierre Semard: tel: 46 41 50 50*. Luggage lockers and café. The station is a 10-min walk from town via the tourist office in the *le Gabut* quarter – ahead along *av. de Gaulle*, left to *le Gabut* then follow the *quais* via the swing footbridge. Heading south by train, look out for the coach-building sheds where the new EuroStar carriages are built.
Tourist Office: *le Gabut, pl. Petit Sirène, 17000 La Rochelle; tel: 46 41 14 68*, in a new small complex of shops and cafés between the SNCF station and town centre. Accommodation booking service: reservations are *essential* in summer. A leaflet with map and hotel listings costs FFr.2, but you can get one free of charge from tourist offices in nearby towns.

Getting Around

In tackling the problems of a street-plan laid out before the motorcar, La Rochelle has become famous for its yellow municipal bicycles, used by locals and visitors alike. Rental is free for the first 2 hrs and FFr.6 an hour thereafter, seven days a week, 0930–1230, 1330–1900. The cycle tracks (*pistes cyclables*) out of town are particularly useful if you are staying at les Minimes. There are several options for travelling by boat (see Sightseeing, below).

Accommodation

Extremely busy in summer: it is well worth booking ahead. Hotel chains include: *Ca, Ib, IH, Me, Nv*. One- and two-star hotels are scattered all around the *vieux port* (old port) and up towards *pl. Verdun*. **HI: Les Minimes**, *tel 46 44 43 11*; **Camping:** *Le Soleil, Port des Minimes, tel: 46 44 42 53* (open May–Sept). Bus no. 10 from town or water taxi – *Bus de Mer* – from *cours des Dames*.

Sightseeing

Behind the cheerful bustling quais the *Grosse Horloge* gateway leads to bustling streets. But as the towers guarding the *vieux port* suggest, this was not always a pleasure port, and a long history of trading, religion and siege is revealed in the town's museums and monuments. All three **towers** can be visited. Opposite the **Tour St-Nicholas**, the **Tour de la Chaine** houses a model of the town before Richelieu's fateful siege (open 1000–1200, 1400–1830 Apr–Nov, adults FFr.18, children under 14 FFr.10), the town walls continue to the **Tour de la Lanterne,** used as a prison in the early 19th century, and to the small town beach beyond.

La Rochelle from Eleanor of Aquitaine to

World War II is depicted in wax at the **Musée Grévin** on *cours des Dames* (0900–1900, 2300 in summer, adults FFr.27, children FFr.18), while relics from the events themselves can be seen at two Renaissance masterpieces: the **Maison Henri II** (*r. des Augustins*, open 1000–1200, 1400–1800 July–Aug, admission free), and the magnificent **Hôtel de Ville** (*r. de l'Hôtel de Ville*, guided visits, adults FFr.16, children FFr.10).

For a more detailed explanation of the importance of Protestantism and the role of the English in the siege, the **Temple**, *r. St-Michel*, has a small museum with notes in English and an enthusiastic curator (open Mon–Sat 1430–1800 July–Aug, by request the rest of the year, free admission).

Visitors staying several days can take advantage of the joint museums ticket (FFr.37 for eight days) which includes the **Musée du Nouveau Monde**, housed in the handsome 18th-century Hotel Fleuriau (*10 r. Fleuriau*, Mon–Sat 1000–1230, 1330–1800, Sun 1500–1800, closed Tues, adults FFr.16, children FFr.10), together with the **Musée des Beaux-Arts**, **Musée d'Histoire Naturelle**, the **Musée D'Orbigny-Bernon** and the **Musée Océanographique** (*Port des Minimes*, with seals in an outdoor pool. Closed Mon, adults FFr.16, under-18s free). The **Musée Maritime** at the **Bassin des Chalutiers** has a frigate, *France I*, a tug and a trawler to visit (open daily 1000–1830, adults FFr.38, children FFr.20).

From the water the extent of modern La Rochelle is clear, stretching from the yacht marina at les Minimes to the commercial port at La Pallice. There is a choice of **water transport**, depending on whether you want to take a short trip around the harbour – trips depart regularly from *cours des Dames* – or make a longer visit to the **islands.**

Out of Town

Inter-iles boats offer a choice of itineraries from the *esplanade St-Jean d'Acre*, beyond the Tour de la Chaine, where you can pick up schedules. Trips include the **Île d'Oléron**, the largest of the islands and which is also accessible by coach from Rochefort, the **Île d'Aix**, the smallest, and exile home to Napoleon, and the **Île de Ré**, nearest to La Rochelle and known as *Ré la Blanche* with its whitewashed houses.

For those without sea legs, the Île de Ré is also linked to the mainland by toll-bridge and can be visited by bus (*Ré-Bus*, departs from the SNCF station and town centre, *tel: 46 09 20 15*). Almost 30 km long but only 3 km wide, and mostly flat, the island is crossed with cycle tracks. There are rental outlets in nearly all of the villages. The largest town is **St-Martin**, with a sheltered harbour on the north coast (tourist information *av. Victor Buthillier, tel: 46 09 20 06*).

About 25 mins south of La Rochelle on the main line to Saintes, **Rochefort** is home to one of France's most remarkable museums. Behind the modest façade of *141 r. Pierre Loti*, the extraordinary home of sailor and writer Loti is complete with Gothic hall and mosque. Open daily except Sun, tours start on the hour, admission FFr.30.

SAINTES

Station: *av. de la Marne, tel: 36 35 35 35*. Buffet, lockers. It is a 20-min walk to the centre. Turn left down *av. de La Marne*, then right on *av. Gambetta*, straight on over the river to *cours National*. Bus no. 2 goes to the centre (stop: *Théâtre*). **BUSS**, *tel; 46 92 99 00*, runs the local bus lines. Single fare FFr.5.80, ten tickets for FFr.50.

Tourist Office: *62 cours National, Villa Musso, BP 96, 17103 Saintes; tel: 46 74 23 82.* Open Mon–Sat 0900–1900, Sun 1000–1230, 1530–1800 (June–Sept); Mon–Sat 0930–1230, 1400–1800 (Oct–May). Leaflets. No hotel reservations. Guided tours (in French), June–Sept, on foot, Mon–Fri 1030, FFr.38–50; by mini-bus to local abbeys and châteaux, Mon–Fri 1430, FFr.130–200.

Accommodation and Food

There is a good choice of reasonably priced hotels. Chains include: *Ca, Cl, F1, Ib.* **HI:** *6 r. Pont-Amillion, Saintes; tel: 46 92 14 92.* It is a 10-min walk from the station. Follow *av. de la Marne*, cross *av. Gambetta* to *r. E. Zola*, turn right on *r. G. Martel.* **Camping:** *Au fil de l'Eau, r. de Courbiac, tel: 46 93 08 00.* Bus no. 2, change at *Théâtre* for bus no. 3 (stop: *Port Larousselle*).

There are many restaurants and brasseries matching the glowing pale colours of the old white stone buildings (*cours National* and its off-shoot pedestrian streets).

Sightseeing

This picturesque town, population 28,000, makes an interesting stop. Its Roman origins, medieval abbey and riverside location make it it is so delightful that visitors linger to stroll down pleasant streets, eat in brasseries and restaurants and browse in fashion and antique shops.

All the attractions are within a few minutes' walk. The little street, *r. d'Arc de Triomphe*, connects the **Arc de Germanicus**, a Roman arch by the riverside, with the **Abbaye aux Dames** at the other end at *125 pl. St-Pallais; tel: 46 97 48 48*

The town's museums are housed in fine buildings. **Le Musée Archéologique** (archaeological museum), *esplanade A. Malraux; tel: 46 74 20 97.* Open Mon–Sat 1000–1200, 1400–1800 (Easter–Sept), Mon–Sat 1400–1700 (Oct–Easter). Admission free. Roman carvings and everyday objects are on display in a former abbatoir. **Le Musée du Presidial,** *r. V. Hugo; tel: 46 93 03 94.* Open Wed–Mon 1000–1200, 1400–1800 (summer); Wed–Mon 1000–1200, 1400–1700 (winter) admission free. This fine arts collection includes the Dutch, Flemish and French school of the 17th–18th centuries. **Le Musée de l'Echevinage,** *r. Alsace-Lorraine, tel: 46 93 52 39.* Open Wed–Mon 1000–1200, 1400–1700 (summer); Wed–Mon 1000–1200, 1400–1800; admission free. In this former town hall are 19th–20th century paintings, from landscapes, to Impressionists to current realist work. **Le Musée Dupuy-Mestreau,** *r. Monconseil, tel: 46 93 36 71.* Open Wed–Mon 1100–1730 (Apr–Oct). Guided tours from 1430; FFr.10. Housed in an 18th-century mansion, the costumes, jewels, furniture and head-dresses make up a collection about local life.

Two boats offer cruises with port stops along the Charente. The **Croisiers Inter-Îles** leaves from the *Arc de Germanicus*, information from the tourist office, or *tel: 46 50 55 54*, in La Rochelle.

- - - - - - - - - - - - - - - - - - - -
⌒ Side Tracks from Saintes

There are regular trains making the 30-min journey to the coastal town of **Royan** at the mouth of the River Gironde. **Tourist Office:** *Palais de Congrès, Façade-de-la-Foncillon; tel: 46 38 65 11.* Mostly modern since it was rebuilt after wartime bombing, it has long, sandy beaches and pine-clad cliffs looking out at the Atlantic. There is a casino near the vestige of old town, the **Pontaillac.** To reach both, walk along the scenic road, **Corniche de Pontaillac.**
- - - - - - - - - - - - - - - - - - - -

NICE

Queen of the Riviera, Nice attracts 4 million visitors a year. Since the days when Russian princes and British royalty graced its opulent hotels and casinos, Nice has enjoyed a reputation for luxury and extravagance. With 240 hotels, countless restaurants and clubs it is still a vibrant resort today. Yet the city has a harsher underside – population growth and economic hardship has led to an increase in petty crime, so be careful about valuables and bags.

Tourist Information

Tourist Office: av. Thiers, 06000 Nice (next to the station); tel: 93 87 07 07, turn left on the station steps. 0845–1215, 1400–1745 in winter, 0845–1830 in summer, closed Sun. Hotel reservations, efficient service.
Branch Office: 5 av. Gustave V, near pl. Masséna, tel: 93 87 60 60.

Arriving and Departing

Airport

Nice Côte d'Azur: promenade des Anglais. Airport Information: Tel: 93 21 30 12. Terminal One (East) handles international flights, Air Littoral and TAT; Terminal Two (West) handles internal French flights only.

Airport to City: 6 km. Taxis to the centre cost FFr.100–120. Airport buses run along the promenade des Anglais to the gare routière (main bus station) every 20 mins, the 20 min journey costs FFr.20. Bus no. 23 to Gare SNCF takes 20 mins, costs FFr.8.

Buses run hourly to Cannes (journey time 45 mins, FFr.65) and every 1 hour 30 mins to Monaco and Menton (45 mins/1 hour 30 mins, FFr.75 and FFr.90 respectively).

Heli-Inter offers helicopter transits every 20 mins to Monte Carlo (15 mins) and seven flights a day to St Tropez during the summer.

Car hire companies at the airport include Avis, Budget, Citer, Eurodollar, Europcar and Hertz.

Station

Nice-Ville, av. Thiers; tel: 93 87 50 50, reservations: 93 88 89 93. Information open 0700–2200. For the town centre, turn left from station to av. Jean Médecin, the main thoroughfare, turn right down to pl. Masséna (300 m), right again to the sea. Bus to the airport from outside the station, every 30 mins (FFr.20). Station closed: 0130–0530. Left luggage open 0530–2400; showers: 0600–1900 in the basement (FFr.18).

There are **Thomas Cook** bureaux de change inside and outside the station, open daily, 0700–2200 in summer, 0900–2000 in winter, tel 93 82 13 00. See p.180 for details of others.

Buses

Gare Routière (bus station): promenade de Peillon; tel: 93 85 61 81. At pl. Masséna head north 300 m up blvd Jean Jaurès. Buy tickets on the bus. Local buses to St-Jean Cap-Ferrat, Villefranche, Beaulieu, Cagnes and Menton.

Ferries

Ferries: SNCM, 3 av. Gustave V; tel: 93 13 66 66, by the Ruhl Hotel and McDonalds. Regular crossings to Corsica (FFr. 260 one-way, students FFr.190). Ferries depart from the east end of the port.

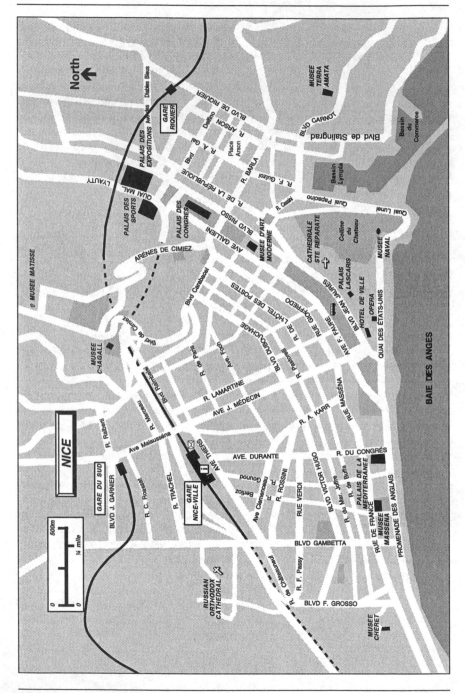

NICE

North ←

GARE RIQUIER

PALAIS DES EXPOSITIONS

PALAIS DES SPORTS

QUAI MAL MAL

PALAIS DES CONGRES

LYAUTY

Av. Diables Bleus

BLVD DE RIQUIER

R. ARSON

Delfino

R. A. Gal

Bvd

Place Arson

R. F. Guizot

R. BARLA

BLVD de Stalingrad

BLVD CARNOT

MUSEE TERRA AMATA

Bassin du Commerce

ARENES DE CIMIEZ

AVE GALIENI

BLVD RISSO

R. DE LA REPUBLIQUE

MUSEE D'ART MODERNE

R. Cassini

Quai Papacino

Quai Lunel

Bassin Lympia

CATHEDRALE STE REPARATE

Colline du Chateau

MUSEE NAVAL

9 MUSEE MATISSE

MUSEE C-HAGALL

Bvd de Cimiez

Bvd Carabacel

AVE F. FAURE

RUE GIOFFREDO

L'HOTEL DES POSTES

BLVD DUBOUCHAGE

RUE PASTORELLI

R. de Foix

BLVD JEAN JAURES

PALAIS LASCARIS

HOTEL DE VILLE

OPERA

QUAI DES ETATS-UNIS

BAIE DES ANGES

R. de Pais

R. LAMARTINE

AVE J. MEDECIN

Bvd Raimbaldi

R. Raiberti

Ave Maleausséna

R. R. KARR

RUE MASSENA

NICE

GARE DU SUD

BLVD J. GARNIER

R. Roussat

R. C. Roussat

R. TRACHEL

AVE THIERS

GARE NICE-VILLE

AVE. DURANTE

Gounod

Berlioz

Ave Clemenceau

R. ROSSINI

RUE VERDI

BLVD VICTOR HUGO

R. de Buffa

R. du Mar. Joffre

R. DU CONGRÉS

PALAIS DE LA MEDITERRANEE

MUSEE MASSENA

RUE de FRANCE

PROMENADE DES ANGLAIS

RUSSIAN ORTHODOX CATHEDRAL

R. de Châteauneuf

R. F. Passy

BLVD GAMBETTA

BLVD F. GROSSO

MUSEE CHÉRET

500m

¼ mile

0

0

Getting Around

Nice is deceptively sprawling, and while it is possible to amble the *promenade des Anglais*, and cover all of the Old Town on foot, getting to all the museums and sights on offer requires bus or taxi transport. Good free city maps are liberally handed out at all tourist offices and many shops. Public transport is excellent.

Renting a car, or motorbike is a popular option, although be warned: prices are high and the reliability of many machines is questionable. Be sure to take all-inclusive insurance, as Niçois drivers are notorious.

Car Hire: Rent a Car, *av. Thiers* opposite the station; *tel: 93 88 69 69.* **Scooter/ motor bike, bike hire: Nicea Location**, *9 av. Thiers* near station; *tel: 93 82 42 71.*

Buses

Local buses run from *pl. Masséna*. Buy tickets on the bus; FFr.8. Alternatively, buy seven-day (FFr.110) or one-day (FFr.25) passes. Information *10 r. Félix Faure; tel: 93 62 08 08.*

Taxis

Taxis are expensive in Nice. Expect to pay FFr.50 for even the shortest trip. A journey to the airport from downtown can cost as much as FFr.200; *tel: 93 80 70 70.*

Staying in Nice

Accommodation

Nice is one of Europe's most popular travel destinations, and as such offers a wide range of hotel accommodation. Hotel chains in Nice include *Ca, Ho, Ib, Md, Me, Nv,* and *Sf.*

It is advisable to book well in advance for the summer season, and for the Nice Carnival period in early Feb.

Nice boasts one of the world's most famous hotels, **Le Négresco**, *37 promenade des Anglais; tel: 93 88 39 51.* This white and pink palace was built for a former Romanian gypsy violinist, Henri Négresco, by the architect of the Moulin Rouge and the Folies Bergères, and abounds with extravagant furnishing and opulent artwork – if you cannot afford a room at least catch a glimpse of the *salon royal* adorned with a Baccarat chandelier made for a Tsar.

For those on more modest budgets, copious good value accommodation is found near the station – *r. d'Angleterre, r. de Suisse, av. Durante, r. Paganini*; in Old Nice, around *pl. St François*, to the north.

HI: Nice has three youth hostels, all far from the centre. **Mt-Alban:** *rte de Mont-Alban; tel: 93 89 23 64.* Four km out of town uphill! (bus no. 5 from the station to *blvd Jean Jaurès*, then no. 14 to hostel). No reservations, open from 1000. Good view over the city.

Clairvallon Youth Hostel: *av. Scudéri; tel: 93 81 27 63*, is up in Cimiez to the north of the centre (bus nos 15 or 22, stop at *Scuderi*). Located in a park with pool.

Magnan: *31 r. Louis-de-Coppet near the airport; tel: 93 86 28 75.* Not the most welcoming of hostels, but clean and efficient. Take bus no. 23 from the station.

Camping is distant, at Villeneuve-Loubet to the west, 10 mins in the train. Sleeping on the beach is not advised: the police have little sympathy if you are mugged.

Eating and Drinking

A culinary paradise, Nice is influenced by its neighbours, Italy and the Mediterranean. The city has many specialities – *Pissaladière* – Niçois onion tart, garnished with anchovies and olives, *Socca* – a traditional lunchtime snack of flat bread made from

---

Getting Around–Staying in Nice

crushed chick peas, served piping hot from the oven, and of course the renowned *Salade Niçoise* – the genuine article containing hard-boiled eggs, tomatoes, anchovies, cucumber, spring onions, broad beans and small artichokes. There's also *Pag Bagnat*, a large bun stuffed with salad niçoise and doused in olive oil.

Vieux Nice (Old Nice) is the best area for restaurants, in particular good value socca joints – try the street leading to the cathedral, *r. Ste Répararte*, and side-streets. North of the old town, *pl. Garibaldi* boasts the best shellfish, and good socca. *Cours Saleya* has sea-food places but is mostly overpriced. The *Zone Piétonne*, off *Jean Médecin*, has pizza places and bistros.

Communications

Post Office: *23 av. Thiers; tel: 93 88 52 52.* It has poste restante, telephones, fax. Open 0800–1900, 0800–1200 Sat.

Money

As well the offices at the station (see p. 177), there is a Thomas Cook bureau de change at *2 pl. Magenta*.

Entertainment

Nice is regarded as the cultural and social capital of the south. Opera, music, dance, theatre and nightlife thrive in happy harmony. **FNAC** (*Fédération Nationale d'Achats des Cadres*) supplies theatre, concert tickets, jazz festival tickets and cultural information at Nice Etoile shopping mall, on *av. Jean Médecin*.

Opera and Music

Nice Opéra, *4 r. St-François-de-Paule; tel: 93 85 67 31.* One of the best in France, putting on operas, concerts and recitals. Chamber and sacred music concerts are held at **Cathédrale Ste-Réparate**, *pl. Rossini.*

CEDAC de Cimiez, *49 av. de la Marne; tel: 93 81 09 09.* Big-league musicians and dancers. **Forum Nice Nord**, *10 blvd Comte de Falicon; tel: 93 84 24 37,* just off the A8 at Nice-Nord is a major venue for modern dance.

Théâtre de Verdure, *Jardin Albert I; tel: 93 82 38 68* for details. From Apr onwards rock, jazz, and other concerts take place in the big tent by the sea off *pl. Masséna.*

Theatre

Théâtre de Nice, *promenade des Arts; tel: 93 80 52 60.* The cavernous new theatre next to the Modern Art Museum puts on grandiose concerts and plays, including opera and ballet.

Théâtre de l'Alphabet, *10 blvd Carabacel; tel: 93 13 08 88.* More classical theatre productions.

Bars and Nightlife

In summer Nice grinds till well past dawn. Bars shut around 0300, when everyone heads to the beach. Saunter along *r. de la Préfecture* in old Nice or side-streets off *pl. Rossetti* by the cathedral. Otherwise stroll the *cours Saleya* at night, and watch the world go by. Clubs are expensive but many bars have music and in summer everyone just dances on the tables.

Events

In Feb the **Nice Carnival** is an overblown parade, ostensibly for the tourists. Information at the **Comité des Fêtes**, *5 promenade des Anglais; tel: 93 87 16 28.*

In July the **Jazz Festival** is not to be missed; great names of world jazz in Nice's Roman amphitheatre and gardens in **Cimiez** (tickets available usually up until the event from FNAC). BB King is a regular, and it was here that Miles Davis gave his last live concert. For information; *tel: 93 37 17 17*.

Shopping

Vieux Nice is the best place to shop, for art, cheap clothes and glorious food at the outdoor markets and local shops. In *cours Saleya*, the morning food and flower market is supplemented on Mon with bric-à-brac; crafts appear on Wed afternoon, and paintings on Sun afternoons.

The pedestrian zone around *pl. Masséna* has scores of clothes shops and boutiques, while in *av. Jean Médecin* you'll find Nice's two biggest department stores, **Galeries Lafayette** and **La Riviera**, as well as **Nice Etoile**, a centre with useful shops like FNAC, The Body Shop and so on.

Sightseeing

Vieux Nice seems more Italian than French (which it was until 1860). Wander the narrow streets to **Palais Lascaris**, *15 r. Droite; tel: 93 62 05 54*, a 17th-century palace/museum (Open 0930–1200 and 1430–1800, closed Mon, Tues in winter). Beyond, steps lead up to the **château**, site of ancient Greek Nikaïa, with a park, small naval museum and breathtaking view.

At sunset, stroll the **promenade des Anglais** as the lights begin to shimmer and the **Negresco** hotel lights up like an elaborate wedding cake.

At the far west end of the promenade near the airport, Nice's most modern (and commercial) attractions are the **Parc des Miniatures**, *blvd Impératrice Eugénie; tel: 93 97 02 02*, containing small-scale models of Riviera landmarks, and the greenhouses of the **Parc Phoenix**, *405 promenade des Anglais; tel: 93 18 03 33*, with 2500 plants in seven tropical and sub-tropical kingdoms.

Museums

Nice boasts some of the best museums in France and they are all free. Most are easily accessible by local bus. Best of the bunch is the newly refurbished **Musée Matisse**; *164 av. des Arènes de Cimiez; tel: 93 13 29 11*, in a 17th-century villa amongst the Roman ruins of Cimiez – beautiful paintings and sketches in a beautiful setting (bus nos 15, 17, 20, 22, from *pl. Masséna*. Open 1100–1900 summer, 1000–1700 Oct–Apr, closed Tues). Next door the **Musée Archéologique**, *160 av. des Arènes de Cimiez; tel: 93 81 59 57*, exhibits the copious finds dug up while excavating the Roman arenas at Cimiez (bus nos 15, 17, 20, 22 to *Arènes*. Open 1000–1200, 1400–1800, closed Sun morning and Tues). Matisse and fellow artist Raoul Dufy are buried in the neighbouring **Couvent des Frères Mineurs**, with a fine view across Nice to the sea. Also in Cimiez, the **Musée Marc Chagall**; *av. du Dr. Ménard; tel: 93 81 75 75*, is a graceful temple to Chagall's genius – beautifully lit to display his huge biblical canvases (bus no. 15, open 1000–1900 summer, 1000–1230, 1400–1730 Oct–June, closed Tues).

In the centre of town, the **Musée d'Art Moderne et d'art Contemporain**; *blvd Jean Jaurès; tel: 93 62 61 62*, is unmistakable: a white marble cliff rising from *blvd Jean Jaurès*. Its squashed cars and pop art are strangely fascinating. Bus nos 5, 17. Open 1100–1800, 1100–2200 Fri, closed Tues. West of the centre is **Musée Masséna**, *65 r. de France, tel: 93 88 11 34*, a splendid old Italianate villa adorned with antiques, traditional artifacts and decorated with paintings by Renoir and local artists. Bus nos 3, 7, 8, 9, 10, 12, 14, 22. Open 1000–1200, 1500–1800 summer; 1000–1200, 1400–1700 winter. To the east of the centre, **Musée Terra Amata**, *25 blvd Carnot; tel: 93 55 59 93* has displays of the prehistoric inhabitants of Nice of 400,000 years ago (bus nos 1, 2, 7, 9, 10, 14. Open 0900–1200, 1400–1800 closed Mon).

Churches

There are two cathedrals in Nice, each in its own way tracing the history of this Riviera settlement. In Vieux Nice, **Cathédrale de Ste-Réparate**; *pl. Rossetti*, is a dimly impressive Catholic masterpiece built with Italian money in the 17th century. To the west the **Cathédrale Orthodoxe Russe St-Nicolas**, *17 blvd du Tzarévitch*, is a mighty five-domed Russian Orthodox church built on the site of a villa where the young Tsarevich Nicholas died. It was completed just five years before the Russian Revolution with royal roubles and remains to this day a symbol of the aristocratic opulence that characterises the Riviera (Open 0900–1200 and 1430–1800 summer, 0930–1200 and 1430–1700, admission FFr.10).

Beaches

The beaches of Nice are disappointingly lacking in sand. In fact there is no sand to the east of Antibes as far as the Italian border, just pebbles. This does not deter the sun-worshippers from overpopulating the *promenade des Anglais* beaches in summer. Whilst private beach clubs cover some of the central section of the *promenade*, charging around FFr.50 for hire of a deck chair, most of the long beach is free. Things are less hectic further west, where the long shore between Cagnes-sur-Mer and Antibes provides space for all. The prettiest of local beaches are found to the east, at **Villefranche** (young, lively crowd), **Beaulieu** (old, sedate crowd) and **St-Jean Cap Ferrat** (well-heeled, laid-back crowd).

Out of Town

Renoir spent the last years of his life in **Cagnes sur Mer**, buying an isolated house in an olive grove overlooking the sea. Today this is the **Musée Renoir**, *chemin les Colettes; tel: 93 20 61 07* (1000–1200, 1400–1700 closed Tues and 15 Oct–15 Nov, admission FFr.20) a delightful tour around the artist's life, with rooms as he kept them eighty years ago (from the rail station, take the bus to Beal-Les Colettes). Above the coast, **Haut de Cagnes** is a medieval citadel, whose **château** is now an art museum; *montée de la Bourgade; tel: 93 20 85 57*, open 0900–1200, 1400–1800 summer, 0900–1200, 1500–1700 Oct–Apr.

There are frequent buses from Nice bus station (hourly) to **St Paul-de-Vence**, one of the coast's most picturesque *villages perchés*, home to artists and tourists. Wander through the narrow medieval streets and sip coffee while watching the *boulistes* argue another round. The most interesting modern art museum in France is here, **The Fondation Maeght**, purpose-built by the Maeghts, who were friends of Matisse; *tel: 93 32 81 63*, open 1000–1230, 1420–1800 winter, 1000–1900 summer, closed mid-Nov to mid-Dec, admission FFr.25). The garden is a quirky sculpture park, designed by Miró.

Three km further up the valley is **Vence**, with a character far-removed from the glitzy settlements of the coast. Here Matisse was nursed by local nuns, and repaid them by designing and building a simple yet breathtakingly beautiful chapel – **La Chapelle du Rosaire**, *av. Henri Matisse; tel 93 58 03 26*. The chapel is open on Tues and Thurs, 1000–1130 and 1430–1700. Matisse considered it his masterpiece, an opinion you will have to judge for yourself.

NICE to DIGNE

Chemins de Fer de Provence (CP) is one of France's few regular private rail services, running the Train des Pignes, a spectacular train ride between Nice and Digne. The ancient route, opened in 1912, takes passengers from the palm trees and glittering buildings of the Côte d'Azur, along the flat bed of the Var with views up to medieval villages perched on mountain peaks, and into the foothills of the Alps.

The train journey of 151 km takes 4 hrs. The train is small, with only 50 seats and room for 24 standing passengers, so get there early. There are no reservations.

Train des Pignes

Shortly before publication, news was received that storm damage had severed the Nice–Digne line in 20 places. A local newspaper, **Nice-Matin**, *214 rte de Grenoble, 06290 Nice*, has launched an appeal to save this line, as it may not be rebuilt without financial assistance.

TRAINS

ETT table: 151d.

→ Fast Track

Four trains a day run from Nice CP to Digne-les-Bains with the journey taking 3¼ hrs. The trains are one class only and do not have refreshment cars.

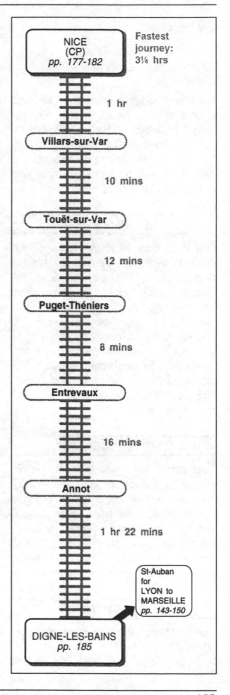

NICE (CP) pp. 177-182

Fastest journey: 3¼ hrs

1 hr

Villars-sur-Var

10 mins

Touët-sur-Var

12 mins

Puget-Théniers

8 mins

Entrevaux

16 mins

Annot

1 hr 22 mins

St-Auban for LYON to MARSEILLE pp. 143-150

DIGNE-LES-BAINS pp. 185

〰⟩ On Track

*Nice–Villars-sur-Var–Touët-sur-Var–
Puget-Théniers–Entrevaux–Annot–
Digne*

The four through trains call at all these stations en route. Nice CP to Villars-sur-Var takes 1 hr, Villars-sur-Var to Touët-sur-Var 10 mins, Touët-sur-Var to Puget-Théniers 12 mins, Puget-Théniers to Entrevaux 8 mins, Entrevaux to Annot 16 mins, and Annot to Digne 1 hr 22 mins.

VILLARS-SUR-VAR

One hour from Nice, the tiny medieval village of Villars already feels like another world. This is the only place in the mountains of *Haute Provence* which boasts an *Appellation Côtes de Provence* wine licence. The vineyards were first planted in the Middle Ages, at the same time the streets were designed – motor vehicles are banned from the village. The local church is the only real 'sight', containing a couple of paintings dating from the early 1500s.

TOUËT-SUR-VAR

Next comes the small village of Touët, clinging to its sheer cliff with great tenacity. Another medieval village, fortress-like in its design, Touët is far from the tourist trail and retains an intimate charm. The station has changed little since the 1950s. Walk up into the old village, where a torrential stream cascades down past the church.

PUGET-THÉNIERS

Tourist Office: Syndicat d'Initiative, *tel: 93 05 02 81.*

Puget comes as a shock – a sizeable settlement in the midst of the imposing mountains. This was the headquarters of the Templar Knights in the 13th century and many of the houses date back to this time, still bearing the insignia of respective lords and knights. One street, *r. Gisclette,* still contains the rings used to thread the chains which barred the road each night. The local church was built by the Templars and restored in the 17th century.

ENTREVAUX

Tourist Office: Syndicat d'Initiative, *Tour du Pontlevis; tel: 93 05 46 73.*

In many ways Entrevaux is the most dramatic sight in this whole region – many passengers ride on the train just to get here. The town has been a place of strategic importance for centuries – it was a fort in Roman days. In the Middle Ages this was the border between the kingdom of France and the estates of the Dukes of Savoy. The present lofty fort, up an impressive series of steps, was built by Louis XIV's illustrious engineer Vauban at the beginning of the 17th century. A 10-franc coin gets you through the turnstiles at the drawbridge (which still works), and then you are free to wander the fort. The climb to the *citadelle* is strenuous – a half-hour up, 10 mins down – but the view out over the Var valley and the sense of history engrained in the walls is worth the slog.

ANNOT

Tourist Office: Syndicat d'Initiative, *Mairie d'Annot; tel: 92 83 23 03.*

Centre de Montagne, *Colle Basse; tel: 92 83 28 14.*

Annot has gone through several transformations in its turbulent history. At the end of the 14th century it was a strategic market town, on the border of Provence, Piedmont and the County of Nice. In the 18th century it was an industrial town, with nut oil distilleries, lavender processing and tile manufacture bringing in wealth and prosperity. With the demise of nut oil the town went into decline, until the advent of tourism. Today, the altitude (705 m) and mild climate have made Annot a highly popular summer mountain resort, with attendant tennis, golf, horse-riding etc.

Yet Annot still manages to retain a Provençal charm, with shady plane trees and ancient tortuous streets.

The relaxed town offers a handful of fine restaurants serving inexpensive local delicacies. The surrounding rocks have been moulded by erosion into weird and wonderful shapes, and provide an interesting walking tour. Otherwise head into the old village and its 16th-century houses built of local stone, fortified church and vaulted passageways.

DIGNE-LES-BAINS

Station: Gare de Digne, *tel: 92 31 01 58.* The town centre is 5 mins walk from the station – turn left at the main road.
Tourist Office: *le Rond-Point, pl. Tampinet, 04000 Digne; tel: 92 31 42 73* (at the entrance to the town by the bus station).

Accommodation and Food

Accommodation can be a problem in Digne in high season, so reserve in advance – the few hotels are clustered around the main street, *blvd Gassendi.* The best restaurants are attached to the hotels, but fast food can be found on *pl. de Gaulle.*

Sightseeing

End of the line, Digne is the epitome of a provincial town, the 'capital' of the sparsely populated Alpes-de-Haute-Provence département. Surrounded by a necklace of mountains, it is a quietly unassuming place, with a few sights but little to stagger the imagination. It is a place in which to stroll and enjoy the isolation.

Digne is small and can be covered in an afternoon's wandering. Start in the main square, the **pl. de Gaulle** with its glitzy **Hôtel de Ville**. From here steps climb up to the old town and its cobbled streets. The **Cathédrale de St-Jérome** dates from the 15th century, but recent excavations have revealed foundations of a 6th-century church.

Digne's most intriguing attraction is the **Fondation Alexandra David Néel**, dedicated to the life of one of the world's greatest travellers. Alexandra David Néel was a Frenchwoman who set out for India in 1891 at the age of 23 and walked across Tibet. Friend of Gandhi and the Dalai Lama, she returned to France at the age of 80 and set up home in Digne, her 'Himalayas in miniature'. She was visited by the Dalai Lama before her death in 1969 at the age of 101. The Foundation, *rte de Nice, 27 av. du Maréchal Juin: tel; 92 31 32 38*, is open for guided tours four times a day (check with the tourist office for details).

- -

🚍 Connection: Digne to St-Auban

SNCF runs three buses a day linking the railway stations at Digne and **St-Auban**. In Digne you can catch the bus from *pl. Tampinet* by the tourist office, or outside the station. The isolated station at St-Auban, surrounded by chemical works and gigantic oil refineries, connects with the main line north to Grenoble and south to Marseille (see Lyon–Marseille route, p. 143).

- -

NICE to MENTON

The Corniche between Nice and the Italian border is one of the most beautiful coastlines in the world, with the tail-end of the Alps plunging dramatically into the Mediterranean, avenues of palm trees decorating small villages, and millionaires' palaces lining the seashore.

The railway hugs the sea, offering stunning views of the Côte d'Azur's finest real estate. Outside Nice are the once sleepy fishing ports of Villefranche and Beaulieu, now wealthy resorts. Jutting from the cliffs is the peninsula of St-Jean Cap-Ferrat, playground of royalty and rock-stars.

The state of Monaco, and its capital Monte-Carlo, is next, the millionaires' fortress. This 7 km stretch of skyscrapers and priceless yachts is an independent country, with its own police force and laws, but there is no border control and French money, telephone and postal services apply.

Finally, on the border between France and Italy lies Menton, one of the Mediterranean's prettiest towns. The influence of Italy is strong – the waterfront houses are Italianate in style, while the markets and shops sell salamis, fresh pasta and biscotti.

TRAINS

ETT table: 164.

→ **Fast Track**

A frequent train service operates between

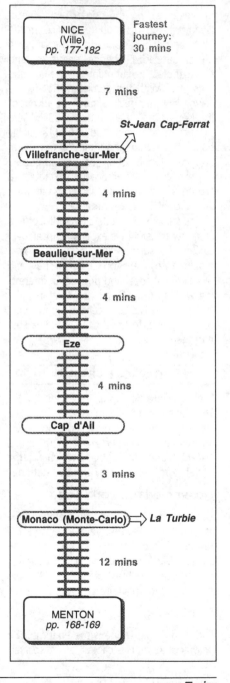

NICE (Ville)
pp. 177-182

Fastest journey: 30 mins

7 mins

St-Jean Cap-Ferrat

Villefranche-sur-Mer

4 mins

Beaulieu-sur-Mer

4 mins

Eze

4 mins

Cap d'Ail

3 mins

Monaco (Monte-Carlo) ⇒ La Turbie

12 mins

MENTON
pp. 168-169

Nice Ville and Menton, with a good local service supplemented by long-distance trains from all over France completing their journeys, as well as international trains starting their journeys into Italy. The journey from Nice to Menton takes around 30 mins.

On Track

Nice–Villefranche–St-Jean-Cap-Ferrat–Beaulieu–Eze-sur-Mer–Cap d'Ail–Monaco-Monte-Carlo–Menton

The local service operates throughout the day between Nice Ville and Menton, stopping at all of these resorts en route.

The journey from Nice Ville to Villefranche-sur-Mer takes 7 mins, Villefranche-sur-Mer to Beaulieu-sur-Mer takes 4 mins, Beaulieu-sur-Mer to Eze takes 4 mins, Eze to Cap-d'Ail also takes 4 mins, Cap-d'Ail to Monaco-Monte-Carlo 3 mins and Monaco-Monte-Carlo to Menton 12 mins.

VILLEFRANCHE

Station: *tel: 93 87 50 50 for information.* **Tourist Office:** *Jardins François Binon, 06230 Villefranche,* near the Basse Corniche; *tel: 93 01 73 68.*

Just outside Nice is Villefranche, one of the deepest ports on the coast, today home to cruise ships and the odd American aircraft carrier. The bay boasts the liveliest beach in the region, conveniently situated right below the rail station. When you have tired of lying in the sun, stroll the Italianesque waterfront and narrow streets – Villefranche is surprisingly relaxed and restaurants in the old town are inexpensive. Artist Jean Cocteau decorated the local chapel, at the town-end of the quay, open 0930–1200 and 1500–1800, admission FFr.12.

 Side Track from Villefranche

ST-JEAN CAP-FERRAT

Tourist Office: *59 av. Denis Séméria, 06230 St-Jean Cap-Ferrat; tel: 93 76 08 90.*

Inaccessible by train, St-Jean Cap-Ferrat is a walk up from Villefranche beach, or a bus ride from Nice bus station. This peninsula contains the prettiest beaches in the region, and some of the world's most expensive homes. Liz Taylor, Joan Collins and Mick Jagger are rumoured to have places here. The port is lined with restaurants, tranquil even in high season, and surprisingly inexpensive. A footpath leads around the peninsula, through pine woods with splendid views back along the coast. On the hump of the hill joining the mainland is one of the Riviera's most attractive museums, the **Villa Rothschild** *tel: 93 01 33 90,* once owned by Béatrice de Rothschild. The house is stunning, but the gardens are what impress most – an eclectic masterpiece of exotic plants with views down to Villefranche and Beaulieu. Not to be missed (open 1000–1800 winter, 1000–1900 summer, admission FFr.30).

BEAULIEU

Station: *tel: 93 87 50 50 for information.* **Tourist Office:** *pl. G. Clémenceau, 06310 Beaulieu* (right outside the station), *tel: 93 01 02 21.*

Beaulieu was christened by Napoleon (meaning 'beautiful place'). Its mild climate has attracted retirees from all over Europe, giving the village a relaxed, if not comatose, air. The beach is pretty, offering views of Cap-Ferrat. Anyone not travelling on to the islands of Greece might want to stop at

Villa Kerylos, *tel: 93 01 01 44*, a replica of the house of a wealthy Athenian, circa 5th-century BC, built by a rich archaeologist at the turn of the century – marbles, ivories, bronzes, mosaics and the Mediterranean lapping at the doorstep. It is open daily 1000–1200 and 1400–1800 winter, 1000–1900 summer, admission FFr.30.

EZE

Station: *tel: 93 87 50 50* for information. **Tourist Office:** *pl. du Gén. de Gaulle, 06360 Eze; tel: 93 41 26 00.*

Perched 427 m above the Mediterranean, the medieval eagle's nest of Eze has a spectacular view. The rail station is by the sea, with steep tortuous steps climbing up the cliff to the village, once trodden by philosopher Friedrich Nietzsche. Once at the top you are greeted by narrow streets, arty boutiques, and a **Jardin Exotique** full of incongruous cacti (*tel; 93 41 10 30*, open 0900–1200 and 1400–1900, summer 0800-2000, admission FFr.10). Yet the real attraction (apart from the shopping in charming but overpriced shops) is the view – the best on the Riviera. On clear days you can see as far as St-Tropez, 100 km away.

CAP D'AIL

Station: *tel: 93 87 50 50* for information.

Cap d'Ail (the 'Peninsula of Garlic') is a popular beach stop along the coast just before Monaco. The beaches in question are shingle and pebbles, but are lively in summer and offer first-rate swimming. Cap d'Ail does boast one of the coast's best youth hostels, perched high above the Mediterranean; **Relais International de la Jeunesse:** *blvd de la Mer; tel: 93 78 18 58.* The maximum stay is three nights, since most people want to stay for a lifetime. There are single-sex dormitories and a midnight curfew.

MONACO

Station: *pl. de la Gare, av. Prince-Pierre; tel: 93 87 50 50*, information 0900–1845. Both the station and luggage lockers are closed 0100–0530.

For the Royal Palace head straight down to *pl. d'Armes*, continue towards the Port and a footpath leads up onto the palace rock. For the Casino turn left at the port along *blvd Albert 1er*, and up the hill along *av. d'Ostende* (500 m). Otherwise take bus no. 4 from the station.

Tourist Office: *2A blvd des Moulins, 98000 Monaco*, near the Casino; *tel: 93 30 87 01* open 0900–1900, 0900–1200 Sun. It provides free maps and makes hotel reservations, although they can be somewhat snooty.

Getting Around

Monaco is not big. You can walk to all sights from the rail station and orientation is simple.

A small motorised train offers hourly tours of Monaco, encompassing all sights. You can get on and off at will. Otherwise the local bus service is very efficient, and for those overwhelmed by the cliff-like hills, a series of free public lifts and escalators whisk tourists between the different levels of streets. Taxis here are more expensive than any in France.

Bike Hire: Auto-moto Garage, *7 r. de la Colle* near the station; *tel: 93 30 24 61.*

Staying in Monaco

Accommodation

Budget accommodation in millionaire city is

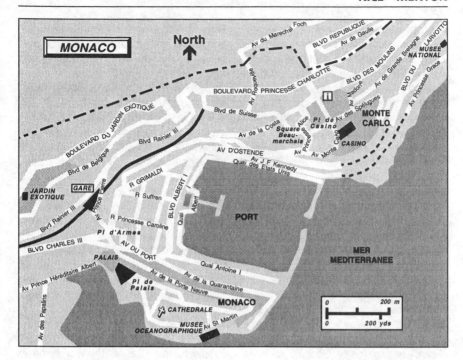

unsurprisingly scarce, although not impossible to find.

To catch a glimpse of where Michael Jackson stays when in town, head to the **Hôtel de Paris**, *pl. de Casino*, by the Casino, one of Europe's most extravagant hotels. Drinks in the bar cost almost as much as a normal hotel room, but worth it if only for the glittering surroundings. Just round the corner on *square Beaumarchais* is its *belle époque* rival, **L'Hermitage**, with spectacular views from its bar-terrace down over the port.

For less ruinous prices try *r. de la Turbie* near the station, where several good, low-budget hotels are congregated.

The **Centre de la Jeunesse Princesse-Stéphanie** youth hostel, *24 av. Prince-Pierre; tel: 93 50 83 20*. 100 m from the station. This excellent hostel, for 16–31

year olds, is a godsend, although as with all low-budget accommodation here, it fills up rapidly in summer months – get here after 0900 and you will not get a bed. Otherwise, most people stay in Nice and visit on day-trips.

Eating and Drinking

You can eat like a prince in Monaco, although usually at a price. Monaco supports a wide range of restaurants, from the most luxurious in Europe to simpler Italian eateries. If you win big at the casino, head across the road to **Restaurant Louis XV** at the Hôtel de Paris. Here, one of the world's top chefs, Alain Ducasse, masterminds menus fit for princesses. This was the favourite dining room of Edward VII when he was Prince of Wales, and present-day patrons include

Pavarotti and Sting, not to mention princesses Stephanie and Caroline. Yet eating with royalty is not the preserve of the wealthy – head to *r. Suffren* up from the port and **Le Texan**, a Tex-Mex restaurant and bar with the cheapest beers in the Principality, good food and the possibility of brushing shoulders with Prince Albert or Boris Becker.

Inexpensive food is not that hard to come by. Proximity to the border means pizzas – again *r. de la Turbie* beckons. For lunchtime fare in the sun by the port head to the terrace bar-restaurants along *quai Albert 1er*. Up on the rock, numerous small restaurants offer set menus for under FFr.100.

Communications

Post Office: *pl. Beaumarchais; tel: 93 50 69 87*, the only place you can buy stamps that you can use nowhere else. French stamps are also on sale. Open 0800–1900, 0800–1200 Sat.

Money

Compagnie Monégasque de Change: *av. Quarantine; tel: 93 25 02 50.*

Entertainment and events

Monaco is synonymous with gambling. There are three casinos, for all tastes. You must be over 21, and they do check, so bring a passport. Granddaddy of them all is the most famous casino in the world, the **Casino de Paris**. You cannot miss it in the centre of *pl. de Casino*, adorned with flags and gold leaf. To get beyond the entrance hall you must pay FFr.50 just for the pleasure of walking into the hallowed halls, and smart dress is required. For free you can pop coins into the slot machines at the entrance, in the *Salle Américain*.

The second money-pit is the **Café de Paris** next door – there is no entrance fee, but it is definitely more tacky. The next best bet after the real thing is **Casino Loess**, down steps at the north end of Casino de Paris. Here a giant slot machine takes FFr.50 tokens, paying out up to FFr.50,000.

Bars in Monaco are fun, but usually expensive. Try side streets off *r. Grimaldi* behind the port. Monaco is an enjoyable wandering ground at night, and watching is free.

To catch a Las Vegas-style show, head to the **Monte-Carlo Sporting Club**, *av. Princesse Grace*, although do not expect to come back with a heavy wallet. Monaco's number one club is **Jimmy Z's**, *26 av. Princesse Grace; tel: 92 16 22 77*, with a strict dress code but free entry. Once inside you are expected to buy a drink, at FFr.100 a shot.

Culturally, Monaco gets the best of the lot. In the **Salle Garnier,** *tel: 93 50 76 54*, behind the main casino, the world's opera stars strut their stuff while the Ballet Russe de Monte Carlo is the resident support act. This opulent theatre was built by Charles Garnier, who was responsible for the opera house in Paris. In its heyday, Picasso and Cocteau were its set designers. Tickets are surprisingly affordable (FFr.75 for student tickets) – ticket office is inside the main casino.

In summer, open-air cinema attracts large crowds at the **Cinema d'Été**, *av. Princesse Grace*, showing a different film in its original language every evening at 2100, from 15 May–30 Sept.

For football fans, Monaco boasts one of Europe's top clubs at the futuristic **Stade Louis II**, Fontvielle. The pitch is actually two storeys above the ground. Tickets are easy to come by, as the team's usual crowd numbers 3000 in the empty cavern of the magnificent 40,000-seat stadium.

In Jan the Monte-Carlo **car rally** includes exciting stages in the hills behind Monaco. Feb sees the international **Circus Festival**.

In Apr the Monte-Carlo **Tennis Open** features top ATP players from the around the world, while in May the Formula One **Grand Prix** motor racing takes place.

July and Aug marks the international **Fireworks Festival**.

Sightseeing

Flash, fast and finely manicured, Monaco will live up to expectations. Do not expect any bargains, but it costs little to wander, look and brush with opulence.

The Principality became an independent state in 1308, when the Grimaldi family bought the 194-hectare site from Genoa. The state grew rich from taxes levied on the lemons and olives of Menton, until the Mentonnais revolted in 1848. Faced with bankruptcy, Prince Charles III decided to open a casino, and the rest is history. So much money poured in that taxes in the state were abolished, and the grateful citizens renamed the hill by the Casino *Monte-Carlo* (Mount Charles). Today the glitter has not worn off, and you are still likely to catch a glimpse of royalty in the street.

The **Casino** is the heart of Monte-Carlo, (the city within the Principality of Monaco) designed by Charles Garnier, and worth a look for the interior gilt alone.

The **Musée National** *17 av. Princesse Grace*, is stuffed full of dolls and figurines (1000–1830 summer, 1000–1200, 1430–1830 winter, admission FFr.26 adults, FFr.15 children). Up on the rock, the **Royal Palace** is small and not-so-regal and the changing of the guard takes place at 1155 precisely. Here too is the **Waxwork Museum**, with waxen Stephanies and Carolines next door to the real thing.

Monaco's most stimulating attraction is the **Musée Océanographique**, *av. St-Martin; tel: 93 15 36 00*, at the southern edge of the rock, open 0930–2000 summer, 0930–1900 Sept–June, admission FFr.60 adults, FFr.30 children. It is one of the world's great aquariums, developed by Jacques Cousteau. Wander the narrow streets of the old town on the rock, admiring the views. The **Cathédrale de Monaco**; *4 r. Colonel Bellando de castro; tel: 93 30 88 13*, contains the tomb of Princess Grace.

Above the skyscrapers, Monaco's botanical garden, the **Jardin Exotique:** *tel: 93 30 33 65*, (take bus no 2) sprouts 7000 tropical plants, and is accessible by public elevator and lift. Admission FFr.34 adults, FFr.17 children.

 Side Track from Monaco

LA TURBIE

Tourist Information: *Mairie; tel: 93 41 10 10*.

La Turbie is accessible by bus from Nice (four a day) and Monaco (one a day). Otherwise take a taxi (FFr.200) or it is a steep bicycle ride.

The culminating point of the ancient Roman Via Aurelia, La Turbie is renown for its huge Roman monument, 'the Trophy of the Alps'. Originally 45 m high, it was inscribed with the names of the 44 Ligurian tribes conquered by the Roman legions. Destroyed by Louis XV in 1705, the monument was rebuilt in 1930 to its present height of 35 m. The only other monument of its kind is in Romania. From the terrace, the view down over Monaco is breathtaking.

PARIS

Despite being a modern, changing capital, Paris maintains and parades its imperial grandeur and bohemian chic. Much of today's city was created by Baron Georges Haussmann, who wiped out large slices of medieval Paris to make way for his broad carriageways and long, straight vistas, designed for easier riot control of the rebellious citizens. They now form part of the city's unique character, along with its cafés and quais, its elegant hotels and town houses, its quirky and controversial new monuments. All combine to create a vibrant capital which can capture the heart of even the most cynical tourist.

Tourist Information

Tourist Office: (Paris Convention and Visitors Bureau), *127 av. des Champs Elysées, 75008 Paris* (near the Arc de Triomphe; metro: *Charles de Gaulle/ Etoile, George V*); *tel: (1) 49 52 53 54*. Open daily all year (except 25 Dec, 1 Jan and 1 May), 0900–2000. Guides, catalogues and phone cards are on sale here, as well as tickets for leisure parks, trips and cabarets, and museum passes. Leaflets on Paris and the rest of France are available on serve-yourself shelves. A *bureau de change* is open in the office Mon–Sat, 0900–1930, and there are SNCF (rail) and Disneyland Paris booking services.

Other offices run by the Paris Convention are based at the main railway terminals:

Gare du Nord (RER lines BD, metro: *Gare du Nord*); *tel: (1) 45 26 94 82*. Open Mon–Sat 0800–2100 (May–Oct); 0800–2000 (Nov–Apr).

Gare d'Austerlitz (RER line C, metro: *Gare d'Austerlitz*); *tel: (1) 45 84 91 70*. Open Mon–Sat 0800–1500.

Gare de l'Est (metro: *Gare de l'Est*); *tel: (1) 46 07 17 73*. Open 0800–2100 (May–Oct), 0800–2000 (Nov–Apr).

Gare de Lyon (RER line A, metro: *Gare de Lyon*); *tel: (1) 43 43 33 24*. Open 0800–2100 (May–Oct), 0800–2000 (Nov–Apr).

Gare Montparnasse (metro: *Montparnasse Bienvenüe*); *tel: (1) 43 22 19 19*. Open Mon–Sat 0800–2100 (May–Oct), 0800–2000 (Nov–Apr).

There is also an office at the **Eiffel Tower** (Tour Eiffel), which opens in high season and sells phone cards and excursion tickets (RER line C, Champ de Mars Tour Eiffel, metro: *Bir Hakeim*); *tel: (1) 45 51 22 15*. Open daily 1100–1800 (May–Sept).

Arriving and Departing

Airports

Roissy-Charles de Gaulle Airport is 26 km north-east of the city on autoroute A1 and has a 24-hr answering service giving flight times, *tel: (1) 48 62 22 80*. A *bureau de change, tel: (1) 48 62 83 11*, operates daily 0630–2330 and there is a hotel booking desk, *tel: (1) 48 62 27 29*, open daily 0700–1900.

A **Roissy Rail** service runs to the Gare du Nord every 15 mins 0530–2330; trains from the city to the airport run on line B3 to *Roissy Aéroport Charles de Gaulle*, 0630–2350, journey time: 35 mins. **Roissy Bus**, *tel: (1) 48 04 18 24,)* runs every 15 mins 0545–2300 from *Opéra Garnier*, journey time: 40 min to 1 hr. **Air France** coaches *tel: (1) 43 23 97 10* run every 12 mins 0540–2300 to *pl. Charles de Gaulle Etoile (av. Carnot)* and *porte Maillot;*

journey time: about 1 hr. Regular buses are slower but cost less – no. 350 runs to the Gare du Nord and the Gare de l'Est, and no. 351 to *pl. de la Nation*.

Orly Airport is 20 km south of the city on autoroute A6, and has its own 24-hour information service: *tel: (1) 49 75 15 15*. There is a *bureau de change* at Orly Sud, *tel: (1) 49 75 79 41*. Orly Rail (RER line C2) runs every 15 mins 0530–2330 to Gare d'Austerlitz and stations along the Left Bank; services to the airport run 0550–2325. A shuttle service, OrlyVal, runs between the airport and Gare Antony (RER line B) every 4 to 7 mins, 0550–2350. Orly Bus connects with *Denfert-Rochereau* metro station every 15 mins, 0630–2330 (from Paris to Orly 0600–2300), journey time 30 mins. Air France coaches, *tel: (1) 43 24 97 10*, travel every 12 mins 0550–2300 to the Gare Montparnasse (*av. du Maine*) and the Gare des Invalides, journey time 35 mins. The RATP (Paris Urban Transport) network has an information line, *tel: (1) 43 46 14 14*, open 0600–2100.

Stations

Paris has six mainline SNCF stations, all of which have tourist information offices, left luggage departments, cafés, restaurants, banks and *bureaux de change*; all are connected with the metro system and RER suburban lines. General information about train times and tickets is available (*tel: 30 64 50 50*); for reservations, *tel: (1) 45 65 60 00*.

Paris-Nord, *r. de Dunkerque*; *tel: (1) 49 95 10 00*, serves the UK, Belgium, Holland, Scandinavia and Boulogne and Calais. Paris-Est, *pl. du 11 Novembre 1918, 75010*; *tel: (1) 40 18 20 00* connects with north-east France, Switzerland, Austria, Germany and Luxembourg. Paris-St-Lazare, *r. d'Amsterdam, 75008*; *tel: (1) 42 85 88 00* serves, Dieppe and Normandy. Paris-Austerlitz, *7 blvd Hôpital, 75013*; *tel: (1) 45 84 14 18*, serves south and south-west France, the Loire Valley, Spain and Portugal. Paris-Lyon, *pl. Louis Armand, 75012*; *tel: (1) 40 19 60 00* serves the Auvergne, Provence, eastern and south-eastern France, the Alps, Italy and Greece. Paris-Montparnasse, *17 blvd de Vaugirard, 75014*; *tel: (1) 40 48 10 00*, connects with Versailles, Chartres, Brittany and the south-west coast.

Getting Around

Although it is possible to see Paris on foot, its worth taking advantage of the public transport system, which is efficient and well co-ordinated. The network is made up of buses, metro (underground/subway) and the RER suburban rail link. Metro stations and some hotels provide free maps of the bus, rail and metro networks; most also have free street maps. The RATP transport system (see map facing back cover) has a general information service *tel: (1) 43 46 14 14*, 0600–2100.

Tickets

Within the city centre, the same tickets can be used on buses, metro and RER. More than one ticket is required to travel through more than one zone; bus journeys usually take up several tickets, as they are split into more zones than metro and RER lines. The best value for a short stay is probably the ten-ticket carnet (booklet), currently FFr.39 (individual tickets are FFr.6.50).

For several journeys on a single day, buy a Formule 1 card at the central tourism office or any metro station. This gives unlimited travel for one day and can cover anything from the city centre (FFr.27) to five zones, taking in the airports (FFr.90), by

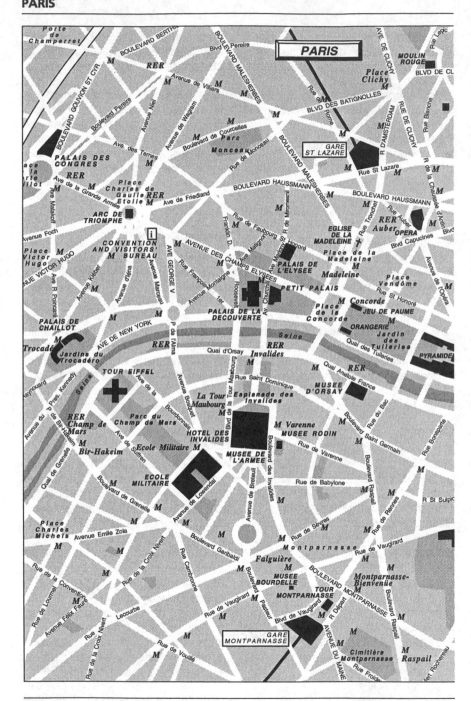

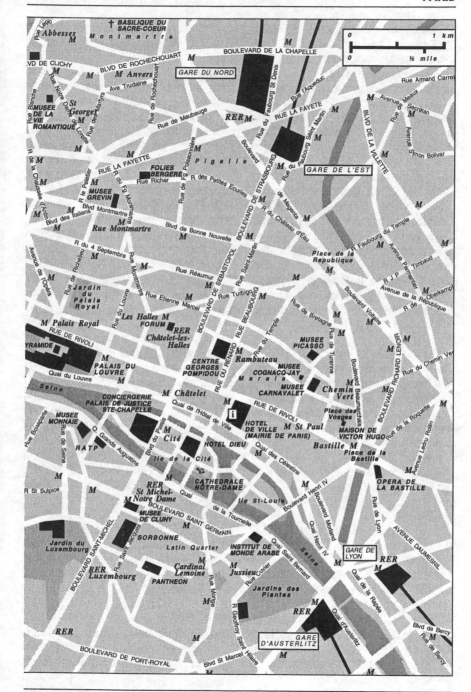

bus (including night buses), metro, RER and SNCF trains. It also includes travel on the Montmartre funicular train.

Paris Visite is a ticket valid for two (FFr.65, zones 1–3) or five consecutive days (FFr.275 for zones 1–5 plus airports), covering the whole RATP, RER, Paris and Île de France SNCF networks. It also includes night buses and airport services (Orly Bus, Orly Rail and Roissy Rail). You can buy it at the central tourism office, metro stations, RER/SNCF stations and airports.

For a weekly or monthly pass (**Carte Orange**), used by many Parisian commuters and available at metro stations, you will need passport-sized photos and identification. The monthly ticket (*coupon mensuel*) is valid from the first day of the month (FFr.219–526), the weekly ticket (*coupon hebdomadaire*) from Monday to Sunday (FFr.59–142).

Metro

The impressive metro system runs every few mins 0530 (first departure) to 0030 (last departure). Lines are known by their final destination, and are coded by colour and number on metro maps. Signs on the platforms indicate connecting lines (*correspondances*). Slot your ticket into the automatic barrier, then retrieve it, to get onto the platform.

Buses

Although you can use the same tickets on the bus as on the metro, you may need to use more, if your journey crosses more than one zone. Buses run 0630 (first departure) to 2030 (last departure), with some lines continuing until 0030.

There are also hourly night buses (*Noctambus*), which follow ten different routes from *pl. du Châtelet*, near the Hôtel de Ville, between 0100 and 0500.

River Journeys

Travelling along the Seine is an undeniably pleasant way of getting a quick look at some of Paris's most famous landmarks (Notre-Dame, the Eiffel Tower and the Louvre among them). There's no shortage of options for sightseeing boat trips, but perhaps the best known are the glass-topped **Bateaux-mouches**, that set out every 30 mins, 1000–1200 and 1330–2230 (summer) from the *pont d'Alma* (metro: *Alma-Marceau*). Winter trips are fewer. The boats travel to the Île-St-Louis and back, and provide running commentaries in several languages (which can be tricky to follow). For bookings *tel: (1) 42 25 96 10*; trips cost FFr.40. Other boat tours are operated by **Bateaux Vedettes de Paris**, *port de Suffren, 75007* (metro: *Bir Hakeim*); *tel: (1) 47 05 71 29* or *45 50 23 79*; trips from 1000, last departure 1900 (FFr.40); **Bateaux Vedettes du Pont-Neuf**, *square du Vert-Galant, 75001* (metro: *Pont-Neuf, Louvre*); *tel: (1) 46 33 98 38*; every half-hour 1000–1200, 1330–1830 (FFr.40); and **Bateaux Parisiens**, *port de la Bourdonnais, 75007* (metro: *Trocadéro*); *tel: (1) 44 11 33 44*, every half-hour 1000–2300 (FFr.45) and *quai Montebello, 75005* (metro: *St-Michel*); *tel: (1) 43 26 92 55*, nine sailings a day 1030–2200 (FFr.40).

The **Batobus** sails Apr–Sept, with no commentary, calling at the Eiffel Tower–Trocadéro; Musée d'Orsay, Passerelle des Arts–Musée du Louvre; Notre-Dame and Hôtel de Ville–Centre Georges Pompidou (FFr.12 each stop, FFr.60 for a day).

Taxis

Day and night fares are shown in the cars, and supplements are charged for journeys to and from stations or airports, fourth passengers, luggage and animals. Fares are generally reasonable; the pick-up charge is FFr.12, and tips of about 15 per cent are expected. Tariffs are divided into three categories: A (0700–1900 in Paris); B (1900–0700 in Paris and 0700–1900 in the suburbs) and C (1900–0700 in the suburbs). Complaints about taxis should be sent to **Service Taxi-Préfecture de Police**, *36 r. des Morillons, 75015, tel: (1) 45 31 14 80.*

Staying in Paris

Accommodation

Finding accommodation in Paris is only a problem in the busiest season (usually May, June, Sept and Oct); there are plenty of options in all price ranges.

Hotel chains in Paris include: *BW, Ca, Ch, Cd, Dm, Ex, GT, Ho, Hn, Hy, Ic, IH, Md, Me, Mp, Nv, Pu, RC, Sf, TH.*

Some of the most expensive hotels in the city have become attractions in their own right. The 18th-century **de Crillon**, *10 pl. de la Concorde, 75008; tel: (1) 44 71 15 00*, is set in a palace and has an opulent, marble-lined restaurant, Les Ambassadeurs; and the **Ritz**, *pl. Vendôme, 75001; tel: (1) 42 60 38 30*, provides up-to-date facilities in a splendid Louis XV setting; and the **Bristol**, *112 r. Faubourg St-Honoré, 75008; tel: (1) 42 66 91 45*, boasts a collection of Gobelin tapestries.

Cheaper accommodation is not hard to find. The Quartier Latin (Latin Quarter) and St-Germain-des-Près, on the Left Bank, have a good range of low to middle priced hotels, and many budget hotels are clustered round the Faubourg Montmartre, in the 9th *arrondissement*. The area around the Gare du Nord can be fairly sleazy and might best be avoided. Self-catering apartments can be arranged by **Paris Séjour**

Réservation, *90 av. des Champs Elysées, 75008; tel: (1) 42 56 30 00*; or **Bed and Breakfast 1**, *7 r. Campagne Première, 75014; tel: (1) 43 35 11 26* (self-catering and bed and breakfast).

The **Fédération Unie des Auberges de Jeunesse**, *27 r. Pajol, 75018; tel: (1) 46 47 00 01*, has a list of youth hostels in Paris and the rest of France. International Accommodation Centres offer sightseeing trips as well as cheap beds; a free list of addresses is provided by **UCRIF (Union des Centres de Rencontres Internationales de France)**, *72 r. Rambuteau, 75001* (metro: *Les Halles*); *tel: (1) 40 26 57 64*. **AJF (Accueil des Jeunes de France)**, opposite the Centre Pompidou, provide beds in the City University during the summer: contact them at *119 r. St-Martin, 75004* (metro: *Châtelet, Hôtel de Ville*); *tel: 42 77 87 80* (open 0900–1800). They also have offices at *139 blvd St-Michel, 75006* (metro: *Port Royal*); *tel: (1) 43 54 95 86* and in the *Gare du Nord; tel: (1) 42 85 86 19*, open Jun–Sept, 0730–2100.

HI: Le d'Artagnan, *80 r. Vitruve, 75020* (metro: *Porte-de-Bagnolet*); *tel: (1) 43 61 08 75* (rooms shut 1000–1400); **Cité des Sciences**, *1 r. Jean-Baptiste Clement, 93310 le Pré St-Gervais* (metro: *Hoche, Porte de Pantin*); *tel: (1) 48 43 24 11*; **Le Jules-Ferry**, *8 blvd Jules Ferry, 75011* (metro: *République*); *tel: (1) 43 57 55 60*; **Rue Marcel Duhamel**, *3 r. Marcel Duhamel, 91290 Arpajon* (RER line C4); *tel: 64 90 28 85*; and **Relais Européen de la Jeunesse**, *52 av. Robert Schumann, 91200 Athis-Mons* (RER line C); *tel: 69 84 81 39*. Rooms cost between FFr.100 and FFr.200 for each person, breakfast included.

For information about campsites near Paris, contact the **Fédération Française de Camping-Caravaning**, *78 r. de Rivoli, 75004; tel: (1) 42 72 84 08* (metro:

Hôtel de Ville), open Mon–Fri, 0900–1230 and 1330–1730.

Eating and Drinking

Despite the Parisian reputation for good food and high living, you are not guaranteed an exquisite meal wherever you go. By the same token, it is possible to eat very well without paying the earth. The vast range and number of restaurants, cafés and other watering holes makes choice the biggest problem, but there are rules of thumb to follow for eating and drinking on a tight budget. Brasseries are open all day and often well into the night; bistros are another alternative, ranging from the trendy and expensive to the cheap and basic. Self-service restaurants sell cheap, hot meals, and fast food of the McDonalds variety is easy to find; a far better lunchtime option is to go for a *crêperie* stand, selling plain or filled pancakes, or to buy picnic ingredients (or a stuffed *baguette*) at a *charcuterie* (delicatessen).

For evening meals, study the set menus displayed outside most restaurants; these often provide a reasonable choice of good food at affordable prices, usually from about FFr.55.

The side streets of Le Marais, Montmartre and Montparnasse are good areas to wander in search of ethnic specialities. North African and East European food can be found in the Jewish Quarter round the *r. des Rosiers*, and in the Latin Quarter on *r. Xavier Privas*. Greek stalls and restaurants line the *r. de la Hachette* and *r. de la Harpe*, near the river, and you will find Asian, Russian, Turkish, Italian, Vietnamese, Moroccan and almost any other national dishes you care to try, just by strolling through the busiest quarters. The weekly listings magazines, *Pariscope*, provides a guide to Paris restaurants by nationality and speciality.

Communications

The main **post office** (*La Poste*) is at *52 r. du Louvre, 75001; tel: (1) 40 28 20 00* (metro: *Louvre, Rivoli*). It opens 24 hrs a day, but only for telephone, emergency cash withdrawal and *poste restante* services after 1900. Stamps can also be bought at stationery and tobacco shops (*tabacs*). Post boxes are yellow and fixed to the wall.

Phone cards can be bought at post offices, tourist offices, SNCF ticket offices, the metro and RER stations, France Telecom offices and *tabacs*. To phone Paris from abroad, dial 33 (France) 1 (Paris) and the number. To phone Paris from elsewhere in France dial 16 + 1 + the number. To phone the French provinces from Paris dial 16 and the number, and to phone abroad from Paris, dial 19 and the country code, followed by the number.

Money

Money can be changed at the banks or at *bureaux de change* dotted throughout the city. **Thomas Cook** bureaux de change locations are listed on p. 199.

Numbers to ring about lost or stolen credit cards are: American Express *tel: (1) 47 77 72 00*; MasterCard/Eurocard *tel: (1) 45 67 84 84*; JCB International *tel: (1) 42 86 06 01*; Diners Club *tel: (1) 47 62 75 00*; Visa International *tel: (1) 42 77 11 90*.

Consulates

Australia: *4 r. Jean Rey, 75015; tel: (1) 40 59 33 00* (metro: *Bir Hakeim*).
Canada: *35 av. Montaigne, 75008; tel: (1) 47 23 01 01* (metro: *Franklin D Roosevelt*).
Republic of Ireland: *4 r. Rude, 75016; tel: (1) 45 00 20 87* (metro: *Etoile*).
New Zealand: *7ter r. L. da Vinci, 75016; tel: (1) 45 00 24 11* (metro: *Victor Hugo*).

UK: *16 r. d'Anjou, 75008* (metro: *Madeleine*); *tel: (1) 42 66 91 42.*
USA: *2 r. St-Florentin, 75001; tel: (1) 42 96 14 88* (metro: *Concorde*).

Entertainment

Organised entertainment generally comes at a cost. Some of the cheapest high-quality events are in the field of classical music; it's also worth looking out for fringe and student entertainment. The monthly *Paris Sélection* and annual *Saisons de Paris* listings are provided at the tourist office, which also has a 24-hr information line: *tel: (1) 49 52 53 56.* Two inexpensive weekly listings are *l'Officiel des Spectacles* and *Pariscope* (with an English language *Time Out* section).

Theatre tickets can be bought at half-price for same-day performances from the kiosks at *15 pl. de la Madeleine, 75008* (metro: *Madeleine*), open Tues–Sat 1230–2000, Sunday 1230–1600; and at RER *Châtelet–Les Halles station, 75001*, open 1230–1930, closed Sun, Mon and public holidays.

Clubs and Discos

The club scene is lively but unpredictable. In the trendier venues, you can be turned away at the door for not looking the part (whatever the part might be); once inside, you may well be expected to pay extortionate prices for drinks. Most places get going after midnight and stay open till dawn. One of the more relatively affordable is **Le Tchatch au Tango**, *13 r. au Maire, 75004* (metro: *Arts-et-Métiers*); *tel: (1) 42 72 17 78*, open Fri–Sat 2300–0500; evening sessions here concentrate on Latin American and African beats.

A pricier institution is **Les Bains**, *7 r. du Bourg l'Abbé, 75003*; (metro: *Etienne–Marcel*) *tel: (1) 48 87 01 80*, open 2330–

Thomas Cook

Thomas Cook bureaux de change in Paris are open seven days a week and have extended opening hours.

As well as encashing Thomas Cook Travellers' Cheques free of commission charges, and providing emergency assistance in the case of lost or stolen Thomas Cook Travellers' Cheques and to holders of MasterCards, they offer foreign exchange facilities. In addition most sell maps and Thomas Cook publications.

Thomas Cook bureaux can be found at the following locations in Paris:

194 r. de Rivoli
4 r. St-Honoré
25 blvd des Capucines
36–42 r. Rambuteau
11 quai St-Michel
4 blvd St-Michel
24 r. St-André des Arts
Port de la Bourdonnais
Tour Eiffel Champs de Mars
52 av. des Champs Elysées
73 av. des Champs Elysées
125 av. des Champs Elysées
Gare St-Lazare
8 pl. de l'Opéra
Gare du Nord
Gare de l'Est
Gare Montparnasse
82 av. de la Grande Armée*
2 r. Lepic
84 blvd de Clichy
14 r. Norvins
8–10 r. Steinkerque

0600 (FFr.140). Set in a former Turkish bath, it still draws the trend-setters and has a restaurant upstairs.

Jazz clubs are very popular in Paris, and range from so-so bands in tiny bars to world-famous names in prestigious venues. Many jazz clubs have quite hefty entrance charges, and seating space is often at a premium. Look round St-Germain-des-Près and the r. des Lombards, where several clubs are based.

Cabarets and Floor Shows

The feathers, sequins and topless, leggy dancing girls passed off as essential Paris are geared to tourists and still attract big audiences. Tickets can include dinner or just the show, and are expensive. The best known names are: **Bal du Moulin Rouge**, 83 blvd de Clichy, pl. Blanche, 75009 (metro: Blanche); tel: (1) 46 06 00 19, from FFr.670; **Crazy Horse Saloon**, 12 av. George V, 75008 (metro: George V); tel: (1) 47 23 32 32, prices ranging from FFr.290–590; **Le Lido de Paris**, 116 bis, av. des Champs Elysées, 75008 (metro: George V); tel: (1) 40 76 56 10, from FFr.670; and the **Folies-Bergère**, 32 r. Richer, 75009 (metro: Cadet/r. Montmartre); tel: (1) 44 79 98 98, from FFr.670 (for dinner).

Classical Music

Free concerts are regular features in churches and museums (check in the listings magazines or at the tourist office for details), and there is a free organ recital at Notre-Dame every Sun at 1745. Otherwise, musical events are surprisingly limited for a major European capital. Concert auditoriums include: **Salle Cortot**, 78 r. Cardinet, 75017 (metro: Malesherbes); tel: (1) 47 63 85 72; **Salle Gaveau**, 45 r. de la Boétie, 75008 (metro: Miromesnil); tel: (1) 49 53 05 07; **Salle Pleyel**, 252 r. du Faubourg-St-Honoré, 75008 (metro: Ternes); tel: (1) 45 61 06 30; **Théâtre Musical de Paris Châtelet**, 2 r. Edouard Colonne, 75001 (metro: Châtelet); tel: (1) 42 33 00 00, and **Théâtre des Champs Elysées**, 15 av. Montaigne, 75008 (metro: Alma Marceau); tel: (1) 49 52 50 51.

Opera is an expensive pursuit, but the cheapest seats are worth considering. The controversial (in design and cost) **Opéra de Paris-Bastille**, 120 r. de Lyon, 75012 (metro: Bastille); tel: (1) 44 73 13 00, has been the venue for major performances since 1990; tickets range from about FFr.60 to FFr.570. Opera can also be heard at the **Opéra-Comique**, Salle Favard, 5 r. Favard, 75002 (metro: Richelieu Drouot); tel: (1) 42 96 12 20.

Ballet is performed by the Ballet de l'Opéra de Paris at the dazzlingly baroque **Opéra de Paris Garnier**, 8 r. Scribe, 75009 (metro: Opéra); tel: (1) 47 42 53 71. Contemporary dance performances are held in several venues, particularly in the Bastille area; try the **Théâtre de la Bastille**, 76 r. de la Roquette, 75011; tel: (1) 43 57 42 14 (metro: Bastille).

Theatre

Classical theatre – Molière, Racine, etc. – is the main repertoire of the **Comédie Française**, Salle Richelieu, 2 r. de Richelieu, 75001 (metro: Palais Royal); tel: (1) 40 15 00 15. Remainder tickets can be bought at a discount for same-day performances. Contemporary theatre is represented by director Ariane Mnouchkine's theatre co-operative, set in an old munitions factory, **Théâtre du Soleil**, La Cartoucherie, rte Champ de Manoeuvres, 75012 (metro: Vincennes); tel: (1) 43 74 87 63; modern theatre (and dance) is also performed at the **Théâtre de la Ville**, 2 pl. du Châtelet, 75004 (metro: Châtelet); tel: (1) 42 74 22 77, and at the **Théâtre de la Bastille** (see Classical Music, above).

Cinema

Finding a good film is no problem in Paris, even if you speak little or no French. The Champs Elysées is lined with cinemas – wander down here to see the new releases, or explore Les Halles and the Latin Quarter. Look for films marked VO (*Version Originale*) and/or *soustitres Français* – these are foreign films shown in their original version, with French subtitles. Seats are cheaper on Mon and there are discounts for children, students and senior citizens Mon–Thurs. Look through the listings magazines for smaller venues, often geared to student audiences, showing old and/or cult films.

If you want to enjoy the cinema as well as the film, visit **La Pagode**, *57 bis r. de Babylone, 75007* (metro: *François Xavier*); *tel: (1) 47 05 12 15*, an oriental extravaganza decorated with dragons and warriors. Old movies are shown daily at the **Cinémathèque Française**, *Palais de Chaillot, pl. du Trocadéro, 75016* (metro: *Trocadéro*); *tel: (1) 45 53 21 86*, and videos covering almost everything you can imagine are run Tues–Sun, 1230–2300, Sat 1000–2300 at the **Vidéothèque de Paris**, *Forum des Halles, porte St-Eustache, 2 Grande Galerie, 75001* (metro: *Les Halles*); *tel: (1) 40 28 93 28*.

Spectator Sports

Details of sporting events and sports clubs are listed in the *Sports-Loisirs* section of the *Pariscope* listings magazine, and on the information line run by **Allô-Sports**, *25 blvd de Bourdon, 75004* (metro: *Bastille*); *tel: (1) 42 76 54 54*.

Soccer and rugby matches are held at **Parc des Princes**, *24 r. du Commandant-Guilbaud, 75016* (metro: *Porte de St-Cloud*); *tel: (1) 42 88 02 76*. Horse races, cycle races and hockey are held at the **Palais Omnisports Paris Bercy**, *8 blvd de Bercy, 75012* (metro: *Bercy*); *tel: 44 68 44 68*.

Events

The most famous annual celebration in Paris is **Bastille Day**, on 13–14 July, when fireworks and parades mark the anniversary of the storming of the city prison in 1789. Other major events include **workers' marches** on May Day (1 May); the **French Tennis Open Championships** at **Roland-Garros**, *2 av. Gordon Bennett, 75016*; *tel: (1) 47 43 48 00* (metro: *Porte d'Auteuil*) in late May–early June; the **Fête de la Musique**, with free concerts, in July; the final of the **Tour de France** along the Champs Elysées on the last Sun of July; and the **Festival de Jazz** in late October.

The tourist office produces a guide, *Saisons de Paris*, giving details of the main events and festivals.

Shopping

Paris is a centre of high fashion and a centre of shopping, and the two combine to create impressive window displays and astronomical price tags. To admire (if not to buy) the designer styles on sale, head for the *r. de Faubourg St-Honoré*, *av. Montaigne* and the *r. de Rivoli*. More reasonable prices can be tracked down at Les Halles and St-Germain-des-Prés. The most famous department stores are **Galeries Lafayette**, *40 blvd Haussmann, 75009*; *tel: (1) 42 82 34 56* (metro: *Chaussée d'Antin*); **Printemps**, *64 blvd Haussmann, 75009*; *tel: (1) 42 82 50 00* (metro: *Havre Caumartin*) and, on the Left Bank, **Au Bon Marché**, *38 r. de Sèvres, 75007*; *tel: (1) 42 60 33 45* (metro: *Sèvres Babylone*).

Markets are big business in Paris –

covered and open-air – the tourist office produces a free list. Perhaps the best-known flea-market is at **porte de Clignancourt**, St Ouen (metro: *St Ouen/Clignancourt*), Sat–Mon, 0730–1900, with 16 separate markets, including Jules-Valles (curios, lace and post cards), Marché Paul-Bert (second-hand goods), Marché Serpette (1900–30 products) and Marché Malik (second-hand clothes and records). The **porte de Montreuil** market (metro: *porte de Montreuil*), either side of the ring road, operates Sun–Mon, 0700–1930, selling pretty well anything. For food, visit the daily street market or **r. Mouffetard** (metro: *Censier Daubenton*) and the **r. de Buci/r. de Seine** (closed Mon; metro: *Mabillon*); or the organic products market on *blvd Raspail*, between *r. du Cherche-Midi* and *r. de Rennes*, on Sun mornings (metro: *Rennes*). A second-hand book market opens at weekends opposite *87 r. Brancion* (metro: *Vanves*).

Sightseeing

As most museums and monuments in Paris charge substantial entrance fees, it's worth investing in a **Carte Inter-Musée**, or Museum Pass, sold at the tourist office, metro stations and the main museums. This gives access to most of the popular museums for one (FFr.60), three (FFr.120) or five (FFr.170) days. Holders of international student identity cards can get in to some places for half price, and reduced rates are available to senior citizens (over 60), who may need their passports as proof of age, and children.

Museums run by the city tend to be closed on Mon, and give free entry to their permanent collections on Sun. National museums usually close on Tues, except the Musée Rodin and the Musée d'Orsay, which shut on Mon.

Daily walking tours of the city's monuments, or on specific themes, are run by the **Caisse Nationale des Monuments Historiques et des Sites**, *Hôtel de Sully, 62 r. St Antoine, 75004; tel: (1) 44 61 21 50* (metro: *St-Paul*). Guided cycling tours of Paris are organised by **Paris by Cycle**, *2 r. de la Jonquière, 75017; tel: (1) 42 63 36 63* (metro: *Porte de Clichy*) and **Mountain Bike Trip**, *6 pl. Etienne Pernet, 75015; tel: (1) 48 42 57 87* (metro: *Félix Faure*).

For the less energetic, bus tours are operated by **Cityrama**, *4 pl. des Pyramides, 75001; tel: (1) 42 60 30 14* (metro: *Palais Royal*) and **France Tourisme/Paris Vision**, *214 r. de Rivoli, 75001; tel: (1) 42 60 30 01* (metro: *Tuileries*) both running hourly 0930–1430; and by **Paris Bus Service**, *20 av. F Roosevelt, 94300, Vincennes; tel: (1) 43 65 55 55*, leaving from the *pl. du Trocadéro* at 1015 and from the Eiffel Tower at 1030 (six buses a day). The **Balabus** takes a route tailored for visitors, passing all the main sights, on Sundays and Public Holidays (15 Apr to 30 Sept), from 1200 to 2100. Its termini are Puteaux–La Défense and Gare de Lyon.

Paris is a relatively compact city, and many of its popular sights are conveniently grouped within walking distance or a short metro-ride. Most of the stately monuments are on the **Rive Droite** (Right Bank); the **Rive Gauche** (Left Bank) has a more casual and intimate character, despite incongruous additions such as the smooth, glass Tour Montparnasse and the new Bibliothèque de France, still mostly under wraps. In the middle of the River Seine, which divides the two banks, are the *Îles* (islands), where the city started life with the first settlement of the Celtic *Parisii* tribe. The **Île de la Cité** and the **Île St-Louis** are linked by a footbridge and provide some of the most elegant of Parisian architecture.

The Right Bank

The **Arc de Triomphe**, *pl. Charles de Gaulle/Etoile* (metro: *Charles de Gaulle Etoile*) is a handy first stop after visiting the tourist centre. Built by Chalgrin to praise the victories of Napoleon, the triumphal arch sits at the head of the Champs Elysées, with 11 other avenues also radiating out from its base. Open 0930–1830, till 2200 Fri (summer), 1000–1700 (winter); FFr.31. At the opposite end of the Champs Elysées is the **pl. de la Concorde**, the largest square in Paris, which was the scene of over a thousand executions during the Revolution. The 23 m-high, 230-tonne pink granite Obelisk was given to King Louis-Philippe by the Viceroy of Egypt in 1831 and is over 3000 years old, having originally been in the Temple of Luxor.

From the *pl. de la Concorde*, the 16th-century **Jardin des Tuileries** (re-landscaped by Le Nôtre in the 17th century) lead up to the Louvre (see below). Don't expect shady lawns and rambling paths – French parks tend to be formal set pieces, with wide walkways, fountains and flower borders. The gardens are the setting for two galleries: the **Jeu de Paume**, *20 r. Royale, Jardins des Tuileries, 75008* (metro: *Concorde*), open Tues 1200–2130, Wed–Fri 1200–1900, Sat and Sun 1000–1900 (FFr.35), which shows changing exhibitions of modern art; and the **Orangerie**, *pl. de la Concorde, Jardins des Tuileries, 75001* (metro: *Concorde*), open 0945–1715, closed Tues (FFr.27), where the Jean Walter and Paul Guillaume Collection includes Renoir, Matisse, Derain, Monet and Picasso. A *grand projet* is still in progress linking the Jardin des Tuileries and the Louvre, making it possible to walk from St-Germain-l'Auxerrois to the *pl. de la Concorde*, and from the river to the Palais de Justice, without interruption.

New subways, with car parks and shops, have already been installed by the **Musée du Louvre**, *cour Napoléon* or *Pavillon de Flore, r. de Rivoli, 75001* (metro: *Palais Royal/Musée du Louvre*), open Wed–Mon 0900–1800, till 2145 on Mon and Wed (FFr.40 till 1500; FFr.20 after 1500 and all day Sun). The Louvre's vast collection of 30,000 works of art covers everything from Greek, Roman and Egyptian antiquities to European art of the 19th century, including the *Mona Lisa*, usually impossible to see for the crowds of masterpiece-spotters. It takes several visits to get the best from the museum – don't expect to do the lot in one go. I M Pei's glass pyramid has formed the Louvre's startling entrance since 1989.

Further to the east of the Louvre is the area known as **Le Marais**, one of the oldest areas of the city, worth exploring for its 17th-century *hôtels* (town houses) and the lovely **pl. des Vosges**, lined with elegant arcades and houses. This is the setting for the **Maison de Victor Hugo**, *Hôtel de Rohan Guémené, 6 pl. des Vosges, 75004* (metro: *Bastille, St-Paul, Chemin Vert*), open Tues–Sun 1000–1745 (FFr.17). The writer lived here from 1832 to 1848 and is recalled with drawings, furniture and memorabilia. Two of the city's best known museums are housed in impressive Le Marais buildings. The **Musée Picasso**, *Hôtel de Juigué-Salé, 5 r. de Thorigny, 75003* (metro: *St-Paul, Chemin Vert*), open Wed–Mon 0930–1800 (summer), 0930–1730 (winter), FFr.27 (FFr.18 on Sun), displays thousands of paintings, sculptures and sketches by the great man in a renovated 17th-century house. The **Musée Carnavalet** is part of the Musée Historique de la Ville de Paris, *23 r. de Sévigné, 75003* (metro: *St-Paul, Chemin de*

Vert), open Tues–Sun 1000–1740 (FFr.27). It occupies a 16th-century mansion, once the home of writer Madame de Sévigné, and traces the history of Paris from its beginnings to the 20th century. Displays relating to the period from 1789 are housed in the next-door Hôtel le Peletier de St-Fargeau. (The tourist office provides a list of the principal town houses in Le Marais).

Between these two museums and the Louvre, on the western edge of Le Marais, is a building in radically different style: the **Centre National d'Art et de Culture Georges Pompidou** (the **Beaubourg**), *r. Rambuteau/r. St-Merri, 75004* (metro: *Châtelet, Les Halles*), open Wed–Mon 1000–2200; Sat, Sun and public holidays 1200–2200; modern art museum till 1800, or 2200 on Fri (FFr.30, free on Sun 1000–1400). This inside-out construction of see-through escalators, pipes and tubes, houses a library, a music and acoustics research institute, an architecture and design centre and the draw for most tourists – the modern art museum, on the fourth floor. This riveting collection includes work by Picasso, Braque, Miro, Dali, Kandinski, Klee, Giacometti and every other major (and the odd minor) force in art since the beginning of the 20th century.

Further to the east of the city, celebrated remains lie in tombs of all shapes, sizes, dates and designs in the huge **Cimetière du Père-Lachaise**, *blvd de Ménilmontant, 75020* (metro: *Gambetta, Père-Lachaise*), open 0800–1730. Some of the biggest draws are Jim Morrison, Edith Piaf, Oscar Wilde and Abélard and Héloïse.

Over to the south-west of the centre, following the river bend, is another clutch of Right Bank sights. Modern and contemporary art is displayed in the **Musée d'Art Moderne de la Ville de Paris**, *11 av.*

du Président-Wilson, 75016 (metro: *Iéna*), open Tues–Fri 1000–1730, Sat and Sun 1000–1900 (FFr.45 for a combined ticket). It also includes a museum specifically for children, and is housed in an enormous colonnaded building, designed for the Universal Exhibition in 1937. Also designed as an exhibition piece in 1937 is the **Palais de Chaillot**, *pl. du Trocadéro, 75016* (metro: *Trocadéro*), adorned with bronze statues and columns, and housing four museums: the Musée du Cinéma (FFr.25), Musée National des Monuments Français (FFr.21), Musée de la Marine (FFr.31) and Musée de l'Homme (FFr.25), and the Théâtre National de Chaillot. The **Musée Marmottan**, *2 r. Louis Boilly, 75016* (metro: *La Muette*), open Tues–Sun 1000–1730 (FFr.35), shows works by artists including Renoir, Pissaro and particularly Monet. Set in a 19th-century house, it sits between the quiet **Jardin du Ranelagh** and the broad sweep of the **Bois de Boulogne** (metro: *Porte Maillot, Porte d'Auteuil*), which encompasses seven lakes and several gardens.

Further Out

North of the river, **Montmartre**, the area once haunted by artists and their hangers-on, climbs to a lookout point with more accessible views of the city than those from the Eiffel or Montparnasse towers or La Défense (see below). Topping the hill are the white cupolas of **Sacré-Coeur**, built at the turn of the century and now besieged by tourists and touts. The **Musée de Montmartre**, *12 r. Cortot, 75018* (metro: *Lamarck-Caulaincourt, Anvers, plus funicular railway*), open Tues–Sun 1100–1800 (FFr.25) traces the history of the quarter.

Out on the north-eastern edge of the city, the **Parc de la Villette** (metro: *Porte de la Villette*) has a collection of facilities, including two concert halls, Cité de la Musique and Le Zénith, and the popular **Cité des Sciences et de l'Industrie**, *30 av. Corentin-Cariou, 75019* (metro: *Porte de la Villette*), open Tues–Sun 1000–1800 (FFr.45), presenting technical innovations in a futuristic setting.

The Left Bank

The Left Bank may have fewer grand monuments than the Right Bank, but it does have a lively, young atmosphere, and one of the most popular and universally recognisable sights of all: the **Eiffel Tower** (Tour Eiffel), *Champ de Mars, 75007* (metro: *Bir Hakeim, Trocadéro*); open 0930–2300 (Sept–June), 0900–2400 (July–Aug). Built by Gustave Eiffel for the 1889 Universal Exhibition, the 307 m-high iron tower was meant to be a temporary structure, but was saved from demolition in 1910 and now attracts about four million visitors every year. Lifts travel up to the third floor for views of Paris and the Île de France. Fees range from FFr.12 for toiling up the stairs to the second floor to FFr.53 for taking the lift to the third.

Following the river upstream, you reach the *Esplanade des Invalides*, at the head of which is the magnificent 17th-century **Invalides**, *av. de Tourville, 75007* (metro: *Latour Maubourg, Invalides*), open 1000–1645 (winter), 1000–1745 (summer). Commissioned by Louis XIV as a home for retired soldiers, the grandiose complex of buildings includes the 'soldiers' church', **Église St-Louis des Invalides**, and the **Église du Dôme des Invalides**, which houses Napoleon's porphyry tomb. In the Hôtel des Invalides itself is the **Musée de l'Armée**, *pl. Vauban, 75007* (metro: *Varenne, Invalides*), open 1000–1700 (summer), 1000–1800 (winter), closed public holidays (FFr.34). Its collection of

military memorabilia includes armour, uniforms and relics associated with Napoleon.

On the eastern side of the Invalides, near the Musée de l'Armée, is the **Musée Rodin**, *Hôtel Biron, 77 r. de Varenne, 75007* (metro: *Varenne*), open Tues–Sun, 0930–1745 (summer), 1000–1700 (winter), FFr.27. Set in an 18th-century house in its own grounds, the museum traces Rodin's career, with several of his sculptures dotted around the beautiful gardens. Continue east along the river to reach the former railway station that now houses the airy **Musée d'Orsay**, *1 r. de Bellechasse, 75007* (metro: *Solférino*), open Tues–Sun, 0900–1800 (summer), 1000–1800 (winter except Sun, from 0900); open till 2145 Thur (FFr.36; FFr.24 on Sun). This wide-ranging display of fine arts covers the period from the 1840s to 1914 including work by Ingres, Delacroix, Gaugin, Cézanne, Manet and Renoir, arranged on three floors spanning a wide central hall.

Further to the east are the arty, historic areas of **St-Germain-des-Près** and the **Latin Quarter**, so-called because it is the home of the **Sorbonne**, once peopled with Latin-speaking scholars, and Papal territory until the 18th century. This is still the heart of the student community and is perfect for wandering through side streets and squares and exploring cafés and little shops. It is also the site of the city's oldest Roman remains and a superb museum of medieval exhibits: the **Musée National du Moyen Age (Musée de Cluny)**, *6 pl. Paul-Painevé, 75005* (metro: *Cluny, Sain-Michel*), open Wed–Mon 0915–1745 (FFr.27, FFr.18 on Sun). The 16th-century mansion housing the collection stands over remains of 2nd-century Roman baths and vaults; above is the absorbing display of medieval tapestries, costumes, jewellery and relics. Guided tours are held on Wed,

Sat and Sun at 1430 (the baths and vaults) and 1600 (the collections).

Two famous gardens skirt the edge of the Latin Quarter. The **Jardin du Luxembourg** is attached to the Palais du Luxembourg, *15 r. de Vaugirard, 75006* (metro: *Luxembourg*). Both were created in the 17th century for Marie de Médicis, the widow of King Henry IV, who wanted an Italianate design to remind her of her native land. The tree-lined avenues, boating pond and strategically placed iron seats are favourites with Parisians in need of a break. On the bank of the Seine is the **Jardin des Plantes**, *57 r. Cuvier, 75005* (metro: *Gare d'Austerlitz*), open 0800–2000 (summer), 0800–1730 (winter). This park was founded by Louis XIII for the cultivation of medicinal plants, and includes a *menagerie*, open 0900–1800 (summer), 0900–1700 (winter) and galleries of palaeontology, anatomy and mineralogy, open Wed–Mon 1000–1700.

Further south of the river, Montparnasse was once known for its literary and artistic associations, but is now dominated by the 209 m steel and glass **Tour Montparnasse**, *33 av. du Maine, 75015* (metro: *Montparnasse Bienvenue*), open 0930–2330 (summer), 1000–2230 (winter), FFr.40 for the viewing floor, FFr.32 for the 56th floor exhibition and film about Paris. Completed in the 1970s, it met with a frosty reception from many Parisians, who saw it as something of a carbuncle. But views from its 59th storey are breathtaking, nevertheless. The nearby **Cimetière du Montparnasse**, *3 blvd Edgar Quinet, 75014* (metro: *Edgar Quinet*) dates from 1824 and is the last resting place of such greats as Baudelaire and Sartre.

The Îles

Between the Right and Left Banks, in the middle of the Seine, are the city's two *Îles* (islands). The **Île St Louis** is mainly composed of 17th-century houses, restaurants and shops; several impressive monuments manage to squeeze onto the large **Île de la Cité**. All road distances in France start at the zero km point in the square of **Notre-Dame**, *Parvis de Notre-Dame, 75004* (metro: *Cité*). The twin-towered Gothic cathedral was conceived by Maurice de Sully and built between 1163 and 1345. Statues, gargoyles and carvings cover the façade and the vast interior includes 37 medieval chapels. Open daily 0800–1900, Sun till 2000. Tours of the cathedral are conducted 0930–1830 (1 Apr–15 Sept), 0930–1730 (16 Sept–31 Oct) and 1000–1700 (1 Nov–31 Mar); FFr.31. The crypt, which houses archaeological items dating from the Gallo-Roman era to the 19th century, is open to the public 1000–1800 (summer), 1000–1700 (winter), closed public holidays.

At the north-western end of the Île de la Cité is the medieval **Palais de Justice**, *4 blvd du Palais, 75001* (metro: *Cité*), open Mon–Fri, 0900–1700, closed public holidays. This was originally the site of the Roman governors' palace, later occupied by Merovingian and Capetian monarchs. Tucked away in its courtyard is the 700-year-old church of **Ste-Chapelle**, open 0930–1800 (summer), 1000–1700 (winter), FFr.26. Built in less than three years (1246–48) for the relics bought by Louis IX during the Crusades, its chief glory is the series of dazzling stained-glass windows, over 600 sq m in all, showing over a thousand scenes from the Bible. A more sinister atmosphere pervades the Capetian **Conciergerie**, *1 quai de l'Horloge, 75001* (metro: *Cité, St-Michel, Châtelet*), open 0930–1800 (summer), 1000–1630 (winter), closed public holidays (FFr.26). Built for

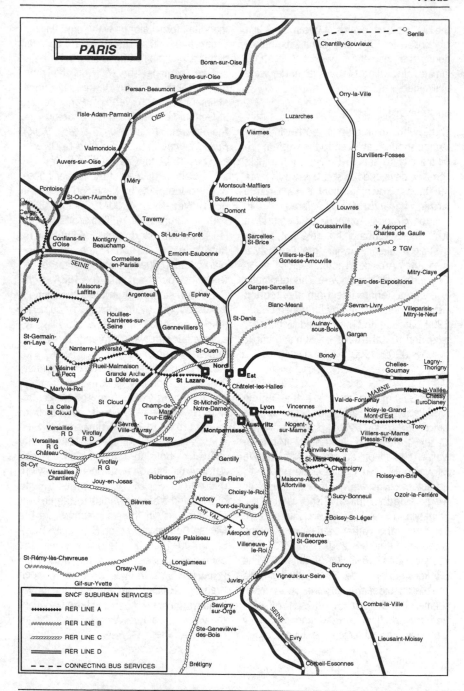

Greater Paris Transport Map

the king's palace guards, it became the first city prison in 1391 and earned its infamy during the Revolution, when half its 4000 inmates (including Marie-Antoinette) were guillotined.

Further Out

Those with an interest in post-war architecture should travel out to the western rim of the city to see La Défense, a business complex developed in spurts since the late 1950s. Its crowning glory is **La Grande Arche**, *1 parvis de la Défense, 92040* (metro: *Grande Arche de La Défense*), a white marble cube with a hole in it, set on a straight alignment, in true Paris style, with the Arc de Triomphe, pl. de la Concorde and the Louvre. This geometry is easier to appreciate from the rooftop viewing point reached by lift. Open 0900–1900, Sat, Sun and public holidays till 2000 (summer); 0900–1800, Sat, Sun and public holidays 0900–1900 (winter, FFr.40).

Out of Town

About 32 km east of Paris is the **Disneyland Paris** theme park; central reservations office: *BP 100, 77777 Marne-la-Vallée, Cedex 4* (RER line A, *Chessy Marne-la-Vallée*; signed off autoroute A4). Despite its well publicised troubles, the resort still attracts crowds and admiration with its Magic Kingdom full of Disney characters, Fantasyland castle, Discoveryland flight simulator and other variations on the escapism theme (FFr.250).

Parc Astérix, *BP8-60128 Plailly* (RER line B3 *Roissy-Charles de Gaulle*, then shuttle bus), is an older theme park, on a French theme. The ancient Gauls Asterix, Obelix and co, originally devised and drawn by Goscinny and Uderzo, are given larger-than-life form along with their village, Greek and Roman towns and associated gimmicks. Open 1000–1900 (FFr.150).

Two genuine survivors of the more recent past can be visited at Rueil-Malmaison, north-west of Paris beyond St-Germain-en-Laye. The **Château de Malmaison**, *1 av. du Château, 92500 Rueil-Malmaison* (RER line A to La Défense and bus 158A to 'Château'); *tel: (1) 47 49 20 07*, is a 17th-century manor-house, given to Josephine by Napoleon in 1799. It opens Wed–Mon, 1000–1200 and 1330–1700 in summer, till 1630 in winter (FFr.27, FFr.18 on Sun). Next to it is the **Château de Bois-Préau**, *1 av. de l'Impératrice Joséphine, 92500 Rueil-Malmaison* (reached via the same route, but take the 158A to the *Bois-Préau* stop). Built in the same century, it was bought by Josephine to house her retinue in 1809 and now has displays associated with Napoleon and his exile on St Helena (open Wed–Mon, 1030–1230, 1400–1730 in summer, till 1700 in winter; FFr.12). The journey to both manors takes about 45 mins to 1 hr from the city centre.

St-Germain-en-Laye itself, 30 mins from Paris en route to Rueil-Malmaison (RER line A1), is the setting for a 12th-century château housing the **Musée des Antiquités Nationales**, open Wed–Mon, 0900–1715 (FFr.21), which traces the life of mankind from his origins to the time of Charlemagne. In the same suburb are the **Musée Debussy**, *38 r. du Pain*, open Tues–Sat, 1400–1800, in the house where the composer was born; and the **Musée du Prieuré**, *2 bis, r. Maurice Den is*, open Wed–Fri, 1000–1730, Sat, Sun and public holidays 1000–1830 (FFr.25), dedicated to the work of painter Maurice Denis and his contemporaries.

PARIS to BRUSSELS

This route links the capitals of France and Belgium, largely travelling through the flat French region of Picardy. The route visits Chantilly and Compiègne, both notable for their châteaux, the ancient cathedral town of Laon, and Mons, close to the World War I battlefields.

TRAINS

ETT table: 18, 101, 203.

→ Fast Track

Jan 1995 saw the introduction of TGV services between Paris Nord and Brussels Midi using the new high-speed line to Lille, although journey times must wait until the new line between Lille and Brussels is completed to see any great improvements. At the moment three TGVs operate each day on this route with journey times of around 2½ hrs. They must be booked in advance and require a supplementary fare. All have buffets. Six or seven traditional trains, including two EuroCity expresses with dining cars, still operate on the old route, with journey times of about 3 hrs.

⤳ On Track

Paris–Chantilly

French Railways (SNCF) trains and RER fast metro trains operate between Paris Nord and Chantilly-Gouvieux. Neither service is,

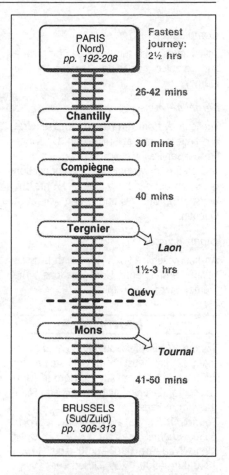

however, very frequent and local time-tables need to be studied carefully to find which train will be most suitable. SNCF trains take 26–27 mins, RER trains (line D) 38–42 mins.

Chantilly–Compiègne

Six trains a day link Chantilly-Gouvieux to Compiègne. This trains are, however confined to the morning and evening peak periods, at other times passengers should change trains at Creil. The journey takes about 30 mins.

Compiègne–Tergnier

Seven trains a day run between Compiègne and Tergnier, averaging 40 mins for the journey.

Tergnier–Mons

The journey from Tergnier to Mons requires a change of train at St Quentin. On Mon–Fri four services are available, on Sat three and on Sun only one. The best connection gives a through journey time of 1½ hrs, the worst a trip of 3 hrs and a long wait at St Quentin.

Mons–Brussels

An hourly service links Mons with Brussels Midi, Central and Nord stations. The journey takes 41–50 mins.

CHANTILLY

Station: Chantilly-Gouvieux, *r. d'Ogremont,* 2 km west of the château. For information contact Gare du Nord in Paris. The station is served by both RER and SNCF trains from Paris.

Tourist Office: *23 av. du Maréchal Foch, 60500 Chantilly; tel: 44 57 08 58.* Open Mon, Wed–Sat 0900–1200 and 1400–1800, Sun 0900–1200, closed Tues (May–Sept); Mon, Wed–Sat 0900–1200 and 1400–1800, closed Tues, Sun (Oct–Apr).

Chantilly, 50 km north of Paris, makes an agreeable day-trip from the capital. Although the name is associated with cream, Chantilly the town has two major attractions, its château and its racetrack. The **Château de Chantilly,** *tel: 44 57 08 00,* is impressive rather than aesthetically pleasing, and rather pales in comparison with Fontainebleau or Versailles. It contains an uneven collection of paintings, the fine examples being somewhat outnumbered by the more ordinary. The **Cabinet des Livres** is noteworthy, however, and displays some exceptional illuminated manuscripts. Château open Mon, Wed–Sun 1000–1800, closed Tues (Apr-Oct); Mon, Wed–Sun 1000–1230 and 1400–1700, closed Tues (Nov–Mar).

Chantilly has long been a centre of equestrian activity, initially hunting and then horseracing. The **Champs de Course** (racetrack), between the rail station and the château, held its first race in the 1830s and still puts on important meetings in the early summer.

COMPIÈGNE

Station: *pl. de la Gare; tel: 44 21 50 50,* north-west of the town centre across the River Oise.

Tourist Office: *Hôtel de Ville, pl. Hôtel de Ville, 60200 Compiègne; tel: 44 40 01 00.* Open Mon–Sat 0900–1200, 1400–1800, Sun 0900–1200, 1430–1730 (summer); Mon–Sat 0900–1200, 1400–1800, Sun 0930–1200 (winter).

Practically all visitors to Compiègne come to see the **Palais National,** *pl. du Gén. de Gaulle,* down *r. des Minimes* past the Hôtel de Ville. The palace was lavishly rebuilt as a 'country cottage' by Louis XIV in the years preceding the Revolution, and then used in turn by Napoleon I and III. Evidence of occupation of the palace by both royal and imperial courts remains. The palace can only be visited on a guided tour. Open Mon, Wed–Sun 0900–1200, 1400–1800, closed Tues (Apr–Sept); Mon, Wed–Sun 0900–1200, 1400–1700, closed Tues (Oct–Mar).

Out of Town

About 6 km east of the town in the **Forêt de Compiègne** is the **Clairière de** l'Armistice, a clearing in the forest where, in a railway car, Maréchal Foch took the German signature of the Armistice ending World War I, at 1100 on 11 Nov 1918. In June 1940, at exactly the same place, the French were obliged to sign the treaty acknowledging the German defeat of France. There is a small museum here housed in a replica railway car.

TERGNIER

Tergnier is the junction for the line to Laon. Around 8 trains a day make the 25-min journey between the two towns. Laon also has a direct service to Paris Nord, taking 2 hrs, and a couple of trains to St Quentin giving connections to Mons and Brussels.

 Side Tracks from Tergnier

LAON

Station: pl. de la Gare; tel: 23 79 10 79, in the Ville Basse (lower town).
Tourist Office: pl. du Parvis, 02000 Laon; tel: 23 20 28 62, by the cathedral. Open Mon–Sat 0900–1200, 1400–1830, Sun 1000–1230 and 1430–1830.

Getting Around

To get from the rail station to the Ville Haute (upper town), a compact collection of narrow streets dominated by the cathedral, walk up the steep steps across from the station or take the high-tech **POMA** cable car.

Sightseeing

The **Cathédrale Notre-Dame** is one of the oldest Gothic cathedrals in France; construction began in 1155. The interior is distinguished by some fine ancient stained glass. Open daily 0800–1900. The **Ville Haute** is a rewarding place for a stroll, especially along the medieval ramparts. Details of self-guided walking tours can be obtained from the tourist office.

MONS

Station: tel: (065) 32 22 10/11, about a 10-min walk west of Grand-Place.
Tourist Office: Grand-Place 20; tel: (065) 33 55 80. Open Tues–Sun 0900–1830, Mon 1000–1830. The tourist guide costs BFr.20 and there are free leaflets about individual attractions. The office also supplies information on tours of the World War I battlefields.

Sightseeing

Every Trinity Sunday morning (that's the one after Whit Sunday) the relics of St Waudru are paraded through the town in the extremely ornate Car d'Or (Golden Coach), a ritual dating back to the 13th century and one of Belgium's major ceremonies. Afterwards, in a tradition almost as old, there's a re-enactment of St George fighting the dragon. This is followed by a three-day folk festival.

With your back to the station, you can see a large Brabantine-Gothic church on a hill: the collegiate church of **Ste-Waudru**. Open Mon–Sat 0900–1200 and 1400–1900; admission free. The church itself contains many works of art, most strikingly the Golden Coach (1780).

When you come out, walk round to the far side of the church and take either road down to Grand-Place. En route is the **Belfry**, from the top of which (there's a lift) you get a panoramic view of the town.

The 15th-century **Hôtel de Ville** (Town Hall), Grand-Place, can be visited only by joining a guided tour (July–Aug; BFr.75):

details and tickets from the tourist office. The arch in the centre leads to *Jardin du Mayeur*, at the far end of which are the **Musées du Centenaire**, several museums, some relating to the World Wars, within one building. Open Tues–Sun 1000–1230 and 1400–1700/1800; BFr.60.

Église Ste-Elisabeth (St Elisabeth's Church), *r. de Nimy*, has a rather lovely altar and some good marble statues; admission free. **Musée des Beaux Arts**, *r. Neuve*, open Tues–Sun 1200–1800; BFr.60, contains mixed-style landscapes and illustrations of how some old paintings have been restored. The upper floor is mostly ultra-modern works. The neighbouring **Musée du Folklore** has themed exhibits and there's a section devoted to the Golden Coach.

 **Side Track from Mons**

TOURNAI

Station: tel: *(069) 22 10 51*, 10–15 mins walk north of the centre. RVW buses (nos 1, 4, 7 and 88) run to *Grand-Place*. Trains make the 40 mins journey from Mons hourly throughout the day.

Tourist Office: *r. du Vieux Marché–aux-Poteries 14* (on *Grand-Place*); tel: *(069) 22 20 45*. Open Mon–Fri 0900–1900, Sat–Sun 1000–1300 and 1500–1800. They provide the free *Guide for a Better Stay*, which outlines the attractions, and it's worth buying the street map (BFr.20) which shows where they are and includes a walking tour (1 hr 30 mins).

Sightseeing

The friendly little town has a dozen churches and chapels, mainly 12th–13th-century. The 72-m **Belfry** is the oldest in Belgium and expected to re-open during 1995 (after restoration). The five towers of **Cathédrale Notre-Dame**, open daily 0900–1200, 1400–1800 (Apr–Oct), 0900–01200, 1400–1600 (Nov–Mar); admission free, overlook the centre. It has a Romanesque nave and transept, a Gothic chorus and the country's biggest collection of 13th-century Romanesque murals. The rich collection in the treasury (open 1015–1145 and 1400–1600/1800) includes two early-13th-century gilt reliquaries and jewel-studded crosses.

The town's museums have standard opening hours: Wed–Mon 1000–1200 and 1400–1730. Each charges BFr.50.

Musée de Folklore, *Réduit des Sions*, displays everything from historical documents to carnival costumes. Tournai's reputation for porcelain is reflected in **Musée d'Histoire et des Arts Décoratifs**, *r. St-Martin 50*. **Musée des Beaux Arts**, *Enclos St-Martin*, is worth visiting for the building alone, custom-designed by Victor Horta in the 1920s, a light, spacious polygonal hall. The impressive and wide-ranging collection of paintings and sculptures spans the 15th to 20th centuries.

Across the courtyard (of the 18th-century Hôtel de Ville) is **Musée d'Histoire Naturelle**, which houses a few live creatures in vivaria as well as exhibits about every form of natural life.

Tournai's importance as a tapestry centre is marked by **Musée de la Tapisserie**, *pl. Reine Astrid*. The exhibits range from 15th- and 16th-century tapestries to ultra-modern ones. **Musée d'Archéologie**, *r. des Carmes 8* (a few blocks on the other side of *Grand-Place*), covers two million years of evolution, while **Musée d'Armes et d'Histoire Militaire**, *r. du Rempart* (not far from the station), is housed in an ancient keep.

PARIS to DIJON

This route links the capital with Dijon in Bourgogne (Burgundy). It visits Fontaine-bleau, renowned for its incomparable château, and the less touristy Burgundian cities of Sens and Auxerre, both distinguished by impressive cathedrals.

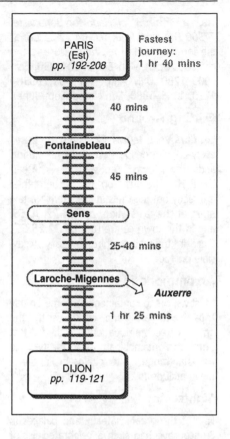

TRAINS

ETT table: 155.

→ Fast Track

Fast TGV trains provide a service roughly every 2 hrs between Paris Gare de Lyon and Dijon Ville. The journey takes around 1 hr 40 mins. The TGVs require a supplement; seats have to be reserved. All have buffets and a few have first-class dining facilities.

⤳ On Track

Paris–Fontainebleau

A suburban service operates between Paris Gare de Lyon and Fontainebleau-Avon, with trains at most hours throughout the day. Journey time is about 40 mins.

Fontainebleau–Sens

Eight or nine trains a day link Fontaine-bleau-Avon with Sens taking around 45 mins for the journey.

Sens–Laroche-Migennes

Around a dozen trains run between Sens and Laroche-Migennes each day. The journey takes 25–40 mins.

Laroche-Migennes–Dijon

Four trains a day travel from Laroche-Migennes to Dijon-Ville with a journey time of 1 hr 25 mins.

FONTAINEBLEAU

Station: Fontainebleau-Avon, off *av. Franklin Roosevelt; tel: 64 22 39 82* or *64 30 50 50*, is 3 km north-east of the town centre. Note that left-luggage costs a remarkable FFr.30 at this station.

Tourist Office: *31 pl. Napoléon Bonaparte, 77300 Fontainebleau; tel: 64 22 25 68,* at the southern end of *r. Grande* close to the château. Open Mon–Sat 0930–1830, Sun 1000–1230 (July–Aug); Mon–Sat 0930–1230, 1345–1800, Sun closed (Sept–June).

Getting Around

Les Cars Vert, *tel: 64 22 23 88,* run buses every 20 mins or so between the rail station and the town centre and château (FFr.8.10). The bus stop (with a timetable) is directly outside the station. There are taxi ranks at the rail station (*tel: 64 22 38 53*) and in the town centre (*tel: 64 22 28 56*). Once in town, everything is easily accessible on foot.

Accommodation

Most visitors to Fontainebleau come on day trips from Paris, and consequently the choice of accommodation is limited. Most hotels in Fontainebleau are in the two- to four-star range. Hotel chains in Fontainebleau include *Ib.*

Sightseeing

Few of the great châteaux and palaces in France have had such a celebrated list of occupants as the **Château de Fontainebleau**. Thirty kings and emperors have lived here, and as the tourist office gushes, 'a tour round Fontainebleau is like a journey through the history of France'. There has been a château on the site since the 12th century; the first monarch to reside here was Louis VI 'the Fat'. The majority of the present buildings were constructed by François I in the 16th century. He developed Fontainebleau as a hunting lodge in order to hunt what he described as 'red and black animals' in the neighbouring forest; subsequent kings maintained the hunting tradition. François patronised a collection of top craftsmen and artists, creating the combination of French and Italian styles known as the First School of Fontainebleau. The buildings were modified and enlarged by, amongst others, Louis XIV and Napoleon.

The self-guided tour to the **Grands Appartements** passes through a succession of outstanding rooms. Particularly noteworthy are: the **François I Gallery**, decorated by Il Rosso with elaborate stucco and wood carvings featuring François' emblems of an 'F', a salamander and three fleurs de lys; the **Ballroom of Henri II**; the overwhelming **Chapelle de la Trinité**; and Napoleon I's throne room. Other fascinating insights into royal and imperial life are provided by the boudoir designed for, but not used by, Marie Antoinette, and Empress Eugenie's bathroom.

The **Napoleon I Museum** and the **Chinese Museum** are also located in the château. The latter consists of a collection of *objets d'art*, some given by Siamese ambassadors, some sequestered by the Anglo-French expedition to China in 1860.

One can pass several pleasant hours in the Fontainebleau's gardens and courtyards. The largest courtyard, the **cours des Adieux** (Farewell Courtyard) or **cours du Cheval Blanc** (Courtyard of the White Horse) features the double horseshoe staircase from where Napoleon departed to exile in Elba. The only surviving tower of the medieval castle forms part of **cours Ovale**. The gardens include the formal, colourful **Jardin Français**, the Grand Canal stretching over towards the railway lines, and **L'Etang des Carpes** (carp pond) where you can hire rowing boats.

Courtyards and gardens open daily from 0800 until between 1700–2030, depending on sunset. Grands Appartements open

Mon, Wed–Sun 0930–1800, closed Tues (July–Aug); Mon, Wed–Sun 0930–1700, closed Tues (June and Sept–Oct); Mon, Wed–Sun 0930–1230, 1400–1700, closed Tues (Nov–May). Admission FFr.31. Napoleon I Museum and Chinese Museum open Mon, Wed–Sun 0930–1230 and 1400–1700, closed Tues. For information *tel: 64 22 27 40* or *60 71 50 70*.

Although Fontainebleau is almost synonymous with the château, the town itself can offer the **Napoleonic Museum of Military Art and History**, *88 r. St-Honoré*. Open Tues–Sat 1400–1700, closed Mon. Surrounding the château and town is the 20,000-hectare **Forest of Fontainebleau**. Many paths and trails criss-cross the forest; ask at the tourist office for details. There are also a number of sandstone outcrops, optimistically called gorges, which provide climbing practice for mountaineers.

SENS

Station: *pl. de la Gare; tel: 86 46 50 50*, 1500 m west of the town centre. Note that there are no left-luggage facilities at this station.
Tourist Office: *pl. Jean Jaurès, 89100 Sens; tel: 86 65 19 49*, just north of the cathedral on *blvd des Garibaldi*. Open daily 0900–1200, 1330–1930 (July–Aug); Mon–Fri 0900–1200, 1330–1815, Sat 0900–1200, 1330–1815, closed Sun (Sept–June).

Getting Around

The centre of Sens is compact and to a large extent pedestrianised. To get to the centre from the rail station, take bus no 1, 2 or 5 (FFr.6). They stop on *blvd des Garibaldi* right opposite the tourist office. Service is relatively infrequent, about three buses per hour. To walk, head down *av.*

Vauban, cross the River Yonne and follow the signs.

Accommodation

There are limited accommodation possibilities in Sens, but prices are reasonable compared to more touristy towns. Hotel chains in Sens include *BW*. There are cheap hotels directly across from the rail station which are convenient for short stays. The tourist office accommodation service (FFr.5) is a good bet given the restricted choice.

Sightseeing

Like many of the cathedrals in France, the **Cathédrale St-Etienne** (St Stephen's) has its own unique claim to importance. Construction began here in 1130, making it the first Gothic cathedral in France. Many of the ancient statues were beheaded during the Revolution, although a 12th-century likeness of St Etienne and some stained glass survives. The most appealing aspect of the cathedral, however, is the **Treasury**. During his flight through France, St Thomas à Becket spent time in Sens, and the treasury contains fragments of his liturgical vestments in addition to other ornaments and robes. Next to the cathedral in the former Archbishops' Palace are the newly renovated Synodal Palace and **Cathedral Museum**. Museums and treasury open Mon, Wed–Sun 1000–1200, 1400–1800, closed Tues (June–Sept); Mon, Thurs, Fri 1400–1800, Wed, Sat, Sun 1000–1200, 1400–1800, closed Tues (Oct–May).

LAROCHE-MIGENNES

Station: for information *tel: 86 46 50 50*.
Tourist Office: *pl. Eugene -Laporte; tel: 86 80 03 70*. Open Mon–Sat 1000–1200 and 1415–1930, closed Sun.

Laroche-Migennes is a rail junction on the Paris–Dijon line. Services between here and Auxerre connect with those between Paris and Dijon.

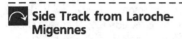

Side Track from Laroche-Migennes

AUXERRE

Station: Auxerre St-Gervais, *r. Paul Doumer; tel: 86 46 50 50*, about 800 m east of town.
Tourist Office: *1--2 quai de la République, 89000 Auxerre; tel: 86 52 06 19*. Open Mon–Sat 0900–1300, 1400–1900, Sun 0930–1300, 1500–1830 (summer); Mon–Sat 1000–1230, 1400–1830, closed Sun (winter).

Getting Around

To walk into the town centre from the station, head down *av. Gambetta* and cross the River Yonne on *pont Paul Bert*. The tourist office is on the west bank of the river. Bus nos 1 and 2 link the town centre and station, but are infrequent. Check the bus map and timetable at the station. Taxis available at the station (*tel: 86 46 91 61*) or the town centre (*tel: 86 52 30 51*).

Accommodation

Auxerre is well-endowed with a wide range of accommodation and there should be few problems finding a room. Hotel chains in Auxerre include *Ib, IH* and *Me*. Hotels are scattered throughout the town. Those with a river view tend to command higher prices.

There are two hostels. **Foyer des Jeunes Travailleurs**, *16 av. de la Résistance; tel: 86 46 95 11* is close to the station across the footbridge. Open May–Aug. The **Foyer**

des Jeunes Travailleuses, *16 blvd Vaulabelle; tel: 86 52 45 38*, is open year round. Both accept men and women.

Eating and Drinking

The most appealing and generally the most expensive places to eat are on the west bank of the Yonne. Up in the town centre there are plenty of brasseries around *pl. des Cordeliers* and *pl. Ch. Lepère*. Try also along *r du Pont*. There is a supermarket in *pl. Ch. Surugue* in the town centre.

Sightseeing

From **Pont Paul Bert** across the River Yonne there are fine views of the two most prominent edifices in Auxerre, the **Cathédrale St-Etienne** and the **Abbaye St-Germain**. The **cathedral** is built on the site of four earlier churches, the earliest being the 5th-century St-Amator church. The crypt survives from an 11th-century Romanesque cathedral and contains a unique ochre fresco of Christ riding a white horse. The cathedral **treasury** contains relics from the cathedral's long history, including manuscripts which can be viewed on video. Crypt and treasury are open Mon–Sat 0900–1200, 1400–1800, Sun 1400-1800. The **abbey** also has impressive crypts adorned with the oldest known frescoes in France, dated to AD 858, which describe the martyrdom of St Stephen. These can be seen only on a guided tour.

Housed in a recently restored part of the monk's old dormitory, the **Musée St-Germain** contains local prehistoric and Gallo-Roman artifacts. Museum and crypt open Mon, Wed–Sun 0900–1200, 1400–1800, closed Tues. Near the Hôtel de Ville in the pedestrianised area is the distinctive 15th-century **Tour de L'Horloge** (clock tower).

PARIS to RENNES

After leaving the Gare de Montparnasse and the south-western suburbs of Paris, this route passes through two towns which have become potent symbols of royal and religious wealth: Versailles and Chartres. It then continues into Brittany, a province which maintains an independence in spirit and culture, and ends in the Breton capital, Rennes.

TRAINS

ETT tables: 125, 125a.

→ Fast Track

A basically hourly TGV service links Paris Montparnasse with Rennes. Journey times vary from just over 1 hr to 1hr 15 mins.

∿ On Track

Paris–Versailles

The best station in Versailles for visits to the Château is Versailles Rive-Gauche. The RER line C has four trains each hour from many central Paris stations, including Austerlitz, St-Michel-Notre-Dame, Musée d'Orsay and Champs de Mars-Tour Eiffel, to Versaille Rive-Gauche. The journey from St-Michel-Notre-Dame takes 37 mins.

Other suburban services operate from Paris Montparnasse to Versailles Chantiers and from Paris St Lazare to Versailles Rive Droite.

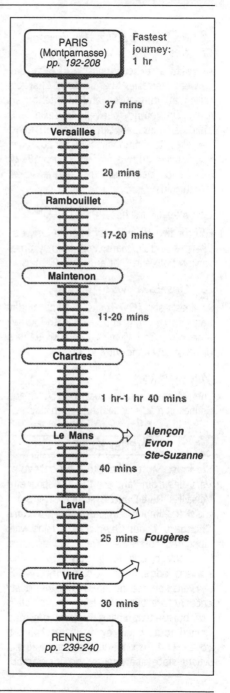

PARIS (Montparnasse) pp. 192-208 — Fastest journey: 1 hr

37 mins

Versailles

20 mins

Rambouillet

17-20 mins

Maintenon

11-20 mins

Chartres

1 hr-1 hr 40 mins

Le Mans ⟹ Alençon / Evron / Ste-Suzanne

40 mins

Laval ⟹

25 mins Fougères

Vitré ⟹

30 mins

RENNES pp. 239-240

Versailles–Rambouillet–Maintenon–Chartres

At least a dozen trains run each day between Versailles Chantiers and Chartres, calling at Rambouillet and Maintenon en route. The journey between Versailles and Chartres takes between 45 and 55 mins, Versailles to Rambouillet takes 20 mins, Rambouillet to Maintenon takes 17–20 mins and Maintenon to Chartres takes 11–20 mins.

Chartres–Le Mans

Four or five trains a day operate between Chartres and Le Mans, with journey times varying between 1 hr and 1 hr 40 mins.

Le Mans–Laval–Vitré

At least six TGV trains run each day between Le Mans and Laval, with journey times of around 40 mins. Five or six trains a day link Laval and Vitré in 25 mins.

Vitré–Rennes

The 30 mins journey between Vitré and Rennes is made by six trains each day.

VERSAILLES

Stations: Most visitors to the **Château** at Versailles from Paris use the RER service to Versailles **Rive-Gauche** station. Trains on the Paris–Rennes line stop at the **Gare Chantiers**, *r. des Chantiers*; 15 mins walk along the *r. des États Généraux* to Louis XIV's palace, built onto Louis XIII's original hunting lodge in the 17th century.

Fleets of coaches park on the dusty château forecourt, where information stalls and bureaux de change are set out, and guided tours begin every day at 1430. It costs FFr.40 to enter the palace itself, where state apartments and the famous Hall of Mirrors are a cold and formal demonstration of the royal ego at its peak. The gardens, which are free, are equally stately, laid out by Le Nôtre with fountains, long paths and lots of symmetry. The royals relaxed in the pink marble **Grand Trianon**; this and Madame de Pompadour's **Petit Trianon** can be visited; but perhaps the most bizarre sight is Marie-Antoinette's hamlet, a kind of bucolic theme park.

Beyond Versailles, the train passes through **Rambouillet**, where the red-brick château, the country seat of the President, can be visited when he is not in residence, Thurs–Mon, and **Maintenon**, whose 16th-century château (with an earlier keep and towers), houses mementos associated with Madame de Maintenon, Louis XIV's second wife.

CHARTRES

Station: *pl. Pierre Semard.*
Tourist Office: *r. Perheronne/pl. de la Cathédrale, 28000 Chartres; tel: 37 21 50 00.*

The great **Cathédrale Notre-Dame** can be seen towering over this hillside town as the train draws in. Walk up the *av. Jehan de Beauce* to reach the tourist office and cathedral, connected by narrow streets of balconied houses. The tourist office has self-guided cassette tours of the old town (1 hr, FFr.35 for one or two people) but your first stop should be the soaring cathedral itself. The original building was destroyed in a fire in 1194; the present version was quickly rebuilt and consecrated in 1260, complete with 10,000 figures in stained-glass and sculptures. Many of the windows are in the process of being cleaned and restored, with dazzling results.

Outside the cathedral, excavations have revealed a public building dating from

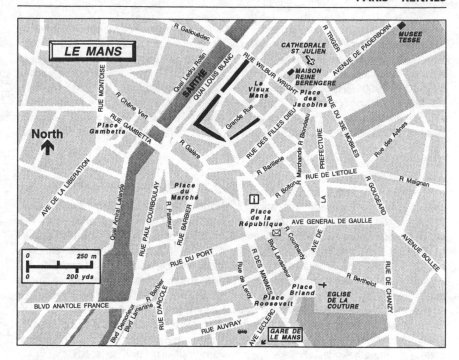

about 70 AD. Behind it is the **Musée des Beaux Arts**, *29 cloître Notre-Dame* (FFr.20), which has good temporary exhibitions. Signs indicate a *circuit touristique*, which leads down to the old town and river. Restaurants here are tourist-geared; cheaper options can be found on the shopping streets leading back towards the station.

LE MANS

Station: *blvd de la Gare; tel: 43 24 50 50.* It is a 20-min walk from the old quarter via *av. du Gén. Leclerc* and *pl. de la République*, or take a bus to the centre. There are direct connections from Le Mans to **Tours** (see p. 270), **Angers** (p. 283) and **Caen** (p. 98).

Tourist Office: Hotel des Ursulines, *r. de l'Étoile; tel: 43 28 17 22.* From *pl. de la*

République follow *r. de Bolton* and bear right for *r. de l'Étoile.*

Accommodation and Food

Several of the cheapest hotels are convenient for the station on *blvd de la Gare* and *av. Gén. Leclerc*, but there are a few more central options around *pl. de la République*, including *r. du Cornet* and *r. Barbier*. As usual, the best choice of restaurants can be found in the more attractive streets of the old quarter, on and around *Grande Rue* and *pl. St-Pierre*. The local speciality here is potted pork, *rillettes du Mans.*

Sightseeing

Le Mans' greatest hour – or 24 hours – is in mid-June when the famous annual motor race takes place just south of town. Enthusiasts who arrive at any other time of year can take bus no. 6 (direction: *Raineries*) from *pl. de la République* to the **Musée Automobile de la Sarthe** at the entrance to the Bugatti racing circuit (open daily 1000–1900 June–Sept, 1000–1800 Oct–May, admission FFr.35. The museum is a short walk from the terminus of the line). There is also a 24-hr motorcycle race in Apr.

The main reason to stop here is to explore the old quarter of *le Vieux Mans* proteced by some impressive Gallo-Roman walls. From *pl. de l'Eperon* the ancient stairs on *r. Boucheries* climb to the south end of **Grande Rue,** the main thoroughfare of *Vieux Mans*, from where you can explore side streets lined with Renaissance houses, several of which have carved and decorated timber façades. At several points, such as the staircase from *r. de Vaux* down to the River Sarthe, you can climb down through the walls to get a better view of them from the other side.

Look out for the the **Maison du Pilier Rouge**, an occasional exhibition centre whose once bright painted pillar has now rather faded. Ahead, *r. de la Reine Bérengère* leads to the vast **Cathédrale St-Julien**, via the 15th-century **Maison de la Reine Bérengère**, now a regional history and art museum (open daily 0900–1200, 1400–1800, admission FFr.14, free on Sun). Several attractive buildings are grouped around *pl. St-Michel* in the cathedral's shadow, including the much-photographed **Maison de la Tourelle**, with its Renaissance turret.

From *pl. des Jacobins* a park leads to the **Musée Tessé**, a fine art museum which includes a piece of 12th-century enamel representing Geoffroi Plantagenet, father of Henry II, who was originally buried in the cathedral (open daily 0900–1200, 1400–1800, admission FFr.14, free on Sun).

Four km east of Le Mans and connected by bus from town, the 13th-century **Abbaye de l'Epau** was founded by Queen Berengaria (Reine Bérengère, see above), wife of Richard the Lionheart. The tour includes the restored abbey buildings and church in which she is buried. Near the abbey is a large park, the **Bois de Changé**.

⌁ Side Tracks from Le Mans

North of Le Mans, 1hr 50 mins on the **Caen** line, **Alençon** is a large market town also on the River Sarthe. Since the 17th century it has been famous for its lace, although today the best place to see any is in the **fine arts museum**, a former Jesuit college on *pl. Foch*. The SNCF station is north-east of the centre. Follow *av. Wilson*, bear left into *r. St-Blaise*, passing the birthplace of St Theresa (see Lisieux, on the Cherbourg–Paris route, p. 100) to reach the **Église Notre-Dame** (church of Our Lady) and the pedestrianised shopping streets. The tourist office is opposite, in the **Maison d'Ozé**, *tel: 33 26 11 36.*

The local train from Le Mans stops at **Evron**, a small town in the quiet Bas-Maine region, with an outstanding **basilica** dating from AD 1000. There are several châteaux in the surrounding villages including the delightful fortified hilltop village of **Ste-Suzanne**. The tourist office at Evron is at *pl. de la Basilique*; *tel: 43 01 63 75.*

LAVAL

Station: *tel: 43 53 50 50*. North-east of the centre. Follow *av. R. Buron* to *r. de la Paix* and cross the bridge, or take bus no 4, 5 or 10.

Tourist Office: *Allée du Vieux St-Louis*

53000 Laval; tel: 43 49 46 46. To the right, off *pl. du 11-Novembre.*

Sightseeing

This industrial and market centre is bisected by the River Mayenne, although most of the buildings of interest are grouped on the west bank in the old quarter.

The early naïf artist Henri Rousseau was a native of Laval, and there is a collection of naïf art in the **vieux château**, whose mighty 12th-century keep overlooks the river (open daily except Mon, 1000–1200 and 1400–1800). From *pl. de la Trémoille, r. des Orfèvres* and *Grande Rue* are lined with over-hanging **timbered houses** and stone Renaissance *hôtels. R. de Chapelle* climbs back up from the river towards the town's surviving medieval gateway and the cathedral.

South of the *vieille ville* (old quarter), the **Jardin de la Perrine** is a pleasant terraced garden, from which there are more views towards the château.

VITRÉ

Station: *pl. Gén. de Gaulle; tel: 99 65 50 50.* Turn left for the tourist office.
Tourist Office: *promenade St-Yves, 35500 Vitré; tel: 99 75 04 46.* Self-guided walking tours on cassette (in English) can be rented for FFr.20. Open daily except Sun 1000–1200, 1330–1800 (Sept–June); daily July and Aug.

Accommodation

This delightful town makes a good base, with some reasonably priced places to stay in the historic centre. As well as a choice of several small hotels (try around *r. Poterie, r. du Guesclin* and *r. Rallon*), you could stay as a guest in a *chambre d'hôte*: ask at the tourist office for details.

Sightseeing

It is not hard to tell that you have crossed into Brittany: an administrative border today, but once a fiercely defended frontier whose legacy is one of the most superb fortified towns in France. Extensive segments of the medieval ramparts enclose narrow streets such as *r. Beaudrarie, r. d'Embras, r. Notre-Dame* and *r. Poterie* which are lined with exquisite stone and timber houses. Protecting it all, and commanding the River Vilaine, is a fortress **château** whose castellated towers are topped with pointed slate roofs. The tour includes **Musée St-Nicholas,** open daily 1000–1230, 1400–1815 (July–Sept), 1000–1200, 1400–1730 (Apr–June), closed Tues and Sat–Mon morning Oct–Mar; admission FFr.26.

⬤ Side Track from Vitré

There are direct SNCF bus connections to **Fougères** from Vitré, Laval or Rennes (see p. 239) – the most frequent service being that from Rennes. Another Breton frontier town, this has an even more astonishing **castle**, guarding the River Nançon below the steep town. From the tourist office, *pl. Aristide Briand (tel: 99 94 12 20), r. Nationale* leads past the small **Musée Emmanuel-de-la-Villéon** (which includes work by this local late-Impressionist painter), to the **Eglisé de St-Léonard** (Church of St Leonard) and a park with superb views. *R. des Vallées* leads down to the **river** and the old quarter of Le Marchix and **Eglisé de St-Sulpice** in front of the castle. If you want to stay and explore further, there is a municipal campsite, *le Parron; tel: 99 99 40 81*, 1.5 km east of town and several good value hotels in the centre.

PARIS to ROUEN

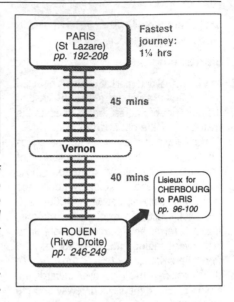

From the capital of France to the capital of Upper Normandy, this route follows the river valley through the Seine Maritime area. It ends at the gateway to the Channel and the Atlantic, with access to the major ports of Le Havre and Dieppe.

TRAINS

ETT table: 115.

Up to 18 trains a day (fewer on Sat and Sun) run between Paris St-Lazare and Rouen Rive Droite, the fastest of them taking around 1¼ hrs.

About eight of the fast trains running between Paris and Rouen call at Vernon. From Paris St-Lazare to Vernon (Eure) takes 45 mins, and from Vernon (Eure) to Rouen Rive Droite takes 40 mins.

VERNON

Station: r. de la Gare. It is a 10-min walk down r. d'Evreux or r. Emile Steiner/r. Ambroise Bully to the town centre (or bus nos 3, 4 or 10 from outside the station).

Tourist Office: pl. Barette, 27200 Vernon, open Mon afternoon, Sat 0930–1200, 1430–1830.

This pretty riverside market town, with its handsome old buildings and lively market square, is worth a visit in its own right, but most tourists stop here for access to the **Jardins Monet** and **Musée**

Américain at Giverny. Buses run there from the station Tues–Sat at 0915, 1315 and 1525 (a 15-min journey), and on Sun at 1212 and 1717 (buy tickets on the bus). Alternatively you can hire a bike at the station for FFr.55 (and a FFr.1000 deposit).

Monet lived in Giverny from 1883 until his death in 1926 and made his exquisite gardens a work of art in themselves (open Wed–Sun 1000–1800; FFr.25 for gardens, FFr.35 for house as well). A main road unfortunately cuts the gardens in two; visitors cross via a subway. The paths are usually heaving with tourists, but the flowers and the water lily pond still maintain a tranquil beauty, against the odds. Monet's house is still decorated in a sequence of strong colours, as he left it.

The **Musée Américain**, a short walk away, was opened in 1992 by US Ambassador Daniel J Terra and his wife Judith, and is dedicated to cultural links between the USA and France (open Tues–Sun, 1000–1800; FFr.30).

PARIS to STRASBOURG

This route links the French capital with Alsace and a city that could claim to be the capital of Europe.. It passes through the heart of Champagne, visiting the two great champagne centres of Épernay and Reims on the way.

TRAINS

ETT tables: 173, 177.

 Fast Track

Six fast expresses each day run between Paris Est and Strasbourg. Three of these are EuroCity expresses, and they and the evening *Orient Express* offer full restaurants, other trains having buffets. The EuroCity trains and a couple of peak hour business expresses require supplementary fares.

There is also an overnight couchette service between Paris Est and Strasbourg. The day expresses take about 4 hrs for the journey, the overnight train taking 6 hrs.

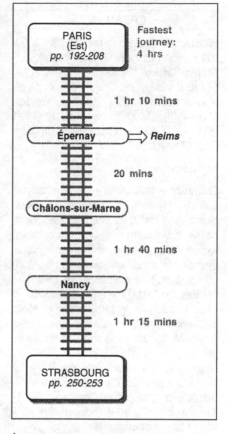

PARIS (Est)
pp. 192-208

Fastest journey: 4 hrs

1 hr 10 mins

Épernay ⟹ Reims

20 mins

Châlons-sur-Marne

1 hr 40 mins

Nancy

1 hr 15 mins

STRASBOURG
pp. 250-253

On Track

Paris–Épernay

About a dozen trains a day link Paris Est to Épernay, the journey taking around 1 hr 10 mins.

Épernay–Châlons-sur-Marne

Four to six trains a day run between Épernay and Châlons-sur-Marne, with the journey time around 20 mins.

Châlons-sur-Marne–Nancy

Five trains a day run between Châlons-sur-Marne and Nancy Ville, taking about 1 hr 40 mins for the journey.

Nancy–Strasbourg

Seven or eight trains a day link Nancy Ville to Strasbourg, taking on average 1 hr 15 mins. Three of the trains are EuroCity expresses and these trains, plus two peak hour business expresses, require supplementary fares.

ÉPERNAY

Station: *pl. Clevedon; tel: 26 88 50 50,* 300 m north-east of the town centre.
Tourist Office: *7 av. de Champagne, 51200 Épernay; tel: 26 55 33 00.* Open Mon–Sat 0930–1230, 1330–1900, Sun 1100–1600 (Easter to mid-Oct); Mon–Sat 0930–1230, 1330–1730, closed Sun (mid-Oct to Easter).

Sightseeing

Champagne is the sole reason to visit Épernay. Some of the world's great champagne *maisons* line *av. de Champagne* beyond the tourist office. Most require advance reservations for tours of their cellars; those where one can just turn up for a tour include Moët et Chandon, Mercier, De Castellane and Demoisselle.

Tours through the chalk cellars of **Moët et Chandon**, *18 av. de Champagne; tel: 26 54 71 11*, last about 45 mins; there are 96 million bottles stored here. Jean-Rémy Moët was an exact contemporary of Napoleon, who took a glass before every battle, except Waterloo. Open daily 0930–1130 and 1400–1630. Closed Sat, Sun (Nov–Mar). Admission FFr.20 including a *dégustation* (tasting).

Mercier, *70 av. de Champagne; tel: 26 54 75 26*, offers a high-tech tour with a jazzy slide display and a laser-guided train to take parties through the cellars. Open Mon–Sat 0930–1130, 1400–1630, Sun 0930–1130, 1400–1730. Admission FFr.20 with a vintage tasting. You can also tour at **De Castellane**, *57 r. de Verdun; tel: 26 55 15 33*, and **Demoiselle**, *42 av. de Champagne; tel: 26 54 91 86*.

Of the dozen or so cham-pagne houses offering tours by appointment only, **Perrier-Jouet**, *26 av. de Champagne; tel: 26 55 20 53*, is arguably the most internationally renowned.

 Side Track from Epernay

REIMS

Station: *blvd Louis Roederer; tel: 26 88 50 50*, about 1 km north-west of the cathedral. A dozen trains a day make the 25–30 min journey from Épernay.
Tourist Office: *2 r. Guillaume de Machault, Reims 51100; tel: 26 47 25 69*, next to the cathedral. Open Mon–Sat 0900–2000, Sun 0930–1900 (July–Aug); Mon–Sat 0900–1930, Sun 0930–1830 (Easter–June and Sept); Mon–Sat 0900–1830, Sun 0930–1730 (Oct–Easter). The office organises tours on foot, by bus and, in summer, by horse-drawn carriage.

Getting Around

To get to the cathedral from the station, head down *r. Thiers* and turn right on *cours J. B. Langlet*. Large parts of the town centre are pedestrianised. Local buses are operated by **TUR**, *6 r. Chanzy; tel: 26 88 25 38*. Tickets cost FFr.5, a *carnet* of ten FFr.28.50. A number of buses run to the centre from the station.

Accommodation

Reims is a city of almost 200,000 inhabitants and finding a place to stay is usually unproblematic, except at the height of the tourist season. Hotel chains in Reims include *Ca, Ch, Ho, Ib, Me, Nv*. There is a cluster of reasonable hotels around *pl. Drouet d'Erlon*, midway between station and town centre. **HI: Centre International de Séjour**, *Parc Léo Lagrange, allée Polonceau; tel: 26 40 52 60*. Take bus nos A, C or D from the rail station.

Sightseeing

Reims is also a major centre of the champagne trade. Champagne *maisons* that give tours of their cellars include **Mumm**, *34 r. du Champs de Mars; tel: 26 49 59 70*, **Taittinger**, *9 pl. St-Nicaise; tel: 26 85 45 35*, and **Piper-Heidsieck**, *51 blvd Henry Vasnier; tel: 26 84 43 44*. The tourist office gives details of other houses which require advance reservations.

Reims – unlike Épernay – offers more than just champagne houses. The awesome **Cathédrale Notre-Dame**, started in 1211, is one of the great masterpieces of Gothic architecture. Over 20 French kings were crowned here. The interior is mesmeric, highlighted by some superb stained glass including a set by Chagall. Open daily 0730–1930. Many of the cathedral's sculptures and tapestries are now housed in the **Palais du Tau**, *pl. du Cardinal Luçon; tel: 26 47 74 39*, next door. Open daily 0930–1830 (July–Aug); daily 0930–1230 and 1400–1800 (mid-Mar–June and Sept–mid-Nov); Mon–Fri 1000–1200, 1400–1700, Sat, Sun 1000–1200, 1400–1800 (mid-Nov to mid-Mar). Admission FFr.26. The **Musée des Beaux-Arts**, *8 r. Chanzy; tel: 26 47 28 44*, contains an eclectic collection of ceramics, early Renaissance paintings and other fine art. Open Mon, Wed–Sun 1000–1200, 1400–1900, closed Tues. Admission FFr.10. The Germans signed the unconditional surrender in World War II on 7 May 1945 in Reims at the **Salle de Reddition**, *12 r. Franklin Roosevelt; tel: 26 47 84 19*. Open Mon, Wed–Sun 1400–1800, closed Tues. Admission FFr.10.

The 11th-century Romanesque **Basilique St-Remi**, about 1 km south-east of the cathedral, is 120 m long but only 28 m wide. Open Mon–Wed, Fri, Sun 0800–1900 or dusk, Thurs, Sun 0900–1900 or dusk. Next door the **Musée-Abbaye St-Remi**, *53 r. Simon; tel: 26 85 23 86*, containing the city's history and archaeology museum is also worth a visit. Open Mon–Fri 1400–1830, Sat–Sun 1400–1900. Admission FFr.10.

— — — — — — — — — — — — — — —

CHÂLONS-SUR-MARNE

Station: *av. de la Gare; tel: 26 88 50 50*, about 1 km west of the town centre.
Tourist Office: *3 quai des Arts, 51000 Châlons-sur-Marne; tel: 26 65 17 80*. Open Mon–Sat 0900–1200, 1330–1900, Sun 1430–1830 (July–Aug); Mon–Sat 0900–1200, 1330–1800, closed Sun (Sept–June).

Châlons-sur-Marne completes the triangle of champagne with Reims and Épernay. Châlons is the least visited of the three, its champagne production vastly diminished. Parts of the town are charming, with restored half-timbered houses set amongst old canals. The **Cathédrale St-Etienne** (St Stephen's) has some fine 13th-century stained glass. More impressive windows can be seen in the Romanesque-Gothic **Église de Notre-Dame-en-Vaux** (Church of Notre-Dame-en-Vaux), *pl. Mgr. Tissier*. The attached Cloister Museum (*tel: 26 64 03 87*) has a reasonable collection of medieval art and sculpture. Open Mon, Wed–Sun 1000–1200 and 1400–1700, closed Tues.

NANCY

Station: *pl. Thiers; tel: 83 56 50 50*, about 600 m west of *pl. Stanislas*.
Tourist Office: *14 pl. Stanislas, 54000 Nancy; tel: 83 35 22 41*. Open Mon–Sat 0900–1900, Sun 1000–1200, 1400–1700 (June–Sept); Mon–Sat 0900–1900, Sun

1000–1300 (Oct–May). May close at 1800 in winter.

Getting Around

To reach *pl. Stanislas* from the station, head through *porte Stanislas* straight down *r. Stanislas*. The majority of Nancy's sights are close to the square.

Sights further afield can be reached on local buses or trolleybuses operated by **CGFTE**, *3 r. du Docteur Schmitt; tel: 83 35 54 54*. Open Mon–Sat 0730–1900, closed Sun. Schedules and maps are also available from the tourist office. A ticket costs FFr.7, a *carnet* of ten FFr.42.

Accommodation

Although there are plenty of visitors to Nancy, there is a decent supply of rooms. Hotel chains in Nancy include *Ca, Ib, Me, Nv.*

Budget hotels are rather scattered, although there is a small cluster around *r. Jeanne d'Arc*, to the west of the station. The area between the station and *pl. Stanislas* is more convenient.

The nearest hostel is the **Centre d'Accueil de Remicourt**, *149 r. de Vandoeuvre, Villers; tel: 83 27 73 67*, 4 km west of town. Take bus nos 26 or 46 to the *Pôle Technologique* stop.

Eating and Drinking

Pl. Stanislas is lined with up-market cafés full of people people-watching. The best places for a meal, though, are off the square. One block north, *r. des Maréchaux*, is a trove of restaurants, each with reasonable fixed-price menus. South of *pl. Stanislas* there are a number of places to eat around *pl. Henri Magnin*.

Sightseeing

Nancy is one of the most stylish towns in eastern France. A good introduction to the town is provided by two self-guided tours available from the tourist office: **Nancy 1900** which concentrates on the art nouveau buildings; and **Nancy Historique**, which visits the monuments in the old town.

Nancy centres around the 18th-century **pl. Stanislas**, constructed by ex-King Stanislas Leszcynski of Poland. The square is completely magnificent, each building, arch and gateway fitting together to form a near-perfect whole. The entire south side is taken up by the **Hôtel de Ville**. In the north-west corner is the **Musée des Beaux-Arts**, (*tel: 83 85 30 72*), with a solid collection of 17th-century and contemporary works. Open Mon 1200–1800, Wed–Sun 1030–1800, closed Tues. Admission FFr.20.

North of *pl. Stanislas* through the Arc de Triomphe is **pl. de la Carrière**, another monumental square.

Probably the most important museum in Nancy is the **Musée de l'École de Nancy**, *36 r. du Sergent Blandan; tel: 83 40 14 86*, which displays the art nouveau work from the School of Nancy movement of the early 1900s. Take bus no 6, 16 or 26 to the *Painlevé* stop. Open Mon, Wed–Sun 1000–1200 and 1400–1800, closed Tues (Apr–Sept); Mon, Wed–Sun 1000–1200 and 1400–1700, closed Tues (Oct–May). Admission FFr.20.

There are nine other museums in and around Nancy. Worth considering are the **Musée Historique Lorrain**, *Palais Ducal, 64 Grande r.; tel: 83 32 18 74*, the **Musée de Zoologie et Aquarium Tropical**, *34 r. Ste-Catherine; tel: 83 32 99 97*, the **Musée de l'Histoire du Fer** (Museum of Metallurgy), *av. du Gén. de Gaulle; tel: 83 15 27 70*, and the **Musée des Arts et Traditions Populaires**, *66 r. Grande: tel: 83 32 18 74*.

PARIS to TOULOUSE

Heading south through the heart of France, the first part of the route crosses the Sologne, doted with lagoons. After built-up Limoges comes rolling countryside, especially past Brive, when the softly-shaped hills become more lushly wooded. There are cornfields, little farms and clusters of houses, until the sheer rock face along the tracks outside Cahors, an ancient red-roofed town set dramatically in a horse-shoe shaped loop of the River Lot.

TRAINS

ETT table: 138.

→ Fast Track

Two TGV trains a day run between Paris Montparnasse and Toulouse Matabiau. Although taking a much longer route, via Bordeaux, than the *classique* services, the journey time is reduced to around 5¼ hrs compared to nearly 7 hrs on the old route via Brive. An overnight service, *l'Occitan*, runs between Paris Austerlitz and Toulouse Matabiau with sleeping cars and couchettes. It takes 8 hrs.

∿ On Track

Paris–Orléans

Six trains a day run between Paris Austerlitz and Orléans, but many more services, often faster, are available by changing trains at Les Aubrais. The journey takes 1–1½ hrs.

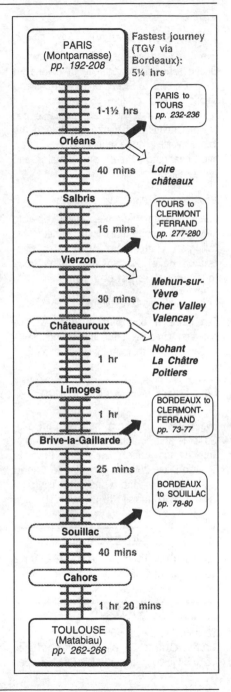

PARIS (Montparnasse) pp. 192-208

Fastest journey (TGV via Bordeaux): 5¼ hrs

1-1½ hrs

Orléans

PARIS to TOURS pp. 232-236

40 mins — *Loire châteaux*

Salbris

16 mins

TOURS to CLERMONT-FERRAND pp. 277-280

Vierzon

30 mins — *Mehun-sur-Yèvre Cher Valley Valencay*

Châteauroux

1 hr — *Nohant La Châtre Poitiers*

Limoges

1 hr

Brive-la-Gaillarde

BORDEAUX to CLERMONT-FERRAND pp. 73-77

25 mins

BORDEAUX to SOUILLAC pp. 78-80

Souillac

40 mins

Cahors

1 hr 20 mins

TOULOUSE (Matabiau) pp. 262-266

Orléans–Salbris–Vierzon

Five or six local trains a day run between Orléans and Vierzon calling at Salbris en route. Orléans to Salbris takes 40 mins and Salbris to Vierzon takes 16 mins.

Many more services are available between Orléans and Vierzon by taking the local *Navette* (shuttle service) to Les Aubrais and changing there onto main line expresses.

Vierzon–Châteauroux–Limoges

Seven or eight expresses a day operate between Vierzon and Limoges Bénédictins, calling at Châteauroux. Vierzon to Châteauroux takes 30 mins and Châteauroux to Limoges takes just over 1 hr.

Limoges–Brive-la-Gaillarde

Ten trains a day offer a good service between Limoges Bénédictins and Brive-la-Gaillarde, with journey times around 1 hr.

Brive-la-Gaillarde–Souillac–Cahors–Toulouse

Five trains a day run between Brive-la-Gaillarde and Toulouse Matabiau calling at Souillac and Cahors en route. Brive to Souillac takes 25 mins, Souillac to Cahors takes 40 mins and Cahors to Toulouse takes 1 hr 10 mins–1 hr 20 mins.

ORLÉANS

See the Paris–Tours Route, p. 233, for a description of Orléans..

VIERZON

Station: *tel: 47 20 50 50.*
Tourist Office: *26 pl. Vaillant-Couturier, 18100 Vierzon; tel: 48 52 65 13,* open

Mon–Fri 0900–1200, 1400–1900, Sat 0900–1200, closed Sun.

Sightseeing

Straddling the Cher and Yèvre rivers and the Canal du Berry, Vierzon is a quiet place whose main interest lies in the fact that this is also the junction of two main rail routes. If you have time to visit the town, head into the centre via *pl. Gabriel Péri* and *r. de la République* to the **Hôtel de Ville** (10–15 mins).

- - - - - - - - - - - - - - - - - - - -

⌁ Side Tracks from Vierzon

Vierzon also lies on the Tours–Clermont-Ferrand route (see p. 277), between **Bourges** and **Tours**.

The local train to Bourges stops at **Mehun-sur-Yèvre**, a small town whose once mighty **château** was the power-base of Jean, duc de Berry, and then Charles VII, who invited Jeanne d'Arc here. Today the castle is an imposing ruin. One of the two towers houses a small museum (open daily 1430–1900, July and Aug; FFr.10). The **tourist office** lies beyond the porte de Bourges clocktower at *pl. du 14-Juillet; tel: 48 57 35 51.*

Heading west to Tours, the local train follows the **Cher valley**, stopping at several small towns and villages including Chenonceaux (see p. 278).

To continue south in a more circuitous way, first head north again on the stopping service to Orléans (occasionally replaced by an SNCF bus) to **Salbris**, where confident timetable jigglers who are are interested in exploring off the beaten track can change onto the *Blanc-Argent* metric gauge train. This crosses the Sologne region via Romorantin to **Valençay** and its fine château with a car museum and animals in the park (open 0900–1900; FFr.32).

From here another SNCF bus connects with **Blois** (on the Paris–Tours route, p. 235) or reconnects with this route at **Châteauroux**. Valençay's tourist office is at *pl. de la Resistance*; *tel: 54 00 04 42.*

CHÂTEAUROUX

Station: *tel: 54 27 50 50.*
Tourist Office: *pl. de la Gare, 36000 Châteauroux; tel: 54 34 10 74.*

Sightseeing

Named after its 15th-century **Château Raoul**, now the Prefecture, this busy industrial town on the Indre has some useful transport connections if you want to explore the region further.

The **Musée Bertrand** in an 18th-century mansion displays Napoleonic memorabilia, fine art, archaeology and local folklore (open daily except Mon). Two km north of town the ruins of the **Abbaye de Déols** include a handsome Romanesque tower.

⌂ Side Tracks from Châteauroux

Many writers were inspired by the landscape of the Centre/Loire region, one of the most famous being **George Sand** who, for 30 years until her death lived, wrote and entertained at a large 18th-century house at **Nohant**; open 0900–1830 (July and Aug), 0900–1115, 1400–1730 (Apr–June and Sept–Oct), 1000–1115, 1400–1530 (Nov–Mar); FFr.26. Guided visits only. There is a museum dedicated to Sand and the *Vallée Noire*, in nearby **La Châtre** (open 0900–1900 (July and Aug), 0900–1200, 1400–1700 (Sept–June); FFr.10. For transport, check with *L'Aile Bleue* buses at the **Gare Routière** in Châteauroux (next to the SNCF station).

A bus connection runs to **Poitiers** (Tours–Bordeaux route, p. 273) via **Argenton-sur-Creuze** and the Romanesque churches at **St-Savin** and **Chauvigny**.

LIMOGES

Station: Gare Bénédictins, *pl. Maison-Dieu; tel: 36 35 35 35.* Buffet, lockers and an automatic cash dispenser. It is a 12-min walk to the centre, straight along *av. du Gén. de Gaulle, pl. Jourdan,* and *blvd du Fleurus.* Bus nos 8 or 10 (stop: *pl. Jourdan*).
Tourist Office: *blvd de Fleurus, 87000 Limoges; tel: 55 34 46 87.* Open Mon–Sat 0900–1200, 1400–1800 (Sept–June); Mon–Sat 0900–2000, Sun 0900–1200 (July–Aug). Guided visits including English. Bureau de change. Information, free maps. Regional information from the **Comité Départemental du Tourisme de la Haut-Vienne,** *4 pl. Denis Dussoubs, 87000 Limoges; tel: 55 79 04 04.* Open Mon–Fri 0900–1200, 1330–1700.

Getting Around

For map and information about local bus network, **Point Bus TCL**, *10 pl. L. Betoulle* (opposite the town hall); *tel: 55 32 46 46.* Single journey FFr.6, a book of ten, FFr.44. Despite its size, Limoges centre is easy for walking to its attractions.

Accommodation and Food

There is a wide range in all price brackets. The closest hotels to the station are at *pl. Jourdan,* a 5-min walk away. Chains include *Ca Ib* and *Nv.* **HI**: *r. Encombe-Vinuse; tel: 55 77 63 97.* Bus no. 2 (stop: *pl. Carnot*).

There are many places to eat, the nicest area being in the old cathedral quarter (*pl. Haute Cité*). There is a greater choice, including food of many nationalities, in the modern centre (around *r. C. Michels, r. J.*

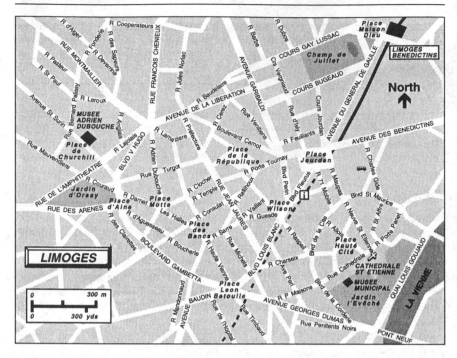

Jaurès, pl. de la République). In this side of town, r. de la Boucherie is charming for outdoor eating.

Sightseeing

Guided tours (including English) take place end-June–mid-Sept, FFr.20. Book in advance at the tourist office. Tours include a 2000-year history, Mon–Fri 1000; and Royal Limoges factory, Tues, Thurs 1000 (not in Aug).

Limoges has some pleasant places to stroll, especially in the **Haut-Cité** around the **Cathédrale St-Étienne**. Here there are cobbled streets and half-timbered houses, illuminated at night, and the **Jardin l'Evêché** (the archbishop's garden) with lovely views over the cliffside and the River Vienne. In its 2000-year history the city grew up in two centres, based in the cité and the castle. The latter is now the modern commercial centre around pl. de la République. Underneath this vast square is the crypt of the former abbey of St-Martial, unearthed in the 1960s. **Crypte St-Martial**, with some 4th-century vestiges, is open daily 0930–1200, 1430–1900; FFr.5.

The city name has been synonymous with fine enamels and porcelain for centuries. There are still master enamellers at work today. The best place to appreciate the history of what is both an industry and an art is **Le Musée National Adrien-Dubouché**, pl. W. Churchill, tel: 55 77 45 58. Open daily 1000–1715 (July–Aug); Wed–Mon, 1000–1200, 1330–1715. FFr.17 (concessions FFr.11). It displays 12,000 pieces of porcelain, not only from Limoges but China, Japan and Persia.

Another must is the **Musée Municipal du Palais de l'Evêché** (in the garden described previously); tel: 55 45 61 75.

Open daily 1000–1145, 1400–1745 (July–Sept); Wed–Mon 1000–1145, 1400–1645 (Oct–May; in June until 1745); admission free. The enamels of Limoges are on display along with an Egyptology collection and Roman archaeological finds. Shop for porcelain around *av. du M. de Lattre de Tassigny, r. A. Thomas, blvd L. Blanc* and *pl. de la Motte.*

 Connection: Souillac to Sarlat

Fom Souillac, a bus goes several time a day to the medieval town of Sarlat, where there are regular trains on a branch line to Bordeaux (see p. 78).

CAHORS

Station: *av. J. Jaurès, tel: 36 35 35 35.* Buffet and lockers. A 10-min walk to the centre along *r. J. Murat.*
Tourist Office: *pl. Aristide Briand* (off *blvd L. Gambetta*), *46004 Cahors; tel: 65 35 09 56.* Open Mon–Sat 1000–1230, 1400–1830, Sun 1000–1230 (June–Sept); Mon–Sat 1000–1200, 1400–1800 (Oct–May). Guided tours (in French).

Accommodation and Food

There is a good choice of moderately priced hotels and some rooms in private homes. Book at the tourist office or call direct using the list in the free town leaflet. Hotel chains include *Ca, Cl, F1* and *IH*.
HI: *r. F. Suisse, tel: 65 35 64 72*, about a 10 min walk from the station. Follow *av. J. Jaurès*, turn left on *r. Wilson*, then left on *r. J. F. Caviole* (which is behind *blvd L. Gambetta*).
Camping: *Rivière de Cabessut, 46000 Cahors, tel: 65 30 06 30.* **Camping Municipal St-Georges**; *tel: 65 35 04 64*, about a 15-min walk from the station

beside the bridge, Pont Louis-Phillippe.
R. Léon Gambetta, is the town's focus, where the restaurants, shops and town hall are located under spreading plane trees. This street has a good choice of food shops and wine merchants' with the famous Cahors wine. **La Chanterie**, *35 r. de la Chantrie; tel: 65 23 97 32*, is a little wine museum. Open daily 1000–1200, 1500–1900 (July–Sept).

Sightseeing

Its position made Cahors a stronghold. It is an ideal town for walking, contained within the River Lot and the remains of city walls. A couple of minutes' walk away from *r. L. Gambetta* is the solid, sun-baked **Cathédrale St-Étienne** (St Stephen's), with two massive domes and a well-depicted Ascension, carved in 1135, on the north door. To the south of the cathedral are early 16th-century cloisters. In this area are quiet streets with houses evocative of past centuries (*r. Lastié, r. Nationale, r. Bergounioux*).

On the other side of town there are more old streets near the 16th-century **Église St-Barthelemy** (Church of St Barthelemy) – *r. Château-du-roi*, and *r. des Soubirous*. Beyond that is **La Barbacane** (barbican), part of the 14th-century wall defences.

A distinctive glory of Cahors is **Pont Valentré**, a six-arched bridge of the 1300s, topped with three towers. The middle one is open and has a historical display. Open daily 1000–1230, 1430–1800 (July–Aug). FFr.12 (FFr.6). Be careful when walking on the bridge, which is busy with traffic and does not allow for pedestrians.

Just 200 m from the bridge is the **Le Petit Train**, which leaves daily for tours the town, 1000–1200 and 1400–1900 May–Sept; FFr.25 (FFr.15).

PARIS to TOURS

From the Gare d'Austerlitz, trains pass the fertile Beauce plain en route to Orléans, once the capital of a royal duchy, whose salvation from the English by Jeanne d'Arc is one of the most treasured and powerful legends of France.

TRAINS

ETT tables: 135, 133, 135a.

→ Fast Track

A few TGV services run directly from Paris Montparnasse to Tours. Many more TGVs call at St-Pierre-des-Corps on the outskirts of Tours, where a local *Navette* train connects with the expresses and makes the 5-min journey into Tours station. The direct trains take around 1 hr, journeys requiring connections at St-Pierre-des-Corps take 1 hr 15 mins. All the TGVs require reservations and supplements

∿ On Track

Paris–Étampes

A half-hourly services operates on RER line C from many central Paris stations, including St-Michel-Notre Dame and Austerlitz, to Étampes. The journey from St Michel-Notre Dame takes 1 hr.

Étampes–Orléans

There are six trains a day between Étampes

and Orléans, although the service is infrequent during the day. The journey takes 40–50 mins.

Orléans–Blois

Eight or nine trains a day link Orléans with Blois, the journey taking about 40 mins.

Blois–Amboise–Tours

Ten trains each day link Blois with Tours

PARIS (Montparnasse/Austerlitz) pp. 192-208

Fastest journey: 1 hr

1 hr

Étampes

40-50 mins

PARIS to TOULOUSE pp. 227-231

Orléans

Châteaudun
Gien
Sully-sur-Loire
Meung-sur-Loire
Beaugency

40 mins

Blois

Chambord
Cheverny
Beauregard
Chaumont

25-30

Amboise

20 mins

TOURS pp. 270-272

---

and all call at Amboise en route. Blois to Amboise takes 25–30 mins, Amboise to Tours takes 20 mins.

ÉTAMPES

Station: Gare SNCF, *pl. Gén. Leclerc*. Trains on the Orléans line stop infrequently at Étampes (one in the early afternoon), but it is worth making the effort to visit this quiet town, especially if you have an interest in Gothic and Renaissance architecture. An alternative route can be taken by RER (line 6), also from Gare d'Austerlitz; the SNCF train to Orléans can then be picked up at Étampes.
Tourist Office: *pl. de l'Hôtel de Ville, 91150 Étampes; tel: 69 92 69 00*, is opposite the late Gothic town hall – look out for the gargoyles on its roof. Open Tues–Sat 0830–1200, 1400–1815; Sun 1400–1700 (July–Sept).

Sightseeing

Just before reaching Étampes, look out for a long avenue leading up to the 17th-century château of **Chamarande**, built on the site of a 9th-century castle. At Étampes itself, the 12th-century **Tour Guinette**, a ruined keep and its watchtower now inhabited by pigeons, overlooks the station on *pl. Gén. Leclerc*. Philippe Auguste kept his wife, Ingeborg, locked up here between 1201 and 1213. Beyond the station, follow the *r. Château* to reach the 15th/16th-century church of **Église de St-Basile**, whose rotting arched portal has carvings of the good flying up to heaven and the damned descending to hell. The main entrance faces a sturdy renaissance house with colonnaded windows, now a municipal library. The *r. de la République* takes you to another church **L'Église de Notre-Dame-du-Fort**, with a 12th-century

castellated tower and spire and fine craftsmanship still evident in the defaced figures carved on its portal. Next door is the **Hôtel Dieu**, whose benefactors have included Louis VI in 1120 and Louis XIV in 1699.

Other gems are the 16th-century church **Église de St-Gilles**, on the long *r. St-Jacques*, and 12th-century **Église de St-Martin**, with a leaning belltower. St-Martin is reached via the *r. St-Martin*, which is lined with a mish-mash of architectural styles, and where a turning leads to the town's second station, on *r. Salvador Allende*; RER trains also stop here.

ORLÉANS

Station: *tel: 38 53 50 50*. Next to a large shopping centre, the *gare routière* (bus station) and the tourist office. *R. de la République* runs straight ahead to *pl. Martroi* at the heart of town. Bicycle rental. (NB Some through services only stop at nearby **Les Aubrais** – with a shuttle (*navette)* into Orléans SNCF.)
Tourist Office: *pl. Albert 1er, 45000 Orléans; tel: 38 53 05 95*. Open Mon–Sat 0900–1830, Sun 0930–1230, 1500–1830 (July–Aug), 1000–1200 (Sept–June). Next to the shopping centre and the station. In summer, there is a programme of full and half-day coach tours to surrounding towns, as well as themed walking tours of town and trips by helicopter and hot-air balloon. Self-guided walking tour leaflets are available in English. Youth information from **Centre Régional d'Information Jeunesse,** *5 blvd de Verdun; tel: 38 54 37 70*.

Accommodation and Food

Orléans is an excellent touring base and has a good selection of one- and two-star hotels throughout town: the tourist office

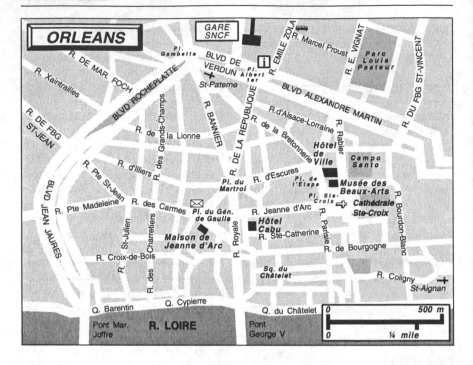

has a full list. Hotel chains include *Ho, Ib, Me, Nv.* **HI:** *14 r. du Fbg-Madeleine; tel: 38 62 45 75* (west of the town centre). Nearest **campsite**: St-Jean-de-Ruelle, *r. de la Roche; tel: 38 88 39 39* (3 km west, open May–Oct). Small restaurants and bistrots are concentrated in the pedestrianised streets known as the Bourgogne quarter around *r. Ste-Catherine* and *sq. du Châtelet*.

Sightseeing

For a city that has been besieged so often, it seems remarkable that so much of Orléans' historic centre still survives. A strategic site at the northern point of the Loire, and occasionally France's capital, Orléans has been attacked from Roman times to World War II, but nothing is commemorated here so much as the

rescue from the English siege of 1429 by Jeanne d'Arc (Joan of Arc). A statue of Jeanne on horseback takes pride of place in the spacious *pl. Martroi*, while on the annual **Fête de Jeanne d'Arc**, May 7–8, a real 'Jeanne' rides through the streets. The nearby **Maison de Jeanne d'Arc** on *pl. du Gén. de Gaulle* is a reconstruction of the house where she stayed, and there is a museum which tells the story of the siege with models (open daily except Mon, 1000–1200, 1400–1800 May–Oct, afternoons only Nov–Apr, adults FFr.12). The city's most impressive monument is **Cathédrale Ste-Croix**, with its mighty twin towers and spire. Across the square the **Musée des Beaux Arts** has a wide-ranging collection including 18th-century pastels and 20th-century art (open daily except Tues 1000–1200, 1400–1800, admission

FFr.16) and nearby are some handsome Renaissance mansions, the **Hôtel Groslot** and **Pavillons d'Escures**. Another restored Renaissance house, the **Hôtel Cabu** on *sq. Abbé Desnoyers* near *r. Royale*, is now home to an Historical and Archaeological museum (open daily except Tues 1000–1200, 1400–1800, admission FFr.11).

South of the river at **Orléans-la-Source**, the River Loiret bubbles up in the middle of a large floral park whose displays change with the season.

⌇ Side Tracks from Orléans

Although the obvious direction from here is south-west along the Loire, SNCF bus services make it possible to explore several more towns and châteaux in the region. To the west, on the smaller Loir river, **Châteaudun** has a mighty fortress which towers high above the plains of the Beauce (open daily 0900-1845 July–mid-Sept, 0930-1145, 1400–1800 Apr–June and mid-Sept–Oct, 1000–1145, 1400–1600 Oct–Mar; admission FFr.26). East from Orléans the SNCF bus service follows the Loire to **Gien** (whose château houses a museum of hunting), via the remarkable Romanesque basilica at **St-Benoît** and the small town of **Sully-sur-Loire** with its magnificent moated château, once home to the duc de Sully and to Voltaire (open daily 1000–1800 mid-June–mid-Sept, 1000–1200 and 1400–1800 mid-Sept–mid-June, admission FFr.12).

Downstream from Orléans, local train and bus services to Blois stop at a couple of interesting riverside towns. **Meung-sur-Loire** has a 13th-century château where the visit includes a tour of the dungeons, open daily 0900–1730 (July–mid-Sept) 1000–1130, 1400–1700 (Apr–June and mid-Sept–mid-Nov), weekends only mid-Nov–Mar, admission FFr.25; and **Beaugency** has a particularly impressive medieval quarter near the attractive tree-lined riverfront. The 15th-century **Château Dunois** houses the *Musée Régional des Arts et Traditions de l'Orléanais* (open daily except Tues 1000–1100, 1400–1730, admission FFr.20). Between the river and the SNCF station, the Renaissance **Hôtel de Ville** is open to visitors on summer weekdays, admission FFr.6.

BLOIS

Station: *tel: 47 20 50 50.* West of the town centre: follow *av. Jean Laigret* for the tourist office and château. Bicycle rental.

Tourist Office: *3 av. Jean Laigret, 41000 Blois; tel: 54 74 06 49.* In the Pavillon Anne de Bretagne.

Sightseeing

Chief town of the *département* of Loir-et-Cher, Blois is smaller than either Tours or Orléans, but makes a good base for exploring the châteaux along this stretch of the Loire valley, as well as having a superb example of its own. The **château** stands at the heart of the steeply terraced town, and its mix of distinct architectural styles reflects the string of royal residents who lived and died here over a period of four centuries. In 1588 the Duc de Guise and his brother were murdered in the château on the orders of King Henri III. You are free to explore the atmospheric rooms, largely unfurnished but with rich decoration. Look out for the royal emblems of bygone inhabitants: Louis XII's porcupine, the ermine of Claude de France and François I's salamander around the famous octagonal staircase. Open daily 0900–1745, adults FFr.30; admission includes

----

entry to the **Musée des Beaux Arts** and the **Musée d'Archéologie** within the château, open daily 1000–1800.

Between the château and the river are the **Musée d'Histoire Naturelle**, open daily except Mon, 1000–1200, 1400–1800 (June–Aug); 1400–1800 (Sept–May), admission free, and the beautiful **Église de St-Nicholas** (Church of St Nicholas), which was originally part of a Benedictine abbey. Towards the **Cathédrale de St-Louis,** in the streets of old Blois, you can see many of the fine Renaissance houses built for the royal courtiers, especially along r. des Papegaults, r. des Juifs and r. du Puits-Châtel.

Being on a slope, Blois has plenty of steps, but also some pretty terraced gardens: the **Jardin du Roi** next to the château and the gardens of the former **bishop's palace** next to the cathedral both have views over the town and the river.

Side Tracks from Blois

This is the heart of the Vallée des Rois and some of the most famous châteaux are within a bus or cycle trip of Blois. Tour buses make regular circuits in summer (the tourist office has details), indeed this is the easiest way to visit mighty **Chambord** which otherwise requires a 17 km bicycle ride. Built for François I, this is the best-known of all the Loire châteaux. With its 400 rooms and famous double spiral staircase, it was built to impress Emperor Charles V. The exterior is most impressive and the enormous hunting park can best be seen from the roof, among the turrets and the 365 chimneys. Open daily 0930–1745 (June–Sept) 0930–1145, 1400–1645 (Sept–June) admission FFr.35.

Sixteen km south west of Blois, classical **Cheverny** is still home to descendants of the original builder, but at only half the distance, and with the alternative of an SNCF bus service to the village of Cellettes, an easier destination is the château of **Beauregard**, with its famous portrait gallery and vast park, which is open daily 0930–1830 (July–Aug), 0930–1145, 1400–1800 (Sept–June), closed Wed Oct–Mar; admission FFr.25. The local train to Tours stops at **Onzain,** from where it is just over 1 km across the river to **Chaumont**. This solid fortress with pointed round towers and interesting stables was Diane de Poitiers' consolation prize when she was forced to swap it for Chenonceau (see p. 278). Open daily 0930–1800 (Apr–Sept), 1000–1630 (Oct–Mar) admission FFr.31.

AMBOISE

Station: tel:47 20 50 50. North of the town, across the Loire: follow r. Jules Ferry to the bridge which crosses the **Île St-Jean** to arrive at the foot of the château. Bicycles are available for rental.

Tourist Office: quai du Gén. de Gaulle, 37400 Amboise; tel: 47 57 01 37. On the riverside to the west of the bridge.

Sightseeing

Amboise was another favourite royal residence. High on its terrace above the town only a portion of the original **château** still stands, including the delightful little **Chapelle of St-Hubert**, but unlike many châteaux, this one is furnished. Open daily 0900–1825 (July–Aug), 0900–1155, 1400–1825 (Sept–June); admission FFr.32. François I invited Leonardo da Vinci to Amboise, and in the lovely house where he stayed (and died), **Manoir de Clos-Lucé**, are models made up from his plans and drawings (open daily 0900–1900; FFr.34).

PERPIGNAN

The capital of French Catalonia, population 113,000, is an enchanting combination of squares and avenues, lined with plane trees and palms and humming with activity. Other ancient streets simply bask silently in the Mediterranean sun. There are old Spanish and French buildings and nice places to stroll. Once a port, it is close to many beaches.

Tourist Information

Tourist Office: *Palais des Congrès, pl. Armand Lanoux, 66000 Perpignan, tel: 68 66 30 30.* Open Mon–Sat 0900–1900, Sun 0900–1300, 1500–1800 (June–Sept); Mon–Sat 0830–1200, 1400–1830 (Oct–May). Hotel reservations, maps, leaflets, guided tours June–Sept. Regional tourist information about the **Pyrenees-Roussillon** area is available at *7 quai de Lattre de Tassigny, Perpignan; tel: 68 34 29 94/95.* No hotel reservations.

Arriving and Departing

Gare SNCF, *av. Gén. de Gaulle; tel: 68 35 50 50* (information) or *68 34 74 11* (sales); from June 1995, *tel: 36 35 35 35.* Facilities include lockers and showers. Taxi rank; *tel: 68 34 59 49.* Bureau de change, *tel: 68 34 63 72.* Open Mon–Sat 0830–1200, 1700–1900, Sun 0830–1100. From opposite the station, bus nos 2, 3 and 12 go to the centre, a 10-min journey. The tourist office outside the station is open Mon–Sat 0900–1900; Sun 0900–1300, 1500–1900 (June–Sept); Mon–Sat 0830–1200, 1400–1830 (Oct–May). It is a 15-min walk straight ahead (*av. Gén. de Gaulle*) to *pl. Catatogne* and the centre beyond. **Gare Routière,** (bus station) is at *av. du Gén. Leclerc; tel: 68 35 29 02.*

Getting Around

CTP bus network has about a dozen lines serving the town. Free route maps and leaflets available at the ticket booth, **Kiosque CTP,** *pl. Péri; tel: 68 61 01 13,* in the centre opposite the Palmarium, open Mon–Fri 0900–1200, 1345–1830, Sat 0900–1200. A single journey ticket is sold on the bus, FFr.6.50; a book of 10, FFr.50.

Staying in Perpignan

Accommodation and Food

From opposite the station to the centre, there is a good choice of hotels of all prices. Chains include: *Cl, F1, Ib* and *Pr.*

HI: *Parc de la Pépinière, av. de Grande-Bretagne; tel: 68 34 63 32.* Closed four weeks (end Dec–end Jan). A 10-min walk from rail station (no bus). **Camping: La Garricole,** *1 r. M. Levy; tel: 68 66 30 22,* bus no. 2 from rail station (stop: *La Garricole*), a 5-min journey.

Eating outdoors along the palm-lined avenues on balmy evenings is one of the great pleasures of Perpignan, added to by the choice of French and Catalan specialities. Most popular is *pl. F. Arago,* a square filled with magnolias, brasseries and cafés.

Communications

Main **post office**, *quai de Barcelone; tel: 68 34 40 65,* has poste restante facilities.

Entertainment

Discos, piano and jazz bars, American theme bars, brasseries and pubs are found in the same area as the shopping streets (ask for the free leaflet *Perpignan La Nuit*).

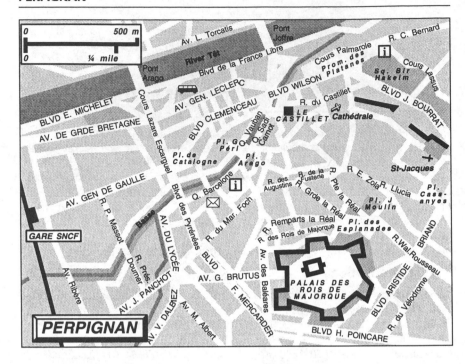

Shopping

The main department stores and other shopping takes place around the *blvd Wilson*. The residents love their markets. There is one every morning at *pl. Cassanyes*; one daily from 0800–1300, 1600–1900 at **pl. de la République**; a flea market every Sun morning outside the **Palais des Expositions** (exhibition hall) and a bric-à-brac market on the second Sat of the month at **promenade des Platanes**.

Sightseeing

Guided walking tours in French (2 hrs) of **Vieux Perpignan** (the old quarter) start at 1500 outside the main tourist office (June–Sept); FFr.20 (concessions FFr.10).

The main attractions are all within walking distance. Just a few amazingly quiet streets away from the centre is the massive fortress on a hill, **La Citadelle**, built in 1642. In the middle are the grand remains of the **Palais des Rois de Majorque** (palace of the kings of Majorca), built in 1276 and still with many Gothic relics. Entrance to both buildings is *2 r. des Archers; tel: 68 34 48 29*; (bus stop: *Archers*). Open daily 1000–1800, (June–Sept); daily 0900–1700 (Oct–May); FFr.20 (FFr.10). There are good views over the **River Têt** and next to it the prettiest walk of all along the **promenade des Platanes**, beside the plane trees planted by the river in 1809.

Out of Town

Bus no. 1 goes to the beach at **Canet Plage** at the mouth of the River Têt on the Mediterranean coast, 3 km away, a 30-min journey. Return ticket is FFr.24.

RENNES

If this gateway to Brittany seems rather like any French city, with its broad straight streets and classical architecture, it is because the heart of medieval Rennes was destroyed by fire in 1720. However, a substantial old quarter of tall, timbered houses still stands and a combination of international music festivals and a large university population help to make this a lively and attractive city.

Tourist Information

Tourist Office: *Pont de Nemours, 35000 Rennes; tel: 99 79 01 78.* A kiosk on the broad *quais* south of the old quarter and north of the SNCF station, open daily 0900–1800 except Mon morning.

The annexe at the SNCF station; *tel: 99 53 23 23*, is open Mon–Fri 0800–2000, Sat–Sun 1000–1300, 1500–1800.

Department Tourist Office *1, r. Martenot; tel: 99 02 97 43*, for information on Île-et-Vilaine and the rest of Brittany.

Arriving and Departing

Station: Gare SNCF, *pl. de la Gare; tel: 99 65 50 50.* Recently emerged from an impressive modernisation programme with shops, cafés and a tourist office. Take bus nos 1, 20, 21, or 22 to *pl. de la République* or walk straight ahead down *av. Jean Janvier* to the river and left along the **Vilaine**. *Pl de la Mairie* and *Vieux Rennes* (Old Rennes) are north of pl. de la République (20–25 mins).

Gare Routière (bus station), *blvd Magenta; tel: 99 30 87 80.* Near the SNCF

station, it has an extensive network of routes.

Getting Around

With the development of the station *quartier* and the Colombier shopping mall south of the old centre, the modern city is growing all the time, but it is still possible to explore the main sights of interest – nearly all north of the river – on foot. The tourist office leaflet *Parcours Historique* is a suggested self-guided walking tour which takes in the main buildings of 18th-century and medieval Rennes.

Staying in Rennes

Accommodation
There is a very good selection of two-star hotels on and around *pl. de la Gare*, but they are not as central as those between *blvd de la Liberté* and the river, and there are very few hotels north of the Vilaine. If you plan to spend two weekend nights enquire about the *Bon-Weekend* promotion, which offers one night free.

International hotel chains include: *Ib, Me.* **HI:** *10–12 Canal St-Martin; tel: 99 33 22 33*, north of the centre, bus nos 20/22 (no. 2 at weekends) to stop: *Coètlogon*.

Eating and Drinking
The area around *pl. de la Gare* has some good fish and seafood restaurants and crêperies abound in *r. St-Thomas, r. Vasselot* near the museums, *r. St-Georges* (off *pl. du Parlement*) and in *pl. Ste-Anne*, north of the centre. The liveliest area at night is in the old quarter between *pl. Ste-Anne* and *pl. St-Michel*: *r. St-Michel* is lined with popular bars.

Entertainment

Rennes is famous for its music festivals, particularly the **Festival des Tombées de**

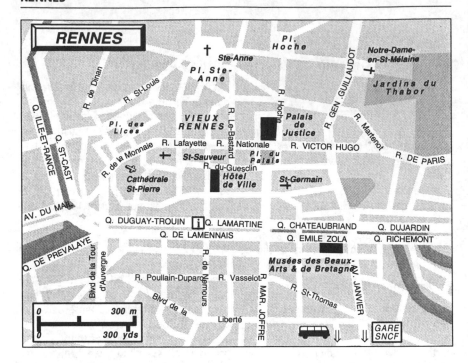

la Nuit in the first week of July, a celebration of Breton and international arts which takes over the whole town. There are rock music events year-round at **L'Ubu**, next to the **Théâtre National de Bretagne** south of the river, and live bands at several of the bars in r. St-Michel and r. St-Malo. The church of **Notre-Dame-en-St-Melaine** has a series of organ recitals throughout the summer.

Sightseeing

The city's two museums are in the same building on quai Émile-Zola, south of the canalised Vilaine river. The **Musée de Bretagne** gives an excellent overview of Breton history and culture from prehistory, via union with France and the Revolution to the present, and upstairs the **Musée des Beaux Arts** also has a wide-ranging

collection from the 14th-century onwards (both open daily except Tues, 1000–1200, 1400–1800, FFr.15 each or joint ticket). Two blocks back from the river, pedestrianised r. Vasselot is a lively street with restaurants and some restored houses.

North of the river, classical Rennes centres on pl. de la Mairie and pl. du Parlement. The 17th-century **Palais de Justice**, former seat of the Breton parliament, survived the 1720 fire but was almost destroyed by fire in 1994. Guided visits are not possible, until further notice. To the east, beyond the abbey church of **Notre-Dame-en-St-Melaine**, is the **Jardins du Thabor**, the third largest park in France.

The city's most attractive quarter, the narrow streets of the medieval town, stretch between pl. Ste-Anne and the **Cathédrale St-Pierre** (St Peter's).

RENNES to NANTES

Instead of heading directly south to Nantes via Redon, a circular tour of Brittany can be made by train, changing at Landerneau or Brest. An extensive network of SNCF buses, replacing discontinued local train services, makes it possible to explore more of the coast and inland countryside.

TRAINS

ETT tables: 134, 121, 130, 126.

→ Fast Track

Three to four through trains run each day between Rennes and Nantes by the direct route with three or four more journeys available by changing trains at Redon. Journey times vary between 1 hr 30 mins and 2 hrs.

⤳ On Track

Rennes–St-Brieuc

Six fast trains a day run between Rennes and St-Brieuc taking 45-50 mins.

St-Brieuc–Guingamp–Morlaix

Eight trains a day make the journey between St-Brieuc and Morlaix, all call at Guingamp. St Brieuc to Guingamp takes 15 mins, Guingamp to Morlaix takes 35 mins.

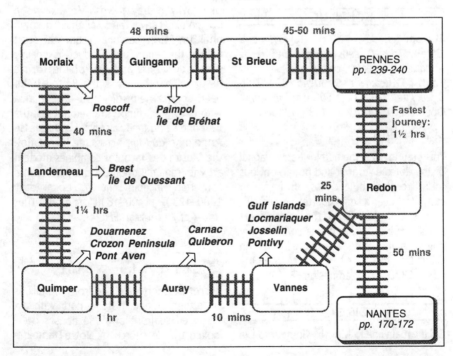

Morlaix–Landerneau

Nine trains a day link Morlaix to Land-erneau, the journey taking about 25 mins.

Landerneau–Quimper

Five or six trains run between Brest and Quimper each day, taking around an hour.

Quimper–Auray–Vannes–Redon

Up to ten trains a day run between Quimper and Redon, calling at Auray and Vannes en route; four of these are TGVs. Quimper to Auray takes 1 hr, Auray to Van-nes 10 mins and Vannes to Redon 25 mins.

Redon–Nantes

At least half a dozen trains run between Redon and Nantes each day with journey times of about 50 mins.

ST-BRIEUC

Station: *tel: 96 94 50 50.* Take *r. de la Gare, r. des Lycéens Martyrs* and *r. de Rohan* to the centre, or bus no. 1.
Tourist Office: *7 r. St-Guéno, 22000 St-Brieuc; tel: 96 33 32 50,* near cathedral. Open daily 0900–1230, 1330–1900.

Sightseeing

This busy town is the administrative capital of the Cotes d'Armour and not an obvious tourist centre, but it has an imposing **cathedral** near a small quarter of medieval houses around *pl. au Lin.* The **Musée d'Art et d'Histoire** reveals the region's history and social life, and stages some interesting exhibitions (open daily except Mon 0930–1145, 1330–1745, admission FFr.15).

GUINGAMP

On the main line to Morlaix, **Guingamp** is a small town with feudal origins where life centres on *pl. du Centre* and its **Plomée fountain**. Inside the **Basilica**, the statue of the Black Virgin is the centrepiece of an annual candlelit *pardon* (religious festival). There is a train connection from here (or a bus from from St-Brieuc) to the port of **Paimpol**, made famous by Pierre Loti's novel *Pêcheur d'Islande* (see Rochefort, p. 175). The bus continues to **Pointe de l'Arcouest** from where the boat leaves for the lovely **Île de Bréhat**.

MORLAIX

Station: *tel: 98 88 50 50.*
Tourist Office: *pl. des Otages, 29600 Morlaix; tel; 98 62 14 94.* Open Mon–Sat 0930–1200, 1400–1800.

Sightseeing

Like many nearby towns, Morlaix was a prosperous canvas and sail-making town until the 19th century. Today the port below the enormous viaduct is mainly visited by yachts and one of the town's best-known products is the Breton bitter beer, *Coreff*. The medieval streets are lined with decorated, timber-framed houses, the best one being the **Maison de la Duchesse Anne** on *r. du Mur*. Across the River Jarlot, the **Musée des Jacobins** combines modern art with regional traditions and history in a converted Jacobin church, open daily 1000–1230, 1400–1830 (closed Tues Nov–Apr), admission FFr.24.

– –

◣ Side Track from Morlaix

Roscoff, a short train ride from Morlaix, is an attractive and historic port with an unspoiled seafront of stone houses over-looked by the church of **Notre-Dame-de-**

Kroaz-Batz and its distinctive Renaissance belfry. It is also a ferry terminal and headquarters of **Brittany Ferries** *(tel: 98 29 28 28)* who sail to the new port of Bloscon, east of town, from **Plymouth** and from **Cork** (see p. 56). Boats leave from the old port every half an hour to make the somewhat shorter crossing to the **Île de Batz**, a small island which can easily be explored by bicycle.

LANDERNEAU

Inland, with frequent trains to Brest, the small town of **Landerneau** on the Elorn river has some very picturesque houses, including those on the 16th-century **Rohan bridge**.

 Side Tracks from Landerneau

BREST

Station: *tel: 98 80 50 50.* Bus to Océanopolis at the *Port de Plaisance,* 4 km west of the centre.
Tourist Office: *pl. de la Liberté, 29200 Brest; tel: 98 44 24 96.* Follow *av. G. Clémenceau* from the SNCF station. Open Mon–Sat 0930–1230, 1400–1830, Sun 1400–1600.

Brest is a large town and important military port. It has not traditionally been a tourist centre, but the new 'sea centre' **Océanopolis** is now a major attraction, exploring the sea and its inhabitants from every possible angle (open daily 1030–1800 June–Sept, 0930–1730 Oct–Apr, closed Mon morning, admission adults FFr.50).

Several buses daily head west from Brest to the fishing village of **Le Conquet** from where ferries depart for the **Île d'Ouessant**

(occasional ferries direct from Brest). Here you can visit a lighthouse museum and folk museum of restored local houses. Both open daily 1030–1830 (June–Sept), daily except Mon 1400–1600 (Oct–May); admission FFr.25.

QUIMPER

Station: *tel: 98 90 50 50.* 10 mins to the cathedral: turn right along *av. de la Gare* and left to follow the River Odet
Tourist Office: *pl. de la Résistance, 29000 Quimper; tel: 98 53 04 05.* On the river beyond the cathedral from the SNCF station.

Sightseeing

Brittany's oldest town makes a very attractive base for exploring southern Finistère – the ancient province of Cornouaille. The sedate **River Odet** flows under 12 small bridges between the station and *pl. St Corentin*, where the beautiful Gothic **cathedral** features a strangely off-centre nave. Next door, the collections of the **Musée Départementale Breton** are well presented in the restored Episcopal Palace (open daily June–Sept 0900–1800, Oct–May daily except Sun morning and Mon 0900–1200, 1400–1700, admission FFr.25) and the outstanding **Musée des Beaux-Arts**, opposite the cathedral, captures the spirit of Brittany on canvas (open daily except Tues 1000–1200, 1400–1800, admission FFr.30). The museum includes many examples of Quimper's most famous product – *faïence*, or earthenware – still manufactured further downstream on the south bank of the Odet with tours of the factories possible. *R. Kéréon* is the main shopping street, with a good view of the cathedral's west end and spires, but take time to explore the rest of the old quarter, particularly *pl. au Beurre*.

 Side Tracks from Quimper

Douarnenez is 45 mins north-west of Quimper by SNCF bus, a working port with an excellent **Port-Musée**, a 'living' museum of boats. The admission price of FFr.60 (FFr.25 for children) includes demonstrations such as boat-building and rope-making. If you plan to visit **Océanopolis** in Brest as well, ask about the special joint ticket. Open daily 1000–1900.

There is also a bus to the **Crozon peninsula**, further north, via the picturesque and touristy village of **Locronan**. At the tip of the peninsula – part of the **Parc Naturel Régional d'Armorique** – **Camaret** is a relaxed small resort where the long sea wall lined with the wooden 'skeletons' of old boats leads to a rose-brick tower built by Vauban. There is a choice of reasonable hotels and a municipal campsite above town if you want to explore the wild coastline at nearby **Penhir Point.**

A relaxing boat trip down the lovely River Odet from Quimper brings you to **Benodet**, a popular small resort with both a quiet marina on the estuary and upmarket hotels around its beach. You can continue by boat to the **Îles Glénan** or to **Concarneau**, a busy fishing port with a medieval *ville close*, a walled citadelle tethered by narrow bridges to the shore. In mid-Aug the town celebrates the **Fête des Filets Bleus**, a Breton arts and music festival which originated as a charitable event for local fishing families.

From Concarneau there are SNCF buses to Quimper or to **Quimperlé**, further west on the main train line. En route is **Pont Aven**, a charming small town on the Aven estuary, made famous by Gauguin whose work here in the 1880s made it popular with a colony of painters. Some of their work can be seen in the **museum** in the main square (open daily 1000–1900 July–Aug, 1000–1230, 1400–1830 Sept–June, admission FFr.25) and there is a pleasant riverside walk through the woods many of them painted, the **Bois d'Amour**.

AURAY

Station: *tel: 97 42 50 50.* A 15-min walk from town.

Tourist Office: *20 r. du Lait, 56400 Auray; tel: 97 24 09 75.* Near the Hôtel de Ville in the town centre, open 0900–1200, 1400–1800;   0900–1800 (June–Sept).

Sightseeing

This small market town clusters around its town hall and the ornate church of **St-Gildas**, but the real attraction is the historic riverside quarter of **St-Goustan**, where Benjamin Franklin landed in 1776 to seek French aid for the American Revolution. *R. du Château* drops down to the stone bridge and immaculate medieval houses on the quay, now mostly restaurants and galleries.

 Side Tracks from Auray

Trains and buses both head south across the narrow isthmus of the Quiberon peninsula, but if you want to explore the famous standing stones at **Carnac** take the bus, via the yachting centre of **Trinité-sur-Mer**. **Quiberon** itself is an extremely popular resort, from where ferries make the crossing to Brittany's largest island, the aptly named **Belle-Île-en-Mer**.

VANNES

Station: *tel: 97 42 50 50.* A good 25 mins north of the centre. Turn right on *av. Favrel* and left along *av. Victor Hugo.* Bear right for *r. Thiers* to go straight to the tourist office, or ahead on *r. Billault* for the town centre.

Tourist Office: *1 r. Thiers, 56000 Vannes; tel: 97 47 24 34.* Near *pl. Gambetta* and the waterfront, it supplies full lists of hotels and campsites.

Sightseeing

At the top of the island-strewn **Gulf of Morbihan** ('little sea' in Breton), Vannes is a lively town with a long history and makes an excellent base for exploring the nearby islands, coast and inland towns. From *pl. Gambetta* you enter the walled old town and the narrow medieval streets around **pl. Henri IV.** At the heart of town between *r. des Halles* and the **Cathédrale de St-Pierre**, the ancient market of **La Cohue** has been restored to form an excellent **museum**, with the old courthouse upstairs converted to combine fine art galleries with natural and local history of the Morbihan, and staging good exhibitions downstairs (open daily 1000–1200 1400–1800, closed Tues out of season, admission FFr.25). Nearby in *r. Noè* there is also a **Musée Archéologique** (open daily except Sun Apr–Sept 0930– 1200, 1400–1800, Oct– Mar 1400–1800, admission FFr.20). Behind the cathedral at **Porte Prison** you can climb a short stretch of the ramparts, but for a better view of the towers walk along by the gardens to the delightful timbered *lavoir* or wash-house. There is a very large **Aquarium** south of town at **Parc du Golfe**, open daily 0900–1900 June–Aug, 0900–1200, 1330–1830 Sept–May; admission FFr.45, children aged 5–12 FFr.25.

Side Track from Vannes

Several companies offer boat tours around the **gulf** with a stop at the largest island, the **Île aux Moines**, but to explore independently take a regular ferry. Boats for Moines leave from nearby Port-Blanc (bus from Vannes) or for the **Île d'Arz** from **Conleau**, near the campsite on the southern edge of Vannes itself (regular buses from the centre). To visit to the huge carved **cairn** on the protected **Île de Gavrinis**, take a guided tour from **Lamor-Baden**, *tel: 97 57 19 38*, adults FFr.55. There are more standing stones at the village of **Locmariaquer** on the south-west tip of the gulf, from where you can also take boat tours (tourist information; *pl. de la Mairie; tel: 97 57 33 05*).

A couple of possible inland destinations from Vannes are **Josselin** and **Pontivy**, both of which have medieval **castles** built by the Rohan family. There are SNCF bus services to each town.

REDON

Station: *tel: 96 65 50 50.* Av. de la Gare, then right under the railway bridge to *r. des Douvres*; the town centre is to the left.

Tourist Office: *pl. du Parlement, 35600 Redon; tel: 99 71 06 04.* Open daily 1000– 1200, 1500–1800; 0930–1800 (15 June– 15 Sept).

Two rivers (the Vilaine and the Oust) and a canal (the Nantes-Brest) meet here, crisscrossing through town under flower-laden bridges. At the heart of the old town the former abbey church of **St-Sauveur** has a central Romanesque belfry and separate Gothic tower. *Grande Rue* and, across the canal, the streets around *r. du Port* have some elegant old houses.

ROUEN

The capital of Upper Normandy meticulously recreated its 'medieval' centre after its devastation in World War II, and even now Rouen's streets are busy with restoration projects. The heart of the city offers a maze of narrow streets and pedestrianised squares, and some of the most impressive Gothic architecture in France.

Tourist Information

Tourist Office:, 25 pl. de la Cathédrale, 76000 Rouen; tel: 35 71 41 77. Open Mon–Sat 0900–1900, Sun 0930–1230, 1430–1800 (May–Sept); Mon–Sat 0900–1230, 1400–1830, Sun 1000–1300 (Oct–Apr). Maps and information are available on the city and Normandy.

Arriving and Departing

Station

Gare SNCF Rouen RD (Rive Droite), pl. Bernard-Tissot. Facilities include an information desk, telephones, shops and a café. Left luggage lockers are available, as well as an office, open Mon–Fri 0815–1945, Sat 0915–1230, 1400–1815.

Buses

The gare routière (bus station) is in r. des Charettes (near the river); tel: 35 71 81 71.

Getting Around

The pedestrianised streets around the pl. de la Cathédrale and r. de Gros Horloge are where the main sights are congregated. Even the **Musée Flaubert** and the **Musée**
des Antiquités (see under 'Sightseeing' on p. 248), further out of the centre, are walkable.

Buses

The bus network (**SIVOM**) extends beyond Rouen's centre and into the sprawling suburbs. A single ticket costs FFr.4.70; the number of tickets needed corresponds to the number of zone boundaries crossed. A Carte Tourisme offers unlimited travel for one (FFr.20), two (FFr.30), or three (FFr.40) days and can be bought at the tourist office or the railway station. The **Métrobus** underground/overground tram system is currently under construction, and the first stage of this system is now open.

Staying in Rouen

Affordable hotels – from around FFr.140 – are easy to find around pl. du Vieux Marché, pl. de la Cathédrale and r. des Juifs. Hotel chains in Rouen include: BW, Ca, Ib, IH, Me, Nv.

HI: Centre de Séjour, 118 blvd de l'Europe, 76100; tel: 35 72 06 45, on the left bank. Campsite: **Camping Municipal** (5 km north-west on the RN27, direction Dieppe), r. Jules Ferry, 76250 Déville-lès Rouen; tel: 35 74 07 59.

Eating and Drinking

Restaurants line the pl. du Vieux Marché, all with set-price menus. There are self-service and fast food restaurants in the r. des Carmes, near the centre, and in the r. du Gros-Horloge. Vegetarian meals are served in converted 16th-century cellars at **Pixie**, 48 r. aux Ours.

Communications

The main **post office** is on r. Jeanne d'Arc (open Mon–Fri 0800–1900, Sat 0800–1200; public holidays 0900–1200).

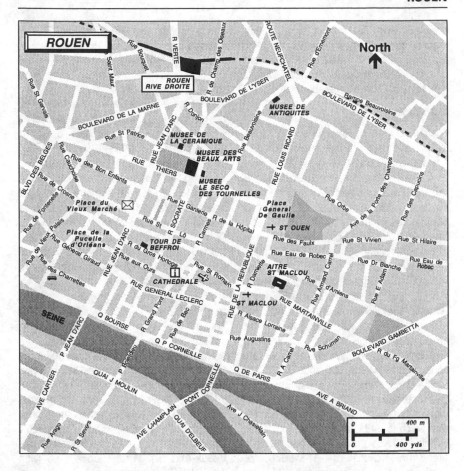

Facilities include poste restante, phones (phone cards are sold here) and Minitel information screens with an English language option.

Entertainment

Mainstream movies are shown at the **UGC Clubs** cinema (four screens), *75 r. de Gén. Leclerc* (near the cathedral); *tel : 35 89 45 57* (answerphone), and the **Gaumont** (seven screens) *28 r. de la République*; *tel: 36 68 75 55*. There are three main theatres: **Théâtre de la Ville**, *16 pl. de la Verrerie, Centre St-Sever; tel: 35 62 313*; **Théâtre des Arts**, *quai de la Bourse*; *tel: 35 71 41 36* and **Théâtre des Deux-Rives**, *48 r. Louis Ricard; tel: 35 70 22 82*.

Details of concerts and temporary art exhibitions in the city can be found in hotels or at the tourist office.

Shopping

Busy shopping streets lead from the centre of Rouen, including supermarkets and bookshops. Across the river are cheaper shops, launderettes and the St-Sever

---

complex, which has budget stores. Decorated ceramics (*faïence*), Rouen's speciality, are sold in the *pl. Barthélemy*. An excellent covered market in the *pl. du Vieux Marché* sells fruit, meat and vegetables.

Sightseeing

Tours in English of Rouen's historic areas leave the tourist office every weekday in July and early Aug at 1400 (FFr.28).

At the heart of the the town centre is the **Cathédrale de Notre-Dame**, *pl. de la Cathédrale* (Mon–Sat 0800–1900, Sun and public holidays 0800–1800), whose west façade was portrayed by Monet in a series of paintings representing the varying light. Dating mainly from the early 13th century, the cathedral suffered badly during World War II, and its lacy exterior still has a battered look. Several effigies, including Richard the Lionheart's, are stored in the ambulatory (40-min tours of the ambulatory, crypt and Chapelle de la Vierge are conducted between 1000 and 1700).

The *r. St-Romain* runs alongside the cathedral and the gutted bishop's palace, where the Church condemned Joan of Arc as a witch in 1431, and where it changed its mind 25 years later. The road leads to the Gothic church of **St-Maclou**, *pl. Barthélemy*, built between 1437 and 1521. An alleyway leads to its cloisters, the **Aître St-Maclou**, once used as a burial ground for plague victims and still surrounded by grotesque wooden carvings of skulls and other morbid subjects.

From St-Maclou, the *r. Damiette* runs to the twin-towered **St-Ouen**, *pl. du Gén. de Gaulle*. Built in the 14th cen-tury, the church is set in small gardens, where Rouen's *boules* players gather. Three blocks west is the originally late-Gothic **Palais de Justice**, *r. aux Juifs*, extensively rebuilt after the war, when little but the

ornate façade was left standing. To the south is the **r. du Gros Horloge**, named after the gatehouse and its 14th-century clock (one-handed), which spans the street; carvings of Christ and his flock decorate the underside of the arch. The belfry next to it, the **Tour du Beffroi** is where the clock was originally displayed (open Thur–Mon, 1000–1145, 1400–1745, Wed pm only (FFr.11); tickets also give access to the Musée des Beaux Arts). In the *pl. du Vieux Marché*, a memorial chapel marks the spot where Jeanne d'Arc (Joan of Arc) was burned at the stake in 1432. Designed by Louis Arretche with a pointed, twisted roof, it houses 16th-century stained glass from the church of St-Vincent, destroyed in 1944.

Museums

Rouen's impressive selection of museums include the quirky wrought-ironwork museum, **Musée le Secq des Tournelles**, in St Lauren church, *r. Jacques Villon* (open Thur-Mon, 1000–1200, 1400–1800, Wed 1400–1800; FFr.11). Its ironwork displays include a Louis XV bannister, shop signs like manic doodles, and orthopaedic corsets. Next door is the **Musée des Beaux-Arts**, *sq. Verdrel* (open Wed–Mon 1000–1900), which has a collection ranging from the 15th to the 20th centuries. A 'passport' can be bought here giving reduced admission to the fine arts museums in Dieppe, Fécamp, Le Havre and Honfleur. Nearby, the **Musée de la Céramique**, *r. Jeanne d'Arc* (open Thur–Mon 1000–1200, 1400–1800, Wed 1400–1800; FFr.11) traces the history of the ceramics industry. Further north, tapestries and Roman mosaics are exhibited at the **Musée des Antiquités**, *198 r. Beauvoisine* (open Mon and Wed–Sat, 1000–1230, 1330–1730; Sun 1400–1800; FFr.10).

Gustave Flaubert's father was a surgeon in the 18th-century Hôtel Dieu, the writer's birthplace (now being restored), west of the *pl. du Vieux Marché*. This is now the **Musée Flaubert et d'Histoire de la Médécine**, *r. de Lecat* (open Tues–Sat 1000–1200, 1400–1800; ring doorbell for admittance), which portrays his childhood and 19th-century hospital life.

_____

⌁ Side Tracks from Rouen

Trains from Rouen to **Le Havre** arrive at the **Gare SNCF**, *cours de la République*. Ferries leave Le Havre for Ireland from *quai Johannes Couvert* and for Portsmouth from *quai de Southampton*. The long *blvd de Strasbourg* leads from the station to the **tourist office**, *Forum de l'Hôtel de Ville*; *tel: 35 21 22 88*, on the central square, a post-war affair with wooden pergolas and fountains. This was the work of Auguste Perret, who designed the rebuilt city after its destruction in World War II. **Église St-Joseph** (St Joseph's Church) is his work, a landmark with its 350 ft steeple, but perhaps the most interesting feature of modern Le Havre is Oscar Niemeyer's **Cultural Centre** on *Espace Niemeyer*, built to look like the huge funnels of a ship, with a giant hand forming a fountain. The excellent **Musée des Beaux-Arts**, *blvd John Kennedy/blvd Clémenceau* includes work by Dufy, Boudin and Monet. Not much was left after the war of the original port, but there are reminders in the Dutch-gabled **Musée l'Ancien Havre**, (Museum of Old Le Havre) on *r. Jérome Bellamato*. A funicular railway at the top of the old town leads to the 625-acre **Forêt de Montgeon**, which has camping facilities (Apr–Sept; *tel: 35 46 52 39*).

There is also a rail service from Rouen to **Dieppe**. The **tourist office**, *pont Jehan Argo*; *35 21 22 88*, is next to the old ferry port. Apart from one disastrous landing by a Canadian force in 1942, Dieppe escaped the effects of Allied invasion and its higgledy-piggledy harbour and attractive old quarter are largely intact. A handsome 15th-century château overlooks the long seafront and pebble beach, where *crêpe* stands and bars stay busy after dark in summer. Climb up to the castle to see the **Musée des Beaux-Arts**, which contains a collection of ivory sculptures and paintings by Braque, Pissarro, Renoir and others who took advantage of the clear coastal light. Shipbuilding, marine biology and fishing are all covered in the extensive **Cité de la Mer**, *37 r. de l'Asile Thomas*. Small restaurants line the *quais Henry IV* and *Duquesne*, but wherever you eat, try the excellent seafood, taken straight from the boats to the stalls outside the tourist office. A new ferry terminal opened in July 1994; shuttle services run there from the tourist office and Stena Sealink office.

Other side tracks worth making are **Fécamp**, where tours of the **Palais Bene-dictine** include an exhibition of relics from the 11th-century abbey and tastings of the Benedictine liqueur; and **Honfleur**, whose past reputation as a magnet for artists is honoured in several galleries. Commemor-ating the man who sparked it all off is the **Musée Eugène-Boudin**, which includes works by Monet, Vallotton, Dufy and Boudin himself (open daily except Tues 1000–1200, 1400–1800 mid-May–Sept, weekdays except Tues 1430–1700, Sat–Sun 1000–1200, 1430–1700 Oct–mid-Mar, admission FFr.20). The ticket includes entry to the wooden belfry of the church of **Ste-Catherine**. To reach Fécamp from Rouen, change at Bréauté-Beuzeville; for Honfleur, take the bus from Rouen to Pont-Audemer and change there (about 2 hrs).

STRASBOURG

Strasbourg, home to the Council of Europe, European Court of Human Rights and European Parliament, can lay claim to be the most 'European' of cities in France.

Strasbourg has been of international importance since Roman times, when the commercial trading route from the Mediterranean to northern Europe passed through the city. Lying only 3 km from the Rhine and the German border, Strasbourg has twice been annexed by Germany – from the Franco-Prussian war until the end of World War I, and during World War II – and the German influence can be seen on the architecture of the city.

Strasbourg has also been a major cultural centre for centuries. Its university is one of the finest in France and numbers Goethe and Napoleon among its alumni. Today Strasbourg is a lively cosmopolitan city of almost half a million inhabitants.

Tourist Information

Tourist Office: 17 pl. de la Cathédrale, 67000 Strasbourg; tel: 88 52 28 28. Open Mon–Sat 0830–1900, Sun 0900–1800 (June–Sept); daily 0900–1800 (Oct–May).

Branch Offices at the rail station, pl. de la Gare; tel: 88 52 28 22, and near the border at pont de l'Europe; tel: 88 61 39 23. Both open Mon–Sat 0830–1900, Sun 0900–1800 (June–Sept); daily 0900–1230 and 1345–1800 (Oct–May). The office at the rail station is currently in a temporary building pending completion of construction work.

Arriving and Departing

Airport

Strasbourg-Entzheim International Airport, tel: 88 64 67 67, about 15 km south-west of the city. Shuttle buses run between the airport and the rail station at pl. de la Gare, and r. du Vieux-Marché-aux-Vins near pl. Kléber.

Station

Strasbourg Gare, Pl. de la Gare; tel: 88 22 50 50, about 1 km west of the cathedral. For seat reservations tel: 88 32 07 51.

Getting Around

Central Strasbourg is compact and concentrated on a small island formed by the narrow **River Ill** and its branch the **Fossé du Faux Rempart**. Most major sights lie on the island, clustered around the cathedral. The centre is largely pedestrianised.

To get to the cathedral from the station, walk across pl. de la Gare down r. du Marie Kuss, crossing the river. Take pedestrianised Grande Rue which leads into r. Gutenberg and the cathedral square.

Buses

You can explore Greater Strasbourg and visit the **Palais de l'Europe** on local buses. These are operated by **Companie des Transports Strasbourgeois (CTS)**, 10 pl. Kléber; tel: 88 77 70 70, open Mon–Fri 0730–1830, Sat 0900–1230, 1330–1700. The central bus station is at pl. des Halles, north of the island, although buses stop within central Strasbourg at pl. Broglie. A ticket costs FFr.7, a carnet of five FFr.27, and a 24-hr pass FFr.22. Passes are available from CTS, the tourist office, the rail station and tabacs.

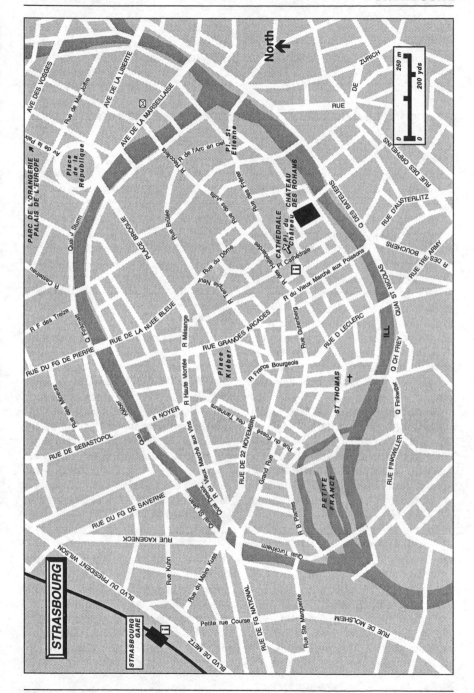

Taxis

There are ranks at the rail station and in town at *pl. Kléber*. Taxis can be ordered by phone, *tel: 88 36 13 13* (24-hr).

Staying in Strasbourg

Accommodation

Strasbourg is something of an anomaly in terms of accommodation in that demand can fluctuate wildly not only with the tourist seasons but also with the sessions of the European Parliament. The parliament meets one week every month except July and Aug: phone ahead to find out whether it is sitting.

Hotel chains in Strasbourg include *Ca, Ho, Hn, Ib, Me, Mp, Nv* and *Sf*. There are many, many hotels in Strasbourg but due to the demand from EU institutions many of them are three-star or higher. However, many of the cheaper hotels are at least conveniently located for rail travellers, in between the rail station and the town centre.

HI: Auberge de Jeunesse Réné Cassin, *9 r. de l'Auberge de Jeunessse; tel: 88 30 26 46*, 3 km from the town centre. Take bus nos 3, 13 or 23 to stop: *Auberge de Jeunesse*. **Auberge de Jeunesse Parc du Rhin**, *r. des Cavaliers; tel: 88 60 10 20*, 4 km from town on the Rhine. Take bus nos 11, 21 or 32 to stop: *Parc du Rhin*.

The non-HI hostel **Centre International d'Accueil de Strasbourg**, *7 r. Finkmatt; tel: 88 32 12 12*, is central.

Eating and Drinking

There are copious restaurants in and around *pl. de la Cathédrale* and *Petite France*, but most of these are tourist-oriented and have inflated prices. For traditional fare, the best bets are the *Winstubs*, eateries that were usually affiliated with particular wine cellars, and which today serve wine, of course, with hearty food. As the name suggests, *Bierstubs* serve beer but usually offer only snacks to accompany it. There are more functional and less touristy restaurants on *pl. Kléber*.

Communications

Main **Post Office**, *8 av. de la Marseillaise; tel: 88 23 44 77*. Open Mon–Fri 0800–1900, Sat 0800–1200, closed Sun. **Branches** at the rail station, *pl. de la Cathédrale* and *pl. des Halles*.

Consulates

Canada: *r. Ried, La Wantzenau; tel: 88 96 25 00*.
USA: *15 av. d'Alsace; tel: 88 35 31 04*.

Entertainment

The tourist office produces a comprehensive guide to events during the summer, many of which are free. These include concerts at the **Pavillon Joséphine**, in the Parc de l'Orangerie, parades of dancing and music in the town centre, and outstanding exterior light shows at the cathedral. In June the city hosts a high-class international **Music Festival**. Throughout the summer, there is folk dancing in the courtyard of the **Palais des Rohans**, folk bands in *pl. des Tripiers*, and organ recitals in the cathedral.

Sightseeing

The rose sandstone **Cathédrale Notre-Dame** dominates the centre of Strasbourg. Intricately ornate, the cathedral was built during the 12th–15th centuries; the 142 m-high spire, completed in 1439, made the cathedral the tallest building in the known world at the time. You can climb up 76 m to the platform from where the spire stretches up the remaining height. The western façade, featuring three doorways ornamented with lacy stonework and the triumphant rose window, provides the finest aspect of the exterior. The stained glass can be most finely appreciated from the interior, although the biggest draw inside is the **horloge astronomique** (astronomical clock), dating from the 16th century. The clock strikes at 1230 every day, to the accompaniment of a procession of carved apostles. Cathedral open daily 0700–1130 and 1240–1900. Admission (FFr.5) to see the clock from about 1150. Platform open daily 0830–1900 (July–Aug); daily 0900–1830 (Apr–June, Sept); daily 0900–1730 (Mar and Oct); daily 0900–1630 (Nov–Feb). Admission FFr.10. There is a sound and light show inside the cathedral daily at 2015 in French and 2115 in German (admission FFr. 26). The exterior floodlighting, which runs from 2200–0100 in July and Aug, is magnificent.

Clustered around the cathedral is a range of museums whose breadth and depth is perhaps unrivalled outside Paris. For information on any of the museums *tel: 88 52 50 00*. Each museum has an admission price of FFr.15.

The **Musée de l'Oeuvre Notre-Dame**, *3 pl. du Château*, has a fine collection of sculpture from AD 1000 to the 1700s. Many of the most outstanding exhibits are the original statues from the cathedral. Open Mon–Sat 1000–1200, 1330–1800, Sun 1000–1700. The 18th-century **Château des Rohans**, or **Palais des Rohans**, *2 pl. du Château*, houses three compact museums. In the basement is the **Musée Archéologique**, which focusses on Alsatian history from 100,000 BC to AD 800, with features on the everyday life of mammoth hunters. On the ground floor, the **Musée des Arts Décoratifs** has installations of royal apartments and some fine ceramics and silver. The **Musée des Beaux Arts** on the first floor has a competent selection of European art from the 14th–19th centuries. Museums open Mon, Wed–Sat 1000–1200, 1330–1800, Sun 1000–1700.

The **Musée d'Art Moderne**, *5 pl. du Château*, has representatives of all the major movements in modern art, from Impressionism through Fauvism and Surrealism. Across the River Ill, the **Musée Alsacien**, *23 quai St-Nicolas*, displays regional crafts (clog-making), costumes and popular art. Both museums open Mon–Sat 1000–1230, 1330–1800, Sun 1000–1700.

Arguably the most picturesque area of Strasbourg is **Petite France** and its old tanners' quarter, which features restored Alsatian houses set amongst locks and bridges. The **ponts couverts** (covered bridges) are topped by 13th-century towers and a Vauban rampart which one can climb for a fine view over the area. Open daily 0900–2000, admission FFr.5 (mid-Mar–mid-Oct); daily 0900–1900, admission free (mid-Oct–mid-Mar). Popular **boat trips** along the River Ill leave from behind the Château des Rohans, daily every 30 mins, 0900–2100 (Apr–Oct); daily at 1030, 1300 and 1430 (Nov–Mar).

North-east of the central island across the Fossé is **pl. de la République**, a wonderful 19th-century square flanked by the National Theatre, National and University Library and Palais du Rhin. Further out to the north-east are the **Parc de l'Orangerie**, Strasbourg's best park by far, and, across *av. de l'Europe*, the **Palais de l'Europe**. Here the European Parliament and Council of Europe meet. To make reservations for a tour, *tel: 81 17 20 07* (parliament) or *tel: 88 41 20 29* (council).

STRASBOURG to DIJON

This route links Strasbourg in Alsace with Dijon in Bourgogne. It winds through the largely gentle Vosges mountains, visiting towns which are off the major tourist trails. Épinal and Lure especially do not attract large numbers of foreign tourists.

TRAINS

ETT tables: 173, 172a, 171, 170.

➡ Fast Track

Only one daily through train links Strasbourg and Dijon Ville and even then with a very late arrival after midnight in Dijon or, in the return direction, a departure time of 0436. During daylight hours the schedule consists of four services each way, each requiring a change of train at Besançon Viotte. The journey takes around 4 hrs. The On Track route takes a much longer meandering route around the Vosges Mountains.

⤳ On Track

Strasbourg–Saverne

The service linking Strasbourg and Saverne varies between fast expresses and slow local trains giving journey times of 25–50 mins.

Saverne–Lunéville

Only three trains a day call at both Saverne and Lunéville, the journey taking 40 mins.

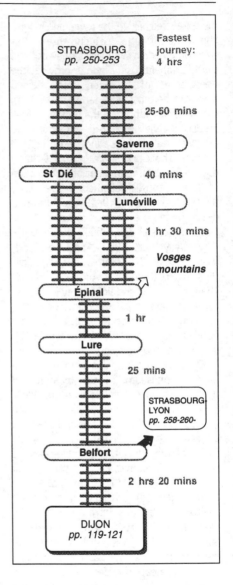

Lunéville–Épinal

The journey between Lunéville and Épinal requires a change of train at Blainville-Damelevières. Although trains are not frequent on either leg of the journey connections are surprisingly good and through journeys average around 1 hr 30 mins. An alternative route for those not wanting to visit Saverne or Lunéville is the line from Strasbourg to Épinal via St Dié, giving more of the flavour of the Vosges Mountains.

Épinal–Lure–Belfort

Three trains are available Mon–Sat but only one on Sun between Épinal and Belfort; they all stop at Lure en route. Journey times between Épinal and Lure are around 1 hr, between Lure and Belfort 25 mins.

Belfort–Dijon

The 'Fast Track' services all call at Belfort (see Strasbourg–Lyon route, p. 260). With the change of trains at Besançon Viotte the journey time to Dijon Ville is around 2 hrs 20 mins.

SAVERNE

Station: *pl. de la Gare, 67700 Saverne; tel: 88 91 33 36,* 400 m north of the town centre.
Tourist Office: *Pavillon du Château des Rohans, pl. Ch. de Gaulle; tel: 88 91 80 47.* Open Mon–Fri 0900–1200, 1400–1800, Sat and Sun 1000–1200, 1500–1800 (June–Sept); Mon–Fri 1000–1200, 1400–1600, Sat 1000–1200, 1500–1700, closed Sun (Oct–May). To get to the tourist office from the rail station, walk down *r. de la Gare,* then turn left on *Grand rue* to reach the Château.

Accommodation

There are a handful of one- and two-star hotels in Saverne, most clustered on *r. de la Gare* and *Grande rue.* The youth hostel is splendidly housed in a wing of the château; *tel: 88 91 14 84.* Open mid-Mar–Oct.

Sightseeing

Saverne sits in the foothills of the Vosges mountains in the valley of the River Zorn, the main route across the Vosges into Alsace. The **canal de la Marne au Rhin** passes right through the centre of town; *Grande rue* crosses over a deep lock. The **Château des Rohan**s, rather optimistically dubbed the Versailles of Alsace, seems forbidding when viewed from the town. However, a right-angled bend in the canal provides a more refined setting for the north-east façade. There is a **Musée Archéologique** in the château. Open Mon, Wed–Sun 1400–1800, closed Tues (June–Sept), closed Oct–May. Admission FFr.8. The pedestrianised section of *Grande rue* contains some fine 17th-century Alsatian houses. The **Roseraie** (rose garden), *Imp. de la Roseraie,* is highly regarded. Open daily 1000–1900, admission FFr.10 (June–Sept); Mon–Fri 0800–1200 and 1400–1700, Sat, Sun closed, admission free (Oct–May).

There is a wide variety of walks and bicycle trails in the surrounding hills. For example, it is possible to cycle along the canal to Strasbourg. Ask at the tourist office for details.

LUNÉVILLE

Station: *pl. Pierre Semard; tel: 83 56 50 50,* about 800 m south of the château.
Tourist Office: *Aile sud du Château, pl. de la 2e D.C., 54300 Lunéville; tel: 83 74 06 55,* at the end of the southern wing of the château. Open daily 0900–1200 and 1400–1800.

Getting Around

What there is of interest to the visitor in Lunéville lies within walking distance of the château. To get there from the station, walk straight along *r. Carnot*, across *pl. Léopold* and straight down *r. du Gén. Leclerc*. At the end one can either cut through to the château gardens, or turn left and pass through *pl. de la Comédie* and *pl. Stanislas* to *r. de Pont Rouge* and the tourist office.

Accommodation

Most visitors to Lunéville come on day trips from Nancy or Strasbourg, and accommodation possibilities are limited. There are a few hotels along *r. d'Alsace* and its continuation *av. Voltaire*; heading from the station on *r. Carnot*, turn right on *r. d'Alsace*.

Sightseeing

Modern suburban Lunéville is drab and unremarkable, and the impressive **château** set in the heart of the town comes as an unexpected surprise. Built from 1703–1720 for Duke Léopold, the château was known as the Versailles of the Last Dukes of Lorraine and Bar. In 1737, the château was taken over by ex-King Stanislas Leszczynski of Poland, the man responsible for *pl. Stanislas* in Nancy (see Paris–Strasbourg route, p. 226). He further improved the château gardens and built some stylish buildings in the immediate surrounding town. In 1766, however, Lorraine was reincorporated into France and the Lunéville court rapidly faded. Today the château appears slightly run-down, although the gardens and **Parc des Bosquets** are still magnificent. The **Musée du Château**, in the south wing along from the tourist office, includes a display of *faïenceries*, enamelled ceramic plates for which Lunéville is apparently famous. Open Mon, Wed–Sun 1000–1200, 1400–1800, closed Tues (Apr–Sept); Mon, Wed–Sun 1000– 1200, 1400–1700, closed Tues (Oct–Mar).

Lunéville is known as *La Cité Cavalière*, due to the number of cavalrymen who came from the region or were barracked here. In the main courtyard of the château is a fine statue of Général LaSalle; his horse has two legs raised, indicating that he was killed in battle.

The tourist office has quirky handwritten guides suggesting tours of 1, 2, or 3 hrs around the town. The **Église St-Jacques** (Church of St Jacques), *pl. St-Remy*, is worth a look. Started by Léopold, it was completed by Stanislas' architect Héré. The appealing interior includes an impressive organ. The baroque **Maison du Marchand**, *15 r. de Lorraine*, also built by Stanislas in distinctive pink sandstone, is arguably the finest building in town. The **Musée du Cycle and de la Moto**, across from the tourist office, is perhaps more for real enthusiasts than casual visitors.

ÉPINAL

Station: *pl. du Gén. de Gaulle; tel: 29 82 50 50*, about 600 m west of the town centre.

Tourist Office: *13 r. de la Comédie, 88000 Épinal; tel: 29 82 53 82*. Open Mon–Sat 0900–1900, Sun 1000–1200, 1500–1800 (July–Aug); Mon–Fri 0900–1230, 1330–1830, Sat 0900–1200, 1400–1700, closed Sun (Sept–June).

Getting Around

To get to the tourist office walk straight across from the station and bear right down to *pl. de 4 Nations*. Keep straight, crossing the canal and Moselle, and then turn right at *pl. des Vosges*.

Accommodation

There should be no problem finding

somewhere to stay in Épinal, although a number of the hotels are located away from the town centre. Hotel chains in Epinal include *BW, Ca, Ib, Me.*

Sightseeing

Due to its position near the borders of the four ancient nations of Lorraine, Burgundy, Champagne and Alsace, Épinal has a history of economic and cultural significance. Although now no longer of any strategic importance and with a population of less than 40,000, Épinal nevertheless has some surprising offerings for visitors.

The **Musée Départemental d'Art Ancien et Contemporain**, *1 pl. Lagarde; tel: 29 82 20 33*, has one of the finest contemporary art collections in France. Fine representatives of Pop Art and Minimal Art are on display. The collection of 17th- and 18th-century paintings includes works from the French movements of classicism and reality painting. The archaeological and ethnographic exhibits are also impressive. The museum is housed in a striking modern building at the tip of the island between the Moselle and the Canal des Grands Moulins. Open Mon, Wed–Sun 1000–1200, 1400–1800, closed Tues (Apr–Sept); Mon, Wed–Sun 1000–1200, 1400–1700, closed Tues (Oct–Mar). Admission FFr.30.

The town itself is a patron of modern art, as evidenced by some eyecatching sculptures in the pedestrianised zone of the town centre, including the unfortunate two bronze fingers of the Freedom sculpture (supposed to be a 'V' for Victory), round the corner from McDonalds.

Épinal's other museum, the **Imagerie d'Épinal**, *42 bis quai de Dogneville; tel: 29 31 28 28*, is also certainly worth a visit. On display are a collection of prints of characters and figures in a style for which Épinal is renowned. Open Mon–Sat 0830–1200, 1400–1830, Sun 1400–1830.

Épinal is set amongst the gentle Vosges mountains and there are plenty of opportunities for hiking in the surrounding forested hills. Épinal itself is the most wooded town in France. In addition it has a reputation for being especially sporty and there are numerous facilites including, most obviously, a white-water canoe course right through the centre of the town.

LURE

Station: *pl. de la gare*, 200 m from the town centre. There are no left-luggage facilities here, although the *chef de service* may oblige.

Tourist Office: *35 r. Carnot, 70200 Lure; tel: 84 62 80 52.* Open Mon–Fri 0900–1200, 1330–1730, Sat 0930–1200, 1400–1700, · Sun closed (July–Aug); Mon–Fri 0900–1200, 1330–1730, closed Sat and Sun (Sept–June). Fom the station, turn right on *r. de la Gare*, then right on *r. Carnot*, crossing the railway tracks.

Sightseeing

Lure is a small relaxed town whose one genuine sight is, bizarrely, the **Musée Historique du Boomerang**, *1 r. Henry Marsot; tel: 84 62 80 80*. It is based in Lure due to the endeavours of Jacques Thomas, a boomerang expert famous throughout the world (of boomerang experts). Open Tues–Sun 1000–1200, 1400–1800, closed Mon (July–Aug); Tues–Sun 1400–1800, closed Mon (Apr–June and Sept–Oct); closed Nov–Mar. Admission FFr.20.

The tourist office can supply details of walks in the Lure environs, including in the **Parc Naturel Régional des Ballons des Vosges**.

Épinal–Lure

STRASBOURG to LYON

This route runs parallel to the German and Swiss borders, through Alsace and Franche-Comté. It visits an exceptionally varied series of towns, including typically Alsatian Colmar, industrial Mulhouse, and wooded Besançon set in the Jura foothills.

TRAINS

ETT tables: 176, 156.

Fast Track

Five trains a day run between Strasbourg and Lyon Part-Dieu, with journey times of around 5 hrs. All trains carry buffets.

On Track

Strasbourg–Colmar

A frequent, but not regular, service runs between Strasbourg and Colmar during the day, although 2-hr gaps between trains do appear in the morning and afternoon. The journey takes 30–35 mins.

Colmar–Mulhouse

The 20-min journey between Colmar and Mulhouse is operated by a frequent service throughout the day.

Mulhouse–Belfort

Nine or ten fast trains run between Mulhouse and Belfort each day. The journey takes 25–30 mins.

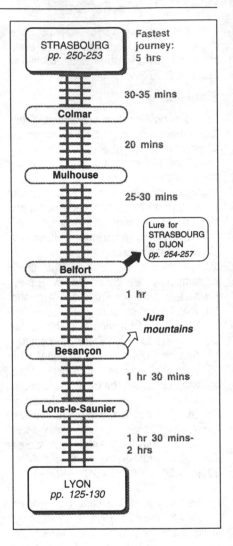

Belfort–Besançon

Six fast trains and a handful of locals operate the service between Belfort and Besançon Viotte each day. The journey takes just over 1 hr.

Besançon–Lons-le-Saunier

Three local trains and one express run

between Besançon Viotte and Lons-le-Saunier on most days, the journey taking around 1½ hrs. An extra lunchtime trip can be made by changing at Mouchard.

Lons-le-Saunier–Lyon

The service between Lons-le-Saunier and Lyon Part-Dieu consists of only a couple of trains in the early morning and two trains in the evening. The journey takes between 1 hr 30 mins and 2 hrs.

COLMAR

Station: *pl. de la Gare; tel: 89 24 50 50*, about 1 km south-west of the town centre. **Tourist Office:** *4 r. d' Unterlinden, 68000 Colmar; tel: 89 20 68 92.* Open Mon–Fri 0900–1900, Sat 0900–1700, Sun 1000–1300, 1400–1600 (July–Aug); Mon–Fri 0900–1200, 1400–1800, Sat 0900–1200, 1400–1700, Sun 1000–1200 (Sept–June).

Getting Around

Virtually all the interesting sights in Colmar are clustered around the pedestrianised area and the tourist office. To get there from the station, walk straight up *av. de la République*. A host of buses run from the station to the main Unterlinden bus station by the tourist office. Details are given at the rail station.

Accommodation

Colmar's quaint Alsatian town centre draws in plenty of crowds in season, and during summer occupancy rates and prices are high.

Hotel chains in Colmar include *Ca, Ch, Ib, Me* and *Nv.* Lower-priced hotels are very limited in number and scattered throughout the town.

HI: Auberge de Jeunesse Mittel-harth, *2 r. Pasteur; tel: 89 80 57 39.* Take bus no.

4 from the rail station to the *Lycée Technique* stop. The non-affiliated hostel **Maison des Jeunes et de la Culture** is at *17 r. Camille Schlumberger; tel: 89 41 26 87.*

Sightseeing

Colmar's old town is crammed with restored medieval houses in the typical Alsatian style: half-timbered with plaster painted in delicate pastel shades. The area from the *Musée d'Unterlinden* to the **Quartier des Tanneurs** and **Petite Venise** (Little Venice) is largely pedestrianised and contains 45 preserved buildings. The tourist office can supply details of a self-guided tour.

The **Musée d'Unterlinden**, *tel: 89 41 89 23*, opposite the tourist office, displays medieval religious art. The pride of the museum and a major draw to Colmar is the *Issenheim Altarpiece*, a three-panelled construction depicting the Crucifixion and biblical tales, painted by Grünewald and sculpted by Nicolas of Hagenau. Schongauer's masterpiece *The Virgin in the Rosebush* is also in the museum. Open daily 0900–1200, 1400–1800 (Apr–Oct); Mon, Wed–Sun 0900–1200, 1400–1700, Tues closed (Nov–Mar). Admission FFr.28.

Auguste Bartholdi, designer of the Statue of Liberty, lived in Colmar, and his former home at *30 r. des Marchands; tel: 89 41 90 60*, is now the **Musée Bartholdi**, housing models of his works and drafts for *the* statue. Open Mon, Wed–Sun 1000–1200, 1400–1800, Tues closed (Mar–Dec), closed Jan, Feb. Admission FFr.20.

Out of Town

The **Route du Vin d'Alsace** winds for 120 km along the eastern edge of the Vosges mountains between Colmar and Strasbourg, passing through quaint villages and the vineyards that have made Alsatian wines famous worldwide. The tourist offices at Colmar and Strasbourg (see p. 250) can supply details of the route, with information on public transportation.

MULHOUSE

Station: *10 av. du Gén. Leclerc; tel: 89 46 50 50*, 400 m south of the town centre.
Tourist Office: *9 av. Foch, 68100 Mulhouse; tel: 89 45 68 31*. Cross *av. Leclerc* from the station and head diagonally to the right. Open Mon–Sat 0900–1900, Sun 1000–1300 (summer); Mon–Fri 0900–1900, Sat 0900–1800, Sun closed (winter).

Sightseeing

Mulhouse is predominantly an industrial town and its major sights derive from its importance as a centre of engineering and manufacturing. There are 12 museums in the city; most are located in the suburbs and can be reached by bus. The **Musée National de l'Automobile** (National Car Museum); *192 av. de Colmar; tel: 89 42 29 17*, comprises over 500 vehicles collected by the Schlumpf brothers. (Take bus nos 1, 4 or 17).

The **Musée Français du Chemin de Fer** (French Railway Museum) and the **Musée du Sapeur Pompier** (Fire Brigade Museum) are located next to each other at *2 r. Alfred de Glehn; tel: 89 42 25 67* (bus no. 17). Museums open daily 1000–1800.

The town centre lacks the appeal of Colmar or Strasbourg, although the tourist office can provide details of a self-guided tour of the highlights. The **Musée de l'Impression sur Etoffes** (Museum of Printed Fabrics), *3 r. des Bonnes Gens*, one of the finest collections of fabrics in the world, is closed until Oct 1995.

BELFORT

Station: *av. Wilson; tel: 84 28 50 50*, 400 m south-west of the town centre.
Tourist Office: *pl. de la Commune de Paris, 90000 Belfort; tel: 84 28 12 23*. Open Mon–Sat 0900–1215, 1345–1900, Sun 1000–1230 (July–Aug); Mon–Sat 0900–1215, 1345–1800, Sun closed (Sept–June). Turn left out of the station and then bear right on *Faubourg de France. Le Petit Geni*, an encyclopaedic guide to all Belfort's offerings, is available free.

Accommodation

Belfort is yet to become the most fashionable of destinations, and rooms are usually easy to find. Hotel chains in Belfort include *BW*. **HI: Foyer de Jeunes Travailleurs Résidence Madrid**, *6 r. de Madrid; tel: 84 21 39 16*.

Sightseeing

Belfort is dominated by its fortified **château**, which occupies most of the eastern section of the city. Built by Vauban in the 17th-century, the château was designed to house 10,000 troops, and commands fine views of the Jura mountains. In front of the fortress is the 22 m-long **Lion of Belfort**, designed by Auguste Bartholdi (see p. 259) to commemorate the resistance in the disastrous 1870 Franco-Prussian war. The **Musée du Château** contains a slightly bizarre collection of military history and modern art. Open daily 1000–1900 (May–Sept); Mon, Wed–Sun 1000–1200, 1400–1700, Tues closed (Oct–Apr). Admission FFr.11. With the construction of the château, a fortified town grew up in its lap. Notable buildings include the **Cathédrale St-Christophe** and the **Hôtel de Ville** on *pl. d'Armes*.

BESANÇON

Station: Besançon Viotte, *av. de la Paix; tel: 81 53 50 50*, about 800 m north-west of the town centre.

Tourist Office: *2 pl. de la 1ère Armée Française, 25000 Besançon; tel: 81 80 92 55*. Open Mon 1000–1900, Tues–Sat 0900–1900 (Apr–Sept); Mon 1000–1800, Tues–Sat 0900–1800 (Oct–May), Sun 1000–1200, 1500–1700 (mid-June–mid-Sept).

Getting Around

Besançon **vieille ville** (old town) is enclosed on three sides by a dramatic meander of the river Doubs. To reach the tourist office from the rail station, walk down steep and busy *av. Maréchal Foch* and then turn left along the river. A number of buses run into town from the station; there is a bus map and timetable in the forecourt.

Accommodation

Finding somewhere to stay in Besançon is relatively easy compared to Colmar or Strasbourg to the north. Hotel chains in Besançon include *Ca, Ib, Me,* and *Nv.*

HI: Foyer Mixte de Jeunes Travailleurs Les Oiseaux, *48 r. des Cras; tel: 81 88 43 11*. **Centre International de Séjour**, *19 r. Martin du Gard; tel: 81 50 07 54.*

Sightseeing

Besançon has twice been voted France's greenest town and commands an impressive setting amid the foothills of the Jura mountains. There is a fine view of the city and its surroundings from the gardens in front of the station. Other than its horticultural attributes, Besançon sports a prominent **citadelle**, another 17th-century construction of Vauban. Inside, the **Musée de la Résistance et la Déportation** (*tel: 81 83 37 14*), is a compelling view of the role of the Vichy government and the Resistance. Admission FFr.30. The **Musée des Beaux Arts**, *1 pl. de la Révolution; tel: 81 81 44 47*, one of the oldest museums in France, has an impressive Renaissance collection. Admission FFr.20. Besançon was a Roman town, and the **Porte Noire**, *r. de la Convention*, dates from this period.

🡖 Side Track from Besançon

South from Besançon, an alternative rail route to Lyon heads through the **Jura mountains**, rather than along the Route des Vins de Jura (see below). The railway passes through an area of lakes and cross-country skiing routes, via the villages of **Champagnole** (tourist office at *Hôtel de Ville; tel: 84 52 43 67*), **Morez** (tourist office *75 pl. Jean Jaurès; tel: 84 33 08 73*) and **St-Claude** (tourist office *1 av. de Belfort; tel: 84 45 34 24*).

LONS-LE-SAUNIER

Station: for information *tel: 84 47 50 50*. **Tourist Office:** *1 r. Pasteur, 39000 Lons-Le-Saunier; tel: 84 24 65 01*. Open Mon–Fri 0830–1200, 1400–1800; Sat 0830–1200, 1400–1700. Also open Sun 1400–1800 (mid-July–mid-Aug).

Lons-Le-Saunier, the capital of Jura, is a picturesque town set on the **Route des Vins de Jura**, which stretches from Arbois in the north via Lons to Beaufort in the south.

Any of the tourist offices in Franche-Comté can provide a guide to the route and its vineyards. Unlike the Alsace route, many of the towns on the Jura route, including Arbois, Poligny and Lons, are accessible by train, although the service is infrequent.

TOULOUSE

The large red-brick city, population 350,000, comes as a pleasant surprise to visitors who expect it to be all hi-tech industry, for which it is justly famous. However, the Canal du Midi, opposite the rail station, shuts out some of the hectic bustle of the ring road traffic, and the River Garonne, beside the historic centre, exudes a gracious, spacious ambience. Toulousains have good places to eat, shop, relax and give the impression of enjoying life to the full.

Tourist Information

Tourist Office: Donjon du Capitole BP 0801, 31080 Toulouse; tel: 61 23 32 00. Housed in a 16th-century tower, the office provides information, guided tours in season, bureau de change facilities (weekends), but no hotel reservations. Open Mon–Sat 0900–1900 (May–Sept), Sun and holidays 0900–1300, 1400–1730 (Oct–Apr); Mon–Fri 0900–1800, Sat 0900–1230, 1400–1800, Sun and hols 1000–1230, 1400–1700 (Oct–Apr).

Regional information available from **Comité Departemental du Tourisme Haute-Garonne**, 14 r. de Bayard 3100 Toulouse; tel: 61 99 44 00. Open Mon–Fri 0900–1700. Wide range of free information with lists of accommodation and activities. No hotel reservations.

Arriving and Departing

Airport
Aéroport de Toulouse-Blagnac; tel: 61 42 44 00; information; tel: 61 42 44 64 or 61 42 44 65. It is 10 km west of the city. **Navette Toulouse-Aéroport**, tel: 61 30 04 89, has a bus every 20 mins. Departs **gare routière** (bus station), behind the rail station, Mon–Fri 0520–2100, Sat 0600–1940, Sun 0600–2100. Departs airport Mon–Fri 0640–2320, Sat 0620–2230, Sun 0540–2320. The last bus waits for the last flight arrival. Fare FFr.23 (concessions FFr.18). The two-storey airport has an information desk, snack bar, restaurant, bars, shops, bank (open Mon–Fri 0900–1900, Sat, Sun and holidays 1000–1200, 1330–1800), post office (open Mon–Fri 1300–1600) and a taxi rank; tel: 61 30 02 54. FFr.100 to city centre.

Station
Gare Toulouse Matabiau; tel: 36 35 35 35. It has automatic cash dispensers, lockers, bath FFr.18, shower FFr.13. Tourist information office open Mon–Sat 0930–2000, Sun 1000–2000, tel: 61 62 50 50. Free maps and leaflets, but no hotel reservations. One of the flamboyant stations of France, the massive building is covered with carved coats of arms. It is a 12-min walk to the city centre, 2 mins by metro.

Buses
Gare Routière (bus station), 20 r. Stalingrad; tel: 62 11 26 99; for information, tel: 61 41 70 70.

Getting Around

It is simple to walk around the centre of Toulouse to its historic quarter, main sights, restaurant and shopping areas. The efficient, extensive bus network is backed by a modern, clean underground metro.

SEMVAT, Espace Transport, 7 pl. Equirol; tel: 61 41 70 70, runs the bus

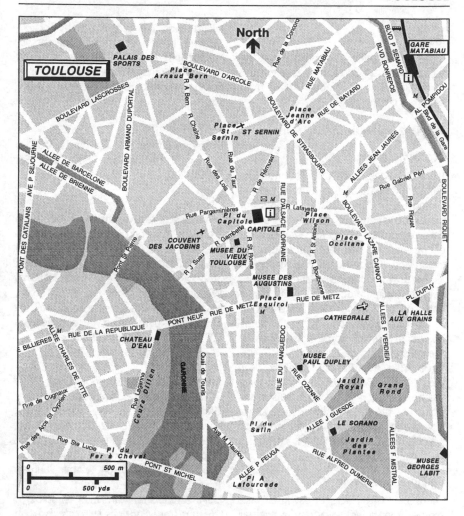

network. There are one and two zone tickets valid for both bus and the new metro, which opened in 1993. One ticket for one zone, FFr.7, is valid for 45 mins after being stamped. One ticket for two zones, FFr.9.50, is valid for 1 hr. A book of ten tickets is FFr.55 for one zone, FFr.75 for two zones. A one-day ticket, on sale at the metro stop within the *Marengo-SNCF* station, is FFr.30, valid for two zones.

Metro

The underground system has a single route, **Ligne A** (Ligne B is under construction), from *Joliment* to *Basso Cambo*. The stop at the rail station is *Marengo-SNCF*. The line is open daily 0500–0030. Ticket machines have buttons to press for instructions in English.

Taxis

There are taxi ranks (day and night) at the rail station, *pl. Wilson* and *pl. Esquirol*; *tel: 61 42 38 38* or *61 21 00 72*. Fare from station to centre: FFr.40.

Staying in Toulouse

Accommodation

There is a wide range of hotels including some apartment hotels and no problem in finding rooms. The tourist office does not make reservations but provides free a very detailed booklet, *Hotels Restaurants*. Most of the modern chain hotels are near the airport and include *Ho, Ib, Me, Nv* and *Sf*.

The town centre is well-dotted with hotels, including a good choice of cheaper hotels off *pl. Wilson* (*r. St-Antoine*) and off *pl. de Capitole* (*r. du Taur*, *r. P. Romiguiéres*). There are some hotels opposite the rail station (*r. de Bayard*).

HI: Villa des Rosiers, *124 av. Jean Rieux; tel: 61 80 49 93*. Closed first three weeks in Jan, it is about 3 km outside the city. From rail station take bus no. 22 via city centre, a 15-min journey to stop: *Leygues* (or take bus no. 14, change at *pl. Dupuy* for bus no. 22).

Eating and Drinking

There are many places to eat in all price ranges. The *r. de Bayard* from the rail station has fast-food bars and take-away restaurants including Tunisian, Chinese, Lebanese and Asian. This leads to the *blvd Strasbourg*, a wide avenue lined with plane trees, open-air brasseries, bistros and restaurants. Set menus can start at FFr.65.

In summer, there are open-air restaurants everywhere, encircling the central fountain of busy *pl. Wilson*, lining the sides of the spacious *pl. du Capitole* and taking over the quieter, pretty *pl. St-Georges*. Local specialities include *cassoulet, pot au feu canard, foies gras, pâtés* and Armagnac brandy. The largest market is at **pl. Victor Hugo**, open Tues–Sun 0600–1300.

Communications

Main **Post Office:** *9 r. Lafayette; tel: 62 15 33 33*. Open Mon–Fri 0800–1900, Sat 0800–1200; poste restante facilities.

Money

The closest bureau de change to the station is at *30 r. du Taur*, near *pl. Capitole*. There are many banks dotted throughout the city including branches of **Barclays**, *2 blvd. Strasbourg; tel: 61 99 41 14*, and **National Westminster**, *34 r. de Metz, 61 52 66 45*. Money-changing facilities are also available at the main tourist office, Sat, Sun, holidays 1030–1200, 1400–1639 (May–Sept).

Consulates

Canada: *30 blvd de Strasbourg; tel: 61 99 30 16.* (bus stop: *Jeanne d'Arc*)
UK: *c/o Lucas Aerospace, Victoria Centre, chemin de Laporte, St-Martin-du-Touch, Toulouse 31300; tel: 61 15 02 02.* (bus stop: the post office at St-Martin-du-Touch; take bus no. 64, 15-min journey, from the *Arènes* metro stop).
USA: *22 cours du Mar. Foch; tel 56 52 65 95.* (bus stop: *Pont des Desmoiselles*).

Entertainment

Toulouse is a busy cultural city with opera seasons at the **Théâtre du Capitole**, *tel: 61 23 21 35;* classical concerts at **La Halle aux Grains**, *pl. Dupuy; tel: 61 23 21 35* and the **Palais des Sports**, *Campans Caffarerelli, blvd Lascrosses; tel: 62 15 14 14*, and dance and dramatic arts at **Le Sorano**, *35 allée Jules Guesde, tel: 61 52 95 50.*

Contemporary, youthful productions are on at **Nouveau Théâtre Jules Julien**, *tel: 61 25 79 92*.

With its large student population, the city has a wide choice of centrally located discos, with one vast club even offering dancing outside by a swimming pool (**L'Apocalypse,** *9 r. Jean Rodier; tel: 61 25 79 92*). For concerts by visiting musicians, the best place to buy tickets is **FNAC,** *16 al. F. Roosevelt; tel: 36 68 91 12*.

Shopping

Toulouse is an excellent shopping city, with many international designer stores and well-known retailing names. Head for *r. Alsace Lorraine*, the backbone of the shopping area, including department stores, and *pl. Wilson*, with off-shoots like *r. St-Antoine du T.*, *r. Lafayette* and *r. Lapeyrouse*. There is a good choice of smart shops in and around *pl. St-Georges* (*r. Boulbonne, r. de la Pomme*).

The narrow streets near St-Sernin have craft and gift shops and a cheaper range of fashion shops. There is a flea market, Sun 0800–1400, beside the St-Sernin basilica and a second-hand book market, Thurs, at the *pl. A. Bernard*. A market takes over *pl. du Capitole* on Wed.

Sightseeing

There are several walking tours on various themes (French only) which leave from the tourist office (July–Sept). A bus tour, 2 hrs, departs daily 1500, FFr.58.

Toulouse is easy to explore on foot because many main attractions are within a few minutes' walk of the grand central hub of the city, **pl. du Capitole** (metro: *Capitole*). One side of the square is dominated by the splendid 18th-century town hall **Le Capitole**, which opens its wing of highly decorated rooms, the **Les**

Salles des Illustres (the room of the illustrious), also used for meetings and receptions; *tel: 61 22 29 22*. Open Wed–Sun, 1300–1900. Admission free.

Leading off the *pl. Capitole* are the narrow picturesque streets of the old town (including *r. du Taur*, *r. Pargaminières Romiguieres*, *r. Gambetta* and *r. St-Rome*). The *r. du Taur* goes to the **Basilique St-Sernin**, the largest Romanesque church in western Europe, built in the late 11th century. Next to it is the **Musée St-Raymond** (a museum of archaeological finds), built as a student hostel in 1523, but now closed for renovations, possibly long-term. The *r. P. Romiguières* leads to the riverside and the **Pont St-Pierre**. From here and along the *prom. H. Martin* to the *Pont Neuf* are fine views of the wide river.

The *r. Gambetta* heads towards another church (on the off-shoot *r. Lakanal*) with a strikingly simple beauty, **Le Couvent des Jacobins** (the Church of the Jacobins), completed in 1385 and dedicated to St Thomas Aquinas, who is buried here. Note the richly coloured rib vaulting of the ceiling. The cloisters have an admission price, FFr.10, which includes entry into the art exhibition, changed monthly, in the refectory.

The *r. St-Rome* goes to form a quaint crossroads with the *r. des Changes* and its corner of half-timbered buildings. Along the way is the **Le Musée du Vieux Toulouse** (museum of old Toulouse), *7 r. du May; tel: 61 13 97 24*. Open Mon–Sat 1500–1800 (June–Sept); Thurs 1430–1730 (May, Oct). FFr.10 (concessions FFr.5). Run by volunteers in an old town mansion which has pottery, ceramics, medals, prints and household objects, it gives a glimpse of Toulousain life over the centuries.

Three other museums to visit include the

important **Musée des Augustins,** *21 r. de Metz, tel: 61 23 55 07.* Open Wed–Sun 1000–1700; Wed until 2100. FFr.10. (metro: *Esquirol*). An impressive former Augustinian monastery houses the municipal collection of paintings and sculptures, with many Romanesque and medieval items which were rescued from other city buildings. (It is just up the street from the city's **Cathédrale St-Etienne**). **Le Musée Paul Dupuy**, *13 r. de la Pleau; tel: 61 22 21 83*, is open Wed–Sun 1000–1700 (Oct–May); Wed–Sun 1000–1800 (June–Sept). FFr.10. (bus stop: *Carmes*). Based on the bequest of one main decorative arts collection, there are clocks, pottery, glassware, silver and gold ornaments and a complete 17th-century apothecary plus paintings, drawings, engravings and altar panels. The **Musée Georges Labit,** *43 r. des Martyrs de la Libération; tel: 61 22 21 84*, is open Wed–Sun 1000–1800 (June–Sept); Wed–Sun 1000–1700 (Oct–May). FFr.10, (bus stop: *Demouilles*). A great collection of treasures from travels to Asia and Japan is housed in a purpose-built, neo-Moorish building which also has sculptures from India, China and Tibet and Egyptian antiques. A multi-entry ticket is available: three museums for FFr.20, six for FFr.30.

On the other side of the Garonne is the **St-Cyprien** district, which has two interesting attractions. Right beside the Pont Neuf is the water tower, built 1822, now converted to hold the **Galerie Château d'Eau**, *pl. Laganne; tel: 61 42 61 72*. Open Wed–Fri, Mon 1200–1800; Sat, Sun 1300–1900. FFr.15–FFr.10. (bus stop: *cours Dillon*). Photographic exhibitions, changed regularly, have been held here for 20 years in tribute to the city's contribution to the early development of photography. A 10-min walk away is the **Centre Municipal de l'Affiche, de la Carte Postale et d l'Art Graphique** (Centre for the Poster, Postcard and Graphic Art), *58 allée Charles de Fitte; tel: 61 59 24 64*. Open Mon–Fri 0900–1200, 1400–1800. Admission free (bus and metro stop: *St-Cyrien République*).

Cruises with commentary, 60–90 min trip, on the Garonne and the Canal du Midi depart all year round (usually 1400 and 1800) aboard the **Cap d'Ambre** from *Port de l'Embouchure* (Ponts Jumeaux). Booking necessary, *tel: 61 71 45 95*. (bus stop: *Ponts Jumeaux*). FFr.70 (FFr.45).

Lunch and dinner cruises on the Canal du Midi aboard **L'Occitana** depart from the *blvd P. Semard*, diagonally opposite the rail station, *tel: 61 63 06 06*. Lunch cruise Tues–Sat 1245–1430, Sun 1245–1530, FFr.180; Sun FFr.230. Afternoon cruise Tues–Sat 1500–1800, FFr.85. Dinner cruise Tues–Thurs 2030–2330, FFr.230. Musical evening cruise Fri, Sat 2030–2330, FFr.260.

Out of Town

All-day guided bus tours (French and English) are available Apr–Nov from **Voyages Fram** (*tel: 61 11 02 22*) at the tourist office. Bookings also taken by phone, *tel: 62 15 17 30*. Tours depart 0800 from *pl. Wilson*, returning between 1900–2030, FFr.160. Themes include castles in the Cathar region; Carcassone and region; Gascony country and fortified villages; Narbonne and Fontfroide Abbey; Moissac and fortified villages; and châteaux in the Lauragais region.

Always an aviation centre, the region is home to **Aérospatiale,** manufacturers of the Airbus and Concorde, *tel: 61 15 44 00*, in the village of Colomiers, 12 km west of Toulouse. Tours of the factory (in French) are available but must be booked in advance – enquire at the tourist office.

TOULOUSE to PERPIGNAN

The flat countryside around Toulouse with its views of farmland changes within an hour as it reaches the walled town of Foix. The wide, rushing waters of the River Ariège appear at frequent intervals. Sheer stone cliffs start closing in on either side of the train and mountains appear in the open stretches. Part of this delightful journey is by an open-sided, narrow-gauge train through tiny hamlets and glorious vistas and with a 'jolly day out' atmosphere. This train goes through many tunnels as it cuts through the Pyrénée mountains on the way to Villefranche and Perpignan.

TRAINS

ETT tables: 163, 144, 143.

→ Fast Track

The fast service between Toulouse Matabiau and Perpignan goes via Narbonne and not through the Pyrenees Mountains. Only one evening train a day makes the through journey, taking 2½ hrs for the run. Other choices are made available by changing trains in Narbonne.

⤳ On Track

Toulouse–L'Hospitalet–La Tour de Carol
Four trains a day run through from Toulouse Matabiau to La Tour de Carol Enveitg each day, calling at L'Hospitalet-près-l'Andorre en route. Toulouse to

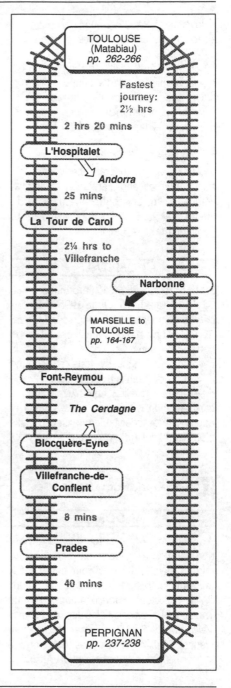

TOULOUSE (Matabiau) pp. 262-266

Fastest journey: 2½ hrs

2 hrs 20 mins

L'Hospitalet
↘ Andorra

25 mins

La Tour de Carol

2¼ hrs to Villefranche

Narbonne

MARSEILLE to TOULOUSE pp. 164-167

Font-Reymou
↘
The Cerdagne
↗
Blocquère-Eyne

Villefranche-de-Conflent

8 mins

Prades

40 mins

PERPIGNAN pp. 237-238

L'Hospitalet takes 2 hrs 20 mins, L'Hospitalet to La Tour de Carol takes 25 mins.

La Tour de Carol–Villefranche

Just a couple of narrow gauge trains run down the line from La Tour de Carol Enveitg to Villefranche-Vernet on most days. Journey time is around 2¼ hrs.

Villefranche–Prades–Perpignan

Six trains a day operate between Villefranche-Vernet and Perpignan calling at Prades-Molitg en route. Villefranche to Prades takes 8 mins and Prades to Perpignan takes 40 mins.

L'HOSPITALET

Station: *tel: 68 35 50 50* (information); *68 34 74 11* (sales). From June 1995, there wil be one number for both services, *tel: 36 35 35 35*. A tiny station with lockers but no buffet. Uniquely, it accepts pesetas in payment for tickets by travellers coming in from Andorra. It is this connection which draws many travellers here. Across the car park, a 2-min walk away, are a couple of hotels with outdoor tables which can make a pleasant spot for admiring the views.

- - - - - - - - - - - - - - - - - - -

 Side Track from L'Hospitalet

ANDORRA

A bus runs from L'Hospitalet-près-l'Andorre station to Andorra all year, 1 hr 40-min journey, with up to four buses a day (mid-July–mid-Sept). The service is run by **SFAT** (*Société Franco-Andorraine de Transports*), *Carrer la Llacuna, Andorra la Vella; tel: 62 8 21 3 72* (when calling from France). FFr.37. The bus goes to Andorra la Vella, the furiously busy capital. Although

no longer isolated from the world, Andorra remains a phenomenon, with mountainous scenery and a duty-free policy which makes its main road traffic-laden with French and Spanish visitors stocking up on alcohol, petrol, ski-wear and electrical goods.

- - - - - - - - - - - - - - - - - - -

LA TOUR DE CAROL

Station: *tel: 68 35 50 50* (information); *68 34 73 11 (sales)* . From June 1995, there will be one number for both services; *tel: 36 35 35 35*. There is a change of trains at this isolated little station which is the terminus. Buffet, no lockers.

Tourist Office: (across the road), *Gare Internationale Enveitg-La Tour de Carol; tel: 68 04 83 58*. Despite its grand address, it is a small office, but has lots of information about the valley of the Carol River, which is popular with hikers.

From this station, the service is by the SNCF narrow-gauge **Petit Train Jaune** (little yellow train), which runs through the **Cerdagne** plateau (see p. 269) as far as Villefranche, an important stronghold in the Middle Ages. This is the Catalan region, a mixture of French and Spanish culture and tradition, which has evolved since the Spanish ceded almost all of it to the French in 1659.

VILLEFRANCHE-DE-CONFLENT

Station: Villefranche-Vernet; *tel: 68 35 50 50* (information); *68 34 74 11* (sales). From June 1995, one number for both; *tel: 36 35 35 35*. The small station has a buffet but no lockers; luggage can be left with the attendant.

Tourist Office: *pl. de l'Église, 66500 Villefranche-de-Conflent; tel: 68 96 22 96*. Information on hiking routes, accommodation, guided tours. Open daily 1000–1800.

Sightseeing

Villefranche-de-Conflent is the actual town at the station. The station name, however, also refers to a town very close by, Vernet-les-Bains. On a hill-top overlooking the station is the enormous stone-built **Fort Liberia**, built by the military engineer, Sebastien Vauban, in 1681. Here there is another change of train, leaving the narrow-gauge track for the train to Perpignan. There is only a 10-min wait for this connecting train. However, there are up to eight trains a day in summer so it is possible to visit the town, a short walk from the station, and catch a later train.

The narrow streets of Villefranche seem transported from the Middle Ages. To get to Fort Liberia, there is a minibus from the gate, **Porte de France**, or, leading from *r. St-Pierre*, there is a path upwards or an underground staircase with 750 steps. The fort, *tel: 68 96 34 01*, is open daily 0900–1900 (Apr–Oct); 1000–1800 (Nov–Mar). FFr.28 (concessions FFr.14).

Travellers who stay in the area might consider trips by jeep to the **Canigou**, the most majestic of the Pyrénée peaks (altitude 2784 m). Contact Jean-Paul Bouzan, *17 blvd des Pyrénées, 66820 Vernet-Les-Bains; tel: 68 05 62 28.*

PRADES

Station: *tel: 68 35 50 50* (information); *68 34 71 11* (sales). From June 1995, *tel: 36 35 35 35.* A tiny station with no buffet or lockers, although luggage can be left.
Tourist Office: *4 r. V. Hugo, 66500 Prades; tel: 68 96 27 58.*

Prades is a town built in layers on steep sides at the foot of Mount Canigou. The town is an international festival centre, thanks to the Spanish cellist Pablo Casals,

The Cerdagne

At a height of 1200 m, the plateau could almost detract from the grandeur of the mountains, the last of the Pyrénées, but they loom too dramatically both as distant vistas and close-up views. The train, bright yellow trimmed with red, whistles energetically as it approaches tunnels and climbs to such towns as **Font-Reymou**, a modern sports resort. At the next stop, **Bloquère-Eyne**, a sign declares that it is the highest station in France with an altitude of 1593 m. From then the train begins its descent through many tunnels, curving tracks, a long suspension bridge, often beside verdant gorges. The line was constructed in 1910–11 to link the isolated villages of the area with the rest of France.

who lived here in exile. Information on the summer concerts from the **Association Festival Pablo Casals**, *r. V. Hugo, 66500 Prades; tel: 68 96 33 07.*

The mountain views along the route continue grandly on the way to Perpignan (see p. 237) which is at the heart of fertile agricultural countryside, the Roussillon plain. Enjoying 325 days of sunshine each year, it produces not only wonderful fruit, but is also France's most southern wine-growing area.

– – – – – – – – – – – – – – – – – – –

⬇ Connection: Perpignan to Narbonne

There are up to a dozen trains from Perpignan to Narbonne, journey time 30–45 mins, to link up with the Marseille–Toulouse route, p. 164.

TOURS

Between the Loire and the Cher at the heart of the 'Vallée des Rois', Tours stands at the centre of the region's rail and bus connections, making it the ideal touring base for independent train travellers. Armed with determination and timetables you can reach many of the most famous and lesser-known châteaux, both of the Loire and of its smaller tributaries. Tours has a rich history of its own to explore and a spacious, big-city feel.

Tourist Information

Tourist Office: 78 r. Bernard Palissy, 37000 Tours; tel: 47 70 37 37, a modern glass building, next to the new Vinci congress centre and diagonally opposite the SNCF station on blvd Heurteloup. Open Mon–Sat 0900–1230, 1330–1800, Sun 1000–1300. There is no accommodation service and the town plan costs FFr.2. The free booklet Pays des Châteaux has useful listings of many of the places to visit in the Centre/Val de Loire region.

Arriving and Departing

Station

The SNCF station is on pl. du Mar. Leclerc; tel: 47 20 50 50, a large and recently renovated station with good facilities. Many long-distance services use the near-by station of St-Pierre des Corps, with a connecting service to and from the main station in Tours. To reach the cathedral and fine arts museum, continue along r. Bernard Palissy (alongside the tourist office) and turn right at the small park (7 mins). For pl. Jean Jaurès, turn left on blvd Heurteloup (5 mins). Cycle rental available.

Getting Around

Despite its spacious feel, Tours can easily be explored on foot, as its main sights all lie north of pl. Jean Jaurès between the boulevards and the Loire.

If you are staying outside the centre, all local bus services stop at pl. Jean Jaurès. For more information the **Aile Bleu Espace Bus** office is in the Galerie Jean Jaurès (tel: 47 66 70 70). Long-distance bus services depart from the **Gare Routière**, (bus station) pl. du Mar. Leclerc; tel: 47 05 30 49, in front of the SNCF station. Ask at the Accueil office (near the platforms) for the leaflet Les châteaux de la Loire en train.

Staying in Tours

Accommodation

There is a wide choice of hotels in all price ranges in the centre of the city, but it is certainly worth making reservations ahead. International chains with hotels in Tours include BW, Ho, Ib, IH, Me.

HI: the nearest is at av. d'Arsonval, Parc de Grandmont; tel: 47 25 14 45 (4km south-east of town at Chambray, bus nos 2 or 6 to stop: Auberge de Jeunesse). **Camping**: nearest is Municipal E Peron; tel: 47 54 11 11 (on the north bank of the Loire, bus no. 7 to Ste-Radegonde).

There are several one- and two-star hotels between the cathedral and r. Nationale (north of pl. Jean Jaurès), although the cheapest area is near the SNCF station and on av. de Grammont (south from pl. Jean Jaurès).

Eating and Drinking

Typical Touraine specialities include rillettes

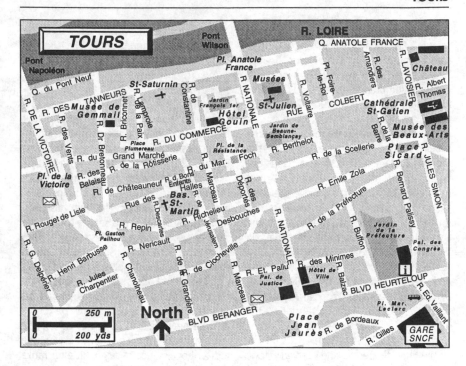

and *rillons* (potted and cubed pork), *friture* (small fried fish from the Loire), and *pruneaux fourrés de Tours* (stuffed prunes) – for the latter try the pâtisserie **Sabat** at *76 r. Nationale* – as well, of course, as Touraine, Chinon, Bourgeil and sparkling Vouvray wines. There are restaurants and brasseries along *av. de Grammont* and *r. Nationale*, including **L'Univers** on *pl. Jean Jaurès*, and several small restaurants around *r. Colbert* which joins the cathedral quarter with the main restaurant area of Tours in the **vieille ville** (old town). The narrow pedestrianised streets of this highly restored quarter centre on **pl. Plumereau**. It is crowded with bars and restaurants and particularly animated at night when the half-timbered houses are illuminated and the pavements and small terraces are buzzing. There is a choice both of prices and types of food, and it is worth investigating the menus in the many side-streets such as *r. de la Paix*, *r. de la Rôtisserie* and *r. du Grand Marché*.

Events

A selection of music festivals take place every summer: the **Florilège Vocal de Tours** in May, the famous **Fêtes Musicales en Touraine** in June and the **Semaines Musicales de Tours** in July.

Sightseeing

Founded by the Romans, and a flourishing trading centre by the 4th century, Tours was the royal capital during the reign of Louis XI and its prosperity continued until the 17th century. Monuments from this long history cluster together between the Loire and *pl. Sicard*.

At the end of this small square the 18th-century Episcopal Palace, in a lovely garden, houses the **Musée des Beaux-Arts**, with an extensive collection including works by Rembrandt, Rubens and Delacroix (open daily except Tues 0900–1245, 1400–1800; adults FFr.30). Next door is the ornate **Cathédrale St-Gatien**, with some superb stained glass windows, and the **Cloître de la Psalette**. Unlike its neighbours along the Loire, Tours is not dominated by its **château**, whose remaining portion, built over **Roman walls**, stands on the corner of *r. Lavoisier* towards the Loire. Today it houses the **Historial de Touraine**, open daily 0900–1800 (July–Aug), 0900–1200, 1400–1800 (Apr–June and Sept–Oct), 1400–1800 (Nov–Mar); adults FFr.31, and the **Tropical Aquarium**, open daily 0930–1900 (July–Aug) 0930–1230, 1400–1800 (Apr–June and Sept–Oct), 1400-1800 (Nov–Mar); adults FFr.28.

The half-timbered and carved stone houses of the **vielle ville** make interesting strolling; at *7 r. du Murier* the **Musée du Gemmail** displays a luminous collection of stained glass above a 12th-century underground chapel, open daily except Mon, 1000–1800 (July–Aug), 1000–1130, 1400–1800 (Sept–June); adults FFr.28, while on *r. du Commerce* the astonishing 16th-century **Hôtel Goüin** has a museum of archaeology, open daily 1000–1900 (May–Sept), 1000–1230, 1400–1830 (Oct–Apr), closed Fri (Oct–Mar); adults FFr.18.

Another pair of museums stands nearby in the St-Julien cloister and cellars on *r. Nationale*. Upstairs, the **Musée du Compagnonnage** is a collection of the 'masterpieces' made by tradesmen before being admitted as master craftsmen by the guilds, open daily except Tues 0900–1800 (mid-June–mid-Sept), 0900–1130, 1400–1630 (mid-Sept–mid-June); adults FFr.20;

downstairs is the **Musée des Vins de Touraine** (same hours, adults FFr.10).

Side Tracks from Tours

Train and bus connections are excellent from here. Many of the châteaux in the region, especially Saumur (see p. 282) and Blois (p. 235) can be reached from Tours.

A delightful detour from the broad, sluggish Loire is to follow the peaceful Indre valley to **Loches**. The train has been replaced by an SNCF bus service (passes are valid as usual) which follows the river with its mills, via the village of **Cormery** and its ruined Benedictine abbey. The charming small town of Loches sits at the foot of the medieval citadel where Charles VII and his mistress Agnès Sorel held court: the tourist office is near the station (*tel: 47 59 07 98*).

South-east from Tours but also on the Indre, Renaissance **Azay-le-Rideau** ranks with Chenonceau (p. 278) as one the most perfect of all the châteaux. Balzac called it 'a diamond cut in facets', open daily 0900–1830 (July–Aug), 0930–1730 (Apr–June and Sept), 0930–1200, 1400–1700 (Oct–Mar), admission FFr.31. Balzac himself stayed 6 km upstream at **Saché**, where he wrote several of his novels (open same hours as Azay, admission FFr.21). Azay station is 2 km from the château, although in the mornings the trip is made by SNCF bus which stops in the village. The service continues to **Chinon** on the Vienne, which stands in stark contrast as a fortress built for defence rather than for pleasure. On Thurs and weekends from late May to early Sept, steam train enthusiasts can make the 21 km trip to **Richelieu**. The statesman's château no longer stands but the grounds are extensive (*tel: 47 58 12 97* for details).

TOURS· to BORDEAUX

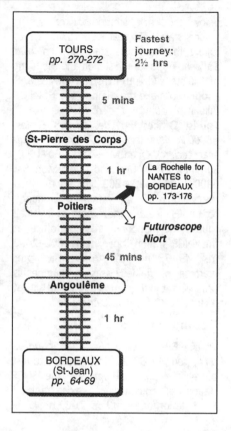

The Tours–Angoulême section of this route passes through the region of Poitou-Charentes, which extends west to La Rochelle (Nantes–Bordeaux route, p. 173), an historic, agricultural region brought closer to Paris since the arrival of the TGV. From Angoulême to Bordeaux the views are striking, owing to the vast swathes of sunflower fields and then almost continuous vineyards stretching along tree-lined countryside. There is the occasional glimpse of a steeple or spire of the little towns on the hills.

TRAINS

ETT table: 136.

 Fast Track

The journey from Tours to Bordeaux involves a change of train at St-Pierre des Corps on the outskirts of Tours. Five TGV services operate from St-Pierre des Corps to Bordeaux St-Jean each day. St-Pierre des Corps is a 5-min minute shuttle train (*Navette*) ride from Tours; from St-Pierre des Corps to Bordeaux takes 2½ hrs.

 On Track

Tours–Poitiers

There are a few through slow trains between Tours and Poitiers but by far the best service involves changing to a TGV at St-Pierre des Corps. Eight connections each

day are available with journey times of around 1 hr.

Poitiers–Angoulême–Bordeaux

Nine or ten TGV trains link Poitiers with Bordeaux, calling at Angoulême en route. Poitiers to Angoulême takes 45 mins, Angoulême to Bordeaux St-Jean takes around 1 hr.

POITIERS

Station: *blvd du Grand Cerf; tel: 49 58 50 50.* In the modern SNCF style, with good facilities and helpful staff, the station lies

---

Trains–Poitiers

below the rock promontory on which Poitiers stands. To reach the town centre, follow the signposts starting from *blvd Solferino* opposite the station and the flight of 140 steps (10–15 mins). Bus nos 3, 6, 8 and 9 also make the climb to the Hôtel de Ville in *pl. du Mar. Leclerc*.

Tourist Office: *8 r. des Grands Écoles, 86000 Poitiers; tel: 49 41 21 24*, (off *pl. du Mar. Leclerc*). Open Mon–Sat 0900–1900, Sun 1130–1800 (July and Aug); Mon–Sat 0900–1200, 1330–1800 (Sept–June). Hotel reservations FFr.10 within the Vienne region, FFr.20 beyond. There is a small tourist information/Futuroscope office at the SNCF station, open daily 0800–2000 (*tel: 49 37 04 18*). An extensive programme of guided visits in summer is organised by the **Service Ville d'Art et d'Histoire**, *1 pl. de la Cathédrale*.

Getting Around

Espace Bus office at *8 r. du Chaudron d'Or; tel: 49 88 23 41* (near the tourist office); *Le Printania* opposite the SNCF station sells bus tickets. **Taxis**: rank at SNCF station or *tel: 49 58 21 37* or *49 88 12 34*.

Accommodation and Food

Hotels and brasseries cluster on *pl. du Mar. Leclerc*, and *r. Carnot*, and around *r. de la Regatterie*. **HI**: *17 r. de la Jeunesse; tel: 49 58 03 05* (bus no. 3 to stop: *Cape Sud*).

Entertainment

The booklet *L'Été à Poitiers*, free from the tourist office, lists all the concerts and events of the summer, including the *Bistrots de l'Été*, free concerts throughout the town.

Sightseeing

An early centre of Christianity in France,

Poitiers combines its ancient architectural heritage with a young university lifestyle. Many a town would blanch at the prospect of shrouding its best-known monument in scaffolding for over three years, but a huge, bright modern mural temporarily covers the astonishing carved 12th-century façade of the church of **Notre-Dame-La-Grande**, and visitors are encouraged to visit the *chantier* (building site). Brochures and videos explain the restoration in minute detail and you can actually climb inside the scaffolding to inspect the difference a blast of sand can make. Inside, the church has painted pillars and frescoes which can be illuminated by a time-switch to the right of the altar.

Also in the *Quartier Notre-Dame* are bustling shopping streets and the **Palais des Comtes de Poitou**, with its vast Gothic hall, now incorporated into the **Palais de Justice**. North of the peaceful quadrangle of the university, **r. de la Chaîne** is lined with half-timbered houses, including the 15th-century **Hôtel Fumé** and, further along, the Renaissance Berthellot mansion.

The long and quiet **r. de la Cathédrale** leads to another fascinating architectural ensemble, the *Quartier Ste-Croix*, which includes the **Cathédrale de St-Pierre**, rather squat from the outside, but light and simple inside; the planetarium at the sleek modern **Espace Mendès France**, (open Tues–Fri 1000–1900, Sat and Sun 1400–1900); and one of France's oldest Christian buildings, the **Baptistère St-Jean**, with frescoes and octagonal font and a small museum (open daily except Tues, 1030–1230, 1500–1800 Apr–Oct, 1430–1700 Nov–Mar: FFr.4). Next door the **Musée Ste-Croix** has an excellent collection of regional ethnography and fine art, in the former abbey of Ste-Croix (open daily except Mon, 1000–1200, 1400–1800, adults FFr.15).

Poitiers also has a couple of attractive parks at either end of the town centre: to the the north, the **Jardin des Plantes,** (open 0700–2000) has a collection of cacti, while at the southern tip of the ramparts the larger **Parc de Blossac** (open 0700–2200) is a traditionally ordered French park with an English garden. Nearby is the unusual **St-Hilaire le Grand**, another early pilgrim church, begun in the 11th century.

↷ Side Tracks from Poitiers

Eight km north of Poitiers, **Futuroscope** is quickly becoming one of France's most popular attractions. A park devoted to the moving and photographic image, the site has its own hotels and restaurants and includes research and teaching facilities, but it is for its collection of modernistic **cinemas** – from Imax and 3-D to *cinéma dynamique*, where the seats move with the action on screen – that it is best known. Every Sat evening from Apr–Oct, and every night in July and Aug, *La Symphonie des Eaux* is a spectacle of water, lasers and projected images (open daily, adults FFr.135, under 16s FFr.100). From the SNCF station take either a *taxi-navette* (FFr.40 round-trip, valid three days) or bus nos 16 or 17.

Heading south from Poitiers there is a delightful view of the town high above the lily-strewn **River Clain**.

Several trains daily connect Poitiers and **La Rochelle** (Nantes–Bordeaux route, p. 174). En route **Niort** stands at the eastern edge of the **Marais Poitevin,** also known as *La Venise Verte* (Green Venice), where the traditional way to travel along the green, algae-covered canals was by flat-bottomed punt. The tourist office publishes a useful guide and offers an accommodation booking service: *pl. de la Poste; tel: 49*

24 18 79, take *r. de la Gare* from the station (where bicycles can be hired) and it is on the right.

The *donjon* (keep) – all that remains of Henry II's castle and now a museum (open daily except Tues 0900–1200, 1400–1800) – stands next to the fine glazed *Halles*, where the daily market is especially busy on Thurs and Sat. Both the *Coulée Verte*, along the **Sèvre Niortaise** River, and the pedestrianised streets around *r. St-Jean* make pleasant wandering.

ANGOULÊME

Station: *pl. de la Gare; tel: 36 35 35 35.* Automatic cash dispenser, buffet and lockers. Tourist information booth outside. **Bus station**: *pl. du Champs de Mars; tel: 45 65 25 25.* **STGA** bus company serves Angoulême and the surrounding communities. From the rail station, bus nos 1 and 2 go to *Champs de Mars* and on to *pl. St-Pierre* in the town centre, journey 15 min. Single ticket FFr.7 (valid for 1 hr); a book of three FFr.18.50, ten for FFr.51. **Taxi**: *tel: 45 95 55 55.*

Tourist Office: *2 pl. St-Pierre, 16000 Angoulême; tel: 45 95 16 84.* Open Mon–Sat 0900–1900; Sun 1030–1230, 1330–1530 (July–Aug); Mon–Fri 0900–1230, 1330–1830; Sat 1000–1200, 1400–1700 (Mar–Apr, May–June, Sept–Oct); Mon–Fri 0900–1230, 1330–1800, Sat 1000–1200, 1400–1700 (Nov–Feb). English leaflets include a walking route.

Regional information from **Comité Départemental du Tourisme de la Charente,** *pl. Bouillard 16021 Angoulême; tel: 45 69 79 09.* This has a booth outside the station in summer. Open Tues–Sat 0900–1200, 1400–1830 (mid-Sept–mid-June; also Mon in summer). Information (no reservations) about hotels, *gîtes* and *chambres d'hôtes*.

Staying in Angoulême

Accommodation

There are about a dozen hotels in the centre in all price ranges and another dozen well outside. Hotel chains include *Ca, Me* and *Nv.*

HI: *Île de Bourgines; tel: 45 92 45 80.* Bus no. 9 from *Champs de Mars*, 10-min journey. (stop: *Font Chaudière*). **Camping:** *Île de Bourgines; tel: 45 92 83 22.* Bus no. 7 (stop: *Bourgines*) or bus no. 9 (stop: *Font Chaudières*); both depart from *Champs de Mars.*

Eating and Drinking

There is a good choice of restaurants and snack bars, especially around the **Hôtel de Ville,** *r. Marengo.*

Shopping

Shopping areas are at *pl. Marengo*, and *r. d'Arcole*. A flea market takes place the third Sun of each month, 0800–1800 (Oct–Mar) at *pl. Mulac*. Free maps from all tourist offices.

Events

An annual international **Comics Festival** takes place in Jan. Information from **Salon International de la Bande Dessinée**, *121 r. de Bordeaux 1600; tel: 45 97 86 50.*

The town's many musical and arts events are featured extensively in a free brochure, in French, called *Programme du Comité de la Ville d'Angoulême.*

Sightseeing

Angoulême is an interesting town, population 43,000, in a cliff-top setting with sweeping views of the Charente Valley. It has made much of its natural, architectural and industrial attractions, but it is a hot,

uphill walk (20-min) from the rail station to the old centre and it needs time to explore. *Walking Around Angoulême* is a free leaflet in English which takes in all the main sights in about 2 hrs.

Sightseeing should include the **Cathédrale St-Pierre,** which dates to 1102, opposite the tourist office. The old quarter is picturesque with half-timbered houses (*r. Beaulieu, r. Soleil*). In an ancient bishop's palace is the **Le Musée des Beaux Arts,** *1 r. Friedland* (next to the cathedral); *tel: 45 95 07 69.* Open Wed–Mon 1000–1200, 1400–1800, closed holidays; FFr.5 (FFr.15).

Off-beat themes are covered at two museums, both on a hectic road by the banks of the **River Charente**, which is at the bottom of a cliff below the picturesque ramparts, a steep 15-min walk down a leafy hillside. The history of paper-making is covered at the **Atelier-Musée du Papier** (a former cigarette paper-making factory), *134 r. de Bordeaux; tel: 45 92 73 43.* Open Wed–Mon 1000–1200, 1400–1800; admission free. The history of comics, especially 150 years of French comics, is on display in a former brewery, the **Musée de la Bande Dessinée CNBDI** (the museum of the strip cartoon), *121 r. de Bordeaux; tel: 45 38 65 65.* Open Wed–Fri 1000–1900, Sat–Sun 1400–1900; FFr.25 (FFr.20) or to include the exhibition which changes regularly; FFr.20 (FFr.30). For both museums, take bus nos 3 or 5 (stop: *NIL-CNBDI*). The ramparts themselves make a delightful walk, including the **Jardin Vert**, with lots of park benches from which to enjoy the view. Look out for the plaque on the walls to local hero Général Résnier, who made man's 'first flight without a motor' in 1806, using an apparatus he had made himself in the town.

TOURS to CLERMONT-FERRAND

Away from the busier tourist trails, this route heads into the heart of France, via the châteaux and small villages of the quiet Cher valley and a string of historic towns, such as Bourges and Vichy, which give fascinating glimpses into France's past.

TRAINS

ETT tables: 128, 145

→ Fast Track

No through trains run from Tours to Clermont-Ferrand, but three services each day are available by changing trains at Moulins-sur-Allier. Journey times are around 4 hrs.

~~> On Track

Tours–Chenonceaux–Montrichard–Selles-sur-Cher–Vierzon

Four fast trains run between Tours and Vierzon each day taking just over 1 hr. Four local trains also operate calling at Chenonceaux-Chisseaux, Montrichard and Selles-sur-Cher en route. The journey from Tours to Chenonceaux takes 35 mins, Chenonceaux to Montrichard takes 10 mins, Montrichard to Selles-sur-Cher 25 mins and Selles-sur-Cher to Vierzon 30 mins.

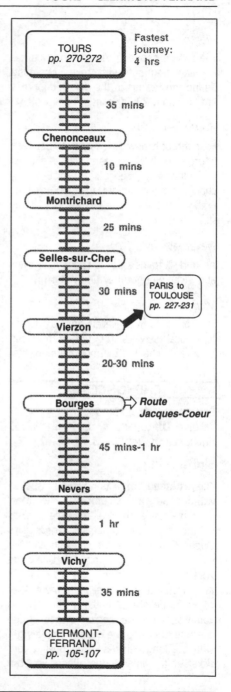

TOURS
pp. 270-272

Fastest journey: 4 hrs

35 mins

Chenonceaux

10 mins

Montrichard

25 mins

Selles-sur-Cher

30 mins

PARIS to TOULOUSE
pp. 227-231

Vierzon

20-30 mins

Bourges

Route Jacques-Coeur

45 mins-1 hr

Nevers

1 hr

Vichy

35 mins

CLERMONT-FERRAND
pp. 105-107

Vierzon–Bourges

The service between Vierzon and Bourges is fairly frequent with trains operating during most hours in the day. The journey time is about 20–30 mins.

Bourges–Nevers

Four through slow trains operate between Bourges and Nevers each day and three additional faster services are available by changing trains at Saincaize. Journey time is about 45 mins with a change and 1 hr by slow train.

Nevers–Vichy

Around six trains a day run between Nevers and Vichy with journey times of 1 hr.

Vichy–Clermont Ferrand

The six trains from Nevers are joined by a few local services for the 35-min run between Vichy and Clermont-Ferrand.

CHENONCEAUX

Station: tel: 47 20 50 50.
Tourist Office: r. du Château, 37150 Chenonceaux; tel: 47 23 94 45.

Sightseeing

The **château of Chenonceau** (spelled without an 'x') is probably the most desirable residence of all the great houses of the region – certainly according to Queen Catherine de Medici, who had her rival, her husband's mistress Diane de Poitiers, removed from here as soon as King Henri II died. Between them they created a delightful château – the mistress commissioning the elegant arched bridge over the Cher and the queen completing it with the long galleries. After buying your ticket at the small lodge, where you can pick up notes in English, you are free to wander in the lovely grounds as well as throughout the château itself, where the many art treasures include Primaticcio's famous portrait of Diane de Poitiers. Open daily, 0900–1900 Mar–Sept, closing at sunset, i.e. slightly earlier, the rest of the year, adults FFr.40, wax-works museum, FFr.10.

MONTRICHARD

Tourist Office: 1, r. du Pont, 41400 Montrichard; tel: 54 32 05 10.

The local stopping train to Vierzon continues along the Cher valley through a string of interesting villages. Worth stopping to look at in particular is **Montrichard**, whose cave-ridden cliffs and old houses are dominated by the 11th-century donjon (tower) of the ruined castle, now housing the town museum, open daily 0930–1145, 1400–1815 June–Sept, adults FFr.20.

SELLES-SUR-CHER

Selles-sur-Cher is famous for its delicious goat's cheese as well as a pretty, small **château** across the river from the SNCF station (open daily 1000–1150, 1400–1750 Apr–Oct, adults FFr.35).

VIERZON

See Paris–Toulouse route, p. 228.

BOURGES

Station: tel: 47 20 50 50; about 1 km north of the city centre – go straight ahead on av. H Laudier and av. Jean Jaurès, then bear left to r. du Commerce and r. Moyenne, the main street. The tourist office and cathedral lie at the far end.

Tourist Office: *21 r. Victor Hugo, 18000 Bourges; tel: 48 24 75 33,* close to the cathedral. Good, free booklet with map, in English.

Accommodation and Food

The heart of Bourges is not bristling with accommodation, although there are some well-placed two-star hotels, and it is advisable to book before you arrive. There are three hotels opposite the SNCF station, a little way out of the centre. International hotel chains include: *Ib, IH.*

HI: *22 r. Henri Sellier; tel: 48 24 58 09,* (south-west of the city centre near the Parc des Expositions); **Centre International de Séjour** *17 r. Félix Chédin; tel: 48 70 25 79* (behind the SNCF station). **Campsite:** *blvd de l'Industrie; tel: 48 20 16 85 .*

There is a better choice of places of eat, with several good restaurants in **pl. Gordaine** and **r. Bourbonnoux** (near the Hôtel Lallement) and a couple of brasseries at the tourist office end of *r. Moyenne.*

Events

Of the several festivals throughout the year, two are particularly interesting: in late April–early May the **Printemps de Bourges** is a very popular world music festival with international rock singers and musicians, while in July and Aug **Balades à Bourges** is a traditional summer *fête* with street entertainment, exhibitions and concerts.

Sightseeing

Bourges is the capital of the historic Berry region, hence the name of its citizens, *Berruyers* (and not, as they would be quick to point out, *Bourgeois*). The power and prosperity of the medieval city is apparent in its beautiful buildings, best seen early in the morning when the streets are empty and atmospheric.

The highlight is the **Cathédrale de St-Etienne,** an exceptional Gothic master-piece with fine carvings around the five west doorways and astonishing stained glass in the soaring interior. You can visit the crypt and tower on a joint ticket. Open daily except Sun morning 0900–1830 (July–Aug), 0900–1115, 1400–1730 (Sept–June); adults FFr.20. To explore more of old Bourges, take *r. Bourbonnoux* north of the cathedral to lively **pl. Gordaine.** En route look out for the the small *promenade des remparts,* along the site of the original Gallo-Roman walls and the **Maison des Trois Flûtes** on the corner with *r. Joyeuse.* The **Hôtel Lallement,** a beautiful Renaissance house at the end of *r. Bourbonnoux,* is now the **Musée des Arts Décoratifs** (open daily except Mon and Sun morning 1000–1200, 1400–1700; FFr.16).

R. Coursarlon, one of the pedestrianised shopping streets, leads towards the *pl. J Coeur* and the **Palais de Jacques-Coeur,** the 15th-century mansion built by a famous local financier, open daily 0900–1900 (July–Aug), 0900–1130, 1400–1730 (Sept–June); adults FFr.26. Nearby, next to the **Palais de Justice,** the **Musée du Berry** is housed in another interesting *hôtel* and covers archaeology, folk art and traditions (open daily except Tues and Sun mornings 1000–1200, 1400–1800, adults FFr.16).

Apart from the gardens of the **Hôtel de Ville,** by the cathedral, the best green spaces are north of the centre. Continue along *blvd de la République* from the market hall to reach the **Près-Fichuaux,** a large pleasant park formed by draining part of the nearby marshes. Just north-east of the town centre, these ancient marshes or *marais* of the Yèvre and Voiselle rivers still irrigate small market garden plots, whose owners, traditionally known as 'water rats', travel by flat-bottom punt to reach them. The best time to visit is during the annual *Fête des Marais* in Sept.

〰 Side Track from Bourges

Bourges lies at the heart of a trail of **châteaux** in the Centre region known as the **Route Jacques Coeur**. They are *almost impossible* to reach without a car, but there is a sporadic SNCF bus service to **Giens** via **Menetou-Salon** and **Aubigny-sur-Nère**. Cariane Centre, from the gare routière (bus station) *r. du Prado; tel: 48 24 36 42.*

NEVERS

Tourist Office is at *31 r. Pierre Bérégovoy; tel: 86 59 07 03.*

More frequent are the several train services a day, either direct or via **Saincaize,** to **Nevers** in neighbouring Burgundy. An historic town on the river Loire near its confluence with the Allier, it was known for its fine *faïence* (porcelain) and has a compact old centre to explore. From the SNCF station, *av. du Gén. de Gaulle* leads to **pl. Carnot**, the centre of life in town, near to the **Cathedral of St-Cyr-et-Ste-Julitte**, the **Ducal Palace** and the **Porte du Croux**, which was part of the town's medieval defences. You may wonder at the many references to Lourdes here: Ste-Bernadette spent the last 29 years of her life as a nun at the **Couvent St-Gilard** (across the park from *pl. Carnot*), and her embalmed body lies in the chapel.

VICHY

Station: *pl de la Gare; tel: 70 46 50 50.* Follow *r. de Paris* to the town centre. **Tourist Office:** *19 r. du Parc, 03200 Vichy;* *tel: 70 98 71 94;* between the Parc des Sources and the Parc Napoléon.

Accommodation

As befits a stylish health resort, Vichy has some luxurious hotels around the spas, including the **Pavillon Sévigné**, *50 blvd Kennedy; tel: 70 32 16 22,* and the new **Steigenberger**, *111 blvd des États-Unis, tel 70 30 82 00,* but there is a wide selection that are less expensive. From the SNCF station, *r. de Paris* and nearby streets such as *r. de l'Intendance* have several one- and two-star hotels. International hotel chains in Vichy include *Ib, IH, Nv.* **HI:** *19 r. du stade, Bellerive-sur-Allier; tel: 70 32 25 14* (open Apr–Oct, across the Allier, via the Pont de l'Europe). **Campsites:** Also across the river at Bellerive, but further south via the pont de Bellerive, two four-star sites both on *r. Claude Decloître:* **Les Acacias au Bord du Lac**, *tel: 70 32 36 22* and the **Camping Beau Rivage**, *tel: 70 32 26 85.*

Sightseeing

For four years the seat of Marshal Pétain's wartime government, this elegant resort of has been updating its image lately. There are still tea dances, but the *Compagnie Fermière* which runs the spas has recently completed a programme of new building and renovation. This is a town for gentle strolling. At the heart of town the lovely **Parc des Sources** takes you from the magnificent **Opera** and **Casino** to the **Hall aux Sources** where you can taste five different spring waters ranging in temperature from 17°C to 43°C, while **Parc d'Allier** stretching along the shores of Lac d'Allier – formed by the widening of the river – leads south to to the smaller **Parc des Celestins** and the older quarter of town, which includes the church of **St-Blaise**.

TOURS to NANTES

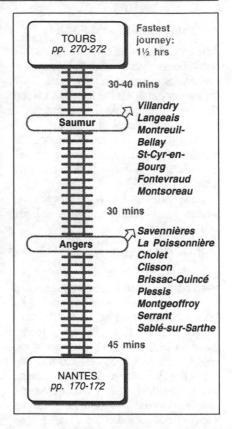

Fastest journey: 1½ hrs

TOURS pp. 270-272

30-40 mins

Saumur

Villandry
Langeais
Montreuil-Bellay
St-Cyr-en-Bourg
Fontevraud
Montsoreau

30 mins

Angers

Savennières
La Poissonnière
Cholet
Clisson
Brissac-Quincé
Plessis
Montgeoffroy
Serrant
Sablé-sur-Sarthe

45 mins

NANTES pp. 170-172

Soon after leaving Tours the train crosses to the right bank of the River Loire and follows it west past vineyards, fruit orchards and a string of attractive towns with grand châteaux. Known today by the rather more functional name of Maine-et-Loire, this is the historic region of Anjou, the old heartland of the Plantagenets who came to rule England.

TRAINS

ETT tables: 127.

Fast Track

Four through trains each day run between Tours and Nantes; additional services are available by changing trains at St Pierre-des-Corps, 5 mins from Tours. Journey times vary between 1½ hrs and 2 hrs.

~~> On Track

Tours–Saumur

Five to seven trains a day operate between Tours and Saumur Rive-Droite, taking 30–40 mins for the journey.

Saumur–Angers

Seven or eight trains a day link Saumur Rive-Droite and Angers St-Laud. The journey takes around 30 mins.

Angers–Nantes

Up to a dozen TGVs run between Angers St-Laud and Nantes each day with the journey taking 45 mins.

SAUMUR

Station: *tel: 41 88 50 50.* Two km from the town centre. To reach the town centre, turn right and cross the two bridges over the River Loire that are separated by the **Île d'Offard**.
Tourist Office: *pl. de la Bilange, 49400 Saumur; tel: 41 51 03 06.* Go straight ahead from the second bridge, *pont Cessart*, and the office is on the left, next to the theatre.

Accommodation and Food

Although only a small town, Saumur has a good choice of accommodation, both near the SNCF station and in town, particularly on the quayside near the forbidding **Hôtel de Ville**. Booking is always recommended. **Centre International de Séjour:** *r. de Verden; tel: 41 67 45 00* on the Île d'Offard. **Campsite:** *r. de Verden; tel: 41 67 45 00* (next to the youth hostel, sharing a swimming pool).

Good streets for restaurant-hunting include *r. St-Nicholas, r. Haute-St-Pierre* and *pl. St-Pierre*.

Sightseeing

Saumur is famous for its sparkling wines, its mushrooms and an élite cavalry school. It also of course has a **château**, which seen from pont Cessart sits high above the roofs of the riverside town, its white towers gleaming in the sun. The path up to the entrance climbs through the old town by the **Église de St-Pierre** (St Peter's Church), whose interior is certainly worth a detour, and past medieval and modern houses standing side by side. The château is an elegant fortress with plenty to see as it houses two museums, the **Musée des Arts Décoratifs** and the **Musée du Cheval** (Equestrian Museum). Visits to these collections are guided, but having bought your ticket you are free explore the **tour de guet** (watchtower) while waiting for the next group to leave.

Another pair of museums, with a more military flavour, commemorate the town's association with the French cavalry school. The **Musée de la Cavalerie** is on *av. du Mal Foch* and there is a collection of international tanks and armoured vehicles in the **Musée des Blindés** on *pl. du Chardonnet*. Every July the vast square is filled with the *Carrousel*, in which the élite riders of the *Cadre Noir* take part. These days they are based outside Saumur at **St-Hilaire-St-Florent** (which can also be visited), along with the producers of sparkling wines and the growers of the other local speciality – mushrooms – which are grown in the caves of the region.

⌔ Side Tracks from Saumur

The route from Tours to Saumur passes several **châteaux** along the Loire, and two of the best-known can be visited by taking the local stopping train from Tours or as side trips back from Saumur. **Villandry** is famous for its magnificent terraced gardens, where vegetables as well as flowers weave intricate patterns in their neat box-hedge borders. It lies a scenic 3.5 km along the River Cher from the nearest SNCF station at Savonnières, open daily 0900–1800 (May–Sept) 0900–1700 (Oct–Apr) admission FFr.40, to visit the gardens only, FFr.26. In contrast, at **Langeais** the château stands in the middle of town, a fortress with a fascinating history and the ruins of Foulques Nerra's original castle at the bottom of the garden, open daily 0900–1830 (mid-Mar–Oct), 0900–1200, 1400–1700 (Nov–mid-Mar); FFr.35.

South of Saumur the SNCF bus service to La Roche-sur-Yon stops at **Montreuil-Bellay**, a charming small town whose 15th-century château overlooks the River Thouet (open daily except Tues 1000–1200, 1400–1730, admission FFr.27). There are several places to stay here but it is worth booking ahead: contact the tourist office, *34 r. du Marché; tel: 41 52 32 35*. En route, at **St-Cyr-en-Bourg** the *caves* of the *Vignerons de Saumur* offer visits and *dégustations*. Local wines include white Côteaux de Saumur and the increasingly popular red Saumur-Champigny.

There are also buses from Saumur to the **Abbey of Fontevraud,** a vast monastic compound which now incorporates a cultural and conference centre alongside its Romanesque kitchens. Several of the Plantagenet monarchs, including Richard the Lionheart, are buried in the abbey church, open daily 0900–1900 (June–Sept), admission FFr.25.

The bus route follows the cliffs of the Loire through Côteaux de Saumur vineyards and the small riverside town of **Montsoreau,** whose château has guarded the Touraine/Anjou border since the 15th century. (**Tourist office** on *av. de la Loire; tel: 41 51 70 22*).

ANGERS

Station: *Angers St-Laud tel: 40 08 50 50.* 10 mins walk from the château, straight ahead to *pl. de l'Academie*, then cross the boulevard to *pl. Kennedy.*
Tourist Office: *pl. Kennedy, 49000 Angers; tel: 41 23 51 11.* Opposite the château. Open Mon–Sat 0900–1900, Sun 1000–1300, 1500–1800 June–Sept; Mon–Sat 0930–1830, Sun 1000–1300 Oct–May. Details of guided half-day tours in the Anjou region and global entrance ticket to château and museums (FFr.45) on sale. Annexe at the SNCF station.

Accommodation

Despite its size there is not a wide choice of places to stay in Angers: the best selection is near the SNCF station. Ask at the tourist office for a list of *chambres d'hôtes.*
HI: Centre d'Acceuil du Lac du Maine *49 av. du Lac de Maine; tel: 41 22 32 10;* part of a leisure complex south west of town where you can also swim or rent

pedaloes and canoes. **Campsite:** *Lac de Maine; tel: 41 73 05 03.* A four-star site. Take the Bouchemaine bus (no. 6) from the town centre.

Events

Lively Angers has a full calendar of annual festivals. Highlights include the **Mois des Jardins** (garden month) in June, during which the horticultural displays in the town's parks and gardens are particulatly impressive. The **Jardin des Plantes** (botanical gardens) is at *pl. Mendès France*, and the **Jardin du Mail** with its enormous fountain is opposite the Hôtel de Ville. The annual **Fête de la Musique** also takes place at venues throughout the town in June. From July to Sept **Angers l'Été** is an arts and music festival during which the château gardens are illuminated by a different guest artist each year, open nightly Aug–Sept 2145–2400, admission FFr.31.

Sightseeing

If the quality of tourist information is a guide, the historic capital of Anjou is happy to welcome its visitors. A walking tour leaflet (published in English) allows you to explore the different quarters of the town at your own pace, while a 'global' entrance ticket (FFr.45) makes it well worth visiting all five monuments and museums which include some world-famous tapestries.

St-Louis' **château**, somewhat sombre with its 17 squat towers striped with white tufa (the local rock) and dark schist, now has colourful flower beds and deer in the dry moat and is floodlit on summer nights (open daily 0900–1900 June–mid-Sept, 0930–1230, 1400–1800 mid-Sept–May, admission FFr.31 but part of the global ticket scheme). Inside, the display of tapestries includes the town's treasure: a

14th-century interpretation of the Apocalypse according to St John, an enormous work of over 70 panels, 100 m long.

Two of the fine arts museums are nearby. In *r. Toussaint*, the **Galerie David d'Angers** is a collection of the local master's casts for his statues, displayed in the airy glass-roofed former Toussaint Abbey, and around the corner on *r. St-Aubin*, the Renaissance Logis Barrault houses the **Beaux Arts** museum. All arts museums open the same hours: daily 0930–1900 (mid-June–mid-Sept); daily except Mon 1000–1200, 1400–1800 (mid-Sept–mid-June), admission FFr.10 or global ticket.

The Far East collection of the **Musée Pincé** is just off the *pl. du Ralliement* at the heart of Angers' shopping streets: en route look out for the famous carvings of the **Maison d'Adam** on *pl. Ste-Croix*. **Cathédrale St-Maurice** has stained glass ranging from the 12th to the 16th centuries and stands at the top of a long flight of steps which lead to the pont de Verdun. Across the Maine in the quarter of **La Doutre** Jean Lurçat's startling 20th-century tapestry *Le Chant du Monde* is displayed in the **Hôpital St-Jean,** a beautiful 13th-century building on *blvd Arago*. Near to the **Museum of Contemporary Tapestry**, on *r. Davier*, the *Centre Régional d'Art Textile* stages exhibitions and workshops and there are several medieval and Renaissance houses in the streets around *pl. de la Laiterie*.

Inspired by the exotic produce arriving at the nearby port of Nantes, Edouard Cointreau invented his orange-flavoured liqueur in Angers at the end of the last century. You can visit the distillery and **museum**, with guided tours available in English on request. Bus no. 7 to stop: *Cointreau*, open on the hour Mon–Fri 1000–1100, 1400–1700; Sat–Sun 1500– 1630 (mid-June–mid-Sept); admission FFr.20 includes tasting.

Side Tracks from Angers

The local train to Nantes and the TER service to Cholet both stop at the riverside villages of **Savennières** and **La Poissonnière,** where some of the best dry white Anjou wine is produced. Before you go, visit the **Maison du Vin de l'Anjou**, *5 bis pl. Kennedy, Angers*, for information on those *caves* which welcome visitors. The 11th-century church at Savennières is the oldest in Anjou.

Cholet is a sizeable industrial and market town with a museum of the Vendéen wars, and tourist information at *pl. Rouge; tel: 41 62 22 35*. There is a train direct to Nantes via **Clisson**, whose château stands at the confluence of the Sèvre Nantaise and Moine rivers (tourist information at *r. du Minage; tel: 40 54 02 95*).

There are several châteaux of note near Angers. Apart from **Brissac-Quincé**, for which you can take *Anjou Bus* no. 9 (to Doué-la-Fontaine and Montreuil-Bellay – see Side Tracks from Saumur, p. 282), the easiest way to visit the 15th-century fortresses of **Plessis-Macé** and **Plessis-Bourré**, classical **Montgeoffroy** or Renaissance **Serrant** is by half-day excursion organised by the tourist office. Prices depend on the number of people in the party.

Frequent train connections north to **Le Mans** (on the Paris–Rennes route, p. 219) follow the valley of the Sarthe river via **Sablé-sur-Sarthe,** a small town with a severe classical château, known for its buttery biscuits. Tourist information is at *pl. Raphael Elize; tel: 43 95 00 60* .

AMSTERDAM

The city's name derives from a 13th-century dam on the River Amstel, the only natural waterway in the city. In the 'Golden Age' (the 17th century) the town followed only London and Paris in importance – and assumed its present shape with the building of three new canals: Herengracht, Keizersgracht and Prinsengracht.

Amsterdam is a delightful city in which to linger: attractive, laid-back, full of tree-lined canals and decorative architecture, with a lively street life that includes many informal performances, notably on colourful barrel-organs. Allow a few days just to meander, on top of plenty of time for the marvellous variety of museums and galleries.

Tourist Information

Tourist Office: VVV, Stationsplein 10 (opposite Centraal, on the other side of the tram terminal); tel: (06) 340 340 66. Open daily 0900–1700. It's invariably very busy and you may queue for some time. They volunteer very little, but can produce leaflets and answer questions on most subjects, if you are specific, and they have a computerised system for last-minute availability of rooms. They charge DG5 per person for making reservations, but their booking service is not restricted to Amsterdam.

There's a booth in **Centraal Station** (in the international area, open daily 0800–2100) and **branches** at Leidsestraat 1 (open daily 0800–1900) and Stadionplein (open daily 0800–1200 and 1300–1600).

Arriving and Departing

Airport

Amsterdam-Schiphol, tel: (06) 350 340 50, is about 14 km south-west of town. The terminal is user-friendly, with several eating places. The duty-free shops have prices which really are low. VVV dispenses free copies of useful telephone numbers and makes hotel reservations (for DG5 per person).

Transfers by train are easily the cheapest and operate every 15 mins 0500–0100 (hourly 0100–0500), the journey between Schiphol and Centraal taking 20 mins.

Stations

Centraal (boards on platform show 'CS') is the terminal for all the city's trains and only 5 mins walk north of Dam. The station building is an ornate 19th-century structure and Stationsplein a hive of activity, so it's easy to become distracted and vulnerable to the opportunistic thieves that hang around there. Exercise caution and leave nothing unattended. There's a manned left luggage facility, as well as lockers, but the luggage area is closed 0100–0500. If you are interested in organised excursions, you will find the **NS Reisburo** office in the station less crowded than VVV, but they dispense no information on other matters.

Amsterdam has several other stations, all outside the centre and (with the exception of **Schiphol**) of little interest to visitors.

Getting Around

Get the free Tourist Guide to Public Transport, which shows all the city transport (except boats) and includes a list of the major attractions and how to reach them. Most tourist literature includes a small map of **Centrum** (the city centre), where everything of major interest is located. If you are

---

Tourist Information–Arriving and Departing–Getting Around　　**285**

staying more than a couple of days it's worth investing in a street map – take time to select the one that best suits your needs.

The city's layout can be confusing when you first arrive, but it doesn't take long to get the hang of things. Bear in mind that *gracht* means 'canal' and that the centre follows the horseshoe shape dictated by the canals. If you're looking for a specific place, remember that odd numbers are on one side of a canal and evens on the other.

Centrum is large and, although it is possible to walk everywhere, it's more sensible to concentrate on one area at a time: get there by public transport and then explore on foot (VVV have leaflets suggesting routes in different areas). The tram network is extensive and services frequent, while the water transport is fun and uses strategically positioned quays.

Tickets

VVV and **GVB** (Amsterdam's public transport company: a few doors from VVV and easily identified by the large yellow signs in the windows) offer a wide variety of passes for city travel, some covering boats and/or museums, so tell them what you'd like to include. Tickets valid several days are better value than the equivalent one-day tickets.

Metro

This is designed primarily for commuters and has few central stops.

Trams

The terminal is just in front of Centraal. Services start Mon–Fri 0600, Sat 0630 and Sun 0730. They stop around midnight. Pressure on the lowest step keeps the door open.

Buses

Buses begin/end just across the canal in front of Centraal, but not all from the same terminal. Buses are less frequent than trams, but go further afield and operate limited night services: look for a black square on the bus stop.

Taxis

The main ranks are at *Centraal, Dam, Rembrandtsplein* and *Leidseplein*; tel: *(020) 677 7777*. They cost around DG2–3 a mile.

Canal Journeys

The canals are an integral part of Amsterdam, freshwater and not tidal. There are locks at both the east and west ends and they are flushed out five times a week to prevent pollution becoming a problem. They offer an excellent way to appreciate the city, so take at least one boat-trip. The boats all have multi-lingual commentaries (usually recordings) and you will learn something about gables and the historical buildings. The norm is to embark at Centraal, but you can usually board at any stop by paying the crew for a single journey.

Watertaxis are available, *Stationsplein 8; tel: (020) 622 2181*, but not cheap: about DG2 a minute.

There are half-hourly **canal cruises**, taking about 1 hr; DG8–12. They are operated by a number of companies. You can get tickets at any quay where the *Rondvaart/Rederij* boats are moored.

Canal buses, *Weteringschans 24; tel: (020) 623 9886*, issue day tickets (DG15) and tickets valid two days (DG22.50), so you can embark and disembark at any stop and as often as you like. They run 1000–1800, with departures every 45 mins or so, and have six stops with red, white and blue canal bus signs. They also run candlelight cruises Fri–Sat, leaving at 2130 (DG39.50); reservations recommended.

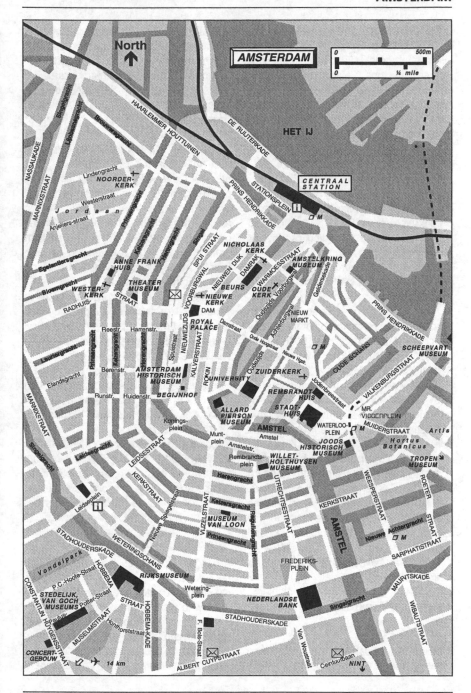

North

AMSTERDAM

0   500m
0   ¼ mile

HAARLEMMER HOUTTUINEN

DE RUIJTERKADE

HET IJ

STATIONSPLEIN

CENTRAAL
STATION

i

M

PRINS HENDRIKKADE

NASSAUKADE
MARNIXSTRAAT
Brouwersgracht

Lindengracht
NOORDER-
KERK

Westerstraat

Anjeliers-straat

J o r d a a n

Egelantiersgracht

Bloemgracht

WESTER-
KERK

ANNE FRANK
HUIS

THEATER
MUSEUM

RADHUIS-
STRAAT

Reestr. Harrenstr.

Berenstr.

Runstr. Huidenstr.

Elandsgracht

Lauriergracht

Prinsengracht

Keizersgracht

Herengracht

Singel

SPUI STRAAT

VOORBURGWAL

NIEUWE
KERK

DAM

ROYAL
PALACE

NIEUWEZIJDS

KALVERSTRAAT

Spuistraat

Damstraat

AMSTERDAM
HISTORISCH
MUSEUM

BEGIJNHOF

ROKIN

ALLARD
PIERSON
MUSEUM

Konings-
plein

Munt-
plein

NICHOLAAS
KERK

NIEUWEN DIJK

DAMRAK

BEURS

OUDE
KERK

WARMOESSTRAAT

AMSTELKRING
MUSEUM

Oudezijds Voorburgwal

Achterburgwal

NIEUW
MARKT

Oude Hoogstraat

Nieuwe Hgst.

ZUIDERKERK

University

STADT-
HUIS

REMBRANDT
HUIS

AMSTEL

Amstel

Amstelstr.

Rembrandte-
plein

Prinsengracht

Keizergracht

Herengracht

VIJZELSTRAAT

Nieuwe Spiegelstraat

MUSEUM
VAN LOON

Reguliersgracht

UTRECHTSESTRAAT

WILLET-
HOLTHUYSEN
MUSEUM

JOODS
HISTORISCH
MUSEUM

WATERLOO-
PLEIN

M

MR.
VISSERPLEIN

MUIDERSTRAAT

Jodenbreestraat

VALKENBURGSTRAAT

OUDE SCHANS

PRINS HENDRIKKADE

SCHEEPVART
MUSEUM

Artis

Hortus
Botanicus

TROPEN
MUSEUM

ROETER

STRAAT

WEESPERSTRAAT

AMSTEL

Nieuwe Achtergracht

M

KERKSTRAAT

SARPHATISTRAAT

MAURITSKADE

WIBAUTSTRAAT

M

Singelgracht

Van Woustraat

Ceintuurbaan

NINT

FREDERIKS-
PLEIN

NEDERLANDSE
BANK

STADHOUDERSKADE

ALBERT CUYPSTRAAT

F. Bols-straat

Wetering-
plein

LEIDSESTRAAT

KERKSTRAAT

Leidseplein

i

STADHOUDERSKADE

WETERINGSCHANS

Singelgracht

MARNIXSTRAAT

Vondelpark

P.C.-Hoole-Straat

HOBBEMA

STRAAT

HOBBEMA-KADE

RIJKSMUSEUM

STEDELIJK,
VAN GOCH
MUSEUMS

Potter-Straat

MUSEUMSTRAAT

Honthorststraat

Paulus-

CONSTANTIJN HUYGENSSTRAAT

CONCERT-
GEBOUW

14 km

Museumboats, *Stationsplein 8; tel: (020) 622 2181*, leave Centraal quay at 45 min intervals, 1000–1700, with five intermediate stops in places convenient for museums. Get a day-ticket (DG19, which includes a number of discounts). The boats are turquoise and the stops are indicated by turquoise signs.

For individual exploration, you can hire **canal bikes**, *Weteringschans 24; tel: (020) 626 5574*. Open daily 0930–2230 (summer); 0930–1900 (spring and autumn). These are pedal-boats for two or four people (respectively DG19.50 or DG29.50 per hr) and there's a folding canopy for protection from the sun/rain. There are four moorings in summer (just Centraal in winter) and you can start at one and finish at another.

Alternatively, hire an **aquarent** (an almost-noiseless, environmentally-friendly motor boat) for six people; DG50 for 1 hr, DG125 for a half day. Available from **Rederij Noord-Zuid**; *tel: (020) 679 1370*.

The low railings you will see bordering most canals were financed largely by insurance companies, who became tired of meeting claims for parked cars that had rolled off the edge.

There are regular (free) **ferries** across the River Ij, linking Centrum with northern Amsterdam, departures from Ruyterkade (behind Centraal). The 5-min crossing provides good views of the harbour. The large *Buikersloterwegveer* operates around the clock, leaving from quay no. 7, while the smaller *IJ-Veer* uses quay no. 8 and runs Mon–Fri 0635–1805.

Staying in Amsterdam

Accommodation

Although Amsterdam has accommodation of every type, it also has countless visitors and (especially for peak season) it's sensible to advance book. If you're stuck, consider commuting from Haarlem/Zandvoort.

Hotels chains in Amsterdam include *FP, GT, Ho, Hn, Ic, Ma, SA*, but the most famous is probably the four-star **American Hotel**, *Leidsekade 97*, once the haunt of artists and writers.

If you fancy being afloat, try the (two-star) **Amstel Botel**, *Oosterdokskade 2–4; tel: (020) 626 4247*, a large, reasonably priced ship-hotel moored in the harbour.

Use the touts at Centraal only as a last resort. They are illegal and many of the places they represent are in the red light district and/or are unlicensed because (among other things) they do not conform with basic fire regulations.

There are two **HI** hostels, both in Centrum: **Vondelpark**, *Zandpad 5; tel: (020) 683 1744* (tram nos 1/2/5 to stop: *Leidseplein*); **Stadsdoelen**, *Kloveniersburgwal 97; tel: (020) 624 6832* (tram nos 4/9 are most frequent: *Muntplein*).

The cheapest place in town is **Eben Haezer Christian Youth Hostel**, *Bloemstraat 179; tel: (020) 624 4717* (tram nos 13/17: *Marnixstraat*).

Campsites: Vliegenbos, *Meeuwenlaan 138; tel: (020) 636 8855* (10 mins from Centraal on bus no. 32); **Het Amsterdamse Bos**, *Kleine Noordijk 1, Aalsmeer; tel: (020) 641 6868* (30 mins on bus nos 171/172).

Eating and Drinking

Amsterdam is a good place to eat, with restaurants in every price range and a wide choice of international cuisine. Cheap food is easy to find, even in the centre: the international fast-food chains are well represented and there are plenty of other takeaways, so you can get by perfectly well without ever setting foot in a restaurant. If you want a real meal for a reasonable price, try one of the many 'brown cafés'.

Amsterdam has two *mensas* (student cafés): at *Oude Zijds Voorburgwal 237* (open Mon–Fri 1200–1400 and 1700–1900) and *Weesperstraat 5* (open Mon–Fri 1700–1925).

Some of the city's trendiest cafés are around Spui, while the areas around Nieuwmarkt, Dam and De Pijp (especially along *Albert Cuyperstraat*) are the best for eastern cuisine.

Beer drinkers should head for **Café In de Wildeman**, *Nieuwe Zijds Kolksteeg 3*, where they can sample 150 types from all over the world. It was founded in 1690, so there's a good atmosphere, and there's a non-smoking room.

Communications

The main **post office** is at *Singel 250–256; tel: (020) 556 3311*. Open Mon, Tues, Wed, Fri 0900–1800, Thur 0900–2000, Sat 0900–1500. It offers a poste restante facility. The branch at *Oosterdokskade 3–5* opens Mon–Fri 0830–2100, Sat 0900–1200.

The telephone code for Amsterdam is 020. At **Telehouse**, *Raadhuisstraat 48/50* (open 24 hrs a day), you can pay for calls after you have finished.

Money

Outside banking hours, the GWK exchanges at Centraal and Schiphol are the best bet: they are open 24 hrs a day.

Thomas Cook bureaux de change are found at *Leidseplein 31A; tel: (020) 626 7000; Dam 23–25; tel: (020) 625 0922;* and *Damrak 1–5; tel: (020) 620 3236.*

Entertainment

The English-language magazine *What's On in Amsterdam* (published every three weeks), is easily the most comprehensive guide to events and also contains pages of useful addresses. It is obtainable from VVV (who can supply tickets, for a fee of DG2.50 each) and bookshops for DG3.50, but you can sometimes get it free from good hotels.

AUB Uit Buro, *Leidseplein 26; tel: (06) 621 1211* (open Mon–Sat 1000–1800), also distribute information about the city's entertainments and make bookings (also for DG2.50 per ticket).

Nightlife

The nightlife is both varied and affordable. Few places have a dress policy and many stay open until 0300/0400. There are countless bars, clubs, discos and casinos. Entrance fees (where they exist) are low, but prices for drinks tend to be inflated. It is around the cafés that most crowds gather and live music is common, especially South American, rock and jazz.

Leidseplein (very touristy) and *Rembrandtsplein* (popular with locals as well as visitors) are lively, noisy centres of evening activity and there's some action in most of the other central squares. The Jordaan area is pleasant for an evening in a less touristy environment.

Theatres, Cinemas and Music

With over a hundred theatres, cinemas and concerts halls, there's plenty of choice.

The **Stalhouderij**, *Bloemdwarsstraat 4; tel: (020) 626 2282*, stages English-language plays and there are other theatres which frequently perform works in English.

Most films are shown undubbed (the exceptions state *Nederlands gesproken* on the listings) and most non-English films have English subtitles. The area of Leidseplein has several multi-screen cinemas.

Classical and chamber music can be found at the **Concertgebouw**, *Concertgebouwplein 2–6; tel: (020) 671 8345*, and ballet and opera at the very modern **Muziektheater**, *Amstel 3; tel: (020) 625 5455*, where backstage tours are possible (except July). In summer both theatres offer regular (free) lunchtime concerts.

De Ijsbreker, *Weesperzijde 23; tel: (020) 668 1805* and **Felix Meritis Theater**, *Keizersgracht 324; tel: (020) 623 1311/(020) 626 2321*, are venues for modern and experimental music.

For traditional jazz, try **Bourbon St Jazz and Blues Club**, *Leidsekruisstraat 6–8*, **Café Alto,** *Korte Leidsedwarstraat 115*, and **Joseph Lam Jazzclub**, *Diemenstraat 242*, while **Bimhuis**, *Oude Schans*, specialises in truly improvised jazz.

Recitals, especially organ concerts, are staged in many of the churches, notably **Oudekerk** and **Nieuwekerk**, and regular carillon performances ring out from their towers.

South of Leidseplein is **Vondelpark** (tram nos 1/2/5), which contains the **Nederlandse Filmmuseum** and the **Openluchttheater**, *tel: (020) 673 1499*, where alfresco performances of diverse types are staged (daily July–Aug), jazz and folk both featuring prominently.

The Fringe

Amsterdam is noted for its enlightened views on, among other things, marijuana and homosexuality and there is a nationwide gay and lesbian organisation based there *(tel: 623 6565; manned 1000–2200)*, which will provide information about gay venues all round the country.

The city has many 'smoking' coffeeshops where hash and pot can be purchased and smoked (usually to the accompaniment of ear-shattering music). This is not legal, but the police usually turn a blind eye. One reason for this tolerance is that it contains the problem, so do not assume that it means you will be all right elsewhere. You can get advice on the local scene; *tel: (020) 626 5115*.

The red light district is a den of thieves, so take as little with you as possible and be careful how you use your camera. Many *habitués* do not appreciate being photographed and your last sight of your camera might well be as it sinks into the nearest canal. There's no need to be frightened, however – if you stick to the well-lit and crowded main canalside streets, you're in little danger.

Events

Amsterdam has several water-related events in the course of each year. The major arts event is the **Holland Festival** (June), while there's **International Showjumping** every Oct/Nov and an **Ice Spectacular** in Dec.

Shopping

Leidsestraat, Kalverstraat, Nieuwendijk, Damrak and *Rokin* are the main shopping streets. For fun shopping, explore the small specialist shops in the alleys linking the main canals, especially in the area between *Leidsegracht* and *Raadhuisstraat*.

The whole Jordaan area is scattered with secondhand shops and boutiques that offer the creations of up-and-coming designers. If antiques and art are your thing, look around the Spiegelkwartier.

The Harrods of Amsterdam is **De Bijenkorf**, *Damrak*: it's enormous, so you can't miss it. If you go for designer labels, try along *PC Hooftstraat, Beethovenstraat* and *Van Baelestraat*. **Magna Plaza**, *Nieuwe Zijds Voorburgwal 182*, is a new shopping gallery just behind the royal palace.

Markets

The city has so many markets that VVV produce a leaflet about them, *Markstad*. The **general market**, *Albert Cuypstraat*, is the largest in the country, held Mon–Sat 0930–1700 (tram nos 4/16/25/25). The **flea market**, *Waterlooplein* (surrounding the Muziektheater), is held Mon–Fri 0900–1700, Sat 0830–1730.

Sightseeing

Amsterdam has nearly 200 museums and art galleries. If you have neither a Museumkaart nor a Kortingkaart, consider buying the **Amsterdam Pass** (DG29.90), which provides free or discounted admission to many attractions.

Amsterdam City of Museums is a free leaflet (available from VVV and some museums) which goes into enough detail for you to decide which will interest you. If you have time to visit only a few, the ones generally regarded as unmissable are the Rijksmuseum, the Van Gogh museum, the Anne Frank house and (less famous) the almost addictive Tropenmuseum. Others are devoted to such diverse subjects as torture, coffee and tea, chess, trams, sex, the Bible, cats and the Dutch Resistance.

The Centre: Dam

From Centraal, Damrak leads directly to **Dam**, site of the original dam (tram nos 1/2/4/5/9/11/13/14/16/17/24/25 to *Dam*), with its distinctive war memorial – a favoured meeting-place for tourists.

Koninklijk Paleis (the royal palace) dominates the square. Open daily 1300–1700 (mid-June–mid-Sept); Tues, Wed, Thur 1300–1600 (mid-Sept–mid-June); DG5. The interior reflects the Golden Age's glory and much of Louis Bonaparte's Empire furniture remains.

The much-rebuilt Gothic **Nieuwekerk** (open daily 1100–1700; admission free) is used for state functions and special exhibitions and regarded rather as an indoor extension of Dam. After a fire in 1645 the now-Protestant church was refurbished in plainer style. It contains an enormous Schonat/van Hagerbeer organ (covered by a painted screen) and the tombs of many notables. The investiture of the Dutch rulers has taken place here since 1814.

Also in Dam is **Madame Tussaud Scenerama**, open daily 0930–1930 (July–Aug); 1000–1730 (Sept–June); DG17, which features waxworks, many of which are brought to life by the latest audio-animatron techniques.

West of Dam

The **Anne Frank Huis**, *Prinsengracht 263* (boat: *Prinsengracht*; tram nos 13/14/17: *Westermarkt*), open Mon–Sat 0900–1900, Sun 1000–1900 (June–Aug); Mon–Sat 0900–1700, Sun 1000–1700 (Sept–May); DG7, was where a Jewish family hid from the Nazis for two years. They were betrayed in 1944 and only the father survived the concentration camps. The 13–14 year-old Anne recorded the family's lifestyle in a moving diary that was discovered after the war and became an international best-seller. You can see the rooms she described and other documents from the period illustrate vividly the horrors of being Jewish at that time.

For a complete change of mood, try the small **Theatermuseum**, *Herengracht 168* (tram nos 13/14/17: *Westermarkt*. Open Tues–Sun 1100–1700; DG5). The ground floor has permanent exhibits, including a model theatre dating from 1781 and a hands-on mock-up of a backstage area.

Nearby is the 17th-century **Westerkerk**,

Westermarkt (tram nos 13/14/17: *Westermarkt*), the largest Protestant church in the country, topped by the gold crown of the Austrian emperor Maximilian. The tower (the city's highest at 85 m) gives one of the few bird's-eye views of the city. Open 1000–1600 (Apr–Sept); DG3.

The Old City: east of Damrak

Across the canal from Centraal is **Nicholaaskerk**, with its largest dome featuring a cross donated by the prostitutes. The notorious **red light district** (*De Walletjes* – Little Walls) is (roughly) the area between Warmoestraat and Gelderskade. There are plenty of ladies in windows, showing what they have to offer, and many visitors like to attend a sex show.

Amstelkring (Our Lord in the Attic), *Oudezijds Voorburgwal 40* (a couple of blocks south of Nicolaaskerk), open Mon–Sat 1000–1700, Sun 1300–1700; DG4.50, was a wealthy merchant's house and the lower floors are furnished in 17th–18th-century style. Above them, three lofts were knocked into one to provide a place of worship for Catholics during the Reformation, a time when they were forbidden to use public places of worship. The lovely little chapel is intact, complete with its organ, a space-saving revolving pulpit, a confessional formed from two cupboards and a superb collection of liturgical items, several jewel-encrusted.

A little further south is **Oudekerk**, *Oudekerksplein 23*. Open Mon–Sat 1100–1700, Sun 1300–1700 (Apr–Oct); Fri–Sun 1300–1500 (Nov–Mar); DG2. It dates from the 14th century and there are carved 15th-century misericordias (seats for choir boys). The great Vater Müller organ (1724) and small 17th-century organ have both been restored. Among the stained-glass windows is the famous 1555 Maria cycle.

South of Dam

The **Amsterdams Historisch Museum**, *Kalverstraat 92* (boats: *Herengracht*; tram nos 1/2/4/5/9/11/14/16/24/25: *Spui*), is open Mon–Fri 1000–1700, Sat–Sun 1100–1700; DG5. Exhibits range from the esoteric to miniature objects fashioned from silver and everyday items like decorative loaves. In the attic you can try your hand at bell-ringing.

Turn right as you leave and signs lead to the **Begijnhof**, once home to pious upper-class women and still a peaceful spot, where a group of mainly 17th–18th-century gabled houses with small gardens surrounds a 15th-century church. The main entrance is off Spui, through a small arch.

A few blocks east, the **Allard Pierson Museum**, *Oude Turfmarkt 127* (tram nos 4/9/14/16/24/25: *Spui*), open Tues–Fri 1000–1700, Sat–Sun 1300–1700; DG5, has impressive sections on Eqypt, Greece, Etruria, Rome, Cyprus and Mesopotamia, including a model of an early marble quarry (with figures of the workers). The well thought-out explanations make it easy to follow developments.

The **floating flower market**, *Singel* (between Muntplein and Koningsplein), takes place Mon–Fri 0900–1800, Sat 0900–1700. The backs of the stalls are on barges, but the fronts are firmly on terra firma and it's only by looking at the back that you realise why it's 'floating'. Nevertheless, the blooms are lovely and there's a pervasive scent of flowers.

Herengracht was the city's grandest canal and the stretch between *Vijzelstraat* and *Leidsestraat* is known as the 'Golden Bend'. This typifies the old city's architecture, when buildings were tall and thin (to minimise taxes based on width) and had protruding gables (still used) to winch up furniture too big for the narrow staircases. The **Willet-Holthuysen Museum**, *Herengracht 605* (tram nos 4/9). Open Mon–Fri 1000–1700, Sat–Sun 1100–1700; DG2.50, enables you to see what life inside was like in the 18th and 19th centuries. Some rooms are furnished in style, others have showcases full of *objets d'art*.

Another canal house (this one 17th-century) is a couple of blocks south-west, the atmospheric **Museum Van Loon**, *Keizersgracht 672* (tram nos 16/24/25). Open Mon 1000–1700, Sun 1300–1700; DG5. It's set up as if still inhabited and there is access to the small formal garden. The few showcases contain useful items like fans and parasols.

The **Technologie Museum, NINT**, *Tolstraat 129* (tram no. 3: *Amsteldijk*; tram no. 4: *Lutmastraat*. Open Mon–Fri 1000–1700, Sat–Sun 1200–1700; DG8), is a fascinating high-tech place that is educational without being dry. Pressing one button, for instance, makes a life-size horse begin to walk.

The Museum Quarter: south-west of centre

Rijksmuseum, *Stadhouderskade 42* (boat: *Singelgracht*; tram no. 16: *Museumplein*), open Tues–Sat 1000–1700, Sun 1300–1700; DG10, ranks as one of the world's great museums. As well as an outstanding collection of Asiatic art, it contains a comprehensive selection of Dutch paintings, the 17th-century section being acknowledged as the world's best and including Rembrandt's *The Night Watch*. The superb applied arts section is extremely varied: exhibits including four-poster beds, delicately engraved silverware, Meissen, tapestries, elaborate jewellery and tiny wooden carvings: there's something to interest everybody.

The **Vincent Van Gogh Museum**, *Paulus Potterstraat 7* (tram nos 2/3/5/15: *Van Baerlestraat*; boats: *Museumplein*). Open daily 1000–1700 (1300–1700 on some public holidays); DG10, owns some 200 of his paintings and 500 drawings covering his whole artistic life (not all shown at the same time). Don't overlook the showcase containing many of his smaller works on the floor above the main display. Exhibits in the rest of the building vary.

At *Paulus Potterstraat 13* is the excellent **Stedelijk Museum**. Open daily 1100–1700; DG7.50. This influential museum of modern art and industrial design displays mainly post-war items and although what's on show usually includes some works by Monet, Cézanne and their contemporaries, Picasso and Chagall are more typical.

Amsterdam has been an important diamond centre since the 16th century and prices are comparatively low, but it's still worth shopping around. Most diamond merchants lay on free tours and hope you will buy. One of the oldest companies is **Coster Diamonds** (who re-polished the Koh-I-Noor in 1852), *Paulus Potterstraat 2–6* (tram nos 2/3/5/15: *Museumplein*). Open daily 0900–1700. Cutting and polishing are demonstrated and you see many finished stones, with an explanation of how to assess their quality. If you want to buy (prices begin at around DG200), you choose your own setting and it's made up on the spot.

Jewish Quarter: south-east of Dam

The Jews played a very important part in the development of Amsterdam and formed 10% of the pre-war population, concentrated in **Jodenhoek**, but less than a quarter survived the Nazis (metro: *Waterlooplein*; boats: *Muziektheater*).

Rembrandthuis, *Jodenbreestraat 4–6* (tram no. 9: *Visserplein)*, is where the artist lived 1639–1658. Open Mon–Sat 1000–1700; Sun 1300–1700; DG5. It isn't very evocative, but does contain most of his engravings and a number of his drawings.

Along the street is a gateway with a skull motif, leading to the **Zuiderkerk**, *Zuiderkerkhof 72*, which is undergoing extensive renovation. The splendid spire is said to have inspired Christopher Wren and contains an exhibition about Amsterdam town planning over the centuries. Open Mon–Fri 1200–1700 (till 2000 Thur); free. The tower can be climbed Wed 1400–1700, Thur–Fri 1100–1400, Sat 1100–1600 (June–Oct).

The nearby **Joods Historisch Museum**, *Jonas Daniel Meijerplein 2* (tram nos 9/14: *Mr Visserplein)*. Open daily (except Yom Kippur) 1100–1700; DG7, is housed in what were four 17th 18th-century Ashkenazi synagogues. It has been rebuilt since the war and is arranged to present (primarily) the happier aspects of Judaism, with some rich religious objects and the chance to learn a great deal about Judaism in the Netherlands.

Across the street is the 17th-century **Portuguese-Israelite Synagogue**, *Mr Visserplein 3*. Open Sun–Fri 1000–1230 and 1300–1600, but not on Jewish holidays; DG5. Still in use, it was once the world's largest, built by Sephardic Jews partly to snub the less powerful, but far more numerous, Ashkenazim.

Artis: east of the centre

Artis, *Plantage Kerklaan 38–40* (special boat from Centraal: Artis Express; tram nos 7/9/14: *Plantage Kerklaan)*, open daily 0900–1700; DG19, is a **zoo** that is part of a complex. The ticket also covers a

planetarium, an aquarium enclosing a zoological museum (closed Mon) and a geological museum. The zoo is home to over six thousand animals, kept in exceptionally pleasant surroundings – you feel that every effort has been made to make them as comfortable as possible.

Across the street, **Hortus Botanicus**, *Plantage Middenlaan 2*. (Open daily 0900–1700; DG6), is a small botanical garden with around 6000 species.

The Docklands: north of Artis

The **Scheepvart Museum**, *Kattenburgerplein 1* (bus nos 22/28: *Kattenburgerplein)*, open Mon–Sat 1000–1700, Sun 1200–1700 (but closed Mon mid-Sept–mid-June); DG10, is an extraordinarily rich maritime museum housed in a 17th-century arsenal. It contains several whole (albeit smallish) vessels, in addition to hundreds of meticulous models (from a submarine to luxury liners) and a comprehensive range of nautical paraphernalia, including such loosely connected items as plates with a whaling motif. You can go aboard an 18th-century East Indiaman, *Amsterdam*, which is moored alongside. She was restored by the unemployed and comes complete with costumed personnel performing shipboard duties.

Further along the waterside is **Museumwert 't Kromhout**, *Hoogte Kadijk 147*. Open Mon–Fri 1000–1600; DG3.50. A genuine shipyard was roofed over in 1890 and is now devoted to restoring historic vessels. You can watch the work.

The ecology-conscious **Tropenmuseum**, *Linnaeusstraat 2* (tram no. 9: *Mauritskade)*, open Mon–Fri 1000–1700, Sat–Sun 1200–1700; DG7.50, is a place where many diverse ethnological exhibits connected with everyday life have been arranged so imaginatively that it feels like you are visiting the areas depicted, from Indian slums and Middle Eastern bazaars to South American rain-forests, all with appropriate background music. There are several hands-on items and so much to take in that you wish you had eyes in the back of your head. Time passes very quickly, so allow plenty. In one wing is the delightful hands-on **Kindermuseum**, designed for children aged 6–12 and barred to adults, unless invited. It has limited opening times, so *tel: (020) 568 8233* for information.

Outside Centrum

Amsterdamse Bos, *Amstelveenseweg 264* (bus nos 170/171/172; there's also a 20-min service by antique trams Apr–Oct; DG4), is an 80-hectare park on the southern fringe of the city which was inspired by the Bois de Boulogne. There are facilities for swimming, rowing, canoeing, cycling and walking. **Bosmuseum**, *Koenenkade 56* (bus nos 125/170/172/194), open daily 1000–1700, admission free; is devoted to the construction of the park and to its flora and fauna.

Aviodome, *Westelijke Randweg 1, Schiphol airport*, open daily 1000–1700 (June–Sept); Tues–Fri 1000–1700, Sat–Sun 1200–1700 (Oct–May); DG7.50, is an aeroplane museum housed in an aluminium dome. Among the real planes is the 1903 Wright Flyer.

◠ **Side Tracks from Amsterdam**

Edam, Marken, Monnickendam and Volendam can be visited in one day-trip: allow 2 hrs each for Edam and Marken, an hour each for the others and about 2 hrs travelling. Bus nos 110/111 go to Monnickendam, no. 110 also serves Volendam and Edam, no. 111 goes to Marken. There

are boats linking Marken to Volendam and Edam, but they are frequent only during July–Aug.

The bus stop in **Edam** is a 5-min walk from the centre. It's worth buying the attractively illustrated *A Stroll Through Edam* from VVV (DG3.50): an excellent souvenir. Across the 'yellow bridge' is the tiny **Museum**, housed in the town's oldest brick building (c.1530), a typically narrow, gabled house with steep winding stairs and low beams. It was inhabited until 1895 and the lower floors still feel lived in. The Wed **cheese market** (1000–1230, July–Aug) is for the benefit of tourists, and the old weigh-house is picturesque. Edam is well worth a visit. It's an attractive place with well-preserved 17th-century architecture, featuring many decorative touches, yet the town has not been swamped by tourists and retains its charm.

If you arrive in **Marken** by bus, cross the car park by the stop to reach the edge of the old village. The harbour is lined with eating places and souvenir shops, but most of Marken remains unspoiled. Cut off from the mainland by 12th-century storms, it remained an island until a 2.5 km causeway was constructed in 1957. The constant danger of flooding meant that many houses were built on stilts and the architecture is extremely picturesque. The people are friendly and many follow the old lifestyle, so traditional dress is not unusual: the whole place is a living museum. **Marker Museum** is tiny, but its slide-show enhances your enjoyment of the costumes and of Marken itself.

At **Monnickendam**, **VVV** is in the old church near the bus stop. The small fishing town offers an 18th-century **town hall** topped by the figure of a monk; a 16th-century **bell tower**; a **music box collection** (in the Stuttenburgh Café, on the waterfront); **De Waegh** (a pancake restaurant occupying the 17th-century weigh-house and full of the old apparatus); and an **eel smokehouse** where you can often watch the work.

The main area of interest in **Volendam** is the harbour, 100 m from VVV. The former fishing village is picturesque, but it has turned to tourism in a big way, which detracts from its charm. The highlight of the **museum** is a mock street featuring a school, shops and domestic scenes. A little west of the town, and on the bus route (5-min drive), is **Alide Hoeve**, a traditional cheese farm.

Enkhuizen (an hour by train) was cut off from the sea when the Zuider Zee was dammed to create Lake Ijsselmeer. VVV (just outside the station) supply tickets for the unmissable **Zuiderzeemuseum** and the ferry to get there: ignore the first stop, which is just a car park. The indoor section, **Binnenmuseum**, contains such things as historic fishing craft and traditional costumes. The open-air section, **Buiten-museum** (closed Nov–Mar), consists of whole streets rescued from fishing villages that were destroyed. You can enter any house with an open door and ask questions if you find someone at home. The Urk section is particularly interesting. If you have time to visit the **Flessenscheepjes Museum**, you will see the world's largest collection of ships in bottles.

Hoorn (40 mins by train, en route to Enkhuizen) is renowned for the extraordinary **Westfries Museum**, crammed with items evoking the 17th century. Exhibits range from a Louis XVI dining-room to detention cells, from embroidery to an altar. Don't miss the tradesmen's loft. **Stads Bierbrouwerij**, newly opened but completely traditional, has a bar offering around a hundred different types of beer,

through which you walk to reach the **Museum van de Twintigste Eeuw** (closed Mon), a fun museum that opened in 1994. It contains everyday objects from the early 20th century: cameras, vacuum cleaners, spectacles and typewriters.

The chief reason to visit the picturesque town of **Medemblik** lies in the actual journey. This begins at Hoorn's **Muzeumstoomtram**, *Van Dedemstraat 8*, where you board a steam train to Medemblik (Apr–Oct). After your visit, you take a ferry to Enkhuizen, then an ordinary NS train to Amsterdam. VVV in Amsterdam can supply schedules and prices.

Alkmaar (30 mins by train) is famous for the colourful alfresco cheese market staged Fri 1000–1200 (mid-Apr–mid-Sept): the place is packed by 0930. The 14th-century market is now strictly for tourists, but the participants enjoy themselves and the crowds are noisily appreciative. VVV is in the newly-renovated **Waag** (on the edge of the market). Above VVV is a cheese museum. The heart of town is **St Laurenskerk**, a cruciform church with a huge pipe organ and a small swallow-organ. **Biermuseum de Boom** is housed in a 17th-century brewery, **Stedelijk Museum** includes a superb assemblage of 19th-century toys and there are several other small museums.

Aalsmeer (about 50 mins by bus no. 172) is the site of **Bloemenveiling** (the world's largest flower auction). It takes place Mon–Fri 0730–1100 (Apr–Sept) and the sheer scale is impressive but, unless you're particularly interested in the mechanics, it's not very inspiring.

The fairy-tale theme park of **Efteling** is a favourite with children (closed Nov–Mar). Take a train to **'s Hertogenbosch** (about 1 hr), then a local bus.

AMSTERDAM to ARNHEM

The emphasis of this route is the 'real Holland', which is epitomised in the north, where the scenery consists almost entirely of totally flat farmland with grazing animals but few trees, criss-crossed by irrigation ditches, lots of windmills and occasional villages centred on old churches. If you have no time for the detour to Schiermonnikoog, one of the Wadden Islands, Groningen and Leeuwarden are connected by train. Contrasting scenery (untypical of the Netherlands) is provided by an extensive forest reserve south-west of Zwolle and Arnhem's wooded hills.

TRAINS

ETT tables: 240, 230, 235.

 Fast Track

The On Track route meanders through northern Holland, but any of the towns mentioned can be reached from Amsterdam by more direct routes. Arnhem can be reached in 58–63 mins by EuroCity trains (supplement payable) from Amsterdam Centraal (CS), nine times each day, or in 1 hr 7 mins by ordinary trains running hourly.

 On Track

Amsterdam–Utrecht

Four fast trains each hour connect Amsterdam CS and Utrecht CS. Journeys take 28 mins.

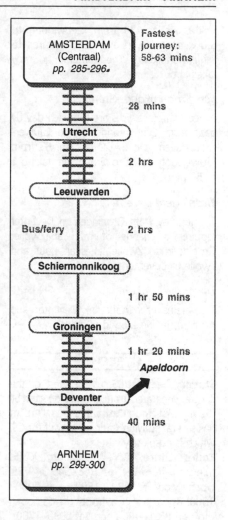

Utrecht–Leeuwarden

An hourly service links Utrecht CS with Leeuwarden, each train taking just less than 2 hrs. Care needs to be taken when boarding the train; one half of the train goes to Leeuwarden and the other half splits off at Zwolle to go to Groningen.

Leeuwarden–Schiermonnikoog

There are two to four journeys a day by

FRAM bus no. 50 from Leeuwarden to Lauwersoog Haven and boat onwards to Schiermonnikoog. The complete journey takes about 2 hrs.

Schiermonnikoog–Groningen

At least three services are run each day by boat from Schiermonnikoog to Lauwersoog Haven, and GADO bus no. 63 from Lauwersoog Haven to Groningen, taking 1 hr 50 mins.

Groningen–Deventer

The journey from Groningen to Deventer requires a change of train at Zwolle. Groningen to Zwolle takes an hour and Zwolle to Deventer takes 20 mins.

Deventer–Arnhem

Two trains each hour link Deventer and Arnhem, taking around 40 mins.

UTRECHT

Station: Centraal/CS, to the west of the centre, separated from the old quarter by the modern **Hoog Catharijne** area. Utrecht has several outlying stations, so wait for CS, which is absolutely vast.
Tourist Office: VVV, *Vredenburg 90* (5-min walk from CS); *tel: (06) 340 340 85.* Open Mon–Fri, 0900–1800; Sat 0900–1600. There's also a **booth** in CS, open Mon–Fri 0830–1800 and Sat 0930–1700.

Sightseeing

Although large, Utrecht is not a major tourist destination. **Domkerk**, *Domplein*, open daily 1000–1700 (May–Sept); Mon–Sat 1000–1600, Sun 1400–1600 (Oct–Apr), is a late-Gothic cathedral with fine stained-glass windows and its 112 m tower, **Domtoren** (DG3.50), gives a marvellous view if you can face 465 steps.

Rijksmuseum het Catherijneconvent, *Nieuwegracht 63* (open Tues–Fri 1000–1700, Sat–Sun 1100–1700; DG5), contains excellent medieval religious paintings and sculptures, while **Centraal Museum**, *Agnietenstraat 1* (open Tues–Sat 1000–1700, Sun 1200–1700; DG5), exhibits items as diverse as a 9th-century Viking ship and a 17th-century doll's house.

Nederlands Spoorweg Museum, (Rail Museum) *Maliebaanstation, Oldenbarneveltlaan 6* (open Tues–Sat 1000–1700, Sun 1300–1700; DG7.50), is a must for train buffs and **Museum van Speelklok tot Pierement**, *Buurkerkhof 10* (open Tues–Sat 1000–1700, Sun 1300–1700; DG6), covers mechanical musical instruments from music boxes to barrel organs.

LEEUWARDEN

Station: a 5-min walk south of the centre. **Tourist Office: VVV** (at the station); *tel: (06) 320 240 60.* Open Mon–Fri 0900–1745, Sat 0900–1400.

Friesland's capital is a friendly place with two claims to fame: *Grote Kerkstraat 28* was Mata Hari's home in her youth, and **Museum Het Princessehof**, *Grote Kerkstraat 11* (bus no. 5. Open Mon–Sat 1000–1700, Sun 1400–1700; DG5), houses the world's largest collection of 15th–17th-century Dutch tiles. The museum is devoted to ceramics and the Far Eastern section ranges from fragments of temple decorations to Western imitations of Oriental designs. The nearby 16th-century **Oldehove** tower, left unfinished because of subsidence, leans at an alarming angle, but you can climb to the top (40 m).

SCHIERMONNIKOOG

The unspoiled island is linked to Lauwersoog by ferries (information: *tel: (05193) 49050*) and Lauwersoog is linked to both Leeuwarden and Groningen by bus. If you want to stay on the island, you must book; contact **VVV,** *Reeweg 5; tel: (05195) 31233* (or HI). The best way to view the natural attractions (including seal colonies) is to hire a bike. The **Visitors' Centre and Nature Museum**, will help you appreciate the island's eight 'environments'.

GRONINGEN

Station: on the southern side of town, about 10 mins walk from VVV.

Tourist Office: VVV, *ged. Kattendiep 6* (5 mins walk from Grote Markt); *tel: (06) 320 230 50.* Open Mon–Fri 0900–1730, Sat 1000–1600.

Grote Markt is the heart of the town and dominated by the 13th-century **Martinikerk**. Open Tues–Sat 1200–1630 (late-May–early-Sept); DG1. The 16th-century paintings in the choir are worthy of note, the ornate 97 m **Martinitoren,** (open daily 1200–1630 Easter–Sept and Sat and Sun the rest of the year; DG2.50), can be climbed and the 49-bell carillon is renowned.

Don't miss the atmospheric **Noordelijk Scheepvaart Museum,** *Brugstraat 24,* west along *A-Kerkhof Nieuwe Zijds* from Grote Markt. Open Tues–Sat 1000–1700, Sun 1300–1700; DG5. It's housed in the city's oldest building and incorporates the fascinating **Niemeyer Tabaksmuseum**: devoted to tobacco from 1600 to the present day.

Groningermuseum (open Tues–Sat 1000–1700, Sun 1300–1700; DG5), is opposite the station, housed in an ultra-modern building with an eye-catching yellow tower. Exhibits range from Chinese porcelain to modern art.

DEVENTER

There is little to detain you in Deventer itself. Instead, make the short side track trip to Apeldoorn.

Side Track from Deventer

Apeldoorn is only 10 mins by train and **VVV** is by the station. The small town is home to two major attractions, which are linked by bus in midsummer. At other times you must walk between them (3–4 km) or return to the station (for bus no. 11 to the palace or bus nos 2 or 4 to Apenheul). The 17th-century **Paleis Het Loo** (closed Mon) has been restored, contemporary records being consulted to ensure accuracy. The old stables contain royal carriages, from sledges to vintage cars, and there are extensive formal gardens. **Apenheul** is basically a monkey zoo, but with a few other species. The primates live in family groups and many types roam free: if you sit quietly, they often climb over you.

ARNHEM

Station: on the north-western edge of town.

Tourist Office: VVV, *Stationsplein 45; tel: (085) 420 330.* Open Mon–Fri 0900–1730, Sat 0900–1600. *Rekreatie Krant* is a free newspaper which includes listings.

Accommodation

The only chain represented is *BW*, but there are other up-market and middle-range hotels, plus a few scattered budget choices. You could try **Pension Warnsborn**, *Schelmseweg 1; tel: (085) 425 994* (bus no. 2).

HI: *Diepenbrocklaan 27; tel: (085) 420*

114, 4 km north of the station (bus no. 3 towards Alteveer: *Gemeente Ziekenhuis)*. You'll see a sign with the HI logo. About 30 m further on are steps leading up a forested hill to the hostel.

There are three **campsites**: **Camping Warnsborn,** *Bakenbergseweg 257; tel: (085) 423 469* (north-west of the centre, bus no. 2); **Camping Arnhem,** *Kemperbergerweg 771; tel: (085) 431600* (bus no. 2 towards Schaarsbergen); and **Kampercentrum De Hoge Veluwe,** *Koningweg 14; tel: (085) 432 272*, a modest site by the Hoenderloo entrance.

Sightseeing

The attractions are scattered, but there's an excellent network of buses.

Burgers, *Schelmseweg 85* (bus no. 3 from the station – or from the hostel – and bus no. 13 in midsummer). Open 0900–1900 (Apr–Sept); 0900–1700 (Oct–Mar); DG20, it is a mixed zoological complex in a giant greenhouse, surrounded by a conventional zoo with safari park.

Nederlands Openlucht, *Schelmseweg 89*, open Mon–Fri 0930–1700, Sat–Sun 1000–1700 (Apr–Oct); DG12.50, is about 500 m from Burgers. This museum, set in delightful woodland, consists of over a hundred reconstructed buildings of all types (including windmills), with appropriate interiors, traditional crafts and farm animals, giving a picture of Dutch rural life spanning two centuries.

The emphasis in the **Gemeentemuseum**, *Utrechtseweg 87* (bus no. 1. Open Tues–Sat 1000–1700, Sun 1100–1700; free except for special exhibitions), is on contemporary Dutch art and applied arts. The archaeological section is along the street at *no. 74*.

The **Airborne Museum**, *Hartenstein, Utrechtseweg 232*, is at **Oosterbeek** (8 km west of the centre – bus no. 1). Open Mon–Sat 1100–1700, Sun 1200–1700; DG4, but free after 1630. This is devoted to *Operation Market Garden*, the Allied débâcle of Sept 1944 immortalised in the film *A Bridge Too Far*.

Out of Town

To the north-west of Arnhem, the delightful 5400-hectare **De Hoge Veluwe National Park** encompasses dunes, fens, moorlands, forests and added attractions ranging from museums to free-ranging animals. It is open daily 0800–sunset (Apr–Oct), 0900–sunset (Nov–Mar); DG7.50 – which covers entrance to its museums (open Tues–Sun 1000–1700). There's a visitors' centre at the **Hoenderloo Gate**; *tel: (08382) 1627* (bus nos 109/110). The other entrances are near **Otterlo** (bus nos 107/110 – also no. 12 in summer) and at **Rijzenburg**, near Schaarsbergen (bus no. 11). Once at a gate, buy a map and (unless you're a very keen walker) borrow a white bicycle (free): there's a lot of ground to cover. The **Kröller-Müller Museum** (a good 35-min walk from the Otterlo entrance, but bus nos 12, 107, and 110 stop there) owns one of Europe's best modern art collections, notably 278 paintings by Van Gogh (including the *Potato Eaters* and *Café Terrace at Night*), although only fifty or so are on show at any one time.

The neighbouring **Sculpture Garden** and **Sculpture Forest** make for a fascinating walk, as they contain works by Rodin, Epstein, Moore, Hepworth (and Dubuffet's extraordinary *Jardin d'Émail*), along with the sort of modernistic work that resembles scrap metal. **Museonder**, near the visitors' centre, is the world's first underground museum, devoted to everything that lives (or lived) beneath ground level.

ARNHEM to LUXEMBOURG

This varied route touches all the Benelux countries. The Dutch section incorporates stops at a series of worthwhile small towns, as well as the culturally mixed city of Maastricht. Liège, in Belgium, has an interesting old area and the southern part of the route passes through the beautiful unspoiled scenery of the Ardennes, which stretches between Belgium and Luxembourg, where rolling forests and rocky outcrops alternate with picturesque hill towns and peaceful agricultural land.

TRAINS

ETT tables: 241, 245, 200, 219.

→ Fast Track

No fast services run on this route.

⤳ On Track

Arnhem–Nijmegen

There are two trains each hour between Arnhem and Nijmegen, taking about 15 mins.

Nijmegen–Venlo–Roermond

An hourly service operates between Nijmegen and Roermond with all trains calling at Venlo. Nijmegen to Venlo takes about 1 hr, Venlo to Roermond takes 26 mins.

Roermond–Maastricht

Two trains each hour operate between

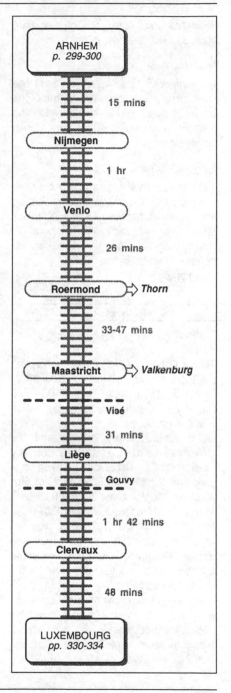

ARNHEM
p. 299-300

15 mins

Nijmegen

1 hr

Venlo

26 mins

Roermond ⇨ *Thorn*

33-47 mins

Maastricht ⇨ *Valkenburg*

Visé

31 mins

Liège

Gouvy

1 hr 42 mins

Clervaux

48 mins

LUXEMBOURG
pp. 330-334

Roermond and Maastricht. The fast train takes 33 mins, the slow 47 mins.

Maastricht–Liège

An hourly service links Maastricht and Liège Guillemins. The journey takes 31 mins. The border between The Netherlands and Belgium is crossed without any formal customs checks.

Liège–Clervaux–Luxembourg

There are seven trains each day between Liège Guillemins and Luxembourg, calling at Clervaux on the way. Liège to Clervaux takes 1 hr 42 mins and Clervaux to Luxembourg takes 48 mins. There are no border controls between Belgium and Luxembourg.

NIJMEGEN

Station: 20-min walk south-west of the centre.

Tourist Office: VVV, *St Jorisstraat 72; tel. (080) 225 440.* Open Mon–Fri 0900–1800, Sat 0900–1600; also Sun 1100–1500 (July–Aug), 25-min walk from the station – or bus no. 6.

The town's history is long and the remains of Barbarossa's fortress (formerly Charlemagne's palace) can be seen in a park near the 11th-century chapel of **Sint Nicolaas**. The **Velorama** (Bicycle Museum), *Waalkade 107* (open Mon–Sat 1000–1700, Sun 1100–1700; DG4.50), has vintage cars as well as antique bicycles. Other museums include **Grootmoeders Keukenmuseum** (grandmother's kitchen) and the **Jukeboxmuseum**.

Nijmegen's two major attractions are away from the centre (special bus July–Aug, otherwise no. 5 gets you close). **Bijbels Museum**, (Bible Museum) *Profeten-laan 2* (open daily 0900–1830 (Easter–Oct);

DG10), depicts Middle Eastern daily life in the biblical era, with half a dozen 'villages' of different types, about 200 m apart and linked by pleasant forest trails and a mini-railway. The **Afrika Museum**, *Berg en Dal*, open Mon–Fri 1000–1700, Sat–Sun 1100–1700 (Apr–Oct); DG7.50, is about 15-mins walk beyond the Bible Museum. The outdoor section recreates three African compounds and features a mini-zoo, while the indoor has a unique collection of African artefacts.

VENLO

Station: in the centre of town.

Tourist Office: VVV, *Koninginneplein 2* (just across the road from the station); *tel: (077) 543 800.*

The attractive small town was inhabited in pre-Roman times and early remains are in **Goltziusmuseum**. Some old buildings survive, including the 15th-century **Sint Martinuskerk** (containing many art treasures), the 16th-century **Huis Schreurs** and the 17th-century **Stadhuis** and **Latijns College**.

ROERMOND

Station: 5-min walk south-east of the old centre.

Tourist Office: VVV, *Kraanpoort 1* (corner of Markt); *tel: (04750) 33205.* Open Mon–Fri 0900–1800, Sat 0900–1600 (May–Sept); Mon–Fri 0900–1700, Sat 0900–1400 (Oct–Apr).

The town is a major junction and watersports centre, with a large marina. VVV's suggested walk takes in what is left of the pleasant old centre. The impressive 15th/16th-century **basilica** is topped by a gilt statue of St Christopher and there are a number of decorative buildings.

Side Track from Roermond

Only 17 km south-west (bus no. 73, taking 45 mins) is the tiny white-painted town of **Thorn**, much of which is now a national monument. It grew around the 10th-century **abbey**, by which it is still dominated. Most of what remains is of later date and the contents include a pure Renaissance altar and an 18th-century organ. Among other places of interest are a 14th-century **water-mill**, a **pottery** and the remains of the abbess's **palace**.

MAASTRICHT

Station: 10-min walk east of the centre.
Tourist Office: VVV, *Kleine Staat 1; tel: (04328) 0830.* Open Mon–Sat 0900–1800 (Sept–June); Mon–Sat 0900–1900; Sun 1100–1500 (July–Aug). Walk straight ahead from the station (along *Stationsstraat*) and across the bridge. There are some large street maps and it's easy to cover the centre on foot.

Accommodation

Hotel chains in Maastricht include *BW, GT, Ho, Me, Nv* and there are plenty of medium-range choices. Cheapish establishments can be found in the station and Markt areas.

HI: *Dousbergweg 4; tel: (043) 434 404*, 4 km from the station. Bus no. 8 to: *Dousberg* (the last stop, beside a swimming pool which is free for hostellers). **Camping: De Dousberg**, 1 km from the hostel.

Sightseeing

The southernmost Dutch city is a very cosmopolitan place, only a stone's throw from Germany and Belgium.

St Servaaskerk, *Vrijthof*, is open Sat–Thur 1000–1700, Fri 1000–1400; admission free. The church has a 10th-century crypt, a painted latticed ceiling and attractive stained glass behind a pretty main altar. Its **treasury**, open daily 1000–1800 (July–Aug); 1000–1600 (Sept–June); DG3.50, reflects the rich patronage of the early days.

The neighbouring 14th-century church **St Janskerk**, Mon–Sat 1100–1600 (Apr–Oct); admission free, is a complete contrast, simplicity being the key.

The lovely Romanesque **Onze-Lieve-Vrouwe-Basiliek** (in a square of the same name) is the most atmospheric of the city's churches. A statue of Mary, Star of the Sea (credited with miraculous powers), is at the entrance and the whole place is full of elaborate decorations, while the **treasury**, open Mon–Sat 1030–1630; Sun 1200–1630 (Apr–Nov); DG3.50, contains an unusually diverse collection.

Just off *Onze-Lieve-Vrouweplein* is **Museumkelder Derlon**, *Plankstraat*. Open Sun 1200–1600; admission free. When the modern buildings above it were being built, remnants of Roman Maastricht were unearthed and it was decided to leave them *in situ*.

South of the square is an attractive old quarter leading to some of the ancient fortifications, including **Helpoort** (the oldest remaining city gate in the Netherlands), but the major remains, notably **Fort Sint Pieter**, are some way south of the city centre.

The **Natuur Historisch Museum**, *De Bosquetplein 6–7* (Open Mon–Fri 1000–1230 and 1330–1700, Sat–Sun 1400–1700; DG3.50), has a peaceful garden with a suitable variety of flora. The exhibits inside range from jewels to gruesome objects in bottles.

Side Track from Maastricht

Ten mins away by half-hourly train, the small town of **Valkenburg** (**VVV**, *Th. Dorrenplein 5; tel: (04406) 13364)* is undeniably touristy, but retains a pleasant atmosphere. It is dominated by a **ruined castle** perched on a marlstone outcrop. Marlstone is soft limestone that has been quarried since Roman times: the man-made labyrinths have been a traditional refuge in times of trouble and now form a series of themed tourist complexes. **Fluweelengrot** is the most atmospheric (especially a chapel created during the French Revolution), while the most extensive is **Gemeentegrot** (with a mini-train for non-walkers). Among the others are **Katakomben** (which reproduces 14 Roman catacombs) and **Prehistoriche Monstergrot** (especially appealing to children).

LIÈGE (LUIK/LUYK/LEUK)

Station: Liège-Guillemins, *tel: (041) 52 98 50*, is the main station, 2 km south of the city centre (bus nos 1 or 4). Facilities there include a manned left-luggage office, eating places and a small exchange office. **Tourist Offices:** at the station (in the train information office); *tel: (041) 52 44 19.* Open Mon–Sat 0900–1200, 1230–1730, Sun 1000–1200, 1230–1600 (Apr–Sept); Mon–Sat 1000–1200, 1230–1600 (Oct–Mar). They don't book accommodation, but do supply a full range of literature about the town and province. This is mostly free, but good maps cost BFr.250. The **Municipal** office, *Féronstrée 92; tel: (041) 21 92 21*, is open Mon–Fri 0900–1800, Sat 1000–1600, Sun 1000–1400 (Apr–Oct); Mon–Fri 0900–1700 (Nov–Mar). **Provincial** office, *blvd de la Sauvinière 77; tel: (041)*

22 42 10, is open Mon–Fri 0830–1730, Sat 0900–1300 (Apr–Sept); Mon–Fri 0830–1700, Sat 0900–1300 (Oct–Mar).

Accommodation

Hotel chains in Liège include *Ho, Ib, Rm*. There are hotels in every category, the cheapest in the area of the station. Non-HI hostels offer cheap dormitories.

Getting Around

The centre is small enough to be walkable (about 3 km to cover the major sights) and there's a day-ticket (BFr.240) that provides unlimited travel on bus no. 4 (a good route) and free entrance to the museums. Single tickets BFr.38, eight-ride tickets BFr.200.

Tours by taxi are available, *tel: (041) 67 66 00*, and there are a variety of boat-trips on the river, *tel: (041) 87 43 33*.

Sightseeing

Although it's a large industrial city, Liège retains some noteworthy churches and has an interesting old centre, with *pl. de la République Française* marking the boundary between the old town and the modern one. Little is left of the original **Citadelle** but, if you can face the climb up **Montagne de Bueren** (373 steps), you will be rewarded with an excellent view.

Cathédrale St-Paul, *r. Bonne-Fortune*, was founded in the 10th century and has a fine interior. Its treasury contains 11th-century items of ivory and a gold reliquary. The nearby **Église St-Denis** (Church of St Dennis) is remarkable for its 11th–12th-century tower (once part of the city's defences) and notable 16th-century Brabant altarpiece. The octagonal **Église St-Jean** (St John's), *pl. Neujean*, contains some good sculptures, while **Église St-Jacques** (St James'), *pl. St-Jacques*, of mixed architectural styles, features some fine

Renaissance windows. The churches are usually open 0900/1000–1200, 1400–1715; admission free.

In a square of the same name, **St-Barthélemy** (open Mon–Sat 1000–1200 and 1400–1700, Sun 1400–1700) is a restored Romanesque church containing a 12th-century bronze baptismal font that is one of Belgium's greatest treasures.

The 16th-century **Palais des Prince-Évêques**, *pl. St-Lambert*, was once a royal home and now houses the provincial government. You can visit two inner courts, one of which has 60 individually carved columns.

Perhaps the most interesting of several museums devoted to different aspects of the region is **Musée de la Vie Wallonne**, (Regional Museum), *cours des Mineurs*, which is rich in ethnological and folkloric exhibits. Open Tues–Sat 1000–1700, Sun 1000–1600; BFr.50. **Musée d'Art Religieux et d'Art Mosan**, *r. Mère-Dieu* (open Tues–Sat 1300–1800, Sun 1100–1600; BFr.50), contains some excellent examples of Mosan (Meuse Valley) craftsmanship, including several jewel-encrusted religious objects. **Musée de Verre**, has thousands of glass items (many very ancient) from around the world at *quai de Maestricht 13*. Open Mon, Thur, Sat 1400–1700, Wed, Fri 1000–1300, second and fourth Sunday of the month 1000–1300; BFr.50 each.

CLERVAUX

Station: a tiny place 10–15 mins walk north-west of the centre.
Tourist Office: *at the castle entrance; tel: 92072.* Open Mon–Sat 1400–1700 (Easter–June), Mon–Sat 0945–1145 and 1400–1800 (July–Sept), Mon–Sat 0945–1145 and 1400–1700 (Oct) also Sun (July–Aug).

Sightseeing

The small medieval town nestles in a wooded valley in the Luxembourg Ardennes and is overlooked by its three major attractions.

The oldest surviving parts of **Château de Lannoy** date from the 12th century. It now houses mixed attractions. One contains models of **Luxembourg castles** and outlines their histories, open Mon–Sat 1300–1700 (June); Mon–Sat 1000–1700 (July–mid-Sept); plus Sun 1300–1700 (mid-Sept–Dec and Mar–May); LFr.40. Another small section contains an atmospheric museum about the **Battle of the Bulge** (same hours; LFr.40), eclectic exhibits ranging from a dangling paratrooper to pin-ups. The **Family of Man** exhibit (open Tues–Sun 1000–1800 (Mar–Dec); LFr.150) consists of photos of people taken all over the world, grouped to illustrate texts about mankind from people as diverse as Homer, Thomas Jefferson, James Joyce, Shakespeare and Anne Frank.

The twin-spired parish church, **Église Paroissiale** (open most days, admission free) is a striking place, constructed in the Rhenish-Romanesque style and decorated with mosaics. The marble apse is topped by a lavishly-decorated dome.

The Benedictine **Abbaye de Sts-Maurice-et-Maur**, with its red-roofed tower visible on a hill to the west, was built in 1909–10. The abbey is still an active monastery and the crypt contains an exhibition about monastic life.

In the town centre is the **Musée du Jouet** (Toy Museum), *9 Grand-Rue*. Open Mon–Fri 1000–1200, 1330–1800, Sat–Sun 1100–1200, 1400–1700 (Easter–Dec); daily 1100–1200, 1400–1700 (Jan–Easter); LFr.95. It contains a wide range of toys and dolls, old and new.

BRUSSELS (BRUXELLES)

Brussels is an exceptionally cosmopolitan city, the headquarters of the EU and NATO, as well as home to a sizeable number of immigrants from around the Mediterranean. This mix is reflected in the varied lifestyles. Most sights are in a smallish area of the centre and visiting them should not take more than two or three days, but allow longer to get the feel of the ancient town and to travel a bit further afield.

The city is officially bilingual and there's often little similarity between the two versions of names (e.g. French Arts-Loi is Flemish Kunst-Wet), so familiarise yourself with both forms. French is the more common.

Tourist Information

Tourist Offices: City: Hôtel de Ville, Grand-Place; tel: 513 89 40. Open daily 0900–1800 (June–Sept); Mon–Sat 1000–1400 (Oct–May). If you make a hotel booking you will get a free map, but the only other thing they will give free is the transport map. The National office is far more helpful. **National:** r. du Marché-aux-Herbes 61; tel: 504 03 90. Open daily 0900–1900 (summer); Mon–Sat 0900–1800, Sun 1300–1700 (winter). They dispense information about the whole country, not just Brussels, and a great deal of it (including a city map with the points of interest marked) is free. Ask them about the Brussels Tourist Passport (BFr.220), which offers a wide range of discounts.

Infor-Jeunes: r. du Marché-aux-Herbes 27, Mon–Fri 1200–1730, is a mine of information about good deals for young people.

Arriving and Departing

Airport

Bruxelles-National/Zaventem, tel: 720 71 67, is 14 km north-east of the centre. There is a tourist information desk, tel: 722 30 00 (open daily 0600–2200) and an exchange office (open daily 0630–2100). An express rail link operates until nearly midnight, with trains every 20 mins or so to all three main stations, the journey taking 15–25 mins. Before you take a taxi, ask the information desk about the approximate cost and ensure the taxi driver agrees.

Stations

Midi/Zuid is the most important station, although it's in a poor immigrant area that is best avoided at night. There are special ticket windows for imminent departures and the train information office (open daily 0630–2230) has a hotel booking desk (open Mon–Fri 0930–2130, Sat–Sun 1100–2030). Bus timetables are displayed in the ticket hall. It's on metro line nos 2/23, so directly linked to Nord.

Nord/Noord, pl. Rogier, is just north of the main ring road, on the edge of the red light district, and is the terminal for many buses. It's on metro line no. 23 (blue): change at Rogier from line no. 2 or at De Brouckère from line no. 1.

Central/Centraal (metro Centrale), blvd de l'Impératrice, is a good place to begin explorations as it's only a 5-min walk from Grand-Place. It's on metro line no. 1.

Other main-line stations are of interest only for local journeys. For all rail enquiries, tel: 219 26 40. Midi/Zuid is to the south,

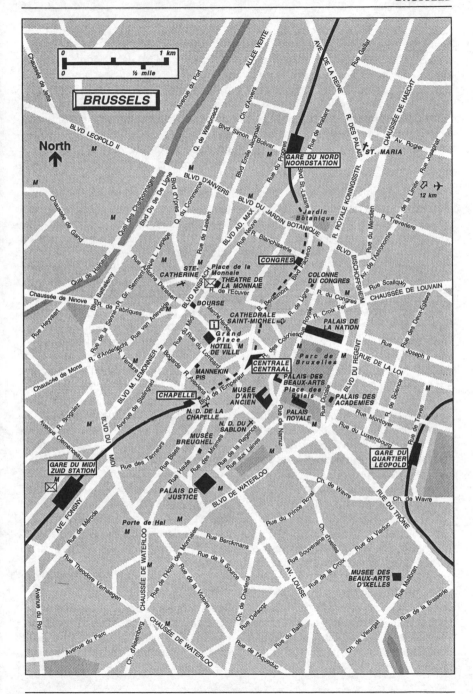

Nord to the north and Central between them. Virtually all long-distance trains stop at both Midi and Nord, but many omit Central. All three stations have luggage lockers, WCs, a variety of eating places, newsagents selling English papers, telephones, train information offices and ticket halls. Both Midi and Nord are undergoing extensive renovation.

Buses

There are two long-distance bus companies: **De Lijn** serve Flemish areas, **TEC** serve French areas. They are primarily for commuters, however, and unlikely to interest visitors – except the TEC service to Waterloo (see p. 313).

Getting Around

The easiest way to get around the most central sights is to walk. Get the *Brussels Guide and Map* (BFr.70 from tourist offices, BFr.100 from bookshops): it's easily the most comprehensive booklet for tourists and well worth the investment. Elsewhere, the metro, bus and tram network is efficiently run by **STIB**. For all city transport information, *tel: 515 20 00*. You can get free route maps from STIB kiosks, metro stations and tourist offices. If stops show *'sur demande'*, raise your hand to the driver as the vehicle approaches. If you want to get off, ring the bell.

Tickets

Tickets covering all city transport can be purchased individually (BFr.50) or you can get a five-trip ticket (BFr.230) or a ten-trip ticket (BFr.305). A tourist pass (BFr.120) gives unlimited travel on all city transport for one calendar day. Multi-ride tickets can be purchased from STIB kiosks, tourist offices, some news-stands and metro stations.

Metro

The terms 'tram' and 'metro' are interchangeable. Metro stations are indicated by a square white 'M' on a blue background. *Loket/guichet* booths for tickets are in all stations. The system is efficient, but assumes you know where you're going, so make sure you do. The essential information is which line(s) you need, where to change (if applicable) and in which direction for each line – only the terminal(s) are indicated on signs. Armed with this information, you should find metro travel easy. Lines are identified by number and colour (nos 1/red and 2/orange being central). Smoking is prohibited throughout the system. Trams run 0600–midnight. Many stations have been decorated by local artists, but don't hang around to admire them late in the evening, as most stations lock automatically when the last tram has gone. Routes of the relevant line are shown on all platforms and trams. Many platforms also have boards showing the whole route and lights indicating the current position of the trams, and every platform has a city map with the metro system superimposed and a light indicating where you are. Doors close automatically (don't use them after the warning buzzer sounds), but you have to open them yourself. The usual system is to exert a little pressure on the handle and let the hydraulics take over. Sometimes, instead of a handle, there's just a thin strip: press it.

Trams and Buses

Both trams and buses have comprehensive networks during the day. They begin around 0600 and stop running from 2200 onwards. After that you must either use the (limited) night service or take a taxi.

Taxis

Ranks are strategically positioned at all the stations and main squares. The basic cost is BFr.38 per km in town, BFr.95 per km outside the city limits.

Staying in Brussels

Accommodation

Hotel chains in Brussels include *BW, Cd, Fo, Hn, Ho, Ib, Mc, Md, Nv, SA, Sf, Sh* and there's a good choice of hotels of every grade, including plenty of budget establishments in the areas of *Ixelles* and *pl. Ste-Catherine*, several hostels (HI and otherwise) and a number of bed and breakfast places (a guide to them costs BFr.100). Nevertheless, advance booking is recommended and is essential in peak periods.

HI: Jacques Brel, *r. de la Sablonnière 30; tel: 218 01 87* (metro no. 2 to stop: *Madou*, direction Simonis, i.e. away from the centre). A sign in the ticket hall indicates the exit: leave by the right-hand stairs and continue straight along the road. Take the second turning left and you'll see the hostel flag on the other side of the large roundabout. **Jean Nihon**, *r. de l'Éléphant 4; tel: 410 38 58*, 2 km from Centraal (metro: *Comte de Flandre* – 500 m). **Heilig Geeststraat**, *Heilig Geeststraat 2; tel 511 04 36*, 300 m from Central (behind Notre-Dame-de-la-Chapelle).

The nearest official **campsite** is at Beersel: *Steenweg 75; tel: 331 05 61*, 9 km to the south. (Tram no. 55: *Uccle*).

Eating and Drinking

The Belgians enjoy eating and there's a huge choice of restaurants serving excellent food. The tourist office has a gourmet guide to restaurants (BFr.80). Prices tend to be high. The best value meals are *plat du jour/dagschotel* (around BFr.295). Many bars sell food and give better value than the restaurants. In the area surrounding *Grand-Place* (noticeably cheaper than establishments in the square itself) is every imaginable type of eating-place, including international fast-food chains. **Wittamer**, *Grand-Sablon 13*, is a renowned patisserie that fully deserves its reputation.

Communications

There's a 24-hr post office at Midi, *av. Fonsny 48*. The main post office in town is *Centre Monnaie, pl. de Brouckère* (upstairs). Open Mon–Fri 0800–2000, Sat 0900–2000, although not for all services. There are also post offices at Central and Nord, open Mon–Fri 0900–1700. The telephone centre at *r. du Lombard 30* is open daily 1000–2200.

The telephone code for Brussels is 02, and that should precede all numbers if you are dialling from outside the city.

Embassies

Australia: *r. Guimard 6; tel: 231 05 96.*
Canada: *av. de Tervuren 2; tel: 735 60 40.*
Republic of Ireland: *r. du Luxembourg 19; tel: 513 66 33.*
New Zealand: *blvd du Régent 47; tel: 512 10 40.*
UK: *r. Arlen 85; tel: 287 62 11.*
USA: *blvd du Régent 27; tel: 513 38 30.*

Money

There are **Thomas Cook** bureaux de change at *4 Grand-Place*, open daily 0900–2000 (summer) Mon–Sat 0900–1900 (winter); and at *19 r. des Bouchers*, open Mon–Fri 1100–2200, Sat–Sun 1100–2215 (summer), daily 1400–2200 (winter).

Midi station has a currency exchange office, open daily 0700–2145, and a *Bancontact* automatic cash dispenser (in the metro hall) which gives cash against Visa and MasterCard. Currency exchange offices at Nord and Central are open daily 0800–2000.

Entertainment

There are many clubs and discos. You can often get in free, but have to buy at least one (expensive) drink. Clustered around *Fernand Cocq* and the lower end of *chaussée d'Ixelles* are lots of bars with music and many stay open until the early hours.

The tourist office publishes a free list of musical performances. Brussels prides itself on its reputation for jazz and there's a wide choice of venues. Operatic productions at **Théâtre Royale de la Monnaie**, *pl. de la Monnaie*, are of international quality. **Cirque Royal**, *r. de l'Enseignement*, hosts touring dance and opera companies, while classical music is performed at **Palais des Beaux Arts**, *r. Ravenstein*, and pop concerts at **Forest National**, *av. du Globe*. Many churches have free Sunday morning concerts.

Unless films are shown as NV (Dutch) or VF (French), they are in the original language. **Kinépolis** (beside Bruparck) is a 24-screen cinema which issues a weekly listing. It also contains **IMAX**, a giant screen (600 sq. m) where you attend performances in your own language: worth going just for the experience (BFr.250). At the **Cinema Museum**, *r. Baron Horta 9* (near Central), there are showings of two silent movies a night, 1730–2230 (BFr.80 for 2 hrs, or BFr.50 if you buy the ticket 24 hours in advance). On summer evenings *Grand-Place* is full of life and there are buskers everywhere.

Events

All major events centre on *Grand-Place*.

These include several jazz festivals, **Ommegang** (a historical pageant in early July) and the **Tapis de Fleurs** (mid-Aug biennial; even years), when the whole square is carpeted with flowers. The **National Holiday** (21 July) offers varied entertainments.

Shopping

Most of the lace shops centre on *Grand-Place*, but ask whether goods offered are Belgian or made in the Far East. Of the many delicious chocolates, **Leonidas** is the brand most popular with the Belgians themselves and their shops are scattered around the city.

South-east of the centre are up-market areas for shopping, near *porte de Namur* and *av. Louise*. Around *r. Neuve* there are many shopping malls that offer a wide range of goods at affordable prices. **Galeries Royales St-Hubert**, which leads off both sides of *r. des Bouchers*, is a vaulted arcade with lots of sculptures and a mixture of shops, including eateries.

Brussels has several markets. **Midi Market** (near the station), resembles an African *souk* and is the place to go for bargains in food and clothes (Sun 0600–1300). There's a **flower market** in *Grand-Place*, open Tues–Sun 0800–1800 (only cut flowers Nov–Mar) and that is also the setting for a **bird market**, Sun 0700–1400. There is an **English bookshop: W H Smith**, *blvd A Max 71; tel: 219 27 08*.

Sightseeing

Chatterbus, *r. des Thuyas 12; tel: 673 18 35*, are a company with a different approach. They run off-beat (multi-lingual) trips with flexible itineraries, usually a walking tour followed by a bus/tram trip. Departures daily at 1000; BFr.300 (less for hostellers).

Grand-Place, with its ornate guild houses, remains the heart of the city. The most imposing building is the Gothic **Hôtel de Ville** (Town Hall), in which there are a succession of impressive rooms (entrance through the archway beside the tourist office). English-language tours: Tues 1130 and 1515, Wed 1515 (all year); also Sun 1215 (Apr–Sept); BFr.75. The neighbouring brewers' house now contains **Musée de la Brasserie** (Brewery Museum), open Mon–Fri 1000–1700, Sat 1000–midnight; BFr.100. Across the square, the neo-Gothic **Maison du Roi**, *Grand-Place*, houses **Musée de la Ville** (open Mon–Thur 1000–1230 and 1330–1700 (closes 1600 Oct–Mar), Sat–Sun 1000–1300; BFr.80), covering every aspect of the city's history. The eclectic exhibits include notable retables, porcelain, silver and ancient documents, but the prize is on the top floor – reached by a wide wooden staircase, lined by stained-glass windows bearing escutcheons. Along with an interesting selection of puppets is the extensive wardrobe of the **Manneken-Pis** (literally 'small man who pisses'), the famous fountain in *r. du Chêne* that was designed by Jerome Duquesnoy in 1619 and has become the city's symbol. Among his more bizarre guises are Dracula, a Viking and a skin-diver.

A bit to the north is **Historium**, *Centre Anspach*, open daily 1000–1800; BFr.190. The Anspach complex stretches between *blvd Anspach* and *pl. de la Monnaie* and the museum is reached by taking the escalator up from the shopping area. It consists of a series of wax tableaux that take you from Roman times to the present. The headphones (in English) adjust themselves to your pace.

Cathédrale St-Michel, *pl. Ste-Gudule* (near Central), is a 13th–16th-century Brabantine-Gothic edifice that has just been restored. The particularly fine stained-glass windows were designed by a 16th-century court painter. Other features include 18th-century carved-oak confessionals and some modern works in copper. Open Mon–Fri 0700–1900, Sat 0730–1900, Sun 0800–1900 (an hour earlier Nov–Mar); admission free.

The home of the Belgian Parliament is **Palais de la Nation**, *r. de la Loi 16* (metro: *Parc*). Guided tours are arranged for groups and individuals can ask if there's a group going that they can join; free. It faces **parc de Bruxelles**, at the far end of which is **Palais Royale**, *pl. des Palais*, open to the public from late July for about six weeks (0930–1530; admission free) and full of rich decorations, including Goya tapestries.

Nearby is **Musées Royaux des Beaux Arts**, where colour-coded sections divide the exhibits into centuries (15th to 20th) and there's a separate section for sculptures. It consists of two sections (ancient and modern), linked by an escalator. When planning which to visit first, bear in mind that they close for lunch at different times. Between them, an audio-visual show is going constantly and you can get English earphones from the desk (admission free). The **Musée d'Art Ancien**, *r. de la Régence 3* (open Tues–Sun 1000–1200, 1300–1700; admission free) is light and well laid-out, containing fine examples of the Flemish school. Around a dozen works by Breughel are scattered through several rooms. Rubens, Jordaens, Cranach and Bosch are also well-represented. The **Musée d'Art Moderne**, *pl. Royale 1* (open Tues–Sun 1000–1300, 1400–1700; admission free), is housed in an interesting modern building designed for the collection: it's underground, but with windows all the way down. Dali's *Temptation of St*

Anthony is there, together with works by such artists as Ernst, Miro and Dubuffet. Walk down and take the lift back up. The 15th-century **Notre-Dame-du-Sablon**, *pl. du Grand-Sablon/r. de la Régence*, once housed a statue of the Virgin said to have miraculous powers. Open Mon–Fri 0900–1800, Sat 0900–1700, Sun 1300–1700; admission free. Across the road, *pl. du Petit-Sablon* features a small ornamental garden (open 0800–2100), the perimeters adorned with statues of figures, each carrying objects connected with their trade), and a fountain depicting two 16th-century counts who opposed Spanish tyranny. On one corner is **Musée Instrumental**. Open Tues–Sun 1430–1630; admission free. Adolphe Saxe, inventor of the saxophone, was Belgian-born and there's a section devoted to him, as well as over a thousand instruments, many unique and some going back to the dawn of time.

Notre-Dame-de-la-Chapelle, *r. des Ursulines 4*, is Brussels' oldest church, a 13th-century structure containing the marble tomb of Breughel the Elder. Open Mon–Fri 1000–1700, Sat 1400–1600, Sun 0930–1300 (June–Sept); admission free.

The neo-classical **Palais de Justice**, *pl. Poelaert* (metro: *pl. Louise*), is fittingly impressive. The 500-step ascent to the cupola is hard but, on clear days, rewarded by an excellent view. Open Mon–Fri 0900–1600; admission free.

Further south is **Musée Victor Horta**, *r. Américain 25, Ixelles* (tram nos 81/92. Open Tues–Sun 1400–1730; BFr.100). Once the home of the noted Belgian architect, the interior is typical of his (Art Nouveau) style.

North-west of the centre

The **Atomium**, *blvd du Centenaire* (metro

nos 1/19/81 to: *Heysel),* (a gigantic model of an iron atom) was constructed in 1958 and has become another symbol of the city. Several of the lower modules are linked (escalators up, easy stairs down) to form a series of exhibits about the human body and medicine. The main attraction, however, lies in the views: primarily from the top module, to which there's a high-speed lift (keep the ticket to get into the museum). Open 1000–1800 (Sept–Mar); 1000–2000 (Apr–Aug); BFr.160. About 100 m away is **Bruparck**, open 0900–2000 (July–Aug); a leisure complex. **Mini-Europe** (open daily 0930–1800 (Apr–June, Sept–Dec); 0930–2000/2100 (July–Aug); BFr.370) is a 2.5 hectare park containing miniaturised (1:25) versions of European landmarks. **Océade** (open Tues–Thur 1400–2200, Fri 1400–2400, Sat 1100–2400, Sun 1000–2000; BFr.480) is an aquatic complex, with pools, saunas and so forth. There are various combi-tickets for Bruparck and the Atomium.

Not far away is the **Planetarium**, *av. de Bouchout 10*, open 0900–1630; BFr.120. For information on shows, *tel; 478 91 06*.

East of the centre

Berlaymont Building, *r. de la Loi* (in Quartier Léopold), is the usual headquarters of the EU, but is empty while renovations are being carried out.

The pleasant **parc Léopold** (metro: *Schuman)* contains **Musée d'Histoire Naturelle**, *ch. de Wavre 260*, where exhibits range from dinosaurs to deadly insects. Open Tues–Sat 0930–1645, Sun 0930–1800; BFr.120.

Parc du Cinquantenaire (metro: *Schuman/Mérode)* surrounds the **Cinquantenaire**, a monumental arch flanked by museums. **Musée Royal de l'Armée et d'Histoire Militaire** (open Tues–Sun 0900–

1200, 1300–1600; admission free) should not be missed by anyone with the slightest interest in things military. As well as an incredible array of weapons and military paraphernalia of every type, there's a whole section devoted to armour, a yard full of armoured vehicles and a hangar full of aircraft (military and otherwise), ranging from a hot-air balloon to jets. **Autoworld**, open 1000–1800 (Apr–Sept); 1000–1700 (Oct–Mar); BFr.150, contains one of the world's best collections of vintage vehicles of all types. **Musée Royaux d'Art et d'Histoire** (entrance on the far side) is open Tues–Fri 0930–1700, Sat–Sun 1000–1700; admission free. This vast and diverse museum has whole galleries devoted to early cultures, from Greek to South American, and other sections cover everything from the cinema to textiles.

South-west of the centre

Beer-lovers should visit **Musée Gueuze**, *r. Gheude 56, Anderlecht* (10 mins walk from Midi), a working brewery with tours that include a sampling. Open Mon–Fri 0830–1630. Open Sat 0930–1300 (June–mid-Oct) or 1000–1800 (mid-Oct–May); BFr.70.

Further away from the centre, **Maison d'Erasme**, *r. de Chapitre 31* (metro: *St-Guidon*. Open Wed–Thur and Sat–Mon 1000–1200 and 1400–1700; BFr.50) was the home of Erasmus and has been authentically restored, with great attention to detail.

◗ Side Tracks from Brussels

There are frequent trains from Brussels to **Leuven**, the journey taking about 30 mins. **Station: Leuven/Louvain** (avoid trains designated 'Leuven/Louvain-La-N-Université'), 10 mins walk from the centre:

straight down Bondgenotenlaan. **Tourist Office:** (in the Stadhuis) *Naamsestraat; tel: (016) 21 15 39.* Open Mon–Fri 0800–1700, Sat–Sun 1000–1700. Get *What's On In Leuven* (BFr.25), which is a run-down of everything the town has to offer and includes a map. The university was founded in 1425 and the pleasant old town itself is the main attraction, a place to wander rather than sightsee, although it does have a handful of interesting museums. The façade of the **Stadhuis** (Town Hall), incorporates over two hundred statues of famous historical figures. In the crypt is **Brouwerijmuseum** (Brewery Museum). The Gothic church of **St-Pieterskerk**, which is being renovated, contains a museum of religious art and the **Stedelijk Museum** (Municipal Museum), *Savoyestraat*, is devoted to fine and applied arts.

Trains from Centrale to **Waterloo** are hourly and take 30 mins, but it's a good 15-min walk from the station. To get directly to the site, take TEC Bus W from Brussels (leaving *pl. Rouppe* every half-hour and taking 40 mins). The **Visitors' Centre**, *rte du Lion 252–254; tel: (02) 385 19 12,* opens daily 0930–1830 (Apr–Oct); 1030–1600 (Nov–Mar). Ask for a combi-ticket if you intend to visit all the sites. Everything of interest is connected with the 1815 battle between Wellington and Napoleon, which is re-enacted regularly on (or close to) 18 June. You can get a panoramic view of the battlefield (*Braine l'Alleud*) if you climb 40 m (226 steps), up the **Lion Mound** (open 0930–1830; BFr.40). See the free show at the centre first. Among several museums are **Musée Wellington,'** **Musée Provincial du Caillou** (Napoleon's HQ), **Panorama of the Battle** and the **Waxwork Museum**.

BRUSSELS to AMSTERDAM

This route between Belgium and the Netherlands is absolutely crammed with interest, incorporating several important cities and many smaller places of great interest, as well as visiting the prime tulip-growing area, which stretches between Haarlem and Leiden, centering on Lisse and the fabulous Keukenhof Gardens.

TRAINS

ETT tables: 18, 205, 220.

→ Fast Track

An hourly rail service links Brussels Midi and Nord to Amsterdam Centraal (CS) calling at Mechelen, Antwerp, Rotterdam, The Hague and Leiden en route, taking 3 hours 5 mins. Four express trains to and from Paris also serve this route; they are not much quicker, but do have buffet cars. The border between Belgium and The Netherlands is crossed with little formality and the trains do not stop.

∿→ On Track

Brussels–Mechelen–Antwerp

There are four trains each hour from Brussels Midi and Nord to Antwerp Berchem and Centraal via Mechelen. Brussels Midi to Mechelen takes 21–24 mins, Mechelen to Antwerp Centraal takes 18–22 mins.

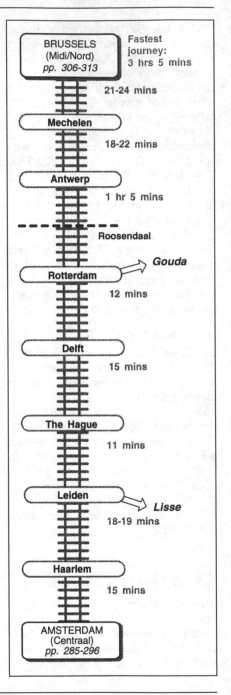

BRUSSELS (Midi/Nord) pp. 306-313

Fastest journey: 3 hrs 5 mins

21-24 mins

Mechelen

18-22 mins

Antwerp

1 hr 5 mins

Roosendaal

Rotterdam → Gouda

12 mins

Delft

15 mins

The Hague

11 mins

Leiden → Lisse

18-19 mins

Haarlem

15 mins

AMSTERDAM (Centraal) pp. 285-296

Antwerp–Rotterdam

An hourly train service takes 1 hr 5 mins to travel between Antwerp Centraal and Rotterdam Centraal (CS).

Rotterdam–Delft

There are four trains each hour taking about 12 mins.

Delft–The Hague

Three trains each hour operate between Delft and The Hague HS and CS stations, with journey times of about 15 mins.

The Hague–Leiden–Haarlem– Amsterdam

Four trains each hour run from The Hague HS to Amsterdam Centraal (CS) via Leiden; two of these trains serve Haarlem and the others go via Schiphol Airport. Additional local trains increase the Haarlem to Amsterdam service to six trains each hour. The Hague to Leiden takes 11 mins, Leiden to Haarlem 18-19 mins and Haarlem to Amsterdam 15 mins.

MECHELEN

Stations: Central and **Nekkerspoel** *tel: (015) 41 59 11.* The platform boards at Central say only 'Mechelen' and that's where most long-distance trains stop, but Nekkerspoel is just as close to the centre: about 10 mins walk either way.

Tourist Office: *Grote Markt* (in the modern wing of the Stadhuis); *tel: (015) 29 76 55.* Open Mon–Fri 0800–1800, Sat–Sun 0930–1700 (Apr–Sept); Mon–Fri 0800–1700, Sat 1000-1700 (Oct–Mar). Well organised, they have a wide range of free multi-lingual literature. A fairly detailed town map costs BFr.20, as does a colour brochure that makes a good souvenir.

Grote Markt is flanked by medieval buildings, including the multi-style **Stadhuis** (Town Hall). The Brabantine-Gothic chuch of **St-Rombout** dominates the centre and provides fine views (514 steps, but you can stop to explore en route). The interior is largely black and white marble, with sumptuous chapels, and Van Dyck's *Crucifixion* amongst the works of art. The two carillons (each with 49 bells) are used by campanologists from all over the world.

Museum Hof van Busleyden is housed in a 16th-century mansion. The grotesque wooden doll by the entrance, *Op Signoorke*, is a traditional focus of rivalry between Antwerp and Mechelen. In one building are a variety of exhibits, including items connected with Mechelen's guilds. Across the courtyard is a superb carillon section.

The enchanting **Speelgoedmuseum** (Toy Museum), open Tues–Sun 1000–1700; BFr.120, is crammed with toys of every description and is a real nostalgia trip. Your weight on the floor brings some of them to life. Another magical place is the tiny **Horlogerie en Klokkenmuseum**, crammed with antique clocks, but unfortunately the owners are often away.

The church of **St Pieter-Paulus** is rich with carved oak and enormous religious paintings. The altars are largely black and white marble, with gold ornamentation decorating the main one. **Sint-Janskerk** has a magnificent altar triptych by Rubens, the *Adoration of the Magi*, and many other baroque paintings.

Tapestry has been a Flemish craft for centuries and **Manufactuur Gaspard De Wit** has fine displays. There are 45-min tours of the (working) tapestry mill.

Planckendael, an extension of Antwerp Zoo, is used for breeding rare and threatened species. You can get a combination ticket that covers both zoos.

ANTWERP
(ANTWERPEN/ANVERS)

Stations: The main station, **Antwerpen-Centraal** tel: (03) 233 70 15, is 2 km east of the centre, but linked by metro-tram. The marble and gold-decorated station is worth a visit in its own right. Some international trains stop at **Bechem**, 2 km to the south; local services link the two.

Although there are no signs, there are baggage lockers at platform level: through the double doors on either side of the central exit. As well as a small train information kiosk on the main concourse, there's a large office downstairs, off the ticket hall. The bookstand there stocks UK newspapers and there's an exchange office. Many buses stop just outside the station and the **De Lijn** bus company office is in Centraal's metro-tram stop, Diamant. **Tourist Office:** Grote Markt 15; tel: (03) 232 01 03. Open Mon–Sat 0900–1745, Sun 0900–1645. From Centraal, take metro nos 2/15 to Groenplaats (direction Linkeroever), then walk past the cathedral and continue along the side street facing you – that leads to Grote Markt.

A free leaflet on **Rubens** covers the many things in town connected with him. There's a good publication called Antwerp Flanders Belgium, for BFr.20. You can get a free transport map, but street maps cost BFr.10. There's a combi-ticket for entrance into any three of the ten state museums.

The **Thomas Cook** bureau de change is at 33 Koningin Astridplein.

Accommodation

The tourist office get good discounts on hotels. Chains in Antwerp include BW, GT, Hn, Hy, Ho, Ib, Nv, SC, Sf and there are hotels in every grade, including some cheap ones near Centraal, but be wary because some rent by the hour. Bed and breakfast places are scarce.

HI: Jeugdherberg, Eric Sasselaan 2; tel: (03) 238 02 73, 5 km from Centraal. Tram no. 2, Bouwcentrum, direction Hoboken (away from the centre) stops about 500 m from the hostel (half of it through the park in which it's located). You can stay free in return for doing 3 hours' work, provided they don't already have enough people on that basis. East of the hostel is the **campsite:** Vogelzanglaan; tel: (03) 238 57 17.

Getting Around

You can get maps and tickets from the **De Lijn** office, Diamant: open Mon–Fri 0810–1230, 1330–1600. Single tickets cost BFr.40, ten-trip tickets BFr.250 and tourist cards (valid for one calendar day) BFr.100.

Most major sights are within easy walking distance of Centraal or Groenplaats. The tourist office produce booklets recommending town walks (BFr.30 each).

The tram system is efficient and buses fill the gaps in the network. Some tram lines run underground in the centre, forming a metro system, and stations are marked with a sign resembling a stylised blue mushroom on a yellow background. The system is well signed and easy to use if you know the terminal for your tram. Platforms have destination boards with lights showing the progress of trams along the route and large plans show where you can connect with other trams and buses.

Tours are possible by **taxi**, tel: (03) 238 38 38, or **horse-drawn carriage**, tel: (03) 324 60 01 or (03) 353 82 70. Rather cheaper (BFr.100) is the **tourist tram** departing from Groenplaats hourly 1100–1800: a 50-min multi-lingual circuit.

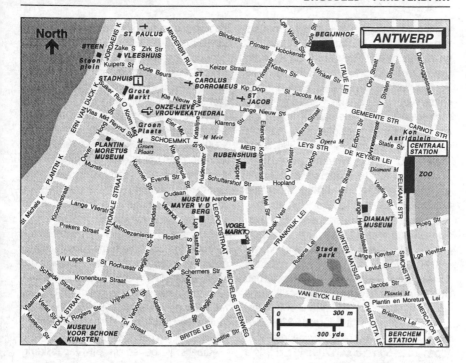

Flandria, *Steenplein 1; tel: (03) 231 31 00*, run a whole range of river excursions (departures hourly), starting at BFr.240 for a 50 min trip – for which you do not need a booking, but you must book for the longer cruises.

Sightseeing

Antwerp, on the River Scheldt, is Europe's second largest port. It is full of street entertainers and has a rich legacy of art and architecture. *Cultural Bulletin* (free) is published twice yearly (in English) with details of special events.

Dierentuin Zoo, *Kon. Astridplein 26* (beside Centraal), open 0900–1830 (closing 1645 in winter); BFr.390 includes admission to the **Planetarium** and **Dolphinarium**, but prices for refreshments are inflated. The **Diamantmuseum**, *Lange*

Herentalsestraat 31 (easily walkable from Centraal. Open 1000–1700 with cutting demonstrations Sat 1330–1630; admission free), covers all aspects of the diamond trade.

The base metro for exploring the centre is *Groenplaats*. This is a large square boasting a statue of the ubiquitous Rubens and overlooked by the 123 m spire of **Onze-Lieve Vrouwekathedral**, entrance on *Handschoenmarkt*. Open Mon–Fri 1000–1700, Sat 1000–1500, Sun 1300–1600; BFr.60, which includes free tours in several languages (times are posted outside). It's a beautiful building that took 170 years to complete (1352–1521). Most of the current stained-glass windows are 19th century. Rubens' *Assumption of Mary*, topped by a 17th-century baroque sculpture of God the Father and God the Son waiting to welcome her into Heaven, is flanked by two enormous Rubens' triptychs: *Raising the Cross* and *Descent from the Cross*. A fourth Rubens, *The Resurrection*, adorns the Moreto side chapel, but he is not the only artist represented: the whole place is a veritable art gallery. Current restoration is revealing unexpected treasures: in mid-1994 some 15th-century frescos were discovered.

The main square is **Grote Markt**, home of the 19th-century **Brabo Fountain** (which depicts the legend of the city's founding), guild houses topped by golden figures and the Renaissance **Stadhuis** (Town Hall). Open Mon, Tues, Wed, Fri 0900–1500, Sat 1200–1530; BFr.30. On 15 Aug each year Grote Markt is turned into a 17th-century market (the stallholders dressing accordingly) in honour of Rubens.

The unique **Plantin-Moretus Museum/ Stedelijk Prentenkabinet**, *Vrijdagmarkt 22* (open Tues–Sun 1000–1700; BFr.75), is a well-preserved 16th-century printer's works and home.

Head west, towards the river, to the medieval **Steen** (Castle), *Steenplein 1*, a 13th-century structure with 16th-century embellishments that houses the **National Scheepvartmuseum**. Open Tues–Sun 1000–1700; BFr.75. Unusually, most of the explanations have an English version and, in addition to the usual types of exhibit, there are such curiosities as a 'painting' made of stamps and a list of naval superstitions. Outside you can board the barge *Lauranda* (covered by the ticket), which has many of the original fittings. A variety of other vessels can be admired in an adjoining boathouse.

Heading away from the river, you come to the striking **Vleeshuis** (Butchers' Guild Hall), *Vleeshouwerstraat 38/40*, which is now an applied arts museum with exhibits that include some excellent wood-carvings. Open Tues–Sun 1000–1700; BFr.75. On the upper stories are superb sets of china and old musical instruments, lots of ticking grandfather clocks and an explanation of Egyptian hieroglyphics.

A little to the north is the Dominican **Sint-Pauluskerk**, *Veemarkt* (open daily 1400–1700 (May–Sept); 1000–1200 (Oct–Apr); BFr.50), a flamboyant Gothic structure with a baroque tower and furnishings. Among other treasures, it contains some magnificently carved wood and three works by Rubens.

Rubens was the major influence in the baroque design of the former Jesuit church of **Sint-Carolus Borromeus**, *Hendrik Conscienceplein 12* (to the south-east), which was badly damaged by an 18th-century fire. Open Tues–Sun 0930/1015–1215/ 1245 and wildly differing afternoon hours: check locally; BFr.20.

Rubens is buried in **Sint-Jacobskerk**, *Lange Nieuwstraat 73*, a few blocks to the east. Open Mon–Sat 1400–1700 (Apr– Oct); 0900–1200 (Nov–Mar); BFr.50. This is a 15th-century Gothic structure with 17th-century Baroque ornamentation and many art treasures.

Antwerp's 16th-century **Begijnhof**, *Rodestraat 39* (metro: *Opera*. Open 0900– 1700; free), with its 19th-century church, is a restful area of cobbled streets and small houses where pious lay women lived while devoting their lives to serving the community.

Rubens spent the last 30 years of his life in **Rubenshuis**, *Wapper 9* (about halfway between Centraal and *Grote Markt*; metro: *Meir*). Open Tues–Sun 1000–1700; BFr.75 (plus optional Walkman; BFr.100). It's an evocative place, reconstructed in 17th-century style, but contains only minor examples of his work.

A couple of blocks west (bus nos 7/8/9) is the **Mayer Van den Bergh Museum**, *Lange Gasthuisstr.19* (open Tues–Sun 1000–1700; BFr.75), which contains an important collection of antiques and paintings, notably by Breughel.

On Sun mornings, the **Vogelmarkt** (bird market), *Oude Vaartplaats,* to the south of Rubenshuis, does sell birds – plus animals, plants, antiques and almost everything else.

Museum Voor Schone Kunsten (Royal Museum of Fine Arts), *Leopold de Wael-plaats,* (bus nos 8/23. Open Tues–Sun 1000–1700; BFr.100), is a neo-classical building housing one of Belgium's best collections of paintings, including over twenty works by Rubens and a superb collection of 14th–17th-century Flemish art, as well as works of the Impressionist and Expressionist schools.

South-east of town, near Berchem station, is the residential *Jugendstil* district, where **Cogels-Osylei** is an avenue full of extraordinary (often overdone) 19th-century architecture. Further examples are found in the surrounding streets.

The **Openluchtmuseum Voor Beeldhouwkunst** (Sculpture Museum), *Middelheim Park,* is further south, just beyond the ring road (bus nos 18/17). Open Tues–Sun 1000–1900 (Apr, Sept); 1000–2000 (May, Aug); 1000–2100 (June–July); 1000–1700 (Oct–Mar); admission free, except for exhibitions. It's dotted with sculptures, notably by Rodin and Moore.

ROTTERDAM

Station: Centraal/CS: on the northern edge of the centre (the blue/green metro line).
Tourist Office: VVV, *Coolsingel 67* (5-mins walk from Centraal); *tel: (010) 413 6000.* Open Mon–Thur 0900–1730, Fri 0900–

2100, Sat 0900–1700; also Sun 1000–1600 (Apr–Sept). **Kiosk in the station:** open Mon–Sat 0900–2200, Sun 1000–2200. *Inside Out* is a free monthly listing and there's a weekly list of films.

There is a **Thomas Cook** bureau de change, offering foreign exchange facilities, at *Meent 74.*

Getting Around

Things of interest tend to be in clusters, so take public transport between the clusters and then walk. It's worth getting a street map unless your stay is very short.

Tickets

RET (*Stationsplein* and *Zuidsplein)* and VVV sell good-value tickets for unlimited city travel over one, two or three days.

Metro

Stations are indicated by a large squarish yellow M. The metro is fast, frequent, easy to understand (the basic system is simple and there are route maps everywhere) and user-friendly (not at all claustrophobic). There are several colour-coded lines but, unless you leave the centre, there are only two for practical purposes: blue/green runs roughly north–south and red/yellow/mauve runs east–west, so all you need worry about is heading in the right direction: note the final destination on 'your' line and follow the signs. If you need to change lines, they intersect at only one stop, where you walk from the Beurs platform to the Churchillplein platform (or vice versa). *Strippenkaarten* are validated in the yellow boxes in ticket halls (two strips).

Trams and buses

Efficient **trams** fill the gaps in the metro. The numbers shown after the names of stations on metro maps indicate the trams

---

and buses with stops close to that station. **Buses** are most use away from the centre.

Boats

Boat tours are operated by **Spido**, *Willemsplein; tel: 413 5400* (metro: *Leuvehaven*, tram no. 5). The basic harbour tour lasts 1 hr 15 mins and tells you all you will ever need to know about containers and Rotterdam harbour. The longer cruises offer more diverse attractions. All have multi-lingual commentaries.

Accommodation and Food

Hotel chains in Rotterdam include *BW, GT, Hn, Ho, Ib, Nv* and there are plenty of middle-range establishments. There are two areas with some cheap hotels: about 1 km south-west of CS (try *'s Gravendijkwal* and *Heemraadsingel*) and just north of CS (try *Provenierssingel*).

HI: *Rochussenstraat 107; tel: (010) 436 5763* (metro: direction *Marconiplein*: *Dijkzigt* stop). Take the Nieuwbinnen exit, do a U-turn at the top of the steps and you're on *Rochussenstraat* – turn left and the hostel is about 30 m away.

Campsite: *Kanaalweg 84*, west of CS (bus no. 33). There is usually dormitory accommodation (mid-June–mid-Aug) at **Sleep In**, *Mauritsweg 291*, 5 mins walk south of CS. This is arranged from year to year, however, so check with VVV.

There's every type of eating-place imaginable in the city and the cuisine of many countries is represented. For traditional Dutch, try the **Delfshaven** area.

Entertainment

There's no shortage of entertainment venues of every kind. **IMAX Theatre**, *Leuvehaven 77* (tram no. 6), is a huge cinema with the largest screen in the country (English earphones available).

Shows are Tues–Sun at about 1400, 1500, 1930 and 2030; DG14.

Tropicana, *Maasboulevard 100* (metro: *Oostplein*, tram nos 3/6/7. Open Mon–Fri 1000–2300, Sat 1000–1800, Sun 1000–1900; DG13, but public holidays are different), is a sub-tropical water complex.

On midweek evenings there's not much activity after 2300. At weekends most nightspots stay open until about 0300. A lively area very popular with students is *Oude Haven*, around the harbour, which is full of cafés with live music. A similar area, considered a little pretentious and regarded as a good place for pick-ups, is *Stadhuisplein*. There are plenty of rock/punk cafés around *Binnenweg*.

Sightseeing

As Rotterdam was virtually flattened by the Germans in World War II, most of it is postwar and it's noted for imaginative modern architecture. Situated at the delta of the Rivers Rhine, Meuse and Waal, it has been a major harbour since the 14th century and **Europoort** is the world's largest container port, but there are many attractions unconnected with maritime activities.

Don't miss the enormous **Museum Boymans-Van Beuningen**, *Museumpark 18/20* (metro: *Eendrachtsplein*, but tram no. 5 gets you much closer). Open Tues–Sat 1000-1700, Sun 1100–1700; DG6. The collection covers medieval times to the present and what is on show varies, but it always represents four areas; Applied Art and Design, Modern and Contemporary, Old Masters, and Prints and Drawings.

Maritiem Museum Prins Hendrik, *Leuvehaven 1* (metro: *Beurs/Churchillplein*; tram nos 3/6/7. Open 1000–1700; DG6), is the oldest and probably the most comprehensive maritime museum in the country, a vast place containing every

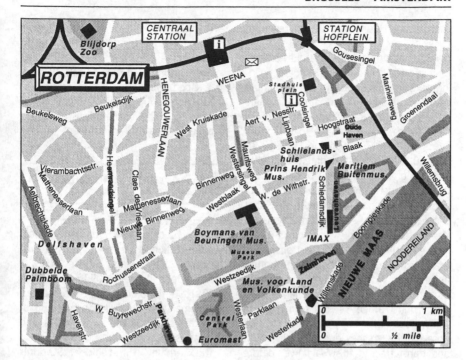

conceivable type of nautical paraphernalia, including whole vessels (old and otherwise) and 1400 models. Upstairs is *Professor Plons*, a hands-on section for children. Outside, you can board the *Buffel*, a well-restored 1863 warship.

Maritiem Buitenmuseum, *Leuvehaven 50*, is along the waterfront. Open Mon–Fri 1000–1230 and 1330–1500, Sun 1200–1600; DG6. This open-air maritime museum is the place to see historic barges, port cranes and old steamships.

Museum voor Land en Volkenkunde, *Willkemskade 25* (metro: *Leuvehaven*; tram no.5: *Willemsplein*. Open 1000–1700; DG6), is an ethnological museum that hosts temporary exhibitions from all over the world.

The 185 m **Euromast**, *Parkhaven 20* (tram no. 6: *Euromast*. Open Tues–Sat 1000–2230, Sun–Mon 1000–1900 (July–Aug); daily 1000–1900 (Apr–June, Sept); daily 1000–1700 (Oct–Mar); DG14.50, towers over the trees and the 5-min walk is through **Central Park**. There's a wooden footbridge over the major road on the other side which leads to the foot of Euromast, the highest structure in the Netherlands and a member of the exclusive World Federation of Great Towers (only 19 members). The original tower, opened in 1960, was 104 m high. It was raised to its present height in 1970 and the Space Adventure was added in March 1994. Even from the first platform you have panoramic views of the 37 km-long waterfront. You can go right to the top by taking the Space Adventure, a simulated rocket flight: after blast-off you go into orbit and have breathtaking views as the

Rotterdam

capsule ascends slowly to the top, revolving as it goes.

Around **Oude Haven**, the old harbour, is where the most striking modern buildings are located, notably the fascinating complex of **Kijk Kubus** futuristic cube houses (metro: *Blaak*, tram nos 3/6/7). One, *Overblaak 70*, is open to the public Tues–Fri 1000–1700, Sat–Sun 1100–1700; DG2.50. It's rather disorientating, but with interesting views (the value of each house depends largely on the view). A couple of doors away (at no. 76) is a little shop that should not be missed by cat lovers, **De Katten Kadowinkel**.

The neighbouring district is **Delfshaven** (tram nos 4/6), which escaped the bombs and where old warehouses have been attractively converted into up-market flats. The Pilgrim Fathers set sail from here in 1620, but their ship proved to be unseaworthy, so they docked at Plymouth and transferred to the *Mayflower* before attempting the Atlantic crossing.

Schielandshuis, *Korte Hoogstraat 31* (metro: *Beurs/Churchillplein*, tram nos 3/6), is a monumental 17th-century building that houses a museum devoted to the city's development and includes a variety of historical everyday objects. **De Dubbelde Palmboom Museum**, *Voorhaven 12*, its sister establishment, is devoted to the history of the delta: exhibits include an Iron Age farm and a traditional blacksmith's shop. Both open Tues–Sat 1000–1700, Sun 1300–1700; DG6.

Toy Toy Museum, *Groene Wetering 41*, (tram nos 3/7/9) contains a collection of rare toys from Europe and Japan that date from 1700 to 1940. It opens only Sun–Mon 1100–1600 (Sept–June); DG6.

There is also a **National School Museum**, *Nieuwemarkt 1a* (metro: *Blaak*, tram nos 3/7. Open Tues–Sat 1000–1700,

Sun 1100–1700; DG3.50) that traces Dutch education from the Middle Ages to the 1950s.

Zoo Blijdorp, *Van Aerssenlaan 49* (tram no.3. Open 0900–1800 (Oct–Mar), 0900–1700 (Apr–Sept); DG17.50), covers 18 hectares and the animals live, as far as possible, in a natural environment.

_ _ _ _ _ _ _ _ _ _ _ _ _ _ _ _ _ _ _ _

 Side Track from Rotterdam

GOUDA

Gouda is 25 mins from Rotterdam by train and the station is 10 mins stroll north of the centre. **VVV:** *Markt 27; tel: (01820) 13666*. Open Mon–Fri 0900–1700, Sat 1000–1600. It's a quaint place that exemplifies small-town Holland, with a ring of quiet canals around ancient buildings, and the main sights cluster around *Markt*.

The ornate 15th-century **Stadhuis** (Town Hall) contains carved fireplaces and 17th-century tapestries. **Waag**, the old weigh-house, opens for trading on Thur morning (July–Aug) and suitably costumed farmers weigh cheeses by traditional methods.

The church of **Sint Janskerk**, just south of Markt, open Mon–Sat 0900–1700 (mid-Mar–mid-Nov); 1000–1600 (mid-Nov–mid-Mar); 1300–1700 (holidays); DG2.50, is famous for its length (123 m) and superb stained-glass windows, the best of which are 16th-century and have biblical themes. The 17th-century bells ring out 45 mins and there are regular 49-bell carillon concerts on Thur (1000–1130) and Sat (1130–1230). There are also frequent concerts on the great 3856-pipe organ.

Across the road is the ornate **Lazaruspoortje** (1609), once leading to a hospital for lepers and now the back entrance to the unmissable **Catharina Gasthuis**, a complex of 14th–17th-century hospital buildings which houses the fascinating **Stedelijk Museum**. Open Tues–Sat 1000–1700, Sun 1200–1700; DG3.50. Among the rooms reproduced are a nursery, a torture chamber, a dispensary (where a dried alligator swings above your head), three rooms in a row furnished respectively in 17th- (Louis XIV), 18th- (rococo) and 19th-century (Empire) style, and an 18th–19th-century school. The **De Moriaan Museum** (across the canal from the front entrance and covered by the same ticket) opens the same hours, except Sat: 1000–1230, 1330–1700. It's an 18th-century tobacco shop displaying an amazing variety of earthenware items and pipes.

Other attractions include **De Roode Leeuw**, a restored flour-mill, and **Pottenbakkerij Adrie Moerings,** where you can watch pottery and pipes being produced.

DELFT

Station: 5-min walk south of the centre.
Tourist Office: VVV, *Markt 85; tel: (015) 126 100.* Open Mon–Fri 0900–1800, Sat 0900-1700, Sun 1000–1500 (Apr–Sept); Mon–Fri 0900–1800, Sat 0900–1700 (Oct–Mar).

In the 17th century Chinese porcelain reached Delft and the inspiration it provided led to the blue and white designs that made the town famous. At a few places still using traditional methods you can learn about the processes and watch the work. The best-known are **De Porceleyne Fles**, *Rotterdamsweg 196*, and **De Delftse Pauw**, *Delftweg 133*, but the most central is **Atelier de Candelaer**, *Kerkstraat 14*, just off *Markt*; all free.

The **Stedelijk Museum/Het Prinsenhof** (the prince's court), *St Agathaplein 1* (open

Tues–Sat 1000–1700, Sun 1300–1700; DG3.50), has a large section devoted to the struggle against the Spanish. William of Nassau/Orange, who led the fight for independence, was assassinated here (in July 1584) and the bullet marks can still be seen. Other exhibits include silverware, tapestries, paintings and Delftware. Across the road (and covered by the ticket) is **Nusantara Museum**, which has a rich collection of art from the former Dutch East Indies.

Oude Kerk, (Old Church) *Heilige Geestkerkhof*, open Mon–Sat 1000–1700 (Apr–Oct); DG2.50 (DG3.50 to include Nieuwekerk), has an alarmingly leaning tower, a number of impressive sarcophagi and 27 stained-glass windows, mostly modern. **Nieuwekerk**, *Markt*, open Mon–Sat 0900–1700 (Apr–Oct); Mon–Sat 1100–1600 (Nov–Mar); DG2.50, houses the enormous black and white marble mausoleum of Prince William of Orange, an enormous pipe organ and some rich stained glass. The 109 m spire provides great views.

At the other end of **Markt** is the **Stadhuis**. Open Mon–Fri 0900–1200 and 1400–1700; free.

THE HAGUE (DEN HAAG)

Stations: Centraal/CS is 5 mins walk from the centre (and serves most Dutch cities), but fast services for Amsterdam and Rotterdam use **Hollandse/HS** (1 km south): CS and HS are linked by frequent trains and also by tram nos 9/12. The Hague's other stations are suburban.
Tourist Office: VVV, *Koningin Julianaplein 30; tel: (06) 340 350 51.* Leave the station with the GWK office on your right and turn right: VVV is in the block facing you. Open Mon–Sat 0900–1800, Sun 1000–1700

(Apr–mid-Sept); Mon–Sat 0900–1800, Sun 1000–1700 (mid-Sept–Mar). *Den Haag Info* is a free monthly covering everything of interest. The free weekly *Over Uit* concentrates on films, theatres and music. **Thomas Cook** bureau de change, *Plein 14.*

Getting Around

If you don't enjoy walking, invest in a proper street map, because the small-scale ones are very deceptive and things that appear to be a block or two away can involve a long walk – unnecessarily, as there's an excellent bus and tram network.

Accommodation

Hotel chains in The Hague include *GT, Ib, IC, Me, Nv, Sf* and (in Scheveningen) *Ib.* If money is a consideration, it's better to base yourself at Scheveningen or ask VVV about private rooms.

HI: *Monsterseweg 4; tel: (07039) 70011,* 10 km west of CS near Kijkduin beach: bus nos 122/123/124 from CS plus a 10-min (signposted) walk: tell the driver you want the hostel. Close to it are a small cheap hotel and a campsite.

Sightseeing

The administrative capital is a pleasant town with wide boulevards and a noticeably cosmopolitan atmosphere. The city centre is the **Binnenhof**, the home of the Dutch parliament (trams nos 3/7/8; bus nos 4/5/22). Open Mon–Sat 1000–1600; admission free. The 13th-century **Ridderzaal** (Knights' Hall) is of particular note and the scene of many official ceremonies.

Mauritshuis Museum, *Korte Vijverberg 8* (tram nos 1/4/7/12/22. Open Tues–Sat 1000–1700, Sun 1100–1700; DG7.50), is a magnificent Renaissance mansion on a lake, housing much of the royal collection: Rembrandt, Vermeer, Ruysdael, Hals,

Cranach, Holbein, Breughel, van Dyck and Rubens are all represented. If you want more, the rest (included in the same ticket and only a short walk away) is in the **Schildergallerij Prins Willem V**, *Buitenhof 35* (open Tues–Sun 1100–1600; DG2.50), which is virtually wallpapered with paintings (one room contains 120 of them).

The neighbouring **Rijksmuseum Gevangenpoort**, *Buitenhof 33A* (tram nos 3/7/8, bus nos 4/5. Open Mon–Fri 1000–1700, Sun 1300–1700; DG5), is in a gatehouse that was a prison for over four centuries and contains a gruesome range of instruments of torture.

Panorama Mesdag, *Zeestraat 65* (tram nos.7/8, bus nos 4/5/13/22. Open Mon–Sat 1000–1700, Sun 1200–1700; DG4), consists of a realistic circular view of Scheveningen painted by Hendrik Mesdag, his wife and some friends in 1881 and it's well worth seeing. Ask at the desk for the English tape to be played.

Gemeentemuseum (the municipal museum), *Stadhouderslaan 41* (bus nos 4/14. Open Tues–Sun 1100–1700; DG8), is a higgledy-piggledy place that mixes temporary exhibitions with the permanent collection and you're sure to find something that appeals to you. **Museon,** in the same building (open Tues–Fri 1000–1700, Sat–Sun 1200–1700; DG5), concentrates on popular science, ranging from the origins of the planet to modern technology – with hands-on exhibits.

The unmissable 1990s version of a panorama, at **Omniversum**, *President Kennedylaan 5* (tram nos 8/10, bus nos 4/14/65/66 – or through the small garden to the rear of Gemeentemuseum), is a stunning spectacle with a wrap-around screen that makes you feel like a participant in the action. There are English earphones and performances are usually

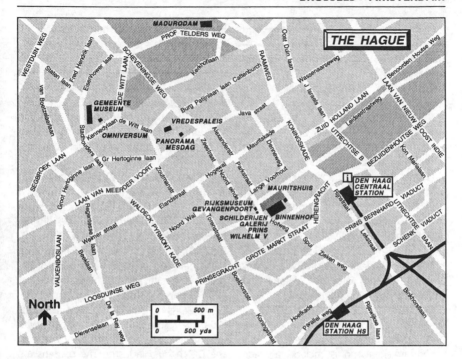

hourly Tues–Sun from 1100 until mid-evening; DG16: booking office open daily 0900–1200; *tel: (070) 354 5454.*

Most of the city's palaces can be viewed only from the outside. An exception is the huge **Vredespaleis** (Peace Palace), *Carnegieplein 2*, which houses the International Courts of Justice and Arbitration, and is a strange architectural mishmash, with a display of items donated by various world leaders. Except when the Court is in session, there are tours Mon–Fri at 1000, 1100, 1200, 1400 and 1500 (also 1600 May–Sept); DG5.

A number of small museums with limited opening hours are worth a look if you are there at the right time (check locally). These include **Museum voor het Poppenspel** (Puppet Museum), **Brandweermuseum** (Fire Brigade Museum) and **Openbaar Vervoer Museum** (Public Transport Museum).

Out of Town

Madurodam, *Haringkade 175* bus no. 22; tram nos 1/9. Open 0900–evening (Easter–early-Jan); DG14), is the world's largest miniature town, which includes models of the nation's landmarks.

The North Sea resort of **Scheveningen** is about 4 km from the city centre (tram nos 1/7/8/9/10/11) and regarded as part of it, although it has its own **VVV:** *Gevers Deynootweg 1134* (telephone and hours as for The Hague office). Hotels here are cheaper than in town, but prices in the promenade eateries are inflated. The resort centres on the 19th-century **Kurhaus Hotel** (in which there's a casino) and offers a long sandy beach and wide promenade.

LEIDEN

Station: 10-mins walk north-west of the centre.
Tourist Office: VVV, *Stationsplein 210; tel: (07114) 6846.*

The delightful little town of Leiden is well worth a visit, with over a dozen user-friendly museums. The medieval quarter centres on the vast **St Pieterskerk**.

Hortus Botanicus, *Rapenburg 73* (open Mon–Sat 0900–1700, Sun 1000–1700; DG3.50), is among the world's oldest botanical gardens. **Van Oudenheden**, *Rapenburg 28* (open Tues–Sat 1000–1700, Sun 1200–1700; DG5), is an excellent archaeological museum with many objects from early Greece and Rome and an amazing array from ancient Egypt.

De Lakenhal, *Oude Singel 32* (open Tues–Fri 1000–1700, Sat–Sun 1200–1700; DG5), covers the history of the town: the period-furnished rooms include a traditional kitchen and various guild rooms, while van Leyden's triptych of the *Last Judgment* is among the fine paintings.

Nearby is **Molenmuseum de Valk**, *Binnenvestgracht 1* (open Tues–Sat 1000–1700, Sun 1300–1700; DG3.50), a windmill that is a museum.

Voor Volkenkunde, *Steenstraat 1* (open Tues–Fri 1000–1700, Sat–Sun 1200–1700; DG5), is the home of temporary exhibitions from around the world and is noted for its excellent displays.

The **Stadhuis** has an incredibly ornate exterior and its bell-tower sounds the passing time.

In the **Boerhave**, *St Agnietenstraat 10* (open Tues–Sat 1000–1700, Sun 1200–1700; DG3.50), is an anatomical theatre, complete with skeletons and displays of early medical paraphernalia.

Rembrandt was born in Leiden and lived here for 26 years, but there is virtually no trace of him in the town.

LISSE

The Bulb District is an area which stretches roughly from Leiden to Haarlem and you can get a good view of the fields from trains between them – a better one from bus nos 50/51, which stop en route at the tiny town of **Lisse**, **VVV:** *Grachtweg 53; tel: (02521) 14262/15263.* Open Mon–Fri 0900–1700, Sat 0900–1600. About 50 m from VVV is **Museum voor de Bloembollenstreek** (open Tues–Sun 1300–1700; DG2.50), which is devoted to bulbs. The permanent section covers all aspects of the history and cultivation of tulips and plants.

The prime reason for visiting Lisse, however, is to see **Keukenhof Gardens** (10 mins by local bus), a 70-acre park, with 16 km of paths, which is the showcase of the Dutch bulb industry. The gardens are open only for two months (late-Mar–late-May 0800–1930, last tickets sold at 1800; DG15) and the peak is April, so it's pot luck how much there is to see in March and May. The gardens are noted for tulips, narcissi and hyacinths and there are pavilions featuring flower arrangements. Take a picnic, the cafés are invariably over-crowded. In season, special bus no. 54 goes from Leiden directly to the gardens.

HAARLEM

Station: 10-mins walk north of the centre. It was built in 1908 and in art deco style.
Tourist Office: VVV, *Stationsplein 1; tel: (023) 319 059.* Open Mon–Sat 0900–1730 (Apr–Sept); Mon–Fri 0900–1730, Sat 0900–1600 (Oct–Mar). The *UIT Loper* is a free listing, published every two or three weeks.

Getting Around

The major sights are close to *Grote Markt*, with the notable exception of the old wing of the **Frans Hals Museum**, which is about 15 mins walk south. To get there (and further afield) there's a good network of buses. Various **boat trips** are available from **Rondvaart Rederij Noord-Zuid**, *tel: (023) 357 723 or 356 491*, departing from *Spaarne 11A*, near *Wildemans-brug*.

Accommodation

Haarlem has a few up-market hotels (including *GT*), but Zandvoort (see Out of Town below) offers more choice.

HI: *Jan Gijzenpad 3; tel: (023) 373 793*, 3 km north of the station, 10 mins on bus nos 2/6 (closed Nov–Feb). The **campsite**, *Liewegje 17; tel: (023) 332 360*, is not very convenient. In spring and summer you can camp in the dunes along Zeeweg (bus no.81: *Bloemendaal-aan-Zee*).

Sightseeing

The **Stadhuis**, *Grote Markt*, was a 13th-century hunting lodge and expanded over the centuries. The lavish interior can often be viewed by arrangement. The late-Gothic **St Bavo/Grote-Kerk** (open Mon–Sat 1000–1600 (Apr–Aug); 1000–1530 (Sept–Mar); free), was completed in the mid-16th century and became a popular subject for painters. Inside is the world-famous Christian Müller baroque pipe-organ, an enormous affair that was played by the young Mozart and is still used for regular concerts. Other features of St Bavo are the tomb of Frans Hals and a 16th-century rood screen and choir stalls.

The town's main draw is the **Frans Hals Museum**, *Groot Heiligland 62*. Open Mon–Sat 1100–1700, Sun 1300–1700; DG6. Although he is not the only artist repre-sented, the highlight of the collection is a group of Hals' paintings depicting militia companies.

A once-private collection that first went on view in 1784 can be seen at **Teylers Museum**, *Spaarne 16*. Open Tues–Sat 1000–1700, Sun 1300–1700; DG6.50. The eclectic exhibits include old scientific instruments, fossils, gem-stones, coins and drawings – some by Raphael, Michelangelo and Rembrandt.

Corrie Ten Boommuseum, *Barteljoris-straat 19* (open Tues–Sat 1000–1630 (Apr–Oct); 1000–1530 (Nov–Mar); free, but there's a box for donations), was founded by Willem Ten Boom in 1837 as a clock shop, and a watch-maker still works there (Mon–Sat 0900–1800). Successive genera-tions committed themselves to helping the needy and this tradition extended to the Jews in World War II. They were betrayed in 1944 and most perished in the camps, but Corrie Ten Boom survived and the house is maintained as a monument to the family, a tribute to courage and a charity.

Out of Town

Zandvoort (10 mins by train and frequent buses in summer) is the beach for Haarlem and has plenty of cheap pensions. **VVV**, *Schoolplein 1; tel: (02507) 17947*, can supply information. Open Mon–Sat 1000–1230 and 1330–1700 (but only to 1600 on winter Saturdays). It's a large resort with good facilities, including a car race-track, a dolphinarium and an ultra-modern casino. The long, sandy beaches (including one for nudists) begin 200 m from the station.

Zaanse Schans (train to Koog Zaandijk, from where it's a 10-min walk) is a typical (if touristy) 17th/18th-century village, of-fering five working windmills, a cheese farm, a bakery museum, hand-crafts and much more.

BRUSSELS to LUXEMBOURG

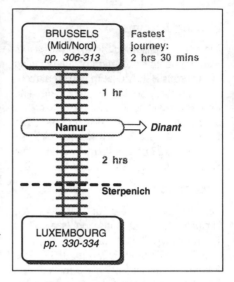

BRUSSELS (Midi/Nord) *pp. 306-313*	Fastest journey: 2 hrs 30 mins

1 hr

Namur ⟹ *Dinant*

2 hrs

--- **Sterpenich**

LUXEMBOURG *pp. 330-334*

It's worth breaking the journey betwen Brussels and Luxembourg in order to visit the attractive old town of Namur, which is the capital of Wallonia and full of interest. The south-eastern end of the route runs through the glorious unspoiled scenery of the Ardennes, characterised by thickly forested hills.

TRAINS

ETT table: 210.

 Fast Track

Ordinary trains run every hour from Brussels Midi and Brussels Nord to Luxembourg, taking nearly 3 hrs for the journey. Three international expresses with restaurant cars also make the journey each day, with a shorter journey time of about 2½ hrs.

 On Track

Brussels–Namur

Two trains each hour operate between Brussels and Namur taking 1 hr for the journey.

Namur–Luxembourg

Trains run every hour between Namur and Luxembourg. It takes just less than 2 hrs to make this scenic journey through the Ardennes.

NAMUR

Station: *av. de la Gare; tel: (081) 25 21 11*, a 3-min walk north of the centre.
Tourist Offices: Municipal, *pl. Leopold* (about 300 m from the station); *tel: (081) 22 28 59*. Open daily 0900–1800, but often closes an hour earlier and for lunch out of season (usually 1230–1300). They have a free brochure about the province's attractions (including Namur itself) and a useful street map for only BFr.10. Various combi-tickets exist. **Provincial:** *r. Notre-Dame 3; tel: (081) 22 29 98*. Open Mon–Fri 0900–1200 and 1300–1700.

Accommodation

Although it's a small place, there are a few hotels. **HI:** *av. Félicien Rops, 8 La Plante; tel: (081) 22 36 88*, 3 km from the station: bus nos 3 or 4 to stop: *Marronnier*.

Sightseeing

The town is overlooked by a medieval **Citadel**, which began life as a Celtic hill fort. Open daily 1100–1900 (Apr–Sept), but last visit 1730; BFr.195. You can wander at will around the 15th–19th-century complex, which is on several levels, but the entrance fee covers a mini-train ride, a good video (in French) and a guided walking tour (allow 2–3 hrs for the full tour), the latter taking you through areas of the old fortifications that you could not otherwise see. It's usual to ascend by the cable-car and to walk down (follow the road until you see a cannon, then take the steps which start on the right: rougher, but quicker, than following the road). The cable-car provides stunning views – better than the citadel. It leaves from *Pied-du-Château*: 1000–1900; BFr.160 single, BFr.195 return.

Musée Archéologique, *r. du Pont* (open Mon, Wed–Fri 1000–1700, Sat–Sun 1030–1700; BFr.40), contributes to archaeological explorations in the Meuse Valley and some of the finds are among its exhibits.

Musée de Groesbeeck de Croix, *r. Joseph Saintraint 3*, exhibits mainly 18th-century *objets d'art* from the region and includes period rooms. Tours Wed–Mon, 1000, 1100, 1400, 1500 and 1600; BFr.80.

The 18th-century **Cathédrale St-Aubin** (admission free) is beautifully proportioned, with half-domes to three sides of the main one, carved wooden confessionals, lots of attractive marble and a main altar surrounded by Baroque paintings. Its treasury, **Musée Diocésain**, *pl. du Chapitre*, is alongside: open Tues–Sat 1000–1200 and 1430–1800 (Easter–Oct); 1430–1630 (Nov–Easter); BFr.50.

Some way south of the centre is **Musée de la Forêt**, *rte Merveilleuse 9*, which is devoted to the Ardennes flora and fauna. Open Sat–Thur 0900–1200 and 1400–1700 (Apr–Oct); also Fri mid-June–mid-

Sept; BFr.50. **Musée de la Fraise** (Strawberry Museum), *chaussée de Dinant, Wépion*, is housed in what used to be the town hall. This once central spot is now on the outskirts, about 15 mins by bus no. 4 from the current centre. Open Wed and Sun 1500–1800 (Easter–Aug); BFr.80.

 Side Track from Namur

DINANT

Station: *tel: (082) 22 28 60*. South of the river, 5 mins walk from the centre (on the north bank). The ticket office supplies a free map which includes useful information. **Tourist Office**: *r. Grande 37*; *tel: (082) 22 28 70*. Open daily 0900–1900.

This tiny town is very pretty, lining the banks of the River Meuse and overlooked by a towering escarpment. Trains from Namur take less than 30 mins and there are about ten a day. In summer full-day river excursions from Namur allow you about 2 hrs in Dinant.

The main attraction is **Grotte la Merveilleuse**, a beautiful complex of caves full of white stalactites and waterfalls. Open 1000–1800 (Mar–Nov); at other times on request; BFr.160, which covers a 50-min tour of the complex and a 45-min boat trip on the River Meuse. The **Citadel** (reached by cable-car) houses an arms museum and a war museum, while **Mont-Fat** (reached by chair-lift) is a pleasure ground that incorporates such natural features as a maze of underground passages, prehistoric caves (halfway up the cliff and connected to the tower by underground passages) and hanging gardens. Open 1030–1900 Easter–Oct; BFr.150.

LUXEMBOURG CITY

The eponymous capital is the only real city in the Grand-Duchy and worth visiting primarily for its dramatic setting on a gorge cut by the rivers Alzette and Pétrusse, although it also has a handful of sights.

The town falls naturally into three sections. The old centre, on the north of the Pétrusse gorge, is home to most of the sights. The station and modern city are south of the gorge. Grund is the valley settlement, currently the scene of extensive restoration.

Tourist Information

Tourist Office: Municipal, *pl. d'Armes; tel: 22 28 09*, is in the old town and has information only about the city. Open Mon–Fri 0900–1900; Sat 0900–1300, 1400–1900; Sun 1000–1200, 1400–1800 (mid-June–mid-Sept); Mon–Sat 0900–1300 and 1400–1800 (mid-Sept–mid-June). All the general literature is free, but they charge LFr.50 to book accommodation. **National**, *pl. de la Gare* (in the Luxair office, right as you exit); *tel: 48 11 99*, has free information about the whole country and books accommodation (without charging). Open daily 0900–1900 (July–mid-Sept); Mon–Sat 0900–1200, 1400–1830; Sun 0900–1200 and 1400–1830 (mid-Sept–June, but closed Sun Nov–Mar).

Arriving and Departing

Airport

Luxembourg-Findel, *tel: 47 98 23 11*, is 6 km to the east of town. A tourist information and hotel booking desk *(tel: 48 11 99)* is open Mon–Fri 1000–1430 and 1600–1900, Sat 1000–1345, Sun 1000–1430 and 1530–1830. The exchange office is open whenever there are flights.

Bus no. 9 (runs every 15–20 mins – less frequent Sun) connects the airport and the station, the journey taking about 30 mins. **Luxair** buses are faster (about 20 mins), but run primarily to connect with major flights (LFr.120). A taxi should cost about LFr.700, plus LFr.20 per case if you have more than one.

Station

Gare Centrale, *tel: 49 24 24*, is a neo-baroque building dating from 1907. It's about 15-min walk south of the centre, the most direct route being over the 19th-century **pont Passerelle** (with great views), but there are lots of buses. Platform 3 is level with the station services. Platforms 1–2 are at one end of Platform 3, the other platforms are linked by tunnels. There are lifts, but the stairs are more central. Few trains take up the whole platform, so keep an eye on the platform departure boards to make sure you're at the right end.

The manned left-luggage office is open daily 0600–2200 (LFr.60 per item for two days, then LFr.60 per item per calendar day) and the baggage-forwarding office will accept left-luggage outside these hours. There are also lockers for LFr.60/80/100 (depending on size) per 24 hrs (max. 48 hours). As well as a variety of eating places and shops, the station offers showers (LFr.40) and baths (LFr.60).

Train and long-distance bus enquiries, hotel bookings and *télécartes* are all handled by the **CFL** office in the station, which does not take credit cards. Open daily 0700–2000.

Getting Around

Ask the tourist office for a street map and *A walk through the green heart of Europe*, which details two routes that cover everything of interest in the capital. Both are free.

If you prefer to be guided, there are a number of options. As well as conventional conducted tours, you can **Walk with a Walkman** at your own speed – available daily 1000–1500 (Apr–Oct); LFr.190. The **Pétrusse Express** (a misnomer: it's slow-moving) departs from *pl. de la Constitution* hourly 1000–1700 (Apr–Oct); LFr.220. It's a small tourist train which takes just under an hour and has multi-lingual headphones. Both are worthwhile for the commentary alone: a highly-dramatised account of history and legend, with martial music, cannon fire and sketches.

Tickets

Single bus tickets cost LFr.35. They and the day-cards are available from drivers. CFL sell the **Oeko-Carnet** and ten-ride tickets (LFr.270). The latter are also available from post offices – and anywhere else displaying an Autobus sticker.

Buses

The tourist office can supply a (free) route guide for the city buses. The terminal for many is the station, but some go further and don't enter the station yard – so get off at the stop across the street.

Taxis

There are ranks at the station and in *av. Monterey* (beside the post office) or *tel: 48 00 58*. The usual rate is LFr.30 per km in town, LFr.60 outside the city limits, with surcharges at night (ten per cent) and on Sun (25 per cent).

Staying in Luxembourg

Accommodation

Hotel chains in Luxembourg City include *BW, GT, Ib, Ic, Me, Sf* and *Sh*. There's quite a wide range of accommodation, most of the cheaper places being around the station. City hotel prices include a five per cent overnight tax.

HI: *2 r. du Fort Olisy* (3 km from the station); *tel: 22 68 89*. Bus no. 9: *Vallée d'Alzette* (150 m from the stop, down a steep hill). If you can't get a small room and object to showering in public, go somewhere else. Meals there are good value.

Kockelscheuer campsite, *tel: 47 18 15*, is south of the centre, 4 km from Centrale and 500 m from the no. 2 bus stop.

Eating and Drinking

Some of the tacky eating-places in the station area are not noticeably cheaper than the much better middle-range ones in the old centre. *Pl. d'Armes* is full of eateries, with open-air entertainment on most summer evenings. If you want to do your own thing, there's a regular food market in *pl. Guillaume* (Wed and Sat 0800–1200).

Communications

There are two major **post offices**. The one in *pl. de la Gare* (in front of the station and to the left as you exit) opens daily 0600–2000, holidays 0800–2000. The one at *25 r. Aldringen (pl. Hamilius)*, opens Mon–Fri 0700–2000, Sat 0700–1900. Both offer an international telephone service.

Money

The exchange office inside the station opens Mon–Sat 0830–2100, Sun 0900–2100. On the exterior wall of the post office in *pl. de la Gare* there's a Postomat

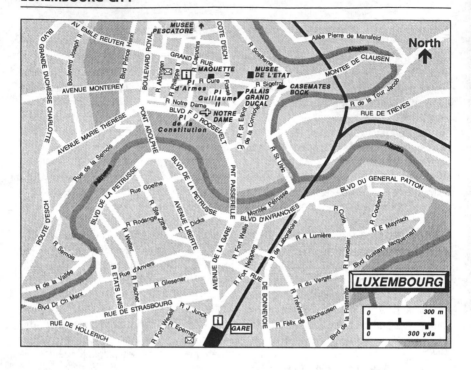

machine (operational 24 hrs a day) which gives cash against credit cards and Giro-bank cards.

Embassies

UK: *14 blvd Roosevelt; tel: 22 98 64.* The UK Embassy represents Commonwealth citizens. **USA:** *22 blvd E Servais; tel: 46 01 23.* **Ireland:** *28 r. d'Arlon; tel: 45 06 10.*

Entertainment

The nightlife is pretty tame, but there are lots of convivial bars and cafés, notably in the Grund and Clausen districts. *La semaine à Luxembourg* is a free weekly listing, which includes films and specifies which language the film is in.

Events

Marché-aux-Poissons is (on the morning of Easter Monday) the setting for the **Emaischen Festival**, a colourful spectacle in which young lovers present each other with whistling clay birds and there's folk dancing and singing.

On 22 June (the eve of National Day) a torchlight parade through the city is followed by fireworks and dancing in the squares.

Shopping

The main shopping streets are *Grand-Rue, av. de la Liberté* and *av. de la Gare*. Popular souvenirs are Luxembourg chocolates (*Knippercher*) and the local Villeroy and Boch porcelain.

Sightseeing

The **Monument de la Solidarité Nationale**, *pl. de la Constitution*, is topped by a golden woman and dedicated to the volunteers (alive and dead) who fought in both world wars.

Across the road, **Cathédrale Notre-Dame**, a 17th-century Jesuit church, is of mixed architectural styles. Inside the simple stone crypt is the tomb of Duke John the Blind, backed by statues of mourners. Bronze lions flank a gate through which can be seen the burial chapel of the Grand-Ducal family, with its marble floor and mosaic walls. At the other end are stained-glass windows of Christ flanked by the apostles. Open daily (usually 0800–1200 and 1400–1900); admission free.

From *pl. de la Constitution*, there is access to two of the **Pétrusse casemates**: underground passages that formed part of the city's original defences. Open Easter, Whitsun and July–Sept; LFr.50. Tours usually leave hourly, but check the notice-board at the top of the steps. The guides are multi-lingual and tours take about 45 mins, beginning with a dark descent of 132 uneven steps – if you find this a strain, forget the ascent and drop out at the bottom. You can take your time to follow the valley paths back to the top and there are benches en route. Nobody who is claustrophobic, unfit or has heart problems should participate.

The similar casemates at **Rocher du Bock** are less of a strain. The entrance is on *r. Sigefroi*, the site where Count Siegfried built the original fortress. It was expanded by later rulers, especially the French, who made it one of the strongest-defended cities in 17th-century Europe. There is not much to see inside the complex, but it provides great views. Open daily 1000–1700 (Mar–Oct); LFr.50.

There are guided tours of the royal residence, the Spanish-Renaissance style **Palais-Grand-Ducal**, when the Grand Duke is away (usually mid-July–early-Sept): get details and tickets from the city tourist office.

Maquette, *Rathskeller, r. du Curé*, is a small museum showing the fortress-city at various stages of its history. Open Mon–Sat 1000–1220, 1400–1800 (Easter–mid-Oct); LFr.40.

Exhibits in the **Musée de l'État**, (National Museum) *Marché-aux-Poissons*, (open Tues–Fri 1000–1200, 1300–1700, Sat 1400–1800, Sun 1000–1200, 1400–1600; admission free) which occupies 120 rooms in converted 16th-century mansions, range from the Stone Age to the 20th century. There's an eclectic and good fine arts section.

Musée Pescatore has a modest permanent collection of fine art that is on display July/Aug. At other times there are temporary exhibitions. Usually open Mon, Wed, Thur, Fri 1300–1800, Sat–Sun 0900–1200 and 1500–1900; admission free.

Plateau Kirchberg, north of the centre and reached by crossing the *Pont Grande-Duchesse-Charlotte* (with spectacular views), is a modern area that houses the European Court of Justice and other EU offices. The European Parliament is in Luxembourg's only skyscraper.

◪ Side Tracks from Luxembourg

About 30 mins by (frequent) train north of the capital, **Ettelbrück** (**tourist office** in a corner of the station building; *tel: 82068)* is a major junction and the place from which to take buses to the more interesting towns in the area.

Only 3 km from Ettelbrück is **Diekirch** (**tourist office:** *pl. Guillaume; tel: 80 30 23)*, a very old settlement, with a 15th-century church on Roman foundations. **Musée Mosaiques Romaines** has well-preserved Gallo-Roman floor mosaics and **Musée Historique** details the Battle of the Bulge, during which the town suffered greatly.

A noted beauty spot, **Vianden** (20-mins scenic drive from Ettelbrück) is interesting as well as lovely, and well worth a visit. The **tourist office, 37 r. de la Gare; tel: 84257,** (open 0930–1200, 1400–1800 Apr–Oct, but closed one day a week, usually Tues) is 5 mins walk from the bus terminal and contains a small museum about **Victor Hugo,** who sometimes stayed there. If you want to stay for a while to explore the beautiful countryside, there are hotels, a hostel and nearby riverside campsites.

The obvious way to explore is to start at the top, by taking the **télésiège** (chair-lift) up to 440 m. There are superb views from the top and a choice of footpaths to the castle: you can descend steeply by rough woodland tracks or follow the easier (longer) paved path. The formidable **château** dates from the 5th century and extensive excavations have unearthed much of interest. Current restorations reveal many different periods and are supplemented by diverse displays, so it's far more varied than most such strongholds. The town begins just below the castle, the main road winding downhill to the river. On the way you pass the **Musée d'Art Rustique et des Poupées,** a delightful place containing rustic rooms in period style and hundreds of dolls, teddy bears and toys. There are several little churches, notably **Église des Trinitaires,** built in 1248 and recently renovated; pride of place going to a spectacular silver, gold and enamel altar. The cloister encloses a small garden and is adorned with ancient stone carvings. In Oct there's a **walnut market,** music accompanying the sale of fresh nuts and all manner of items containing them.

An exceptionally lovely 45-min bus ride through the Ardennes from Ettelbrück (also linked by bus to Vianden in July–Aug), **Echternach** is a pleasant little town with a somewhat medieval atmosphere and some unique attractions. The bus terminal is a 5-min walk from the **tourist office:** *Porte St-Willibrord* (near the Basilica); *tel: 72230.*

The town grew around the Benedictine **Abbaye,** founded in 698 by St Willibrord, an English missionary monk who was famed for curing epilepsy. His white marble sarcophagus is in the crypt of the **basilica** and there are some 11th-century frescos in the vault. One wing of the complex houses the **Musée de l'Abbaye,** which should not be missed. The major exhibits concern illuminated manuscripts (of which it has many examples) and the techniques involved. Star of the fascinating collection is the *Codex Aureus of Echternach*: the gospels decorated in gold and bound in a superb 10th-century gold cover encrusted with enamel and gems – this is one of the greatest examples of medieval art still in existence. Other attractions in town are **Église-Sts-Pierre-et-Paul** (Church of St Peter and St Paul), thought to be the oldest Christian sanctuary in the country, and the small **Musée de Préhistoire**.

Every Whit Tuesday at 0900 there's a day-long **dancing procession** in St Willibrord's honour, the participants linked by white handkerchiefs in a ritual which can be traced back to the 15th century, and is believed to have its origins in pagan rites. Nowadays it attracts thousands of pilgrims and spectators. Another annual excitement is a month-long **Festival**, which begins in late May and draws international classical musicians for concerts in the abbey, the basilica and the church.

– – – – – – – – – – – – – – – – – – – –

OSTEND to BRUSSELS

This route between the North Sea coast and the Belgian capital incorporates two of the country's most interesting cities, Bruges and Ghent, both very Flemish and stuffed with historical buildings and good museums. If you're in search of a beach, the Belgian coastline is one long stretch of sand, with a string of resorts: Zeebrugge is the most famous, but that's due to its proximity to Bruges and it is less attractive to visitors than some of the others.

TRAINS

ETT tables: 200.

→ Fast Track

An hourly service links Ostend with Brussels Midi and Nord, the journey takes about 1 hour 15 mins. All trains call at Bruges and Ghent en route.

⁓⁓ On Track

Ostend–Bruges

It takes 14 mins to travel between Ostend and Bruges and there are three trains each hour.

Bruges–Ghent

Three fast trains each hour link Bruges and Ghent Sint-Pieters, taking around 22 mins.

Ghent–Brussels

Two trains each hour operate between

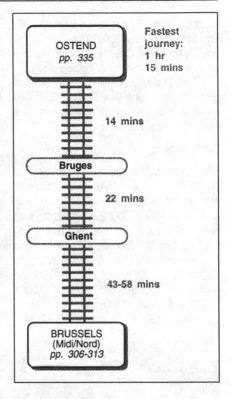

Ghent Sint-Pieters and Brussels Midi and Nord; the journey takes 43–58 mins.

OSTEND (OOSTENDE)

Station: tel: (059) 70 08 81. The ferries and trains share a building, 10 mins walk from the tourist office (or bus no. 5). There are several eateries and lots of seats. Baggage trolleys require a 20-franc coin and baggage can be checked an hour before vessels leave.

Tourist Office: *Monacoplein 2; tel: (059) 70 11 99 (open Mon–Sat 0900–1900, Sun 1000–1900; closes at 1800 Oct–May):* walk right from the station and along the sea-front, then take the last turning left before the front curves. Purchase the A–Z brochure (BFr.10) and town map (BFr.5). The hotel brochure (BFr.10) is free if you book from it and *Oostende Events* is a free annual listing. There's an Ostend day-pass (BFr.100) and one covering several resorts (BFr.350, late-June–Aug only). Tours by horse-drawn carriages and boats are available along the front.

Sightseeing

The three-master *Mercator*, a training vessel in authentic style, now houses a **maritime museum**. Open daily 1000–1300 and 1400–1800/1900 (Easter–Sept); Sat–Sun 1100–1300 and 1400–1700 (Oct–Easter); BFr.75. **Noordzeeaquarium** (on the front) displays the flora and fauna of the North Sea. Open daily 1000–1230 and 1400–1800 (June–Sept); Mon–Fri 1000–1200 and 1400–1700, Sat–Sun 1000–1230 and 1400–1800 (Apr–May); BFr.50.

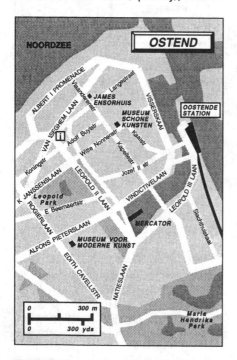

The studio where the Expressionist James Ensor worked has become a museum devoted to him: **James Ensorhuis**, *Vlaanderenstraat 27*. Open Wed–Mon 1000–1200 and 1400–1700 (June–Sept): BFr.50. Many of Ensor's possessions are among the exhibits in **Museum voor Schone Kunsten** (Fine Arts), *Cultuurpaleis, Wapenplein*, open Wed–Mon 1000–1200, 1400–1700; BFr.50. **PMMK (Museum voor Moderne Kunst)** (Modern Art), *Rome-straat 11*, open Tues–Sun 1000–1800; BFr.100, contains modern paintings and sculptures and is very wide-ranging within the genre.

A feature of the pleasant **Leopoldpark** is a floral clock that includes the date.

_____

Side Track from Ostend

The **De Lijn Coastal Tram** can be boarded by the station. It runs the length of the coast (75 km of dunes and wide sandy beaches), with Ostend in the middle of the route. Minor stops are marked by a pole with a red square saying 'tram' and the name of the stop. The tram stops only on demand, so ring the bell when your stop is approaching (you can check progress on the route map in the tram).

Several of the (13) resorts are quiet places, providing little other than watersports. Others, notably **Blankenberge** and **Knokke**, are sizeable towns. The Ostend tourist office supplies a free brochure about the resorts and every type of accommodation is available, from four-star hotels to campsites.

_____

BRUGES (BRUGGE)

Station: *tel: (050) 38 23 82*, 20 mins walk south of the centre. Buses stop in front of the station: get tickets and a free route

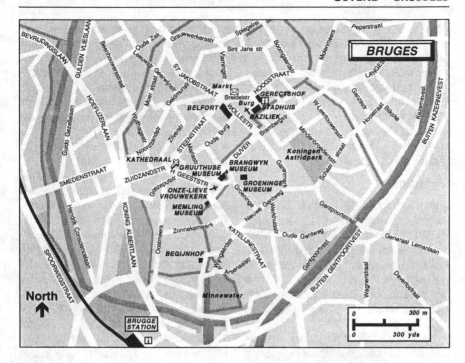

map from the **De Lijn** kiosk there (open Mon–Fri 0730–1800, Sat 0900–1800, Sun 1000–1800). To the right as you leave the station is a branch of the tourist office which offers a full service.

Tourist Office: Municipal, *Burg 11; tel: (050) 44 86 86.* Open Mon–Fri 0930–1830, Sat–Sun 1000–1200 and 1400–1830 (Apr–Sept); Mon–Fri 0930–1700, Sat 0930–1245 and 1400–1745 (Oct–Mar). *Brugge* (price BFr.20), is a comprehensive brochure (in several languages) that includes walks and a map. *Agenda Brugge* is a free monthly detailing local events.

Accommodation

Hotel chains in Bruges include *BW, GT, Ho, Ib, IH, Nv, Pu, Sf.* Accommodation of all types is available, but book ahead. **HI: Europa,** *Assebroek, Baron Ruzettelaan*

143; tel: (050) 35 26 79, is about 1.5 km east of the station (2 km south of Markt); bus no. 2: *Wantestraat* – 100 m away. It's a friendly place in its own grounds. To reach the centre (or the station), wait at the stop for bus no. 2, but board no. 1!

Among the private hostels is **Bauhaus**, *Langestraat 135; tel: (050) 34 10 93* (bus nos 6/16: *Kruispoort)*: good value and the bar is popular locally. The nearest **campsite** is *St-Michiel, Tillegemstraat 55; tel: (050) 38 08 19,* 3 km south-west of the station (bus no. 7).

Getting Around

A boat-trip on the extensive canal system is an excellent introduction to the town, with frequent departures from quays along Dijver: BFr.150 for about 30 mins. After that, explore on foot: most places of

---

interest are in a small area around **Markt** and **Burg**. The tourist office can supply a Walkman guide in English for BFr.300.

The basic 30-min tour by the horse-drawn carriages available in Burg costs BFr.800 and you can extend the time for BFr.400 per 15 mins.

Bus-stops show the **De Lijn** logo. Single tickets are BFr.40, eight-ride tickets BFr.200 and ten-ride tickets BFr.250.

Sightseeing

Markt is surrounded by guild buildings. **Belfort**, open daily 0930–1700 (Apr–Sept); 0930–1230 and, 1330–1700 (Oct–Mar); BFr.100, is an octagonal 88 m belfry, is mainly 13th-century, but the top storey was added in the 15th century. There are 366 steps to the top, and regular concerts take place on the 47-bell carillon (including 1415 Sun all year).

Burg, the other main square, features monumental buildings spanning several centuries. Don't miss **Baziliek van Het Heilig Bloed** (Basilica of the Holy Blood), open Thur–Tues 0930–1200 and 1400–1800, Wed 0930–1200 (Apr–Sept); Thur–Tues 1000–1200 and 1400–1600, Wed 1000–1200 (Oct–Mar); admission free. At ground level there's an atmospheric early-12th-century stone chapel, little changed by time. Upstairs is a magnificent 16th-century chapel, every inch decorated; the side chapel contains a marble altar with a silver-gilt tabernacle, behind which is kept a drop of Christ's blood. Every Ascension Day this is paraded through the streets in a magnificent 1617 shrine: a gloriously elaborate affair of jewel-encrusted gold and silver that's among the items in the treasury (admission BFr.40).

Other buildings include the Renaissance **Civiele Griffie** (recorder's house) and the neo-classical **Gerectshof** (Court of Justice), which contains **Provinciaal Museum Het Brugse Vrije** (open Tues–Sun 1000–1200 and 1330–1700; BFr.20), worth visiting for the superb Renaissance chimney-piece (1529). The Gothic **Stadhuis** (Town Hall) has sandstone turrets and a magnificent hall with a polychrome vaulted ceiling and historic murals. Open daily 0930–1700 (Apr–Sept); 0930–1230 and 1400–1700 (Oct–Mar); BFr.60.

Dijver is the central canal. *Dijverstraat* (scene of a weekend antiques and flea market) is home to several museums. **Groeningemuseum** (open daily 0930–1700 (Apr–Sept); Wed–Mon 0930–1230 and 1400–1700 (Oct–Mar); BFr.130) houses a fine collection of Flemish art from the 15th century to date, notably Primitive and Expressionist. **Gruuthuse-museum** (open daily 0930–1700 (Apr–Sept); Wed–Mon 0930–1230 and 1400–1800 (Oct–Mar); BFr.130) was a 16th-century palace and the decor reflects that time. Room 17 looks into **Onze-Lieve** (see below): the king attended services without leaving home. The diverse exhibits include a guillotine, chairs of office, musical instruments and spinning-wheels. **Brang-wyn Museum** (open daily 0930–1700 (Apr–Sept); Wed–Mon 0930–1230 and 1400–1700 (Oct–Mar); BFr.80) is noted for its collection of lace, among other items.

Onze-Lieve Vrouwekerk (Church of Our Lady), *Katelijnestraat* (open Mon–Sat 0900/1000–1130 and 1430–1600/1700, Sun 1430–1600/1700; BFr.30), is an architectural mishmash, incorporating Belgium's highest spire (122 m). Among its treasures are a marble *Madonna and Child* by Michelangelo, impressive mausoleums and 13th–14th-century painted tombs.

The peaceful **Béguinage** is now home to Benedictine nuns. A typical old-style

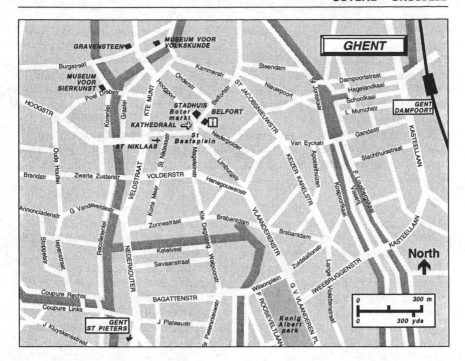

béguine's house is open daily 0930/1045–1200 and 1345–1800; BFr.60. It consists of a simple dwelling with a cloister surrounding a well and evidence of religious belief everywhere.

St-Janshospitaal en Memlingmuseum, *Mariastraat 38* (next to Onze-Lieve), is open daily 0930–1700 (Apr–Sept); Thur–Tues 0930–1200 and 1400–1700 (Oct–Mar); BFr.130. Hans Memling was a patient and it's now a museum devoted to his work, incorporating the 17th-century dispensary.

Not far away, the enormous **Kathedraal St-Salvator** (free), contains Gobelins tapestries, a rood-loft organ, 15th-century carved stalls, a Louis XVI-style pulpit and dozens of side altars. The treasury is open Mon–Sat 1000–1130 and 1400–1700, Sun 1500–1700 (July–Aug); closed mornings and Sun (Sept–June) plus Wed (Oct–Mar);

BFr.60. Contents include the silver shrine of St-Eligius, early frescos, a 6th-century ivory crozier and a 13th-century gold one.

Out of Town

Quasimodo Tours, *Poortersstraat 47*, open 0700–2300, run an English-language daytrip round the major **World War I battlefields,** which includes visits to the picturesque town of **Damme**, castles and a chocolate manufacturer; BFr.1300 (less for backpackers).

GHENT (GENT)

Station: The main station is **Gent-St-Pieters** (*tel: (09) 222 44 44*), 2 km south of the centre (tram nos 1, 10, 11, 12: *Korenmarkt*). **De Lijn** bus/tram information is to the left as you exit (open Mon–Fri

0700–1900). Trams to the centre leave from immediately in front of the station.
Tourist Offices: Municipal, *Botermarkt* (in the Stadhuis crypt); *tel: (09) 224 15 55.* Open daily 0930–1830 (Easter–Oct); 0930–1630 (Nov–Easter). **East Flanders**, *Kon. Maria-Hendrikaplein 64* (across the road from the station); *tel: (09) 222 16 37.* Open Mon–Fri 0830–1200 and 1315–1645. They provide information about Ghent as well as Flanders.

Sightseeing

Ghent is a deeply Flemish town, steeped in culture, yet very lively during the university year. For ten days in July, **Gentse Feesten** (traditionally a holiday for factory workers) dominates the town, with lots of cheap food, high beer consumption and street entertainments, as well as a variety of more formal performances.

Sint-Baafskathedraal is open Mon–Sat 0930–1200 and 1400–1800, Sun 1300–1800 (Apr–Sept); Mon–Sat 1000–1200 and 1430–1600, Sun 1400–1700 (Oct–Mar); admission free. It contains an incredible 18th-century marble and wood pulpit, an enormous baroque organ, marble statues and ornate guild chapels. Van Eyck's masterpiece *The Adoration of the Mystic Lamb* is concealed behind a screen, and covered by the same ticket (BFr.50) as the Romanesque crypt, which contains medieval tombs, 15th–16th-century Romanesque frescos and 12th–18th-century examples of local stonework. It has bags of atmosphere. The 90 m **belfort** (belfry), *Sint-Baafsplein*, opens 1000–1230, 1400–1730; BFr.100: there's a lift to the top.

The 13th-century Flemish-Gothic **St-Niklaaskerk**, *Korenmarkt* (open Mon–Thur 1000–1200, 1400–1700, Fri 1400–1830; admission free), is relatively plain, but bits of early ceiling paintings are partially visible – restoration proved too difficult. The central altar is magnificent and the church has its full quota of old religious paintings.

Gravensteen, *Sint-Veerleplein*, the 12th-century Castle of the Counts, opens daily 0900–1800 (Apr–Sept); 0900–1700 (Oct–Mar); BFr.80. Its museum displays a selection of gruesome instruments of torture, with illustrations and explanations of how they were used. The basic circuit includes a variety of rooms and displays and you can also walk round the ramparts and explore the castle grounds.

The **Stadhuis** (Town Hall), *Botermarkt*, has a flamboyant exterior, with architectural styles ranging from Gothic to baroque.

In **Museum Voor Sierkunst** (decorative arts museum), *Jan Breydelstraat 5*, (open Tues–Sun 0930–1700; BFr.80), you can compare styles from the Gothic era to the present. Exhibits include furniture, glass, ceramics, silver and textiles, all displayed in suitable settings.

Allow plenty of time for the fascinating folk museum, **Museum Voor Volkskunde**, *Kraanlei 65*, open daily 0900–1230, 1330–1730 (Apr–Oct); 1000–1200, 1330–1700 (Nov–Mar); BFr.50, which spreads through three converted almshouses. It portrays the town's lifestyle at the turn of the century and is crammed with everyday items, from toys to flat irons, hats to hurricane lanterns, as well as tableaux of various craftsmen.

In Citadel Park is **Museum voor Schone Kunsten** (Museum of Fine Arts), *Nicolaas de Liemaeckereplein 3.* Open Tues–Sun 0930–1700; BFr.80. It contains an impressive collection of ancient and modern art in all fields and from all over Europe, although the emphasis is on Flemish paintings.

SPECIAL TRAINS

LITTLE RAILWAYS

The following is a selection of minor lines, sometimes operated by steam train, which head off the beaten track into areas of spectacular scenery. There are many more such lines in France and the Benelux – specialist operators and enthusiasts' clubs can suggest other examples.

The narrow-gauge line from **La Tour de Carol** to **Villefranche** (see p. 268) is one of the highlights of train travel in France, with excellent mountain views and a rustic charm. In summer there are special open carriages. Services run throughout the year with connecting trains running from Villefranche to **Perpignan** (see p. 237).

Also narrow-gauge, but privately operated, is the line from **Nice**, which follows the Var valley before striking through the mountains to reach the small town of **Digne** (see p. 183), however severe weather has severed the line in many places and its future operation is in some doubt.

For mountain scenery the narrow gauge railway running from **St Gervais** and **Chamonix** (p. 137) over the border to **Martigny** in Switzerland takes some beating. Services operate in the shadow of Mont Blanc and the journey takes 2½ hrs.

If travelling back in time appeals the hour long journey from **Bayonne** (p. 72) to the small Pyrenean town of **St Jean Pied de Port** has much to recommend it. Three or four trains run up the valley each day .

The Mediterranean Island of **Corsica** has a rail system all of its own, with small trains trundling through the countryside linking Ajaccio and Calvi to the port of Bastia, where ferry services link to mainland France at Marseille and Nice.

For preserved steam enthusiasts the **Vivarais Railway** at Tournon (station Tain-Hermitage-Tournon on the main line south of Lyon) holds much of interest. Steam and diesel trains operate at weekends Mar–Oct (daily July and Aug).

Not far away at St Georges de Commiers (south of Grenoble) the **La Mure** railway operates electric trains on a 30 km long scenic line from April to Oct.

The main railway museum in France is situated at **Belfort** (see p. 260) in eastern France and contains an impressive collection of engines and rolling stock. In the Netherlands a similar museum is found in **Utrecht** (p. 298).

VENICE–SIMPLON ORIENT EXPRESS

The original Orient Express began on its long journey from Paris to Istanbul in 1883 and achieved an almost legendary status. However, World War II nearly killed it off, and the advent of cheap air travel and the descent of the Iron Curtain finished it in 1977. The journey has been resurrected in the form of the Venice–Simplon Orient Express, the opulent privately run cruise train, formed from restored carriages that were in use in the 20s and 30s.

From Paris the train service can be used to travel to London, via the SeaCat service between Boulogne and Folkestone, or to Venice via Basel, Zurich, Innsbruck and Verona. There are also services to Vienna and Budapest. **Information and booking (UK):** Venice–Simplon Orient Express, *Sea Containers House, 20 Upper Ground, London SE1 9PF; tel: 0171-928 6000.*

CONVERSION TABLES

INCHES AND CENTIMETRES

Unit	Inches	Feet	Yards
1mm	0.039	0.003	0.001
1cm	0.39	0.03	0.01
1metre	39.40	3.28	1.09

Unit	mm	cm	metres
1 inch	25.4	2.54	0.025
1 foot	304.8	30.48	0.304
1 yard	914.4	91.44	0.914

To convert cms to inches, multiply by 0.3937
To convert inches to cms, multiply by 2.54

24 HOUR CLOCK

Midnight = 0000	12 noon = 1200	6 pm = 1800	
6 am = 0600	1 pm = 1300	Midnight = 2400	

WEIGHT

Unit	Kg	Pounds
1	0.45	2.205
2	0.90	4.405
3	1.35	6.614
4	1.80	8.818
5	2.25	11.023
10	4.50	22.045
15	6.75	33.068
20	9.00	44.889
25	11.25	55.113
50	22.50	110.225
75	33.75	165.338
100	45.00	220.450

1 kg = 1000 g
100 g = 3.5 oz
1 oz = 28.35 g
1 lb = 453.60 g

FLUID MEASURES

Litres	Imp. gal.	US gal.
5	1.1	1.3
10	2.2	2.6
15	3.3	3.9
20	4.4	5.2
25	5.5	6.5
30	6.6	7.8
35	7.7	9.1
40	8.8	10.4
45	9.9	11.7
50	11.0	13.0

1 litre (l) = 0.88 imp.quarts
1 litre (l) = 1.06 US quarts
1 imp. quart = 1.14 l
1 imp. gallon = 4.55 l
1 US quart = 0.95 l
1 US gallon = 3.81 l

DISTANCE

km	miles	km	miles
1	0.62	30	21.75
2	1.24	40	24.85
3	1.86	45	27.96
4	2.49	50	31.07
5	3.11	55	34.18
6	3.73	60	37.28
7	4.35	65	40.39
8	4.97	70	43.50
9	5.59	75	46.60
10	6.21	80	49.71
15	9.32	90	55.92
20	12.43	100	62.14
25	15.53	125	77.67

1 km = 0.6214miles
1 mile = 1.609 km

METRES AND FEET

Unit	Metres	Feet
1	0.30	3.281
2	0.61	6.563
3	0.91	9.843
4	1.22	13.124
5	1.52	16.403
6	1.83	19.686
7	2.13	22.967
8	2.44	26.248
9	2.74	29.529
10	3.05	32.810
14	4.27	45.934
18	5.49	59.058
20	6.10	65.520
50	15.24	164.046
75	22.86	246.069
100	30.48	328.092

LADIES' SHOES

UK	Europe	USA
3	36	4.5
4	37	5.5
5	38	6.5
6	39	7.5
7	40	8.5
8	41	9.5

MENS' SHOES

UK	Europe	USA
6	40	7
7	41	8
8	42	9
9	43	10
10	44	11
11	45	12

LADIES' CLOTHES

UK	France	Italy	Rest of Europe	USA
10	36	38	34	8
12	38	40	36	10
14	40	42	38	12
16	42	44	40	14
18	44	46	42	16
20	46	48	44	18

MENS' CLOTHES

UK	Europe	USA
36	46	36
38	48	38
40	50	40
42	52	42
44	54	44
46	56	46

MENS' SHIRTS

UK	Europe	USA
14	36	14
15	38	15
15.5	39	15.5
16	41	16
16.5	42	16.5
17	43	17

TEMPERATURE

°C	°F	°C	°F
-20	-4	10	50
-15	5	15	59
-10	14	20	68
-5	23	25	77
0	32	30	86
5	41	35	95

Conversion Formula
°C x 9 ÷ 5 + 32 = °F
1 Deg. °C = 1.8 Deg. °F
1 Deg. °F = 0.55 Deg. °C

BRITRAIL PASSES
Unlimited travel in England, Scotland & Wales
Prices effective Jan. 1, 1995 – Prices are U.S. $

BRITRAIL PASS – Unlimited travel every day

Validity Period	Adult		Senior (60 +)		Youth (16 - 25)
	First	Standard	First	Standard	Standard
8 Days	❑ $315	❑ $230	❑ $295	❑ $209	❑ $189
15 Days	❑ $515	❑ $355	❑ $479	❑ $320	❑ $280
21 Days	❑ $645	❑ $445	❑ $585	❑ $399	❑ $355
1 Month	❑ $750	❑ $520	❑ $675	❑ $465	❑ $415

BRITRAIL FLEXIPASS – Travel any days within 1 Month

4 Days / 1 Month	❑ $259	❑ $195	❑ $235	❑ $175	❑ $160*
8 Days / 1 Month	❑ $399	❑ $275	❑ $360	❑ $250	❑ $225*
15 Days / 1 Month	❑ $590	❑ $405	❑ $535	❑ $365	❑ $319*

*Youth pass valid for 2 months

FREEDOM OF SCOTLAND TRAVEL PASS
8 Days ❑ $159 15 Days ❑ $220

FREEDOM OF SCOTLAND FLEXIPASS
Any 8 Days of Travel in 15 Days ❑ $185

ENGLAND / WALES PASS
Any 4 Days ❑ $205 First
in 1 Month ❑ $155 Standard

BRITIRELAND PASS
Includes round trip ticket on Stena Line Ferry between Britain and Ireland.

Validity	First	Standard
Any 5 Days in 1 Month	❑ $389	❑ $289
Any 10 Days in 1 Month	❑ $599	❑ $419

BRITFRANCE PASS
Does not include travel across English Channel or through Eurotunnel.

Validity	First	Standard
Any 5 Days in 1 Month	❑ $359	❑ $259
Any 10 Days in 1 Month	❑ $539	❑ $399

Eurostar – We are official agents for Channel Tunnel tickets and reservations. Passenger services from London operate non-stop to Paris and Brussels in 3 Hr. & 3:15 respectively. All seats require advance reservations and tickets. Various prices and 14-Day advance discounts available. Call for latest rates and reservations.

LONDON EXTRA
Combines a BritRail Flexipass good in S.E. England only and a London Visitor TravelCard (LVTC).

Validity	First Class	Standard
3 Days in 8 Pass Plus 3 Day LVTC	❑ $105	❑ $85
4 Days in 8 Pass Plus 4 Day LVTC	❑ $145	❑ $115
7 Days in 15 Pass Plus 7 Day LVTC	❑ $219	❑ $175

Call for children's rates

LONDON SERVICES
LONDON VISITOR TRAVEL CARD
Unlimited Inner Zone on Underground and red buses.

Duration	Adult	Child
3 Days	❑ $25	❑ $11
4 Days	❑ $32	❑ $13
7 Days	❑ $49	❑ $21

GATWICK EXPRESS
Non-stop from Gatwick Airport to Victoria Station every 15 miniutes. Takes only 30 minutes. Fastest way to London! Round trip – buy two one-ways.
❑ First Class $21 One-way
❑ Standard $14 One-way

SLEEPERS – We can confirm overnight sleepers on Anglo-Scottish and West Country routes. Accommodation supplement is $50 per person First Class and $40 per person Second Class. **CHILDREN'S RATES** (5 - 15) are half fare for most passes. **SEAT RESERVATIONS, GROUP RATES, CROSS-CHANNEL SERVICES, IRISH SEA SERVICES** – call for rates.

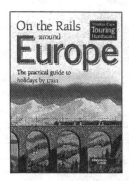

READER SURVEY
Fill in this form and you can win a full-colour guidebook!

If you enjoyed using this book – or if you didn't – please help us to improve future editions, by taking part in our reader survey. Every returned form will be acknowledged, and to show our appreciation for your help we will give you the chance to win a Thomas Cook Travellers illustrated guidebook for your travel bookshelf. Just take a few minutes to complete and return this form to us.

When did you buy this book?

Where did you buy it? (Please give town/city and if possible name of retailer)

Did you/do you intend to travel in France, Belgium, Netherlands or Luxembourg by train this year?
☐ Have travelled   ☐ Will travel this year   ☐ Not this year

If so, which countries did you/do you intend to visit?

In which month did you/do you intend to travel?

For how long (approx.)?

Did you/will you travel on: ☐ An Inter-Rail pass?   ☐ A Eurail pass?
                                ☐ Other passes or ticket(s)? Please specify:

Did you/do you intend to use this book:
☐ For planning your trip?   ☐ During the trip itself?   ☐ Both?

Did you/do you intend to also purchase any of the following travel publications for your trip?
☐ Thomas Cook European Timetable
☐ Thomas Cook New Rail Map of Europe
☐ Thomas Cook European Rail Travellers' Phrasebook
☐ Other guidebooks/maps. Please specify:

Please rate the following features of On the Rails around Europe for their value to you
(Circle the 1 for "little or no use," 2 for "useful," 3 for "very useful"):

The themed itineraries on pages 51–54	1	2	3
The "Travel Essentials" section on pages 12–21	1	2	3
The "Travelling by Train" section on pages 23–30	1	2	3
The "Country by Country" section on pages 31–50	1	2	3
Information on rail routes and trains	1	2	3
The rail route diagrams	1	2	3
Information on towns and cities	1	2	3
The city maps	1	2	3

Please use this space to tell us about any features that in your opinion could be changed, improved, or added in future editions of the book, or any other comments you would like to make concerning the book:

Your age category:
☐ Under 26   ☐ 26–50   ☐ over 50

Your name: Mr/Mrs/Ms   (First name or initials)
(Last name)

Your full address (please include postal code or zip code):

Your daytime telephone number:

Please detach this page and send it to: The Project Editor, On the Rails around France and Benelux, Thomas Cook Publishing, PO Box 227, Peterborough PE3 6SB, United Kingdom.

North American readers: Please mail replies to: E. Taylor, On the Rails around France and Benelux, Passport Books, 4255 West Touhy Avenue, Lincolnwood (Chicago), Illinois 60646-1975, USA.

Ten guidebooks to be won!

All surveys returned to us before the closing date of 31 October 1995 will be entered for a prize draw on that date. The senders of the first **ten** *replies drawn will each be invited to make their personal selection of any book from the Thomas Cook Travellers* range of guidebooks, to be sent to them free of charge. With 36 cities and countries to choose from, this new, full colour series of guides covers the major tourist destinations of the world. Each book, retail price £7.99/$14.95*, offers 192 pages of sightseeing, background information, and travel tips.*

*North American readers please note: in the United States this range is published by Passport Books under the name "Passport's Illustrated Guides from Thomas Cook". North American winners will receive the US edition of their selected book.

Prizewinners will be notified as soon as possible after the closing date and asked to select from the list of titles. Offer is subject to availability of titles at 1 November 1995. A list of winners will be available on receipt of a stamped self-addressed envelope.

INDEX

This index lists place names and topics in one alphabetical sequence. All references are to page numbers. **Bold** numbers refer to map pages. To find routes between cities, see pp 8–10.

KEY TO SYMBOLS
ROUTE DIAGRAMS

CITY BEGINNING OR ENDING ROUTE
(Name of station where necessary)
Page reference to description of city
Fastest train time between start and end of route

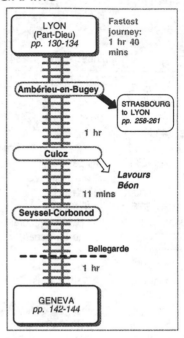

CONNECTING
ROUTE
*Page reference to
route*

Connection in
this city with
another route
in the book

Fastest journey time between each pair of cities

*Side-trip
destination*

Side-trip
opportunity (not
necessarily by rail)
mentioned in route
description

Town or city on the route
(NB not all trains will necessarily stop at every city
shown: check route description and timetables)

Name of border station
– – – – – – – –

Border crossing
point between
countries; border
station may be
some way from
actual frontier

CITY MAPS

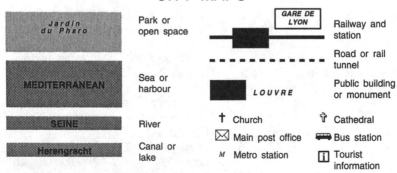

Park or
open space

GARE DE
LYON

Railway and
station

Road or rail
tunnel

Sea or
harbour

LOUVRE

Public building
or monument

River

† Church

✠ Cathedral

Canal or
lake

✉ Main post office

🚍 Bus station

M Metro station

[i] Tourist
information

COLOUR MAPS
Black lines show railways.
Red lines show high speed lines.
Lines on a green background are scenic.
Purple lines show selected bus routes.